Handbook of Research on Embedded Systems Design

Alessandra Bagnato
Softeam R&D, France

Leandro Soares Indrusiak
University of York, UK

Imran Rafiq Quadri
Softeam R&D, France

Matteo Rossi
Politecnico di Milano, Italy

A volume in the Advances in Systems Analysis,
Software Engineering, and High Performance
Computing (ASASEHPC) Book Series

An Imprint of IGI Global

Managing Director:	Lindsay Johnston
Production Editor:	Jennifer Yoder
Development Editor:	Erin O'Dea
Acquisitions Editor:	Kayla Wolfe
Typesetter:	Thomas Creedon
Cover Design:	Jason Mull

Published in the United States of America by
Information Science Reference (an imprint of IGI Global)
701 E. Chocolate Avenue
Hershey PA, USA 17033
Tel: 717-533-8845
Fax: 717-533-8661
E-mail: cust@igi-global.com
Web site: http://www.igi-global.com

Library of Congress Cataloging-in-Publication Data

Handbook of Research on Embedded Systems Design / Alessandra Bagnato, Leandro Soaores Indrusiak, Imran Rafiq Quadri, and Matteo Rossi, editors.
    pages cm
  Includes bibliographical references and index.
   ISBN 978-1-4666-6194-3 (hardcover) -- ISBN 978-1-4666-6197-4 (print & perpetual access) -- ISBN 978-1-4666-6195-0 (ebook) 1. Embedded computer systems. I. Bagnato, Alessandra, 1974- II. Indrusiak, Leandro Soares, 1974- III. Quadri, Imran Rafiq, 1981- IV. Rossi, Matteo.
  TK7895.E425253 2014
  006.2'2--dc23
                                       2014013826

This book is published in the IGI Global book series Advances in Systems Analysis, Software Engineering, and High Performance Computing (ASASEHPC) (ISSN: 2327-3453; eISSN: 2327-3461)

British Cataloguing in Publication Data
A Cataloguing in Publication record for this book is available from the British Library.

All work contributed to this book is new, previously-unpublished material. The views expressed in this book are those of the authors, but not necessarily of the publisher.

For electronic access to this publication, please contact: eresources@igi-global.com.

Advances in Systems Analysis, Software Engineering, and High Performance Computing (ASASEHPC) Book Series

Vijayan Sugumaran
Oakland University, USA

ISSN: 2327-3453
EISSN: 2327-3461

MISSION

The theory and practice of computing applications and distributed systems has emerged as one of the key areas of research driving innovations in business, engineering, and science. The fields of software engineering, systems analysis, and high performance computing offer a wide range of applications and solutions in solving computational problems for any modern organization.

The **Advances in Systems Analysis, Software Engineering, and High Performance Computing (ASASEHPC) Book Series** brings together research in the areas of distributed computing, systems and software engineering, high performance computing, and service science. This collection of publications is useful for academics, researchers, and practitioners seeking the latest practices and knowledge in this field.

COVERAGE

- Engineering Environments
- Network Management
- Parallel Architectures
- Storage Systems
- Human-Computer Interaction
- Performance Modelling
- Computer Networking
- Distributed Cloud Computing
- Metadata and Semantic Web
- Computer System Analysis

IGI Global is currently accepting manuscripts for publication within this series. To submit a proposal for a volume in this series, please contact our Acquisition Editors at Acquisitions@igi-global.com or visit: http://www.igi-global.com/publish/.

Titles in this Series

For a list of additional titles in this series, please visit: www.igi-global.com

Handbook of Research on Architectural Trends in Service-Driven Computing
Raja Ramanathan (Independent Researcher, USA) and Kirtana Raja (IBM, USA)
Information Science Reference • copyright 2014 • 759pp • H/C (ISBN: 9781466661783) • US $515.00 (our price)

Contemporary Advancements in Information Technology Development in Dynamic Environments
Mehdi Khosrow-Pour (Information Resources Management Association, USA)
Information Science Reference • copyright 2014 • 410pp • H/C (ISBN: 9781466662520) • US $205.00 (our price)

Systems and Software Development, Modeling, and Analysis New Perspectives and Methodologies
Mehdi Khosrow-Pour (Information Resources Management Association, USA)
Information Science Reference • copyright 2014 • 365pp • H/C (ISBN: 9781466660984) • US $215.00 (our price)

Handbook of Research on Emerging Advancements and Technologies in Software Engineering
Imran Ghani (Universiti Teknologi Malaysia, Malaysia) Wan Mohd Nasir Wan Kadir (Universiti Teknologi Malaysia, Malaysia) and Mohammad Nazir Ahmad (Universiti Teknologi Malaysia, Malaysia)
Engineering Science Reference • copyright 2014 • 686pp • H/C (ISBN: 9781466660267) • US $395.00 (our price)

Advancing Embedded Systems and Real-Time Communications with Emerging Technologies
Seppo Virtanen (University of Turku, Finland)
Information Science Reference • copyright 2014 • 502pp • H/C (ISBN: 9781466660342) • US $235.00 (our price)

Handbook of Research on High Performance and Cloud Computing in Scientific Research and Education
Marijana Despotović-Zrakić (University of Belgrade, Serbia) Veljko Milutinović (University of Belgrade, Serbia) and Aleksandar Belić (University of Belgrade, Serbia)
Information Science Reference • copyright 2014 • 476pp • H/C (ISBN: 9781466657847) • US $325.00 (our price)

Agile Estimation Techniques and Innovative Approaches to Software Process Improvement
Ricardo Colomo-Palacios (Østfold University College, Norway) Jose Antonio Calvo-Manzano Villalón (Universidad Politécnica De Madrid, Spain) Antonio de Amescua Seco (Universidad Carlos III de Madrid, Spain) and Tomás San Feliu Gilabert (Universidad Politécnica De Madrid, Spain)
Information Science Reference • copyright 2014 • 399pp • H/C (ISBN: 9781466651821) • US $215.00 (our price)

Enabling the New Era of Cloud Computing Data Security, Transfer, and Management
Yushi Shen (Microsoft, USA) Yale Li (Microsoft, USA) Ling Wu (EMC, USA) Shaofeng Liu (Microsoft, USA) and Qian Wen (Endronic Corp, USA)
Information Science Reference • copyright 2014 • 336pp • H/C (ISBN: 9781466648012) • US $195.00 (our price)

www.igi-global.com

701 E. Chocolate Ave., Hershey, PA 17033
Order online at www.igi-global.com or call 717-533-8845 x100
To place a standing order for titles released in this series, contact: cust@igi-global.com
Mon-Fri 8:00 am - 5:00 pm (est) or fax 24 hours a day 717-533-8661

List of Contributors

Table of Contents

Section 1
Research Perspective: Software and Hardware Design

Chapter 1
Collaborative Development of Dependable Cyber-Physical Systems by Co-Modeling and Co-
Simulation 1
John Fitzgerald, Newcastle University, UK
Ken Pierce, Newcastle University, UK
Peter Gorm Larsen, Aarhus University, Denmark

Chapter 2
UML MARTE Time Model and Its Clock Constraint Specification Language 29
Frédéric Mallet, Université Nice Sophia Antipolis, I3S, UMR 7271, CNRS, INRIA, 06900
Sophia Antipolis, France
Marie-Agnès Peraldi-Frati, Université Nice Sophia Antipolis, I3S, UMR 7271, CNRS, INRIA,
06900 Sophia Antipolis, France
Julien Deantoni, Université Nice Sophia Antipolis, I3S, UMR 7271, CNRS, INRIA, 06900
Sophia Antipolis, France
Robert de Simone, INRIA Sophia Antipolis Méditerranée, 06900 Sophia Antipolis, France

Chapter 3
Symbolic-Based Monitoring for Embedded Applications.. 52
Pramila Mouttappa, Institut Mines-Telecom, France
Stephane Maag, Institut Mines-Telecom, France
Ana Cavalli, Institut Mines-Telecom, France

Chapter 4
Designing Resource-Constrained Embedded Heterogeneous Systems to Cope with Variability.........75
Ian Gray, University of York, UK
Andrea Acquaviva, Politecnico di Torino, Italy
Neil Audsley, University of York, UK

Section 2
Development Methodologies and Tool Suites

Section 3
Industry Perspective and Applications

Detailed Table of Contents

Section 1
Research Perspective: Software and Hardware Design

Chapter 1

John Fitzgerald, Newcastle University, UK
Ken Pierce, Newcastle University, UK
Peter Gorm Larsen, Aarhus University, Denmark

The pace of innovation in Cyber-Physical Systems (CPSs) drives the need for multi-disciplinary methods and tools to support rapid and accurate assessment of design alternatives. In this chapter, the authors describe collaborative models (co-models) that link Discrete-Event (DE) models of control software with Continuous-Time (CT) models of controlled plant. They present methods and tools for co-modeling using VDM as the DE formalism, and bond graphs on the CT side, using the Crescendo platform to link existing simulators (Overture for VDM and 20-sim for bond graphs). The authors discuss the exploitation of co-models within the design flow, including their use with SysML, and the roles of Software-in the-Loop and Hardware-in-the-Loop simulation on the way to realising co-models in cyber and physical media. The authors identify research challenges in providing sufficient model fidelity and the evidence needed to support the engineering of certifiably dependable systems.

Chapter 2

Frédéric Mallet, Université Nice Sophia Antipolis, I3S, UMR 7271, CNRS, INRIA, 06900 Sophia Antipolis, France
Marie-Agnès Peraldi-Frati, Université Nice Sophia Antipolis, I3S, UMR 7271, CNRS, INRIA, 06900 Sophia Antipolis, France
Julien Deantoni, Université Nice Sophia Antipolis, I3S, UMR 7271, CNRS, INRIA, 06900 Sophia Antipolis, France
Robert de Simone, INRIA Sophia Antipolis Méditerranée, 06900 Sophia Antipolis, France

The UML Profile for MARTE extends the UML with constructs dedicated to the modeling and analysis of real-time and embedded systems. Its time profile provides a rich model of time based on the notion of logical clocks that can be used consistently through all modeling elements/diagrams. The MARTE time profile comes with a companion language, called CCSL. CCSL is a formal declarative language used to handle the MARTE logical clocks and schedule the execution of the different parts of a model. This chapter gives a snapshot on modeling and analysis facilities that have been developed specifically around the time profile of MARTE and CCSL. A second objective is to show how MARTE can be combined with other profiles such as EAST-ADL. The last objective is the use of CCSL as a common language for specifying the semantics of models to allow their execution in a common framework. The MARTE and EAST-ADL constructs are illustrated on an example of a simplified cruise control. The example starts with a description of functional and timing requirements captured using a specific profile called EAST-ADL dedicated to the automotive domain. Then some of the requirements are refined with UML state machines and activities adorned with MARTE stereotypes. All these models rely on MARTE clocks. The semantics of these diagrams is given by a CCSL description that is automatically derived from the models. The resulting CCSL specification can be used to execute the UML/EAST-ADL specification, to animate the model, or to perform various kinds of analyses.

Chapter 3

Pramila Mouttappa, Institut Mines-Telecom, France
Stephane Maag, Institut Mines-Telecom, France
Ana Cavalli, Institut Mines-Telecom, France

Testing embedded systems to find errors and to validate that the implemented system as per the specifications and requirements has become an important part of the system design. The research community has proposed several formal approaches these last years, but most of them only consider the control portion of the protocol, neglecting the data portions, or are confronted with an overloaded amount of data values to consider. In this chapter, the authors present a novel approach to model protocol properties of embedded application in terms of Input-Output Symbolic Transition Systems (IOSTS) and show how they can be tested on real execution traces taking into account the data and control portions. These properties can be designed to test the conformance of a protocol as well as security aspects. A parametric trace slicing approach is presented to match trace and property. This chapter is illustrated by an application to a set of real execution traces extracted from a real automotive Bluetooth framework with functional and security properties.

Chapter 4

Ian Gray, University of York, UK
Andrea Acquaviva, Politecnico di Torino, Italy
Neil Audsley, University of York, UK

As modern embedded systems become increasingly complex, they also become susceptible to manufacturing variability. Variability causes otherwise identical hardware elements to exhibit large differences in dynamic and static power usage, maximum clock frequency, thermal resilience, and lifespan. There are currently no standard ways of handling this variability from the software developer's point of view, forcing the hardware vendor to discard devices that fall below a certain threshold. This chapter first presents a review of existing state-of-the-art techniques for mitigating the effects of variability. It then presents the toolflow developed as part of the ToucHMore project, which aims to build variability-awareness into the entire design process. In this approach, the platform is modelled in SysML, along with the expected variability and the monitoring and mitigation capabilities that the hardware presents. This information is used to automatically generate a customised variability-aware runtime, which is used by the programmer to perform operations such as offloading computation to another processing element, parallelising operations, and altering the energy use of operations (using voltage scaling, power gating, etc.). The variability-aware runtime affects its behaviour according to modelled static manufacturing variability and measured dynamic variability (such as battery power, temperature, and hardware degradation). This is done by moving computation to different parts of the system, spreading computation load more efficiency, and by making use of the modelled capabilities of the system.

Chapter 5

  Norbert Druml, Graz University of Technology, Austria
  Manuel Menghin, Graz University of Technology, Austria
  Christian Steger, Graz University of Technology, Austria
  Armin Krieg, Infineon Technologies Austria, Austria
  Andreas Genser, Infineon Technologies Austria, Austria
  Josef Haid, Infineon Technologies Austria, Austria
  Holger Bock, Infineon Technologies Austria, Austria
  Johannes Grinschgl, Independent Researcher, Austria

Due to the increase in popularity of mobile devices, it has become necessary to develop a low-power design methodology in order to build complex embedded systems with the ability to minimize power usage. In order to fulfill power constraints and security constraints if personal data is involved, test and verification of a design's functionality are imperative tasks during a product's development process. Currently, in the field of secure and reliable low-power embedded systems, issues such as peak power consumption, supply voltage variations, and fault attacks are the most troublesome. This chapter presents a comprehensive study over design analysis methodologies that have been presented in recent years in literature. During a long-lasting and successful cooperation between industry and academia, several of these techniques have been evaluated, and the identified sensitivities of embedded systems are presented. This includes a wide range of problem groups, from power and supply-related issues to operational faults caused by attacks as well as reliability topics.

Chapter 6

  David de Andrés, Universitat Politècnica de València, Spain
  Juan–Carlos Ruiz, Universitat Politècnica de València, Spain
  Jaime Espinosa, Universitat Politècnica de València, Spain
  Pedro Gil, Universitat Politècnica de València, Spain

The steady reduction of transistor size has brought embedded solutions into everyday life. However, the same features of deep-submicron technologies that are increasing the application spectrum of these solutions are also negatively affecting their dependability. Current practices for the design and deployment of hardware fault tolerance and security strategies remain in practice specific (defined on a case-per-case basis) and mostly manual and error prone. Aspect orientation, which already promotes a clear separation between functional and non-functional (dependability and security) concerns in software designs, is also an approach with a big potential at the hardware level. This chapter addresses the challenging problems of engineering such strategies in a generic way via metaprogramming, and supporting their subsequent instantiation and deployment on specific hardware designs through open compilation. This shows that promoting a clear separation of concerns in hardware designs and producing a library of generic, but reusable, hardware fault and intrusion tolerance mechanisms is a feasible reality today.

    Haoyuan Ying, Technische Universität Darmstadt, Germany
    Klaus Hofmann, Technische Universität Darmstadt, Germany
    Thomas Hollstein, Tallinn University of Technology, Estonia

Due to the growing demand on high performance and low power in embedded systems, many core architectures are proposed the most suitable solutions. While the design concentration of many core embedded systems is switching from computation-centric to communication-centric, Network-on-Chip (NoC) is one of the best interconnect techniques for such architectures because of the scalability and high communication bandwidth. Formalized and optimized system-level design methods for NoC-based many core embedded systems are desired to improve the system performance and to reduce the power consumption. In order to understand the design optimization methods in depth, a case study of optimizing many core embedded systems based on 3-Dimensional (3D) NoC with irregular vertical link distribution topology through task mapping, core placement, routing, and topology generation is demonstrated in this chapter. Results of cycle-accurate simulation experiments prove the validity and efficiency of the design methods. Specific to the case study configuration, in maximum 60% vertical links can be saved while maintaining the system efficiency in comparison to full vertical link connection 3D NoCs by applying the design optimization methods.

Section 2
Development Methodologies and Tool Suites

    Alessandra Bagnato, SOFTEAM, France
    Imran Quadri, SOFTEAM, France
    Etienne Brosse, SOFTEAM, France
    Andrey Sadovykh, SOFTEAM, France
    Leandro Soares Indrusiak, University of York, UK
    Richard Paige, University of York, UK
    Neil Audsley, University of York, UK
    Ian Gray, University of York, UK
    Dimitrios S. Kolovos, University of York, UK
    Nicholas Matragkas, University of York, UK
    Matteo Rossi, Politecnico di Milano, Italy
    Luciano Baresi, Politecnico di Milano, Italy
    Matteo Carlo Crippa, Txt e-Solutions, Italy
    Stefano Genolini, Txt e-Solutions, Italy
    Scott Hansen, The Open Group, UK
    Gundula Meisel-Blohm, Airbus Defence and Space, Germany

This chapter presents the EU-funded MADES FP7 project that aims to develop an effective model-driven methodology to improve the current practices in the development of real-time embedded systems for avionics and surveillance industries. MADES developed an effective SysML/MARTE language subset, and a set of new tools and technologies that support high-level design specifications, validation, simulation, and automatic code generation, while integrating aspects such as component re-use. This chapter illustrates the MADES methodology by means of a car collision avoidance system case study; it presents the underlying MADES language, the design phases, and the set of tools supporting on one hand model verification and validation and, on the other hand, automatic code generation, which enables the implementation on execution platforms such as state-of-the-art FPGAs.

Chapter 9

    Laura Baracchi, Intecs, Italy
    Alessandro Cimatti, FBK-Irst, Italy
    Gerald Garcia, Thales Alenia Space, France
    Silvia Mazzini, Intecs, Italy
    Stefano Puri, Intecs, Italy
    Stefano Tonetta, FBK-Irst, Italy

The development of complex computer-based systems poses two fundamental challenges. On one side, the architectural decomposition must be complemented by a suitable refinement of the requirements. On the other side, it is fundamental to provide the means for component reuse in order to limit development costs. In this chapter, the authors discuss the approach taken in FoReVeR, a project funded by the European Space Agency (ESA), where these two issues are tackled in the setting of space systems. The approach taken in FoReVeR is based on the idea of contracts, which allow one to formally specify the requirements of components at different levels of abstraction and to formally prove the correctness of requirements decomposition. In particular, the authors show how system-level requirements can be progressively refined into software requirements and how the contract-based framework supports the reuse of the components of a reference architecture under development by ESA. The authors discuss how the proposed solution has been integrated in a space development process and present the results of case studies.

Chapter 10

    Sara Tucci-Piergiovanni, CEA, LIST, 91191 Gif-sur-Yvette CEDEX , France
    DeJiu Chen, KTH Royal Institute of Technology, Sweden
    Chokri Mraidha, CEA, LIST, 91191 Gif-sur-Yvette CEDEX , France
    Henrik Lönn, Volvo Technology, Sweden
    Nidhal Mahmud, University of Hull, UK
    Mark-Oliver Reiser, Technische Universität Berlin, Germany
    Ramin Tavakoli Kolagari, Nuremberg Institute of Technology G. S. Ohm, Germany
    Nataliya Yakymets, CEA, LIST, 91191 Gif-sur-Yvette CEDEX , France
    Renato Librino, 4S s.r.l., Italy
    Sandra Torchiaro, Centro Ricerche Fiat, Italy
    Agnes Lanusse, CEA, LIST, 91191 Gif-sur-Yvette CEDEX , France

Modern cars have turned into complex high-technology products, subject to strict safety and timing requirements, in a short time span. This evolution has translated into development processes that are not as efficient, flexible, and agile as they could or should be. Model-based design offers many potential solutions to this problem. This chapter presents the main aspects and capabilities of a rich model-based design framework, founded on EAST-ADL, and developed during the MAENAD project. EAST-ADL is an architecture description language specific to the automotive domain and complemented by a methodology compliant with the ISO26262 standard. The language and the methodology set the stage for a high-level of automation and integration of advanced analyses and optimization capabilities to effectively improve development processes of modern cars.

Chapter 11

Michel Bourdellès, Thales Communications and Security, France
Shuai Li, Thales Communications and Security, France
Imran Quadri, Softeam, France
Etienne Brosse, Softeam, France
Andrey Sadovykh, Softeam, France
Emmanuel Gaudin, PragmaDev, France
Frédéric Mallet, INRIA, France
Arda Goknil, University of Luxembourg, Luxembourg
David George, Rapita Systems Ltd., UK
Jari Kreku, VTT Technical Research Centre, Finland

In most industrial embedded systems development projects, the software and the hardware development parts are separated, and the constraint requirements/capabilities are informally exchanged in the system development phase of the process. To prevent failures due to the violation of timing constraints, hardware components of the platform are typically over dimensioned for the capabilities needed. This increases both cost and power consumption. Performance analysis is not done sufficiently at early stages of the development process to optimize the system. This chapter presents results of the integration of tools and extra modeling to offer new performance analysis capabilities in the early stages of the development process. These results are based on trace generation from code instrumentation. A number of enhancements were made, spanning the system modeling stage down to the execution stage (based on an ARM dual core Cortex A9-based target board). Final results taken from a software-based radio case study (including the analysis and validation stages) are presented.

Chapter 12

Katrina Falkner, The University of Adelaide, Australia
Vanea Chiprianov, The University of Adelaide, Australia
Nickolas Falkner, The University of Adelaide, Australia
Claudia Szabo, The University of Adelaide, Australia
Gavin Puddy, The University of Adelaide, Australia

Autonomous, Distributed Real-Time Embedded (DRE) defense systems are typically characterized by hard constraints on space, weight, and power. These constraints have a strong impact on the non-functional properties of the final system, especially its performance. System execution modeling tools permit early prediction of the performance of model-driven systems; however, the focus to date has been on the practical aspects and creating tools that work in specific cases, rather than on the process and methodology applied. In this chapter, the authors present an integrated method to performance analysis and prediction of model-driven DRE defense systems. They present both the tools to support the process and a method to define these tools. The authors explore these tools and processes within an industry case study from a defense context.

Section 3
Industry Perspective and Applications

Chapter 13

Norbert Druml, Graz University of Technology, Austria
Manuel Menghin, Graz University of Technology, Austria
Christian Steger, Graz University of Technology, Austria
Armin Krieg, Infineon Technologies Austria, Austria
Andreas Genser, Infineon Technologies Austria, Austria
Josef Haid, Infineon Technologies Austria, Austria
Holger Bock, Infineon Technologies Austria, Austria
Johannes Grinschgl, Independent Researcher, Austria

Embedded systems that follow a secure and low-power design methodology are, besides keeping strict design constraints, heavily dependent on comprehensive test and verification procedures. The large set of possible test vectors and the increasing density of System-on-Chip designs call for the introduction of hardware-accelerated techniques to solve the verification time problem. As already described earlier, emulation-based methodologies based on FPGA evaluation platforms prove capable of providing a solution compared to traditional system simulation. This chapter gives an introduction into a multi-disciplinary emulation-based design evaluation and verification methodology that is based on various techniques that have been presented in chapter 5. Test and verification capabilities are enhanced by the augmentation of this approach using model-based analysis units: gate-level-based power consumption models, power supply network models, event-based performance monitors, and high-level fault modes. The feasible usage of this verification methodology in the field of contactlessly powered smart cards is finally demonstrated using several industrial case studies.

Chapter 14

Naim Harb, Polytechnic Faculty of Mons, Belgium
Smail Niar, LAMIH-University of Valenciennes Le Mont Houy, France
Mazen A. R. Saghir, Texas A&M University at Qatar, Qatar

Embedded system designers are increasingly relying on Field Programmable Gate Arrays (FPGAs) as target design platforms. Today's FPGAs provide high levels of logic density and rich sets of embedded hardware components. They are also inherently flexible and can be easily and quickly modified to meet changing applications or system requirements. On the other hand, FPGAs are generally slower and consume more power than Application-Specific Integrated Circuits (ASICs). However, advances in FPGA architectures, such as Dynamic Partial Reconfiguration (DPR), are helping bridge this gap. DPR enables a portion of an FPGA device to be reconfigured while the device is still operating. This chapter explores the advantage of using the DPR feature in an automotive system. The authors implement a Driver Assistant System (DAS) based on a Multiple Target Tracking (MTT) algorithm as the automotive base system. They show how the DAS architecture can be adjusted dynamically to different scenario situations to provide interesting functionalities to the driver.

Automotive infotainment applications are examples of embedded systems in which a heterogeneous software stack is used, which most likely comprises a real-time operating system, an automotive-grade Linux, and possibly Android. Thanks to the availability of modern systems-on-a-chip providing multicore computing platforms, architects have the possibility of integrating the entire software stack in a single chip. Embedded virtualization appears an interesting technology to achieve this goal, while providing the different operating systems the capability of exchanging data as well as optimizing resource usage. Although very well known in server-class systems, virtualization is rather new to the embedded domain; in order to leverage its benefits, it is therefore mandatory to understand its peculiarities and shortcomings. In this chapter, the authors illustrate the virtualization technologies with particular emphasis on hypervisors and Linux Containers. Moreover, they illustrate how those technologies can cooperate to fulfill the requirements on automotive infotainment applications. Finally, the authors report some experimental evidence of the performance overheads introduced when using embedded virtualization.

Current information systems used for data collection and to generate information on the state of the roads have two drawbacks: the first is that they have no ability to identify target-detected vehicles; the second is their high cost, which makes them expensive to cover the secondary road network, so they are usually located just on main routes. Thus, a new low-cost information system to monitor the traffic in real-time is proposed in this chapter. This system is based on scanning Bluetooth devices that are near the detection node. A large amount of data from passes of Bluetooth devices by different nodes (movements or displacements) have been collected. From this data, the frequency of appearance, average speed, or the number of devices that pass a certain site each day (on both working or non-working days) can be determined. The analysis of collected data has given statistics and indicators about the use of vehicles by the population of the monitored area. Specifically, the authors have obtained information about the total number of vehicles that each node has detected, on weekdays or holidays, information on traffic density by time range, on individual movements, the average speed on a section delimited by two consecutive nodes, and what demonstrates the power and features of the developed system.

Chapter 17

Stefano Genolini, TXT e-solutions, Italy
Matteo Crippa, TXT e-solutions, Italy

While analyzing currently available international research about embedded system development, it seems that as the complexity of embedded systems is continuously increasing, the major problems regarding their development remain always the same: vague requirements, insufficient time to develop, lack of resources, and complexity management. With the focus on the development process, it is shown, with examples coming from 20 years of experience, the industry perspective of a company managing such problems by adopting a consolidated set of good practices.

Chapter 18

Gokhan Tanyeri, Clarinox Technologies Pty Ltd
Trish Messiter, Clarinox Technologies Pty Ltd
Paul Beckett, RMIT University, Australia

Debugging embedded systems is almost guaranteed to cause headaches. Embedded systems, and especially portable embedded systems, are becoming increasingly complex and have unique constraints that make them hard to debug. Traditional static debugging tools provided by the embedded development tool chains are important but are only part of the story. Time-dependant issues cannot be debugged by such tools. Embedded environments have to provide efficient mechanisms for managing a range of issues such as thread interaction, control of timers, semaphores and mutexes, IPC message passing, event handling, and finite-state machine organizations. This chapter looks at issues of escalating complexity in modern heterogeneous embedded systems and their impact on debugging techniques and advocates a framework approach to manage this complexity. Using the ClarinoxSoftFrame® Suite framework as an illustrative example, this chapter describes how a modular and open approach to debugging can aid the rapid development of robust wireless-enabled embedded systems that employ a variety of operating systems and platforms. The overall objective in this type of approach is to leverage prebuilt code infrastructure plus existing development skills as much as possible, thereby avoiding the need for engineering staff to learn and re-learn a range of compilers, operating systems, and the like. Overall, debug time can be greatly reduced by improved visibility into the complex interactions between cooperating processes within the code. Collateral benefits can include a reduction in the size of the necessary development team with a reduction in skills specialization.

Chapter 19

Emmanuel Gaudin, PragmaDev, France

The increasing complexity of embedded systems calls for verification techniques to make sure the systems behave properly. When it comes to safety-critical systems, this aspect is even more relevant and is now taken into consideration by certification authorities. For that matter, property verification is accepted to be done not only on the system itself but also on a representative model of the system. This chapter first introduces the different properties and how they could be expressed. Then associated modeling languages characteristics are discussed to describe the systems on which the properties can be verified. Finally, different technologies to verify the properties are presented, including some practical examples and existing tools. This last part is illustrated by several research projects such as the PRESTO ARTEMIS European project and the exoTICus System@tic Paris Region competitiveness cluster project.

Preface

The idea behind this book came during a group meeting in a European R&D project. We came to a realization that while there exists a plethora of research articles that detail activities related to embedded systems design, they usually do not show the whole picture. The academic research articles are more visible as compared to design activities and practices present in the embedded systems industry, which are not often brought to light, either due to confidentiality reasons or because the results are usually presented in industrial exhibitions and conferences, which may not be accessible to academia. It is for this reason that we decided to go ahead with the idea of editing a book that targets not only current academic practices but also relevant industrial trends for embedded systems design in order to provide valuable insight to embedded systems designers, developers, and students about the whole spectrum of embedded systems design covering various topics such as model-based methodologies, software optimisation techniques, hardware implementation strategies, and general design choices that result in existing embedded systems.

BACKGROUND

Real-Time Embedded Systems (RTES) are omnipresent in our personal and professional daily lives: from physical/environmental monitoring via Wireless Sensor Networks in the field of telecommunications to the domains of medicine, defense, avionics, and transport; it is difficult to find a place where RTES have not made their mark.

Low power and energy consumption factors have become critical to the design and implementation of these systems in order to ensure maximum battery life, while providing adequate balance between performance and system lifetime. According to the ITRS roadmap, "power defines performance" and is the single most important factor for the design of future RTES (ITRS, 2011).

In addition to these critical factors, rapid evolution and continuous technological advances in RTES, along with a sharp increase in targeted application domains, have led to new challenges in the specification, design, and implementation of these systems, like increased development life cycles, non-recurring engineering costs, and poor synergism between the different development teams related to hardware and software development, resulting in decreased productivity. Therefore, effective design methodologies and efficient design tools are needed to address the above-mentioned challenges while resolving issues related to system complexity, power consumption, and verification.

It is thus evident that in the near future embedded systems will become more difficult to develop unless new and effective methodologies are developed to combat the above-mentioned issues. New domains such as Cyber-Physical Systems (Foundations for Innovation in Cyber-Physical Systems, 2013) can be viewed as the next generation of embedded systems that couple the latter with physical processes, along with human-in-the-loop. These complex systems will benefit from effective methodologies targeting real-time and embedded systems.

In recent years, numerous research works have been carried out to reduce the above-mentioned challenges related to RTES: task scheduling for power management, software power optimizations (for example code compression and coding), and low-power communication techniques. Effective Network-on-Chip communication-based architectures have been proposed among other diverse approaches at various levels of abstraction, from the electronic Register Transfer Level (RTL) up to the system design level, to address these issues (Lee, et al., 2006).

It has been observed that a high abstraction-level design methodology produces more effective impacts, due to increased degree of flexibility, as compared to tighter constraints applicable at either transactional-level modeling (via SystemC) or RTL (Cai & Gajski, 2003). Hence, high-abstraction-based system design approaches such as Model-Based Design (MBD) or Model-Driven Development (MDE) (Selic, 2003) have been developed, which enable system specification via graphical notations or languages like UML (Unified Modeling Language) (OMG, 2011a) to reduce system complexity, and to effectively partition the system design according to the classical Y-chart hardware/software co-design paradigm (Gajski & Kuhn, 1983). Additionally, MDE integrates different tools, technologies (like the Eclipse Modeling Framework or EMF), and standards (UML and related profiles for high-level system specifications, such as SysML [OMG, 2012] and MARTE [OMG, 2011b]). Finally, Model Transformations can automatically generate executable models or code from these high-level design models (Sendall & Kozaczynski, 2003).

High-abstraction model-based design methodologies have some crucial advantages. The abstraction achieved by a modeling approach permits one to abstractly emphasize the overall system structure, while bypassing details related to implementation and associated technologies. This enables conception and development of huge complex systems in a speedy and efficient manner. These approaches enable representing a system or a part of the system with different points of view, which permit system separation by aspects related to specific domain views. These approaches can also be found in Aspect-Oriented Programming (AOP) and Domain-Specific Languages (DSLs) (Mernik, et al., 2005).

The European research initiative has also taken up the challenge for real-time and embedded development processes, and many research efforts have been carried out during the last few years in many European-funded R&D projects (such as EU FP7, ARTEMIS, and EU members' national projects) related to embedded systems, to decrease time-to-market and to address issues related to increasing costs, complexity, and productivity.

This book presents an overview of the results of various R&D projects in order to provide a reference text that addresses system engineering principles for embedded systems to disseminate them in the embedded system developers and user communities.

The book provides contributions from practitioners of the embedded systems community, both from industry as well as academia, involved in European Research projects targeting real-time and embedded systems. These projects focus on a wide spectrum of design principles related to these complex systems, ranging from their specification at high abstraction levels using standards such as UML and related profiles (SySML, MARTE, EAST-ADL [East-ADL Association, 2014], AUTOSAR [2014], etc.) to intermediate design phases related to verification, timing, scheduling, and performance analysis, down to low-level implementation details related to the underlying execution platforms, such as synthesis, placement, and routing on FPGAs, System-on-Chips (SoCs), and Network-on-Chips (NoCs). In particular, the book covers the research carried out to address specific embedded system constraints related to hard timing constraints, limited memory and power use, predefined hardware platform technology, and hardware costs.

The book provides an overview of different approaches developed out in the embedded systems domain in academia and industry. The topics covered in the book are extremely current as they tackle issues related to increasing design productivity, lowering energy consumption levels, increasing performance, and decreasing the overall time-to-market, all aspects that have been identified as core in the Horizon2020 EU R&D program as well as in the INCOSE 2020 vision for systems engineering.

The book tackles various interesting and relevant aspects: from model-based design (such as requirements management, model transformations and adoption of high-level standards such as EAST-ADL, SysML, and MARTE) resulting in early design space analysis, verification, and automatic code generation for implementation of embedded systems, to topics such as development of low-power embedded systems and emulation techniques, fault tolerance, software development techniques such as aspect-oriented programming, virtualization techniques, to hardware implementation techniques like dynamic reconfiguration of embedded systems to manage system configurations and failures.

TARGET AUDIENCE

The target audience of this book are designers of embedded software, academicians, students, practitioners, professionals, and researchers working in the field of real-time and embedded systems development. This book is a rich source of information covering theoretical analysis, algorithms, and practical applications of software engineering for real-time and embedded systems.

The book will also be of great advantage to a reader interested in gaining a basic understanding of embedded systems design perspectives in research and industry and at which level the current standardization efforts in the field have been used. This could be, for example, the design and development manager in an organization, a system architect, or a researcher interested in learning the current embedded system design perspectives in both industry and academia.

CHAPTER OUTLINES

The chapters of the book are organized in three sections. The first focuses on design techniques addressing specific issues in the development of embedded systems; they range from simulation of early system models to optimization of hardware components. The second includes chapters presenting complete development methodologies that have been defined as the result of collaborations among academic and industrial partners in various projects. The third comprises chapters providing a more industrial and application-oriented view on the development of embedded systems.

Section 1: Research Perspective – Software and Hardware Design

The first three chapters of Section 1 deal with modeling and verification in the broad sense of the term of the control logic in embedded and cyber-physical systems.

In Chapter 1, "Collaborative Development of Dependable Cyber-Physical Systems by Co-Modeling and Co-Simulation," Fitzgerald, Pierce, and Larsen explore the challenges related to the simulation of complex cyber-physical systems and propose a method developed in the European project DESTECS for the simulation of heterogeneous systems through the combination of different tools for different parts of the system.

In Chapter 2, "UML MARTE Time Model and its Clock Constraint Specification Language," Mallet, Peraldi-Frati, Deantoni, and de Simone present an approach to the modeling and analysis of timing constraints in real-time embedded systems based on the UML MARTE profile and on its notion of clocks.

In Chapter 3, "Symbolic-Based Monitoring for Embedded Applications," Mouttappa, Maag and Cavalli introduce a formal approach, which was applied in the DIAMONDS European project, for checking the conformance of execution traces of an implemented embedded system with respect to its specification.

The final four chapters of Section 1 cover design issues that are closer to the hardware platform level and address hardware-related metrics and properties, such as energy dissipation or fault tolerance.

Chapter 4, "Designing Resource-Constrained Embedded Heterogeneous Systems to Cope with Variability" by Gray, Acquaviva, and Audsley, considers the upcoming problems resulting from the performance and energy dissipation variability introduced by the latest silicon manufacturing processes at the nano-dimensions. It proposes a model-based flow that facilitates the creation of a runtime environment that is aware of the variability effects and that is able to mitigate those effects by remapping computation to different processors, parallelizing operations, and optimizing the energy dissipation by dynamically scaling voltage.

In Chapter 5, "Vulnerabilities of Secure and Reliable Low-Power Embedded Systems and their Analysis Methods: A Comprehensive Study," by Druml, Menghin, Steger, Krieg, Genser, Haig, Bock, and Grinschgl, a number of power analysis and minimisation techniques are discussed, followed by a review of security threats that can explore power-related vulnerabilities, such as power profile side channel attacks and fault injection attacks.

Chapter 6, "An Aspect-Oriented Approach to Hardware Fault Tolerance for Embedded Systems" by de Andrés, Ruiz, Espinosa, and Gil, presents a meta-programming approach to extend an HDL-based design flow aiming to facilitate the optimization and evaluation of fault-tolerance and security features in hardware IP cores.

In Chapter 7, "Optimized System Level Design Methods for NoC-Based Many Core Embedded Systems," Ying, Hofmann, and Hollstein present a methodology and respective tool flow to optimise performance and energy dissipation of the 3D XHiNoC network-on-chip. It does that by relying heavily on search-based heuristics to tune task mapping, core placement, network topology, and routing.

Section 2: Development Methodologies and Tool Suites

The second section of the book includes chapters that look at several phases and activities in the development of embedded systems, either by defining methodologies that span over them, or by describing tool suites that support them.

In Chapter 8, "MADES FP7 EU Project: Effective High Level SysML/MARTE Methodology for Real-Time and Embedded Avionics Systems," Bagnato, Quadri, Brosse, Sadovykh, Soares Indrusiak, Paige, Audsley, Gray, Kolovos, Matragkas, Rossi, Baresi, Crippa, Genolini, Hansen, and Meisel-Blohm present the model-driven approach to the development of embedded systems that was the outcome of the MADES European project; the approach covers many aspects, from high-level modeling, verification and simulation, to the allocation of functions on the target hardware, to the automated generation of code tailored to the target platform.

In Chapter 9, "Requirements Refinement and Component Reuse: The FoReVer Contract-Based Approach," Baracchi, Cimatti, Garcia, Mazzini, Puri, and Tonetta describe the mechanisms developed in the FoReVer project, funded by the European Space Agency, to develop complex systems in a modular, component-based manner through the notion of "contracts" among modules; the proposed approach allows designers to formally verify the correctness of the decomposition of requirements when moving through the different development phases of a space system and in particular, from system-level to software requirements.

In Chapter 10, "Model-Based Analysis and Engineering of Automotive Architectures with EAST-ADL," Tucci-Piergiovanni, Chen, Mraidha, Lönn, Mahmud, Reiser, Kolagari, Yakymets, Librino, Torchiaro, and Lanusse introduce the model-based development approach of automotive systems based on EAST-ADL defined in the MAENAD European project; in particular, the chapter describes how different analysis techniques (for studying functional, safety and timing properties of the system, and for its optimization) are integrated and automated in the MAENAD approach.

In Chapter 11, "Fostering Analysis from Industrial Embedded Systems Modeling," Bourdellès, Li, Quadri, Brosse, Sadovykh, Gaudin, Mallet, Goknil, George, and Kreku present the tool suite developed in the PRESTO ARTEMIS project for the validation of non-functional properties of embedded systems from the early phases of development; the tool suite allows developers to generate execution traces from instrumented code, specify the functional and non-functional properties of interest, and then verify that the generated traces have the desired properties.

In Chapter 12, "A Model Driven Engineering Method for DRE Defense Systems Performance Analysis and Prediction," Falkner, Chiprianov, Falkner, Szabo, and Puddy describe a tool suite that allows embedded systems developers to analyze and predict the performances of the designed system from the early development phases.

Section 3: Industry Perspective and Applications

The third section of the book includes chapters that look at embedded systems on one hand from the point of view of the applications and on the other hand from the point of view of industries involved in the field.

In Chapter 13, "Industrial Applications of Emulation Techniques for the Early Evaluation of Secure Low-Power Embedded Systems," Druml, Menghin, Steger, Krieg, Genser, Haid, Bock, and Grinschgl build on the results presented in Chapter 5 and apply them to evaluate and verify designs of contactless smart cards.

In Chapter 14, "Dynamically Reconfigurable Embedded Architectures for Safe Transportation Systems," Harb, Niar, and Saghir show how the features of modern FPGAs, and in particular Dynamic Partial Reconfiguration, can be leveraged to tailor the functions offered by a Driver Assistant System (DAS) according to different situations, for example to increase the accuracy of obstacle tracking algorithms when the density of obstacles increases (e.g., during rush hour).

In Chapter 15, "Embedded Virtualization Techniques for Automotive Infotainment Applications," Violante, Macario, and Campagna study the features of several virtualization technologies that are available for the embedded systems domain; with particular reference to the automotive domain, where they can be used to build infotainment systems that include functions requiring different OSs. The chapter shows the benefits and drawbacks of each possible solution.

In Chapter 16, "Studying Individualized Transit Indicators using a New Low-Cost Information System," Castillo, Fernández-Ares, Garcíia-Fernández, Garcia-Sánchez, Arena, mora, Rivas, Asensio, Romero, and Merelo describe the realization of a low-cost embedded system that exploits the Bluetooth devices that are available on modern cars to track the passages of vehicles at specific locations around a region; the system has been deployed around the city of Granada, and the chapter describes some statistics retrieved through it.

In Chapter 17, "Mission Critical Embedded System Development Process: An Industry Perspective," Genolini and Crippa summarize their experiences gained in several decades of work on development of embedded systems; they outline key critical aspects and offer some lessons learned.

In Chapter 18, "Framework-Based Debugging for Embedded Systems," Tanyeri, Messiter and Beckett illustrate, through the use of an industrial tool suite, a modular and open approach to the problem of debugging embedded systems that rely on several different OSs and platforms; the approach hides the details of the underlying hardware and operating system, thus facilitating the debugging activities of the development team.

In Chapter 19, "Industrial Experiments in IMS, ATC, and SDR projects of Property Verification Techniques," Gaudin explores the issues concerning the verification, in an industrial setting, of properties of interest of a system under development; in particular, it outlines the application of verification techniques to several industrial case studies.

CONCLUSION

In conclusion, this book is interesting for current and future embedded systems designers and developers. It covers a wide spectrum of issues related to embedded systems design ranging from high-level methodologies, software development techniques, and hardware implementation on execution platforms. The book not only summarizes current results in the design of embedded systems, but, also sheds light on the future of such systems , towards so-called cyber-physical systems. The book can thus provides insight on current practices, related issues, and their solutions, and how these solutions are giving rise to the next evolutionary trend for embedded systems design.

Alessandra Bagnato
Softeam R&D, France

Leandro Soares Indrusiak
University of York, UK

Imran Rafiq Quadri
Softeam R&D, France

Matteo Rossi
Politecnico di Milano, Italy

REFERENCES

AUTOSAR. (2014). *AUTOSAR specifications 4.1*. Available from http://www.autosar.org/index.php?p=3&up=0&uup=0&uuup=0

East-ADL Association. (2014). *East-ADL Specifications*. Available from http://www.east-adl.info/Specification.html

Gajski & Kuhn. (1983). Guest editor introduction: New VLSI-tools. *IEEE Computer, 16*(12), 11–14.

International Technology Roadmap for Semiconductors. (2001). *2011 edition*. Retrieved from http://public.itrs.net/

Lee, K., et al. (2006). Low-power network-on-chip for high-performance SoC design. *IEEE Transactions on VLSI Systems, 14*(2). Cai & Gajski. (2003). Transaction level modeling: An overview. In *Proceedings of Int. Conference on HW/SW Codesign and System Synthesis* (CODES-ISSS), (pp. 19-24). CODES-ISSS.

Mernik, et al. (2005). When and how to develop domain-specific languages. *ACM Computing Surveys, 37*(4), 316–344.

Object Management Group (OMG). (2011a). *Unified modeling language 2.4.1*. Available from http://www.omg.org/spec/UML

Object Management Group (OMG). (2011b). *UML MARTE profile 1.1*. Available from http://www.omg.org/spec/MARTE/1.1/

Object Management Group (OMG). (2012). System modeling language specification v1.3. Available: http://www.omg.org/spec/SysML/1.3/

Selic. (2003). The pragmatics of model-driven development. *IEEE Software, 20*(5), 19–25.

Sendall & Kozaczynski. (2003). Model transformation: The heart and soul of model-driven software development. *IEEE Software, 20*(5), 42–45.

Acknowledgment

The research presented in this book is partially funded by the European Community's Seventh Framework Program (FP7/2007-2013) under grant agreement no. 248864 (MADES), grant agreement no. 248821 (ENOSYS), and by the PRESTO project (ARTEMIS-2010-1-269362), which is co-funded by the European Commission under the ARTEMIS Joint Undertaking Programme.

Alessandra Bagnato
Softeam R&D, France

Leandro Soares Indrusiak
University of York, UK

Imran Rafiq Quadri
Softeam R&D, France

Matteo Rossi
Politecnico di Milano, Italy

Section 1
Research Perspective: Software and Hardware Design

Chapter 1

Collaborative Development of Dependable Cyber–Physical Systems by Co–Modeling and Co–Simulation

John Fitzgerald
Newcastle University, UK

Ken Pierce
Newcastle University, UK

Peter Gorm Larsen
Aarhus University, Denmark

ABSTRACT

The pace of innovation in Cyber-Physical Systems (CPSs) drives the need for multi-disciplinary methods and tools to support rapid and accurate assessment of design alternatives. In this chapter, the authors describe collaborative models (co-models) that link Discrete-Event (DE) models of control software with Continuous-Time (CT) models of controlled plant. They present methods and tools for co-modeling using VDM as the DE formalism, and bond graphs on the CT side, using the Crescendo platform to link existing simulators (Overture for VDM and 20-sim for bond graphs). The authors discuss the exploitation of co-models within the design flow, including their use with SysML, and the roles of Software-in the-Loop and Hardware-in-the-Loop simulation on the way to realising co-models in cyber and physical media. The authors identify research challenges in providing sufficient model fidelity and the evidence needed to support the engineering of certifiably dependable systems.

1. INTRODUCTION

Cyber-Physical Systems (CPSs) are groups of collaborating computational elements controlling physical entities (Rajkumar, Lee, Sha, & Stankovic, 2010; Lee, 2010). They present exciting opportunities for innovative product development, with examples ranging from body-area networks for medical monitoring to "smart" power grids and transport networks. Enabled by advances in

DOI: 10.4018/978-1-4666-6194-3.ch001

mobile and wireless networking, as well as by rapid improvements in processor capability and power consumption, the pace of innovation in both the market for and the technology of CPSs mean that multi-disciplinary methods and tools are needed to support rapid but accurate exploration of design alternatives.

Although there is great potential in CPS technology, the challenges facing developers are also significant (Marwedel, 2010; Broy, Cengarle, & Geisberger, 2012). The presence of multiple distributed, mobile and heterogeneous components, and the need to accommodate change and reconfiguration, make it difficult to demonstrate the levels of dependability required in many applications. CPSs will typically interact with other systems and human beings, so that they may be considered as Systems of Systems (SoS) involving a wide range of stakeholders and engineering disciplines in their design and operation. For example, development of a CPS for rail transport management might require collaboration between control engineers, mechanical engineers, power transmission specialists and software developers.

Model-based design is increasingly recognised as a way to master complexity and support the collaboration of engineering teams (France & Rumpe, 2007). For the development of CPSs, the greatest challenge lies in bridging the gaps between the distinct computational models underpinning the disciplines involved (Henzinger & Sifakis, 2007). Although model-based methods and tools require formal foundations in order to support consistent analysis, models must nevertheless be accessible to engineering practitioners and domain experts, be capable of integration with established techniques and processes (Woodcock, Larsen, Bicarregui, & Fitzgerald, 2009), and support multiple views covering different system facets.

The challenge that we address in our work is that of creating methods and tools to support multi-disciplinary (and hence multi-paradigm) model-based development. In this chapter, we focus on the development and use of *collaborative models (co-models)* linking discrete-event (DE) models of control software with continuous-time (CT) models of controlled plant. The focus will be on *embedded control systems* in which a cyber (computing hardware plus software) controller interacts with a physical plant. We first illustrate the construction of co-models and co-simulation for embedded control systems using technology developed in the DESTECS[1] project described by Broenink el al. (2010). This combines VDM as the DE formalism (Fitzgerald, Larsen, Mukherjee, Plat, & Verhoef, 2005) with bond graphs as the CT formalism (van Amerongen, 2010). Using the approach proposed by Fitzgerald, Larsen, Pierce, Verhoef, & Wolff (2010), we show how models developed in these two diverse formalisms have been linked within the open tools platform *Crescendo* which supports co-simulation. We introduce methodological aspects of co-model construction (Fitzgerald, Larsen, Pierce, & Verhoef, 2013), and the use of co-models in "design space exploration" (DSE).

This chapter continues with a discussion of the background in co-modeling and co-simulation (Section 2). We then introduce basic concepts, terms and alternative co-simulation approaches (Sections 3.1-3.3) and, using a line-following robot as an example (Section 3.4), show the elements of a VDM/20-sim co-model and co-simulation using Crescendo. Drawing on several industrial applications of co-modeling using Crescendo (Section 3.5), we discuss the integration of co-modeling into established development processes (Section 4), and the steps needed to move from embedded control systems towards fully fledged cyber-physical systems (Section 5). Finally we briefly discuss the prospects for the collaborative model-based approaches presented in the chapter (Section 6). Full details of the methods and tools developed in DESTECS and implemented in Crescendo are provided in a forthcoming text (Fitzgerald, Larsen, & Verhoef, in press).

2. BACKGROUND

In this section, we briefly survey some of the leading approaches to co-modeling embodied in contemporary tools, and then introduce the DE and CT modeling formalisms that we bring together in our approach.

Approaches to Heterogeneous Modeling

In order to realise the potential of model-based methods in the successful development of CPSs, it is essential to provide the means to encompass models expressed in semantically distinct formalisms. Hardebolle and Boulanger (2009) identify several approaches to heterogeneous modeling. These include: translating models between formalisms; composing modeling languages to create a new composed language; composing models themselves; composing modeling tools; and providing a unifying semantics. It is instructive to compare contemporary methods and tools against this scheme.

A *hybrid system* is a dynamic system that exhibits both continuous and discrete dynamic behaviour (Alur et al., 1995). The term is often (wrongly) used interchangeably with *embedded system* or *cyber-physical system*. Hybrid systems are often described using transition systems that lend themselves to model checking, the major challenge here being to have a meaningful notion of time progression that can align with simulation of CT elements so that there is reasonable fidelity to the physical phenomena being modelled. A hybrid system can be described by means of a hybrid automaton consisting of a finite automaton with continuous dynamics. Each discrete state includes initial conditions for time and values of the continuous state, differential equations that describe the flow of the continuous state, and invariants that describe regions of the continuous state-space where the system stays at the discrete state. The modeling of hybrid systems has also

been investigated using UML, for example in the work on HybridUML described by Berkenkötter, Bisanz, Hannemann, & Peleska (2004), introducing structure diagrams similar in some respects to the Internal Block Diagrams subsequently introduced in SysML, and providing for multiple views over a model. Hybrid systems approaches tend to fall into the "composition of modeling languages" category. Here the combination of continuous and discrete time in the models is typically carried out in an ad-hoc manner. However, if a modeling problem fits the constraints of a specific approach, it is generally very efficient.

Modelica[2] (Fritzson & Engelson, 1998) is a non-proprietary, object-oriented, equation-based language intended to model complex physical systems. Both commercial and free Modelica simulation environments exist. The Modelica Association is a non-profit organisation with members from Europe, U.S.A. and Canada. Since 1996, its simulation experts have been working to develop an open standard and an open source standard library. Modelica has a comprehensive collection of components in its libraries, including components that enable the simulation of delays in network components. The DE modeling primitives lie closer to the abstraction level found in programming languages than the DE formalism we present in this chapter.

Ptolemy[3] (Eker et al., 2003; Bae, Öleczky, Feng, & Tripakis, 2009) has studied modeling, simulation and design of concurrent, real-time embedded systems, using a mixture of models of computation using an actor-oriented modeling approach. Ptolemy takes a "composition of models" approach in that it permits coherent coupling of heterogeneous models. The models are organised into hierarchical layers, where each layer has one Model of Computation (MoC). To our knowledge, Ptolemy is the approach which supports the widest range of MoCs.

Matlab/Simulink[4] created by MathWorks is one of the most widely used tools for creating CT models. Matlab is a modeling language and interactive environment which lets the user create models more rapidly than is the case using traditional programming languages. Simulink is an environment for multi-domain simulation and model-based design for dynamic and embedded systems. It provides an interactive graphical environment and a customisable set of block libraries which let the user design, simulate, implement, and test a variety of time-varying systems, including communications, controls, signal processing, video processing, and image processing.

TrueTime is an extension of Matlab/Simulink that enables to study detailed timing models of computer-controlled systems (Cervin, Henriksson, Lincoln, Eker, & Arzen, 2003). This enables both timing delays for both the computing node and the network communications between them in a network control systems setting.

In our work, we aim to enable CT and DE experts to collaborate while being able to use established notations and tools that are familiar to them and are regarded as natural for their work. In Hardebolle and Boulanger's terms, we are not composing modeling languages or models, but our work is based on "joint use of modeling tools", with a "unifying semantics" – in our case an operational semantics – that describes the interaction between DE and CT simulators participating in a co-simulation.

Discrete-Event Baseline Modeling Language

The *Crescendo* tool supports co-modeling using VDM as the DE formalism supported by the model construction and simulation capabilities in the open-source Overture[5] (Larsen et al., 2010). VDM is a model-oriented formal technique that supports the construction of models based on abstract data types, constants, functions, operations and additional integrity constraints such as invariants, pre- and post-conditions (Bjørner & Jones, 1978). The ISO-standard VDM-SL notation

(Fitzgerald & Larsen, 2009) has been extended to allow the description of object-orientation and concurrency (Fitzgerald et al., 2005) and the specification of distributed and embedded systems (Verhoef, Larsen, & Hooman, 2006).

VDM has been used in a series of industry applications from experimental (Larsen, Fitzgerald, & Brookes, 1996) to full-scale commercial use, including the firmware of the Felica Near-Field-Communication chip used for mobile secure payment transactions (Kurita, Chiba, & Nakatsugawa, 2008). The VDM modeling language allows software deployment architectures to be modelled, which permits the assessment of the impact of a given deployment on overall performance and timing (Fitzgerald, Larsen, Tjell, & Verhoef, 2007).

To give a flavour of the modeling language, the following extracts present some snippets of a VDM model that controls a line following robot. The example is explained in more detail in Section 3.4. The first extract shows the definition of an enumerated type, called ModeID. The values of this type are restricted to the seven listed. The angle brackets define quote types, which can only be compared for equality. Note also that VDM specifications are divided into sections that indicate the kinds of definitions that will appear. As shown in this example, types must be defined in a section preceded by the keyword types:

```
types
public ModeID = <Wait> | <Calibrate>
| <FindLine> | <Follow> |
<LostLine> | <Idle> | <FollowSingle>
```

In addition to enumerated and quote types, VDM also provides other basic types, including various numerical types and the Boolean type; and compound types, including sets, sequences, maps, and record types with named entries. Types may also be *restricted* using an invariant; in the following example, a type called Percent is defined to be a real number, but restricted to the range (-1,1):

-- restricted to (-1,1)
public Percent = real
inv p == -1 <= p and p <= 1;

Top-level specifications in VDM consist of classes that contain various definitions. In addition to types, classes may define a state (in the form of one or more *instance variables*) and operations that modify that state. In the following example, a partial definition for a class called Abstract-Controller is given. This class has a mode that determines how it operates. The state comprises two parts: a mapping from ModeID (introduced above) to objects of the class Mode (not shown) recording all possible modes of the controller; and a single ModeID indicating the current mode.

An operation is shown that changes the current mode by updating the mode instance variable; the mode is changed to the value of the parameter, m. The operation does not return a value, indicated by the empty parentheses in the signature. Note that before the mode is updated, the Exit operation (defined in the Mode class) is called on the current mode. This operation allows the current mode to perform any final actions before the mode changes. The operation has a pre-condition that requires that the mode is in the domain of the mapping, which ensures that mode is updated to a known mode:

```
class AbstractController
instance variables
-- current mode and map of all possible modes
protected modes: map ModeID to Mode;
protected mode: ModeID;
operations
public ChangeMode: ModeID ==> ()
ChangeMode(m) == (
-- call exit on the current mode
modes(mode).Exit();
-- change mode
mode:= m;
...
)
pre m insetdom modes;
end AbstractController
```

In addition to the assignment and operation call statements shown in the example above, VDM supports many other statements that will be familiar from other languages, including conditional statements and looping constructs. Classes may also define values (constants), functions and threading and synchronisation constructs in other sections (not shown here). Classes may be instantiated as objects using the *new* keyword. Note that in these examples the keywords *public* and *protected* allow their associated definitions to be available to all other classes and to only subclasses, respectively. Additionally, the *private* keyword can restrict a definition to only the defining class (the default visibility for a definition is private).

Continuous-Time Baseline Modeling Language

The *Crescendo* tool supports co-modeling using bond graphs on the CT side, supported by the commercial 20-sim[6] (Kleijn, 2006) tool. The tool offers a graphical interface for building models from blocks (also called *submodels*). Blocks may define one or more input or output ports that allow them to be connected to other blocks, thus forming more complicated models. Blocks may be built from scratch by the modeller, or imported from the large, open source library of domain specific sub-models available for mechanical, pneumatic, hydraulic and electrical components. The 20-sim simulator automatically converts these blocks into differential equations that are handled by a numerical solver. Furthermore, 20-sim offers a 3D mechanics editor in which a virtual mock-up is created that can be directly coupled to the simulation model, which provides powerful visualisation capabilities.

To demonstrate how a typical 20-sim model might look, Figure 1 shows the top-level model for a small, two-wheeled robot with two infrared (IR) sensors on the front. This example is explained in more detail in Section 3.4. The model has a block representing the body of the robot, which internally is modelled as a mass with a

Figure 1. CT model of R2G2P plant

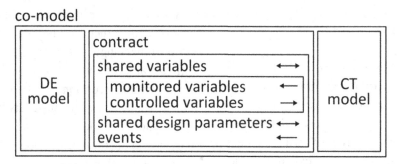

position and rotation. Blocks representing the wheels, rotational encoder and servo motors are connected to the main body block; these models specify how the body should be moved in space (by altering the translation and rotation). At the bottom of the model, a block representing the controller is included, which sends signals to the servos (to move the body) and receives feedback from the encoders and IR sensors (seen at the top of the model).

Blocks in 20-sim may be implemented in several ways. First, they may contain further graphical models, allowing for a hierarchy of submodels to be created. Alternatively, blocks may contain (textual) equations expressed using a language called SIDOPS+. Finally, blocks may be implemented using bond graphs.

Bond graphs offer a domain-independent description of a physical system's dynamics, realised as a directed graph. The vertices of these graphs are idealised descriptions of physical phenomena, with their edges (*bonds*) describing energy exchange between vertices. The energy exchanged is the product of *effort* and *flow*, which map to different concepts in different domains, for example voltage and current in the electrical domain.

Bonds are bi-directional, meaning that connecting two bond graph blocks affects them both. Therefore there are two types of connection in a 20-sim model: bonds, and simple connections called signals. In Figure 1, for example, the connections to the controller are all signal-level

(solid arrowhead) and are used to send data to and from the sensor and actuator blocks (IR sensors and encoders, and the servos). The connections between the servos, encoders, wheels and body are bonds (note the distinctive one-sided arrowhead) because these blocks are modelled internally using bond graphs.

By connecting two elements with a bond, they can affect each other. For example, the rotational inertia of the body in Figure 1 will affect the wheels. The causality between bond graph elements is calculated automatically, meaning bond graph models are compositional. While Newton's equations of motion could be captured using equation blocks to model the robot, if additional blocks are added, each block must be connected together and the equations updated manually to take account of the new element. For bond graphs this process is automatic and therefore a good choice for modeling physical processes.

3. CO-MODELING AND CO-SIMULATION IN CRESCENDO

The collaborative development of an embedded control system requires productive interaction between engineers from very different backgrounds. Control engineering and software engineering have matured over many decades, each with its own philosophy, methods and terminology, and so it is necessary to clarify the common ideas that underpin co-modeling and co-simulation. This section introduces the Crescendo concepts and technology, including the ideas of models, co-models, and co-simulation. In order to put the collaborative modeling approach in context, it also describes the possibility of aligning co-modeling and co-simulation with existing practice.

Basic Concepts: Co-Models and Co-Simulation

For our purposes a *system* is a group of interacting or interdependent items forming a coherent whole, and a *model* is an abstract description of reality or a putative system (van Amerongen, 2010). The act of creating models is called *modeling*. A system model may contain representations of the system's internal elements, the entities in its environment and the stimuli that they generate. A model should not be unnecessarily complex, but it should describe all of the important properties of the system with sufficient accuracy to serve its declared purpose, and this in turn implies that "a clear purpose is the single most important ingredient for a successful modeling study." (Sterman, 2000, p. 89). The main purpose of models in our approach is to permit analysis of system properties at an early development stage, in particular allowing the selection of optimal designs, or the elimination of infeasible ones. Models may be analysed by inspection or by formal mathematical analysis. Many models are also *executable* in that they may be performed as a sequence of instructions on a computer; such an execution is termed a *simulation* because the behaviour exhibited is intended to simulate that of the system of interest. A *design parameter* is a property of a model that affects the model's behaviour but which remains constant during a given simulation. A *variable* is part of a model that may change during a given simulation.

Our approach focuses on multi-disciplinary system models that are composed of a DE model (typically of a controller) and a CT model (typically

of controlled plant). The DE and CT models are referred to as *constituent models*; the combined model is termed a *co-model*. Interaction between the DE and CT models is achieved by executing them simultaneously and allowing information to be shared between them. This is termed a *co-simulation*. In a co-simulation, *a shared variable* is a variable that appears in and can be accessed from both the DE and CT models. Design parameters that are common to both models are called *shared design parameters*. An *event* is an action that is initiated in the one model that leads to an action in another model. Events can be scheduled to occur at a specific time (time events) or can occur in response to a change in a model (state events). State events are described with *predicates* (Boolean expressions), where the changing of the local value of the predicate during a co-simulation triggers the event. In our approach, events are referred to by name and can be propagated from the CT model to the DE model within a co-model during co-simulation.

Shared variables, shared design parameters, and events define the nature of the communication between models. These elements are recorded in an interface *contract*. We use a fairly simple form of contract, but the approach could be extended to encompass more elaborate contracts as in Derler, Lee, Torngren, and Tripakis (2013). Only one constituent model (either the DE model or the CT model) may have write access to a shared variable. Shared variables written by the DE constituent model are called *controlled variables* and those written to the by the CT constituent model are termed *monitored variables* (Figure 2). A co-model thus comprises a DE model, a CT model and a contract. Note that a co-model is itself a model and that a co-simulation can therefore be described succinctly as simulation of a co-model.

Co-simulation requires a reconciled operational semantics for the cooperating simulation tools from different domains. The operational semantics are given by Coleman, Lausdahl, & Larsen (2012). Figure 3 gives an outline view of the synchronisa-

Figure 2. A co-model contains a DE model, contract, and CT model

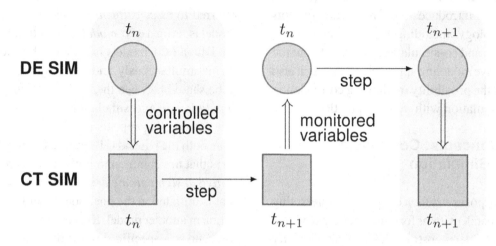

Figure 3. Outline synchronisation scheme for co-simulation

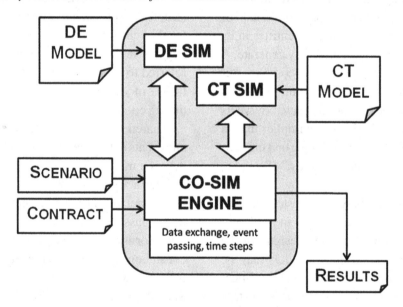

tion scheme underlying co-simulation between a DE simulation of a controller (top) and a CT simulation of the plant (bottom). Each simulator maintains its own local state and internal simulation time, but the co-simulation engine explicitly synchronises the shared variables, events and the simulation time in the linked simulators. At the start of a co-simulation step, the two simulators have a common simulation time. The granularity of the synchronisation time step is always determined by the DE simulator. The scheme does not require

resource-intensive roll-back of the simulation state in either of the simulator, though roll-back may occur inside the CT simulator in order to catch the precise time requested.

At the start of a co-simulation step (t_n in Figure 3), the DE controller simulation sets the controlled variables, and proposes a duration by which the CT simulation should, if possible, advance. The co-simulation engine communicates this to the CT simulator. The CT simulator then tries to advance its simulation time. If an event occurs before the proposed step time is reached, the CT simulator stops early so that the DE simulator can be notified of the event. Once the CT simulator has paused (reaching internal time t_{n+1}), the monitored variables and the actual time reached in the CT simulation are communicated back to the DE simulator. The DE simulation then advances so that both DE and CT are again synchronised at the same simulation time.

Co-modeling and co-simulation open up the possibility of exploring the space of designs with computing and physical elements as a single space, rather than as separate activities. We use the term *design space exploration (DSE)* to refer to an activity undertaken by one or more engineers in which they build and evaluate co-models in order to reach a design from a set of requirements.

Related Co-Simulation Approaches

A distinctive feature of our approach to co-simulation is the stress on decoupling the semantics of the separate tools, in contrast to using unified hybrid models such as those underpinning interchange formats (Sonntag, Schiffelers, van Beek, Rooda, & Engell, 2009). Our priority has been to deliver robust tools for co-simulation, rather than to provide a new co-simulation semantics. However, it is worth taking account of the considerable interest in the technology of co-simulation (Carloni, Passerone, Pinto, & Sangiovanni-Vincentelli, 2006). A discussion of related co-simulation methods can be found in Coleman, Lausdahl and Larsen (2012), so we here identify other relevant approaches for interested reader.

Perhaps the work most closely related to ours is the general framework of Nicolescu et al., for which semantics (for the co-simulation part) are given by Gheorghe, Bouchhima, Nicolescu, and Boucheneb (2006, 2007) and Gheorghe (2009), implemented over the simulation tools Simulink and SystemC (Nicolescu, Bouchhima, & Gheorghe, 2006).

Work on hybrid systems has the potential to provide an underlying semantic framework for co-simulation (Henzinger, 1996; Tudoret, Nadjm-Tehrani, Benveniste, & Strömberg, 2000; Lee and Zheng, 2005). The Ptolemy framework introduced in Section 2.1 above addresses heterogeneous modeling (Liu, Liu, Eker, & Lee, 2003; Lee and Zheng, 2007; Lee and Seshia, 2011), and has been compared with our work in Wolff, Pierce and Derler (2013). ModHel'X[7] is inspired by Ptolemy, but with component interface specification reminiscent of our approach. A co-simulation of the hybrid process algebra, Chi, and Simulink models has been described by van Beek, Hofkamp, Reniers, Rooda, and Schiffelers (2007). Although the baseline formalisms differ, the basic approach to co-simulation is similar to ours in allowing the DE simulation to advance and then allow the CT part is allowed to simulate over the same interval.

Crescendo: Tool Support for Co-Modeling and Co-Simulation

One of the principal objectives of Crescendo is to allow DE and CT engineers to develop their respective models using the tools most suited to the relevant formalisms, yet supporting collaborative analysis through co-simulation. Thus the DE models are developed using Overture and the CT models using 20-sim, with Crescendo providing the co-model management, defining shared variables and design parameters. Figure 4 shows the architecture of the Crescendo co-simulator. The Crescendo tool acts as a master simulator, managing timing across the two simulators (Overture and 20-sim), following the coordination scheme described above. It also maintains the sharing of design parameters, variables and the handling of events defined in the contract. To predict a system's behaviour using a co-model, it is often desirable to try out a number of *scenarios*, in which certain aspects are varied, including the setup of the modelled system, simulated user inputs and faulty

Figure 4. Co-simulator architecture

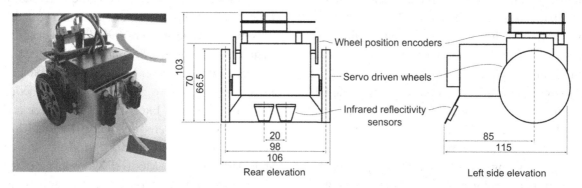

behaviours. Scenarios are realised through two mechanisms: co-model settings and scripts. Co-simulation settings include selection of alternative components from within the co-model, setting of design parameters, and various tool settings such as co-simulation duration and choice of integration method. A *script* may influence a co-simulation during execution by changing selected values in the co-model. Scripts can be used for fault activation and for mimicking, or triggering models of, user inputs.

We use the term a*utomated co-model analysis* (ACA) to refer to the facilities that support design space exploration in Crescendo. Ranges of values for co-model settings can be defined, with the tool then running co-simulations for each combination of these settings. Results are stored for each simulation and can be analysed afterwards. One way to analyse these results is to define a ranking function that assigns a value to each design based upon its ability to meet the requirements defined by an engineer. After the co-simulation runs are complete, the ranking function can be applied to the test results.

Example Co-Model and Design Space Exploration

We have introduced the basic theory of co-modeling and co-simulation. Let us briefly consider how this looks in practice using a small example based on a simple two-wheeled robot (Pierce, Gamble,

Ni, & Broenink, 2012) equipped with sensors that are able to detect variations in the light reflected by the surface on which the robot moves. The wheels are driven by a pair of continuous rotation servos that allow both their direction and speed to be set and maintained (Figure 5). We will illustrate the co-modeling and co-simulation of the robot with a controller designed to permit the robot to follow a black line printed on the surface[8].

The CT model describes the physical robot and its behaviour. Recall that the top-level structure, as modelled in 20-sim, was shown in Figure 1. The body submodel is shown in Figure 6. In this bond graph, the "MTF" node at the centre represents the mass of the body. The wheel left and wheel right inputs may cause a rotation or translation of the body, which are computed in the "Theta" and "Position" blocks respectively. These rotation and translation elements can be connected to a 3D visualisation, allowing the movement of the robot model to be seen intuitively.

Below we show an extract from the contract, indicating some of the shared design parameters (SDP), monitored and controlled variables. Design parameters include the robot's wheel radius and the exact positioning of the infrared sensors with respect to the centre of the robot's body. These parameters would remain fixed for a given co-simulation run, but we may wish to vary them across multiple runs, for example in order to determine the sensor configuration that delivers the most accurate or most energy-efficient performance. We

Figure 5. The R2-G2P line following robot

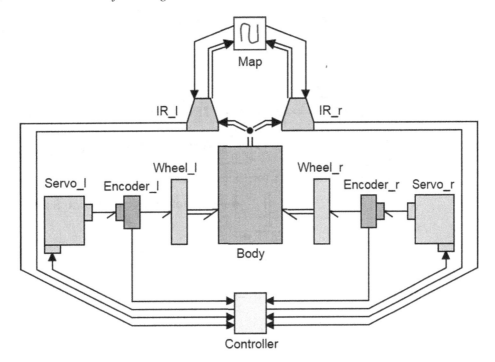

could even trade off several design parameters, looking at the effect of wheel radius on optimal sensor positioning, for example. The monitored and controlled variables record the data read and written by the DE controller model.

```
-- shared design parameters
sdp real wheel_radius;
sdp real line_follow_x; -- x offset
of line follow sensor
sdp real line_follow_y; -- y offset
of line follow sensor
-- encoders
monitored real encoder_left; -- position
 of left wheel
monitored real encoder_right; -- position
of right wheel
-- line-following sensors
monitored real lf_left; -- left line
sensor reading
monitored real lf_right; -- right line
sensor reading
-- servos
```

```
controlled real servo_left; -- setting of
left wheel servo
controlled real servo_right; -- setting of right
wheel servo
```

The controller is multi-modal. Modes are required for calibration of the sensors, and for handling specified defects. For example, a failure of one line sensor leads to a special single-sensor mode; failure of both sensors moves the controller to an idle state. The DE controller model uses object-oriented structuring features from VDM, allowing us to utilise common patterns such as those defined by Gamma, Helm, Johnson, & Vlissides (1995). Here we use a structure based on the state pattern. An abstract modal controller class defines a state variable that contains the current mode and a mapping from the names of all modes to subclasses that describe the functionality for that particular mode. Each mode offers entry and exit methods and the top-level control loop checks for and performs model changes when required. An extract from the abstract modal controller follows.

Figure 6. Bond graph model of R2G2P robot body

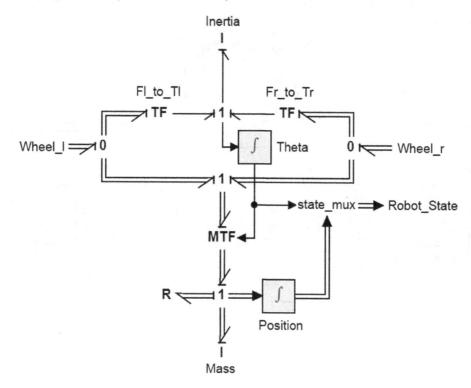

```
types
public ModeID = <Wait> | <Cali-
brate> | <FindLine> | <Follow> |
<LostLine> | <Idle> | <FollowSingle>
instance variables
-- current mode and map of all possible modes
protected mode: Mode;
protected modes: map ModeID to Mode;
operations
-- main control loop
public Step: () ==> ()
Step() == (
if init then (
-- initial mode
modes(mode).Enter();
init:= false
);
-- check if a mode change is needed
let m = CheckModeChange() in
if m <>nilthen ChangeMode(m);
-- delegate output to current mode
-- change mode if it requests
```

```
let m = modes(mode).Step() in
if m <>nilthen ChangeMode(m);
);
-- change mode
public ChangeMode: Mode ==> ()
ChangeMode(m) == (
-- call exit on the current mode
modes(mode).Exit();
-- change mode
mode:= m;
-- call entry on new mode
modes(mode).Enter();
)
pre m insetdom modes;
```

For example, the <Follow> mode offers simple step functionality whereby the monitored variables are checked and cause a course adjustment by invoking left or right turn functionality. The variable con refers to the abstract controller described above.

```
-- control loop
public Step: () ==>
[AbstractModalController`Mode]
Step() == (
-- black to the right, go right
if con.GetLeftBW().IsWhite() and
con.GetRightBW().IsBlack()
then con.TurnRight();
-- black to the left, go left
if con.GetLeftBW().IsBlack() and
con.GetRightBW().IsWhite()
then con.TurnLeft();
-- no internal mode change
return nil;
);
```

The ability to describe multiple controller modalities is particularly significant in dealing with error detection and recovery. DE modeling languages such as VDM lend themselves more naturally to this than CT notations such as those of 20-sim; this is one of the prime motivations for collaborative modeling and co-simulation in the first place. The mode change decision logic is in the CheckModeChange operation. For example:

```
public CheckModeChange: () ==> [Mode]
CheckModeChange() == (
...
-- once the line is found, start following
if mode = <FindLine> and modes(mode).Done()
then return <Follow>;
-- once the line is lost, stop the robot
if mode = <LostLine> and modes(mode).Done()
then return <Idle>;
-- failure in one sensor
if (mode = <Follow> or mode = <LostLine>) and
(GetLeftLF().HasFailed() or Get-
RightLF().HasFailed())
then return <FollowSingle>;
...
);
```

In order to describe the real-time properties of the controller within the DE model, we define a "system" class that sets up the DE-side versions of the shared variables and explicitly models the deployment of the controller process to a CPU with specified scheduling strategy and capacity in terms of instructions per second. In this case we assume a fixed priority scheduler offering one million instructions per second. An extract follows:

```
system System
instance variables
-- sensors
public static encLeft: Encoder:= new Encoder();
public static encRight: Encoder:= new Encoder();
public static lfLeft: IRSensor:= new IRSensor();
public static lfRight: IRSensor:= new IRSensor();
-- actuators
public static velLeft: SpeedServo:= new
SpeedServo();
public static velRight: SpeedServo:= new
SpeedServo();
-- controller
public static controller: [AbstractController]:= nil;
-- cpu
cpu: CPU:= new CPU(<FP>, 1E6)
operations
public System: () ==> System
System() ==
(
controller:= new Controller();
-- deployment
cpu.deploy(controller);
cpu.deploy(lfLeft);
cpu.deploy(lfRight);
cpu.deploy(encLeft);
cpu.deploy(encRight);
cpu.deploy(velLeft);
cpu.deploy(velRight)
)
end System
```

Figure 7 shows the search space of an ACA on this example, in this case exploring only the behaviour of one line-following controller design with a range of physical sensor positions – varying the x and y offsets among the shared design parameters defined in the interface contract above.

Figure 7. An automated co-model analysis over R2G2P

		Longitudinal sensor offset		
		0.01m	0.07m	0.13m
Lateral sensor offset	0.01m	(a)	(b)	(c)
	0.03m	(d)	(e)	(f)
	0.05m	(g)	(h)	(i)

Experience Applying Crescendo

In the DESTECS project, co-modeling methods and tools were applied experimentally on three substantial industrial case studies and a larger group of smaller-scale applications. Chess Embedded Technology[9] in the Netherlands developed a personal transporter, similar to the famous Segway, with one controller for each wheel and a distributed safety monitor.

Verhaert[10] has developed a scale model of a dredging excavator with operator assistance, capable of digging trenches with perfectly level bottoms. Neopost[11] produced models of a new document inserting system that folds stacks of documents and inserts them into envelopes, fully automatically and at high speed. Analysis of fault resilience was the prime focus point for all these case studies. Details of the case studies can be found in a DESTECS report (Verhoef et al., 2012).

The tools and methodology were additionally exposed to challenge problems obtained from an industrial interest group. Crisplant[12] used Crescendo to explore the behaviour of packets on their tilting conveyor belt system. Terma[13] produced models of a weapons countermeasure flare dispensing system for military aircraft. For the European Space Agency, an existing CT model of a planetary rover was adapted to allow combinations of specific rover movements ("gaits") to be described and studied, which was previously infeasible.

The seven case studies demonstrated that co-simulation is a valuable tool to support the multi-disciplinary design dialogue, starting from the conceptual stages of the product development. We have used 20-sim and VDM-RT in Crescendo, but the Crescendo tool has an open architecture and a well-defined semantics that is essentially technology-agnostic. Any tool with a semantics that is compatible with the Crescendo co-simulation engine can be used. For example, we have demonstrated within the project that MATLAB/Simulink can be used instead of 20-sim (Kleijn & Visser, 2012). Nevertheless, Crescendo is not a "silver bullet": simulation speed is rarely going to be as fast as a user wants, and simulation does not provide complete answers, as the state space of the model is not exhaustively covered.

The case studies demonstrated that it is possible to create models that are both abstract and competent. These models remain lightweight and compact, giving us the ability to play "what-if" scenarios at relatively low cost. The insight gained by these simple experiments rapidly raises confidence in the models because design decisions are continuously validated. Implicit choices and hidden assumptions are exposed, which replaces "gut feelings" by credible, objective and quantitative information that now can be assessed by all designers involved. This typically gives direction, depth and momentum to the design effort because the potential of certain designs and the likelihood and impact of potential risks can be determined very fast and without large upfront investments. Last but not least, the models are not produced in vain, as they can either form the basis for more advanced verification studies or as a reference for the implementation phase of development.

Practical experience with a range of case studies has allowed us to develop a set of methods to accompany co-modeling and co-simulation tools. These include approaches to co-model construction (Fitzgerald et al., 2013). For example, we may begin "DE-first", starting with models of the DE side using discrete approximations of the CT elements, before replacing these with higher fidelity CT models in 20-sim. A "CT-first" process begins from the model of the physical elements, using CT "stubs" for digital elements, replacing these with more expressive DE models at a later stage. Finally, one may begin with the interface contract, developing both sides around an initial division of responsibilities. Which process is correct for a given project depends on the characteristics of the development problem and of the available skills in the development team. For example, a project with relatively simple physics but sophisticated multi-moded control with a need for digital fault tolerance would lend itself to a DE-first approach.

In DESTECS, we were able to develop a methodology for co-modeling and co-simulation, including initial patterns for building and structuring co-models, and in particular dependability-related features such as the modeling of faults and fault-tolerance mechanisms, as well as providing guidance in other methodological areas such as ensuring consistency between constituent models. The Crescendo tool enabled co-simulation and design space exploration to a certain degree, and we validated the approach in several industry case studies. Nevertheless, there remain several

important areas in which further work is required in going from co-models "in the small" to co-models of cyber-physical systems "in the large". We concentrate here on two: the place of co-modeling in the wider product development process, and the scaling of the approach from embedded to cyber-physical systems. We discuss these in Sections 4 and 5 respectively.

4. CO-MODELING AND CO-SIMULATION IN THE DESIGN FLOW

We have discussed co-modeling and co-simulation based on single DE models of controllers coupled with single CT models of controlled plant and environment, but this is only of practical value if it can be successfully integrated with the core activities of system development. There are many well-established standards that identify these activities, including ISO/IEC and IEEE standards 15288 (IEEE, 2008a) and 12207 (IEEE, 2008b), the ECSS standards ECSS-E-40 on Space Software (ECSS, 2009a) and ECSS-Q-80 on Space Software Product Assurance (ECSS, 2009b), and the Rational Unified Process (RUP) (Rational Software Corporation, 1998).

The standards mentioned above typically identify activities including requirements definition, requirements analysis, architectural design, detailed design, implementation/integration, operation and maintenance. We would expect to see applications of collaborative modeling and co-simulation in several of these areas. Defining the stakeholder requirements involves the development of representative use cases that help to elicit requirements that may not have been explicitly stated. Co-models and co-simulation can help subsequent analysis and maintenance of stakeholder requirements to identify areas of ambiguity or incompleteness, and the communication back to the stakeholders of these deficiencies. A collaborative model allows system elements to be expressed in the most appropriate formalism and this in turn may make the model easier to communicate to stakeholders. In requirements analysis a representation of a technical system (for example, a co-model) that meets the requirements is built. Here we expect co-models to be valuable in considering alternative boundaries and functions. IEEE 15288 states that "System requirements depend heavily on abstract representations of proposed system characteristics and may employ multiple modeling techniques and perspectives to give a sufficiently complete description of the desired system requirements" (IEEE 15288, Clause 6.4.2.3). Architectural design involves the allocation of responsibilities to units in a solution architecture. Alternative design solutions, expressed as co-models, can form the basis of trade-off and risk analyses. In detailed design, the constituent models of the selected co-model can then be used to explore the detailed design of the chosen solution and co-simulation used to test the evolving design.

Although co-modeling has considerable potential to benefit the activities discussed above, several factors need to be considered before embarking on co-model construction. First, it is essential to have an explicitly defined *purpose* of the co-model, since the purpose governs the key abstraction decisions and sets the requirements for the model's competence. Second, having a structural description of the system is an advantage in selecting a modeling approach (DE-/CT- or contract-first) because it gives an indication of where complexity and development risk lie. Such system structural models are often expressed using notations such as UML and SysML. We focus on the latter here, and consider how SysML can be used upstream of detailed co-modeling to help define the structure and content of co-models themselves.

SysML (Friedenthal & Moore, 2008) is an extension to UML defined and maintained by the Object Management Group with the International Council on Systems Engineering (INCOSE). SysML is widely used in industry to manage and

track requirements, link test cases to requirements, decompose systems into more manageable components and allocate requirements to the responsible system components. A similar integration between SysML and Simulink has also been made in Palachi, Cohen, and Takashi (2013).

The purpose of the model can be described using natural language or at a high-level with use cases. Once the purpose has been explicitly articulated, requirements can be expressed using SysML requirements diagrams. As an example, consider the line-following robot described above. Suppose that it must be tolerant to several possible failures: excessive ambient light that hinders the ability to determine black from white; noise introduced by the analogue-to-digital (A/D) conversion process; and broken sensors that simply return a constant value. Figure 8 shows how these three fault management requirements are expressed in a SysML requirements diagram.

Once the model purpose and requirements have been determined, the system must be decomposed into its main parts. A block definition diagram (BDD) can be used to show the elements of the system that is to be developed and its environment. To add levels of detail, an internal block diagram (IBD) can be made for each of the main parts of the system. In these diagrams, the child blocks, their interfaces and interconnections are described using SysML ports. An IBD of the robot and its environment is shown in Figure 9. The robot's body is connected to two wheels and two motors. The motors, along with two encoders and two infrared sensors, are connected to a controller. In this diagram, the line being followed is the only relevant element of the robot's environment.

The controller's ports correspond to the data passed between the DE and CT sides of the co-model, and so this IBD can be used for systematic (even automatic) generation of the co-model contract.

SysML permits the definition of blocks defining constraints on a system. In this case, we create a separate BDD defining the constraints on the

Figure 8. SysML requirements diagram describing the required faulty scenarios

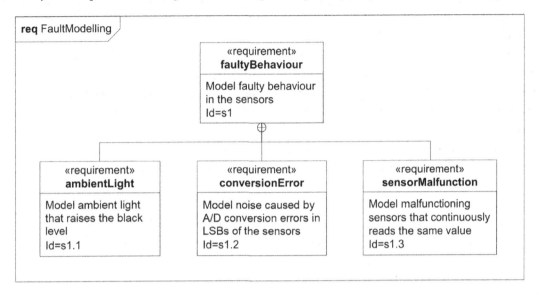

Figure 9. SysML internal block diagram (IBD) of the robot and its environment

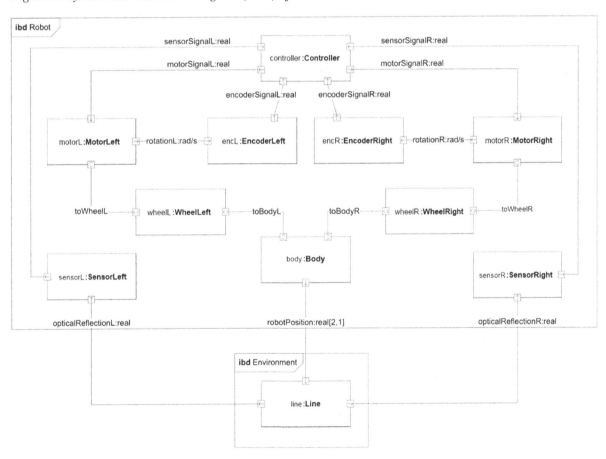

physical system and these will therefore apply to the CT model. This diagram can be seen in Figure 10, showing the constraints on the forces acting on the robot body. Such constraints can also be used to identify critical performance parameters.

The BDD in Figure 10 does not show relationships between the constraints; these can be shown in a parametric diagram. Parametric diagrams show how the constraint block parameters are bound to value properties of a parent block, its parts, or the parameters of other constraints. A parametric diagram for the line-following robot is shown in Figure 11. It demonstrates the causal relationships between the constraints defined in Figure 10, showing how the total force acting on the robot's body is a result of the forces generated by the motors on the left and right sides. Such causal relationships are calculated automatically by 20-sim; parametric diagrams like this could be used to check such calculations, or to gener-

ate causal information for tools connected to the co-simulation engine that cannot automatically generate it.

A suite of SysML models developed in the way described here can be of considerable value in determining both the interface contract and the constraints to be embedded in the CT model, easing the transition from informally expressed requirements to a functioning co-model, and providing traceability through the process.

5. FROM EMBEDDED TO CYBER-PHYSICAL SYSTEMS

We have so far looked at co-simulation "in the small" as a means of exploring the design space for systems that are most appropriately described in terms of both discrete and continuous elements. As we move from single embedded systems to CPSs,

Figure 10. SysML block definition diagram (BDD) describing the physical constraints on the robot

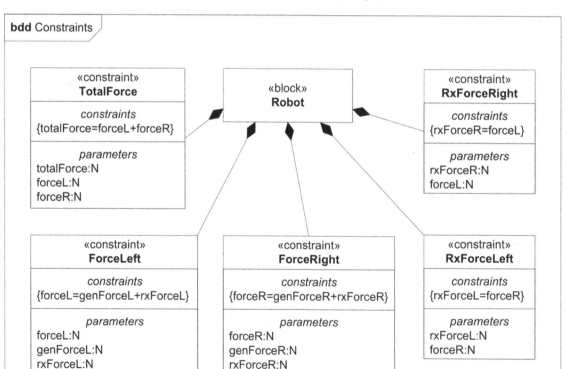

Figure 11. SysML parametric diagram describing the relationships between the physical constraints of the robot

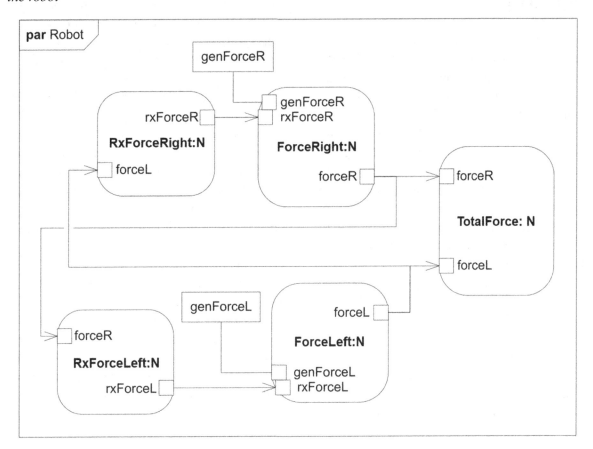

the need arises to describe and analyse multiple networked cyber elements interacting with each other and with a physical environment. The DE and CT elements in CPSs may be independently owned and managed, and reliance may be placed on both their emergent collective and individual behaviours. The development of a CPS is likely to be as much about integration of existing systems as about ab initio design. Further, guidance is needed in determining whether a model's fidelity is sufficient for its purpose. Can co-modeling and co-simulation help us to explore the emergent behaviour of these larger-scale networked CPSs?

As stakeholders come to depend on the services provided by CPSs, it becomes important to consider the production of evidence sufficient to justify reliance being placed upon them. The broad concept of using an assessment of criticality to moderate the level of assurance and evidence required is well-established in some domains. Today, the creation of such evidence is typically based on the final realisations of devices and software, and on documentation of the development process, and not on the results of model-based development activities. For destructive tests (in which the physical devices may be damaged) in particular, it would be a substantial advantage if some analysis could be carried out on models rather than implementation. If the models represented reality with sufficient fidelity, such an approach could be a major cost saver in industries where assurance of CPS behaviour is needed (Jackson, 2009).

Supporting Realisation: Model Fidelity

The (co-)models developed and analysed during the design of a CPS need to be managed in such a way that a large and complex design space can readily be explored at each stage from requirements to code.

Figure 12 illustrates the role of co-modeling and co-simulation in such a process. Alongside co-modeling, Software-in-the-Loop (SiL) and Hardware-in-the-Loop (HiL) simulations enable a gradual transition of DE or CT elements from models to their realisations. In order for this to work, co-models not only require competence, but also fidelity. On the DE side, refinement theories provide a formal basis for relating models to one other. However, on the CT side such notions are not well-established and CT models will always be approximations of real-world behaviour for any non-trivial system. So the challenge here is to determine when a model is sufficiently close to the corresponding realisation to permit the use of simulation results as evidence needed for assurance.

We can envision SysML being used to construct requirements and architecture models for a CPS. Requirements diagrams link requirements to CPS elements and provide a basis for demonstrating traceability. The composition of a CPS from constituent elements can be described using BDDs and IBDs. At the lowest level, each of these can be represented either as DE or as CT elements. Thus it should be possible to derive automatically the contracts that link the constituents together, yielding information that can be used in simulations. Developers need to be able to move gradually from models to their realisations. DE elements are typically realised as source code and to automate this process, it is necessary to have code generation support. CT elements are typically represented as physical devices interacting with the environment. In order to be able to use co-simulation as a source of assurance evidence, the fidelity of the models must be sufficient to provide confidence in global properties. In the future it may be possible to partly automate the realisation of prototypes of physical elements using 3D printers, but it is not realistic to be able to fully automate the transition from CT models to their final realisations.

Figure 12. CPS design flow from requirements to realisations

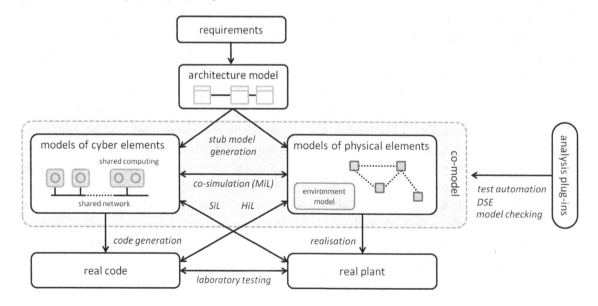

Combining Collections of DE and CT Models

Combining collections of DE models into a single DE model, or collections of CT models into a single CT model, is conceptually straightforward if the topology of components can statically be determined. However, for many CPSs the topology is likely to evolve dynamically, for example in models of smart transportation, further increasing the complexity of the modeling task. In order to properly describe dynamic evolution, the BDDs and IBDs currently offered by SysML are insufficient, because they cannot describe dynamic behaviour. One solution would to introduce a new type of 'dynamic evolution' diagram to SysML however this would likely increase the complexity of models significantly. Therefore adding such diagrams would only be worth the increased effort if the level of assurance required merited it.

In order to support dynamic evolving topologies at the modeling level it is necessary to be able to express dynamic reconfiguration in the modeling language (Nielsen, 2010; Mazzara & Bhattacharyya, 2010). The handling of time in CPSs is absolutely essential (Lee, 2009, 2010; Eidson, Lee, Matic, Seshia, & Zou, 2012; Broman, Derler, & Eidson, 2013). CPSs demand that timing is a correctness criterion and not just a quality factor. Hence time, mobility and dynamic topologies would all be essential elements of a reconciled operational semantics for co-simulation of CPSs.

Opening Co-Simulation

In general, CPSs involve cyber elements interacting not only with a full range of physical behaviours (electrical, mechanical, hydraulic, for example), but with people. If we wish to model the effects of a particular control system in a public transport network, for example, it may be necessary to include agent-based models of human behaviour within a co-simulation (Bonabeau, 2002; Schirner, Erdogmus, Chowdhury, & Padir, 2013), or stochastic descriptions of such behaviours. This potential

for a wide range of constituent model types means that co-simulation platforms like Crescendo need to be both open and extensible.

One option for more open co-modeling than is currently available in Crescendo would be to utilise the platform-independent Functional Mock-up Interface (FMI[14]) (Blochwitz et al., 2012) to create tool-specific Functional Mock-up Units (FMUs) that can be used in heterogeneous co-simulation. FMI comes with two flavours: FMI for Model Exchange (FMI-ME) and FMI for Co-simulation (FMI-Co). FMI-ME provides a mathematical description of a model. FMI-Co additionally includes a numerical solver to allow a co-simulation.

CPSs are in general distributed and in many cases they form an SoS where different stakeholders have responsibility of the individual constituent systems. European research projects such as COMPASS[15] and DANSE[16] are developing modeling and validation methods for such SoSs in the discrete domain.

Research Challenges

The research challenges for CPSs are a subject of current debate (Lee, 2008; Lee & Seshia, 2011; Broy et al., 2012). Domain-specific analyses have been by Gupta, Mukherjee, Varsamopoulos, and Banerjee (2011) on energy-sustainable CPSs and by Lee et al. (2012) on medical applications. There are many open research challenges in the field, including:

- **Modeling CPSs:** We have chosen specific formalisms for modeling DE and CT constituent elements, but there are many other potential candidates each with limitations and advantages. Methodical steps for engineering of CPSs are important (Jensen, Chang, & Lee, 2011).
- **Verifying CPSs:** We have chosen to focus on simulation based techniques for creating evidence about the properties of CPSs, but there are techniques available includ-

ing theorem proving. The question of whether full verification will ever be possible for fully fledged CPSs is an open one. Wan, Hughes, Man, and Krilavičius (2010) elaborate the challenges of ensuring compositionality of analysis results for CPSs. Magureanu, Gavrilescu, and Pescaru (2013) attempt to verify CPSs from a purely DE perspective whereas others, such as Sanwal and Hasan (2013), focus on the CT elements. For the latter, the scalability of the approach is still uncertain.

- **Demonstrating Robustness of CPSs:** DESTECS developed patterns and guidelines for fault-tolerance in embedded systems, but there are many other aspects of dependability that also need exploring in CPSs. Sztipanovits et al. (2012) aim to address challenges of dependable integration in part by automating the synthesis of the schedulers for the software components using constraint solving techniques with assumptions of the uncertainties of timing of the tasks and the communication. Miclea and Sanislav (2011) provide general considerations about how to increase the dependability of CPSs.

- **Achieving Security in CPSs:** Security aspects of CPSs have received only limited attention from the model-based engineering community, but the more critical personalised applications that are developed, the more significant security aspects become. Wan and Alagar (2011) attempt to address CPS security issues by considering trust levels in a service-oriented setting.

- **Achieving Safety in CPSs:** CPSs are typically more open than a traditional safety-critical system and this has significant consequences for the construction of the safety cases required by regulators. Trapp, Schneider, and Liggesmeyer (2013) have proposed a roadmap for CPS safety incorporating run-time features to cope with open and adaptive systems. Banerjee,

Venkatasubramanian, Mukherjee, & Gupta (2012) consider both security and safety with a focus on context awareness.

6. CONCLUDING REMARKS

We have described the concept of collaborative modeling and co-simulation between discrete-event and continuous-time systems, and shown how this can be applied to the design of embedded systems. The viability of the approach has been confirmed using independent modeling and simulation environments for VDM and bond graphs, harnessed together by the Crescendo tool. We have given a brief example of the approach applied to co-modeling of a line-following robot, but the methods and tools have been employed in several industry pilot studies.

We have argued that the kind of collaborative working supported by Crescendo could be extended to allow the early-stage modeling and analysis of cyber-physical systems (CPS). We see CPSs as having some of the characteristics of "Systems of Systems" (SoSs) as well as the close coupling of computing and physical domains exhibited in embedded products.

Rather than see long debates about whether a system is really "cyber-physical" or not, we prefer to concentrate on support for "cyber-physical thinking" during product development. This is characterised by the ability to readily trade off concerns across the boundary between the computing and physical, human or other elements of the system. Exercising cyber-physical thinking on products of modern scale and complexity entails having semantically well-founded support for the integration of a wide range of models, not just those of control software and the environment. Providing sound methods and robust tools to support such thinking has enormous potential benefit in systems development and engineering, from theories up to the provision of libraries of pragmatic patterns for models, system architectures and verification.

ACKNOWLEDGMENT

The work reported here was carried out under the EU Framework 7 projects DESTECS and COMPASS. The work of Fitzgerald and Pierce is additionally supported by the UK EPSRC Platform Grant on Trustworthy Ambient Systems. We are particularly grateful to our collaborators in these projects, especially Carl Gamble, who contributed substantially to the R2-G2P robot pilot study, Sune Wolff who prepared the SysML models, and Marcel Verhoef for many helpful discussions on the content of this paper.

REFERENCES

Alur, R., Courcoubetis, C., Halbwachs, N., Henzinger, T. A., Ho, P.-H., & Nicollin, X. et al. (1995). The algorithmic analysis of hybrid systems. *Theoretical Computer Science*, *138*, 3–34. doi:10.1016/0304-3975(94)00202-T

Bae, K., Öleczky, P. C., Feng, T. H., & Tripakis, S. (2009). Verifying Ptolemy II Discrete-Event Models Using Real-Time Maude. In *Proceedings of the 11th International Conference on Formal Engineering Methods: Formal Methods and Software Engineering* (ICFEM'09) (LNCS) (vol. 5885, pp. 717-736). Rio de Janeiro, Brazil: Springer.

Banerjee, A., Venkatasubramanian, K. K., Mukherjee, T., & Gupta, S. K. S. (2012). Ensuring Safety, Security, and Sustainability of Mission-Critical Cyber–Physical Systems. *Proceedings of the IEEE*, *100*(1), 283–299. doi:10.1109/JPROC.2011.2165689

Berkenkötter, K., Bisanz, S., Hannemann, U., & Peleska, J. (2004). SoftSpez Final Report. In Executable HybridUML and Its Application to Train Control Systems (LNCS) (vol. 3147, pp. 145-173). Berlin: Springer.

Bjørner, D., & Jones, C.B. (1978). *The Vienna Development Method: The Meta-Language* (LNCS) Vol. 61). Berlin: Springer-Verlag.

Blochwitz, T., Otter, T., Akesson, J., Arnold, M., Clauß, C., & Elmqvist, H., … Viel, A. (2012). Functional Mockup Interface 2.0: The Standard for Tool independent Exchange of Simulation Models. In *Proceedings of the 9th International Modelica Conference*. Academic Press.

Bonabeau, E. (2002). Agent-based modeling: Methods and techniques for simulating human systems. *Proceedings of the National Academy of Sciences of the United States of America*, *99*(Suppl 3), 7280–7287. doi:10.1073/pnas.082080899 PMID:12011407

Broenink, J. F., Kleijn, C., Larsen, P. G., Jovanovic, D., Verhoef, M., & Pierce, K. (2010). Design support and tooling for dependable embedded control software. In *Proceedings of the 2nd International Workshop on Software Engineering for Resilient Systems*. ACM.

Broman, D., Derler, P., & Eidson, J. (2013). Temporal Issues in Cyber-Physical Systems. *Journal of the Indian Institute of Science*.

Broy, M., Cengarle, M. V., & Geisberger, E. (2012). Cyber-Physical Systems: Imminent Challenges. In *Proceedings of the Monterey Workshop 2012* (LNCS) (vol. 7539, pp. 1–28). Berlin: Springer.

Carloni, L., Passerone, R., Pinto, A., & Sangiovanni-Vincentelli, A. (2006). Languages and tools for hybrid systems design. *Foundations and Trends in Design Automation*, *1*(1), 1–204. doi:10.1561/1000000001

Cervin, A., Henriksson, D., Lincoln, B., Eker, J., & Arzen, K. (2003). How does control timing affect performance? Analysis and simulation of timing using Jitterbug and TrueTime. *Control Systems, IEEE*, *23*(3), 16–30. doi:10.1109/MCS.2003.1200240

Coleman, J.W., Lausdahl, K.G., & Larsen, P.G. (2012). *Co-simulation Semantics, DESTECS Project Deliverable D3.4b*. Retrieved from http://www.destecs.org/

Derler, P., Lee, E. A., Torngren, M., & Tripakis, S. (2013). Cyber-Physical System Design Contracts. In *Proceedings of ICCPS '13: ACM/IEEE 4th International Conference on Cyber-Physical Systems*. ACM/IEEE.

ECSS. (2009a). *Std ECSS-E-ST-40C Space engineering—Software*. ECSS.

ECSS. (2009b). *Std ECSS-Q-ST-80C Space product assurance—Software product assurance*. ECSS.

Eidson, J. C., Lee, E. A., Matic, S., Seshia, S. A., & Zou, J. (2012). Distributed Real-Time Software for Cyber–Physical Systems. *Proceedings of the IEEE, 100*(1), 45–59. doi:10.1109/JPROC.2011.2161237

Eker, J., Janneck, J. W., Lee, E. A., Liu, J., & Liu, X. … Xiong, Y. (2003). Taming Heterogeneity – the Ptolemy Approach. *Proceedings of the IEEE, 91*(1), 127-144.

Fitzgerald, J., Larsen, P. G., Pierce, K., Verhoef, M., & Wolff, S. (2010). Collaborative Modeling and Co-simulation in the Development of Dependable Embedded Systems. In D. Méry & S. Merz (Eds.), Integrated Formal Methods 2010 (LNCS) (vol. 6396, pp. 12-26). Nancy, France: Springer.

Fitzgerald, J. S., & Larsen, P. G. (2009). *Modeling Systems - Practical Tools and Techniques in Software Development* (2nd ed.). Cambridge University Press. doi:10.1017/CBO9780511626975

Fitzgerald, J. S., Larsen, P. G., Mukherjee, P., Plat, N., & Verhoef, M. (2005). *Validated Designs for Object-oriented Systems*. Springer.

Fitzgerald, J. S., Larsen, P. G., Pierce, K., & Verhoef, M. (2013). A Formal Approach to Collaborative Modeling and Co-simulation for Embedded Systems. *Mathematical Structures in Computer Science, 23*(4), 726–750. doi:10.1017/S0960129512000242

Fitzgerald, J. S., Larsen, P. G., Tjell, S., & Verhoef, M. (2007). *Validation Support for Distributed Real-Time Embedded Systems in VDM++*. Paper presented at the High Assurance System Engineering Symposium. Dallas, TX.

Fitzgerald, J. S., Larsen, P. G., & Verhoef, M. (Eds.). (in press). *Collaborative Design for Embedded and Cyber-Physical Systems*. Springer.

France, R., & Rumpe, B. (2007). Model-driven Development of Complex Software: A Research Roadmap. In *Proceedings of Future of Software Engineering (FOSE'07)*. IEEE.

Friedenthal, R. S., & Moore, A. (2008). *A Practical Guide to SysML*. Morgan Kaufman OMG Press.

Fritzson, P., & Engelson, V. (1998). Modelica - A Unified Object-Oriented Language for System Modeling and Simulation. In *Proceedings of the 12th European Conference on Object-Oriented Programming*, (pp. 67-90). Springer.

Gamma, E., Helm, R., Johnson, R., & Vlissides, J. (1995). *Design Patterns. Elements of Reusable Object-Oriented Software*. Addison-Wesley Publishing Company.

Gheorghe, L. (2009). *Continuous/Discrete Co-simulation interfaces from formalization to implementation*. (PhD thesis). University of Montreal, Montreal, Canada.

Gheorghe, L., Bouchhima, F., Nicolescu, G., & Boucheneb, H. (2006). Formal definitions of simulation interfaces in a continuous/discrete cosimulation tool. In *Proceedings of the Seventeenth IEEE International Workshop on Rapid System Prototyping*, (pp. 186–192). IEEE Computer Society.

Gheorghe, L., Bouchhima, F., Nicolescu, G., & Boucheneb, H. (2007). A formalization of global simulation models for continuous/discrete systems. In Proceedings of SCSC'07, (pp. 559–566). SCSC.

Gupta, S. K. S., Mukherjee, T., Varsamopoulos, G., & Banerjee, A. (2011). Research directions in energy-sustainable cyber–physical systems. *Sustainable Computing: Informatics and Systems, 1*(1), 57–74.

Hardebolle, C., & Boulanger, F. (2009). Exploring Multi-Paradigm Modeling Techniques. *Simulation, 85*(11-12), 688–708. doi:10.1177/0037549709105240

Henzinger, T. (1996). The theory of hybrid automata. In *Proceedings of the 11th Annual Symposium on Logic in Computer Science (LICS)*, (pp. 278–292). IEEE Computer Society Press.

Henzinger, T., & Sifakis, J. (2007). The Discipline of Embedded Systems Design. *IEEE Computer, 40*(10), 32–40. doi:10.1109/MC.2007.364

IEEE. (2008a). *International Standard ISO/IEC 15288:2008(E), IEEE Std 15288-2008 (Revision of IEEE Std 15288-2004) Systems and software engineering — System life cycle processes*. ISO/IEC and IEEE Computer Society.

IEEE. (2008b). *International Standard ISO/IEC 12207:2008(E), IEEE Std 12207-2008 (Revision of IEEE/EIA 12207.0-1996) Systems and software engineering — Software life cycle processes*. ISO/IEC and IEEE Computer Society.

Jackson, D. (2009, April). A direct path to dependable software. *Communications of the ACM, 52*(4), 78–88. doi:10.1145/1498765.1498787

Jensen, J. C., Chang, D. H., & Lee, E. A. (2011). A model-based design methodology for cyber-physical systems. In *Proceedings of Wireless Communications and Mobile Computing Conference (IWCMC)*, (pp. 1666-1671). IWCMC.

Kleijn, C. (2006). Modeling and Simulation of Fluid Power Systems with 20-sim. *Intl. Journal of Fluid Power, 7*(3).

Kleijn, C., & Visser, P. (2012). Extension to MATLAB/Simulink. *DESTECS Project Deliverable D3.5*. Retrieved from http://www.destecs.org/

Kurita, T., Chiba, M., & Nakatsugawa, Y. (2008). Application of a Formal Specification Language in the Development of the "Mobile FeliCa" IC Chip Firmware for Embedding in Mobile Phone. In Proceedings of Formal Methods (LNCS) (pp. 425-429). Berlin: Springer-Verlag.

Larsen, P. G., Battle, N., Ferreira, M., Fitzgerald, J. S., Lausdahl, K. G., & Verhoef, M. (2010). The Overture Initiative - Integrating Tools for VDM. *ACM SIGSOFT Softw. Eng. Notes, 35*(1), 1. doi:10.1145/1668862.1668864

Larsen, P.G., Fitzgerald, J.S., & Brookes, T (1996). Applying Formal Specification in Industry. *IEEE Software, 13*(3), 48 – 56.

Lee, E. A. (2008). *Cyber physical systems: Design challenges* (Tech. Rep. UCB/EECS-2008-8). EECS Department, University of California, Berkeley.

Lee, E. A. (2009). Computing needs time. *Communications of the ACM, 52*(5), 70–79. doi:10.1145/1506409.1506426

Lee, E. A. (2010). CPS foundations. In *Proceedings of the 47th Design Automation Conference (DAC '10)*. ACM.

Lee, E. A., & Seshia, S. (2011). Introduction to Embedded Systems: A Cyber-Physical Systems Approach. Academic Press.

Lee, E. A., & Zheng, H. (2005). Operational semantics of hybrid systems. In Hybrid Systems: Computation and Control (HSCC), (LNCS) (vol. 3414, pp. 25–53). Berlin: Springer-Verlag.

Lee, E. A., & Zheng, H. (2007). Leveraging Synchronous Language Principles for Heterogeneous Modeling and Design of Embedded Systems. In *Proceedings of EMSOFT '07*. ACM.

Lee, I., Sokolsky, O., Chen, S., Hatcliff, J., Jee, E., & Kim, B. … Venkatasubramanian, K.K. (2012). Challenges and Research Directions in Medical Cyber–Physical Systems. *Proceedings of the IEEE, 100*(1), 75-90.

Liu, X., Liu, J., Eker, J., & Lee, E. A. (2003). Heterogeneous modeling and design of control systems. In *Software-Enabled Control: Information Technology for Dynamical Systems*. IEEE Press. doi:10.1002/047172288X.ch7

Magureanu, G., Gavrilescu, M., & Pescaru, D. (2013). Validation of static properties in unified modeling language models for cyber physical systems. *Journal of Zhejiang University Science C, 14*(5), 332–346. doi:10.1631/jzus.C1200263

Marwedel, P. (2010). *Embedded System Design -- Embedded Systems Foundations of Cyber-Physical Systems*. Springer.

Mazzara, M., & Bhattacharyya, A. (2010). On Modeling and Analysis of Dynamic Reconfiguration of Dependable Real-Time Systems. In *Proceedings Third International Conference on Dependability* (DEPEND 2010), (pp. 173–181). DEPEND.

Miclea, L., & Sanislav, T. (2011). About dependability in cyber-physical systems. In *Proceedings of Design & Test Symposium (EWDTS)*, (pp. 17-21). EWDTS.

Nicolescu, G., Bouchhima, F., & Gheorghe, L. (2006). CODIS – A Framework for Continuous/Discrete Systems Co-Simulation. In C. G. Cassandras, A. Giua, C. Seatzu, & J. Zaytoon (Eds.), *Analysis and Design of Hybrid Systems* (pp. 274–275). Elsevier. doi:10.1016/B978-008044613-4.50051-3

Nielsen, C. B. (2010). *Dynamic Reconfiguration of Distributed Systems in VDM-RT*. (Master's thesis). Aarhus University.

Palachi, E., Cohen, C., & Takashi, S. (2013). Simulation of cyber physical models using SysML and numerical solvers. In *Proceedings of Systems Conference (SysCon)*, (pp. 671-675). IEEE.

Pierce, K., Gamble, C., Ni, Y., & Broenink, J. F. (2012). Collaborative Modeling and Co-simulation with DESTECS: A Pilot Study, In *Proceedings IEEE 21st International Workshop on Enabling Technologies: Infrastructure for Collaborative Enterprises (WETICE)*, (pp. 280—285). IEEE.

Rajkumar, R., Lee, I., Sha, L., & Stankovic, J. (2010). Cyber-physical systems: the next computing revolution. In *Proceedings of the 47th Design Automation Conference* (DAC '10). ACM.

Rational Software Corporation. (1998). *Rational Unified Process - Best Practices for Software Development Teams*. IBM.

Sanwal, M.U., & Hasan, O. (2013). Formal Verification of Cyber-Physical Systems: Coping with Continuous Elements. *ICCSA,* (1), 358-371.

Schirner, G., Erdogmus, D., Chowdhury, K., & Padir, T. (2013). The Future of Human-in-the-Loop Cyber-Physical Systems. *IEEE Computer, 46*(1), 36–45. doi:10.1109/MC.2013.31

Sonntag, C., Schiffelers, R. R. H., van Beek, D. A., Rooda, J. E., & Engell, S. (2009). Modeling and simulation using the compositional interchange format for hybrid systems. In *Proceedings of MATHMOD 2009 - 6th Vienna International Conference on Mathematical Modeling*, (pp. 640–650). MATHMOD.

Sterman, J. D. (2000). *Business Dynamics: Systems Thinking and Modeling for a Complex World*. Irwin Professional Pub.

Sztipanovits, J., Koutsoukos, X., Karsai, G., Kottenstette, N., Antsaklis, P., & Gupta, V., ... Wang S. (2012). Toward a Science of Cyber–Physical System Integration. *Proceedings of the IEEE, 100*(1), 29-44.

Trapp, M., Schneider, D., & Liggesmeyer, P. (2013). A Safety Roadmap to Cyber-Physical Systems. In J. Münch & K. Schmid (Eds.), Perspectives on the Future of Software Engineering, (pp. 81-94). Berlin: Springer.

Tudoret, S., Nadjm-Tehrani, S., Benveniste, A., & Strömberg, J.-E. (2000). Co-simulation of hybrid systems: Signal-simulink. In M. Joseph (Ed.), FTRTRT 2000 (LNCS) (pp. 134–151). Berlin: Springer-Verlag.

van Amerongen, J. (2010). *Dynamical Systems for Creative Technology*. Enschede, The Netherlands: Controllab Products.

van Beek, D. A., Hofkamp, A. T., Reniers, M. A., Rooda, J. E., & Schiffelers, R. R. H. (2007). Co-simulation of chi and Simulink models. In *Proceedings of the 6th EUROSIM Congress on Modeling and Simulation*. EUROSIM.

Verhoef, M., Bos, B., van Eijk, P., Remijnse, J., Visser, E., De Paepe, M., ... Van Lembergen, R. (2012). Industrial Case Studies – Final Report. *DESTECS Project Deliverable D4.3*. Retrieved from http://www.destecs.org/

Verhoef, M., Larsen, P. G., & Hooman, J. (2006). Modeling and Validating Distributed Embedded Real-Time Systems with VDM++. In *Proc. 14th Intl. Symposium on Formal Methods* (LNCS) (vol. 4085). Berlin: Springer-Verlag.

Wan, K., & Alagar, V. (2011). Dependable Context-Sensitive Services in Cyber Physical Systems. In *Proceedings of Trust, Security and Privacy in Computing and Communications* (TrustCom). IEEE.

Wan, K., Hughes, D., Man, K. L., & Krilavičius, T. (2010). Composition challenges and approaches for cyber physical systems. In *Proceedings of Networked Embedded Systems for Enterprise Applications* (NESEA). IEEE.

Wolff, S., Pierce, K. G., & Derler, P. (2013). *Multi-domain modeling in DESTECS and Ptolemy – a Tool Comparison* (Technical Report ECE-TR-15). Dept. of Engineering, Aarhus University.

Woodcock, J., Larsen, P. G., Bicarregui, J., & Fitzgerald, J. (2009). Formal Methods: Practice and Experience. *ACM Computing Surveys, 41*(4), 1–36. doi:10.1145/1592434.1592436

KEY TERMS AND DEFINITIONS

Co-Model: Collaborative models (co-models) are composed of a DE model of a controller, a CT model of a plant and a contract connecting them (see *Figure 2: A co-model contains a DE model, contract, and CT model*).

Contract: Shared variables, shared design parameters, and events define the nature of the communication between CT and DE models. These elements are recorded in a contract acting as the glue for the co-simulation engine.

Co-Simulation: Interaction between the DE and CT models is achieved by executing them simultaneously and allowing information to be shared between them. This is termed a co-simulation. In a co-simulation, a shared variable is a variable that appears in and can be accessed from both the DE and CT models. Design parameters that are common to both models are called shared design parameters.

Cyber-Physical System (CPS): A CPS is a system of collaborating computational elements controlling physical entities. Unlike more traditional embedded systems, a full-fledged CPS is typically designed as a network of interacting elements with physical input and output instead of as standalone devices.

Embedded Control System: This is a device, or set of devices, that manages, commands, directs or regulates the behaviour of one or more physical devices or other device(s) or system(s) mostly without human intervention.

ENDNOTES

[1] www.destecs.org

[2] www.modelica.org

[3] ptolemy.berkeley.edu/publications/index.htm

[4] www.mathworks.com

[5] www.overturetool.org

[6] www.20sim.com

[7] http://wwwdi.supelec.fr/software/Mod-HelX/

[8] Videos of the robot and the output of its co-simulation can be found on the DESTECS YouTube channel (www.youtube.com/user/DestecsVideos).

[9] www.chess.nl

[10] www.verhaert.com

[11] www.neopost.com

[12] www.crisplant.com

[13] www.terma.com

[14] www.fmi-standard.org

[15] www.compass-research.eu

[16] www.danse-ip.eu/home

Chapter 2
UML MARTE Time Model and Its Clock Constraint Specification Language

Frédéric Mallet
Université Nice Sophia Antipolis, I3S, UMR 7271, CNRS, INRIA, 06900 Sophia Antipolis, France

Julien Deantoni
Université Nice Sophia Antipolis, I3S, UMR 7271, CNRS, INRIA, 06900 Sophia Antipolis, France

Marie-Agnès Peraldi-Frati
Université Nice Sophia Antipolis, I3S, UMR 7271, CNRS, INRIA, 06900 Sophia Antipolis, France

Robert de Simone
INRIA Sophia Antipolis Méditerranée, 06900 Sophia Antipolis, France

ABSTRACT

The UML Profile for MARTE extends the UML with constructs dedicated to the modeling and analysis of real-time and embedded systems. Its time profile provides a rich model of time based on the notion of logical clocks that can be used consistently through all modeling elements/diagrams. The MARTE time profile comes with a companion language, called CCSL. CCSL is a formal declarative language used to handle the MARTE logical clocks and schedule the execution of the different parts of a model. This chapter gives a snapshot on modeling and analysis facilities that have been developed specifically around the time profile of MARTE and CCSL. A second objective is to show how MARTE can be combined with other profiles such as EAST-ADL. The last objective is the use of CCSL as a common language for specifying the semantics of models to allow their execution in a common framework. The MARTE and EAST-ADL constructs are illustrated on an example of a simplified cruise control. The example starts with a description of functional and timing requirements captured using a specific profile called EAST-ADL dedicated to the automotive domain. Then some of the requirements are refined with UML state machines and activities adorned with MARTE stereotypes. All these models rely on MARTE clocks. The semantics of these diagrams is given by a CCSL description that is automatically derived from the models. The resulting CCSL specification can be used to execute the UML/EAST-ADL specification, to animate the model, or to perform various kinds of analyses.

DOI: 10.4018/978-1-4666-6194-3.ch002

INTRODUCTION

The Unified Modeling Language (UML) (OMG, 2009b), and its SysML profile/variant have originally been conceived by recognizing and adopting common modeling concepts frequently used in practice for design: Components/structured classes for structural description, behavioral models for concurrent hierarchical finite state-machines, dataflow streaming diagrams, sequence and timing diagrams are well-known examples. Variants of such models were widely used in various forms before the advent of UML/SysML, which have then captured them as modeling artifacts. Still, despite their overall familiar look, most of these diagrams adopt distinct or unclear interpretations in their various forms, very often for good reasons (and some time for no reasons at all). This may lead to an incorrect or a context-dependent interpretation of a model and the impossibility to perform a strict verification. This point is a limitation for using plain UML in the domain of real-time and embedded systems. An even more important problem, in the case of real-time embedded systems, is the non-functional performance aspects. It soon appeared that extra specific annotations were needed to express the timing properties and constraints in a formal way, with appropriate syntax and expressivity. Time constraints could be used to define the precise timely semantics of a given profiled model, or the general description of a scheduling requirement setting, or the intrinsic time features of a given individual model.

MARTE 0, the dedicated UML profile for Modeling and Analysis of Real-Time Embedded systems and its Time Model (André et al., 2007) were specifically defined to serve this goal. They provide extensions for dealing with a multiform notion of Time, where local Logical Clocks may be completely, partially, or not inter-related at all. The central concern of scheduling can be then seen as the means to organize the ticks of these various clocks (of time threads) so as to respect provided constraints. This view (harmonizing local times provided by design into a consistent global

solution) is strongly indebted to the theory of synchronous/polychronous languages (Benveniste et al., 2003)0, and of Tag Systems (Edward & Sangiovanni-Vincentelli, 1998).

MARTE 0 provides also as an annex a candidate language for expressing the relevant constraints, called the Clock Constraint Specification Language (CCSL) (André, 2009). In a collection of articles (Goknil et al., 2013a) we have shown in the past how the CCSL language could represent many distinctive patterns used for the definition of timed semantics of domain-specific Architecture Description Languages (e.g., AADL or EAST-ADL) (Peraldi-Frati et al., 2012), or for prominent scheduling policies, or again for Timed Processes formal analysis tools (such as UppAal for Timed Automata) (Goknil et al., 2013b). We address here an example to show how the different pieces can be put together and how the logical clocks are used to bring consistency between the different parts of the models, captured with different complementary formalisms.

This chapter is structured into four sections. The first section gives the theoretical foundations of the MARTE Profile and its companion language CCSL, motivating the use of logical time and its inspirations from the theory of concurrency. The second section presents a cruise control system example. The third section is the main contribution where we combine UML, MARTE, EAST-ADL (EAST-EEA, 2004 & EAST_ADL Language Specification, 2013) and its timing extension TADL2 (Timing Augmented Description Language) (TIMMO-2-USE deliverable D11, 2012) to build a model for the example. Some methodological rules are given on a possible usage for MARTE in conjunction with a domain specific language for automotive systems. Section four is dedicated to the analysis and the interpretation of this composition of models and proposes to encode UML/MARTE and EAST-ADL /TADL2 with CCSL. CCSL and logical clocks are used to build links between those models, ensure the consistency of the different views and give an operational semantics to those models. Additionally, this section opens the discussion to more fundamental aspects related to the recently developed analysis capabilities. The last section gives an overview of some works related to this approach.

THE UML PROFILE FOR MARTE

Overview

The Unified Modeling Language (UML) is a general-purpose modeling language specified by the Object Management Group (OMG). It proposes graphical notations to represent all aspects of a system from the early requirements to the deployment of software components, including design and analysis phases, structural and behavioral aspects. As a general-purpose language, it does not focus on a specific domain and maintains a weak, informal semantics to widen its application field. However, when targeting a specific application domain and especially when building trustworthy software components or for critical systems where life may be at stake, it is absolutely required to extend the UML and attach a formal semantics to its model elements. The simplest and most efficient extension mechanism provided by the UML is through the definition of profiles. A UML profile adapts the UML to a specific domain by adding new concepts, modifying existing ones and defining a new visual representation for others. Each modification is done through the definition of annotations (called stereotypes) that introduce domain-specific terminology and provide additional semantics. However, the semantics of stereotypes must be compatible with the original semantics (if any) of the modified or extended concepts, *i.e.,* the base metaclass.

The UML profile for MARTE extends the UML with concepts related to the domain of real-time and embedded systems. It supersedes the UML profile for Schedulability, Performance and Time (SPT) that was extending the UML 1.x and that had limited capabilities. UML 2.0 has introduced a simple (or even simplistic) model of time and has proposed several new extensions that made SPT unusable.

MARTE has three parts: *Foundations*, *Design* and *Analysis*.

The *foundation* part is itself divided into five chapters: *CoreElements*, *NonFunctionalProperties* (NFP), *Time*, *Generic Resource Modeling* (GRM) and *Allocation*. *CoreElements* defines configurations and modes, which are key parameters for analysis. In real-time systems, preserving the non-functional (or extra-functional) properties (power consumption, area, financial cost, time budget...) is often as important as preserving the functional ones. The UML proposes no mechanism at all to deal with non-functional properties and relies on mere strings for that purpose. *NFP* (Non Functional Properties) offers mechanisms to describe the quantitative as well as the qualitative aspects of properties and to attach a unit and a dimension to quantities. It defines a set of predefined quantities, units and dimensions and supports customization. NFP comes with a companion language called VSL (Value Specification Language) that defines the concrete syntax to be used in expressions of non-functional properties. VSL also recommends syntax for user-defined properties. Time is often considered as an extra-functional property that comes as a mere annotation after the design. These annotations are fed into analysis tools that check the conformity without any actual impact on the functional model: *e.g.,* whether a deadline is met, whether the end-to-end latency is within the expected range. Sometimes, though, time can also be of a functional nature and has a direct impact on what is done and not only when it is done. All these aspects are addressed in the *time* chapter of MARTE. The next section elaborates on the time profile. The *GRM* (Generic Resource Modeling) chapter provides annotations to capture the available resources on which the applicative part shall be deployed. The allocation chapter gives a SysML-compatible way to make this deployment. In MARTE, we use the wording allocation since the UML deployment usually implies (in people's minds) a physical distribution of a software artifact onto a physical node. *Allocation* in MARTE goes further. It encompasses the physical distribution of software onto hardware, but also of tasks onto operating system processes, and, more importantly, it covers the temporal distribution (or scheduling) of operating parts that need to share a common resource (e.g., several tasks executing on a single core processor, several communications sharing a TDMA bus).

The *design* part has four chapters: *High Level application modeling*, *Generic component modeling*, *Software Resource Modeling*, and *Hardware Resource Modeling*. The first chapter describes real-time units and active objects. Active objects depart from passive ones by their ability to send spontaneous messages or signals, and react to event occurrences. Normal objects, the passive ones, can only answer to the messages they receive or react on event occurrences. The three other parts provide a support to describe resources used and in particular execution platforms on which applications may run. A generic description of resources is provided, including stereotypes to describe communication media, storages and computing resources. Then this generic model is refined to describe software and hardware resources along with their non-functional properties.

The *analysis* part also has a chapter that defines generic elements to perform model-driven analysis on real-time and embedded systems. This generic chapter is specialized to address schedulability analysis and performance analysis. The chapter on schedulability analysis is not specific to a given technique and addresses various formalisms like the classic and generalized Rate Monotonic Analysis (RMA), holistic techniques, or extended timed automata. This chapter provides all the keywords usually required for such analyses. Finally, the chapter on performance analysis, even if somewhat independent of a specific analysis technique, emphasizes on concepts supported by the queueing theory and its extensions.

MARTE extends the UML for real-time and embedded systems but should be refined by more specific profiles to address specific domains (avionics, automotive, silicon) or specific analysis techniques (simulation, schedulability, static analysis). The three examples addressed here consider different domains and/or different analysis techniques to motivate the demand for a fairly general time model that has justified the creation of the MARTE time subprofile.

We have briefly reviewed here the whole specification of MARTE. However, MARTE is not expected to be used as a whole on a single specification, as his usage chapter states. It is expected to be the base of several complementary methodologies that cover different aspects of a system. In this chapter, we have selected a subset of it that we combine with the EAST-ADL profile, dedicated to the specification of automotive applications, to show how we can treat them both in a consistent way through the notion of clock.

The Time Profile

Time in SPT is a *metric* time with implicit reference to physical time. As a successor of SPT, MARTE supports this model of time. UML2, issued after SPT, has introduced a model of time called *SimpleTime*. This model also makes implicit references to physical time, but it is too simple for use in real-time applications, and was initially devised to be extended in dedicated profiles.

MARTE goes beyond SPT and UML2. It adopts a more general time model suitable for system design. In MARTE, Time can be *physical*, and considered as continuous or discretized, but it can also be *logical*, and related to user-defined clocks. Time may even be multiform, allowing different times to progress in a non-uniform fashion, and possibly independently to any (direct) reference to physical time.

In MARTE, time is represented by a collection of *Clocks* (see Andre et al. (2007)). The word *Clock* comes from synchronous languages. They may be understood as a specific kind of events on which constraints (temporal, hence the name, but also logical ones) can be applied. Each clock specifies a totally ordered set of instants, *i.e.*, a sequence of event occurrences. There may be dependence relationships between the various occurrences of different events. Thus this model, called the MARTE time structure, is akin to Tagged Systems (Edward, & Sangiovanni-Vincentelli, 1998). To cover continuous and discrete times, the set of instants associated with a clock can either be dense or discrete. In this paper, most clocks are discrete (*i.e.*, they represent discrete time). In this case the set of instants is indexed by natural numbers. For a clock c, $c[k]$ denotes its kth instant. The MARTE Time profile defines one central stereotype *Clock* that extends the UML metaclass *Event*. A *Clock* carries more specific information such as its actual *unit*, and values of quantitative (resolution, offset, etc.) or qualitative (time standard) properties, if relevant.

TimedElement is another stereotype introduced in MARTE. A timed element is explicitly bound to at least one clock, and thus closely related to the time model. For instance, *TimedProcessing* is a specialization of *TimedElement*, which extends the UML metaclass *Action*. It defines a *start* and a *finish* event for a given action. These events (which are usually clocks) specify when the action starts or when it finishes. *TimedProcessing* also specifies the duration of an action. Duration is also measured on a given logical or physical clock.

In a MARTE model of a system, the stereotype *TimedElement* or one of its specializations is applied to model elements which have an influence on the specification of the temporal behavior of this system. The expected behavior of such *TimedElement*s is controlled by a set of *ClockConstraint*s. Those constraints specify dependencies between the various occurrences of events. The Clock Constraint Specification Language (CCSL), which is defined in an annex of MARTE, can be used to specify those constraints formally. CCSL is further described in the following subsection.

The MARTE Time subprofile also provides a model library named *TimeLibrary*. This model library defines the enumeration *TimeUnitKind* which is the standard type of time units for chronometric clocks. This enumeration contains units like *s* (second), its submultiples, and other related units (*e.g.*, minute, hour). The library also predefines a clock called *IdealClock*, which is a dense chronometric clock with the second as time unit. This clock is assumed to be an ideal clock, perfectly reflecting the evolutions of physical time. It should be imported in user's models with references to physical time concepts (*e.g.*, frequency, physical duration).

The Clock Constraint Specification Language (CCSL)

The Clock Constraint Specification Language has first been defined as an annex of MARTE. Its formal operational semantics has been defined separately in a research report (Andre, 2009). It provides a concrete syntax for handling logical clocks attached to modeling elements. It defines a set of constraints, derived from patterns frequently used in the domain, to define the synchronization schemes between those clocks, and thus between the modeling elements attached to them.

A clock is an ordered set of instants. In MARTE, clocks can be dense but most of usages only consider discrete clocks. Thus, we restrict the discussion to discrete logical clocks, *i.e.*, sequences of logical instants. More information on dense aspects can be found in a separate article (Liu et al., 2013). If c is a clock, $c[i]$ denotes its ith instant in the sequence, for all natural number i.

CCSL combines two kinds of orders on clocks. A pre-order (reflexive and transitive) called *precedence* and denoted $\leq$, that captures a causality relation or temporal precedence inherited from asynchronous languages and process network theory. Another pre-order called *subclock* and denoted $\subseteq$ inherited from the synchronous languages mainly used to define repetitive behaviors.

In the following, we use a precedence (*a precedes b*, also denoted a ≤ b) to represent causality relations, for instance a loss-less communication through an infinite FIFO queue, such that, for all natural number *i*, the ith instant of *a* (*a[i]*), representing the sending of a data, must occur before the ith instant of *b* (*b[i]*), representing the reception of the same data through a FIFO queue.

Regarding the subclock pre-order, we mainly use a simple version to represent periodic executions:

a is periodic on b period P. This states that, for all natural number *i*, *a[i]* is synchronous (must occur simultaneously) with *b[i*P]*, which is a particular scheme where *a* is a subclock of *b*. For instance, T_Req11 explained below uses this pattern as *BrakePedalPressed is periodic on UniversalTime period 10 ms* to express a repetition constraint. Both *BrakePedalPressed* and *UniversalTime* are considered as clocks. The former represents (logical) instants when the brake pedal is pressed. The latter represents (more physically-related) instants when the universal time clock ticks.

With these two basic schemes, we can build most of the patterns generally found in real-time system specifications (deadline, jitter, periodic repetitions, sporadic activations…).

EXAMPLE: SPECIFICATION OF THE CRUISE CONTROL SYSTEM

This section describes informally the running example used to illustrate the MARTE/CCSL capabilities discussed in this chapter.

Informal Description

A Cruise control is a system that regulates a vehicle speed. The Cruise control (CC) system helps to improve driver comfort by relieving the driver of maintaining speed of the vehicle constant in a phase requiring moderate attentiveness (non-congested traffic). The driver sets the desired speed and the CC takes over the throttle of the car to maintain the speed. The driver can always override the automatic control at any time. When the accelerator is pressed, the vehicle responds in a normal way and when the accelerator is released, the cruise control resumes its control and forces the vehicle to the predefined cruising speed. The CC is deactivated when the brake pedal is pressed.

The CC requires information from the engine management and the brake control system (current speed, acceleration/deceleration parameters, and throttle). Conversely, the implementation of the CC instructions is operated by those systems. The CC integrates different inputs (switches) to control the CC systems and different outputs (displays) to control what is visualized and when. The CC can only be activated under certain circumstances defined as preconditions, e.g., the vehicle speed must be higher than the minimum possible cruise speed setting (30km/h), and the brake pedal must not be pressed.

From this general textual functional description and after an analysis process based on this functional description, we built a more detailed specification of the CC system. This specification defines the input/output interface of the system, identifies the possible states of the system and lists the functional and non-functional requirements.

Requirements of the Cruise Control System (CC)

The functional interface of the CC system contains multiple inputs/outputs described below.

Inputs (Information and Commands from the Environment of the Cruise Control):
- **Activate:** Boolean value that switches the cruise control ON/OFF;
- **SetSpeed, IncreaseSpeed, DecreaseSpeed:** Boolean value that respectively sets the reference speed to the current speed of the vehicle, increments and decrements the reference speed;

- **Resume:** To resume the control of the cruise control that becomes responsible for controlling the speed according to the set cruise speed;
- **AccelerationRequest:** Numerical value that represents the positive (acceleration) or negative (deceleration) acceleration requested. Based on this, it is possible to inform the system when the accelerator pedal is pressed or released;
- **BrakeTorque:** Numerical value that represents the torque requested according to the position of the brake pedal. Based on this, it is possible to inform the system when the brake pedal is pressed;
- **VehicleSpeed:** Numerical value that gives the current speed of the vehicle.

Outputs (Instructions to the Environment of the Cruise Control):

- **Throttle:** Numerical value that specifies the throttle level;
- **GreenSignState:** Boolean value that indicates whether the cruise control is visualized as being ON or OFF;
- **DashBoardLightState:** Boolean value that indicates that the CC reference speed is highlighted.

The cruise controller has four main states:

- **CC_Disable:** The system is not in operation;
- **CC_Enable:** The system has been switched ON but the cruise speed has not been selected;
- **CC_Passive:** The system has been switched ON and the cruise speed has been selected but the controller is not active and the speed is controlled by the driver. This happens, for instance, when the driver uses the accelerator or the brake pedals. The system remains passive until the button resume is pressed;
- **CC_Active:** The cruise controller is in operation and is in charge of regulating the vehicle speed.

The following list presents, informally, the requirements on the CC system. Those requirements are captured in a more formal way in the next sections. F_ReqXX denote functional requirements, whereas T_ReqXX denote time requirements.

F_Req0: The CC has to be enabled /disabled by master switches CC_ON/CC_OFF;

F_Req1: Pressing button *setSpeed* (*i.e.*, *setSpeed* is true) sets the current speed as being the desired cruise speed. The value of the actual speed is assigned to a reference speed variable (RSV). It generates an event and the CC goes to the *CC_Passive* mode;

F_Req2: In *CC_Passive*, the system is ready for the control;

F_Req3: In *CC_Passive* mode, button *increaseSpeed* (resp. *decreaseSpeed*) allows the increment (resp. decrement) of the reference speed variable RSV;

F_Req4: CC goes from *CC_passive* to *CC_active* when the accelerator is released;

F_Req5: In the active mode, an acceleration request shall suspend the speed regulation that is automatically reactivated when the accelerator pedal is released;

F_Req6: In the active mode, pressing the brake pedal shall suspend the regulation. It can be resumed by setting the *resume* signal to true;

F_Req7: When the CC goes to *CC_Active*, a visual confirmation shall be given by switching ON the *GreenSign*;

T_Req8: Cruise control should be deactivated within 100ms after any deactivation request;

T_Req9: When activated, the CC should display the reference speed highlighted during 10 seconds;

T_Req10: the Human Machine Interface (HMI) must be cyclically polled at a period of 80ms;

T_Req11: Sensor acquisitions and interpretations for the brake and accelerator should be performed every 10ms;

Figure 1. Excerpt of MARTE time profile

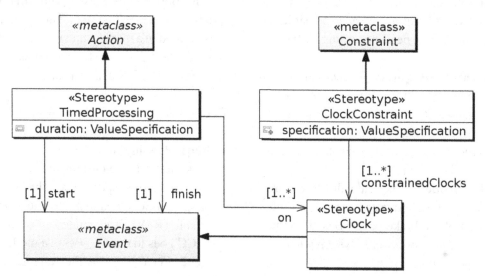

T_Req12: The CC can resume its activity only if it has been suspended before (by pressing the brake pedal for instance).

T_Req13: When the driver activates or resumes the cruise control, the throttle should be calculated and the set value displayed within 500 ms.

MODELING WITH MARTE/ CCSL AND EAST-ADL

In this section we illustrate–on the Cruise Control system–how the different MARTE/CCSL and EAST-ADL constructs are combined to capture within a single model the requirements, the functional parts and behavioral parts of a system.

Methodology

Figure 2 gives an overview of our proposal. All these notions are further explained in the following sections. Here, we briefly introduce their role in our proposition.

Some structural aspects are captured with UML classifiers and EAST-ADL function prototypes. In EAST-ADL, *function prototypes* are associated

with *function triggers* that specify when the function should be executed. Triggers in EAST-ADL play a similar role of clocks in MARTE/CCSL. In our proposition, clocks are automatically defined based on the EAST-ADL triggers.

The EAST-ADL function prototypes come with TADL functional and non-functional requirements. TADL2 has extended TADL with a notion of time bases that is identical to the notion of clocks in MARTE/CCSL. In our proposition, we automatically generate clocks for each TADL time base and each of the three kinds of TADL2 time requirements is captured as a CCSL specification that gives its formal semantics.

The behavioral part of the system is captured with *UML state machines* and *activities*. The MARTE profile has extended those concepts to introduce a notion of *TimedProcessing* (as described in the subsection on MARTE Time profile). This notion introduces clocks to specify when a *behavior* must start and finish its execution. Clocks can also be used to trigger the transitions of *UML state machines*.

Finally, since requirements models, structural and behavioral models all rely on the notion of clock, we propose to use MARTE/CCSL as a specification language for the composition of

Figure 2. Overview of our proposal

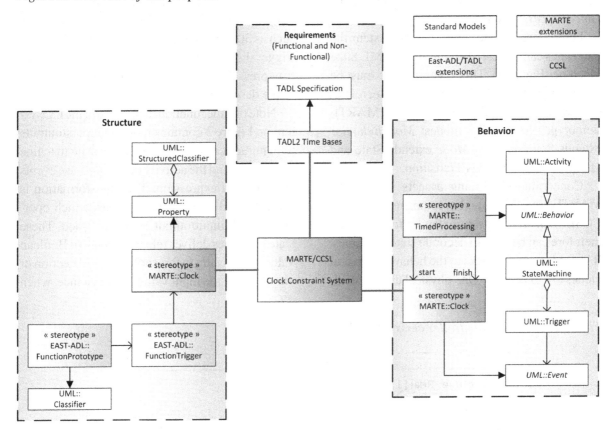

these models. Having a single model at the center of this specification allows for a global coordination of the models. Since CCSL has a formal operational semantics, this semantics can be used (by TimeSquare) to execute the models. This is, per se, a contribution of its own since UML, as a language, does not specify any methodological consistency between the different modeling parts (structural and behavioral) and neither EAST-ADL nor TADL2 have a formal definition.

Those models being coordinated by CCSL also opens the path to exhaustive verification techniques that are briefly discussed in the last section. However, the first kind of verification targeted here is to check the consistency of the global model and specification. Inconsistent CCSL specifications can be detected by TimeSquare. Even though, TimeSquare can be used to compare a CCSL specification to an implementation,

this is not the goal of this paper. Conducting more exhaustive verifications would require, for instance, having an implementation of the target system, producing execution traces and comparing it with the CCSL specification. We do have neither such an implementation nor the traces for the cruise controller.

Modeling the Behavior with MARTE UML Constructs

The first step in modeling with UML MARTE is the description of the main classes, their operations and their ports, which participate to their interface.

Figure 3 shows the main class for the cruise controller. The cruise control inputs and outputs are represented by ports. The behavioral part can be either a UML state machine or an activity or an interaction. MARTE extends these elements with timing aspects by applying the stereotype *TimedProcessing* on these behavioral models

For example in the cruise controller system, the four states can be described through a UML State Machine (Figure 3). This state machine must be adorned with MARTE stereotypes to better reflect the expected semantics. First, we use MARTE stereotypes to describe modes: *ModeBehavior* extends StateMachine, *Mode* extends State and *ModeTransition* extends Transition.

Concerning the timing aspects we use the MARTE Time Profile and its companion language CCSL. *TimedProcessing* extends *Behavior* and therefore can be used to decorate state machines. It is used to attach clocks to the behavior. Several clocks are to be used. One physical clock (Ideal-

Clock) is used to represent the physical time. This clock serves as a base to express speed constraints such as 30 km/h. Other clocks can also be used to trigger the execution of the timed processing and to express durations. We discuss more this aspect in the description of the activity (Figure 5).

Note that the functional interface of the CC system on Figure 3 contains multiple inputs/outputs with numerical values whereas the state machine on Figure 4 and the activity on Figure 5 use events and Boolean expression. This transformation is given by additional state machines which operate on each input/output of the interface. These state machines deliver relevant events or Boolean values, according to threshold values detection or variations of the input values. For instance, when

Figure 3. The cruiseController class and behaviors

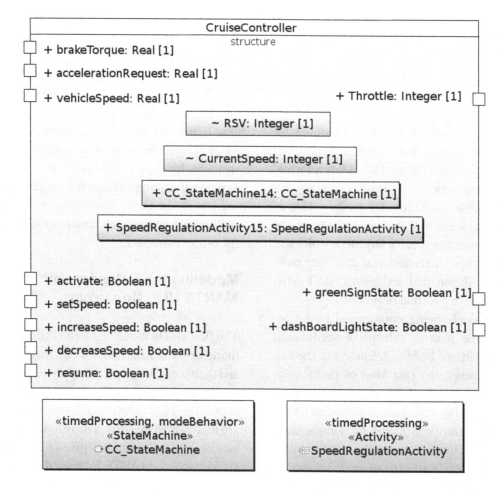

Figure 4. State-machine for the cruise control

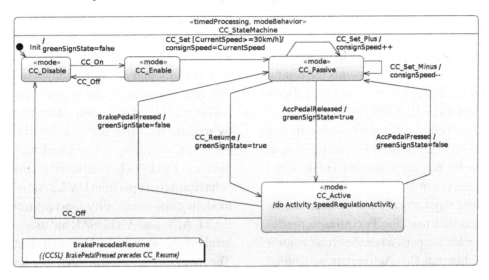

Figure 5. Activity for the speed regulation

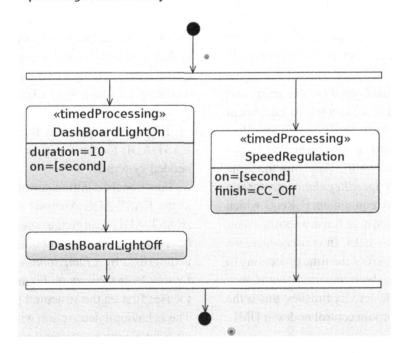

the *setSpeed* value changes from *false* to *true*, a *CC_Set* event occurs.

In MARTE one can capture relevant events of the system by considering them as logical clocks.

For instance on Figure 4, *BrakePedalPressed* and *CC_Resume* are logical clocks[1], whose ticks are the respective occurrences of these events. Applying the stereotype *Clock* to those events makes them qualified to be used in clock constraints. As an example, a clock constraint is shown at the bottom left of Figure 4. This constraint is specified as an opaque expression where the language used is CCSL. This constraint implements the timing requirement T_Req12, which would be difficult to capture in plain UML. CCSL relation *precedes* expresses a precedence between events. In this case, the system can resume its control only if the brake pedal has been pressed before (thus suspending the control).

Not all the requirements can be satisfied by using only this state machine. For instance, the description of what happens when the cruise control is active (within state CC_Active) can be detailed with a UML activity (see Figure 5). Here again, this activity is adorned with MARTE stereotypes to adapt the semantics to the closest of the expected requirements. Stereotype *timedProcessing* is used again on both the activity and its internal actions. In this activity, this stereotype uses clocks either based on the *IdealClock* to specify *duration* of an action and/or logical clocks to define *start* or *finish* events of an action (see Figure 1). This stereotype is applied on the *DashBoardLightOn* action and specifies a duration of 10 seconds to implement the time requirement T_Req9, which specifies the time the dashboard must be highlighted when activating the cruise control. Applying the same stereotype to action *SpeedRegulation* captures a part of the functional requirement F_Req0, which specifies that the action must finish when the event/ clock *CC_Off* occurs/ticks. In consequence, we specify the finish clock of the time processing to be *CC_Off*. Note that both concurrent paths must end before the whole activity finishes, this is the normal semantics of join control nodes in UML.

Modeling Timing Requirement with EAST-ADL

For the last 10 years, the automotive industry has fully invested in the AUTOSAR standard (AUTOSAR, 2013) and EAST-ADL (ATESST Consortium, Deliverable D3.1, 2007) as supports for the development of embedded automotive systems. These standards provide supports for a multi-level development process based on different abstraction levels allowing a separation of concerns between hardware and software parts. Additionally, it helps abstracting the hardware by making intensive use of common interfaces for buses, operating systems and reusable components. The EAST-ADL inherits structural and behavioral concepts from UML2 and requirement modeling and traceability concepts from SysML. EAST-ADL and AUTOSAR are used at different levels of the so-called EAST-ADL methodology. The methodology is structured into four abstraction levels: vehicle level, analysis level, design level and implementation level.

After introducing EAST-ADL, we show how EAST-ADL formalizes functional and non–functional requirements, especially the timing requirements with a TADL2 (Time Augmented Description Language) specification to obtain a global model for timing constraints. We use the cruise control example as running example for illustrating the functional and timing requirements modeling.

This section presents the main features of EAST-ADL for the functional modeling of embedded systems.

Functional definitions are modeled and refined at the EAST-ADL Analysis and Design Levels (EAST-ADL Language specification, 2013) (Cuenot et al., 2007). At both levels, the system is described by a *FunctionalArchitecture* (called *CruiseControlSystem* on Figure 6). EAST_ADL focuses first on the structural part of the system. The behavioral description with MARTE can be associated with a structural part.

The functional architecture is composed of a number of interconnected *FunctionPrototypes* where each prototype instantiates a *FunctionType*. The most important one is *cruiseController*. Sensors and actuators are modeled as *FunctionalDevices* and represent the interactions with the

Figure 6. EAST ADL model for the cruise control

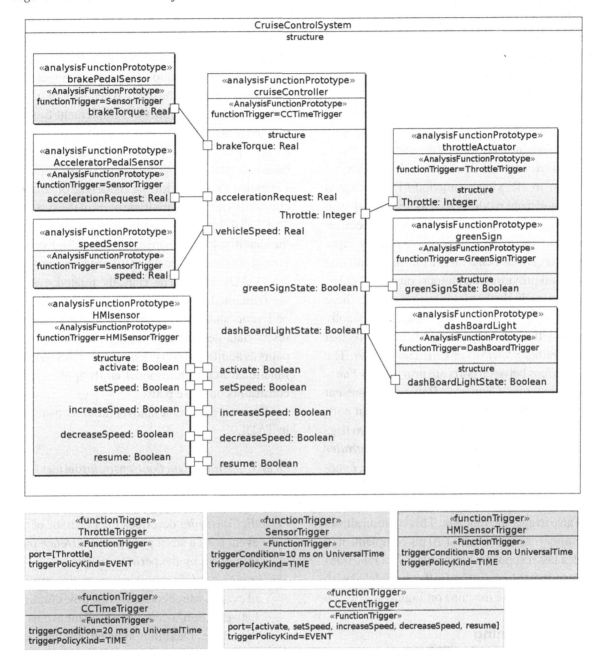

environment through acquisition of information and actuation of devices. In the Cruise control system, we have several *FunctionalDevices* such as the brake pedal and the accelerator pedal which provide their state. These sensors are managed by other functions of the vehicle. The cruise control only needs information about state changes in these sensors. The third device delivers the current speed of the vehicle. The last one, called *HMISensor*, factorizes the switches used by the driver for setting parameters to the cruise control. Concerning the outputs, the cruise controller calculates the throttle for the engine. This part is modeled with the *FunctionalDevice* called *ThrottleActuator*, the other output switches the dashboard light or the green sign.

The behavior of a *FunctionType* is provided by a *FunctionBehavior* that can be either a simple transfer function or an external model (*e.g.,* SIMU-LINK, ASCET, MARTE). The *FunctionTrigger* specifies when a function and the associated *FunctionBehavior* should be executed. It is a flexible mechanism allowing a function to be activated in a time-driven mode as well as an event-driven mode. In both modes, *triggerCondition* specifies when to trigger the function, *i.e*, reading input ports, execute the behavior in a run-to-completion mode and providing the outputs on output ports.

To provide the communication among these functions, the function types and consequently their function prototype instances have ports that can be either *FlowPort* or *ClientServerPort*. The connections between ports are provided by *FunctionConnectors*. Connected flow ports represent shared data from an output port to an input port.

In the example on Figure 6 we have two trigger policies assigned to the *cruiseController* (*CCTimeTrigger* and *CCEventTrigger*). The *FunctionPrototype* is time-driven with a rate of 20 ms and a change on some ports (*activate*, *setSpeed*) can also trigger the function. This solution allows a minimal execution rate of 20 ms complemented with a fast response when needed. The *FunctionBehavior* of the *cruiseController* is modeled with the MARTE state machine on Figure 4.

Modeling Timing Requirements with TADL2

Expressing the behavior and the timing requirements on an EAST-ADL structural view is a key point to perform timing analysis on an EAST-ADL model. The state machine on Figure 4 and the activity diagram on Figure 5 enriched with MARTE stereotypes provide an internal behavioral model

for the *cruiseController*. They cover functional requirements (requirements F-Req0 to F_Req7) and timing requirements (F_Req9) of the cruise control system. The *functionTrigger* of EAST-ADL and their execution strategy participate to the formalization of the internal behavior of functions. These trigger functions implement timing requirements T_Req10 and T_Req11.

EAST-ADL also provides a timing model based on the Timing Augmented Description Language (TADL2) for the modeling of timing constraints involving multiple parts of the system. The TADL2 timing constraints mostly constrain the identifiable state changes formulated as Events. Events are sending/receipt of information through EAST-ADL ports. The causally related events are contained as a pair by *EventChains*. Based on Events and *EventChains*, it is possible to represent data dependencies and critical execution paths as additional constraints for an EAST-ADL functional architecture model, and to apply timing constraints on these paths.

There are three basic kinds of timing constraints in TADL2:

DelayConstraint/ReactionConstraint defines how long after the occurrence of a stimulus a corresponding response must occur.

PeriodicConstraint describes the behavior of an event with a strict periodic occurrence pattern given by the period attribute.

SynchronizationConstraint is a constraint on a set of events, which constrains the time duration between the nth occurrence of all the events in the set (*i.e.*, maximum allowed time between the arrival of the event occurrences).

All event occurrences in TADL2 are measured on an explicit time base.

Timing constraints have timing attributes like upper, lower, tolerance and period. These attributes are given as Timing Expressions. There are three types of timing expressions: Value, Variable and

Symbolic. Value and Variable stand for free variables and constants. Symbolic Timing Expressions integrate basic arithmetic and relation operators associated with timing values.

Timing constraints can be attached to the cruise controller. One of these constraints is about periodic sensor acquisition (T_Req10, T_Req11). Another constraint is a reaction constraint between ports (T_Req8, T_Req13).

Figure 7 gives examples of a TADL2 specification for modeling the timing requirements T_Req9, T_Req11 and T_Req13. The first thing to do is to capture events used for specifying the constraints. These are directly derived from the UML figures by extracting the CCSL clocks. For instance, *CC_On* is the trigger described on Figure 4 that is emitted when the input signal *activate* (Figure 6) holds true. *DBLOn* (respectively *DBLOff*) is an event associated with the

Figure 7. Three examples of requirements in TADL2

Event CC_On
Event DBLOn
Event DBLOff
Event BrakeTorque
Event Throttle

ReactionConstraint T_Req9{
source   : DBLOn
target   : DBLOff
minimum = 10 s on universalTime
maximum = 10 s on universalTime
}

PeriodicConstraint T_Req11{
event BrakeTorque
period = 10 ms on UniversalTime
}

ReactionConstraint T_Req13{
source CC_On
target Throttle
lower = 500 ms on universalTime
}

start of action *DashBoardLightOn* (respectively *DashBoardLightOff*) shown on Figure 5. Every time the MARTE stereotype *TimedProcessing* is used, it implies a start and a finish event (see Figure 1). Event *BrakePedalPressed* is derived from the value of the input port *brakeTorque on* Figure 6. Finally, event *Throttle* occurs whenever the value changes on the output port *Throttle* (see Figure 6).

After listing the events, the constraints are specified as a one to one mapping from the requirement constraints. In the following listing, examples are given for one reaction constraint (T_Req9) and two periodic constraints (T_Req11 and T_Req13).

Event CC_On
Event DBLOn
Event DBLOff
Event BrakeTorque
Event Throttle
ReactionConstraint T_Req9{
source : DBLOn
target : DBLOff
minimum = 10 s on universalTime
maximum = 10 s on universalTime
}
PeriodicConstraint T_Req11{
event BrakeTorque
period = 10 ms on UniversalTime
}
ReactionConstraint T_Req13{
source CC_On
target Throttle
lower = 500 ms on universalTime
}

ANALYSIS AND INTERPRETATION OF MODELS

UML gives the standard basic support to capture the main model elements. Its extensions (MARTE and EAST-ADL) add constructs to capture specific time properties, requirements, or resource descriptions. Our first objective was to show how to combine the different models of MARTE state machine and activity, TADL2 and EAST-ADL. However, we go further than just a mere modeling of the requirements and we give a formal operational semantics to the models in order to make them executable, run simulations, conduct analyses on both the UML MARTE and EAST-ADL/TADL2 models and their associated timing constraints.

To that aim, we have built a transformation flow, which relies on MARTE Clock Constraint Specification Language (CCSL) as a common language to give and compose the semantics of these different models and to analyze or simulate the whole specification in a common UML-based environment.

Our flow to make the models executable is sketched on Figure 8. Generic transformation rules are expressed with ECL (Event Constraint Language) at the metamodel level. ECL is further described in the following subsection. From these rules, we generate a QVTo (operation Query Value Transformation) specification that can take any model conforming to the selected metamodel and generate the CCSL constraints according to the rules defined in ECL. Once the CCSL model has been generated, we use TimeSquare[2], the development framework dedicated to the simulation and analysis of MARTE/CCSL models, to perform analyses. This is further described in the following subsections.

The Event Constraint Language (ECL)

The model is built in UML/MARTE and the semantics is given by the CCSL specification. However, the CCSL specification is automatically derived from the UML/MARTE model through a model transformation. We use the Event Constraint Language (ECL) to capture a set of rules that capture the semantics of State Machines, the semantics of Activities, but also the semantics of EAST-ADL requirements and TADL2 expressions. Just like OCL constraints that are specified at the meta-model level and checked on any model, the ECL works at the meta-model level and describes generic behavior for a set of meta-elements. From this meta-description, we use a high-order transformation engine to automatically generate the CCSL specification. This action mainly consists in instantiating each of the high-order rules, defined at the metamodel level, on each model element. This process guarantees that the rules are described once and for all and are then applied in a systematic way whatever the actual model.

For what follows it does not matter whether the CCSL specification has been generated automatically from generic ECL rules or whether it has been manually specified by someone knowing the actual syntax of CCSL.

Figure 8. Exogenous transformation from EAST-ADL / TADL2 to CCSL

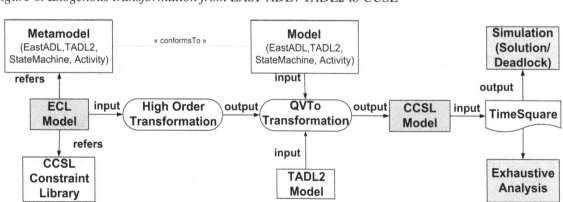

Executable Specification of MARTE and EAST-ADL/TADL2 with CCSL

We have described the various EAST-ADL and TADL2 elements that we rely on. Logical clocks of CCSL are used as handles to activate and co-ordinate the different elements from the various models. Some clocks are attached to the UML models (*e.g.,* to trigger state machine transitions), some others to the EAST-ADL models (*e.g.,* to trigger the execution of the functions) and some are attached to TADL2 constraints (see Figure 2).

More precisely we denote formally in CCSL (i) the causal and synchronization semantics of EAST-ADL reflected by the definition of the design and/or analysis functional architecture, (ii) the timed and causal semantics of TADL2 to augment the functional architecture with the temporal constraints imposed by real-time distributed systems, (iii) the behavior model semantics of the MARTE state machine and activity and the functional behavior of EAST-ADL.

The result is an operational framework (TimeSquare) which is able to conduct simulations and formal analyses of EAST-ADL/TADL2 models. Some details about this transformation are given in the following subsection.

Simulation with TimeSquare

The first kind of analyses provided by TimeSquare is a model simulation capability. TimeSquare simulation highlights disabled constraints and identifies dead clocks. Under-specification results in many possible solutions to satisfy the constraints. TimeSquare then attempts to find one valid solution amongst the set of valid solutions. When several simulation runs result in different solutions, the system is considered as underspecified. Finding either satisfying solutions or falsifying ones helps refining the constraint system until the specification matches the expectations. Dead clocks highlights inconsistent specifications, where this is no solution for a given problem.

This is only possible with a formal specification and cannot be achieved by traditional informal EAST-ADL models.

The CCSL specification is attached to the UML model. The CCSL specification gives the semantics of the model. The simulation steps are computed one by one so as to satisfy the CCSL specification. Depending on those simulation steps, the model can be animated. A first example for illustrating the TimeSquare capabilities is given on Figure 9. Based on the Cruise control state machine model (Figure 4) we automatically generate a CCSL specification, executable in the TimeSquare environment. On the left hand side of the Figure 9, the list of clocks is given, then on the right hand side, a trace denoting the simulation is displayed. The cruise control is initially disabled, then when *CC_On* occurs, the transition t1 from the state machine is triggered and the cruise control enters the state *CC_Enable*. This is a typical illustration of the use of logical clocks. TimeSquare brings the model to life and shows the exact interpretation of the modeling elements and the requirements.

Multiple runs of the CCSL state machine specification can be executed. Some of these runs can lead to an execution path and a complete execution. Some others can lead to a deadlock. This is typically the case if the T_Req12 is not satisfied i.e: if the clock *CC-Resume* ticks whereas *BrakePedalPressed* has not ticked before. In this case, one of the CCSL constraints is violated, meaning that the specification should be refined.

The second example of simulation derived from the case study is given on Figure 10. It highlights the concurrency and synchronizations of the different actions in the activity diagram. For instance, the *DashBoardLightOn* action starts after the 1st second and the action *SpeedRegulation* starts at the 2nd second (after the activity started). The actions are then executing concurrently. At the 11th second after the activity beginning, the *DashBoardLightOn* stopped. It is executed during 10 seconds as specified by the *TimedProcessing* stereotype (see Figure 5). Additionally, the *SpeedRegulation* action stopped when the *CC_Off* event occurred, as specified in the *TimedProcessing* stereotype. Finally, this simulation also highlights that the natural semantics of UML activity is preserved since some actions are concurrent, some other sequential and all of them are executed during the execution of the activity as specified by the diagram of Figure 5. The MARTE stereotypes act as additional constraints over the ones given by the UML.

Exhaustive Verification

The second kind of analyses supported by TimeSquare is through exhaustive analysis as opposed to simulation that only explores one possible scenario. At this level, the CCSL specification can play two very different roles: either as a *specification language* or as a *verification language*.

As a *specification language*, CCSL gives a high-level formal executable view of what the behavior of the system is expected to be. This specification can be used by TimeSquare to establish properties on the model. It can be done for instance by model-checking the CCSL specification. An example of classical property that can be established by model-checking is whether deadlocks can happen in the specification. Deadlocks would denote problems with the actual specification and would require a modification of the requirements. In presence of timing requirements CCSL deadlocks often expose violations of timing constraints, i.e., behaviors where a given timing constraint cannot be satisfied. When a constraint is violated, the model checker proposes a path in the execution that leads to the deadlock and therefore shows a scenario where the requirements cannot be satisfied.

Figure 9. Simulation of the UML State Machine with TimeSquare

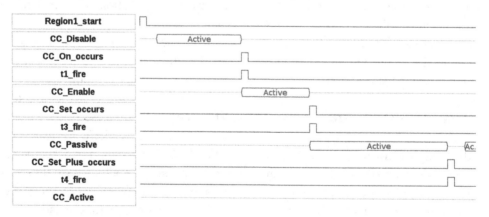

Figure 10. Simulation of the UML Activity with TimeSquare

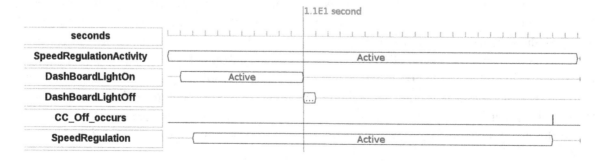

To conduct model-checking on CCSL speci-fication, it must first be transformed into a lan-guage more adequate. For instance, TimeSquare can transform a CCSL specification into a SPIN program which can then be model-checked using Promela (Ling et al., 2011). When CCSL is trans-formed into Promela, only the logical aspects are captured since there is no support for physical time in Promela. Real-Time extensions around Real-Time SPIN could be used to capture the physical time constraints. More recently, we have shown that it could also be transformed into a network of Timed Automata and then model-checked using UPPAAL 0. This second transformation is more interesting to capture the physical properties like T_Req11 or T_Req13.

In both cases, properties to be verified must be captured using temporal logics and model-check-ing can only be performed when the specification is finite. However, it is very easy to build infinite CCSL specifications and underspecified constraint systems are usually infinite. Finiteness of CCSL specifications also called safety is decidable 0.

As a *verification language*, CCSL does not represent the whole behavior but only a set of expected properties from the system under design. In this role, CCSL takes the place of temporal logic languages. Even though the expressiveness of CCSL is different from languages like CTL 0, it provides a set of predefined patterns to express timing properties (deadlines, causal relationships, jitter constraints). So it is expected to be easier to be used by engineers that are not always willing to invest in learning temporal logic languages. When used as a specification language, the CCSL specification can be used to verify properties of existing implementations. A thorough example from General Motors also related to the automo-tive domain and focusing only the model-checking aspect based on interaction diagrams can be found in (Millo et al., 2013).

On the cruise control example, we are at a specification level and there is no actual imple-mentation of this system. In that case, TimeSquare should merely be used to execute the model and check the consistency of the various elements (state machines constraints with respect to TADL2 requirements).

RELATED WORK

Executable UML0) defines, among other things, a model of causality for UML that is at the core of various scenario-based analysis methods. It was a first attempt to provide an operational semantics for UML. However, this is no operational frame-work that actually allows for executing it, only a set of code generation patterns that can be applied if we restrict to this well-founded subset. It does not apply to MARTE nor to EAST-ADL that did not exist at that time. More recently, there have been actions at the OMG to work on Foundational UML and a specific action language called ALF. To the best of our knowledge it does not address MARTE or EAST-ADL constructs and no opera-tional framework is available yet.

Some attempts have been conducted to ex-tend the simulation and verification capabilities around the EAST-ADL language. For instance the ViTAL tools 0 expresses the functional EAST-ADL behavior as timed automata which have a precise semantics allowing a formal verification of EAST-ADL model. Additionally, supports for model transformation from EAST-ADL be-havioral models to analysis tools include SPIN Matlab/Simulink and modelica. General mapping rules are defined between EAST-ADL behavior constructs and PROMELA language for logical model checking with SPIN. These approaches ap-plied on a subset of EAST-ADL and do not offer a support to combine it with TADL2 or MARTE models. In our approach the idea is to use clocks as a gluing element between the various models, just as tagged models (Edward, & Sangiovanni-Vincentelli, 1998) are used on a theoretic point of view to compose heterogeneous models of computation.

Some approaches, like Ptolemy (Buck et al., 1994) or ForSyDE (Sander, & Jantsch, 2004) focus on the composition of heterogeneous models but do not address specifically EAST-ADL or MARTE aspects.

Another approach (Walker et al., 2013) focuses only on the analysis of EAST-ADL models and is therefore complementary.

CONCLUSION

This chapter has given a snapshot of current modeling and analysis facilities that have been developed around the MARTE Time Profile and its companion language, the Clock Constraint Specification Language. We have not attempted to give a comprehensive formal definition or a more theoretical view of the mathematical models that have motivated the definition of the profile and of CCSL. Rather we have tried to give a practical view with a concrete example on how the logical clocks advocated by MARTE Time Profile can be used on different kinds of UML models. Since our example comes from the automotive domain, we have also shown how MARTE could be combined with another specific profile called EAST-ADL. Clocks are used in both EAST-ADL and MARTE to describe the way the different UML elements are orchestrated. The semantics and orchestration of both the EAST-ADL and UML/MARTE models are given through an automatic transformation into CCSL. CCSL can then be used to execute the specification and conduct analyses. Additional references are given for the readers willing to explore more the foundational aspects, the theoretical aspects or the different kinds of analyses that can be performed.

REFERENCES

André, C. (2009). *Syntax and Semantics of the Clock Constraint Specification Language (CCSL)* (Research Report RR-6925). INRIA.

André, C., Mallet, F., & De Simone, R. (2007). Modeling Time(s). In *Proceedings of ACM/IEEE Int. Conf. on Model-Driven Engineering Languages and Systems (MoDELS/UML'07)*, (LNCS) (vol. 4735, pp. 559-573). Berlin: Springer.

ATESST Consortium, ATESST Deliverable D3.1. (2007). The Modeling Approach: Overview of the EAST-ADL2. *ITEA, Tech. Rep., 2007, deliverable D.3.1*. Available from http://www.atesst.org

AUTOSAR AUTomotive Open System Architecture. (2013). Retrieved from http://www.autosar.org/download/R4.1/Main.zip

AUTOSAR Specification of Timing Extensions, 1.1.0. (n.d.). *AUTOSAR Release 4.0.2, 2010-11-03*. AUTOSAR Development Cooperation.

Benveniste, A., Caspi, P., Edwards, S. A., Halbwachs, N., Le Guernic, P., & de Simone, R. (2003). The synchronous languages 12 years later. *Proceedings of the IEEE, 91*(1), 64–83. doi:10.1109/JPROC.2002.805826

Buck, J. T., Ha, S., Lee, E. A., & Messerschmitt, D. G. (1994). Ptolemy: A Framework for Simulating and Prototyping Heterogenous Systems. *International Journal in Computer Simulation, 4*(2).

Cuenot, P., Frey, P., Johansson, R., Lönn, H., Papadopoulos, Y., Reiser, M.-O., … Törngren, M. (2007). The EAST-ADL Architecture Description Language for Automotive Embedded Software. In Model-Based Engineering of Embedded Real-Time Systems (pp. 297-307). Academic Press.

East-ADL Consortium. (2013). *EAST ADL language specification*. Retrieved from http://www.east-adl.info/Specification/V2.1.11/EAST-ADL-Specification_V2.1.11.pdf

EAST-EEA Project. (2004). *Definition of language for automotive embedded electronic architecture*. ITEA.

Edward, A. L., & Sangiovanni-Vincentelli, A. L. (1998). A framework for comparing models of computation. *IEEE Trans. on CAD of Integrated Circuits and Systems*, *17*(12), 1217–1229. doi:10.1109/43.736561

Enoiu, E. P., Raluca Marinescu, R., Seceleanu, C., & Pettersson, P. (2012). ViTAL: A Verification Tool for EAST-ADL Models using UPPAAL PORT. In *Proceedings of 17th IEEE International Conference on Engineering of Complex Computer Systems*, (pp. 328-337). IEEE.

Gascon, R., Mallet, F., & DeAntoni, J. (2011). Logical time and temporal logics: Comparing UML MARTE/CCSL and PSL. In *Proceedings of Int. Symp. on Temporal Representation and Reasoning (TIME'11)* (pp. 141-148). Lubeck, Germany: TIME.

Goknil, A., DeAntoni, J., Peraldi-Frati, M.-A., & Mallet, F. (2013a). Tool Support for the Analysis of TADL2 Timing Constraints using TimeSquare. In *Proceedings of 18th Inter. Conf. on Engineering of Complex Computer Systems,* (pp. 145-154). Academic Press.

Goknil, A., Suryadevara, J., Peraldi-Frati, M.-A., & Mallet, F. (2013b). Analysis Support for TADL2 Timing Constraints on EAST-ADL Models. In *Proceedings of European Conference on Software Architecture* (LNCS) (vol. 7957, pp. 89-105). Berlin: Springer.

Ling, Y., Mallet, F., & Liu, J. (2011). Verification of MARTE/CCSL Time Requirements with Promela/SPIN. In *Proceedings of 16th Int. Conf. on Engineering of Complex Computer Systems* (ICECCS'11), (pp. 65-74). IEEE.

Liu, J., Ziwei, L., He, J., Mallet, F., & Ding, Z. (2013). Hybrid MARTE statecharts. *Frontiers of Computer Science*, *7*(1), 95–108. doi:10.1007/s11704-012-1301-1

Mallet, F., Millo, J.-V., & De Simone, R. (2013). Safe CCSL specifications and Marked Graphs. In Proceedings of MemoCode'13, (pp. 157-166). Academic Press.

Mellor, S. J., & Balcer, M. (2002). *Executable UML: A foundation for model-driven architectures*. Addison-Wesley Longman Publishing Co., Inc..

Millo, J.-V., Mallet, F., Couadou, A., & Ramesh, S. (2013). Scenario-based verification in presence of variability using a synchronous approach. *Frontiers of Computer Science*, *7*(5), 650–672. doi:10.1007/s11704-013-3094-6

OMG. (2009a). *UML Profile for MARTE, v1.0., Novembre 2009*. Object Management Group, formal/2009-11-02.

OMG. (2009b). *Unified Modeling Language, Superstructure, v2.2, February 2009*. Object Management Group, formal/2009-02-02.

Peraldi-Frati, M.-A., Goknil, A., Deantoni, J., & Nordlander, J. (2012). A timing model for specifying multi clock automotive systems: The Timing Augmented Description Language V2. In *Proceedings of International Conference on Engineering of Complex Computer Systems*. IEEE.

Sander, I., & Jantsch, A. (2004). System modeling and transformational design refinement in ForSyDe. *IEEE Trans. on CAD of Integrated Circuits and Systems*, *23*(1), 17–32. doi:10.1109/TCAD.2003.819898

Suryadevara, J., Seceleanu, C., Mallet, F., & Pettersson, P. (2013). Verifying. MARTE/CCSL Mode Behaviors Using UPPAAL. In *Proceedings of Software Engineering and Formal Methods* (SEFM'13), (LNCS) (vol. 8137, pp. 1-15). Berlin: Springer.

TIMMO-2-USE project, Deliverable D11. (2012). *TADL2 language semantics and metamodel V2*. Retrieved from https://itea3.org/project/ workpackage/document/download/850/09033-TIMMO-2-USE-WP-2-D11Languagesyntax,se mantics,metamodelV2.pdf

Walker, M., Reiser, M.-O., Tucci Piergiovanni, S., Papadopoulos, Y., Lönn, H., & Mraidha, C. et al. (2013). Automatic optimisation of system architectures using EAST-ADL. *Journal of Systems and Software*, *86*(10), 2467–2487. doi:10.1016/j. jss.2013.04.001

ADDITIONAL READING

André, C., Deantoni, J., Mallet, F., & De Simone, R. (2010) The Time Model of Logical Clocks available in the OMG MARTE profile. Synthesis of Embedded Software: Frameworks and Methodologies for Correctness by Construction, Chapter 7, Springer Science+Business Media, LLC 2010 (pp. 201-227).

André, C., & Mallet, F. (2009). Specification and Verification of Time Requirements with CCSL and Esterel. In Languages, Compilers, and Tools for Embedded Systems, Dublin, Ireland. ACM SIGPLAN/SIGBED, ACM SIGPLAN Notices, 44 (pp. 167-176).

André, C., Mallet, F., & De Simone, R. (2007). Modeling of Immediate vs. Delayed Data Communications: from AADL to UML MARTE. In *ECSI Forum on specification & Design Languages (FDL)*, Barcelona, Spain. ECSI (pp. 249-254).

André, C., Mallet, F., & De Simone, R. (2008). Modeling AADL data-communications with UML MARTE. Embedded Systems Specification and Design Languages, chapter 11, LNEE 10, Springer (pp. 150-170).

André, C., Mallet, F., & Peraldi-Frati, M.-A. (2007). Multiform Time in UML for Real-time Embedded Applications. In *IEEE Int. Conf. on Real-Time Computing Systems and Applications (RTCSA)*, Daegu, Republic Of Korea, IEEE (pp. 232-237).

Combemale, B., DeAntoni, J., Vara Larsen, M., Mallet, F., Barais, O., Baudry, B., & France, R. B. (2013). Reifying Concurrency for Executable Metamodeling. In *Int. Conf. on Software Language Engineering* (SLE'13), IN, US, Springer LNCS 8225 (pp. 365-384).

Deantoni, J., & Mallet, F. (2012). TimeSquare: Treat your Models with Logical Time (2012) In *50th International Conference on Objects, Models, Components, Patterns -*, Prague, Czech Republic. LNCS 7304, Springer (pp. 34-41).

Dubois, H., Peraldi-Frati, M.-A., & Fadoi, L. (2010). A model for requirements traceability in an heterogeneous model-based design process. Application to automotive embedded systems. In *15th IEEE Int. Conference on Engineering of Complex Computer Systems*, (pp. 233-242).

Glitia, C., Deantoni, J., & Mallet, F. (2012). In T. J. J. Kaźmierski & A. Morawiec (Eds.), System Specification and Design Languages, LNEE 106 (pp. 223–238). Springer.Logical Time @ Work: Capturing Data Dependencies and Platform Constraints doi:doi:10.1007/978-1-4614-1427-8_14 doi:10.1007/978-1-4614-1427-8_14

Glitia, C., Deantoni, J., Mallet, F., Millo, J.-V., Boulet, P., & Gamatié, A. (2012). *Design Automation for Embedded Systems*, Springer Science+Business Media. *LLC*, *16*(2), 137–169. Progressive and explicit refinement of scheduling for multidimensional data-flow applications using UML MARTE

Goknil, A., & Peraldi-Frati, M.-A. (2012). In 2nd Int. Model-Driven Requirements Engineering (MoDRE) Workshop (pp. 49–57). Chicago, United States: IEEE. A DSL for Specifying Timing Requirements doi:doi:10.1109/MoDRE.2012.6360074 doi:10.1109/MoDRE.2012.6360074

Kuntz, S., Peraldi-Frati, M.-A., Blom, H., & Karlsson, D. (Mar 2012). Design Automation. Dresden, Germany: Test in Europe. Timing Modeling with AUTOSAR. Current State and Future Directions

Le Tallec, J. F., Deantoni, J., De Simone, R., Ferrero, B., Mallet, F., & Maillet-Contoz, L. (2011) Combining SystemC, IP-XACT and UML/MARTE in model-based SoC design. In *Workshop on Model Based Engineering for Embedded Systems Design (M-BED 2011)*, Grenoble, France.

Mallet, F. (2011). Logical Time @ Work for the Modeling and Analysis of Embedded Systems *LAP LAMBERT Academic Publishing, Jan. 2011, 978-3-8433-9388-1.*

Mallet, F., & Millo, J.-V. (2013) Boundedness Issues in CCSL Specifications. In 15th International *Conference on Formal Engineering Methods.* LNCS 8144, Springer (pp. 20-35).

Mallet, F., Peraldi-Frati, M.-A., & André, C. (2009). Marte CCSL to execute East-ADL Timing Requirements. *Int. Symp. on Object/component/service-oriented Real-time distributed Computing (ISORC'09),* Tokyo, Japan. IEEE (pp. 249-253).

Peraldi-Frati, M.-A., Goknil, A., Adedjouma, M., & Gueguen, P.-Y. (2012). Modeling a BSG-E Automotive System with the Timing Augmented Description language. In *5th Int. Symp. On Leveraging Applications of Formal Methods, Verification and* Validation, Amirandes, Héraklion, Greece. Springer, LNCS 7610, Springer (pp. 111-125).

Peraldi-Frati, M.-A., & Sorel, Y. (2008). From high-level modeling of time in MARTE to real-time scheduling analysis. In *Int. Workshop on Model Based Architecting and Construction of Embedded Systems,* Toulouse, France. CEUR 503 (pp. 129-144).

KEY TERMS AND DEFINITIONS

CC: Cruise Control, the running example used in this chapter.

CCSL: Clock Constraint Specification Language, a companion language defined as an annex of MARTE.

CTL: Computation Tree Logic, a branching time temporal logic.

EAST-ADL: A domain-specific language defined by a succession of European projects and dedicated to the design of automotive systems.

ECL: Event Constraint Language, an OCL extension with events and synchronization constraints.

MARTE: Modeling and Analysis of Real-Time and Embedded systems, an OMG UML Profile.

OCL: The Object Constraint Language, an OMG specification.

OMG: The Object Management Group.

UML: The Unified Modeling Language, an OMG specification.

SysML: The System engineering Modeling Language, an OMG UML Profile.

TADL: Timing Augmented Description Language.

ENDNOTES

[1] Note that the Clock stereotype applied to the events is not displayed by the environment we used to capture the UML diagram. This avoids overloading the figure and making it difficult to read.

[2] TimeSquare is available for download as a standalone application or through an Eclipse update site at http://timesquare.inria.fr.

Chapter 3
Symbolic–Based Monitoring for Embedded Applications

Pramila Mouttappa
Institut Mines-Telecom, France

Stephane Maag
Institut Mines-Telecom, France

Ana Cavalli
Institut Mines-Telecom, France

ABSTRACT

Testing embedded systems to find errors and to validate that the implemented system as per the specifications and requirements has become an important part of the system design. The research community has proposed several formal approaches these last years, but most of them only consider the control portion of the protocol, neglecting the data portions, or are confronted with an overloaded amount of data values to consider. In this chapter, the authors present a novel approach to model protocol properties of embedded application in terms of Input-Output Symbolic Transition Systems (IOSTS) and show how they can be tested on real execution traces taking into account the data and control portions. These properties can be designed to test the conformance of a protocol as well as security aspects. A parametric trace slicing approach is presented to match trace and property. This chapter is illustrated by an application to a set of real execution traces extracted from a real automotive Bluetooth framework with functional and security properties.

INTRODUCTION: HOW IT ALL BEGAN

Embedded systems are becoming increasingly ubiquitous, controlling a wide variety of popular and safety-critical devices. Testing is the most commonly used method for validating software systems, and effective testing techniques could be helpful for improving the dependability of these systems. However, there are challenges involved in developing such techniques. So, how is this testing performed ? Usually, testing is performed by executing experiments on the implementation, by making observations during the execution of the tests and by subsequently assigning a verdict about the correct functioning of the system. This method is called *active testing*. But, this is not always possible for systems that operate continuously and where direct interfaces are not provided. Further, interfering with such systems can result in

DOI: 10.4018/978-1-4666-6194-3.ch003

misbehavior of the system. To compensate for the limitations of active testing techniques, we have another interesting technique called *passive testing* or *monitoring*. Passive testing can be considered as one of the promising technologies to meet the challenges imposed on software testing.

Passive testing (or Monitoring) consists of recording the trace (i.e., sequence of exchange of messages) produced by the implementation under test and mapped to the property to be tested or specification if it exists. This technique has proved to be a powerful technique for reactive systems (like communication protocols, embedded systems, etc.) testing by observing its input/output behaviors (implementation traces) without interrupting its normal operations. Passive testing helps to observe abnormal behavior in the implementation under test on the basis of observing any deviation from the predefined behavior. This deviation can also sometimes match with certain attack patterns. As the systems evolve, network protocol messages become richer with data values. They are defined as control and data portions. Nevertheless, many works on passive testing are focused only on checking the control portion of the message without taking into account the data part which may result in producing false positive verdicts as explained in (Che, Lalanne, & Maag, 2012).

In this chapter, we introduce a new passive testing methodology based on the integration of symbolic execution of an IOSTS and parametric trace slicing techniques. From the literature we see that most of the work (Bentakouk, Poizat, & Zaidi, 2011; Weiglhofer, Aichernig, & Wotawa, 2010; Gaston, Le Gall, Rapin, & Touil, 2006) is based on active testing using a symbolic execution approach. IOSTS are used here for modeling communicating systems interacting with their environment (behavior or attack). The most important aspect of this IOSTS formalism is that the parameters and variable values are represented by *symbolic values* instead of *concrete data values*, which helps in avoiding the necessity for data enumeration.

The IOSTS model is symbolically executed to obtain a tree-like structure with different branches constituting the behavior or attack scenario. The branches or the behaviors of the symbolic tree are monitored against the real system trace using passive testing approach.

The technique of parametric trace slicing (Chen & Rosu, 2009) is used for trace analysis. Trace analysis plays a very important part in passive testing. A parametric trace is defined as a trace containing events with parameters that have been bound to a concrete data value (i.e., valuation) and parametric trace slicing is defined as a technique to slice (or cut) the real protocol execution trace into various slices based on this valuation. We then apply the symbolic execution of properties on the trace slices to provide a test verdict. This approach has been applied to passively test the traces of the Bluetooth protocol implemented in an embedded system dedicated to an automotive framework experimented through the ITEA2 DIAMONDS1 project.

More precisely, the main contributions of this chapter include:

- We briefly define how to formally model the embedded system properties and possible attacks using IOSTS formalism and also discuss the advantages of symbolic passive testing over other existing passive testing or monitoring methodologies.
- The definition of an algorithm for parametric trace slicing by taking into account the data portions contained in the trace events.
- The definition of a novel algorithm to check whether an IOSTS property is satisfied on a real execution trace. We also demonstrate that security attacks can be monitored by this approach.
- Demonstrations on real execution traces extracted from an embedded automotive Bluetooth system have been conducted with a prototype tool.

The remaining parts of the chapter are divided in the following way. First, we present the background of conformance testing as well as the formal testing techniques. In the related works section, we discuss and compare with the other passive testing techniques. The proposed approach is discussed in the symbolic monitoring methodology section. The definition of the adapted symbolic formalism and how it can be applied to model the system behavior and their evaluation logic is discussed in this section. Application of the methodology to a Bluetooth protocol is discussed in the industrial experimentation and results section. Finally, we present future works and conclude the chapter.

BACKGROUND

What is Conformance Testing?

Testing determines whether a system meets the functional requirements. The intent of system test is to find defects and correct them before go-live. There is no approach or method to guarantee that a system is completely free of defects. The notion of conformance, according to (ISO/IEC, 1996), links to implementations under test (IUT) and specifications. Conformance testing checks whether the IUT conforms to its specification. Conformance can be defined as a relation between the observable behavior of the IUT and the behavior of the corresponding model, which serves as a system specification. An IUT conforms to its specification if both, the IUT and the specification, show the same behavior. The internal structure of the IUT (the code) is not known. Hence, in conformance testing, the IUT is considered to be a black-box, which means, only the observable behavior of the IUT (i.e., the interactions of the IUT with its environment) is testable.

Conformance testing is broadly classified into two main testing families: active testing and passive testing. Each of these two families encompasses various approaches, and each approach contains different testing techniques.

Active Testing Technique

Figure 1 shows how the tester tries to show the conformance relation by executing a set of test scenarios on an implementation under test and verifies whether its behavior matches with the specified requirements. In this type of test, the tester interacts directly with the IUT via its interfaces (external). According to the testing community, it is referred to as black-box testing as there is no information about the internal structure of the implementation.

However, sometimes this activity becomes difficult and even impossible to perform. Nevertheless, most of the formal testing approaches consist in the generation of test cases that apply

Figure 1. Active testing approach

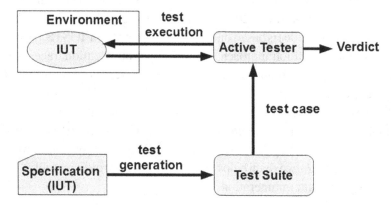

to the implementation in order to check its correctness with respect to a specification. However, this is not always possible for large systems that are running continuously and cannot be shutdown or interrupted for a long period of time and also when direct interfaces are not provided. Indeed, interfering with such systems can result in misbehavior of the system. In these situations, there is a particular interest in using other types of validation techniques such as passive testing.

Passive Testing Technique

Passive testing consists in analyzing the traces (i.e., the input and output events) recorded from the IUT and trying to find a fault by comparing these traces with either the complete specification or with some specific requirements (or properties) during normal runtime. As the name implies, it does not disturb the natural run-time of an IUT. It is sometimes also referred to as *monitoring*. The record of the event observation (input/output) is called an *event trace*. This event trace will be verified against the specification (or requirements) in order to determine the conformance relation between the implementation and the specification and based on that a final verdict is produced. We can distinguish two different approaches: Online and Offline. In the former, the passive tester tries to detect a fault during the execution of the system, whereas, in the latter, the evaluation of the system is done by collecting the recorded traces. In the approach herein presented, offline testing is performed. Figure 2 shows the general passive testing architecture.

In order to minimize wrong interpretations of the specification, it is preferable to describe them with the help of a formal language or formal model. According to the literature, we find that most of the passive testing approaches are based on such formal models or specifications. We present in the following the important works and methodologies in this area.

Finite State Machine representation (FSM), has been widely used in the system specification of various areas, like network protocols, high level software design, real-time reactive systems, etc. Although, the FSM has been used to model simple systems they quickly become complex or impractical to use for complex systems. In addition, it has the provision to model only the control portion of a protocol. As an extension of the FSM, extended FSM (EFSM) was developed. EFSM- based testing considers the observable (input/output events) behavior of the model as the control portion and the variable and parameter

Figure 2. Passive testing approach

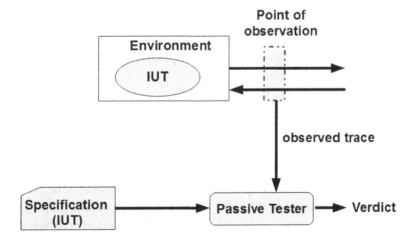

values as the data portion. Although an EFSM considers data portion checking, an enumeration of all the data values is still required to formally test large reactive systems which may be complex.

An invariant-based passive testing is another interesting approach where, a set of properties are extracted from the EFSM specification or standard, and then the trace resulting from the implementation is analyzed to determine whether it validates this set of properties. These extracted sets of properties are called invariants because they have to hold true at every moment. In this aspect, a Horn logic based approach was proposed to test data-centric protocols (Lalanne & Maag, 2013). While this approach also avoids the enumeration of parameters, nevertheless, it cannot be valuated as in our approach but just compared. Furthermore, the approach requires checking all the traces before providing a verdict.

Symbolic Testing Technique

Most of the test generation techniques (active testing, model-based testing, etc.) enumerate the specification's state space and are thus limited by the state space explosion problem. This work uses symbolic techniques in order to avoid this problem. It is based on Input Output Symbolic Transition Systems (IOSTS), which extend Input Output Labeled Transition Systems (IOLTS) by the use of variables and parameters. System specifications as well as test purposes/behaviors, which are used in conformance testing to specify what aspects of the system have to be tested, are defined as IOSTS. However, almost all the related works on symbolic execution are based on active testing, i.e., it is possible to generate test cases without enumerating the specifications state space. The resulting test cases are symbolic and can be made executable by instantiation of their variables. The approach presented in this chapter is different from the others in a way that the behavior/property is modeled in the form of IOSTS and symbolically executed to perform the passive testing.

Trace Analysis Technique

In the literature there are several techniques that have been proposed to analyze parametric traces, but they have limitations: some in the specification formalism, others in the type of traces they support. Parametric trace slicing (Chen & Rosu, 2009) provides solutions to parametric trace analysis that is unrestricted by the type of parametric property or trace that can be analyzed. Trace slicing is actually a transformation technique that reduces the size of execution traces for the purpose of testing and debugging. Based on the appropriate use of antecedents, trace slicing tracks back reverse dependencies and causality along execution traces and then cuts irrelevant information that do not influence the data observed from the trace. Other approaches that have been proposed to specify and monitor parametric properties are Tracematches (Avgustinov, Tibble, & Moor, 2007), J-LO (Bodden, 2005) and LSC (Damm & Harel, 2001) but they support a limited number of parameters, and each has its own approach to handle parameterization specific to its particular specification formalism. On the contrary, the parametric trace slicing technique is generic in the specification formalism, and supports unlimited number of parameters.

To the best of our knowledge, there are currently no works tackling passive testing of functionality and security aspects of a system based on IOSTS without any awareness on the status of the execution traces. We thus present in the following related works in the area but mainly focusing on the passive testing techniques.

RELATED WORK

Among the researches in passive testing techniques, we can cite the following ones. (Andrés et al., 2008) proposed a formal framework to perform passive testing of distributed systems, assuming that the formal specifications of both the web services and the interaction between them are given. The specifications are modeled by timed automata and the properties are expressed as invariants. The main drawback is that the authors focus only on checking the control portion.

In (Lee et al., 2002; Ural & Xu, 2007), data portion testing is approached by evaluation of traces in EEFSM (Event-driven Extended Finite State Machine) and SEFSM (Simplified Extended Finite State Machine) models, testing the correctness through the specification states and the internal variable values. Although the authors check the data values, these approaches assume to have a specification model. In this chapter, it is not assumed the existence of a specification and test protocol properties directly on the trace. The knowledge of the property that we monitor is obtained from the Bluetooth developer. Moreover, it is usually considered that the implementation is taken without knowledge of its internal state, that is to say that we do not consider the event trace to start from the initial state or some predefined state. In another work (Alcalde, Cavalli, Chen, Khuu, & Lee, 2004), the authors have proposed a backward checking method that analyses in a backward fashion the input/output trace. It checks both the control and data portion of a protocol system. Although, the approach seems to be interesting, in our approach we are not dependent on any formal specifications.

The author of (Stolz, 2010) proposed a parameterized proposition to include data. The propositions contain formulas, but the data values in these formulas are considered to be fixed. Thus the data values must be enumerated leading to a huge amount of data which is avoided by the symbolic technique. In (Lalanne & Maag, 2013), a Horn logic based approach is proposed to test data-centric protocols. Interesting syntax and semantics are defined to write clauses between data carried by protocol packets. While this approach also avoids the enumeration of parameters, nevertheless, it cannot be valuated as in our approach but just compared Furthermore, the approach requires checking all the trace before providing

a verdict. We do not have this constraint by using the slicing technique defined in this chapter.

In (Oostdijk, Rusu, Tretmans, Vries, & Willemse, 2007), the authors propose learning from implementation to complete a partial specification using IOSTS. But, learning here is done by interacting with the implementations. In this chapter, the symbolic execution is derived from the IOSTS property and the finite symbolic traces are verified against the trace slices without interacting with any models or implementations. From our knowledge, there are currently no works tackling passive testing of functionality and security aspects of network protocols based on IOSTS without any awareness on the states of the execution traces.

The authors of (Gall, Rapin, & Touil, 2007) propose a conformance testing based approach to check a refinement relation between reactive system specifications. The systems are modeled using the IOSTS formalism. Like in traditional conformance testing, some properties or behaviors (observable traces) are selected from the abstract specification and are submitted to the concrete specification to get a verdict about the refinement relation. However, contradicting to conformance testing techniques, the execution of selected behaviors is not a black box procedure but a white box procedure based on static analysis called symbolic execution technique with constraints solver.

In (Nguyen, Poizat, & Zaidi, 2012) the authors propose a conformance checking framework based on symbolic models and an extension of the symbolic bisimulation equivalence. In this approach, the global specification and implementation description are provided as input to the framework and are transformed into Symbolic Transition Graphs (STGs). Later the STGs (comprising the STG from specification and implementation) are checked for conformance. This leads to the generation of a large Boolean formula which is then verified using SMT solver to reach a conformance verdict. Although this approach is interesting as it avoids state space explosion issues but still, complex constraints cannot be resolved and also it depends on a complete formal specification.

The same authors as an improvement in (Nguyen, Poizat, & Zaidi, 2012) discuss an interesting online verification of service choreographies considering complex data constraints. However, they assume that the IUT conforms to the model (which is based on Symbolic Transition Graph with Assignments (STGA)) and also they prove the scalability of their approach for a maximum of 20,000 packets. But, in our approach we consider only an informal specification to define the properties and do not depend on any model. In addition, we have proved the scalability of our approach to very large traces ($> 10^6$).

From the literature we see that most of the works stated above and also to mention few others (Bentakouk, Poizat, & Zaidi, 2011; Weiglhofer, Aichernig, & Wotawa, 2010) are based on active testing using symbolic execution approach. However, in our work we represent the system behavior or property in the form of IOSTS and symbolically execute to obtain a treelike structure. The branches or the behaviors of the symbolic tree are monitored against the real system trace using passive testing approach.

Several Model-based testing techniques have been carried out to test the embedded system in the past that are suitable for state based systems. Some of them are based on Formal or semi-formal description languages which includes EFSM and Specification Description Language (SDL). A set of tools has been developed based on these techniques to generate system level test suites from system models. However, an assumption here is that we do not have any system model or formal specification.

SYMBOLIC MONITORING METHODOLOGY

This section details the monitoring methodology based on symbolic models. It is composed of three subsections following three main phases:

- **Symbolic Modeling of System Properties:** This description consists of a set of properties modeled using IOSTS (Input-Output Symbolic Transition Systems) formalism that the embedded system has to satisfy or respect. These IOSTS are symbolically executed to obtain a tree-like structure which represents the symbolic behavior of the system. These branches/properties can express both behavioral or security attacks.
- **Trace Slicing Technique:** A parametric trace slicing technique is proposed to trace analysis which is an important concept in passive testing techniques. The real-time trace is split into different trace slices based on certain parameters of interest.
- **Property Evaluation Methodology:** A verdict PASS is obtained if the system satisfies the requirement, a FAIL if the property is not satisfied by the system implementation, an ATTACK-PASS if the attack scenario is satisfied by the system and an INCONCLUSIVE is deduced, if the system cannot decide on the verdict (for example, in the case of very short system trace).

Based on a real case study (Bluetooth in automotive), a detailed description of each step above mentioned is given in the following sections.

Symbolic Modeling of System Properties

IOSTS (Input-Output Symbolic Transition Systems) formalism is adapted to formally model the system behaviors and security related attacks. We would like to focus on the IOSTS formalism to model the system behavior mainly because:

- IOSTSs introduce the concept of attribute variables. That is, instead of enumerating all possible real data when modeling systems, an IOSTS uses these attribute variables (also called as *fresh variables or symbols*). This abstraction of real data helps to avoid *the state explosion problem* in large reactive systems like communication protocol, embedded systems, etc.

- Reduction of non-determinism. IOSTSs introduce the concept of *guards*, which are conditions of the transitions. Thus, when there are two transitions leaving from the same state, one can easily find out which one of the two transitions is executed.
- IOSTSs are a general abstraction of the IOLTSs. The semantics of an IOSTS are also given by means of an IOLTS.

Since the IOSTSs introduce the notion of attribute variables to represent concrete data they seem to fit well with the symbolic execution technique. The symbolic execution trees resulting from the symbolic execution of an IOSTS represents all the possible behaviors in the system, it suffices to find concrete data for the different symbols in the corresponding branch satisfying the guard conditions accordingly, so one can reach a specific state. Additionally, to verify the system behaviors we also monitor certain attack scenarios, which may be a deviation from the expected behavior.

IOSTS Formalism

Definition 1: Syntax of IOSTS (Constant, Jeron, Marchand, & Rusu, 2007)

An IOSTS M is a tuple $\langle D, I, L, l^0, \Sigma, T \rangle$ where:

- $D = V \cup P$ *is a finite set of typed data which consists of the set V of variables and set P of parameters.*
- *I is the initial condition, a Boolean expression on V.*
- *L is a non-empty, finite set of locations.*
- $l^0 \in L$ *is the initial location.*
- $\Sigma = \Sigma^? \cup \Sigma^! \cup \Sigma^\tau$ *is a non-empty, finite alphabet of actions which consists of three*

mutually disjoint alphabets of output actions $\Sigma^!$, input actions $\Sigma^?$, and internal actions Σ^τ, i.e.,

$$(\Sigma^? \cap \Sigma^! = \varnothing) \wedge (\Sigma^? \cap \Sigma^\tau = \varnothing) \wedge (\Sigma^! \cap \Sigma^\tau = \varnothing).$$

- *T is a finite set of symbolic transitions. Each symbolic transition is a tuple $t = \langle l, a, G, A, l' \rangle \in T$ consisting of:*
  - *A location $l \in L$, the origin of the symbolic transition.*
  - *An action $a \in \Sigma$ called the action of the transition.*
  - *A guard G on $V \cup P$, which is a Boolean expression containing the truth values true, false.*
  - *A set of assignment A, each assignment is of the form $\left(x := A_x \right)_{x \in V \cup P}$, such that, for each $x \in V \cup P$, the right-hand side A_x of the assignment is an expression on $V \cup P$. These assignments are well-typed, that is, the expressions A_x returns a data type which is the same as that of x.*
  - *A location $l' \in L$, the destination of the transition.*

Note: Here, we consider only the observable behaviors of the system, i.e., $\Sigma^\tau = \varnothing$. In order to distinguish an input from an output action, we may respectively attach the '?' and '!' symbols to the actions.

Definition 2: Semantics of an IOSTS

The semantics of an IOSTS $\langle D, I, L, l^0, \Sigma, T \rangle$ is an Input-Output Labeled Transition Systems (IOLTS)
$\langle S, S_0, \Lambda, \rightarrow \rangle$ defined as:

- *The set of states is $S = L \times V$, where V is the set of valuation for the variables V. Formally a state is a pair*

$\langle l, v \rangle$ *where* $l \in L$ *is a location and* $v \in (V_x)_{x \in V}$.

- *The set of initial states is* S_0, *an initial state*

$s^0 = \langle l^0, v^0 \rangle$ *such that* $l^0 \in L$ *is the initial location and* v^0 *is the valuation of the variables that satisfies the initial condition* I, *i.e.*, $\{ S_0 = \langle l^0, v^0 \rangle \mid I(v^0) = true \}$ *and* $v, v^0 \in V$.

- *The set of valued actions* $\Lambda = \{ \langle a, v \rangle \mid a \in \Sigma, v \in \Pi_{sig(a)} \}$, *where* a *is an (input, output) action and* v *is a valuation for the parameter(s) carried by the action* a. *The set of valued parameters* P *is given by* Π.

- $\Pi_{sig(a)}$ *corresponds to the all possible valuations for the parameters seen in the action* a.

- *Is the transition relation, which is a 3-tuple* $\langle s, \alpha, s' \rangle$ *where,* $s = \langle l, v \rangle, s' = \langle l', v' \rangle$ *are the source and destination states respectively and* $\alpha = \langle a, v \rangle$ *is a valued action, where* $a \in \Sigma$ *is the action of the symbolic transition* t *and* v *is a valuation of the parameters carried by the action* a.

Note: Valuation in general means assigning concrete values to V or P. In this approach, the concrete input values and initialization values of variables are replaced by symbolic ones, called fresh variables. We represent the set of fresh variables by F, where $F \cap V = \varnothing$.

To illustrate the IOSTS formalism, we describe in the following a real case study based on the Bluetooth protocol used in an automotive environment. Then, we provide a basic property of the Bluetooth protocol and an attack scenario taken from the Bluetooth specifications[1]. Like many other communication technologies, Bluetooth is composed of a hierarchy of components referred to as a stack. Here, we only consider the host

controller interface (HCI) layer messages (collected from one device) to describe the device discovery and connectivity behavior between the Bluetooth devices.

AUTOMOTIVE CASE STUDY – BLUETOOTH PROTOCOL

Overview of Bluetooth Protocol

Bluetooth (Miller & Bisdikian, 2000) is a technology for short range wireless data and real-time two-way voice transfer providing data rates up to 3 Mb/s. Moreover, Bluetooth networks are formed by radio links, which means that there are additional security aspects whose impact is not yet well understood. Almost any device can be connected to another device by using Bluetooth.

Bluetooth devices that communicate with each other form a *piconet*. The device that initiates a connection is the piconet master. One piconet can have a maximum of seven active slave devices and one master device. All communication within a piconet goes through the piconet master. The clock of the piconet master and frequency hopping information are used to synchronize the piconet slaves with the master. Two or more piconets together form a *scatternet*, which can be used to eliminate Bluetooth range restrictions. A scatternet environment requires that different piconets must have a common device, called a scatternet member, to relay data between the piconets. Many kinds of Bluetooth devices, such as mobile phones, headsets, PCs, laptops, printers, mice and keyboards, are widely used all over the world.

Just like any other protocol a Bluetooth Stack is well-defined. The Bluetooth stack is primarily divided into a Controller part and a Host part. Between the Host and the Controller there is a *Host/ Controller Interface (HCI)*, whose messages are mainly considered in the analysis of the case study.

Passive Testing Module

The System Under Test (SUT) is an automotive connectivity module, which provides the driver an ability to connect a mobile phone to the infotainment system. The module itself is connected via the controller area network (CAN) bus to the vehicle. The phone can be linked via the Bluetooth technology. In this case study the Bluetooth specification 2.1[2] was used.

An overview of the SUT is shown in Figure 3. As mentioned before, it is shown that the SUT is connected to the vehicle bus via the CAN network. The connection to a mobile phone is possible over the Bluetooth network, whereas additional USB devices can be attached via a USB interface. In this section, we discuss how the Bluetooth session establishment and Bluestabbing attack scenario are monitored using the symbolic passive testing methodology.

Examples of IOSTS Model

Connection Establishment Property in Bluetooth Protocol

Figure 4 shows the message sequences captured from the HCI layer of the master (car's Bluetooth device) while trying to achieve the Bluetooth connectivity with the slave device (mobile phone). Each Bluetooth device has a device local name, a user-friendly name to identify the different Bluetooth devices. This device name can be initially configured by each host by sending an *hci-change-local-name* message to the host controller (HC/ LM-A). A Bluetooth device in *discoverable* mode can communicate or be visible to other Bluetooth devices. If it does not prefer to be visible, it could be in *non-discoverable* mode. Devices which are in discoverable mode are only eligible to participate in the session. So when one Bluetooth device wants to connect to another one, it must go through certain steps to learn and authenticate with the remote device. The master first finds the other devices which are in "*discoverable*" mode, and then performs an inquiry on each device by sending an *hci-inquiry* message. Thus the inquiry process gives the master a list of hardware addresses called bd-addr which are available to be connected and the important device feature information. The bd-addr is a unique address of a Bluetooth device, similar to the MAC address of a network device. This address is needed for further communications with a device. Having received the slave addresses, the master can establish an actual connection with one or more of the devices it found via the *paging* process. During the paging process the master sends an *hci-create-connection* message to establish a connection with a particular slave (based on the parameter bd-addr). The connection is successfully established upon

Figure 3. Overview of the SUT

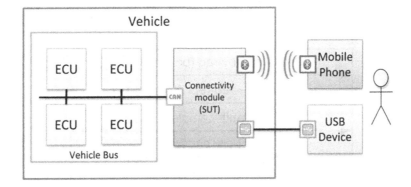

receiving an *hci-connection-complete* message. Authentication can be explicitly executed at any time after a connection has been established by an *hci-auth-req* message. The established connection can be anytime detached by the master device by an *hci-disconnect message*.

Bluetooth Attack: Bluestabbing

Usually, the list of discovered Bluetooth devices displays only the name of the located device, and it does not show the actual Bluetooth address. If the slave devices are familiar with the located device name they are in discoverable mode else invisible. This local name can be changed anytime by anyone, hence prone to Bluestabbing attack (Browning & Kessler, 2009) as shown in Figure 4.

In the Bluestabbing attack, the attacker impersonates as a legitimate user and modifies the Bluetooth device name of a legitimate user by resending an *hci-change-local-name* message with a badly formatted device name thereby causing the slave device to confuse during the device discovery phase (Inquiry). But this attack could be more severe, if the Bluetooth attacker modifies

Figure 4. Sequence diagram - Bluetooth connection establishment and bluestabbing attack

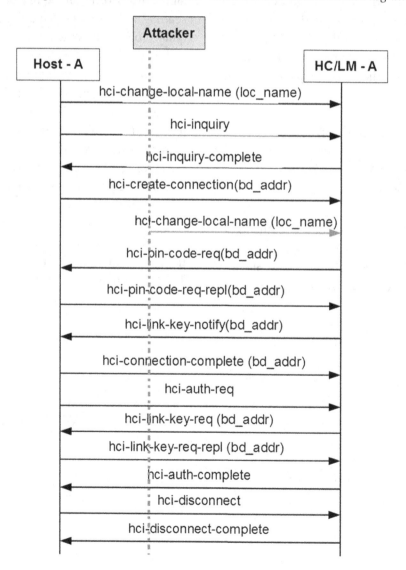

his own local device name as a legitimate user's device name, and tries to establish a connection with the other Bluetooth device by capturing the passwords and sensitive information from the device.

For a better understanding of the IOSTS formalism, we represent the Bluetooth behavior along with the attack scenario in Figure 5. We observe that there is a transition from state l5 to state l5.1, a deviation from the regular scenario due to *the hci-change-local-name* message inserted by the attacker, during the device inquiry phase, resulting in the Bluestabbing attack. For an explanation

we have considered only few parameters *bd-addr, loc-name* corresponding to the Bluetooth protocol, but in practice there is no limitation in considering the number of parameters.

In Figure 5, *vloc_name* and *v_bd_addr* belongs to set of system variables V and *loc_name0* and *bd_addr0* constitutes the set of formal parameters P. In an IOSTS, all the values of the parameters and variables are represented symbolically. For instance, the IOSTS tuple for the symbolic transition $t \in T$ from l0 to l1 can be expressed as below.

t: ⟨l0, (hci-change-local-name), true, ((vloc_name:= loc_ name_ i)), l1⟩

Figure 5. Equivalent IOSTS model - Bluetooth Connection establishment and Bluestabbing attack

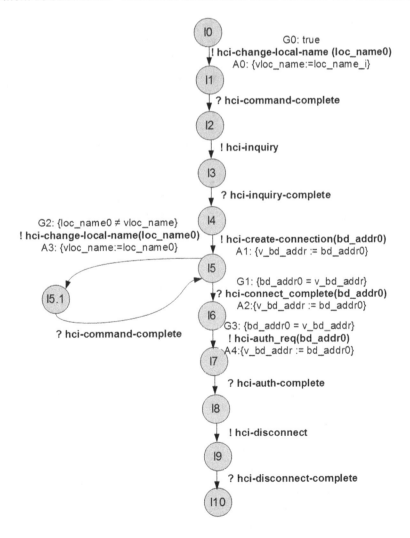

In the next section, we introduce the syntax-related notions of the symbolic execution, as well as the symbolic execution of IOSTS. Then we define the semantics associated with a symbolic execution and an example based on the Bluetooth protocol.

Symbolic Execution

The symbolic execution (SE for short) of IOSTS serves two main objectives: (i) to use symbolic values for action messages and initialization val-

ues for IOSTS variables instead of concrete data values (ii) to obtain a tree-like structure which represents all the behaviors accepted by the IOSTS in a symbolic way.

In Figure 6, the symbolic execution of an IOSTS (defined in Figure 5) is represented as a tree with different branches in which the vertices are symbolic extended states and edges are labeled by symbolic communication actions (Gaston, Gall, Rapin, & Touil, 2006). The branches depict the session establishment and security attack in Bluetooth as explained in the previous section. In

Figure 6. Symbolic execution of IOSTS

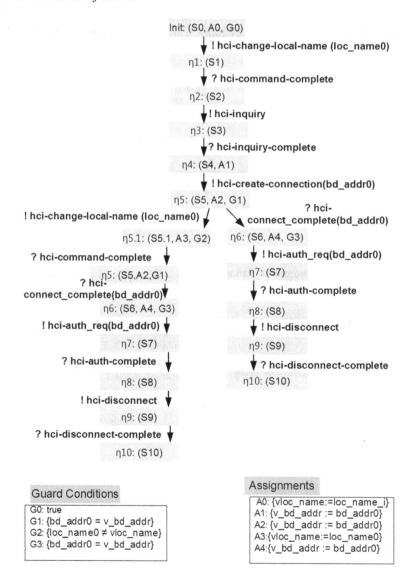

this section we provide the definitions related to symbolic execution of the IOSTS.

Note: Also, to be noted that, based on the above mentioned definition, some of the state triples have been discarded by the execution since they are related to transitions or assignment statements that are not guarded by the path condition.

Technical Background

Definition 3: Symbolic Extended States

Let M be an IOSTS. A symbolic extended state for an IOSTS is a triple given by $\eta = (s, A, G)$ where $s \in S$, A is a set of assignments and G a set of guard conditions. η is said to be an acceptable symbolic state if its guard condition G, which is a Boolean expression, is satisfiable. K_{sat} is the set of all acceptable symbolic states.

Definition 4: Symbolic Execution of an IOSTS

Let M be an IOSTS. The symbolic execution SE(M) of an IOSTS is defined by (init, R_{sat}), where init = $(S_0, A_0, true)$ and $R_{sat} \subseteq K_{sat} \times \Lambda_F \times K_{sat}$ is the symbolic execution of the transitions of M, where Λ_F is the set of valued communication actions obtained by assigning fresh variables F as values for the parameters.

We define the behaviors of a symbolic execution by means of its symbolic traces.

Definition 5: Traces of a Symbolic Execution

Let $t_1 \ldots t_n$ be a finite sequence of symbolic executions of the transitions of M such that $t_i = (\eta_i, \alpha_i, \eta_i') \in R_{sat}$, $\eta_1 = init$ and $\eta' = \eta_{i+1}$, $i \in 1 \ldots n$. A symbolic trace in SE(M) is the ordered sequence of valued actions $\alpha_1 \ldots \alpha_n$.

Trace(SE(M)) is the set of all symbolic traces of SE(M).

Definition 6: Traces Projection

Let $\alpha = \langle a, v \rangle \in \Sigma \times \Pi_{sig(a)}$ be a valued action. The projection CP(α) is defined as the projection of the valued actions on Σ, i.e. CP(α)=a. Consequently, we name CP[Trace(SE(M))] the projection of all the traces of SE(M) describing the set of traces without the valuated parameters (only the Control Portions of the actions (Σ) are kept).

Example 1: Let us consider the symbolic execution tree in Figure 6 representing the session establishment and Bluestabbing attack in Bluetooth protocol. For readability reasons, the assignments and guard conditions are not directly shown inside the symbolic states but in separate frames. In this symbolic execution tree we have two different paths. The symbolic traces are given by:

Trace(SE(M))={

!hci-change-local-name(loc_name0)?hci-command-complete!hci-inquiry?hci-inquiry-complete!hci-create-connection(bd_addr0)?hci-connect-complete(bd_addr0)!hci-auth-req(bd_addr0)?hci-auth-complete!hci-disconnect?hci-disconnect-complete, !hci-change-local-name(loc_name0)?hci-command-complete!hci-inquiry!hci-change-local-name(loc_name0)?hci-command-complete?hci-inquiry-complete!hci-create-connection(bd_addr0)?hci-connect-complete(bd_addr0)!hci-auth-req(bd_addr0)?hci-auth-complete!hci-disconnect?hci-disconnect-complete}

The set of traces with only the control portion of the action is given by:

CP[Trace(SE(M))]={

!hci-change-local-name?hci-command-complete!hci-inquiry?hci-inquiry-complete!hci-create-connection?hci-connect-complete!hci-auth-req?hci-auth-complete!hci-disconnect?hci-disconnect-complete,!hci-change-local-name?hci-command-complete!hci-inquiry!hci-change-local-name?hci-command-complete?hci-inquiry-complete!hci-create-connection?hci-connect-complete!hci-auth-req?hci-auth-complete!hci-disconnect?hci-disconnect-complete}

In this section we have obtained the traces of the symbolic execution of an IOSTS representing a protocol property with a possible eventual attack scenario, in the next section we explain the parametric trace slicing approach to passively test these symbolic traces on real network traces.

Trace Slicing Technique

Trace slicing is a widely used technique for analyzing a real system trace (Chen & Rosu, 2009). The parametric trace slicing technique simplifies the real protocol execution trace into different slices based on the data portions of each event (i.e., packet) in the trace. The events corresponding to a particular valuation are grouped in the order they appear in the trace in a particular slice, and all the other events that are unrelated to the given valuation are dropped. We begin this section by defining parametric traces and then some terminology related to the parametric trace slicing algorithm.

Technical Background

Definition 7: Non-Parametric and Parametric Traces

A non-parametric trace is an element in Σ^*, that is a sequence of actions (as defined by Definition 1) without data portions. A parametric trace is a word in the set of valued actions Λ^*.

Example 2: Consider three valued actions $\langle a1, \upsilon' : (x \to 1, y \to 2) \rangle$, $\langle a2, \upsilon'' : (x \to 1, y \to 2, z \to 3) \rangle$ and $\langle a3, \upsilon''' : (x \to 1) \rangle$. τ defined as $\tau : \langle a1, \upsilon' \rangle \langle a2, \upsilon'' \rangle \langle a3, \upsilon''' \rangle$ is a parametric trace.

Definition 8: Less and More Informative Valued Actions

Let $Q \subseteq P$ be a set of parameters in an IOSTS. We denote by Π^Q the set of valued parameters Q. Let υ', $\upsilon \in \Pi^Q$ be two valuations of the parameters Q, we say that υ' is less informative than υ (or υ is more informative than υ'), denoted by $\upsilon' \sqsubseteq \upsilon$, if for any $q \in Q$, if $\upsilon'(q)$ is defined it implies $\upsilon(q)$ is also defined and $\upsilon(q) = \upsilon'(q)$.

Example 3: Let us represent two valuations υ': $\langle x \to 1, y \to 2 \rangle$ and υ: $\langle x \to 1, y \to 2, z \to 3 \rangle$

Here, υ' is less informative than υ since all the parameters (x, y) defined in υ' are also defined in υ and υ carries additional information (parameter z).

Definition 9: Trace Slicing

Let $\tau = (\langle a_i, \upsilon_i \rangle, (\langle a_2, \upsilon_2 \rangle, ..., \langle a_n, \upsilon_n \rangle) \in \Lambda^*$ be a parametric trace, and $\upsilon \in \Pi^Q$ be a valuation. We define recursively (for i = 1 to n) the function $\tau \upharpoonright_\upsilon$ such as:

$$\tau \upharpoonright_\upsilon = \begin{cases} <> & if \tau = <> \\ (\langle a_i, \upsilon_i \rangle), (\langle a_2, \upsilon_2 \rangle, ..., \langle a_n, \upsilon_n \rangle) \upharpoonright_\upsilon & if \upsilon_i \sqsubseteq \upsilon \\ (\langle a_2, \upsilon_2 \rangle, ..., \langle a_n, \upsilon_n \rangle) \upharpoonright_\upsilon & if \upsilon_i \not\sqsubseteq \upsilon \end{cases}$$

It means that for a finite parametric trace τ represented by $\tau' \langle a_i, \upsilon_i \rangle$, the trace slice for υ can be obtained under two different cases. If υ_i is less informative than υ, then the action a_i is added at the end of the trace slice else we leave the trace slice undisturbed as defined above.

Algorithm for Parametric Trace Slicing

The parametric trace slicing takes the trace τ in event order (i.e., from the first event to the last one) as input and provides *ts*, the set of all possible trace slices of τ as output. $ts \in \Sigma^*$ is obtained by the table L: $\Pi \rightarrow \Sigma^*$ analyzing the valuation of parameters observed in τ as defined in Definition 8.

The Algorithm 1 is defined as follows. The outer for-loop (lines 2-11) takes each event $\langle a, \upsilon \rangle$ incrementally in the trace τ and the existence of the valuation of the current event is checked in θ using the inner for-loop (lines 3-9). If the valuation υ' is less informative than υ observed in the outer for-loop as per line 4, then the action a is added at the end of the trace slice as per line 5, if not, the action is not added to the trace slice. The procedure described for the inner for-loop is continued until all the parametric instances in θ are evaluated against $\langle a, \upsilon \rangle$ in the outer for-loop. Later, θ is updated with the new instance υ as per line 10. Now, the next event in the outer for-loop is taken and the whole procedure is repeated until line 10. This procedure is continued until we reach the end of the trace τ in the outer for-loop. At the end, we obtain a table L with all possible trace slices *ts* and θ with all possible valuations contained in the trace.

The proposed slicing algorithm computes trace slices for all the parametric instances observed in the trace rather than computing all possible combinations of parametric instances. The complexity of the slicing algorithm is $O(n \times m)$ where n is the number of messages in the trace and m is the number of available parametric instances in the monitored trace. In the worst-case, the number of observed parametric instances m can be equal to the trace length n. Hence, the worst-case time complexity is given by $O(n^2)$ where $m = n$. However, we do not consider all possible combinations of parametric instances, the number of slices would be significantly reduced thereby improves the evaluation time complexity.

Example 4: Consider a sample Bluetooth trace.

$\tau = $!hci- inquiry

?hci-inquiry-complete

!hci-create-connection(bd_addr1)

!hci-create-connection(bd_addr2)

?hci-connect-complete(bd_addr1).

For simplicity we represent only the parameter values when writing valuations, that is, instead of $\langle bd\_addr \rightarrow bd\_addr1 \rangle$ we denote by $\langle bd\_addr1 \rangle$. Applying the trace slicing algorithm on τ based on the parameter *bd_ addr* we obtain the Table 1.

In this section, we have defined how we can obtain the trace slices by applying the trace slicing algorithm. In the next section, we discuss how the obtained parametric trace slices are used for evaluating a Bluetooth property defined as an IOSTS.

Algorithm 1. Parametric trace slicing algorithm

Input: *parametric trace* $\tau \in \Lambda^*$.
Output: *A table L:* $\Pi \rightarrow \Sigma^*$
1: *Initialization:* $L \leftarrow \epsilon$; $\theta \leftarrow \{\epsilon\}$
2: *for each ordered event* $\langle a, \upsilon \rangle$ *in* τ *do*
3: *for each parametric instance* υ' *in* θ *do*
4: *if* $\left(\upsilon' \sqsubseteq \upsilon \right)$ *then*
5: $L(\upsilon) \leftarrow \tau \restriction_\upsilon a$
6: *else*
7: $L(\upsilon) \leftarrow \tau \restriction_\upsilon$
8: *end if*
9: *end for*
10: $\theta \leftarrow \theta \cup \{\upsilon\}$
11: *end for*

Table 1. Trace slice table for sample Bluetooth trace τ

Valuation (v)	ts – the v -trace slice
$\langle$bd_addr1$\rangle$	!hci-inquiry?hci-inquiry-complete!hci-create-connection?hci-connect-complete
$\langle$bd_addr2$\rangle$	!hci-inquiry?hci-inquiry-complete!hci-create-connection

PROPERTY EVALUATION METHODOLOGY

The objective is to check an expected behavior formally specified as an IOSTS property *P* against an execution trace slice in *ts*. We also target here the test of deviant behaviors for security testing. It means that if our conformance property is not satisfied on real traces, we check the presence of an eventually defined security attack in the monitored trace. As illustrated by Figure 5, we observe a security attack sequence (the deviation in the model to state S5.1) within the global conformance property. To perform the proposed approach, the *symbolic tester* requires two different input files as shown in the Figure 7:

- The *raw trace files* (in .txt format) collected from the network analyzer.
- The *symbolic state property details* like guard-conditions, assignments, symbolic trace information, etc.

Once the symbolic tester receives the raw trace file, it performs the following tasks:

- **Trace Parsing:** Filtering the trace files keeping only the relevant information for the protocol(s) under test. The basic idea is to keep in the traces only the messages and parameters corresponding to the specified properties to check.
- **Trace Slicing:** Traces are sliced based upon the specific parameters of interests. For example, for the Bluetooth proto-

col, *bd-addr* the parameter that identifies a unique Bluetooth device was selected. Based on the Algorithm 1 discussed in the Trace Slicing Technique section the slicing was performed.

- **Evaluation Engine:** This module receives the output from the trace slicing logic and the symbolic state details which was provided as one of the inputs and then, based on the evaluation logic, the verdicts *Pass/ Fail/Inconclusive/Attack-Pass/Attack-Fail* is obtained for each trace slices which provide a final verdict of the tested property on the trace.

Evaluation of a Property on Trace Slices

In the evaluation approach, we evaluate the control and the data portions of the messages observed in the symbolic traces. *CP[Trace(SE(M))]* and *L(v)* are used to check the control portion. For the data portion, we check the guard conditions associated with each state in the symbolic execution of the IOSTS. The evaluation is done for each slice against the symbolic traces. Based on the value of the variable *AttackSeq* we differentiate the conformance property (*AttackSeq* = 0) from the attack sequence (*AttackSeq* = 1). The verdicts *Pass* and *Fail* are provided for the test of the conformance property while *Attack-Pass* and *Attack-Fail* are dedicated to the test of the security property. *Inconclusive* is emitted if we cannot firmly decide (e.g. in case of a too short execution trace).

- Pass
  - The control portions are identical for two sequences in $L(v)$ and $CP[Trace(SE(M))]$
  - The data portions are *accepted* (all states in $SE(M)$ are acceptable, Definition 2).

$\forall ts_i \in ts,\ (\exists X \in CP[Trace(SE(M))],\ X = L(v_i)\ \wedge$
$\forall \eta \in SE(M),\ \eta \in K_{sat},\ AttackSeq = 0)$

- Fail
  - The control portions are identical.
  - The data portions are not *accepted*.

$\forall ts_i \in ts,\ (\exists X \in CP[Trace(SE(M))],\ X = L(v_i)\ \wedge$
$\exists \eta \in SE(M),\ \eta \notin K_{sat},\ AttackSeq = 0)$

- Attack-Pass
  - The control portions are identical for the two sequences: it exists one slice $ts_i \in ts$ identical to one element of $CP[Trace(SE(M))]$ holding the attack sequence.
  - The data portions are *accepted*.

$\forall ts_i \in ts,\ (\exists X \in CP[Trace(SE(M))],\ X = L(v_i)\ \wedge$
$\forall \eta \in SE(M),\ \eta \in K_{sat},\ AttackSeq = 1)$

- Attack-Fail
  - The control portions are identical for the two sequences like the *Attack-Pass* above.
  - The data portions are not *accepted*.

$\forall ts_i \in ts,\ (\exists X \in CP[Trace(SE(M))],\ X = L(v_i)\ \wedge$
$\exists \eta \in SE(M),\ \eta \notin K_{sat},\ AttackSeq = 1)$

- *Inconclusive*, if the control portions are not identical. Indeed, the execution trace has eventually been extracted from the IUT starting from a time t that does not correspond to the initial state (reset). Thus, the obtained finite trace may not be practically sufficient to prove the property or attack on the trace slice, which results in an *inconclusive* verdict. Since the control portion is not satisfied, we do not check the data portions.

$\forall ts_i \in ts,\ (\nexists X \in CP[Trace(SE(M))],\ X = L(v_i),$
$AttackSeq = 0\ or\ 1)$

Figure 7. Symbolic tool framework

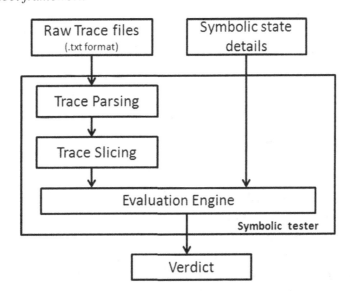

Algorithm for Evaluating the Property on the Trace Slices

In order to evaluate the conformance or security properties on the trace slices, two steps are performed: control portion must be checked and then we verify the data portion. An Algorithm 2 is defined for this purpose. In line 4, the control portion is checked by comparing $L(v_i)$ and X_k. If the sequences are identical and if the verdict is not *Pass*, then we process the lines 5-17, else it returns *Inconclusive* and skips the data-portion checking.

In the if-loop, we check for the type of sequence. If *(AttackSeq = 0)*, then it is a conformance property sequence and the data portion is verified using the function *data-check-fn*. In *data-check-fn*, the set of assignments A corresponding to each state is performed and the guard conditions are evaluated. If the function returns a *Pass*, then the output verdict is *Pass* else *Fail*. If *(AttackSeq ≠ 0)* it is an attack sequence and the data portions are evaluated using the same function. If the function returns a *Pass*, then the output verdict is *Attack-Pass* else *Attack-Fail*.

Finally, based on the verdicts obtained on the slices, we may define the final verdict of the property testing on the entire real trace by:

- Pass, if $(\forall Verdict(ts_i) = Pass)$.
- Attack-Pass, if $(\exists Verdict(ts_i) = Attack\text{-}Pass)$.
- FAIL, if $[(\exists Verdict(ts_i) = Fail) \wedge (\exists Verdict(ts_i) \neq Attack\text{-}Pass)]$.
- Inconclusive otherwise.

INDUSTRIAL EXPERIMENTATIONS AND RESULTS

The approach has been implemented using SQL. SQL is used to process the huge amount of data contained in the captured traces. We specifically used its efficiency to perform the trace slicing approach. This section reports some experiments with the tool and its application to an automotive case study in order to test an embedded Bluetooth entity and eventual security attack depicted in Figure 4. In this section we illustrate the results obtained for symbolic passive testing approach by its application to a set of real execution traces extracted from a real automotive Bluetooth framework with functional and security properties as described in the IOSTS section.

Passive Testing Results

For the experiments, Bluetooth traces collected from the Bluetooth framework depicting the session establishment was provided. A sample of the results obtained for 10 Bluetooth traces are shown in Table 2. Each of the Bluetooth trace obtained had a different device local name. In order to evaluate the efficiency of the implemented prototype tool, we performed the experiments in two ways: with

Algorithm 2. Evaluation logic for each slice

Input: *A table Trace(SE(M)), set of G for all* $\eta \in K$

AttackSeq), $ts_i \in ts$
Output: *verdict(ts_i) = Pass/Fail/Inconclusive/Attack-Pass/Attack-Fail*
1: *Initialization:* $i \leftarrow 0$ *to n, verdict(tsi)* $\leftarrow$ ''
2: *for each* $\left(ts_i \in ts\right)$ *do*
3: *for each* $\left(X_k \in CP\left[Trace\left(SE\left(M\right)\right)\right]\right]$ *do*
4: *if* $(L(v_i) = X_k)$ *(verdict(ts_i ≠ Pass) then*
5: *if (AttackSeq = 0) then*
6: *if data-check-fn(ts_i;G) = Pass then*
7: *verdict(ts_i)* $\leftarrow$ *Pass*
8: *else*
9: *verdict(ts_i)* $\leftarrow$ *Fail*
10: *end if*
11: *else*
12: *if data-check-fn(ts_i,G) = Pass then*
13: *verdict(ts_i)* $\leftarrow$ *Attack-Pass*
14: *else*
15: *verdict(ts_i)* $\leftarrow$ *Attack-Fail*
16: *end if*
17: *end if*
18: *else*
19: *verdict(ts_i)* $\leftarrow$ *Inconclusive*
20: *end if*
21: *end for*
22: *end for*

unmodified traces and by manually introducing errors and also by introducing few fake messages to create an attack scenario in the real trace. For example, in the traces 1,3,5,9 we tried to modify manually the parameter *bd-addr* in a Bluetooth message like *hci-connect-complete* so that we can obtain *Fail* verdict. Introducing error in the message caused the guard conditions associated with the symbolic state $\eta 5$ to *Fail,* as shown in Figure 6. Also, note that these manual modifications could also be performed automatically by applying a fuzzy testing approach (Takanen., DeMott & Miller, 2008) or a mutation technique (Dadeau, Heam & Kheddam, 2011).

In addition, in order to detect the attack scenario explained in the IOSTS section, we introduced few fake messages to the traces 2,4,6,7,8,10 to create a Bluestabbing attack scenario. For example, as shown in the Figure 3 we manually introduced fake message like *hci-change-local-name* before the inquiry complete phase in the real-time trace obtained. The attacks introduced were also correctly detected by our tool which indicates the correctness of the prototype tool. The verdicts obtained before and after introducing the errors are provided in the Table 2. The evaluation time to passively test the sample traces were approximately less than 1 second for each trace. The prototype and the sample files used for the experiments can be found at http://www-public. it-sudparis.eu/~mouttapp/TestSym.html.

FUTURE RESEARCH DIRECTIONS

As future work, fuzzing approaches could be applied to modify the traces automatically instead of manually as performed in this approach. Time constraints could also be included. They are indeed needed in the definition of several properties of real-time embedded systems. Moreover, timing constraints could certainly reduce the number of inconclusive verdicts by limiting the evaluation algorithm to a set of well defined slices.

Online testing, i.e., evaluation of properties as the implementation is being run, might also be a desired improvement, for instance for the detection of certain attacks and abnormal behavior of the implementation. The proposed methodology could also be adapted to bigger systems to study its scalability. Although, the experimentations were carried out in simple scenarios in this chapter, this could help extend this methodology to passively test more complex systems as future works.

Table 2. Tool results on sample Bluetooth traces

Trace	No. Messages	No. Slices	Trace Output without Errors				Trace Output with Errors and Attacks				
			P	F	I	Final O/P	P	F	I	AP	Final O/P
1	81	2	1	-	1	I	-	1	1	-	F
2	89	3	1	-	2	I	-	-	2	1	AP
3	81	2	1	-	1	I	-	1	1	-	F
4	81	2	1	-	1	I	-	-	1	1	AP
5	81	2	1	-	1	I	-	1	1	-	F
6	81	2	1	-	1	I	-	-	1	1	AP
7	81	2	1	-	1	I	-	-	1	1	AP
8	81	2	1	-	1	I	-	-	1	1	AP
9	81	2	1	-	1	I	-	1	1	-	F
10	81	2	1	-	1	I	-	-	1	1	AP
Note: P: Pass, F: Fail, I: Inconclusive, AP: Attack-Pass											

CONCLUSION

This chapter proposes a symbolic monitoring approach to detect functional and security flaws in embedded network systems by taking into account the control and data portions of real protocol traces. The presented methodology depends upon two important techniques: (i) the specification of properties defined using IOSTS formalism. The IOSTS is then symbolically executed to obtain a tree-like structure wherein the branches represent both the functional and security attack scenarios. (ii) and a trace slicing technique to perform real-time trace analysis.

The integration of symbolic execution combined with a parametric trace slicing technique allows to provide a testing verdict of a property on real execution traces. The evaluation scheme of the property on the trace slices is provided and experiments of the proposed approach on Bluetooth traces are performed. An advantage is that it can be applied to any text-based or message-based protocol. Interesting results on the conformance of the protocol as well as in the detection of a potential attack have been obtained.

REFERENCES

Alcalde, B., Cavalli, A.R., Chen, D., Khuu, D., & Lee, D. (2004). Network Protocol System Passive Testing for Fault Management: A Backward Checking Approach. In *Formal Techniques for Networked and Distributed Systems* (pp. 150-166). Academic Press.

Avgustinov, P., Tibble, J., & de Moor, O. (2007). Making trace monitoring feasible. In R. P. Gabriel (Ed.), *ACM Conference on Object-Oriented Programming, Systems and Languages* (pp. 589-608). ACM Press.

Bentakouk, L., Poizat, P., & Zaidi, F. (2011). Checking the behavioral conformance of web services with Symbolic Testing and an SMT solver. In *Proceedings of the 5th International Conference on Tests and Proofs* (pp. 33-50). Academic Press.

Bluetooth specification, version 2.1 + edr [vol 0] 1999.

Bodden, E. (2005). *J-lo, a tool for runtime-checking temporal assertions.* (Unpublished Master's thesis). RWTH Aachen University.

Browning, D., & Kessler, G. (2009). Bluetooth hacking: A case study. In *Proceedings of the Conference on Digital Forensics, Security and Law* (pp. 20-22). Academic Press.

Che, X., Lalanne, F., & Maag, S. (2012). A Logic-based Passive Testing Approach for the Validation of Communicating Protocols. In *Proc. 7th International Conference on Evaluation of Novel Approaches to Software Engineering* (pp. 53-64). Academic Press.

Chen, F., & Rosu, G. (2009). *Parametric Trace Slicing and Monitoring. In Proceedings of 15th Tools and Algorithms for the Construction and Analysis of Systems (pp. 246-261).* York, UK: Springer-Verlag.

Constant, C., Jeron, T., Marchand, H., & Rusu, V. (2007). Integrating formal verification and conformance testing for reactive systems. *IEEE Transactions on Software Engineering*, *33*(8), 558–574. doi:10.1109/TSE.2007.70707

Dadeau, F., Heam, P. C., & Kheddam, R. (2011). Mutation-Based Test Generation from Security Protocols in HLPSL. In *Proceedings of International Conference on Software Testing, Verification and Validation (ICST)*. ICST.

Damm, W., & Harrel, D. (2001). LSCs: Breathing life into message sequence charts. *Formal Methods in System Design*, *19*(1), 45–80. doi:10.1023/A:1011227529550

Gaston, C., Le Gall, P., Rapin, N., & Touil, A. (2006). Symbolic Execution Techniques for Test Purpose Definition. In Proceedings of 18th IFIP Testing of Communicating Systems (pp. 1-18). New York, NY: Springer Berlin Heidelberg.

Lalanne, F., & Maag, S. (2013). A formal data-centric approach for passive testing of communication protocols. *IEEE/ACM Transactions on Networking, 21*(3), 788–801. doi:10.1109/TNET.2012.2210443

Lee, D., Chen, D., Hao, R., Miller, R. E., Wu, J., & Yin, X. (2002). A Formal Approach for Passive Testing of Protocol Data Portions. In *Proceedings of 10th IEEE International Conference on Network Protocols* (pp. 122-131). IEEE.

Martijn, O., Vlad, R., Jan, T., De Vries, R. G., & Willemse, T. A. C. (2007). Integrating verification, testing, and learning for cryptographic protocols. In *Proceedings of the 6th International conference on Integrated formal methods* (pp. 538-557). Academic Press.

Miller, B. A., & Bisdikian, C. (2000). Bluetooth Revealed: The Insider's Guide to an Open Specification for Global Wireless Communications. Upper Saddle River, NJ:Prentice-Hall.

Nguyen, H. N., Poizat, P., & Zaidi, F. (2012a). Online verification of value-passing choreographies through property-oriented passive testing. In Proceedings of the 2012 IEEE 14th International Symposium on High-Assurance Systems Engineering (pp. 106-113). Washington, DC: IEEE Computer Society. doi:10.1109/HASE.2012.15

Nguyen, H. N., Poizat, P., & Zaidi, F. (2012b). A symbolic framework for the conformance checking of value-passing choreographies. In *Proceedings of the ICSOC*, (pp. 525-532). ICSOC.

Stolz, V. (2010). Temporal Assertions with Parametrized Propositions. *Journal of Logic and Computation, 20*(3), 743–757. doi:10.1093/logcom/exn078

Takanen, A., DeMott, J., & Miller, C. (2008). *Fuzzing for software security testing and quality assurance. Norwood, MA:* Artech House, Inc.

Ural, H., & Xu, Z. (2007). An EFSM-Based Passive Fault Detection Approach. Tallinn, Estonia: Springer-Verlag.

Weiglhofer, E. J. M., Aichernig, B. K., & Wotawa, F. (2010). When BDDs Fail: Conformance Testing with Symbolic Execution and SMT Solving. In *Proceedings of 3rd International conference on Software Testing, Verification and Validation* (pp. 479-488). Academic Press.

ADDITIONAL READING

Andrés, C., Merayo, M. G., & Nunez, M. (2012). Formal Passive Testing of Timed Systems: Theory and Tools. *Software Testing, Verification & Reliability, 22*(6), 365–405. doi:10.1002/stvr.1464

Bannour, B., Gaston, C., Lapitre, A., & Escobedo, J. P. (2012). Incremental Symbolic Conformance Testing from UML MARTE Sequence Diagrams: Railway Use Case. In *14th International Symposium on High-Assurance Systems Engineering* (pp. 9-16).

Bayse, E., Cavalli, A., Nunez, M., & Zaidi, F. (2005). A passive testing approach based on invariants: application to the WAP. *Computer Networks and ISDN Systems, 48*(2), 247–266. doi:10.1016/j.comnet.2004.09.009

Beizer, B. (1990). Software Testing Techniques . New York, NY:Van Nostrand Reinhold Co.

Constant, C., Jéron, T., Marchand, H., & Rusu, V. (2007). Integrating formal verification and conformance testing for reactive systems. *IEEE Transactions on Software Engineering, 8*(33), 558–574. doi:10.1109/TSE.2007.70707

Escobedo, J. P., Gaston, C., Le Gall, P., & Cavalli, A. (2010). Testing Web Service Orchestrators in Context: A Symbolic Approach. In Software Engineering and Formal Methods (pp. 257-267). Pisa: IEEE Computer Society.

Faivre, A., Gaston, C., & Le Gall, P. (2007). Symbolic Model Based Testing for Component Oriented Systems. In Testing of Software and Communicating systems (pp. 90-106). Talinn, Estonia:Springer Berlin Heidelberg.

Gaston, C., Aiguier, M., Bahrami, D., & Lapitre, A. (2009). Symbolic Execution Techniques Extended to Systems. In *4th International Conference on Software Engineering Advances* (pp. 78-85).

Gaston, C., Le Gall, P., Rapin, N., & Touil, A. (2013). Symbolic Execution-Based Techniques for Conformance Testing. In J.-P. Babau, M. Blay-Fornarino, J. Champeau, S. Robert, & A. Sabetta (Eds.), *Model-Driven Engineering for Distributed Real-Time Systems: MARTE Modeling, Model Transformations and their Usages (pp. 73-103)*. Hoboken, NJ, USA: John Wiley & Sons, Inc. doi:10.1002/9781118558096.ch4

Jéron, T. (2009). Symbolic Model-based Test Selection. *Electronic Notes in Theoretical Computer Science, 240*, 167–184. doi:10.1016/j.entcs.2009.05.051

Jéron, T., Veanes, M., & Wolff, B. (2013). Symbolic Methods in Testing . Dagstuhl, Germany: Schloss Dagstuhl—Leibniz-Zentrum fuer Informatik.

Le Gall, P., Rapin, N., & Touil, A. (2007). Symbolic execution techniques for refinement testing. In *Proceedings of the first international conference on Tests and proofs* (pp. 131-148).

Mouttappa, P., Maag, S., & Cavalli, A. (2013). Using passive testing based on symbolic execution and slicing techniques: Application to the validation of communication protocol. *Computer Networks, 57*(15), 2992–3008. doi:10.1016/j.comnet.2013.06.019

Rusu, V., Du Bousquet, L., & Jeron, T. (2000). An approach to Symbolic Test Generation. In Proceedings of the Second International Conference on Integrated Formal Methods (pp. 338–357). UK:Springer-Verlag.

Salva, S. (2011). Passive testing with proxy tester. *International Journal of Software Engineering and its Applications, 5*(4).

KEY TERMS AND DEFINITIONS

BD-ADDR: Bluetooth device address. The bd-addr is a unique address of a Bluetooth device, similar to the MAC address of a network device.

CAN: Controlled Access Network used to connect the different ECU's (Electronic Control Unit) in the car's vehicular network.

HCI: Host Controller Interface layer lies between the host part and the controller part of the Bluetooth stack.

IOSTS: Input-Output Symbolic Transition System is an automata defined to model system and behaviors.

Passive Testing: Method to test an IUT, without interfering with its normal operations. Traces collected from the IUT are analyzed based on some functional and security requirements described in a formal specification.

SE: Symbolic Execution of IOSTS results in a tree-like structure . Each branch corresponds to a behavior or attack.

SUT (IUT): System Under Test (Implementation Under Test).

ENDNOTES

[1] http://www.itea2-diamonds.org/index.html.
[2] Bluetooth specification, version 2.1 + edr [vol 0]," 1999.

Chapter 4
Designing Resource-Constrained Embedded Heterogeneous Systems to Cope with Variability

Ian Gray
University of York, UK

Andrea Acquaviva
Politecnico di Torino, Italy

Neil Audsley
University of York, UK

ABSTRACT

As modern embedded systems become increasingly complex, they also become susceptible to manufacturing variability. Variability causes otherwise identical hardware elements to exhibit large differences in dynamic and static power usage, maximum clock frequency, thermal resilience, and lifespan. There are currently no standard ways of handling this variability from the software developer's point of view, forcing the hardware vendor to discard devices that fall below a certain threshold. This chapter first presents a review of existing state-of-the-art techniques for mitigating the effects of variability. It then presents the toolflow developed as part of the ToucHMore project, which aims to build variability-awareness into the entire design process. In this approach, the platform is modelled in SysML, along with the expected variability and the monitoring and mitigation capabilities that the hardware presents. This information is used to automatically generate a customised variability-aware runtime, which is used by the programmer to perform operations such as offloading computation to another processing element, parallelising operations, and altering the energy use of operations (using voltage scaling, power gating, etc.). The variability-aware runtime affects its behaviour according to modelled static manufacturing variability and measured dynamic variability (such as battery power, temperature, and hardware degradation). This is done by moving computation to different parts of the system, spreading computation load more efficiency, and by making use of the modelled capabilities of the system.

DOI: 10.4018/978-1-4666-6194-3.ch004

INTRODUCTION

It is becoming increasingly difficult to efficiently exploit complex Multiprocessor Systems-on-Chip (MPSoC) architectures using existing programming languages and approaches. This is due to two main issues:

1. Modern MPSoC platforms have a very complex programming model, but the languages commonly used to develop software for them (C, C++ etc.) present a very simple view of hardware. This is the "programming model gap."
2. Hardware variability causes systems that were designed as regular architectures to become irregular once they are manufactured, and to change over time.

Commonly used languages such as C, Java and C++ all assume a homogeneous implementation architecture with a uniform, shared memory space. This is incompatible with the application-specific, heterogeneous architectures of MPSoCs – specifically parallelism, non-uniform memory architectues (NUMA) and non-standard communications (i.e. on-chip networks). This problem is compounded when variability is considered.

Variability is the observation that as the manufacture of integrated circuits moves to lower and lower process nodes, the transistors become increasingly variable. This gate-level variation leads to large differences in the performance of the final design. Therefore, multiple copies of the same design may exhibit considerable differences in static and dynamic power consumption, lifespan and clock frequency. A system designed as a homogenous MPSoC will be heterogeneous after manufacturing variability is considered. This is a major challenge for the development of both the hardware and software of future embedded systems.

This chapter begins by describing in detail the kinds of variability that exist in modern embedded systems. The chapter then discusses existing approaches that attempt to mitigate the effects of such variability. The next sections detail the approach taken in the ToucHMore project, an EU FP7 research project which is focussed on the development of variability-aware systems. Finally, the chapter summarises potential areas for future work in this area and concludes.

BACKGROUND: VARIABILITY IN MULTICORE SYSTEMS

Due to the increasing demands placed on modern embedded devices, multicore devices are now commonplace. They are deployed to address the high performance and energy efficiency requirements imposed by audio, video, mobile telephony, and gaming applications. Moreover, multicore systems are becoming widespread in the automotive infotainment and power-train domains; especially in the context of hybrid and electric vehicles where energy efficiency is critical.

Technology scaling has traditionally offered advantages to embedded systems in terms of reduced energy consumption and increased performance without requiring significant additional design effort. Developers could expect performance improvements "for free". However, scaling to and past the 22 nm and 14 nm technology nodes brings a number of problems. Random intra-die process variability, reliability degradation mechanisms, and their combined impact on system-level quality metrics (i.e. power consumption or maximum clock speed) are prominent issues that will need to be tackled in the next few years. In particular, due to aggressive technology scaling, sub-65 nm CMOS technology nodes are increasingly affected by variation phenomena, and multicore architectures are impacted in many ways by the variability of the underlying silicon fabrics (Flamand, 2009) (Tiwari & Torrellas, 2008).

Variability causes significant perturbations to the performance and power consumption of multicore platforms. This is of particular interest to multicore systems (Bowman, Alameldeen, Srinivasan, & Wilkerson, 2007) (Humenay, Tarjan, & Skadron, 2007) (Sylvester, Blaauw, & Karl, 2006) because it leads to systems that were designed as homogeneous multicore systems but in which each core runs at a different speed and uses a different amount of power to do so. For example, a recent study (Gottscho, Kagalwalla, & Gupta, 2012) found that supposedly identical DRAM chips from the same wafer of the same production run may vary in write power consumption by up to 22%. Furthermore, variations may increase at runtime due to aging and wear-out phenomena. This may cause failure of single components, when the speed of the circuits becomes too slow to be properly sampled by the clock signal. In the rest of this section we provide details about both static and dynamic sources of uncertainty in modern multicore systems. In the next section we will outline current countermeasures adopted to face these issues.

Static Uncertainty: Process Variability

The progress and scaling of CMOS technology has encountered a number of walls. The most obvious is the fact that the dimensions of silicon devices are approaching the atomic scale and are hence subject to atomic uncertainties. According to the International Technology Roadmap for Semiconductors (ITRS, 2012), this becomes of concern at 45nm, and becomes critical at the 22nm technology node and below. Other issues impair technology scaling even before this. Lithography resolution, photo resist and electrical field limits (due to power supply voltage fluctuations, thin oxide breakdowns, etc.) are critical issues for 65nm and 45nm technologies.

Two different types of process variations have different impacts on multicore architecture design. Intra-die process variations result in significant core-to-core frequency variations (Cao &

McAndrew, 2007) (Herbert & Marculescu, 2008) (Bowman, Alameldeen, Srinivasan, & Wilkerson, 2007). Simultaneously, global variations lead to inter-die variability. The result is that overall performance differs from the nominal design, and varies across multiple instances of the fabricated chips (Ndai, Bhunia, Agarwal, & Roy, 2008). In the produced chips, critical paths can be faster or slower than designed, meaning that the clock frequency of each core needs post-fabrication calibration. Faster cores are overclocked and slower cores are clocked at a lower frequency.

Statistical variability introduced predominantly by the discrete nature of the electron charge and the granularity of matter has become a major limitation to MOSFET scaling and integration. It already adversely affects the yield and reliability of SRAM, causes timing uncertainty in logic circuits and exacerbates on-chip power dissipation problems. Figure 1 illustrates the variability introduced by random discrete dopants and line edge roughness in a 35 nm gate length MOSFET.

Runtime Uncertainty: Wear-Out Effects

New technology nodes will also be increasingly affected by runtime uncertainty of performance and power consumption values. This dynamic uncertainty is mainly due to wear-out phenomena and temperature-related effects. Temperature itself may accelerate wear-out and chip degradation in a non-uniform way, especially in the presence of hot-spots.

As a consequence, embedded MPSoCs fabricated in upcoming nanometer technologies will be increasingly affected by aging mechanisms, leading to threshold voltage increase (Karl, Blaauw, Sylvester, & Mudge, 2008) which implies circuit slowdown. Typically, guardbands (GB) are inserted to compensate for circuit delay. These GB will shrink during core activity until their complete consumption will lead to timing violations. In the absence of correction mechanisms,

Figure 1. (Left) 3D simulation of a 35 nm MOSFET fabricated under the effects of variability. (Right) Illustration of the potential distribution in such a device (Fujitsu).

these violations will result in system failure. In multicore platforms an additional reliability issue is that both the initial GB margin and its consumption rate are not uniform across the cores. Thus, nominally homogeneous cores will have drastically different lifetimes. Preventing the less reliable core from dictating the entire system lifetime requires the GB consumption to be equalized as much as possible. At the system level this can be obtained by monitoring the GB consumption (Agarwal, Paul, Zhang, & Mitra, 2007) (Eireiner, Henzler, Georgakos, Berthold, & Schmitt-Landsiedel, 2007) and slowing down the aging process of less reliable cores (Tiwari & Torrellas, 2008).

The strategy to slow down the aging of cores depends on the considered aging effect. The main aging phenomena affecting nanometer devices are Negative Bias Temperature Instability (NBTI) and Hot Carrier Injection (HCI), for which wear-out takes place only during activity periods. In particular, NBTI has gained much attention from recent research because it is considered a dominant effect (Krishnan, Reddy, Chakravarthi, Rodriguez, John, & Krishnan, 2003). NBTI is due to the dissociation of Si-H bonds along the silicon-oxide interface in presence of a negative bias (Vgs = −Vdd) on PMOS transistors, which causes the generation of traps. These traps lead to the increase in the threshold voltage. Recent

studies demonstrate that NBTI leads to up to a 10% voltage increase over a three year lifetime (Kang, Park, Roy, & Alam, 2007).

The NBTI degradation model is characterized by a recovery effect, caused by the reduction of interface traps when the negative bias is removed. As a result, the threshold voltage decreases. Thus, NBTI-induced aging can be partially compensated by imposing a virtual ground (i.e. a logical "1") to PMOS transistors gates for a certain period of time (the recovery period) where the core is idle from a functional viewpoint. As a result, it is possible to slow-down GB degradation by interleaving core activity with idle periods where the core is placed in a recovery state. The impact of NBTI does not depend on the granularity and distribution of stress / recovery periods but only on their total duration (Kumar, Kim, & Sapatnekar, 2006). This makes it possible to efficiently distribute the required idleness with convenient granularity.

In the next section we will describe the main techniques used to compensate for NBTI through runtime task allocation.

Runtime Uncertainty: Temperature Effects

Aggressive MPSoC scaling exacerbates thermal effects. Power densities are increasing due to transistor scaling, thereby reducing the chip surface available for heat dissipation. Also, in an MPSoC the presence of multiple heat sources increases the likelihood of temperature variations over time and chip area rather than just a uniform temperature distribution across the entire die (Mulas, D.Atienza, Acquaviva, Carta, Benini, & De Micheli, 2009). Overall, it is critically important to control temperature and bound the on-chip gradients to preserve circuit performance and reliability in MPSoCs.

Challenges

Given the issues outlined above, the reality of modern multicore platforms is that each core must be characterized by its own clock frequency, static power, and dynamic power, and that these values can vary from the nominal value at runtime depending on wear-out and temperature conditions. Without any compensation and knowledge at software and application level, the consequences on quality of service (QoS) can be severe. Parallel algorithms for video processing, for instance, assume a symmetric workload distribution amongst the cores. However, the heterogeneity caused by variations will cause an asymmetric distribution of execution times of the various threads, leading to the situation where the slowest thread, running on the slowest core, determines the overall execution time.

The next key challenge in this area, therefore, is to integrate process technology into the architecture and system software tool flows. To achieve this target, a deep rethinking is needed of system architectures and design methodologies. In particular, the software development flow should take into account underlying platform uncertainties and at the same time exploit the presence of capabilities to monitor them. Variation-tolerant multicore platforms require circuits to monitor static and dynamic variations. The software must be able to decide when and how to apply compensation in response to static and dynamic perturbations of the nominal operating characteristics.

Software counter-measures are effective in reshaping application workload to account for variability in the underlying multiprocessor fabric. In this context, countermeasures at the software level have to be taken to optimize QoS and energy consumption by selectively allocating workload to the more efficient cores, depending on the target metric. However, such policies may greatly worsen platform lifetime as a side effect, as the most used cores will age faster and dominate the Mean Time To Failure (MTTF). Hence, workload allocation strategies are needed that optimize energy consumption and performance while preserving reliability by adapting allocation to wear-out conditions. Such compensation policies are presented in the following section.

CURRENT APPROACHES

The problems caused by variability must be addressed at multiple levels of abstraction, from the circuit (Drake, Senger, Singh, Carpenter, & James, 2008) (Rebaud, Belleville, Beigne, Robert, Maurine, & Azemard, 2009) to the architectural level (Mutyam, et al., 2009) (Palermo, Silvano, & Zaccaria, 2009) (Verghese, Rouse, & Hurat, 2008). At the software level, a number of solutions have been recently proposed. The aim of these approaches is to hide the effects of both static and runtime variations on the running applications. Most existing systems are runtime-only and tend to be based on a library or middleware layer. There are also "whole-stack" approaches that include the design and compilation of the system. The ToucHMore approach, presented later in this chapter, is one such example.

Research has led to the development of a number of approaches which may be characterized as follows:

- Runtime approaches apply decisions at runtime, even if these decisions are taken offline. For example, a scheduler may be created offline which can change the allocation of tasks at runtime according to certain variability metrics.

- Compiler-assisted approaches extend this by bringing variability awareness into another piece of the software development toolchain, customizing the compiler itself, or by making code generation variability-aware.

- Finally whole-stack approaches go further still and involve all aspects of software development.

Runtime Approaches

To cope with variability, knowledge of platform degradation is of key importance. This implies that it is possible to measure the GB degradation, static power and dynamic power for each core. While static information about these quantities can be characterized at post-fabrication time, wear-out and temperature effects require on-line monitors.

Such online monitors have been proposed to expose core-by-core variability in power and performance at the software level (Drake, Senger, Singh, Carpenter, & James, 2008) (Rebaud, Belleville, Beigne, Robert, Maurine, & Azemard, 2009). Consequently, policies exploiting these monitors have been developed (Chandra, Lahiri, Raghunathan, & Dey, 2007) (Eyerman & Eeckhout, 2010). For instance, if the user has information about per-core frequency, they may change supply voltage and clock frequency to improve system lifespan. However, this will greatly impact performance because in many embedded platforms, core frequency selection is very coarsely-grained and only provides a small selection of disparate speeds.

Another approach exploits task allocation. Tasks may be assigned to cores such that the amount of workload executed by each core compensates for their degradation. This approach depends on the cost function to be minimized. For example, when targeting performance, task allocation aims at compensating for speed differences amongst cores by allocating the fastest core to the largest workload. This avoids bottlenecks, but faster cores are also the most power consuming ones so this is not the best solution to minimize energy use. Equally, a non-uniform workload allocation may result in one core failing before the others because of wear-out effects. Policies which try to improve lifespan are based on allocation of idleness to cores, such that more idleness is experienced by more degraded cores.

In other work (Teodorescu & Torrellas, 2008), variation-aware task scheduling algorithms are proposed with different power / performance objectives. In their study, the authors consider various platform configurations in which processors may have differing clock frequencies and may or may not support dynamic voltage and frequency scaling (DVFS). DVFS allows the voltage or core clock frequency of processors to be altered during runtime. A core may be slowed down at times of low system load to reduce overall power consumption and system wear. The work uses a ranking approach where tasks are first ranked by either power consumption or Instructions Per Cycle (IPC) and then mapped on the cores depending on the selected metric. Power consumption minimization is achieved by mapping the most power-consuming threads onto the lowest power cores. Maximizing performance is achieved by mapping the highest IPC threads to the highest frequency cores. When DVFS is supported, the authors explore the possibility to maximize the performance with a given power budget by an efficient distribution of voltage levels among cores. In particular, they formulate the problem using linear programming, where the result is the best selection of N voltage levels for N cores to maximize the throughput with a given power constraint. This policy however cannot be applied online due to the time overhead to compute the solution. In similar approaches (Paterna, Acquaviva, Papariello, Desoli, & Benini, 2009), a two-stage heuristic composed of a linear programming step and a bin packing step was proposed which gives a suboptimal solution to the allocation problem. However, the solution is again too expensive to be applied online.

An alternative approach uses an online technique to extract the process variation map of an MPSoC (Zhang, Bai, Dick, Shang, & Joseph, 2009). The estimation is based on temperature and power sensors. This information is exploited to perform task allocation to meet a time constraint and with minimum energy consumption. The problem is formulated using integer linear programming. Even though this is optimal, this solution cannot be computed online and thus cannot be applied on embedded systems. Other similar task allocation approaches have been recently proposed (Hong, Narayanan, & Kandemir, 2009) (Huang & Xu, 2010) (Huang, Yuan, & Xu, 2009) (Paterna, Acquaviva, Papariello, Desoli, Olivieri, & Benini, 2009).

Finally, recent work (Paterna, Acquaviva, Papariello, Caprara, Desoli, & Benini, 2012) in the domain of multimedia processing has applied information from runtime sensors but also application-level time constraints to perform task allocation. A time-constrained, variability-aware, task allocation methodology which compensates for core-level performance and power variations is applied to meet the real-time constraints imposed by the frame rate of the multimedia system, whilst minimizing energy as a secondary objective.

Compiler-Assisted Techniques

Compiler-level techniques introduce variability- and reliability-awareness into the compiler. In particular, various approaches have been proposed to extend existing parallel compilers to make their parallel decomposition variability-aware.

Consider the fork-join parallel processing model, in which each processing core works on a portion of a data structure and must synchronize with the others on a barrier. OpenMP is the de-facto standard for such a parallel execution model, and

it features a number of MPSoC-suitable implementations (Marongiu & Benini, 2009) (Jeun & Ha, 2007). In the OpenMP model, the compiler can manage idleness insertion at the granularity of a single iteration (or chunks of iterations). This allows very fine control over the actual duration of idle and active periods, and thus on the stress and recovery time applied to cores. Longer idle periods are allocated to processors with smaller GB. The impact of the inserted idleness on loop execution time can be evaluated so that iteration redistribution among the cores can be exploited to minimize it. Performance loss can be compensated for by reallocation of workload to cores depending on the idleness distribution.

Whole-Stack Approaches

Compiler-assisted approaches are promising, however recently more holistic approaches that exploit code generation from a high-level system model have also been proposed (Gauthier, Gray, Larkam, Ayad, Acquaviva, & Nielsen, 2013). This enables the insertion of variability-awareness throughout the software and hardware development process. Such an approach is pursued in ToucHMore project, in which variability and energy-aware information is used at all development stages, from system modeling, to application software, to the runtime and compiler. The ToucHMore approach is described in the next section.

The ToucHMore Approach

The ToucHMore project argues that the programming of heterogeneous MPSoCs cannot currently be handled entirely at any one level of abstraction. Effectively targeting modern MPSoCs in the presence of variability requires the use of a customisable tool flow-based approach. The approach combines existing runtime and compile-assisted techniques with model-driven engineering (MDE), code generation and customisable compilers.

A key contribution of the toolflow is the ability to make use of model-driven engineering to control the implementation of software with regards to variability. The model-driven flow uses a set of models to describe the target hardware, not just in terms of its architecture or topology, but in terms of the variability aspects present in the system. The model also describes the variability mitigation options that are available, such as voltage scaling or power gating capabilities. Equally, the input software is modelled in a way that allows the programmer to express their optimisation metrics (power saving, performance etc.) and to identify key areas of the software for special attention. From this model, a customised, variability-aware runtime is generated that is specifically targeted towards mitigating variability on the target platform for the modelled input application.

The toolchain of the project is shown in Figure 2.

The input to the flow is a SysML (Weilkiens, 2011) model which describes the target hardware and the structure of the input software. From this model, code generation is used to generate Java code. The toolflow may either generate the full source code or simply an application structure, depending on the complexity of the input system model. The software may then be completed using more traditional development methodologies. The model is used to generate files that guide the customisation of the runtime to support the application software. Finally, the generated code is processed through a custom software flow in order to generate the output binaries for the target architecture.

Figure 2. The ToucHMore toolflow

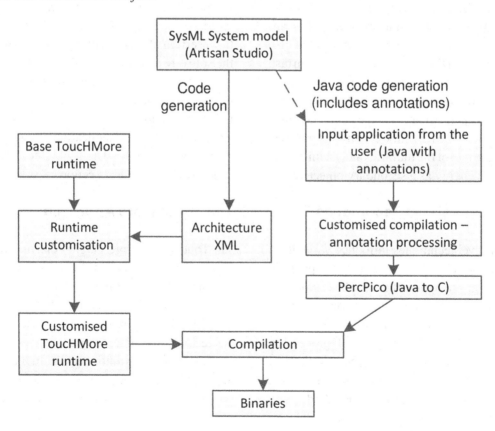

Running Example

Throughout the rest of this chapter, a small example function called sum_data will be referred to in order to show how various aspects of the toolchain operate. sum_data is a simple vector sum operation, in which the input is an array of integers and the result of the operation is a single integer which is the numerical sum of all the elements of the array. This function will be generated from the system model, offloaded to other processing cores, parallelised and run in a power-saving mode. This example is very simple for the purpose of clarity, but through the context of the ToucHMore project the approach has also been successfully applied to an automotive case study in which the computation of audio processing functions is moved automatically in response to system temperature, and a large set of synthetic case studies including a heterogeneous 12-core system built on the Xilinx Zynq-7000 SoC (Xilinx Corporation, 2014).

ToucHMore Methodology

The language used in this project is JSR302-compliant Java, known as *Safety-Critical Java* or *SCJ* (Schoeberl, 2007). This is a form of Java that is applicable for use in embedded, safety-critical software environments. These are the domains in which variability-awareness is currently most important due to their tendency to use non-standard architectures, battery power, limited cooling, long lifespans, and slower CPUs which demand efficient software. However, this methodology would also be very applicable to almost any embedded development process.

The ToucHMore flow is based around the concept of *operations*. Operations are elements of the input software which are modelled in the system model and represent the smallest unit of software of which the programmer can control the implementation. Operations are allocated to processing elements for execution. This model is illustrated in Figure 3.

The input application is a set of Java classes. Each class may potentially contain a number of methods that are modelled as operations. The target hardware is a set of processing elements, which are defined as hardware capable of executing Java. (Note that in the ToucHMore project the Java code is translated to C and compiled before deployment. Other approaches may choose to use a standard JVM.) One of these processing elements is the *master* processing element which will host the Java classes. Other processing elements are *target* processing elements which can optionally host a set of operations. One target may contain multiple operations, and each operation can be mapped to a set of targets. These mappings are specified by the programmer in the system model and carried into this toolflow as arguments to the @Offload annotation.

Note that this computational model does not prevent multiple applications executing at the same time on the same architecture. Indeed this is the most common model used to target complex MPSoCs because most programming languages cannot describe a single application that can execute over a heterogeneous architecture without

Figure 3. ToucHMore software model

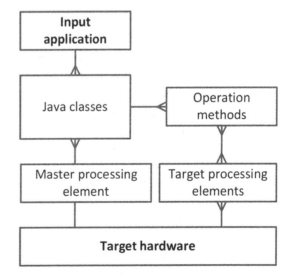

shared memory (and Java is no different). Rather than attempt to redefine the accepted industrial methodology, this approach seeks to augment it with variability-awareness.

Operation Annotations

The operations of the input application may be tagged with three ToucHMore-specific annotations which affect the way in which code should be generated. These annotations may be added manually by the programmer, or carried into the code from the system SysML model (described in Sections 5.1.1 to 5.1.3). The meanings of these annotations are described later whilst this section concentrates on the general transformation approach. The annotations are:

- **@Offload:** Applied to an operation (method) to mark the method as suitable for offloading from the master to a target computation resource (such as a DSP).
- **@Parallel:** Applied to an operation tagged with @Offload to mark the method as suitable for parallel offload.
- **@Energy:** Applied to an operation to allow the programmer to control the energy usage characteristics of the operation.

All of these annotations are implemented with a combination of two approaches:

1. **Bytecode Transformation:** The standard Java compiler is used to generate class files from the Java source code. These class files are then parsed and transformed using the ASM bytecode library (Bruneton, 2002) to change their behaviour. In the ToucHMore project, annotations do not change the functional meaning of the code, only its non-functional properties. If all annotations are removed the code will still produce the same result (assuming well-formed code without data races).

2. **Code Generation:** The annotations customise the behaviour of the ToucHMore runtime. The runtime support required for each annotation is described in their respective sections.

MODEL-DRIVEN ENGINEERING IN TOUCHMORE

The ToucHMore project uses model-driven engineering to integrate variability-awareness into its toolchain. The developer creates the following three models:

- A model of the target platform, describing its structure, communication, and the variability aspects of the hardware.
- A model of the source application in terms of the operation model described previously.
- A deployment model of the application on to the platform.

From these models the developer uses automatic model transformations and code generation to perform the following actions:

- Create Java code which implements the source application. This may be complete code generation, or class and method stubs which are filled in manually.
- Generation of configuration files to customise the behaviour of the ToucHMore variability-aware runtime.
- Generation of annotations for the Java code to mark that, for example, a given operation should be offloaded to a slave, or executed in a low-power state.

The chosen modeling language is SysML. SysML is already well-established in industrial use and models both hardware and software resources equally well. A commonly-cited weakness of UML is that it was initially software-centric. MARTE (The Object Management Group, 2011) is another common choice for embedded development but its specification is very large and complex. It covers much greater detail than is required by the ToucHMore toolflow.

The next three sections briefly give examples of the three kinds of modeling in the project.

Target Platform Modeling

The aim of the target platform model is to describe three main elements:

- The processor cores in the platform (and their capabilities).
- The connections between the cores - in terms of shared memory, busses, or on-chip networks.
- The variability capabilities of the modelled hardware elements.

The target platform hardware is modelled using SysML blocks. In order to provide a generic way to extend the hardware properties that can be modelled without the need for additional profiles, inheritance is used to identify the subtype of a SysML block. Figure 4 shows this using an example of a Block Definition Diagram (BDD) describing the GENEPY platform (Lemaire, Thuries, & Heiztmann), a heterogeneous network-on chip-based architecture.

The BDD defines the existence of various hardware types and some simple value properties representing hardware capabilities. It does not define how the more complex hardware types are constructed from the SysML blocks. The SysML Internal Block Diagram (IBD) shows the internals of a SysML block, potentially in terms of parts typed by other SysML blocks. An example IBD from the GENEPY platform is shown in Figure 5.

The target platform model also describes hardware capabilities and variability. Capabilities currently modelled by the ToucHMore flow are:

- Power saving capabilities of a component.
  - Clock gating.
  - Voltage gating.
  - Voltage or frequency scaling (DVFS).
- Sensing abilities to measure:
  - Temperature.
  - Supply voltage.
  - Current power consumption.
  - Memory latencies (core to memory).
  - Communication latencies (core to core).
  - Current maximum clock frequency (using wear sensing).
  - Current battery levels (if present).
- Offload capabilities.
  - Ability to offload computation to this component.

Figure 6 shows how (a subset of) the capabilities are modelled in a SysML BDD.

Source Application Modeling

The ToucHMore approach does not restrict the modeling language used to model the source application. The only requirement is that enough of the application is modelled such that a Deployment mapping can be built. In practice, this means that all offloadable computation (operations) should be modelled.

Deployment Modeling

A deployment map is used to identify which processor core types a given operation is built for and to which it should be offloaded. Each map is represented by a stereotyped package with dependencies on exactly one platform model and exactly one application model. Each map connects n elements, where elements can be operations, classes or whole packages of the application, to m processor core instances within the context of the target platform. This indicates that those n elements of the application (and anything scoped

Figure 4. Example of a SysML Block definition diagram describing the elements of the GENEPY platform

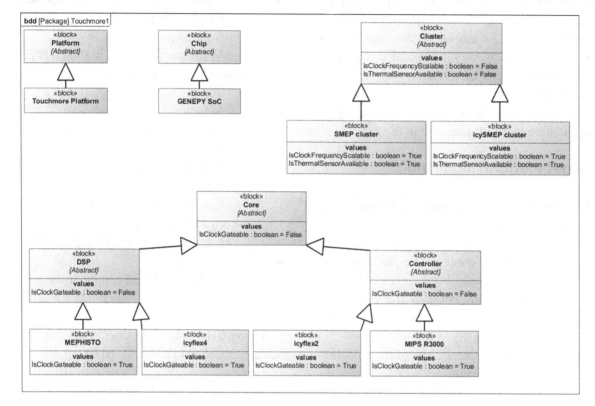

by them unless another mapping overrides at a lower level) will be built and deployed on each of the *m* processor cores of the target platform. It is also possible to map operations to all processors of a given type, rather than individual processors.

Figure 7 shows an example mapping for the sum_data example to an example architecture. In this mapping, all operations of the class IcfxExample except sum_data are built and deployed on the MIPS processor in the SMEP cluster at location 10. The operation sum_data is built and deployed on the same MIPS processor but also built for the two Mephisto processors in the SMEP cluster at location 10.

Model Transformation and Code Generation

There are two kinds of code generation that are used in the ToucHMore toolchain:

1. Generation of Java code for implementation on the target platform.
2. Customisation of the variability-aware runtime.

Generation of Java code is handled by standard model transformation tools which transform software models into stub code for completion by the developer. The generated code is then passed to the software toolchain.

Code generation also customises the variability-aware runtime according to the description of variability in the platform and the deployment mappings. An XML file is generated which contains this information. This is then linked in to the runtime to customise its behaviour. A complete description of this process is outside the scope of this chapter, but the following list describes the kinds of features that are affected:

Figure 5. Example of a SysML Internal Block definition

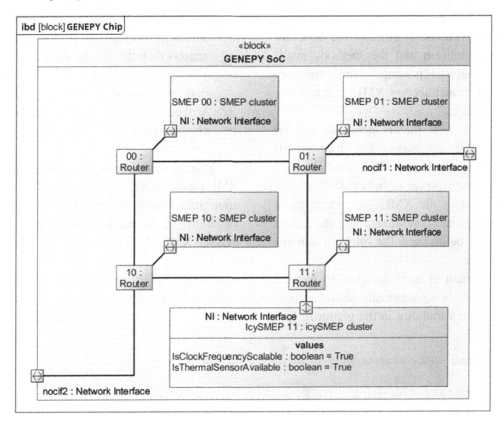

Figure 6. Subset of the capabilities described in the ToucHMore flow

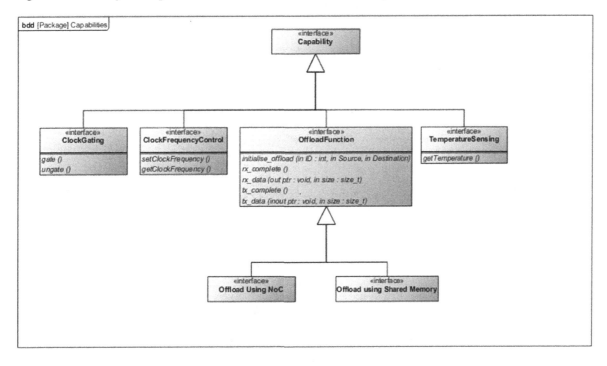

- The runtime handles offloading computation to remote processors. In order to do this, the runtime must know the structure of the platform and the methods available (message passing, shared memory etc.). The architecture XML contains this information.

- The user code merely needs to call an offloadable operation. The location of where to offload and when (i.e. "always", "only when power is below $X\%$" etc.) is contained in the XML. To change these mappings and conditions, only the model needs to be updated, the software remains the same.

- The amount of work assigned to parallel operations is automatically scaled according to the variability in the platform. In a platform without runtime monitoring, this is static according to the model. If the XML details the presence of runtime monitoring sensors then this can be dynamic.

- The ToucHMore API exposes to application software all the sensors that are described in the XML, and all the power and clock gating features present.

Figure 8 shows a fragment of the generated XML for one of the ToucHMore project's evaluation architectures. Observe that the structure and variability of the architecture are both encoded into the XML.

Figure 7. Sample application mapping for the sum_data example

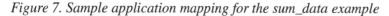

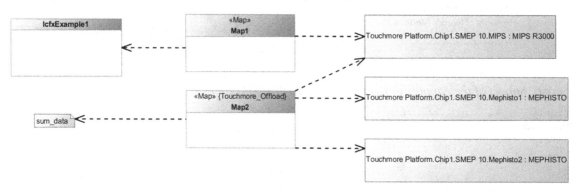

Figure 8. Edited fragment of generated architecture XML

```
<Platform name="ToucHMore Platform" id="1">
    <Chip name="Chip1" type="GENEPY SoC" id="2">
        <Connector end1="3" end2="18" id="5" latency="none"
            Type="GENEPYNoC">
        <Router name="00" id="17"></Router>
        <Cluster name="SMEP00" type="SMEPcluster" id="21"
            IsClusterClockGatable="true"
            IsClusterClockScalable="true"
            IsClusterTemperatureMonitorable="false"
            IsClusterVoltageGatable="false"
            IsClusterVoltageScalable="false">
            <Core name="Mephisto1" type="Mephisto" id="28"
                ClockScalingDelay="none"
                CoreClockFrequencyCurrent="manufacture"
                ...
```

THE TOUCHMORE SOFTWARE TOOLCHAIN

As was discussed, the ToucHMore project uses Java's annotation system to annotate operations and thereby allow the programmer to configure the deployment and runtime behaviour of code. These annotations impart information about variability-awareness to the software toolchain.

The software flow is shown in Figure 9. Recall that the input application may be generated from the system SysML model, or coded directly using traditional software development.

Operations in Software

As can be seen in Figure 9, the input Java application is passed through a standard Java compiler and then a string of transformations are applied to implement the ToucHMore variability annotations.

Operations are implemented as Java methods with the following restrictions:

- Static, non-variadic, methods only.
- No recursion.

Figure 9. Customised compilation in the ToucHMore tool flow

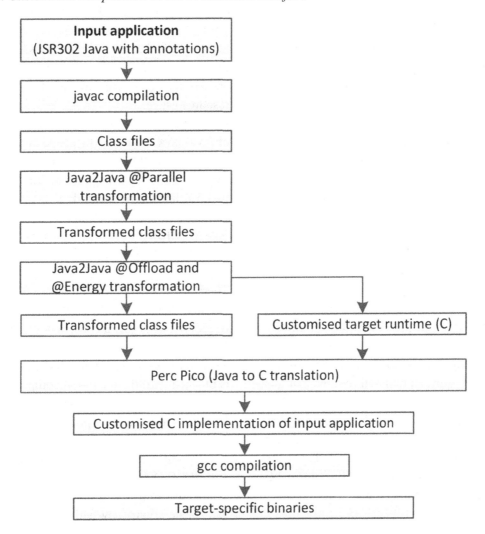

- May only reference static fields from their own class.
- No dynamic memory allocation.
- No synchronization.
- Cannot throw exceptions.
- Arguments must be primitive types, or arrays thereof.
- May not call other @Offload-annotated methods. May call other methods if those methods also obey these restrictions.

Arguments to operations can be annotated to assist with optimisation of data movement:

- *Input arguments* will be read, so their contents must be passed in to the operation. Without this annotation the runtime may omit this copy phase.
- *Output arguments* will be generated by the operation, so their contents should be read out after completion. Without this annotation the runtime may discard the contents of the argument.
- *InOut* is the default state of an argument, and implies both input and output.

These transformations are applied by a tool called *Java2Java*.

Source Transformation: The Java2Java Tool

The Java2Java tool transforms Java class files using the ASM bytecode transformation framework. It can support any Java code that conforms to the ToucHMore system model and that obeys the restrictions. It requires a minimal runtime, but this runtime is designed to be compliant with Safety Critical Java and so has bounded execution time and memory use. In the toolchain, after Java2Java is complete a Java to C compiler is used to create C code which is finally compiled by a normal C compiler to produce target binaries.

Java2Java implements a *master-slave* computation model for computation offloading. The *master* processing element is where the majority of the application's classes execute. A *slave* is a processing element to which operations may be offloaded for calculation. Thus, Java2Java transforms the user's annotated application into several executables; one version for the master and one version for each of the designated targets for offloading.

On the master, Java2Java's runtime implements a thread pool that it uses to implement parallel method offloading. This means that the user's application will require more threads than are specified in the initial source code. Any real-time schedulability analysis must be performed on the output of Java2Java rather than the input. The thread pool implementation is compliant with Safety Critical Java. For the slaves, Java2Java's runtime only implements a minimal bootloader and so does not have any significant effect on resource usage.

A full discussion of the internal operations of Java2Java is outside the scope of this chapter. However, the following sections describe the specific transformations that are implementation by Java2Java in more detail.

Annotations for Offloading: @Offload

There are a range of limitations on the Java code that may be part of an @Offload-tagged method. In addition to these, for consistency with the input Java, the implemented offloading mechanism uses a synchronous model in which the calling thread is blocked until the operation completes.

The @Offload annotation is implemented by Java2Java in three main phases.

1. Modification of the class files containing the @Offload methods.
2. Generation of new class files for each target.
3. Generation of new native files for each target.

For each @Offload method, the transformation performs the following:

- The original @Offload method is transformed into a static method and is renamed. This part will be executed by the slave side to perform the actual computation.

- A new native static method with the original @Offload method's name is created. It embeds generated C code to implement the master side of the offloading mechanism. This side makes calls into the variability-aware runtime to determine whether or not an offload should take place, and if so, to where the computation should be offloaded.

An example of this transformation for the sum_data example is shown in Figure 10.

In addition to the transformation, a new C file is generated for each target. It contains a loop in which it waits for incoming offload requests, calls the appropriate native function to perform the requested computation, and returns the results. An example of this transformation is shown in Figure 11.

Annotations for Parallel Execution: @Parallel

The @Offload annotation does not imply parallel execution. During the execution of an operation tagged with @Offload the thread of control moves

Figure 10. An example of @Offload-annotated method transformation. Original method (above) and its transformation (below).

```
/* Original user-annotated method */
public static sum_data([S[I]V
@Loffload/Offload;(targets={"Mips"},id=2201,sharedMemory=Loffload/Offload$S
haredMemory;.RUNTIME_DECISION)
    @Loffload/In;() // parameter
    @Loffload/Out;() // parameter
  L0
    LINENUMBER 51 L0
    ICONST_0
    ISTORE 2
    //bytecode continues...


/* Original method transformation */
public static native sum_data([S[I]V
@com.percpico.util.mc.NativeMethodImpl(nativeCode="native_implementation")
@com.percpico.util.mc.NativeMethodDep(depends={@com.percpico.util.mc.Native
MethodDep.Dependency(clazz=SumData, methods={"sum_data_2201([S[I]V"})})
    @Loffload/In;() // parameter
    @Loffload/Out;() // parameter

public static sum_data_2201([S[I]V
@Loffload/Offload;(targets={"Mips"},id=2201,sharedMemory=Loffload/Offload$S
haredMemory;.RUNTIME_DECISION)
    @Loffload/In;() // parameter
    @Loffload/Out;() // parameter
  L0
    LINENUMBER 51 L0
    ICONST_0
    ISTORE 2
    //bytecode continues...
```

Figure 11. Native C function to implement offload communication on the target side for the sum_data example

```
int do_offload_2201(int channel_id, jint shared_memory_flag) {
    // Receive arg1
    jobject arg1;
    if(shared_memory_flag) { // Receive only the array address:
        offload_receive(channel_id, &arg1, sizeof(arg1));
    } else { // Receive array length
        jint arg1_length;
        offload_receive(channel_id, &arg1_length, sizeof(arg1_length));
        if (arg1_length >= 0) {
            // Allocate array in local stack:
            // ...detail omitted...
            // Receive array content
            offload_receive(channel_id, arg1, arg1_length * sizeof(jshort));
        }

    // Receive arg2
    // ...detail omitted...

    //Call the actual offloaded code
    _pico_SumData2_sum_1data_12201___3S_3I(arg1, arg2);

    // Send back @Out parameters content
    if(!shared_memory_flag) {
        // Send back arg2
        offload_send(channel_id, arg2, PICO_arrayLength(arg2)*sizeof(jint));
    }

    // End
    return 0;
}
```

from the host computing element to the target element and only returns once the operation is complete. The purpose of @Parallel is to avoid this, and to allow a single operation to be offloaded to multiple targets concurrently. The work of the operation is split amongst the targets according to the variability parameters provided from the XML generated.

@Parallel may only be applied to methods tagged with @Offload. The restrictions that are already applied to operations are sufficient to ensure that the translated code will maintain functional correctness. The developer, however, should be aware that a single call to a @Parallel method may result in multiple threads of computation being spawned throughout the application. They can control this through the deployment map in the system model.

Parallel Execution Model

The use of SCJ in the toolflow places some restrictions on the parallel execution model.

- Memory use is strictly controlled in SCJ. New object instances are created in specific *allocation contexts*, each of which is specified with hard limits on their maximum size. Overflowing any allocation context results in a runtime exception.

- Garbage collection is not present in an SCJ system, meaning that memory is only reclaimed when an allocation context is destroyed.

- These points imply that the programmer must be able to analyse any library or framework they use and statically analyse the total number of allocations made.

Consequentially, the parallel computation model is described as follows:

- The @Parallel annotation is used by the programmer to mark methods that are considered for parallel execution. When @Parallel is applied to a method, every invocation of that method may result in a number of concurrent invocations of the method at runtime. Computation may be executed on other slaves of the architecture. Shared memory is neither required nor assumed, but will be used if present to reduce communication overhead.

- These invocations are identical, except for their parameters. Scalar parameters are copied to all invocations. Array parameters may be passed in their entirety, but more commonly they will be passed as sub-arrays (termed *chunks*) with different invocations receiving different chunks.

- At the point of the method invocation, the invoking thread is suspended and a set of threads spawned to execute the concurrent invocations of the method. For clarity, these threads are called *threadlets*.

- The variability-aware runtime is queried to determine how many threadlets should be used (and therefore the number of chunks that array parameters are split into).

- The invoking thread remains suspended until all the threadlets have completed and the results of the work have been aggregated (un-chunked). This is an implied barrier synchronisation on the completion of the method.

Work-stealing is not used. Work is balanced by the variability-aware runtime at the point of invocation but once execution has started it is not redistributed. This allows a much tighter bound on the worst-case response time of an operation.

The presented model is designed to be small, predictable, and analysable. Consequently it does not allow the same rich parallel constructs available in the Java 8 concurrency framework. Instead it is designed to be a first step to variability-aware, low-overhead concurrency in an embedded domain.

Method Parameters

Most parallel methods will operate on large arrays of data. Rather than pass the entire array to each threadlet, it is usually optimal to split arrays into chunks and pass only a subset of the chunks to each threadlet. The @Parallel annotation marks every array parameter with an integer chunkSize which describes the smallest amount of each array which is required by any given threadlet. The programmer can assume that after chunking, the length of array parameters to the @Parallel method will be at least their chunkSize, but they are likely to be longer. The exact length will be a multiple of the chunkSize, may vary between different invocations at runtime, and is adjusted by the variability-aware runtime according to runtime parameters. For example, if the runtime is offloading a parallel operation to two remote DSPs, it may choose to pass a larger volume of data to the DSP which is cooler, or which due to design-time variability is slightly faster or has a lower power usage than the other.

An example of the @Parallel annotation used to perform the sum_data example in parallel is shown in Figure 12.

Implementation of @Parallel

The parallel annotation framework uses an application-wide static thread pool to spawn the threadlets of the parallel method. After the transformation, these threadlets will execute concurrently and call @Offload-tagged methods. The @Offload transformation will then transform these methods. Currently there is no standard thread pool in SCJ so the framework includes an implementation of one. The thread pool uses

Figure 12. An example of the @Parallel annotation

```
@Parallel
@Offload{targets = {"Mips"}}
public void sum_data(@In(chunkSize = 1) int[] input, int[] output) {
    for(int i = 0; i < input.length; i++) {
        output[0] = output[0] + input[i];
    }
    return total;
}

public void main(void) {
    //Create the arrays
    int[] input = ...
    int[] output = ...

    //Call the parallel method
    sum_data(input, output);

    //Total the collected return values
    int total = 0;
    for(int i = 0; i < output.length; i++) {
        total = total + output[i];
    }
}
```

instances of javax.safetycritical.MangedThread, which is part of SCJ level 2. The size of the thread pool is fixed, determined by the programmer, and specified during the build process. The thread pool can serve threadlets to multiple concurrent parallel invocations.

The transformation process modifies the main() method to create a global immortal instance of ThreadPool for use by the parallel methods. Each @Parallel-annotated method is renamed to add '_Threadlet' to the end of its name, and a replacement method added which does three operations. It calls the runtime to find out how many threadlets to use and where they should be offloaded to. It splits the input parameters of the parallel method into a set of sub-arrays; one for each threadlet. Finally, it then creates an array of Runnable instances which will perform the actual parallel work. These Runnables are then submitted to the global thread pool.

The threadlet method is still annotated with @ Offload after this transformation, which is then processed as described in Section 6.3.

Annotations for Energy Awareness: @Energy

The deployment model can define the execution characteristics for operations. These include goals such as 'energy minimization', 'power minimization' and 'hotspot reduction'. The @Energy code annotation captures these goals and passes them to the Java2Java translator. The generation of customization information from the hardware platform model allows the runtime to implement these goals based on decisions which depend on the energy, power and thermal characteristics of the platform.

These features of the target platform are passed through the customization path of the toolchain (the generated XML) and not through the @Energy annotation itself. The purpose of this annotation is to define whether or not a certain method is to be given specific "care". The customization path provides to the runtime the instruments which allow it to implement decisions in a platform-dependent way. For example, the customization path may inform the runtime about average dynamic and static power consumption of cores, presence and quantity of temperature sensors. This can then be used to offload computation to minimise power use or similar. Since minimization of energy, power or temperature may degrade performance, the flow allows the programmer to define bounds in terms of timing constraints and QoS degradation. This information is passed through the annotation.

As with the other annotations in the presented toolflow, Java2Java processes the @Energy annotation. The processing adds calls to the variability-aware runtime at the entry and exit of the annotated method to set and reset execution characteristics that are specified by the programmer. An example of this is shown in Figure 13 in which the sum_data example is annotated to be executed with energy minimisation optimisations.

If used alone, @Energy instructs the runtime to apply a frequency and voltage scaling policy. In order to define the minimum frequency level, the runtime will exploit any time constraint information that is passed in the @Energy annotation. Also, the @Energy annotation (when minimising energy use) attempts to deactivate as many system components as possible. This relies on the variability-aware runtime. The techniques that are employed are described in Section 3. Section 5.1.4 described how the system model is transformed into an XML file which details the variability capabilities of the system. This file is used by the variability-aware runtime to determine what system components can have their power disconnected, which do not support it, and which do support it but are currently in use (perhaps from an @Offload, or @Parallel method) and so they should be deactivated later.

When used together with @Offload and @ Parallel, the @Energy annotation indicates to the runtime how the decision of where to offload to must be performed. This impacts the target task allocation. When using @Offload and @Energy, the target is selected to minimize energy or minimize temperature hotspots. Energy and temperature optimization are not always the same. For instance, a hotspot reduction policy may execute code in two cores which are physically far apart from each other, even if this consumes more energy through communication than two closer cores.

The annotation supports deadline and QoS parameters that are used as inputs to the defined optimizations. Frequency and voltage scaling and workload to core allocation are currently used, but many other potential policies are possible, as discussed in Section 3.

Time constraints and QoS bounds are used to tune the aggressiveness of energy and temperature policies. There is a trade-off between performance and energy or thermal optimisation because such optimisation often requires clock frequency reduction or because it imposes additional delays for component shut-down. Many state-of-the-art

Figure 13. The sum_data example transformed by @Energy. The two italicised lines have been added to pass energy optimisation information to the runtime.

```
@Energy(energyMinimization=true)
@Offload(targets = {"Mips"}, id = 2201, sharedMemory = RUNTIME_DECISION)
public static void sum_data(@In short[] data, @Out int[] result) {
    TouchmoreRuntime.energy(true, false, false, 0, 0, 0);

    int sum = 0;
    for (int i = 0; i < data.length; i++) {
        sum += data[i];
    }
    result[0] = sum;

    TouchmoreRuntime.energy_end();
}
```

policies concerning joint variability and energy optimization require some performance constraint information in order to achieve the best trade off between energy and performance. The use of such an annotation can assist the programmer in the investigation of this trade off because changing parameters and deployments requires only changing the SysML model, no software needs to be altered.

FUTURE RESEARCH DIRECTIONS

There are a number of areas of future research that could be followed from the work discussed in this chapter.

The purpose of the ToucHMore project was to investigate how to integrate variability-awareness into the embedded development flow. Consequentially, the programming model used is not as expressive as some existing systems. To extend the applicability of the toolflow, the following extensions could be explored:

Asynchronous Offload Semantics

Currently offloaded methods are synchronous, meaning that when an offload is called, the caller is blocked until the method completes. This is consistent with the basic Java model and so is the approach taken. However, Java also has support for asynchronous method invocations through the use of the Future interface (Oracle Corporation, 2013). Futures represent the result of a computation that may not yet have completed. They are returned immediately from an asynchronous call, and will be updated with the result asynchronously once the computation completes.

Asynchronous semantics may help the programmer to use their available hardware more fully, and are used in a number of languages such as Go (Google, 2014) and Javascript (The jQuery Foundation, 2014). Interesting future work would investigate extending the programming model to support such semantics.

Extending the Parallel Programming Model

In order to better concentrate on the variability issues explored by the ToucHMore toolchain, the current parallel programming model is very simple. In order to extend the applicability of the approach, the model should be unified with an existing parallel programming framework such as OpenMP (Chandra R., 2001). The use of GPUs and other powerful accelerators could be tackled through the integration of OpenACC (OpenACC-Standard.org, 2013). Neither of these frameworks are currently variability-aware.

Online Energy Profiling

It is very challenging to develop accurate models of the power usage of modern embedded SoCs. This is because of both their complexity, and because of industrial secrecy. Often the approach taken is to attempt to measure the power consumption of a subset of operations (such as the opcodes of a processor) and then develop a power model from those measurements. However this can be time-consuming and inaccurate, and crucially does not account for variability between devices. Currently, this limits the accuracy of the profiles implemented by the @Energy annotation.

A possible solution to this is to use online profiling to learn about how the target system is actually performing, and then to feed this information back into the runtime for use by an adaptive energy profile. This could lead to a power-aware runtime with greater accuracy and predictive power than can be currently achieved.

CONCLUSION

Due to increasing consumer demands, modern embedded architectures are becoming increasingly complex, leading to the adoption of designs based around the use of heterogeneous, multiprocessor systems on chip. These designs require billions of transistors on a single die but with minimal power consumption, thereby motivating the use of smaller and smaller fabrication processes. As fabrication moved from the 90nm process, through 45nm, 32nm, 22nm and smaller, manufacturing variability became an increasingly significant issue. At these smaller scales, the variation in transistors that should be identical is so large that designs exhibit large deviations from their designed power consumption, clock speed, and lifespan. It has therefore become necessary to design systems with variability in mind.

This chapter has described the sources of variability in modern systems and summarised many existing state-of-the-art approaches to addressing the problems that it causes. One such approach is the customisable toolflow that is implemented as part of the ToucHMore project. The tool flow uses model-driven engineering to describe the target architecture in terms of its variability, and to deploy the user's application over it.

The toolchain allows the programmer the use of three special annotations to perform the following actions:

- Optionally offload computation to a remote processing node, depending on variability parameters.
- Parallelise multiple offloaded computations for simultaneous execution, adjusting parallelism according to variability.
- Adjust the execution of software in response to features such as battery life, temperature, or silicon wear.

These annotations are supported by a customisable ToucHMore runtime which is generated automatically from the model-driven flow to be variability-aware. This means that the runtime can affect the operation of the above features in response to manufacturing variability. For example, if in a multicore system, one processor is slightly faster due to manufacturing variability

(or runtime degradation), then it may receive a correspondingly higher amount of computation from offloads and parallel operations. Similarly, a programmer may provide multiple offload locations for a given offloadable operation and allow the runtime to decide where to offload to given the variability of the system.

Together, these approaches allow the programmer to target complex architectures in the presence of variability in an efficient and portable way.

REFERENCES

Agarwal, M., Paul, B., Zhang, M., & Mitra, S. (2007). Circuit failure prediction and its application to transistor aging. In *Proceedings of the 25th IEEE VLSI Test Symposium*, (pp. 277-286). IEEE.

Bowman, K. A., Alameldeen, A. R., Srinivasan, S. T., & Wilkerson, C. B. (2007). Impact of Die-to-Die and within-Die Parameter Variations on the Throughput Distribution of Multi-Core Processors. In *Proceedings of the ACM/IEEE International Symposium on Low Power Electronics and Design*, (pp. 50-55). ACM/IEEE.

Bruneton, E. (2002). *ASM 4.0: A Java bytecode engineering library*. Retrieved from http://download.forge.objectweb.org/asm/asm4-guide.pdf

Cao, Y., & McAndrew, C. (2007). Mosfet Modeling for 45 nm and Beyond. In *Proceedings of the IEEE International Conference on Computer-Aided Design*, (pp. 638-643). IEEE.

Chandra, R. (2001). *Parallel programming in OpenMP*. Morgan Kaufmann.

Chandra, S., Lahiri, K., Raghunathan, A., & Dey, S. (2007). System-on-Chip Power Management Considering Leakage Power Variations. In *Proc. ACM/IEEE Design Automation Conference*, (pp. 877-882). ACM/IEEE.

Drake, A., Senger, R., Singh, H., Carpenter, G., & James, N. (2008). Dynamic Measurement of Critical-Path Timing. In *Proc. IEEE Conf. Integrated Circuit Design and Technology and Tutorial*, (pp. 249-252). IEEE.

Eireiner, M., Henzler, S., Georgakos, G., Berthold, J., & Schmitt-Landsiedel, D. (2007). Delay characterization and local supply voltage adjustment for compensation of local parametric variations. *IEEE Journal of Solid-State Circuits, 42*(7), 1583–1592. doi:10.1109/JSSC.2007.896695

Eyerman, S., & Eeckhout, L. (2010). A Counter Architecture for Online DVFS Profitability Estimation. *IEEE Transactions on Computers, 59*(11), 1576–1583. doi:10.1109/TC.2010.65

Flamand, E. (2009). Strategic Directions Toward Multicore Application Specific Computing. In *Proc. IEEE Conf. Design, Automation and Test in Europe*, (p. 1266). IEEE.

Gauthier, L., Gray, I., Larkam, A., Ayad, G., Acquaviva, A., & Nielsen, K. (2013). Explicit Java Control of Low-Power Heterogeneous Parallel Processing in ToucHMore. In *Proceedings of International conference on Java Technologies for Real Time Embedded Systems*. Academic Press.

Google. (2014). *The Go Programming Language*. Retrieved January 2014, from http://golang.org/

Gottscho, M., Kagalwalla, A., & Gupta, P. (2012). Power Variability in Contemporary DRAMs. *IEEE Embedded Systems Letters, 4*.

Herbert, S., & Marculescu, D. (2008). Characterizing Chip-Multiprocessor Variability-Tolerance. In *Proc. ACM Conf. Design Automation Conference*, (pp. 313-318). ACM.

Hong, S., Narayanan, S., & Kandemir, M. (2009). Process Variation Aware Thread Mapping for Chip Multiprocessors. In *Proceedings of IEEE Design Automation and Test in Europe*, (pp. 821-826). IEEE.

Huang, L., & Xu, Q. (2010). Energy-Efficient Task Allocation and Scheduling for Multi-Mode MPSoCs under Lifetime Reliability Constraints. In *Proceedings of IEEE Design, Automation and Test, Europe*, (pp. 1584-1589). IEEE.

Huang, L., Yuan, F., & Xu, Q. (2009). Lifetime Reliability-Aware Task Allocation and Scheduling for MPSoC Platforms. In *Proceedings of IEEE Design, Automation and Test, Europe*, (pp. 51-56). IEEE.

Humenay, E., Tarjan, D., & Skadron, K. (2007). Impact of Process Variations on Multicore Performance Symmetry. In *Proc. Conf. Design, Automation and Test in Europe*, (pp. 1653-1658). Academic Press.

ITRS. (2012). Retrieved from http://www.itrs.net/Links/2012ITRS/Home2012.htm

Jeun, W.-C., & Ha, S. (2007). Effective OpenMP implementation and translation for multiprocessor system-on-chip without using OS. In *Proceedings of Asia and South Pacific Design Automation Conference*, (pp. 44-49). ASP-DAC.

Kang, K., Park, S., Roy, K., & Alam, M. (2007). Estimation of statistical variation in temporal NBTI degradation and its impact on lifetime circuit performance. In *Proceedings of the 2007 IEEE/ACM international conference on Computer-aided design*, (pp. 730-734). IEEE/ACM.

Karl, E., Blaauw, D., Sylvester, D., & Mudge, T. (2008). Multi-mechanism reliability modeling and management in dynamic systems. *IEEE Transactions on Very Large Scale Integration (VLSI). Systems, 16*(4), 476–487.

Krishnan, A., Reddy, V., Chakravarthi, S., Rodriguez, J., John, S., & Krishnan, S. (2003). NBTI impact on transistor and circuit: models, mechanisms and scaling effects. In *Proceedings of IEEE International Electron Devices Meeting*, (pp. 14.5.1–14.5.4). IEEE.

Kumar, S., Kim, C., & Sapatnekar, S. (2006). An analytical model for negative bias temperature instability. In *Proceedings of the 2006 IEEE/ACM international conference on Computer-aided design*, (pp. 493-496). IEEE.

Lemaire, R., Thuries, S., & Heiztmann, F. (2012). A flexible modeling environment for a NoC-based multicore architecture. In *Proceedings of High Level Design Validation and Test Workshop (HLDVT)*, (pp. 140-147). Huntington Beach, CA: IEEE.

Marongiu, A., & Benini, L. (2009). Efficient OpenMP support and extensions for MPSoCs with explicitly managed memory hierarchy. In *Proceedings of the 12th International Conference on Design, Automation and Test in Europe*, (pp. 809–814). Academic Press.

Mulas, F., Atienza, D., Acquaviva, A., Carta, S., Benini, L., & De Micheli, G. (2009). Thermal Balancing Policy for Multiprocessor Stream Computing Platforms. Transactions on Computer-Aided Design of Integrated Circuits And Systems, 28.

Mutyam, M., Wang, F., Krishnan, R., Narayanan, V., Kandemir, M., & Xie, Y. et al. (2009). Process-Variation-Aware Adaptive Cache Architecture and Management. *IEEE Transactions on Computers, 58*, 865–877. doi:10.1109/TC.2009.30

Ndai, P., Bhunia, S., Agarwal, A., & Roy, K. (2008). Within-Die Variation-Aware Scheduling in Superscalar Processors for Improved Throughput. *IEEE Transactions on Computers, 57*, 940–651. doi:10.1109/TC.2008.40

OpenACC-Standard.org. (2013, June). *The OpenACC Application Programming Interface, Version 2.0*. Author.

Oracle Corporation. (2013). *Java Platform, Standard Edition 7 API Specification - Future Interface*. Retrieved from http://docs.oracle.com/javase/7/docs/api/java/util/concurrent/Future.html

Palermo, G., Silvano, C., & Zaccaria, V. (2009). Variability-Aware Robust Design Space Exploration of Chip Multiprocessor Architectures. In *Proceedings of the IEEE Asia and South Pacific Design Automation Conference*, (pp. 323-328). IEEE.

Paterna, F., Acquaviva, A., Papariello, F., Caprara, A., Desoli, G., & Benini, L. (2012). Variability-Aware Task Allocation for Energy-Efficient Quality of Service Provisioning in Embedded Streaming Multimedia Applications. *IEEE Transactions on Computers*. doi:10.1109/TC.2011.127

Paterna, F., Acquaviva, A., Papariello, F., Desoli, G., & Benini, L. (2009). Variability-Tolerant Workload Allocation for MPSoC Energy Minimization under Real-Time Constraint. In *Proc. IEEE Workshop Embedded Systems for Real-Time Multimedia*, (pp. 134-142). IEEE.

Paterna, F., Acquaviva, A., Papariello, F., Desoli, G., Olivieri, M., & Benini, L. (2009). Adaptive Idleness Distribution for Non-Uniform Aging Tolerance in Multiprocessor Systems-on-Chip. In *Proc. IEEE Conf. Design, Automation and Test in Europe*, (pp. 906-909). IEEE.

Rebaud, B., Belleville, M., Beigne, E., Robert, M., Maurine, P., & Azemard, N. (2009). An Innovative Timing Slack Monitor for Variation Tolerant Circuits. In *Proc. IEEE Conf. IC Design and Technology*, (pp. 215-218). IEEE.

Schoeberl, M. (2007). A Profile for Safety Critical Java. In *Proceedings of 10th IEEE International Symposium on Object and Component-Oriented Real-Time Distributed Computing, ISORC '07*, (pp. 94-101). IEEE.

Sylvester, D., Blaauw, D., & Karl, E. (2006). Elastic: An Adaptive Self-Healing Architecture for Unpredictable Silicon. *IEEE Design & Test of Computers, 23*, 484–490. doi:10.1109/MDT.2006.145

Teodorescu, R., & Torrellas, J. (2008). Variation-Aware Application Scheduling and Power Management for Chip Multiprocessors. *ACM SIGARCH Computer Architecture News, 36*(3), 363–374. doi:10.1145/1394608.1382152

The jQuery Foundation. (2014). *The jQuery API Documentation - Deferred*. Retrieved January 2014, from http://api.jquery.com/jQuery.Deferred/

The Object Management Group. (2011, June). *UML Profile for MARTE: Modeling and Analysis of Real-Time Embedded Systems*. Retrieved from http://www.omg.org/spec/MARTE/1.1/PDF/

Tiwari, A., & Torrellas, J. (2008). Facelift: Hiding and Slowing Down Aging in Multicores. In *Proceedings of the IEEE/ACM International Symposium on Microarchitectures*, (pp. 129-140). IEEE/ACM.

Verghese, N., Rouse, R., & Hurat, P. (2008). Predictive Models and CAD Methodology for Pattern Dependent Variability. In *Proceedings of the IEEE Asia and South Pacific Design Automation Conference*, (pp. 213-218). IEEE.

Weilkiens, T. (2011). *Systems engineering with SysML/UML: modeling, analysis, design*. Burlington, MA: Morgan Kaufmann.

Xilinx Corporation. (2014, January). *Zynq-7000 All Programmable SoC*. Retrieved from http://www.xilinx.com/products/silicon-devices/soc/zynq-7000/

Zhang, L., Bai, L., Dick, R., Shang, L., & Joseph, R. (2009). Process Variation Characterization of Chip-Level Multiprocessors. In *Proceedings of the ACM Conference of Design Automation*, (pp. 694-697). ACM.

ADDITIONAL READING

Audsley, N., Gray, I., Matragkas, N., Indrusiak, L. S., Kolovos, D., & Paige, R. Embedded and Real Time System Development: A Software Engineering Perspective, Springer-Verlag, 2014. András Vajda, Programming Many-Core Chips, Springer, 2011.

H. Aydin, R. Melhem, D. Mossé, and Pedro Mejia Alvarez, *Dynamic and Aggressive Scheduling Techniques for Power-Aware Real-Time Systems*, Real-Time Systems Symposium, London, England, Dec 2001.

Balmelli, L., Brown, D., Cantor, M., & Mott, M. (2006, July). Model-driven systems development. *IBM Systems Journal, 45*(Issue 3). doi:10.1147/sj.453.0569

Bathen, L. A. D., & Dutt, N. D. *E-RoC: Embedded Raids-on-Chip for Low Power Distributed Dynamically Managed Reliable Memories*, UC Irvine. Proc., IEEE/ACM 2011 Design, Automation and Test in Europe.

Faugère, M., Bourbeau, T., de Simone, R., & Gérard, S. *MARTE: Also an UML Profile for Modeling AADL Applications*, proceedings of ICECCS 2007, IEEE Computer Society, Auckland, New Zealand, July 11-14, 2007.

M. Gottscho, A. A. Kagalwalla, and P. Gupta., *Power Variability in Contemporary DRAMs*, IEEE Embedded Systems Letters.

Guerin, X., & Petrot, F. *A System Framework for the Design of Embedded Software Targeting Heterogeneous Multi-core SoCs*, IEEE International Conference on Application-Specific Systems, Architectures and Processors, pp. 153-160, 2009.

Jerraya, A. (2010). *Wayne Wolf, Multiprocessor Systems-on-Chips, Morgan Kaufmann, 2004. Michael Hübner and Jürgen Becker, Multiprocessor System-on-Chip: Hardware Design and Tool Integration*. Springer.

Mosterman, P. *Model-Based Design of Embedded Systems*, Proceedings of International Conference on Microelectronic Systems Education 2007.

Piguet, C. (2006). Ultra-Low Power Processor Design. In V. Oklobdzija, & R. Krishnamurthy (Eds.), *High Performance Energy-Efficient Microprocessor Design* (pp. 1–30). Springer. doi:10.1007/978-0-387-34047-0_1

Poletti, F., Poggiali, A., Bertozzi, D., Benini, L., Marchal, P., Loghi, M., & Poncino, M. (2007). Energy-Efficient Multiprocessor Systems-on-Chip for Embedded Computing: Exploring Programming Models and Their Architectural Support. *IEEE Transactions on Computers, 56*, 606–621. doi:10.1109/TC.2007.1040

Schattkowsky, T., & Muller, W. Model-based design of embedded systems, Proceedings of Object-Oriented Real-Time Distributed Computing, pp. 113-128 2004.

Shih, C., Wu, C.-T., Lin, C.-Y., Hsiung, P.-A., Hsueh, N.-L., Chang, C.-H., et al. *A Model-Driven Multicore Software Development Environment for Embedded System*, Computer Software and Applications Conference, Annual International, pp. 261-268, 2009 33rd Annual IEEE International Computer Software and Applications Conference, 2009.

Wellings, A. (2004). *Concurrent and Real-Time Programming in Java*. Published by Wiley.

KEY TERMS AND DEFINITIONS

Code Generation: The automatic generation of software (or another form of computer input language) from a higher-level description. Used to accelerate development by reducing the effort required by developers, and reducing the possibility for errors.

Embedded System: A generic term for a computer system that is part of a larger system. Unlike a desktop or laptop computer, an embedded system will operate either wholly or partly as a component of a larger device, for example an aeroplane or car. Embedded systems are generally size, cost, and power constrained.

Guardband: In semiconductor manufacture, one way of accounting for uncertainty in the design and manufacturing process is to weaken the guarantees on certain design criteria (such as power consumption or minimum clock speed). This weakening creates a 'margin of error' known as a guardband.

Model-Driven Engineering: A development process which makes use of high-level abstract models to aid development and communication between team members, rather than focussing solely on the creation of software and hardware.

SysML: Systems Modeling Language. A general-purpose modeling language for systems engineering applications. SysML supports the specification, analysis, design, verification and validation of a broad range of systems.

Technology Node: A term used in semiconductor device fabrication to describe the size of the features in the finished product. Quoted in terms of nanometres (or larger for earlier nodes), the node name refers to half the distance between identical features in a memory cell. However, for many process nodes this is not a precise measurement and should be understood to be indicative only. Smaller nodes are more recent.

Variability: The observation that features in fabricated silicon devices that were designed as identical will not be identical after manufacture. A wide range of effects contribute to variation in the features' power consumption, maximum clock frequency, and lifespan.

Yield: In semiconductor manufacture, after manufacture and testing, the ratio of products which meet their designed specification against the total number produced. A high yield is important to ensure minimal wastage and a cost-efficient design.

Chapter 5

Vulnerabilities of Secure and Reliable Low–Power Embedded Systems and Their Analysis Methods:
A Comprehensive Study

Norbert Druml
Graz University of Technology, Austria

Manuel Menghin
Graz University of Technology, Austria

Christian Steger
Graz University of Technology, Austria

Armin Krieg
Infineon Technologies Austria, Austria

Andreas Genser
Infineon Technologies Austria, Austria

Josef Haid
Infineon Technologies Austria, Austria

Holger Bock
Infineon Technologies Austria, Austria

Johannes Grinschgl
Independent Researcher, Austria

ABSTRACT

Due to the increase in popularity of mobile devices, it has become necessary to develop a low-power design methodology in order to build complex embedded systems with the ability to minimize power usage. In order to fulfill power constraints and security constraints if personal data is involved, test and verification of a design's functionality are imperative tasks during a product's development process. Currently, in the field of secure and reliable low-power embedded systems, issues such as peak power consumption, supply voltage variations, and fault attacks are the most troublesome. This chapter presents a comprehensive study over design analysis methodologies that have been presented in recent years in literature. During a long-lasting and successful cooperation between industry and academia, several of these techniques have been evaluated, and the identified sensitivities of embedded systems are presented. This includes a wide range of problem groups, from power and supply-related issues to operational faults caused by attacks as well as reliability topics.

DOI: 10.4018/978-1-4666-6194-3.ch005

INTRODUCTION

Tremendous steps forward in improving the density of silicon integration in recent years have introduced significant challenges for system engineers. An increasing number of new features have been integrated while development and implementation cycles have simultaneously decreased. This System on Chip (SoC) design complexity trend for portal devices is highlighted by Figure 1, as presented by the International Technology Roadmap for Semiconductors (ITRS Working Group, 2012, ITRS). Apart from consumer electronics, such highly integrated portable SoCs are also used in critical fields with high reliability and security demands. Because of this ever-increasing complexity, exhaustive test coverage of novel designs is difficult to achieve. As a consequence, support of system designers is needed during the whole design phase to test new hardware and software designs for possible weaknesses, as outlined by Ravi et al. (2004).

In addition to design flaws caused by complexity, there is the increasing fault probability provoked by deep sub-micron silicon integration technologies, as outlined by the latest ITRS report (ITRS Working Group, 2012, ITRS). This is a major issue especially for high safety applications (e.g., automotive, space, aviation). Therefore, a wide variety of fault injection techniques have been developed during the last few years to test the resistance of hardware/software designs against random faults, cf. for example Leveugle (2007).

The portable SoCs' trend of complexity increase is accompanied by an increase of power consumption, as depicted by Figure 2. This power consumption increase introduces major problems in several aspects. For example, mobile devices come with a limited power budget due to the limitations of batteries: the higher the power consumption, the lower the operational time. As another example, state-of-the-art integrated circuits use low supply voltage levels. This low-voltage approach causes high changing electrical currents, which requires sophisticated power supply networks to cope with the dynamic impedance of the chip. This is especially a problem for energy harvesting systems such as contactless reader / smart card systems.

In addition to complexity and power consumption challenges, secure embedded systems face the problem of the potential leak of critical information through side channels. A device's power consumption, for example, may disclose such crucial information, because of its data dependency. Thus, an adversary is able to deduce the internal secrets simply by observing the device's power consumption.

Figure 1. Design complexity trend of portable SoCs

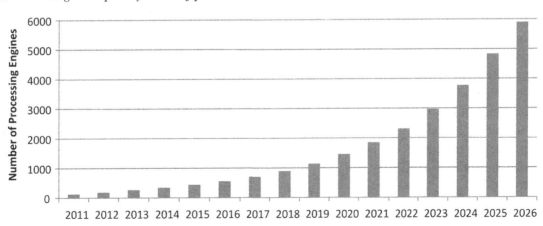

Figure 2. Power consumption trend of portable SoCs

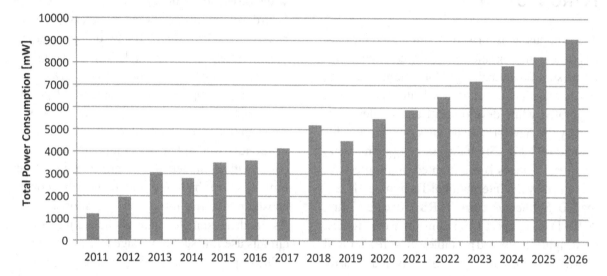

OBJECTIVES

Given all these complexity, power consumption, and security related issues, system engineers face difficult design challenges these days. Therefore, the objective of this chapter is to present an extensive study of recent challenges in designing low-power and secure embedded systems. Furthermore, this chapter will highlight state-of-the-art design evaluation methodologies used in the industry and will propose some industry-proven design recommendations used to cope with the outlined design challenges.

BACKGROUND

The background of this chapter outlines state-of-the-art methods in the fields of power analysis, supply voltage analysis, performance and benchmarking analysis, as well as fault resistance analysis. With the help of these methods, an embedded system's vulnerabilities in these mentioned fields can be identified. Based on this knowledge, design optimization techniques can be proposed to counteract these vulnerabilities.

Power Analysis

With the advent of low-power digital design techniques, power profiling has emerged as a standard method in order to evaluate their effectiveness. Power profiling can be performed in manifold ways that can be subdivided in two main categories, (i) measurement-based and (ii) estimation-based methods.

If prototypes are available, measurement-based methods benefit from taking actual physical measurements, which results in high accuracy compared to all other methods. However, additional measurement equipment is required.

Estimation-based power profiling makes expensive measurement equipment obsolete by modeling the power consumption of embedded systems, even before sample implementations of the embedded system are available. Power modeling is usually less accurate compared to pure measurements and requires more computational effort. However, it provides more flexibility, since power modeling can be carried out on multiple layers of abstraction.

Measurement-Based Methods

In Flinn (1999), PowerScope gives an energy profiling tool for mobile applications. A run-time measurement is automatically carried out by a digital multimeter. Measurement data is transferred to a host computer to be processed for further analysis.

Texas Instruments has proposed another measurement power profiling technique (Texas Instruments, 2002). They developed a proprietary visualization in order to display current measurement data in their software development environment.

Estimation-Based Methods

Estimation-based methods for power analysis can be carried out on multiple levels of abstraction influencing estimation accuracy. Furthermore, the level of abstraction impacts on computational effort. In the following, an overview on academic and industrial research contributions is given tackling challenges accompanying the diverse field of power estimation.

Power estimation started with simulation-based methods by executing algorithms in simulators in order to acquire power information by evaluating power models integrated into these simulators. In recent years, an increasing number of hardware-accelerated methods have emerged that diminish a major drawback of estimation-based methods: their increased run-time compared to measurement approaches. Power models are integrated into hardware, which can yield power profiling speedups of multiple factors compared to purely simulation-based approaches. Real-time power profiling is limited to hardware-accelerated approaches.

Industry state-of-the-art power estimation tools operate on a low level of abstraction, e.g., gate- or register transfer level (RTL) (Flynn et al., 2005). This requires extensive computational

effort, which is the reason that these simulations are most often performed on server farms. Estimation accuracies are comparably high, however the extensive run-times limit this approach to organizations that can afford to provide this high degree of computational power. Hence, raising the level of abstraction by compromising the estimation accuracy has been a recent way in order to relieve this burden and provide power estimation tools to embedded software developers as well.

Tiwari et al. (1994) proposed a simulation-based power estimation method on instruction-level. The implemented power model considers base costs and circuit state overhead costs, which translates to the power consumption during instruction execution and the power consumption during the transition of two consecutive instructions, respectively. Additional micro-architectural effects, in order to improve the instruction-level power model, are considered by Sami et al. (2002). The authors extended the power model by means of pipeline awareness for Very-Long-Instruction-Word (VLIW) architectures. Lajolo et al. (2002) introduced a co-simulation approach for power estimation for System-on-Chips (SoCs). The power estimation is performed on system-level. If higher accuracy is required, various system components can be simulated on a lower-abstraction level. Another SoC power estimation approach is proposed by Lee et al. (2006). Power models are implemented for the processor, memories, and custom IP blocks. The simulator provides power values cycle-accurately in a dedicated power profile viewer.

Hardware-accelerated power estimation migrates power models from software to hardware. These power models map states of hardware blocks (CPU idle/active, memory read/write, etc.) to dedicated power values, which have been determined during a power characterization process.

Bellosa (2000) implemented hardware event counters in order to derive thread-specific energy information from operating systems. According to

Joseph et al. (2001) the system's power consumption is derived by exploiting performance counters of a microcontroller. A coprocessor dedicated for power estimation has been proposed by Haid et al. (2003). The central controller tracks energy sensors deployed in the system. It requires extra hardware but also speeds up power estimation compared to simulation-based methods.

Finally, power emulation has emerged as an alternative approach for hardware-accelerated power estimation. A system equipped with power estimation hardware is deployed on an FPGA-platform. These platforms can then be used to carry out not only functional verification but also real-time power estimations.

The power emulation principle has first been proposed by Coburn et al. (2005) claiming run-time improvements of about 10x to 500x compared to commercial state-of-the-art power estimation tools. Moreover they proposed hardware overhead reduction techniques. Ghodrat et al. (2007) extended this approach to a hybrid power estimation methodology for complex SoCs by combining simulation and emulation techniques. This reduces power profiling times by a large amount. Power emulation in order to guide process migration between different cores has been proposed by Bhattacharjee et al. (2008).

Supply Voltage Issues, Analyses, and Countermeasures

The fact that embedded systems grow in complexity means that the number of simultaneously switching transistors during operation grows as well. At the same time, the operational voltage level of high-end integrated circuits decreases. As a consequence, such high-end integrated circuits provoke significant electrical current changes during a relatively small amount of time. This situation introduces several problems for power supply networks and the integrated circuit itself:

1. Using a low supply voltage reduces the noise margin. Thus, the integrated circuit's vulnerability against voltage drops increases and, e.g., the following hazardous affects may arise: false triggering logic, missing clocked pulses, or double clocking.

2. Power supply networks come with significant parasitic inductances, due to wires, pins, etc. Electrical current changes across an inductance cause voltage variations, according to (1), as demonstrated by Grochowski et al. (2002). If these voltage variations exceed a certain limit, the electronics may malfunction. This issue is referred to as the di/dt problem.

$$V = L \cdot \frac{di}{dt} \tag{1}$$

3. Voltage variations are caused within power and ground busses if a high electrical current flows between these busses. According to Bai et al. (2001), the gate delay and thus the critical path are affected by these voltage variations. This is a problem especially for integrated circuits that are operated at high clock frequencies.

4. Energy harvesting embedded systems (e.g., contactlessly powered smart cards) obtain their electrical energy from the environment. Since this very limited available electrical energy is buffered within capacitors, sharp electrical current changes of the electronics may cause hazardous supply voltage drops.

Supply voltage issues can be coped with either during design-time or during run-time. For example, by using semi-asynchronous architectures or by adding decoupling capacitors, supply voltage hazards can be reduced during design-time. A simulation approach was presented by Grochowski et al. (2002). Based on a current simulator and a detailed power supply network model, the supply voltage behavior is estimated. A feedback loop is then used to control the supply voltage by means of activating/deactivating processor components and deactivating the clock. The presented approach was also tested on a processor die. Only little performance and power degradation was introduced. Hardware emulation solutions were proposed by Genser et al. (2011) and Druml et al. (2013). The design-under-test, which was integrated into an FPGA prototyping board, was augmented with model-based power and supply voltage analysis units. Thus, supply voltage estimates were gathered in real-time and for each clock cycle.

During run-time, hazardous supply voltage drops can be measured with on-die circuits as Holtz et al. (2008) demonstrated. By injecting electrical current into selected nodes, supply voltage drops can be reduced. Analog-to-digital converters and voltage comparators represent further sensing approaches. However, the sensor delay is a drawback that limits their efficiency. Grochowski et al. (2002) proposed shift registers to delay clock gated processor components. As a result, the number of simultaneously switching transistors was reduced and a reduction of voltage alterations was achieved. A predictive approach was presented by Reddi et al. (2009). First, signatures (program path sequences and micro architectural events such as cache misses, etc.) of programs which provoked hazardous voltage drops were collected. During runtime, if the currently executed program's signature matched an emergency signature, the processor was throttled. This approach detected 90% of the tested emergency situations but introduced a high amount of overhead. An estimation-based technique to reduce supply voltage drops was presented by Druml et al. (2012). The authors enhanced the design of a contactlessly powered smart card with model-based analysis units at low hardware overhead costs. If a supply voltage hazard was detected, the smart card's processor was throttled.

Performance Analysis and Benchmark Characterization

In order to carry out performance measurements and activity analyses, hardware performance counters (HPCs) are commonly used in modern processor systems and embedded systems. Typically, an HPC consists of a counter and dedicated trigger logic, which monitors the hardware component or circuitry of interest. This approach enables the analysis of low-level processor events (e.g., cache misses, pipeline stalls) without the need for time-consuming simulations at RTL level. Sweeney et al. (2004) demonstrate the importance of providing software developers with low-level activity and performance information by means of the Java virtual machine. With the help of such analysis data, software/hardware issues can be found which violate real-time constraints or worst-case execution time requirements. In addition, software-based performance optimization can be explored. HPCs are also used in computing centers, as outlined by the Ganesan et al. (2008). They measured the workload of IBM's Blue Gene supercomputer. Based on such workload analysis data, software developers can then optimize the workload distribution to increase the overall computing performance. Apart from pure performance analyses, HPCs are also used to estimate the momentary power consumption of embedded systems with the help of power models, as presented for example by Bhattacharjee et al. (2008).

The generation of well-balanced power models and accurate fault models is based on the characterization of the system using benchmark applications. Generic benchmark applications are used for the performance evaluation of high-level system properties and hence, are usually done at a very high software level, where system calls, instructions, and runtimes are evaluated. First basic rules for the task of benchmark characterization have been described by Conte et al. (1991). In this work, several benchmarks and the corresponding evaluation results are shown for different cache configurations and physical memory sizes. Micro-architecture dependent and independent characteristics are described in the work introduced by John et al. (1998). Further investigations specializing in the temporal and spatial locality properties of selected applications have been presented. Still, small embedded systems were not well covered in literature concerning workload characterization. Therefore, Guthaus et al. (2001) introduced the MiBench suite directly targeting such implementations. The characterization methodology is still the same as used in applications used for larger scale systems. For the sake of completeness we would also like to mention the new EEMBC benchmark suite introduced by Poovey et al. (2009), which has also been characterized for memory activity, parallelism, and branch efficiency.

Concerning fault and power modeling there is therefore still significant work needed to lay a foundation for the generation of accurate models.

Fault Injection for the Evaluation of Reliable and Secure Systems

Systems operated in very harsh environments, such as radioactive or space flight applications, are prone to suffer from reliability issues caused by operational faults. These problems lead to the publication of a wide range of works concerning test techniques using fault injection techniques. The system level on which such fault injection runs are applied can be varied depending on the evaluation target. Depending on this abstraction level different injection methods are needed, e.g., completely manufactured devices can be attacked using radiation. Early stage testing during the design phase can be realized using manipulation of the hardware description.

Simulation techniques for high-level hardware descriptions can be applied at very early stages when only very rough models exist. This advantage can also be exploited for the implementation of fault injection using standardized simulation tools.

MEFISTO was a first attempt to implement a fault-aware simulation methodology for VHDL models, cf. Jenn et al. (1998). To integrate saboteur and mutant models into such a simulation-based setup, the principle has been enhanced using automatized insertion strategies in the VFIT tool (Baraza et al., 2005). In addition to improvements of the injection simulation performance, emulation approaches have been shown in the work of Valderas et al. (2007).

While simulation certainly provides a high grade of flexibility, the need for higher fault injection coverage made it necessary to increase research activity on hardware-accelerated emulation methodologies. The expected significantly higher injection rates of such implementations have been shown (Leveugle et al., 2000). Emulation promises and also enables the possibility to evaluate more possible fault configurations than using simulation. The introduction of novel partial reconfiguration capabilities of certain new FPGAs allowed fault injection without modification of the system hardware description, as described by Antoni et al. (2003). Performance and practicality of this approach have been continuously improved in many following publications, such as the works by Zheng et al. (2008) and Daveau et al. (2009). While previous techniques mostly relied on the emulation of RTL-level descriptions, the work presented by Guzman-Miranda et al. (2009) showed how the import of netlists into an FPGA-based evaluation platform can be done. Furthermore, proximity information is used for correct and fast Multi-Bit Upset (MBU) robustness investigations.

Up to this point, the main reason behind these works has been reliability evaluations using random fault patterns. If this random fault model is replaced by the model of an adversary that intentionally injects faults into a system, (security) evaluations result in more complex fault scenarios. This is first caused by the possibility that such an attacker injects multiple faults at once. Such an MBU scenario now has to be considered for modern deep sub-micron process technologies as well. Hence, Leveugle et al. (2007) suggested considering multiple fault models. Contrary to dependability testing, such security investigations also have to handle cases where an adversary knows where to place faults to gain best results; the worst case is the most likely one.

In the automotive industries domain, hardware-accelerated emulation-based system fault testing is already widely accepted (Abke et al., 1998). Gate-level fault emulation is often the first choice, which has the advantage of being very accurate but on the other hand can only be applied at a late stage which could be unwanted for early software evaluations. Especially for automotive communication systems the work presented by Corno et al. (2004) and Armengaud et al. (2008) introduced systematic high-level methodologies. A parallelized approach, as presented by Daveau et al. (2009), can help to increase emulation capacity and performance, but still the authors of this work only considered random fault distributions and single hardware modules. Hence, a bridge between low-level hardware and higher level system verification needs to be created to avoid possible evaluation gaps.

Therefore, the introduction of hybrid platforms combining the advantage of state-of-the-art verification systems (Baronti et al., 2011), multi-level testing environments (Entrena et al., 2012), and deep low-level emulation methodologies (Myaing et al., 2011), is needed. If information leakage is an evaluator's primary concern, our work presented by Krieg et al. (2011a) highlighted the importance of using accelerated evaluation techniques for software security verification.

SENSITIVITY OF LOW-POWER EMBEDDED SYSTEMS

Secure and reliable low-power embedded systems face important sensitivity issues that a system designer must be aware of, e.g., peak power consumption and consequently supply voltage drops,

as well as fault induced security and reliability interferences. This section highlights these sensitivity issues and outlines commonly used techniques used in industry to deal with these issues.

Sensitivity to Power and Supply Voltage

The adequate availability of supply voltage and power is a major requirement to ensure reliable embedded systems operation. However, sharp changes of an embedded system's electrical current consumption caused, for example, by a high number of simultaneously switching transistors, may provoke hazardous supply voltage drops. If the supply voltage drops below a certain threshold, the hardware's operational stability is compromised. As a consequence, the analysis of the hardware's power consumption and supply voltage behavior are of high importance, especially in the field of resource constrained embedded systems.

As a well-known example for low-power embedded systems, this section highlights the power and supply voltage vulnerabilities of an industrial smart card. Applications for smart cards have increased drastically during the last years. Applications can be found in our everyday life, for example, in the fields of payment, loyalty and coupons, transportation, healthcare, logistics, and access control. However, a secure, RF-powered, contactless smart card is very constrained in terms of power supply and computational resources: power is transferred from a reader device to the smart card by means of a time-varying magnetic field. The induced electrical voltage is rectified and electrical energy is then buffered within a capacitor. A shunt resistor protects the smart card's electronics from power surges and reduces security-related side channel footprints. Data is transferred by means of Amplitude Shift Keying (from reader to smart card) and load modulation (from smart card to reader). Because of the smart card's low power budget, it may face hazardous supply voltage drops and power starvation periods, e.g., due to the following reasons. For example, variations in the magnetic field's strength or changes of the smart card's orientation within the magnetic field can cause a loss in harvestable electrical power. As a consequence, the smart card's internal capacitor discharges and the voltage which is supplied to the electronics drops accordingly. Another example of supply voltage emergency is depicted in Figure 3. The smart card performs a certain benchmark application. During the processor's peak power consumption, more electrical power is consumed than electrical power can be harvested from the magnetic field. As a consequence, the smart card's capacitor discharges and the electronics' supply voltage drops hazardously below a level of 1 V. If a certain threshold is crossed, then the operational stability is lost.

Besides operational stability concerns, an embedded system's data dependent power consumption analysis is of high interest for security-related side channel evaluations, such as Simple Power Analysis (SPA) or Differential Power Analysis (DPA) methodologies. SPA and DPA techniques can be used, e.g., to extract internal secrets from an embedded system's power profile while performing cryptographic operations. In addition, significant changes of the embedded system's power consumption may reveal security relevant countermeasures (e.g., security traps or hardware resets) against intentionally provoked hardware faults. Thus, an attacker may detect when security critical code is executed. Figure 4 illustrates an example of applying the DPA technique on an embedded system's power profile while the embedded system performs cryptographic operations. As highlighted by the figure, DPA can successfully extract the embedded system's secret key, if the system is not properly protected. This example demonstrates the worst possible scenario for a supposed 'secure' embedded system, because internal secrets, like cryptographic keys, must not be disclosed.

Recommendation: Power Analysis and Power Management Techniques

Given the described power and supply voltage vulnerability of low-power and secure embedded systems, several improvements and solutions have

Figure 3. Supply voltage emergencies during peak power consumption

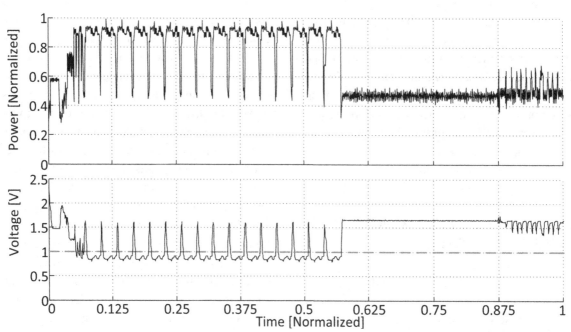

Figure 4. DPA-based key extraction from power profiles

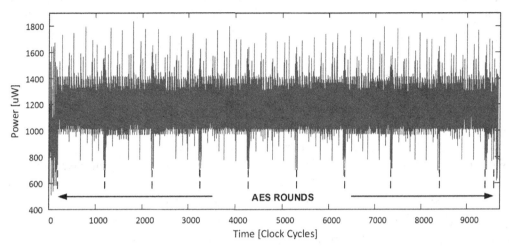

A.) Cropped power trace from RTL simulation of an unprotected AES implementation

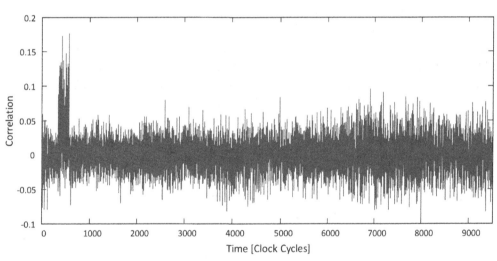

B.) Correlation result for the first key byte (correct guess using 800 traces)

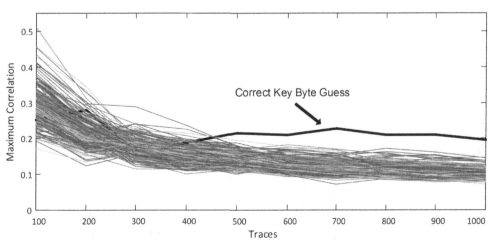

C.) Maximum correlation for the first key byte over the amount of used traces

been developed in recent years. Here we outline the most important and most commonly used industry-proven techniques.

Dynamic Power Management

Dynamic power management encompasses techniques to adapt a system's power consumption during runtime. Dynamic power management methods often use an observer / controller approach, as summarized by Benini et al. (2000). The observer monitors the system's performance, load of computation, power consumption, etc. Based on this information, certain system parameters are manipulated by the controller with the help of a dedicated control algorithm. Various control techniques are used in state-of-the-art embedded systems. A very well-known way to control an embedded system's power consumption is the dynamic scaling of its voltage or frequency parameters (DVFS). According to (2), voltage and frequency alterations have a cubic impact on the power consumption of a CMOS-based system. However, voltage and frequency cannot be assigned arbitrary values. There are certain constraints that need to be considered when designing a system featuring the DVFS technique (e.g., when setting a certain frequency value, a minimum voltage level is required to operate the circuitry properly).

$$P_{CMOS}(t) \approx V^2(t) \cdot f(t) \qquad (2)$$

In the past, a lot of observer techniques have been proposed and implemented. A common technique is the modeling and definition of system power states. For example, an embedded system's idle state may define minimized computational activities. If the system enters this state, unused system components (e.g., coprocessors, peripherals) may be reduced in their clock speed or switched off completely. Another commonly implemented observer approach is the usage of

fast analog comparators. If the comparator detects a power or supply voltage emergency, the system's clock is throttled or paused completely until the emergency is resolved.

Offline Power Analysis Techniques

Besides online power management techniques, offline analysis methodologies are commonly also used. Such simulation-based and emulation-based techniques can be used early during a product's development cycle. They are able to estimate power consumption profiles based on the executed source code and power models. Then, analyses can be carried out to detect source code regions which provoke power or supply voltage hazards. If such critical source code regions are detected, engineers can then resolve these issues using the following techniques given as example: by modifying the source code or by throttling the processor core while being in this critical code region. As an example of application, Figure 5 illustrates an emulation-based power estimation approach, according to Genser et al. (2009) with extensions. Power models are used to estimate the embedded system's state dependent (SD) and data dependent (DD) power consumption hardware accelerated while performing a benchmark application. Estimation errors of less than 9% can be achieved. Emulation-based supply voltage analysis techniques, as presented for example by Druml et al. (2012), achieve estimation errors of approximately 2%.

Side Channel Information Suppression

It is of high importance for a secure embedded device to prevent internal secrets to be leaked to adversaries through side channels, such as the power consumption profile. This field of research is moving at a high pace because novel attack methods and corresponding countermeasures are being constantly developed.

Figure 5. Model-based power estimation technique used for offline analyses

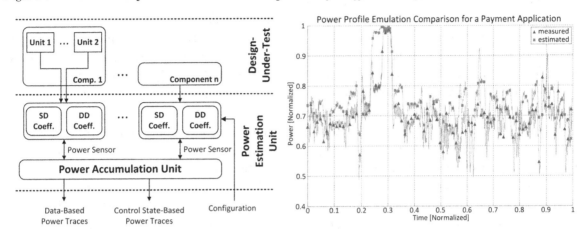

A commonly used method of hiding an embedded system's data dependent power profile works as follows. The embedded system adds a variable amount of power consumption to its original changing power consumption to achieve permanently constant total power consumption. This approach makes it complicated for an adversary to extract data dependent side channel information. However, as a drawback, the total embedded system's power consumption increases.

Another commonly used and easy to implement side channel suppression method was demonstrated by Krieg et al. (2011b). The power profile is randomly scrambled with the help of available on-chip units. For example, during security critical calculations cache flushes are randomly provoked or unused processor units are activated or deactivated. As a consequence, an adversary requires a lot more effort to extract internal secrets. This side channel suppression method requires no additional hardware components, but as a drawback the embedded system's performance may be reduced.

Sensitivity to Fault Attacks and Semiconductor Reliability Issues

The continuous increase in semiconductor implementation density has been strongly driven by the shrinkage of technology nodes to a level where

isolation thickness decreases to few atomic layers. With the exception of leakage power (which is significantly worsened if manufacturing techniques such as Silicon-on-Insulator (SOI) are not used), small transistor sizes have a positive effect on power consumption. On the other hand, available chip integration space, thinner isolation, and shorter transistor channels introduce problematic reliability issues. Novel problems also include accelerated device aging and process variability that impact operation stability of modern processing systems. The significance of the latter is visualized in Figure 6 showing fault probabilities based on data from the latest ITRS report (ITRS Working Group, 2012, ITRS).

A wide variety of research concerning fault detection, recovery, and fault-robust devices has been triggered by this development. In high-reliability, security, and safety implementations system-level duplication, such as triple-module-redundancy, is still the preferred choice. In low-cost embedded systems though, the additional hardware effort cannot be spent, hence, novel strategies for such system-level techniques that do not rely on duplication are strongly needed.

Processes, as described above, are of a random nature, unlike faults resulting from fault attack scenarios. This results from the fact that an attacker deliberately injects faults into a system to change the system behavior while having knowledge where an attack is the most efficient. Therefore, significant precautions have to be taken as such attacks can be easily applied because of the huge number of external parameters an attacker has access to. As introduced earlier, intensive research has provided a wide variety of different tools to simulate or emulate fault scenarios during early design phases. Particularly, the influence of fault sources on the design can be evaluated using fault emulation in a very efficient way. Especially the tremendously increasing capacity of modern FPGAs provides the flexibility that is needed to make FPGA-based investigation platforms a reasonable alternative to simulation-based approaches.

Until recently, system emulation came with the disadvantage of not being able to allow the concurrent investigation of the power consumption side-channel while performing fault injections. As shown in Figure 7, this side-channel can give information to an adversary if the attack had a successful effect on the system or not. As described beforehand, the introduction of power emulation made the concurrent evaluation of the attack and its side-channel finally possible.

Modern reliability or fault attack evaluations call for a multi-bit fault model resulting in significantly more complex fault interdependencies than in SEU models. In the case of attacks, the

Figure 6. Fault probabilities for deep sub-micron technologies

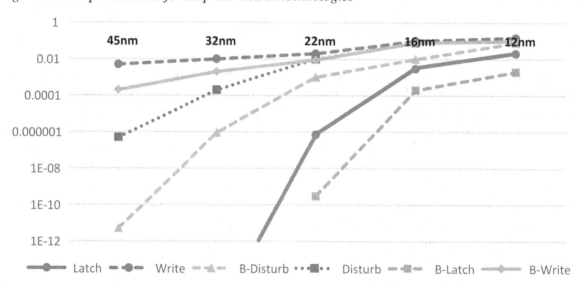

Figure 7. Power consumption side-channel during fault attacks

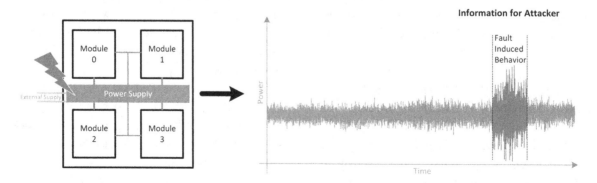

time frame and location space of such faults is even larger as these have to be considered as being of a non-random nature. Thus, in dependability evaluations, similar types of sensitive sub-circuits will much likely fail at the same time. In security analyses, this dependency is defined by the attack scheme of the adversary.

Recommendation – System-Level Fault Detection and Recovery

Under the assumption that faults can threaten system integrity at any point of time, the detection of operational faults during the execution of critical software sequences is urgent. Hence, this topic has been a very active field of research for many decades. For this work, we will mainly consider signature-based approaches to detect and manage faults on three different abstraction levels: only the software-level using software-based signature mechanisms, on the hardware-level using hardware-based signature mechanisms, and complete hardware-software co-design solutions.

Software-Based Signature Mechanisms

The automatic or semi-automatic generation of source-code signatures is the technique of choice if signature checking is to be done on the software-level. Based on these signatures, changes in the program control flow, resulting from tampering or environmental influences, can be detected. While directly embedding them into the executed binaries allows the checking procedure itself to be done using processor internal resources, this could detrimentally influence the program run-time.

The application of extensive redundancy was the first choice to achieve software fault detection and recovery. Additionally, control flow checking can be applied to recognize unforeseen execution behavior. By generating these signatures during compile time, no hardware needs to be involved in any stage of the generation process. On the other hand, software-only approaches have the significant disadvantage of influencing the execution performance (up to 40 - 600% performance and memory overhead). From a security perspective such software checks have also to be considered as an additional risk in security critical systems, as they could be manipulated by an adversary.

Hardware-Based Signature Mechanisms

Historically, integrity checking of hardware blocks has been commonly solved by the integration of hardware monitors. The applicability of this approach depends highly on the way in which precomputed signatures are stored while the hardware implementation can be done in highly efficient way. On the other hand when large memories are needed for storage, this is often not affordable in low-cost designs. Also, the current state-of-the-art does not sufficiently cover the selection of the monitored system region. The heterogeneous nature of modern System-on-Chip designs calls for approaches that cover more than only a processor's pipeline. If hardware monitors are to be used in such configurations, system complexity could be dramatically increased, decreasing area efficiency.

Another point that has to be considered concerning monitoring hardware blocks is the impact of the monitoring process on the execution performance. In order to significantly reduce it, direct access to hardware resources needs to be granted. Therefore, dedicated monitoring hardware has been introduced to enable control flow-monitoring implementations. Initially watchdog-type modules have been used for dedicated monitoring purposes. The integration of specialized monitoring circuits has been described by Mao et al. (2010) and Lukovic et al. (2010) specifically targeting sensitive parts of the system.

Contrary to techniques that rely on an external view of the supervised elements, on-line control flow evaluation methods make use of the modification of a processor's pipeline. Such techniques are very effective when evaluating applications that mostly rely on a central processor, but again, lack proper applicability for heterogeneous System-on-

Chip implementations. These could be System-on-Chips that include various different processing units like coprocessors or dedicated DSPs.

Hardware/Software Co-Design Solutions

Wide fault detection coverage in recent years has resulted in various hardware/software co-design based methodologies. These techniques make use of the possibility to adapt both software and hardware layers to solve the detection coverage problem with low memory overhead and performance degradation. Application-specific instruction-set processors (ASIP) are by design optimal for the direct integration of fault detection functionality, as introduced by several publications such as Patel et al. (2011). For other than in ASIP-based architectures such methodologies can only be used in cases of highly adaptable target architectures or when strong interventions in existing development flows are allowed because of an early stage in the design process.

An alternative, if these changes in the design flow cannot be applied, is the generation of representative signature values to enable tracking of control changes. There are various different possible sources for these values, for example the test infrastructure such as scan-out-chains. Unfortunately, the on-line testing property is only partially applicable in case of test reuse, because periodic tests influence the operational performance (although the hardware area overhead is quite low). If the architectural state needs to be directly analyzed, fingerprinting techniques based on system hash-values can be applied. The high frequency of the changing hash-values in high performance systems leads to high demands on circuit bandwidth that cannot always be provided. Large chip multi-processors require additional improvements and extensions to this technique such as those introduced by Khan et al. (2011).

We have shown (Krieg et al., 2012) that emulation-based power estimation infrastructure can also be used as a source for the on-line generation of operation signatures. These signatures can then be checked during operation in order to detect execution variations that could have been a result of an attack or a reliability issue. Such architecture is depicted in Figure 8, but different implementations are possible depending on the target system.

Figure 8. Power estimator-based fault detection

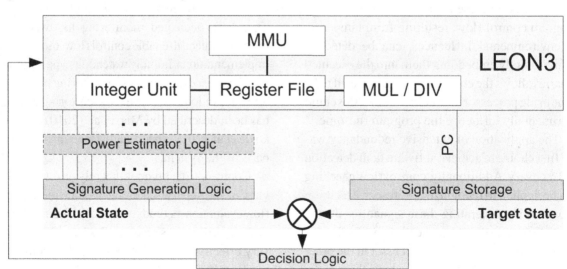

FUTURE RESEARCH DIRECTIONS

Variability Analysis

As shown in Figure 6 and described in previous sections the fault sensitivity of circuits increases tremendously with the reduction of the semiconductor feature size. A novel problem that has been identified in state-of-the-art System-on-Chips is strong process variations not only between different chips, but inside large heterogeneous SoCs. A very good overview is given by Gupta et al. (2013) over the many problems resulting from this issue.

As the evaluation of System-on-Chip implementations as well as the corresponding software is of highest priority, first steps to conquer this problem have been taken in recent years. Kozhikkottu et al. (2011) introduced a novel methodology to enable the evaluation of variability effects on an FPGA-based evaluation platform.

Thermal Analysis Management for 3D-Integration

The limits of 2D-silicon integration density are about to be reached. 3D-integration is one of those technologies which enables a further density and performance increase. However, 3D-integration introduces major challenges in handling the generated heat, because computational elements are stacked above each other. The heat density increases, but standard heat sinks are insufficient to remove the generated heat; cf. Coskun et al. (2009).

A very important future research field is the thermal understanding of 3D-integrated circuits. This includes, for example, thermal modeling and thermal simulation of 3D-integrated chips while running dedicated benchmark applications to detect hazardous thermal hot spots. With the help of this analysis data, novel heat sink techniques (e.g., integration of mini heat pipes within the package)

are about to be integrated. Furthermore, novel task distribution and power management algorithms are required to regard the 3rd dimension and to reduce these hazardous thermal hot spots. If these methods are applied properly, the circuit's reliability and lifetime can be significantly increased.

CONCLUSION

The integration capability of the semiconductor industry has increased tremendously during the last years. Thanks to these improvements, the supported features of recent embedded systems have increased exponentially. However, this increase in complexity introduces problems that a system engineer needs to be aware of: a high amount of simultaneously switching transistors causes abruptly changing electric currents; deep submicron silicon integration technology is prone to random faults that need to be coped with during runtime, etc.

In this chapter, we presented a comprehensive study of issues that engineers face when developing embedded systems. We described design analysis methodologies that were presented in recent years, and we outlined state-of-the-art techniques from industry to cope with the presented issues. These topics were discussed with a focus on reliable and secure low-power embedded systems, which play an important role in our more and more mobile environment.

ACKNOWLEDGMENT

The authors would like to thank the Austrian Federal Ministry for Transport, Innovation, and Technology, which funded the POWERHOUSE, POWER-MODES, and META[:SEC:] projects under the corresponding FIT-IT contracts FFG 815193, 825749, and 829586.

REFERENCES

Abke, J., Böhl, E., & Henno, C. (1998, July). Emulation based real time testing of automotive applications. In *Proceedings of 4th IEEE International On-Line Testing workshop* (pp. 28-31). IEEE.

Antoni, L., Leveugle, R., & Fehér, B. (2003, October). Using run-time reconfiguration for fault injection applications. *IEEE Transactions on* Instrumentation and Measurement, *52*(5), 1468–1473.

Armengaud, E., Steininger, A., & Horauer, M. (2008, August). Towards a systematic test for embedded automotive communication systems. *IEEE Transactions on* Industrial Informatics, *4*(3), 146–155.

Bai, G., Bobba, S., & Hajj, I. N. (2001). Static Timing Analysis Including Power Supply Noise Effect on Propagation Delay in VLSI Circuits. In *Proceedings of the 38th Design Automation Conference* (pp. 295-300). IEEE.

Baraza, J. C., Gracia, J., Gil, D., & Gil, P. J. (2005, November). Improvement of fault injection techniques based on VHDL code modification. In *Proceedings of High-Level Design Validation and Test Workshop, 2005. Tenth IEEE International* (pp. 19-26). IEEE.

Baronti, F., Petri, E., Saponara, S., Fanucci, L., Roncella, R., & Saletti, R. et al. (2011, March). Design and verification of hardware building blocks for high-speed and fault-tolerant in-vehicle networks. *IEEE Transactions on* Industrial Electronics, *58*(3), 792–801.

Bellosa, F. (2000, September). The benefits of event-driven energy accounting in power-sensitive systems. In *Proceedings of the 9th workshop on ACM SIGOPS European workshop: beyond the PC: new challenges for the operating system* (pp. 37-42). ACM.

Benini, L., Bogliolo, A., & De Micheli, G. (2000, June). A survey of design techniques for system-level dynamic power management. *IEEE Transactions on* Very Large Scale Integration (VLSI) Systems, *8*(3), 299–316.

Bhattacharjee, A., Contreras, G., & Martonosi, M. (2008, August). Full-system chip multiprocessor power evaluations using FPGA-based emulation. In *Proceedings of Low Power Electronics and Design (ISLPED),* (pp. 335-340). IEEE.

Coburn, J., Ravi, S., & Raghunathan, A. (2005, June). Power emulation: a new paradigm for power estimation. In *Proceedings of the 42nd annual Design Automation Conference* (pp. 700-705). ACM.

Conte, T. M., & Hwu, W. M. (1991, January). Benchmark characterization. *Computer, 24*(1), 48–56. doi:10.1109/2.67193

Corno, F., Esposito, F., Sonza Reorda, M., & Tosato, S. (2004, October). Evaluating the effects of transient faults on vehicle dynamic performance in automotive systems. In *Proceedings of Test Conference,* (pp. 1332-1339). IEEE.

Coskun, A.K., Ayala, J.L., Atienza, D., Rosing, T.S., & Leblebici, Y. (2009, April). Dynamic thermal management in 3D multicore architectures. In *Proceedings of Design, Automation & Test in Europe Conference & Exhibition* (pp. 1410-1415). IEEE.

Daveau, J. M., Blampey, A., Gasiot, G., Bulone, J., & Roche, P. (2009, April). An industrial fault injection platform for soft-error dependability analysis and hardening of complex system-on-a-chip. In *Proceedings of Reliability Physics Symposium,* (pp. 212-220). IEEE.

Druml, N., Menghin, M., Steger, C., Weiss, R., Genser, A., Bock, H., & Haid, J. (2013, February). Emulation-Based Test and Verification of a Design's Functional, Performance, Power, and Supply Voltage Behavior. In *Proceedings of 21st Euromicro International Conference on Parallel, Distributed, and Network-Based Processing* (pp. 328-335). IEEE.

Druml, N., Steger, C., Weiss, R., Genser, A., & Haid, J. (2012, March). Estimation Based Power and Supply Voltage Management for Future RF-Powered Multi-Core Smart Cards. In *Proceedings of Design Automation and Test in Europe Conference and Exhibition* (pp. 358-363). IEEE.

Entrena, L., Garcia-Valderas, M., Fernandez-Cardenal, R., Lindoso, A., Portela, M., & Lopez-Ongil, C. (2012, March). Soft error sensitivity evaluation of microprocessors by multilevel emulation-based fault injection. *IEEE Transactions on* Computers, *61*(3), 313–322.

Flinn, J., & Satyanarayanan, M. (1999, February). Powerscope: A tool for profiling the energy usage of mobile applications. In *Proceedings of Mobile Computing Systems and Applications,* (pp. 2-10). IEEE.

Flynn, J., & Waldo, B. (2005). *Power management in complex soc design.* Synopsys White Paper.

Ganesan, K., John, L., Salapura, V., & Sexton, J. (2008, September). A Performance Counter Based Workload Characterization on Blue Gene/P. In *Proceedings of 37th International Conference on Parallel Processing* (pp. 330-337). IEEE.

Genser, A., Bachmann, C., Haid, J., Steger, C., & Weiss, R. (2009, July). An Emulation-Based Real-Time Power Profiling Unit for Embedded Software. In *Proceedings of International Conference on Embedded Computer Systems: Architectures, Modeling and Simulation* (pp. 67-73). IEEE.

Genser, A., Bachmann, C., Steger, C., Weiss, R., & Haid, J. (2011, April). Voltage Emulation Platform for DVFS Voltage Drop Compensation Explorations. In *Proceedings of International Symposium on Performance Analysis of Systems and Software* (pp. 129-130). IEEE.

Ghodrat, M. A., Lahiri, K., & Raghunathan, A. (2007, June). Accelerating system-on-chip power analysis using hybrid power estimation. In *Proceedings of Design Automation Conference,* (pp. 883-886). ACM.

Grochowski, E., Ayers, D., & Tiwari, V. (2002, February). Microarchitectural simulation and control of di/dt-induced power supply voltage variation. In *Proceedings of High-Performance Computer Architecture,* (pp. 7-16). IEEE.

Gupta, P., Agarwal, Y., Dolecek, L., Dutt, N., Gupta, R. K., & Kumar, R. et al. (2013, January). Underdesigned and opportunistic computing in presence of hardware variability. *IEEE Transactions on* Computer-Aided Design of Integrated Circuits and Systems, *32*(1), 8–23.

Guthaus, M. R., Ringenberg, J. S., Ernst, D., Austin, T. M., Mudge, T., & Brown, R. B. (2001, December). MiBench: A free, commercially representative embedded benchmark suite. In *Proceedings of Workload Characterization,* (pp. 3-14). IEEE.

Guzman-Miranda, H., Aguirre, M. A., & Tombs, J. (2009, May). Noninvasive fault classification, robustness and recovery time measurement in microprocessor-type architectures subjected to radiation-induced errors. *IEEE Transactions on* Instrumentation and Measurement, *58*(5), 1514–1524.

Haid, J., Kaefer, G., Steger, C., & Weiss, R. (2003, January). Run-time energy estimation in system-on-a-chip designs. In *Proceedings of the 2003 Asia and South Pacific Design Automation Conference* (pp. 595-599). ACM.

Holtz, M., Narasimhan, S., & Bhunia, S. (2008, December). On-Die CMOS Voltage Droop Detection and Dynamic Compensation. In *Proceedings of the 18th ACM Great Lakes symposium on VLSI* (pp. 35-41). ACM.

Texas Instruments. (2002). *Analyzing Target System Energy Consumption in Code Composer Studio IDE.* Texas Instruments, Application Report

Jenn, E., Arlat, J., Rimen, M., Ohlsson, J., & Karlsson, J. (1994, June). Fault injection into VHDL models: the MEFISTO tool. In *Proceedings of Fault-Tolerant Computing,* (pp. 66-75). IEEE.

John, L. K., Vasudevan, P., & Sabarinathan, J. (1999). Workload characterization: Motivation, goals and methodology. *Workload Characterization: Methodology and Case Studies,* 3–14.

Joseph, R., & Martonosi, M. (2001, August). Run-time power estimation in high performance microprocessors. In *Proceedings of the 2001 international symposium on Low power electronics and design* (pp. 135-140). ACM.

Khan, O., & Kundu, S. (2011, September-October). Hardware/software codesign architecture for online testing in chip multiprocessors. *IEEE Transactions on* Dependable and Secure Computing, *8*(5), 714–727.

Kozhikkottu, V. J., Venkatesan, R., Raghunathan, A., & Dey, S. (2011, March). VESPA: Variability emulation for System-on-Chip performance analysis. In *Proceedings of Design, Automation & Test in Europe Conference & Exhibition (DATE)* (pp. 1-6). IEEE.

Krieg, A., Bachmann, C., Grinschgl, J., Steger, C., Weiss, R., & Haid, J. (2011, June). Accelerating early design phase differential power analysis using power emulation techniques. In *Proceedings of Hardware-Oriented Security and Trust (HOST), 2011 IEEE International Symposium on* (pp. 81-86). IEEE.

Krieg, A., Grinschgl, J., Steger, C., Weiss, R., Genser, A., Bock, H., & Haid, J. (2012, May). Characterization and handling of low-cost micro-architectural signatures in MPSoCs. In *Proceedings of Test Symposium (ETS),* (pp. 1-6). IEEE.

Krieg, A., Grinschgl, J., Steger, C., Weiss, R., & Haid, J. (2011, July), A side channel attack countermeasure using system-on-chip power profile scrambling. In *Proceedings of On-Line Testing Symposium (IOLTS),* (pp. 222-227), IEEE.

Lajolo, M., Raghunathan, A., Dey, S., & Lavagno, L. (2002, June). Cosimulation-based power estimation for system-on-chip design. *IEEE Transactions on* Very Large Scale Integration (VLSI) Systems, *10*(3), 253–266.

Lee, I., Kim, H., Yang, P., Yoo, S., Chung, E.-Y., Choi, K.-M., et al. (2006, January). PowerViP: Soc power estimation framework at transaction level. In *Proceedings of the 2006 Asia and South Pacific Design Automation Conference* (pp. 551-558). IEEE.

Leveugle, R. (2000, October). Fault injection in VHDL descriptions and emulation. In *Proceedings of Defect and Fault Tolerance in VLSI Systems,* (pp. 414-419). IEEE.

Leveugle, R. (2007, October). Early analysis of fault-based attack effects in secure circuits. *IEEE Transactions on* Computers, *56*(10), 1431–1434.

Lukovic, S., Pezzino, P., & Fiorin, L. (2010, April). Stack Protection Unit as a step towards securing MPSoCs. In *Proceedings of Parallel & Distributed Processing, Workshops and Phd Forum (IPDPSW),* (pp. 1-4). IEEE.

Mao, S., & Wolf, T. (2010, June). Hardware support for secure processing in embedded systems. *IEEE Transactions on* Computers, *59*(6), 847–854.

Myaing, A., & Dinavahi, V. (2011, January). FPGA-based real-time emulation of power electronic systems with detailed representation of device characteristics. *IEEE Transactions on* Industrial Electronics, *58*(1), 358–368.

Patel, K., Parameswaran, S., & Ragel, R. G. (2011, September). Architectural Frameworks for Security and Reliability of MPSoCs. *IEEE Transactions on* Very Large Scale Integration (VLSI) Systems, *19*(9), 1641–1654.

Poovey, J. A., Conte, T. M., Levy, M., & Gal-On, S. (2009, August). A benchmark characterization of the eembc benchmark suite. *Micro, IEEE, 29*(5), 18–29. doi:10.1109/MM.2009.74

Reddi, V. J., Gupta, M. S., Holloway, G., Wei, G., Smith, M. D., & Brooks, D. (2009, February). Voltage Emergency Prediction Using Signatures to Reduce Operating Margins. In *Proceedings of 15th International Symposium on High Performance Computer Architecture* (pp. 18-29). IEEE.

Sami, M., Sciuto, D., Silvano, C., & Zaccaria, V. (2002, September). An instruction-level energy model for embedded VLIW architectures. *IEEE Transactions on* Computer-Aided Design of Integrated Circuits and Systems, *21*(9), 998–1010.

Sweeney, P. F., Hauswirth, M., Cahoon, P., Cheng, A., Diwan, A., Grove, D., & Hind, M. (2004). Using hardware performance monitors to understand the behavior of java applications. In *Proceedings of the 3rd USENIX Virtual Machine Research and Technology Symposium* (pp. 57-72). ACM.

Tiwari, V., Malik, S., & Wolfe, A. (1994, December). Power analysis of embedded software: a first step towards software power minimization. *IEEE Transactions on* Very Large Scale Integration (VLSI) Systems, *2*(4), 437–445.

Valderas, M. G., Garcia, M. P., Cardenal, R. F., Lopez Ongil, C., & Entrena, L. (2007, June). Advanced simulation and emulation techniques for fault injection. In *Proceedings of Industrial Electronics,* (pp. 3339-3344). IEEE.

Zheng, H., Fan, L., & Yue, S. (2008, December). FITVS: A FPGA-based emulation tool for high-efficiency hardness evaluation. In *Proceedings of Parallel and Distributed Processing with Applications,* (pp. 525-531). IEEE.

ADDITIONAL READING

Bachmann, C., Genser, A., Haid, J., Steger, C., & Weiss, R. (2010, September). Automated Power Characterization for Run-Time Power Emulation of SoC Designs. *13th Euromicro Conference on Digital System Design* (pp. 587-594). IEEE.

Baraza, J., Gracia, J., Blanc, S., Gil, D., & Gil, P. (2008, June). Enhancement of fault injection techniques based on the modification of VHDL code. *IEEE Transactions on Very Large Scale Integration Systems, 16*(6), 693–706. doi:10.1109/TVLSI.2008.2000254

Grinschgl, J., Krieg, A., Steger, C., Wei, R., Bock, H., & Haid, J. et al. (2013, March). Case study on multiple fault dependability and security evaluations. *Elsevier. Microprocessors and Microsystems, 37*(2), 218–227. doi:10.1016/j.micpro.2012.05.016

Kocher, P., Jaffe, J., & Jun, B. (1999, January). Differential power analysis. In Advances in Cryptology—CRYPTO'99 (pp. 388-397). Springer Berlin Heidelberg.

Mangard, S., Oswald, E., & Popp, T. (2007). *Power analysis attacks: Revealing the secrets of smart cards* (Vol. 31). Springer.

KEY TERMS AND DEFINITIONS

Error: An error describes a deviation from the expected system behavior caused by a fault. Therefore, an error is a final consequence after a fault was activated and the result is stored by internal or external resources.

Fault: A fault constitutes a deviation of normal internal system states or signals. Such deviation could lead to the generation of wrong results, but it could also be masked by the current system state.

Fault Attack: A fault attack is an intentional manipulation of the integrated circuit or its state, with the aim to provoke an error within the integrated circuit in order to move the device into an unintended state. The goal is to access security critical information or to disable internal protection mechanisms.

Hardware Emulation: Hardware emulation is a technique that integrates a hardware design into a reconfigurable (e.g. FPGA-based) prototyping platform in order to allow the functional testing of a design-under-test including its firmware. This way both hardware and software can be evaluated in a realistic performance setting.

Power Emulation: Power emulation extends the hardware emulation technique with power sensors and corresponding power models in order to gather estimated power analysis data of the design-under-test.

Smart Card: A smart card is a device with an integrated circuit including its own memory and central processing unit. Besides a standard contact-based interface, it can also be powered contactlessly by means of an alternating and modulated magnetic field, through which contactless communication is also enabled.

System-on-Chip: A System-on-Chip (SoC) is an integrated circuit integrating all circuits and electronics (such as analog, digital, mixed-signal, or RF components) necessary for a system on a single chip.

Vulnerability: Vulnerability describes a certain inability of a system to withstand the effects of an attack in a hostile environment.

Chapter 6
An Aspect–Oriented Approach to Hardware Fault Tolerance for Embedded Systems

David de Andrés
Universitat Politècnica de València, Spain

Jaime Espinosa
Universitat Politècnica de València, Spain

Juan–Carlos Ruiz
Universitat Politècnica de València, Spain

Pedro Gil
Universitat Politècnica de València, Spain

ABSTRACT

The steady reduction of transistor size has brought embedded solutions into everyday life. However, the same features of deep-submicron technologies that are increasing the application spectrum of these solutions are also negatively affecting their dependability. Current practices for the design and deployment of hardware fault tolerance and security strategies remain in practice specific (defined on a case-per-case basis) and mostly manual and error prone. Aspect orientation, which already promotes a clear separation between functional and non-functional (dependability and security) concerns in software designs, is also an approach with a big potential at the hardware level. This chapter addresses the challenging problems of engineering such strategies in a generic way via metaprogramming, and supporting their subsequent instantiation and deployment on specific hardware designs through open compilation. This shows that promoting a clear separation of concerns in hardware designs and producing a library of generic, but reusable, hardware fault and intrusion tolerance mechanisms is a feasible reality today.

INTRODUCTION

Current embedded VLSI (Very Large Scale Integration) systems are widespread and operate in multitude of applications in different markets, ranging from life support, industrial control, or avionics to consumer electronics. Benefits of current manufacturing capabilities, in terms of at-

tainable logic density, processing speed and power consumption, become threats to systems dependability, causing higher temperatures, shorter timing budgets and lower noise margins (Narayanan & Xie, 2006). In addition, deep-submicron technologies have both decreased the probability of manufacturing defect-free devices, and increased the likelihood of wear-out related problems and

DOI: 10.4018/978-1-4666-6194-3.ch006

the susceptibility to radiated particles (Constantinescu, 2003). Likewise, communications among devices expose hardware embedded systems to a number of external threats, especially when they are manufactured as an aggregation of off-the-self (OTS) Intellectual Property (IP) cores developed by third, and sometimes untrusted, parties. Nonetheless, reusing these components offers a reduction in time-to-market costs and a rapid integration of technology innovations while minimizing the risk of designs that integrate millions of gates (Rosenstiel, 2004; Vörg, 2003). It is unquestionable that critical systems require different degrees of fault and intrusion tolerance, given the human lives or great investments at stake. However, nowadays, the consideration of resilience in modern VLSI designs, understood as the ability of the system to ensure acceptable levels of dependability and security despite changes, is a requirement even in the industry of non-critical applications, as the occurrence of unexpected failures in consumer products may negatively affect the reputation of manufacturers and undermine the success of new products in the market.

The dependability and security communities widely accept that involving unskilled designers in the development of non-functional strategies (such as fault- and intrusion-tolerance and security) may actually have a negative impact on the global resilience of the deployed solution (Fabre & Pérennou, 1998). There is therefore an emerging requirement for frameworks supporting the separate design of non-functional and system core (functional) mechanisms, and their subsequent integration. In other words, fault and intrusion tolerance mechanisms must be developed by experts, but hardware designers with limited expertise in dependability and security must be able to integrate such mechanisms in their designs to make them resilient to faults and attacks.

How to support such separation of concerns during the design of dependable VLSI solutions remains an open challenge today. Aspect orientation (Kiczales, et al., 1996) provides interesting means

to cope with this issue from the first steps of the system design flow, when integrated circuit models become available. The vast majority of modern solutions to digital circuit design revolve around the use of HDL (Hardware Description Language) models. Using such languages, hardware designers program circuits in a modular and hierarchical way. By modifying such models, related circuits can be accordingly adapted and evolved. The notion of metaprogramming, defining programs that automatically reason about and customize the structure of other programs, encompasses this idea. If this customization is specialized for fault tolerance (Taïani, Fabre, & Killijan, 2005), metaprogramming becomes a valuable technique to develop dependable strategies, which can be later (automatically and transparently) deployed onto HDL models following an open compilation process.

This chapter explains how an open compilation process can be established to support i) the implementation of fault tolerance and security techniques as metaprograms, and ii) their subsequent application to HDL-based models of integrated circuits. Additionally, this process must be seamlessly integrated into the regular design flow typically followed for HDL-based hardware systems, thus offering a great potential to increase the productivity of designers and reduce their error proneness. Other asset is that it can be applied as soon as a model is ready to simulate, even if it is not synthesizable yet. Hence, this opens the chance to study the impact of the applied modifications in the early stages of the design cycle, thus reducing the costs associated to late corrections. By enabling the automated integration of non-functional mechanisms and system functional mechanisms, the old idea of providing libraries of dependability and security mechanisms that could be reused in different contexts and deployed on different components could become a reality.

The rest of the chapter introduces first the basic concepts about aspect orientation and metaprogramming, and existing approaches to translate those concepts into hardware design in general, and the deployment of fault tolerance and security strategies in particular. After that, an already existing framework is used to describe a procedure for metaprogramming hardware fault tolerance and its integration into the hardware design flow. Taking this procedure as a guide, two examples of different metaprograms implementing time-redundant and symmetric encryption mechanisms are detailed in depth. The feasibility of the proposed approach is demonstrated by automatically deploying the implemented strategies onto a PIC microcontroller core and analyzing both the benefits obtained in terms of dependability and security, and the cost to pay in terms of silicon area, throughput and energy consumption overhead. Finally, different open challenges for further research are discussed.

RELATED WORK

Although aspect orientation and metaprogramming have been applied to the development of fault-tolerant software during years, they have not been fully considered yet for their integration in the regular hardware design flow. Academia and industry research has mainly focused on metaprogramming a restricted number of commonly used fault tolerance strategies, but no framework supporting the metaprogramming of any required type of fault and intrusion tolerance mechanism has been considered yet. These concepts and current efforts towards provisioning metaprogramming and aspect orientation to hardware design are next presented.

Metaprogramming and Aspect Orientation

"Computational reflection is an activity performed by a system when doing computation about (and by that possibly affecting) its own computation" (Maes, 1987, p. 147). When reflection is applied to compilers, it is possible to modify the code

analysis performed at compile-time and influence the code generation process, i.e. programs (named *metaprograms* or *aspects* in this context) can analyze and customize the structure of conventional programs as needed. This idea was initially applied to compilers by (Shigeru, 1995) and later by (Kiczales, et al., 1996) as a mean to express and deploy transversal (non-functional) mechanisms on object-oriented programs.

As a result, a metaprogram is associated to a compiler in order to customize its compilation process through a number of analysis and transformation rules. An exchange of information thus takes place at compile-time between the compiler and its metaprogram. The compiler reifies structural information about the input program, let's name it P, to the metaprogram. That metaprogram then uses intercession mechanisms to apply code modifications resulting from the analysis and customization process it carries out. This is how the input program P is transformed into a different output program, named P'. By default, the metaprogram applies an identity transformation to the input program P, i.e. the output program P' is equivalent to P. However, the user can modify such behavior by refining the implementation of the default metaprogram, i.e. by adapting existing or specifying new transformation rules. Such compilers are called *open compilers* (OC) after their ability to modify the default compilation rules by means of metaprograms. It is worth mentioning that in aspect-oriented programs, metaprograms are named aspects, since they express cross-cutting features of programs, and open compilers are called weavers, since they weave the functional code provided by programs with the non-functional one provided by aspects. Despite the difference of notation, the goal of both metaprogramming and aspect-oriented programming remains the same, i.e. promote a clear separation of mechanisms in programs. What is important in this chapter is that the underlying specialization process can be applied to generate a library of mechanisms that, if focused on providing fault and intrusion tolerance, can constitute a library of resilience mechanisms like those created for software systems (Alexandersson & Öhman, 2010; Fabre & Pérennou, 1998).

Hardware Fault and Intrusion Tolerance Automation

Due to current stringent time-to-market constraints, the traditional manual development, adaptation, and deployment of the required mechanisms is no longer an option. Therefore, it seems just natural that both academia and industry had devoted great efforts towards defining methodologies and tools for the automatic generation and deployment of fault detection and tolerance mechanisms into hardware designs.

One of such suitable methodologies relies on aspect-oriented programming (AOP) concepts that, although being applied to object-oriented high-level programming languages for years, have been seldom used for hardware design (Engel & Spinczyk, 2008). This survey constitutes a seminal work that identifies crosscutting concerns in hardware descriptions and provides a first definition of possible join-points and pointcuts for HDLs. Other preliminary works applying AOP concepts to the design of digital hardware focused on the design of a SystemC-based synthesizable resource scheduler at RTL (Mück, Gernoth, Schröder-Preikschat, & Fröhlich, 2011), and the definition of an aspect-oriented extension of VHDL, named AspectVHDL (Meier, Hanenberg, & Spinczyk, 2012). As can be seen, the adoption of AOP concepts for hardware design is still in its infancy and, to the best of our knowlegde, no work has focused yet on the application of AOP for the provision of fault detection and tolerance capabilities for hardware designs.

Other methodology consists in providing separation of concerns implemented via metaprogramming for the design of customizable components (Štuikys, Damaševičius, Ziberkas, & Majauskas, 2002). This work discussed the use of just the target

HDL or in combination with another metalanguage as metaprogramming paradigms for higher flexibility, reusability and customizability. These paradigms enabled the massive hardware replication through Triple Modular Redundancy (TMR) and error detection/correction codes for registers protection (Entrena, López, & Olías, 2001), and tolerating single bit-flips in a state register and multiple faults in the next state computation logic (Leveugle, 2002). The automatic insertion of detection and fault tolerance mechanisms in high-level HDL descriptions, like Finite State Machines (FSM) or Register-Transfer Level (RTL), instead of at a lower (gate) level, allowed the early insertion and validation of the considered mechanisms at the cost of losing control over the generated hardware and increasing the overhead in terms of area, performance, and power consumption.

Following this paradigm, a number of different tools have emerged to provide alternative solutions for improving the dependability and security of hardware designs.

vMAGIC (VHDL Manipulation and Generation Interface) constitutes an automatic code generation tool, developed by the University of Paderborn, that makes use of a Java library to read, manipulate, and write VHDL code (Pohl, Paiz, & Porrmann, 2009). Although it has not been specifically designed with dependability in mind, the inclusion of this tool in the hardware design flow improves code reliability and reduces the development time. A similar approach, but dealing with EDIF (Electronic Design Interchange Format) netlists instead of VHDL code, is implemented by the BYU EDIF Tools (Brigham Young University, 2013). These tools work at a lower level, thus circumventing all the issues related to the optimizations performed by synthesis tools during the implementation process, although a high level of expertise is required to precisely define the required transformations to obtain the desired circuit. This set of tools includes an Automated TMR application to automatically deploy hardware replication. This same idea of providing a library of already defined fault detection and tolerance components and mechanisms is exploited by CODESH (Ruiz, de Andrés, Gil, & Blanc, Using Open Compilation to Simplify the Design of Fault-Tolerant VLSI Systems, 2008), an open compilation process for the design of dependable and secure high-level HDL descriptions. The default library provided by CODESH contains the N-Modular Redundant hardware replication strategy (Ruiz, de Andrés, Blanc, & Gil, 2008), and an error detection and correction Hamming approach for information stored on registers (Ruiz, de Andrés, & Gil, Design and Deployment of a Generic ECC-based Fault Tolerance Mechanism for Embedded HW Cores, 2009). It is to note that this is the only recent tool from academia specifically developed to define and automatically deploy components and mechanisms for dependability and security.

On the industry side and with TMR as its main dependability strategy too, XTMR Tool was the first commercial development tool to address the special requirements of programmable logic devices in high-radiation environments (Xilinx Inc., 2010). It automatically builds TMR into Xilinx FPGA (Field-Programmable Gate Arrays) designs, thus increasing designer productivity but limiting its applicability to just this particular strategy and only for Xilinx's products. Mentor Graphics' Precision Hi-Rel (Do, 2011) offers a more generic approach by automatically adding TMR or safe FSM encoding at synthesis time, so targeting a wide variety of devices and manufacturers. However, it has been deemed International Traffic in Arms Regulation (ITAR) controlled by the US Department of State, so it can only be provided to United States Persons within the United States.

This brief survey seems to support the notion that "AOP is a goal, for which reflection (metaprogramming) is a powerful tool" (Kiczales, et al., 1996, p. 239). Indeed, Kiczales et al. (1996) started by developing simple metaobject protocols with which prototype imperative language aspect programs. Later, with a better knowledge of what the aspect programs should do, more explicit aspect language support was developed. This empirical process exactly describes how academia and industry are adopting the AOP concepts for the automatic development of hardware systems. Nowadays, and as previously presented, the stronger current still focuses on metaprogramming the required rules to customize components and systems to include predefined components and mechanisms for dependability and security. The next and more ambitious step of developing HDL extensions for AOP support, not just for dependability but also for any other non-functional concerns, still requires further research to reach a stage mature enough to transfer this approach to the industry.

Accordingly, next sections will unfold the details of how to articulate a metaprogramming approach for the design of hardware systems as implemented by CODESH, the most up to date non-commercial tool that specifically focuses on the definition and deployment of fault detection and tolerance components and mechanisms.

METAPROGRAMMING THE DESIGN OF DEPENDABLE AND SECURE HDL-BASED EMBEDDED SYSTEMS

HDLs are description languages specifically designed to model the behavior of synchronous digital circuits in terms of the flow of information between hardware registers (Register Transfer Level), or specify the behavior of the circuit by means of logic equations or logic gates and their interconnections (gate level). Similarly to other programming languages, HDL models are processed by specific design compilers, called synthesizers, in charge of transforming the HDL code listing into a physically realizable gate netlist. This netlist can take one of many forms, like a simulation-oriented netlist with gate delay information, or a standard EDIF format, which can be later used to either implement the design on reconfigurable hardware devices like FPGAs or manufacture silicon-based circuits.

Hence, as hardware faults occur at the physical level, it is necessary to understand how these faults manifest at higher HDL levels (gate or RTL) to determine the kind of fault detection and tolerance mechanisms that could be considered and how they could be deployed into the HDL model of the system. As different types of faults can induce the same type of errors, it is enough that these faults induce similar behaviors (fault models). Transient faults appear during the normal operation of the circuit for a short period of time after which they disappear again. They usually result from the interference or interaction of the circuitry with its physical environment (Karnik, Hazucha, & Patel, 2004), such as transients in power supply, crosstalk, electromagnetic interferences, temperature variation, alpha and cosmic radiation, etc. The resulting fault models at RTL and gate levels are the *bit-flip* (reverses the logic state of a memory cell), *pulse* (reverses the logic state of a combinational logic element), *indetermination* (undetermined logic value between the high- and low-logic thresholds), and *delay* (increases de propagation delay of a line). Permanent faults are due to irreversible physical defects in the circuit. They usually appear as a result of the manufacturing process or the normal operation of the system. In this latter case, sometimes they initially reveal as intermittent faults until some long-term wearout mechanisms cause the occurrence of a permanent fault (Gil, et al., 2002). The fault models derived at RTL and gate level include the *stuck-at* (fixes the logic value of a logic element), *stuck-open* (fixes the logic value of a logic element for a retention time, and to '0' afterwards), *short* (short-circuits two lines), *open-line* (splits a line into two parts), *bridging* (special combination of open-line and short), *indetermination* and *delay*.

Accordingly, the challenge of metaprogramming the design of dependable HDL-based hardware systems is two-folded. On the one hand, it

is necessary to articulate the metaprogramming approach to ease the definition and deployment of RTL and gate level fault tolerance mechanisms as metaprograms. On the other hand, this process should be engineered in such a way that it could be easily integrated in the common design flow for both programmable logic devices and standard cells. CODESH (Ruiz, de Andrés, Gil, & Blanc, Using Open Compilation to Simplify the Design of Fault-Tolerant VLSI Systems, 2008), a framework providing an open compilation process for the design of dependable and secure HDL-based systems, will be taken as an example of how to meet these two requirements.

Open Compilation to Support the Customization of Hardware Systems

The common open compilation flow has been customized by CODESH to ease the definition and deployment of dependable and secure components and mechanisms for HDL-based hardware designs. The resulting open compilation process is depicted in Figure 1.

The very first step consists in processing the input HDL model to obtain an abstract tree-form representation, or Abstract Syntax Tree (AST), of all the HDL constructs occurring in that model. Each node of this tree embeds the information related to the particular HDL construct it represents. For instance, an AST node for the component instantiation statement shown in the Input HDL Model of Figure 1 will provide syntactical information about the instantiated unit (*HalfAdder*), its name (*ha1*), and the mapping established between its ports (*a*, *b*, *c*, and *s*) and the signals they connect to (*a*, *b*, *carry1*, and *sum*). In particular, CODESH has been developed using ANTLR (Parr, 2103) and thus all AST nodes inherit from the CommonNode class, which is specialized for each existing HDL construct.

Once the AST generated, a parser is in charge of walking through the obtained data structure. For each identified construct (component instan-

Figure 1. Open compilation process defined by CODESH

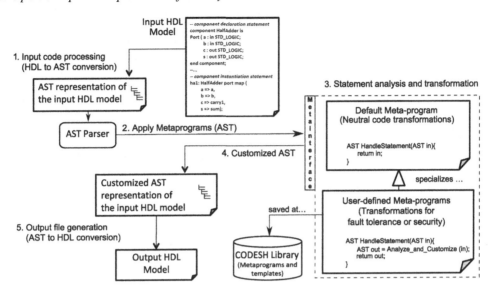

tiation statement, for instance), a metaprogram has the chance of analyzing and customizing the AST representation of such construct (step 2 in Figure 1). The communication between the open compiler and the metaprogram is performed through a well-known interface implemented by the *Metainterface* class. Metaprograms must implement that part of the Metainterface related to those constructs they are willing to customize. The AST node representing the construct to be handled is systematically provided to the suitable metaprogram, which is thus activated (step 3 in Figure 1).

The variety of actions a metaprogram can carry out, defined by means of analysis and transformation rules, will obviously vary according to the considered resilience strategy. In fact, the implementation of the default metaprogram follows a neutral transformation approach, meaning that no actual transformation takes places onto the original HDL construct represented by the input AST. This behavior can be specialized through inheritance, so non-neutral metaprograms should overload those methods required for their specific purpose, such as removing constructs or modifying their internal structure, either by changing their internal elements (like identifiers or types) or by introducing

new ones. It must be noted that the way in which analysis and transformation rules are applied to input HDL models also rely on the structure of such models. Accordingly, as each metaprogram could customize just a particular construct of the input HDL model, a whole set of metaprograms could be required to implement a given fault tolerance mechanism. In fact, these rules can be viewed as templates that are used to adapt the implementation of resilience mechanisms to each particular hardware component structure. Hence, each newly defined metaprogram, or set of metaprograms, integrates CODESH library of components and mechanisms for dependability and security. The customized AST node resulting from applying those analysis and transformation rules implemented by the metaprogram is finally returned back to the open compiler (step 4 in Figure 1), thus replacing the original AST.

Once this approach is recursively applied to all the nodes in the AST, the open compiler finally generates an output file reflecting all model transformations (step 5 in Figure 1).

As an example, Figure 2 details the process followed for replacing a non-fault-tolerant component by its Triple Modular Redundant (TMR) version. TMR is a well-known strategy consisting

Figure 2. CODESH open compilation process in action: a TMR case

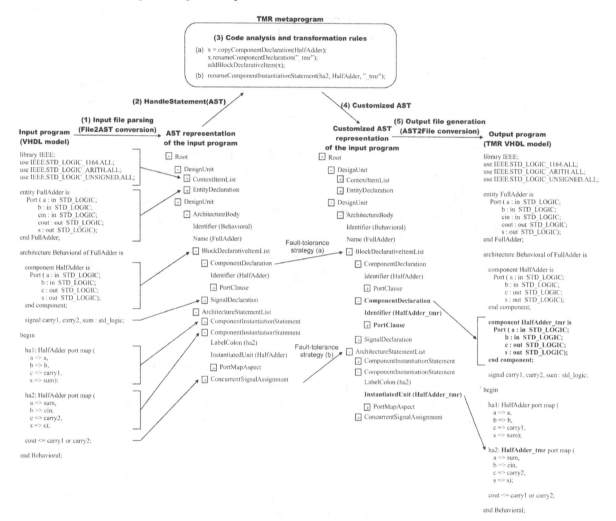

in physically replicating the hardware component to be protected, and obtaining the right output of the system by majority voting the outputs of all the replicas (Avizienis, 1969). The leftmost column of the figure lists the structural definition of a FulllAdder in terms of two internal HalfAdders. The AST obtained after parsing the VHDL model (step 1 in Figure 2) is shown in the second column of the figure, with arrows mapping VHDL statements to AST nodes. Steps 2 to 4 apply a TMR strategy to *ha2* HalfAdder through transformations (a) and (b), thus affecting different nodes of the AST (shown in boldface in the third column of the figure). Finally, the rightmost column in Figure 2 lists the TMR enhanced version of the original model after step 5 takes place. This schema tolerates any number of transient faults, as long as they affect just one replica at a time and disappear before any other fault occurs, and just one permanent fault affecting one replica. This approach is greatly favored when protecting hardware components due to its simplicity and good tolerance capabilities, although it has a large cost in terms of silicon area, making it more suitable to critical-systems rather than consumer electronics.

Architecting Hardware Fault Tolerance Mechanisms as Metaprograms

Currently, CODESH library of fault tolerance mechanisms contains a set of metaprograms enabling i) the deployment of spatial redundancy through N-Modular Redundancy (Ruiz, de Andrés, Blanc, & Gil, 2008), ii) the detection and correction of errors on registers via Hamming codes (Ruiz, de Andrés, & Gil, Design and Deployment of a Generic ECC-based Fault Tolerance Mechanism for Embedded HW Cores, 2009), and iii) the detection of errors on buses throuch Cyclyc Redudant Checks (Espinosa, de Andrés, Ruiz, & Gil, 2011). After careful analysis, experience has demonstrated that fault tolerance strategies for hardware designs can be defined as metaprograms responsible for i) generating the required logic infrastructure, ii) encapsulating this logic with the original core within a new component, and iii) integrating this new component into the original model.

Any fault tolerance or security strategy for hardware systems needs to make use of multitude of different common components used in hardware design, like registers or multiplexers, and specific components to detect or tolerate faults, like comparators or majority voters. Particular metaprograms should be developed in order to generate this infrastructure according to the requirements of the given strategy. Once developed, these metaprograms will integrate the library of predefined components and strategies for fault tolerance, so they could be reused by any other strategy requiring them. It must be noted that metaprogramming the whole HDL model of any new component (a majority voter, for instance) is not a simple task. That is why it is recommendable to reuse the proposed open compilation approach to define some HDL *templates*. These templates (input HDL models in this case) should contain as much as possible of the required structure and only those parts that must be adapted to the particular strategy or hardware under consideration will be dynamically generated by means of smaller and much simpler metaprograms (like the size of the input/output ports, for instance).

After the required infrastructure has been generated, it is usually encapsulated with the original target component (or system), which retains its original functional capabilities, to introduce the new non-functional capabilities (fault detection and tolerance in this case). This can be seen as a kind of *wrapper* producing a fault-tolerant and/or secure version of the original component. Metaprograms will be in charge of i) configuring and instantiating as many components as required, and ii) interconnecting all these elements to implement the selected strategy. To achieve this goal it is essential to parameterize the whole process according to the particular strategy and, in many cases, the target component. When those components are delivered in the form of HDL models (*soft IP cores*), or when reusing components developed in-house, it is possible to access their internal structure (white box approach) and precisely determine the required customizations. However, third party cores are usually delivered as *hard IP cores*, which are already implemented (synthesized, placed and routed) and ready for manufacturing. This black box approach prevents designers from getting any knowledge about the internals of the component, thus limiting the available information to that provided by the manufacturer. Newer approaches enabling and easing the reflection on hard IP cores are then in need.

Finally, once the fault-tolerant and/or secure version of the target component has been obtained, another metaprogram will replace the original component by this customized version. In case the target component was the top-level component of the system, there is no replacement, but the new component is the one to be used from now on in the rest of the design process.

Integration within the Regular Hardware Design Flow

The common digital hardware design process, depicted in Figure 3, involves several steps to obtain a final product from initial specifications. Verification is usually performed after each step of the design (considering a respectable design size) to prevent any undetected error from causing further delays. This general design flow has been enriched to include the open compilation process required to introduce metaprogramming

as a technique to generate and deploy fault detection and tolerance mechanisms in the model of the system under development. The newly added steps shown in Figure 3 are highlighted in light grey to ease their identification.

The first step takes a set of functional and non-functional specifications to act as an input for the design of a system meeting these requirements. From these specifications, an HDL model describing the behavior and/or structure of the final system is defined. The design entry, although mostly done using HDL files, could also take into

Figure 3. Integrating the proposed open compilation process into the regular hardware design flow

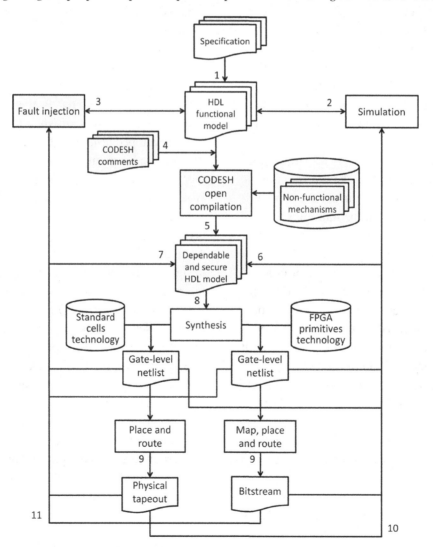

account acquired off-the-shelf components, which are integrated with other hand-coded components in a hierarchical style.

Step 2 in Figure 3 performs functional simulations of the HDL model of the system to verify its proper behavior in terms of service delivery. It must be noted that, as non-functional mechanisms have not been deployed yet, this simulation just verifies that the correct functionality has been implemented. At this point (step 3 in Figure 3), fault injection could be a useful mean to determine the sensitivity of each component to the fault models considered representative of each particular system. The aim of this process is to determine which mechanisms should be applied, and where they should be deployed, to meet dependability and security requirements. Fault injection may take place at this stage, using a simulation-based tool like VFIT (Gil, Baraza, Gracia, & Gil, 2004). Any problem reported during simulation or fault injection will feedback the design process, thus modifying the HDL model to correct any deviation from the specification.

Provided that end users of CODESH will be HDL designers, and assuming that this community is not intended to know about the subtleties of open compilation and its implementation, an easy to use approach has been implemented to help them to specify where and how to deploy a given metaprogram (dependability and security mechanism) into the system model. This approach consists in inserting a number of HDL comment lines with a special format that has a particular meaning to the CODESH parser (step 4 in Figure 3). The specific comment lines and related parameters for the customization of the deployed components and mechanisms are documented for each metaprogram available in the library. When running the open compiler, comment lines are first parsed to determine which metaprograms must be applied for each HDL construct. The main benefit of this approach is that hardware designers are already familiar with it to specify synthesis

directives in commercial products, like Synopsys' Design Compiler (Synopsys Inc., 2013). Furthermore, as it makes use of actual HDL comments, any Electronic Design Automation (EDA) tool may implement the original model of the system as it is, ignoring those comments that are only meaningful for CODESH.

It is at this point that CODESH open compiler takes the incoming HDL model, which includes all the special comments specifying the parameterization of the different fault tolerance and intrusion mechanisms to be deployed, and applies all the required metaprograms to generate the output HDL model following the previously explained procedure (step 5 in Figure 3). This new model can be then simulated and subjected to fault injection as in the previous step to confirm that all the (functional and non-functional) requirements are still met (steps 6 and 7 in Figure 3). This output model is the one re-injected into the regular design flow for its implementation.

The common hardware design flow typically continues with synthesis (step 8 in Figure 3), which uses specific libraries for the final implementation technology selected (like FPGAs or Standard Cells) and generates a gate-level design adapted to the end target. Following stages (step 9 in Figure 3) include map and place and route to achieve a physical tape-out or configuration file.

Finally, the implemented design is simulated again (step 10 in Figure 3), including extracted timings, to check that the functional requirements are still met. Likewise, emulation-/prototype-based fault injection (step 11 in Figure 3) may be also considered to validate the non-functional requirements (de Andrés, Ruiz, Gil, & Gil, 2008; Kafka, Danek, & Novak, 2007; Parreira, Teixeira, & Santos, 2003). Any deviations from the specifications should be corrected by either parameterizing the implementation (synthesis, mapping, and place and route) process or modifying the HDL model. This may lead to iterate through the design flow until the requirements are finally met.

As shown, the metaprogramming approach followed by CODESH can be seamlessly integrated into the regular hardware design flow. Next section will describe, by means of two case studies, how far more ambitious fault tolerance mechanisms than those commonly considered can be engineered while facing the problem of dealing with white and black box approaches.

DEALING WITH WHITE AND BLACK BOX IP CORES AS CASE STUDIES

As previously presented, third party components could be troublesome, as their degree of openness could limit the visibility of its internal structure and thus the flexibility metaprograms will have to deal with them. To illustrate both cases and show the feasibility of metaprograming to deploy fault tolerance and security mechanisms, two different cases studies have been considered. The first metaprogram will define a fault tolerance strategy to tolerate transient faults via temporal redundancy for white box combinational components. Later on, a second metaprogram will enable the integration of a qualified black box encryption core into an embedded component to secure its communications with other components.

White Box IP Cores: Tolerating Transient Faults via Temporal Redundancy

Temporal redundancy involves the use of additional time to perform tasks related to both software and hardware fault tolerance. It usually requires the repetition of a failed execution using the same resources involved in the initial one. This simple approach may tolerate the occurrence of timing or transient faults, as long as the causes of that fault are already absent prior to the re-execution of the failed task. Otherwise, the re-execution will lead to a failure again. Hence, temporal redundancy could

be a suitable solution for those systems that cannot afford the extra cost of including redundant logic but may easily neglect longer execution times, like mission-critical systems (Pullum, 2001). Although latency-critical applications, like many of those that can be found in nowadays mobile devices, are not so eager to trade timing for area, the inclusion of a hardware core implementing this mechanism in the integrated circuited will alleviate the temporal cost of applying a software-based approach.

Figure 4 shows the generation and customization processes that should be applied to the original model of the system in order to deploy a temporal redundancy mechanism. Solid black lines represent data lines, solid grey lines depict control lines, whereas dotted lines are used for the clock signal distribution. The different generation and customization rules devised for the automatic deployment of such mechanism are described in the following sections.

Generating the Required Infrastructure

Adapting an existing component to exhibit temporal redundancy capabilities involves the generation of some generic infrastructure to store and compare intermediate results (see Figure 4a). As demonstrated in (Ruiz, de Andrés, Blanc, & Gil, 2008), the generation of voting infrastructures (*voters*) can be accomplished via metaprogramming. Accordingly, and following a similar approach, the generation of generic *comparators* can be easily accomplished. Finally, (Ruiz, de Andrés, & Gil, Design and Deployment of a Generic ECC-based Fault Tolerance Mechanism for Embedded HW Cores, 2009) showed how generic pre-designed *registers* can serve as temporal data storage.

All these elements are kept in the CODESH library once generated. Hence, as many different instances of these components as required can be used to enhance the selected target component with temporal redundancy capabilities.

Figure 4. Metaprogramming temporal redundancy

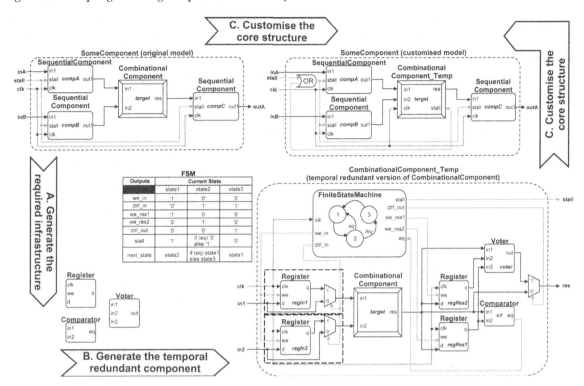

Encapsulating the Temporal Redundancy Mechanism

Providing temporal redundancy relies on processing the incoming inputs a given number of times in order to compare the different outcomes obtained and determine the correct one when discrepancies appear. Figure 4b depicts all the logic required and its interconnection to a given component, in order to expand the non-functional aspects of that component with temporal redundancy capabilities.

It is to note the importance of the component's nature when applying that kind of approach. The outputs provided by a *combinational* component only depend on its current inputs. Accordingly, it is necessary to feed the combinational component with the same inputs for each required re-execution. However, when dealing with a *sequential* component, the obtained outputs not only depend on its current inputs, but also on its current *state*. Hence, when in a black box approach, sequential

components should provide *intercession* capabilities to enable the system to obtain its current state (*getState*) and restore it later (*setState*) for each re-execution. In case those intercession capabilities are absent from the component's interface, it will not be possible to deploy the desired temporal redundancy mechanism. Then, this constraint must be taken into account when designing sequential components that could be considered as candidates for temporal redundancy techniques. If a white box approach is used, intercession could be implemented by inserting in the output of each register a structure as the one surrounded by thick dashed lines (register + multiplexer) in Figure 4b. As this technique can always be applied to combinational components, the description of the proposed approach will consider that kind of component as target.

Following the approach commonly used in the design of digital circuits, all the logic required to control the previously described infrastructure and the different re-execution stages is implemented by means of a FSM. This FSM will comprise a number of states equal to the number of re-executions (usually an odd number). In this example, the FSM consists of *three (3)* different states, and the activation of the signals it controls for each state is listed in the table depicted in Figure 4b. As FSM are synchronous elements that require a clock signal in order to activate the transition from one state to another, when dealing with combinational components it will be required to include a *clock input port* to the interface of the new customized component.

During the first state incoming inputs are registered, so the following re-executions may use these very same data for their operation. Hence, each input of the target component is associated to a *register*. In this first state, the target component directly operates with these incoming data, not the registered ones, to avoid delaying the operation one clock cycle. The outcome of the computation is also stored in another *register* for later use. As several re-executions will take place after this first one, the rest of the system should suspend its normal operation to wait for the right outcome to be provided. Hence, a new *stall output port* should be included to the interface of the customized component. This signal is now activated by the FSM, which proceeds to its second state.

From the second state and on, the target component must operate with the data stored in the incoming registers. Hence, the FSM activates the control signal of those multiplexers in charge of feeding the target component. The outcome of this operation is also stored on a dedicated *register*. Once more than half of the required re-execution have already been performed (3 for 5 executions, 4 for 7 executions, etc.), it is possible to optimize the performance of this component: if all operations have provided the very same result, it is not necessary to continue with the rest of re-executions, since this will be the right outcome for

the considered inputs. Accordingly, a *comparator* is used to determine whether all the previously stored outcomes and the current one are equal. If this is the case, the current outcome is passed onto the outputs of the component, the *stall* signal is deactivated so the system may resume its normal operation, and the FSM proceeds to its first state again. Otherwise, the FSM proceeds to its next state (third state in the figure).

Upon reaching the last (third in the example) state, the last re-execution is performed. As it is not necessary to store the outcome of this operation, a *register* is not required. This outcome, along with those previously stored, are fed to a *voter* to determine the correct output of the component. Finally, the FSM deactivates the *stall* signal to allow the system to resume its operation, and proceeds to its first state.

In summary, and following this reasoning, to re-execute *n* times the operation of a given component with *k* inputs, a FSM with *n* states will be in charge of controlling: *k* registers to store the original inputs, *n-1* registers to store the computed outputs, *k+1* multiplexors, an *(n+1)/2* comparators to optimize the performance of the component, and an *n-inputs* voter. In addition, a *stall* signal will control the execution flow of the rest of the system to wait for the correct outcome. A metaprogram is in charge of deploying and interconnecting all these elements to generate the temporal redundant version of the target component.

Inserting the New Component into the Original Model

The inclusion of the new (customized) component into the original model is usually quite straightforward, just replacing the original component by an instantiation of this new component. However, several other considerations must be taken into account to deploy a temporal redundancy strategy (see Figure 4c).

In first place, the clock signal must also be connected to the *clock input port* of the customized component. This should not pose any problem, except when the original component (SomeComponent in the figure) is combinational (asynchronous). In this case, an input clock port must also be added to the interface of that component, which should be connected to the clock signal of the component on the next (higher) level of the hierarchy. In case the whole system exclusively consists of asynchronous logic, this fault tolerance mechanism cannot be applied.

The second problem appears when considering that the new component may suspend the execution of the rest of components to synchronize them with the computation of the correct output. The best situation is faced when all components have been designed with a *stall input port*. In this case, the current connection of each stall input port may be OR-ed in order to be activated by either the normal flow of the execution or the customized component. This is the approach shown in Figure 4c. If this stall port is missing in any of the components, things get a bit more complex. One possible solution is determined by the existence of a *write enable input port* in these components. If they are designed in such a way that disabling that signal prevents the contents of *all* their registers from being updated, then this write enable port may be also AND-ed with the *NOT stall* signal. Otherwise, the last resort is to apply *clock gating* techniques (Emnett & Biegel, 2000). In this case, *clk AND NOT stall* is added to the clock tree to prevent those components from receiving a clock edge, thus keeping their state until the stall signal is deactivated. This is the less desirable method because of possible race conditions generated in the path.

As an example of how all these considerations are taken into account to customize the original model of the system, Table 1 specifies, in a Java-like pseudo code, the metaprogram interface that implements this approach (Table 1a) and all the required transformation rules (Table 1b).

Black Box IP Cores: Integrating Third Party Cores for Symmetric Encryption

An IP core providing symmetric encryption (McQueen, 2010) has been selected to show the feasibility of using metaprogramming to enhance the non-functional capabilities (security) of a given design and ease the integration of the core in further designs. Let us assume that the outgoing data of very same component previously studied should be encrypted in order to ensure its privacy. Figure 5 shows the generation and customization processes that should be applied to the original model to deploy the requested data encryption mechanism provided by the third party IP core. All the rules devised for the automatic integration of such core are next described.

Generating the Required Infrastructure

As Figure 5a shows, the main infrastructure required is just the IP core to integrate into the system. This is somewhat different from what happens when adding redundancy mechanisms to a target core, which usually require lots of other elements to implement the desired non-functional aspect. In this case, the symmetric encryption mechanism is already implemented by the selected IP core and, hence, very little additional infrastructure is needed.

Encapsulating the Third Party Core

The usefulness of a third party core, in addition to its intended functionality, relies on its ability to be easily introduced into any kind of systems. Therefore, analyzing and enhancing the interface of a given IP core may contribute to ease its reusability and extend its context of use.

For instance, the following assertion may be found in the documentation of the selected symmetric encryption core: "The reset signal is used to set all internal signals to a known state

Table 1. Metaprogram interface (a) and transformation rules (b) required to insert the new component into the original model (customize the core structure)

A. Model customisation metaprogram	B. Required metaprogram rules

```
interface Model_Customisation {

    //Initialisation of local variables

    ComponentDeclaration handleComponenDeclaration(
        ComponentDeclaration cd
    ){
        if (cd.getName().equals(this.targetComponentName) {
            // Generate the new customised component declaration
            ComponentDeclaration newCD =
                        Generation_Rule_g1(cd);
            //Add clk and stall ports to the new component
            Customisation_Rule_c1(
                newCD, "clk", Mode.IN, Subtype.STD_LOGIC);
            Customisation_Rule_c1(
                newCD, "stall", Mode.OUT, Subtype.STD_LOGIC);
            // Append the customised component to the
            list of components
            bdiList.append(newCD);
        }
        return(cd);
    }

    ArchitectureDeclarativePart
        handleArchitectureDeclarativePart(
        ArchitectureDeclarativePart adp
    ){
        BlockDeclarativeItem[] bdiList = adp.getList();
        // Generate the auxiliary stall signals declaration
        SignalDeclaration newSD =
            Generation_Rule_g2({"stall_temp", "stall_ored"});
        // Append the auxiliary signals to the list of signals
        bdiList.append(newSD);
        return(adp);
    }

    ComponentInstantiationStatement
        handleComponentInstantiationStatement(
        ComponentInstantiationStatement cis
    ){
        if (cis.getLabel().equals(this.targetComponentLabel) {
            // Map the new ports in the target instantiation list
            Customisation_Rule_c3(cis, "clk", "clk");
            Customisation_Rule_c3(cis, "stall", "stall_temp");
            // Modify target instance for new component
            Customisation_Rule_c4(cis);
        }
        else {
            // Modify the stall mapping
            Customisation_Rule_c2(cis, "stall", "stall_ored");
        }
        return(cis);
    }

    ArchitectureStatementPart
        handleArchitectureStatementPart(
        ArchitectureStatementPart asp
    ){
        // Generate the stall signal assignment statement
        SignalAssignmentStatement newSAS =
            Generation_Rule_g3(
                "stall_ored", "stall", "stall_temp", LogicOperator.OR);
        // Append the new assignment to the concurrent
            assignments list
        asp.getConcurrentStatementList().append(newSAS);
        return(asp);
    }
}
```

```
ComponentDeclaration Generation_Rule_g1 (
    ComponentDeclaration cd,
) {
    //Generate a clone of the target component
    ComponentDeclaration newCD =
        new ComponentDeclaration(cd);
    newCD.setID(newCD.getID() + "_" + "Temp");
    return(newCD);
}

void Customisation_Rule_c1 (
    ComponentDeclaration cd,
    string pn, // Port name
    Mode pm, // Port mode
    Subtype ps, // Port subtype
) {
    cd.getPortClause().AddPort(
        new InterfaceSignalDeclaration(new Identifier(pn,pm,ps));
}

SignalDeclaration Generation_Rule_g2 (
    string[] snList, // Signal name list
) {
    //Generate a new signal declaration
    SignalDeclaration newSD = new SignalDeclaration(
        new IdentifierList(snList), Subtype.STD_LOGIC);
    return(newSD);
}

void Customisation_Rule_c2 (
    ComponentInstantiationStatement cis,
    string fp // formal part name
    string ap // actual part name
) {
    AssociationElement ae =
        cis.getPortMap().
            FindAssociationElementByFormalPartName(fp);
    ae.getActualPart().setName(ap);
}

void Customisation_Rule_c3 (
    ComponentInstantiationStatement cis,
    string fpn // formal part name
    string apn // actual part name
) {
    cis.getPortMap().Add(
        new AssociationElement(fpn, apn));
}

void Customisation_Rule_c4 (
    ComponentInstantiationStatement cis,
) {
    cis.getInstantiatedUnit().setName(
        cis.getInstantiatedUnit().getName() + "_Temp");
}

SignalAssignmentStatement Generation_Rule_g3 (
    string tn, // Target name
    string se1, // Simple expression name
    string se2, // Simple expression name
    LogicOperator lo,
) {
    //Generate a new signal assignment statement
    SignalAssignmentStatement newSAS =
        new SignalAssignmentStatement(
            tn, new Expression(se1, se2, lo));
    return(newSAS);
}
```

Figure 5. Metaprogramming the integration of a third party core providing symmetric data encryption into a given model

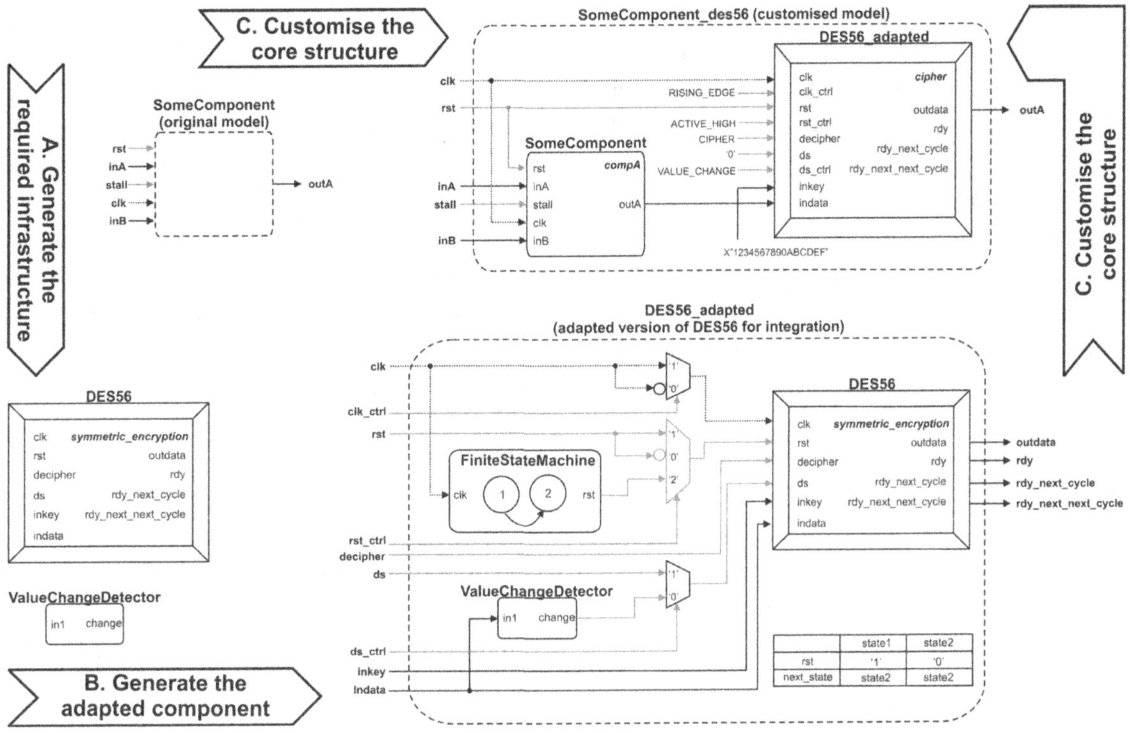

and prepare the core for operation. It should be strobed high at least once after power on and before attempting the first cryptographic operation." (McQueen, 2010). Accordingly, the system integrator should take it into account to feed the reset signal of that component with the expected high logic level. However, it could happen that the original reset signal of the system is active low, or even worse, that it consists of pure combinational logic and so no reset signal is available. In any case, it seems highly convenient to provide the third party core with a parameter (*rst_ctrl*) that can be used to control whether this component will receive an active high or low reset signal, or it should internally generate a reset to initialize the core. That is the purpose of the 3-to-1 multiplexer and the finite state machine depicted in Figure 5b. This new control signal will prevent system integrators from forgetting to properly feed the reset signal of the third party core, as no input

maybe left unconnected and only meaningful values like *ACTIVE_HIGH*, *ACTIVE_LOW*, and *RST_NOT_AVAILABLE*, are accepted.

Something similar can be said about the clock signal. In this case, no information can be found on the documentation stating whether the symmetric encryption core operates on rising or falling edges. After checking the core's behavior (*black box* approach), and determining that it operates on rising edges, a 2-to-1 multiplexer has been included to take care of passing the right edge to the core. As in the previous example, it will be mandatory to activate the related control signal (*clk_ctrl*) with one of the two eligible values (*RISING_EDGE*, *FALLING_EDGE*).

Another interesting case is related to the *ds* signal. According to the documentation: "the DS signal is the data strobe. When momentarily strobed high, it indicates the input data set is valid, and signals the core to start a cryptographic operation. Only the rising edge of this signal has meaning: all other states are ignored." (McQueen, 2010). A singular problem arises from the fact that, probably, the system integrating this core does not present any *ready* signal in charge of notifying when new data is available on the output port. One possible solution consists in making use of another component (*ValueChangeDetector* on Figure 5b) that provides a rising edge whenever the data to be cyphered/deciphered changes. Accordingly, the *ds_ctrl* signal will control whether the *ds* input (*DS*) or the *ValueChangeDetector* (*VALUE_CHANGE*) will trigger the encryption/decryption operation.

The development of metaprograms to wrap third party cores in the required additional infrastructure may not only help system integrators, but will enable other metaprograms to automatically deploy these cores into the target model.

Inserting the New Component into the Original Model

Once encapsulated, this customized core may be easily integrated into the original model. As this component was not present in the model, it is necessary to include its declaration (interface) and insert a new instantiation to establish the connections among its input/output ports and the rest of signals and ports of the system. In the example depicted in Figure 5c this is quite simple, since the data to be ciphered comes from the target component, and the actual output of the system is now computed by the symmetric encryption core. The clock and reset signals are directly connected to the corresponding core ports. As the original component do not provide any *output ready* signal, all the *rdy* output ports of the core are left unconnected (*open*).

The last step is properly parameterizing the control signals that have been added to the customized third party core to ease its interconnection. In this example, the *clk* and *rst* signals of the

system follow the same specification as noted in the documentation of the encryption/decryption core and, thus, its corresponding control signals are set accordingly (*RISING_EDGE* and *AC-TIVE_HIGH*, respectively). As the component must encrypt the incoming data, the *cipher* port is set to *CIPHER*. The target component does not provide any information related to new data being available on its output and, hence, the *ds* activation signal must be internally generated by checking the incoming data (*ds* is set to '0' and *ds_ctrl* to *VALUE_CHANGE*). Finally, the key used to encrypt/decrypt the incoming data must be passed to the *inkey* port (*X"1234567890ABCDEF"* in the figure).

The model resulting from the application of the generation rules defined in the proposed metaprogram to automatically integrate the symmetric encryption mechanism is depicted in Figure 6. In this way, the privacy and confidentiality of outgoing data is easily ensured by reusing existing qualified components.

ANALYSIS OF RESULTS AND DISCUSSION

A structural HDL model of a PIC (Programmable Intelligent Computer) 16C5X microcontroller (Romani, 2007), whose family is representative of those commonly used in embedded applications, has been selected to show the feasibility of the proposed approach. The generated metaprograms will be applied to that microcontroller to automatically deploy i) a temporal redundancy mechanism to tolerate transient faults in combinational logic, and ii) a symmetric encryption mechanism to ensure the privacy of data sent by its output ports. The rest of this section presents the considered experimental setup, the proposed solution to be automatically applied by the metaprograms, and the analysis of computed results.

Figure 6. Metaprogram generation rule required to integrate the symmetric data encryption third party component

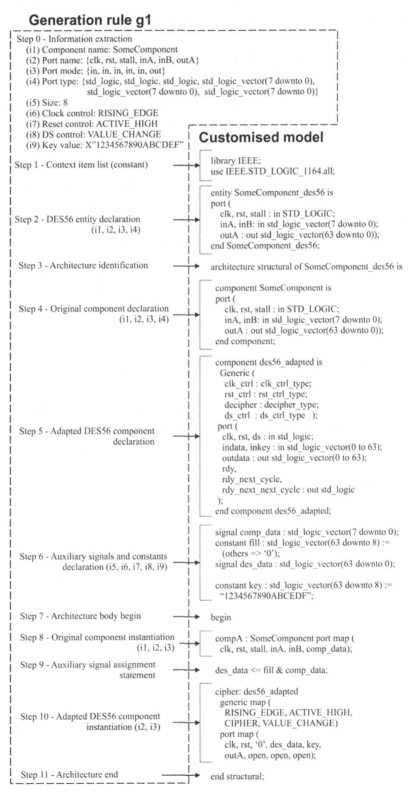

Experimental Setup

In order to perform a fair comparison between the original model of the system and the automatically generated fault-tolerant and secure models, the same implementation technology should be used for all of them. Field-Programmable Gate Arrays (FPGAs), which are very useful for prototyping and testing HDL models in the field, seem a good implementation choice since all these models follow a synthesizable VHDL description. FADES (de Andrés, Ruiz, Gil, & Gil, 2008), an FPGA-based Framework for the Analysis of the Dependability of Embedded Systems, appears as a suitable framework for implementing the models on a programmable device and injecting faults during the experiments execution to analyze the sensitivity and final robustness of the resulting system.

The selected workload consists in a *quicksort algorithm*, which could be representative of those control algorithms typically executed, for instance, in automotive applications (EEMBC, 2013).

Temporal redundancy can deal with transient faults and, as previously stated, this case study specifically focuses on those faults affecting the combinational logic of the system. Hence, the considered faultload comprises *pulses*, *transient indeterminations*, and *transient delays* (Gil, et al., 2002), with just a single fault being injected in each experiment. The number of experiments is determined according to the silicon area devoted to implement the combinational logic of the target component and, thus, the relative area exposed to the considered faults.

The set of considered measures to estimate the robustness of the system includes the percentage of faults being *masked*, remaining *latent* or leading to a *failure*. Other measures related to cost or performance are the *silicon area*, *clock frequency* and *energy consumption*. The detailed process of how to extract all these measures from the observed measurements is described in (de Andrés, Ruiz, & Gil, Using Dependability, Performance, Area and Energy Consumption Experimental Measures to Benchmark IP Cores, 2009).

In a first stage, the design is implemented and prototyped, and faults are injected using the aforementioned fault models to obtain a sensitivity analysis of each available component. This initial study revealed that the most suitable candidate to improve its dependability via temporal redundancy is the *control unit*, whereas communications from *input output ports* should be encrypted. Therefore, these are the target components for the proposed metaprograms. Modified designs are subjected to a new fault injection campaign to assess the improvements, proper functioning and overhead of the inserted strategies. The results from this experimentation are reported in next section.

Analysis of Results

For each fault model, a number of 330 experiments were injected during the sensitivity analysis of the original control unit, and 850 more were required after its customization. As the goal of the encryption mechanism is to ensure the privacy of the generated data, it makes no sense to inject accidental faults into that version of the system. Dependability/security improvements usually come at a price, in terms of increased silicon area, reduced throughput and increased power consumption. The comparison of these results for the original IP core (*PIC*), the version enhanced with a temporally redundant control unit (*TR*), and the version encrypting the outputs (*DES*) is presented in Table 2.

As can be expected, the impact of transient faults on the combinational logic of the system (see Table 2a) is quite low since they can be electrically, temporally and logically masked. Nevertheless, nearly a 10% of pulses and a 7% of indeterminations lead the system to a failure. This rate is reduced to just a 1% in the case of transient delays.

Table 2. Comparison of the original (PIC), temporally redundant (TR), and secured (DES) cores in terms of failures, area, throughput, and energy consumption

A. Impact of Faults			
IP Core	**Pulses Leading to Failure**	**Transient Indeterminations Leading to Failure**	**Transient Delays Leading to Failure**
PIC	9.7%	6.6%	0.9%
TR	3.7%	2.8%	1.3%

B. Area Estimation					
IP Core	**Number of Flip-Flops**	**Number of Look-Up Tables**	**Number of Slices**	**Equivalent Logic Count**	**Area Increment**
PIC	752	457	629	18362	–
TR	880	720	772	20979	+ 14%
DES	1006	1002	984	24051	+ 31%

C. Throughput Estimation					
IP Core	**Clock Period (ns)**	**Number of Clock Cycles**	**Execution Time (us)**	**Throughput (Executions/s)**	**Throughput Reduction**
PIC	33.232	1722	57.225	57.225	–
TR	43.691	3344	146.102	146.102	– 61%
DES	33.922	1722	58.413	58.413	– 2%

D. Energy Consumption Estimation				
PIC Core	**Power Consumption (mW)**	**Execution Time (us)**	**Energy Consumption (mW × s)**	**Energy Consumption Increment**
PIC	366	57.225	0.0209	–
TR	257	146.102	0.0375	+ 79%
DES	399	58.413	0.0233	+ 11%

After protecting the system with the temporal redundancy mechanism, the occurrence of any transient fault within the control unit is completely tolerated. However, the whole set of logic that has been added in order to deploy this mechanism is not protected against these faults and, thus, the percentage of faults leading to a failure (on the whole) is decreased to just near a 4% and 3% for pulses and indeterminations, respectively. The case of transient delays is somewhat special. As the impact of delays is so low, the large amount of additional unprotected logic included is negatively affecting the robustness of the system, and no benefit can be obtained from this strategy. Moreover,

the registers introduced to hold input data may suffer other faults that have not been tested but could add a minor impact in the system. That shows the importance of performing a previous sensitivity analysis to accurately determine which strategies to deploy and which components to target.

However, these benefits in terms of dependability and security do not come for free. As can be seen in Table 2b, and as can be expected, the original core is the one requiring the smallest amount of silicon area for its final implementation. This area, estimated by the number of logic gates required to build and equivalent circuit, increases a 14% when considering the fault tolerance mechanism (additional logic required to store inputs and intermediate results, and to control the re-execution of the operations) and a 31% for the security mechanism (additional logic required to keep tables with information for the next encryption round and to execute the operation in 16 rounds). This somehow estimates the increased cost related to the larger quantity of resources (flip-flops and look-up tables to implement the sequential and combinational logic of the system, respectively) required for implementing any of these mechanisms.

The number of times the system can execute the selected workload per second (throughput) is also estimated in Table 2c. The original core presents the highest clock frequency and the lowest execution time, leading to the highest throughput. As could be expected, deploying the fault tolerance mechanism onto the control unit is highly impacting the critical path of the core and, hence, increasing its clock period. Furthermore, as each instruction of the workload must be executed at least twice, the finally obtained throughput is reduced a 61% with respect to the original core. On the other hand, as the third party encryption core has been designed with a 16-stages pipeline structure, its insertion in the original model barely affects the finally obtained throughput (-2%). This variation is not significant and maybe attributed to the non-deterministic implementation process.

The energy consumed by the three considered versions is reported in Table 2d. Once again, the original core obtains the best results, since it requires the smallest quantity of resources to be implemented, and presents the lowest clock frequency and the shortest execution time for the selected workload. The inclusion of the temporal redundancy mechanism reduces the *power consumption* of the core, as half of the time most of its components are *stalled* to recompute the output signals of the control unit. However, the so long execution time counterbalances this result, leading to an increase in the *energy consumption* of a 79%. Although the original core and the version improved with a security mechanism present very

similar clock frequency and execution times, the latter consumes an 11% more energy due to the larger amount of physical resources required for its implementation.

It must be noted that all these overheads are inherent to the insertion of the different fault tolerance and security mechanisms considered, and are not due to their definition and deployment via metaprogramming. These overheads are very similar to those that can be expected when implementing the very same mechanisms by hand.

Finally, experimental results validate the metaprogram-generated implementation and deployment of both mechanisms. Temporal redundancy increases the robustness of the system against transient faults targeting its combinational logic at the cost of greatly reducing the expected throughput and increasing its energy consumption. Symmetric encryption enhances the security (privacy) of the system by using a large number of physical resources for its implementation and slightly increasing its energy consumption. This hinders malicious attacks based on eavesdropping.

CONCLUSION AND OPEN CHALLENGES

Increasing integration scales, time to market pressure and the use and re-use of third party cores are greatly increasing the likelihood of occurrence of faults in hardware embedded systems. Although once reserved for safety-, mission-, and business-critical systems, fault tolerance and security strategies are nowadays a requirement even to consumer electronics. Accordingly, both academia and industry are currently moving towards the provision of tools for automating the implementation of fault-tolerant and secure components and their subsequent deployment in hardware systems.

This chapter has shown that aspect orientation concepts, which have been successfully used for software development, can also be applied to hardware development. The most common approach to support the separation between functional and non-functional concerns in hardware design is based on metaprogramming and open compilation. In concrete, CODESH, an open compilation process for the design of dependable and secure high-level HDL descriptions, has been used to illustrate how metaprograms could support the design of fault-tolerant and secure hardware by i) developing the required basic infrastructure, ii) encapsulating these elements to define a new fault-tolerant or secure component, and iii) integrating it into the original HDL model. The proposed open compilation approach is seamlessly integrated into the regular hardware design flow, thus enabling hardware designers to apply different fault tolerance and security strategies to any HDL-based design within minutes and avoiding error prone procedures. The feasibility of the approach has been proved through two different case studies, which also showed the importance of properly analyzing the weaknesses of the system so as not to incur in large overheads with negligible benefits.

Despite metaprogramming and open compilation provide a highly flexible approach for the generic development and automatic deployment of fault tolerance and security mechanisms, its use requires a deep technical knowledge of HDL, the metalanguage (Java in the case of CODESH), and the API reflecting the structure of the input HDL model. Latest research in this domain is focusing on instantiating all the concepts related to aspect orientation, like join points, advices and pointcuts, in the domain of HDL. In this way, common HDLs could be extended to support the definition of fault tolerance and security mechanisms as aspects using the same language hardware designers usually employ.

The applicability of this methodology may also be hindered by the openness (white box and black box) of the considered models. *Soft cores*, with a white box approach, can usually be analyzed and modified as desired and, thus, it is possible to add the logic needed to implement the intended functionality. However, performing this analysis to understand the implemented functionality, and modify it accordingly, is not always as straightforward as it could seem. The definition of precise design guidelines to help open compilers and metaprograms to reason about the input model and locate the critical infrastructure necessary to implement the desired interface is necessary. This is very similar to hardware design guidelines to help synthesizers to obtain the right circuit from the input HDL model. When dealing with *hard cores*, with a black box approach, and even under *grey box* approaches, all the implementation details are hidden from the metaprogram and, thus, the responsibility for implementing and properly documenting the required interfaces falls again upon the core designer. This problem could be alleviated by designers adhering to standards supporting the definition of buses for easing the interconnection of cores, and thus their reuse, such as the Advanced Microcontroller Bus Architecture (ARM Ltd., 2013), the Wishbone architecture (OpenCores, 2010), and the OpenCore Protocol architecture (OCP-IO Association, 2013). Thus, components could be provided with a common interface allowing their easy interconnection and interrogation about their configuration parameters and capabilities.

Another interesting point is related to the composition of mechanisms. Up to now, research has mainly focused on showing the feasibility of using open compilers and metaprogramming to automatically deploy fault tolerance and security mechanisms into a given hardware system but, however, the implications derived from its composition have not been considered yet. Obviously, faults will affect differently a *spatially redundant and secure* component and a *secure and spatially redundant* component. So, it could be very interesting to study the composition of available mechanisms, how to deploy them in an efficient and automatic way, the effect of faults and attacks on these combinations and, also, how they impact the area, throughput and energy consumption of the final system. From this study, and by analyzing all the possible combinations with HDL models considered representative of different application contexts (like automotive, aircraft, or consumer electronics), it could be possible to obtain a rough estimation of the benefits and drawbacks of each combination in each application context. This could assist the open compiler user when deciding which mechanisms to deploy on a given system according to cost, performance, and dependability requirements.

Finally, this kind of approaches may be of great interest for the development of adaptive hardware systems. Let us assume, for instance, that to protect a system against faults a *Triple Modular Redundancy* mechanism is deployed, thus increasing the required area for a simple (non-protected) system by around 200% (note again that this overhead is intrinsic to the mechanism and is not due to its metaprogramming). In case a permanent fault occurs, the faulty module is removed from the system and a *Dual System with Comparison* is used instead. Now, when results do not match, they are re-executed once more. This system would increase, with respect to the simple system, the required area by a 100% and the execution time by 100%, but only in presence of faults. In case another permanent fault is detected, the remaining fault-free component can be encapsulated into a *Temporal Redundancy* mechanism, which will increase the execution time by a 200%. If another permanent fault is detected, the system will fail. Although a metaprogram could be developed to handle the deployment of all three mechanisms at once, with the logic required to switch from one mechanism to another, the cost in terms of area, performance and energy consumption will be enormous. However, reconfigurable devices like FPGAs could be used not only as prototyping platforms, but also as the implementation technology for the final system. In this way, the hardware system could change from one defined configuration to another as faults occur, but also as dependability, area, performance, or energy consumption requirements change. For instance, if the reconfigurable device is required to imple-

ment a given function, the system could move to a reduced area implementation (like the temporal redundancy mechanism) sacrificing performance and dependability in favor of area. Once this additional function is no longer needed, the system can change into a more dependable but otherwise conservative configuration, such as the comparison with detection. Finally, when the device detects that the likelihood of occurrence of faults is high, it may switch into a fully dependable configuration in spite of the area taken. As shown, the powerful automation capabilities provided by metaprogramming and open compilation may pave the way towards the actual use of adaptive resilience mechanisms, whose performance and dependability capabilities could evolve depending on faults, attacks and changes in the operation environment.

ACKNOWLEDGMENT

This work has been partially funded by the Spanish Ministry of Economy through the ARENES project (TIN2012-38308-C02-01).

REFERENCES

Alexandersson, R., & Öhman, P. (2010). On Hardware Resource Consumption for Aspect-Oriented Implementation of Fault Tolerance. In *Proceedings of European Dependable Computing Conference* (pp. 61-66). Valencia, Spain: IEEE Conference Publishing Services.

Avizienis, A. (1969). *Design Methods for Fault-Tolerant Navigation Computers*. Pasadena, CA: Jet Propulsion Laboratory.

Berrojo, L., Corno, F., Entrena, L., González, I., López, C., Sonza Reorda, M., & Squillero, G. (2002). An Industrial Environment for High-Level Fault-Tolerant Structures Insertion and Validation. In *Proceedings of 20th IEEE VLSI Test Symposium*, (pp. 229-236). Monterey, CA: IEEE.

Brigham Young University. (2013). *BYU EDIF Tools Home Page*. Retrieved 07 29, 2013, from FPGA Reliability Studies: http://reliability.ee.byu.edu/edif/

Constantinescu, C. (2003). Trends and Challenges in VLSI Circuit Reliability. *IEEE Micro, 4*(23), 14–19. doi:10.1109/MM.2003.1225959

de Andrés, D., Ruiz, J.-C., Gil, D., & Gil, P. (2008). Fault Emulation for Dependability Evaluation of VLSI Systems. *IEEE Transactions on Very Large Scale Integration (VLSI) Systems, 16*(4), 422–431.

de Andrés, D., Ruiz, J.-C., & Gil, P. (2009). Using Dependability, Performance, Area and Energy Consumption Experimental Measures to Benchmark IP Cores. In *Proceedings of Latin-American Symposium on Dependable Computing*, (pp. 49-56). Joao Pessoa, Brazil: Academic Press.

Do, R. D. (2011). *New tool for FPGA designers mitigates soft errors within synthesis*. Retrieved 07 29, 2013, from DSP-FPGA.com Magazine: http://dsp-fpga.com/articles/new-errors-within-synthesis/

EEMBC. (2013). *AutoBench™ 1.1 Benchmark Software*. Retrieved 07 29, 2013, from The Embedded Microprocessor Benchmark Consortium: http://www.eembc.org/benchmark/automotive_sl.php

Emnett, F., & Biegel, M. (2000). *Power Reduction Through RTL Clock Gating*. San José, CA: Synopsys Users Group.

Engel, M., & Spinczyk, O. (2008). Aspects in hardware: what do they look like?. In Proceedings of AOSD workshop on Aspects, components, and patterns for infrastructure software, (pp. 1-6). Brussels, Belgium: AOSD.

Entrena, L., López, C., & Olías, E. (2001). *Automatic Generation of Fault Tolerant VHDL Designs in RTL*. Forum on Design Languages.

Espinosa, J., de Andrés, D., Ruiz, J.-C., & Gil, P. (2011). *Robust communications using automatic deployment of a CRC-generation technique in IP-blocks*. Laguna, Spain: XI Reconfigurable Computing and Applications.

Fabre, J.-C., & Pérennou, T. (1998). A Metaobject Architecture for Fault Tolerant Distributed Systems: The FRIENDS Approach. *IEEE Transactions on Computers, 47*, 78–95. doi:10.1109/12.656088

Gil, D., Baraza, J.-C., Gracia, J., & Gil, P. (2004). VHDL Simulation-Based Fault Injection Techniques. In A. Benso, & P. Prinetto (Eds.), *Fault Injection Techniques and Tools for Embedded Systems Reliability Evaluation* (pp. 159–176). Springer, US. doi:10.1007/0-306-48711-X_10

Gil, P., Arlat, J., Madeira, H., Crouzet, Y., Jarboui, T., Kanoun, K., et al. (2002). *Fault Representativeness*. Retrieved July 29, 2013, from Dependability Benchmarking Project (IST-2000-25425): http://www.laas.fr/DBench

Kafka, L., Danek, M., & Novak, O. (2007). A Novel Emulation Technique that Preserves Circuit Structure and Timing. In *Proceedings of International Symposium on System-on-Chip*, (pp. 1-4). Tampere, Finland: Academic Press.

Karnik, T., Hazucha, P., & Patel, J. (2004). Characterization of Soft Errors Caused by Single Event Upsets in CMOS Processes. *IEEE Transactions on Dependable and Secure Computing, 1*(2), 128–143. doi:10.1109/TDSC.2004.14

Kiczales, G., Irwin, J., Lamping, J., Loingtier, J.-M., Lopes, C. V., Maeda, C., & Mendhekar, A. (1996). Aspect-oriented programming. *ACM Computing Surveys, 28*(4).

Koopman, P., & Chakravarty, T. (2004). Cyclic Redundancy Code (CRC) Polynomial Selection For Embedded Networks. In *Proceedings of IEEE International Conference on Dependable Systems and Networks*, (pp. 145-154). IEEE.

Leveugle, R. (2002). *Automatic Modifications of High Level VHDL Descriptions*. Grenoble, France: Design, Automation and Test in Europe Conference and Exhibition.

Ltd, A. R. M. (2013). *CoreLink System IP and Design Tools for AMBA*. Retrieved July 29, 2013, from http://www.arm.com/products/system-ip/amba

Maes, P. (1987). Concepts and experiments in computational reflection. ACM SIGPLAN Notices, 22(12), 147-155.

McQueen, S. R. (2010). *Basic DES Cryptography Core*. Retrieved July 29, 2013, from OpenCores: http://opencores.org/project,basicdes

Meier, M., Hanenberg, S., & Spinczyk, O. (2012). AspectVHDL Stage 1: The Prototype of an Aspect-Oriented Hardware Description Language. In *Proceedings of 2nd AOSD Workshop on Modularity in Systems Software*, (pp. 3-8). Potsdam, Germany: AOSD.

Mück, T. R., Gernoth, M., Schröder-Preikschat, W., & Fröhlich, A. A. (2011). A Case Study of AOP and OOP Applied to Digital Hardware Design. In *Proceedings of Brazilian Symposium on Computing System Engineering*, (pp. 66-71). Florianopolis, Brazil: Academic Press.

Narayanan, V., & Xie, Y. (2006). Reliability Concerns in Embedded System Designs. *IEEE Computer*, 1(39), 118–120. doi:10.1109/MC.2006.31

OCP-IO Association. (2013). *Open Core Protocol International Partnership (OCP-IP)*. Retrieved July 29, 2013, from http://www.ocpip.org

OpenCores. (2010, Juny 22). *Wishbone System-on-Chip (SoC) Interconnect Architecture for Portable IP Cores*. Retrieved July 29, 2013, from OpenCores: http://opencores.org/opencores,wishbone

OpenCores. (2013). Retrieved July 29, 2013, from http://www.opencores.org

Parr, T. (2103). *The Definitive ANTLR 4 Reference*. The Pragmatic Bookshelf.

Parreira, A., Teixeira, J., & Santos, M. (2003). A Novel Approach to FPGA-Based Hardware Fault Modeling and Simulation. In *Proceedings of IEEE International Workshop on Design and Diagnostics of Electronic Circuits and Systems*, (pp. 17-24). Poznań, Poland: IEEE.

Pohl, C., Paiz, C., & Porrmann, M. (2009). vMAGIC—Automatic Code Generation for VHDL. *International Journal of Reconfigurable Computing*, 1–9. doi:10.1155/2009/205149

Pullum, L. L. (2001). *Software fault tolerance techniques and implementation*. Artech House, Inc.

Romani, E. (2007, July 02). *Structural PIC165X microcontroller*. Retrieved July 29, 2013, from The Hamburg VHDL Archive: http://tams-www.informatik.uni-hamburg.de/vhdl

Rosenstiel, W. (Ed.). (2004). Special Issue on IP and Design Reuse. Integration, the VLSI Journal, 37, 191-356.

Ruiz, J.-C., de Andrés, D., Blanc, S., & Gil, P. (2008). Generic Design and Automatic Deployment of NMR Strategies on HW Cores. *IEEE Pacific Rim International Symposium on Dependable Computing*, (pp. 265-272). Taipei, Taiwan: IEEE.

Ruiz, J.-C., de Andrés, D., & Gil, P. (2009). Design and Deployment of a Generic ECC-based Fault Tolerance Mechanism for Embedded HW Cores. In *Proceedings of IEEE International Conference on Emerging Technologies and Factory Automation*, (pp. 3956-3964). Mallorca, Spain: IEEE.

Ruiz, J.-C., de Andrés, D., Gil, P., & Blanc, S. (2008). Using Open Compilation to Simplify the Design of Fault-Tolerant VLSI Systems. In *Proceedings of Workshop on Compiler and Architectural Techniques for Application Reliability and Security*, (pp. B14-B19). Anchorage, AK: Academic Press.

Shigeru, C. (1995). A Metaobject Protocol for C++. In *Proceedings of Tenth annual conference on Object-oriented programming systems, languages, and applications* (pp. 285-299). Austin, TX: ACM.

Štuikys, V., Damaševičius, R., Ziberkas, G., & Majauskas, G. (2002). Soft IP Design Framework Using Metaprogramming Techniques. In Proceedings of Design and Analysis of Distributed Embedded Systems (pp. 257-266). Springer.

Synopsys Inc. (2013). *Accelerate Design Innovation with Design Compiler*. Retrieved 07 29, 2013, from http://www.synopsys.com/Tools/Implementation/RTLSynthesis/Pages/default.aspx

Taïani, F., Fabre, J.-C., & Killijan, M.-O. (2005). A multi-level meta-object protocol for fault-tolerance in complex architectures. In *Proceedings of IEEE/IFIP International Conference on Dependable Systems and Networks*, (pp. 207-279). Yokohama, Japan: IEEE.

Tanenbaum, A. S. (2002). *Computer Networks*. Prentice Hall.

Vörg, A. (2003). *ToolIP - Tools and Methods for IP*. Retrieved July 29, 2013, from http://toolip.fzi.de

Xilinx Inc. (2010). *XTMR Tool*. Retrieved July 29, 2013, from http://www.xilinx.com/ise/optional_prod/tmrtool.htm

KEY TERMS AND DEFINITIONS

AOP: Aspect-Oriented Programming is a programming paradigm promoting modularization by allowing the separation of cross-cutting concerns.

Dependability: Ability to deliver service that can justifiably be trusted.

FPGA: Field-Programmable Gate Arrays are two-dimensional arrays of configurable logic blocks, interconnected by means of programmable matrices, which are all controlled by a configuration memory.

HDL: Hardware Description Languages enable the specification of the structure and behavior of digital circuits, which can be later synthesized and implemented using logic configurable devices and standard cells.

IP Cores: Intellectual Property cores are reusable hardware components distributed as HDL models (soft cores) or final implementations ready for manufacturing (hard cores).

Metaprogramming: Defining programs able to reason about and manipulate the structure of other programs.

Open Compilation: Source-to-source transformation over which the user has a degree of control.

Temporal Redundancy: Fault tolerance strategy based on re-executing the same operation a given number of times to determine the right output by majority voting.

TMR: Triple Modular Redundant is a fault-tolerance strategy consisting of three replicas of the same component processing the same inputs in parallel to obtain the right result by majority voting.

Chapter 7
Optimized System–Level Design Methods for NoC–Based Many Core Embedded Systems

Haoyuan Ying
Technische Universität Darmstadt, Germany

Klaus Hofmann
Technische Universität Darmstadt, Germany

Thomas Hollstein
Tallinn University of Technology, Estonia

ABSTRACT

Due to the growing demand on high performance and low power in embedded systems, many core architectures are proposed the most suitable solutions. While the design concentration of many core embedded systems is switching from computation-centric to communication-centric, Network-on-Chip (NoC) is one of the best interconnect techniques for such architectures because of the scalability and high communication bandwidth. Formalized and optimized system-level design methods for NoC-based many core embedded systems are desired to improve the system performance and to reduce the power consumption. In order to understand the design optimization methods in depth, a case study of optimizing many core embedded systems based on 3-Dimensional (3D) NoC with irregular vertical link distribution topology through task mapping, core placement, routing, and topology generation is demonstrated in this chapter. Results of cycle-accurate simulation experiments prove the validity and efficiency of the design methods. Specific to the case study configuration, in maximum 60% vertical links can be saved while maintaining the system efficiency in comparison to full vertical link connection 3D NoCs by applying the design optimization methods.

INTRODUCTION

Since NoCs are promoted to be the one of the best interconnect techniques for many core em-

bedded systems, it is important to improve the NoCs performance and to reduce the communication overhead in order to optimize the system configuration. From the perspective of hardware,

DOI: 10.4018/978-1-4666-6194-3.ch007

developing the efficient and complex NoCs routers architectures that support multi-casting communication, various Quality-of-Service (QoS) modes, adaptive routing mechanisms and optimized hardware based flow control methods, *etc.* is the key to the success (Duato, Yalamanchili, & Ni, 2003). However, implementing these functions on hardware certainly leads to more overheads in terms of hardware area and power consumption. Depending on the characteristics of different target software applications, the improvement of performance might be sometimes less than expected. Nevertheless, many NoCs routers architectures with the complex and advanced hardware functions are still proposed and claimed to gain the performance and power advantage for the entire system with the unpredictable running applications such as Chip Multi-Processor (CMP) and soft real-time systems.

On the other hand, if the characteristics of the target applications are known in advance, such as in mobile communication, automation and other hard real-time systems applications, the entire system can achieve excellent performance and cost efficiency by employing proper design optimization methods. Therefore, the hardware implementations of the NoC routers can be simplified. Then, the area and power overhead is reduced accordingly.

Several design configurations such as task mapping, core placement, routing and topology have to be determined to deliver the final system configuration based on the given system specification. Among the various patterns of different design configurations, designers should optimize each design configuration and build the final system configuration at the best trade-off point. The best trade-off point of NoC system is always the most balancing point between communication overhead and performance with respect to the communication bandwidth requirement, NoC transaction latency, communication energy consumption, NoC link throughput and so forth. In this chapter, formalized system level design optimization meth-

ods for NoC based many core embedded systems are introduced and demonstrated. Four design configurations (task mapping, core placement, routing and topology) are optimized in order to deliver the final system configuration at the best trade-off point.

Simulated Annealing (SA), Genetic Algorithm (GA) and Tabu Search (TS) are applied as the design optimization algorithms. All of the three algorithms are meta-heuristic searching algorithms. Hence, the efficient and correct cost functions are needed to lead the optimization to the right direction. In this chapter, four different cost functions such as Link Utility Distribution Degree (LUDD), NoC Communication Energy (ENG), Global Routing Path Length (GRPL) and Guaranteed Bandwidth (GBW) are demonstrated. Different possible combinations of all cost functions and algorithms are employed to optimize the entire NoC system through task mapping, core placement, routing and topology.

A Hybrid Constructive Heuristic (HyCH) algorithm is also introduced in order to optimize the NoC system, because the constructive heuristic is more computation time efficient in comparison to meta-heuristic algorithms. However, the optimization degree is limited by the characteristics of constructive heuristic algorithms when multiple solution elements are floating and to be determined. Therefore, in this chapter, the HyCH algorithm is proposed to optimize single NoC design configuration only. For instance, the HyCH is utilized to optimize the NoC core placement, when the task mapping, routing and topology design configurations are fixed and unchangeable.

Besides introducing the design optimization methods, the utilization flow of the proposed methods are also demonstrated. Four system evaluation metrics as flit latency, flit data rate, NoC area and system efficiency factor (SEF) are applied to evaluate the final determined system configuration. SEF is the novel concept to evaluate the entire NoC system efficiency, which considers both the performance and cost numbers. The detailed explanation of these metrics is given in the following section.

In this chapter, in order to demonstrate our methods clearly, a case study of 3D NoC with irregular reduced vertical link connection topologies running random generated task graphs and benchmark applications is employed. With the increased number of cores, NoCs based communication infrastructures reaches the latency and power bottlenecks. To solve the problem, 3D integrated circuit (IC) is targeted as one of the solutions. Many technologies such as die-to-die bonding, die-to-wafer bonding and wafer-to-wafer bonding are investigated for 3D integration. As an interconnect for 3D integration, Trough Silicon-Via (TSV) technology is one of the best solutions in terms of thermal, power, performance and yield properties (Motoyoshi, 2009).

Referring to the ITRS road map, the expected TSV diameter is in the range of 1.0 µm to 1.5 µm till 2015. During the same period, the area of a 4-transistor logic gate is predicated to reduce from $0.82\,\mu m^2$ to $0.20\,\mu m^2$. Thus, the area ratio of TSVs to logic gates is turned to be in the range of 2.74 (= 2.25/0.82) to 5 (= 1.0/0.20). If the pitch of a TSV (between 3 µm and 5 µm) is considered, the TSV-to-gate-size ratio is further increased. Therefore, minimizing the TSV number saves considerable active area that can be utilized for more transistors. Besides, the thermal issue for 3D ICs is critical as well. One of the best solutions is to place several TSVs between dies to perform as heat sinks with inserted micro-fluidic (Zhang, Dembla, & Bakir, 2013). Therefore, minimizing the number of TSVs that utilized for data communication can save more space for placing heat sink TSVs and the system reliability is improved (Shi, Srivastava, & Bar-Cohen, 2012).

The system performance can be maintained while reducing the number of data communication TSVs (vertical link) between dies in 3D NoCs by applying our design optimization methods. In order to achieve the performance and communication overhead excellence of the entire system,

our design optimization methods are employed through optimizing task mapping, core placement, routing and topology design configurations. All of the optimized 3D NoC system configurations are simulated with GSNoC platform (Ying, Hollstein, & Hofmann, 2013). The simulation results show that up to 60% vertical links (TSVs) can be saved in comparison to full vertical link connected 3D NoC configurations after applying our design optimization methods, while the system efficiency is maintained.

The state-of-art NoC design optimization methods are discussed in the next section. After the discussion, the system level design configurations and problem formulation are given, where all the used definitions and terminologies are explained. Then, SA, GA and TS algorithms and LUDD, ENG, GRPL and GBW cost functions are demonstrated for the 3D NoCs case study. The HyCH algorithm is demonstrated as well for single particular design configuration optimization. After the algorithm demonstrations, the utilization and evaluation flow of these methods are introduced. Four NoC system evaluation metrics and system simulation configurations are described in depth. Two sets of simulations by running the randomly generated task graph and state-of-art benchmark applications are provided to prove the efficiency and validity of our design optimization methods. At the end, the conclusion and future work are presented.

BACKGROUND

A body of research works are demonstrated for optimizing the task mapping, core placement, NoC topologies and routing design configurations at system level. There are several significant works in this domain to generally introduce the state-of-art.

Many research works achieve the task mapping excellence by minimizing the energy consumption and latency. Amory, Marson, and Lubaszewski (2011) demonstrated the task mapping method in

MPSoC with faulty tiles. While avoiding mapping the tasks onto faulty cores in the NoC, minimizing the communication energy and overall execution time are considered as the main optimization points. Also, Hu and Marculescu (2005) presented an idea of mapping tasks onto NoCs in order to minimize the communication energy and to improve the performance by using a branch-and-bound algorithm. The task graph is constructed as a tree and allocated the task-to-task connection transactions to NoC paths. After allocating the transactions, the deadlock-free dedicated routing scheme is calculated. The proposed method is faster than SA for about 2.2 hours.

For NoC architectures, contention and congestion problems are critical to harm the system performance and to increase the power consumption. Chou and Marculescu (2008) demonstrated a task mapping method by employing linear programming algorithm in order to reduce the contention occurrence probabilities. Different from the algorithm above, Zhou, Sheng, Liu, He, and Mao (2011) demonstrated a combined SAGA task allocation method. The GA is utilized at the starting phase to explore a number of possible task allocation solutions. After several rounds, the best solution is passed to the SA phase to perform further optimization. Extending to the 3D NoC domain, Addo-Quaye (2005) demonstrated a GA based thermal aware task mapping algorithm. The key idea in this work is to reduce the peak temperature in the entire 3D NoC over the complete running time.

Choudhary, Gaur, Laxmi, and Singh (2011) presented a GA based NoC topology generation method. Based on the method, the maximal bandwidth capacities for all channels are not allowed exceed, when assigning the network tile placements due to the communication requests. Jin and Watanabe (2010) also demonstrated a GA algorithm based high-level NoC synthesis technique. The idea is to find the minimal accumulation of all communication transaction routing path lengths and to reduce the power consumption

accordingly. Tino and Khan (2011) used Tabu search method with the linear queue numbering (LQN) contention analysis model to deliver the optimized NoC system topology. The LQN can roughly detect the contention occurrences when the routers consume much time on arbitration. The main logic behind the LQN model is that the less narrow arbitration nodes on the routing path, the better performance the system can achieve. However, in some cases irregular NoC topologies are needed to satisfy the system constraints. Todorov, Mueller-Gritschneder, Reinig and Schlichtmann (2013) demonstrated a spectral clustering approach to generate irregular application-specific NoC topologies. According to the characteristics of different applications, the approach clusters different tasks into one core and the tree-based NoC topology can be generated and optimized for the core-to-core communications. Specific to our case study in this chapter, Xu, Liljeberg, and Tenhunen (2011) presented a study for analyzing the efficiency of different vertical link pillar insertion patterns in 3D NoCs.

Once the mapping process is done, the next step is to place different cores onto the NoCs with certain topologies. Hredzak and Diesel (2011) introduced a SA based method to place the NoCs cores. The objective function considers the link bandwidth and latency. Good results can be achieved when distributing the traffic into the network as evenly as possible. Also, Kwon, Pasricha, and Cho (2011) presented a heterogeneous NoC system core placement method at abstract level by considering the communication activities. The combination of area and total communication data volume is set as the cost function. Abderazek, Akanda, Yoshinaga, and Sowa (2007) presented a suitable mathematical model for the NoC core placement design configuration. The key idea is to find the minimal power consumption configuration for the IP placement and layout, meanwhile the performance constraints as latency and port capacities should be maintained. By using the linear programming algorithms characteristics, Zhong,

Chen, Ma, and Yoshimura (2011) presented a four-stage ILP based method for 3D NoC synthesis optimization at system level. The core-to-core communication from the task graph is analyzed and the closed-communication pair network nodes are attempted to be in the same cluster. The data communications TSVs are inserted at the positions where the communication occurrence probability is high. Unlike the meta-heuristic algorithms based core placement methods, Chen, Xie, and Li (2009) presented a constructive heuristic IP placement method (CMAP), which can be separated into two parts, LBMAP (Link-based) and SBMAP (Sort-based). The results showed that the CMAP could achieve both lower communication cost and shorter computation time.

The latest Europe Union (EU) FP7 research project NaNoC that ended at the end of 2012 also addressed system level design optimization problems for mobile applications embedded systems. Although the NaNoC project is focusing more on the vertical design flow from design specifications to tape out the embedded system IC, the task mapping, core placement, topology and routing are properly optimized as a system level firmware (Todorov et al., 2013).

All the above works are briefly introduced to plot the state-of-art system level design optimization methods for NoC based many core embedded systems with respect to task mapping, core placement, routing and topology generation. By referring to these works, readers can be familiar with the contents of this chapter.

OPTIMIZED SYSTEM LEVEL DESIGN METHODS

In this section, the objectives of the design optimization methods are to improve the NoC system performance and to reduce the NoC system communication cost. The average flit latency and flit rate indicate the system performance metrics and the NoC communication energy and the NoC area

represent the system communication cost metrics. Task mapping, core placement, topology and routing NoC design configuration parameters are together considered and optimized to achieve the efficient NoC system design configurations. The applied optimization algorithms such as SA, GA and TS with corresponding cost functions (LUDD, ENG, GBW and GRPL) are introduced after the problem formulation. Besides the general optimization methods, a special case as constructive heuristic algorithm (HyCH) for optimizing the core placement configuration is also demonstrated.

Design Configurations and Problems Formulation

In this chapter we demonstrate the system level NoC design optimization methods through a case study of 3D NoCs with reduced vertical link connection topology configurations.

Figure 1 illustrates the 3D NoC system design configurations. Four design configurations are clearly shown, such as task mapping, core placement, routing and topology. By knowing the target applications (task graphs) in advance, task mapping design configuration defines the clustering pattern of different tasks in different cores. The core placement design configuration defines the placement of these cores on 3D NoC positions. The 3D NoCs have irregular vertical link connection topologies and the routing algorithms should be specific to the customized configurations (vertical link insertion pattern).

There are several definitions should be declared in advance to formulate the design problem.

M: Task mapping NoC design configuration.
P: Core placement NoC design configuration.
T: NoC topology design configuration, for this case study focus on vertical link floor plan patterns.
R: NoC routing algorithms design configuration for the specific NoC topologies.

Figure 1. 3D NoC system design configurations illustration

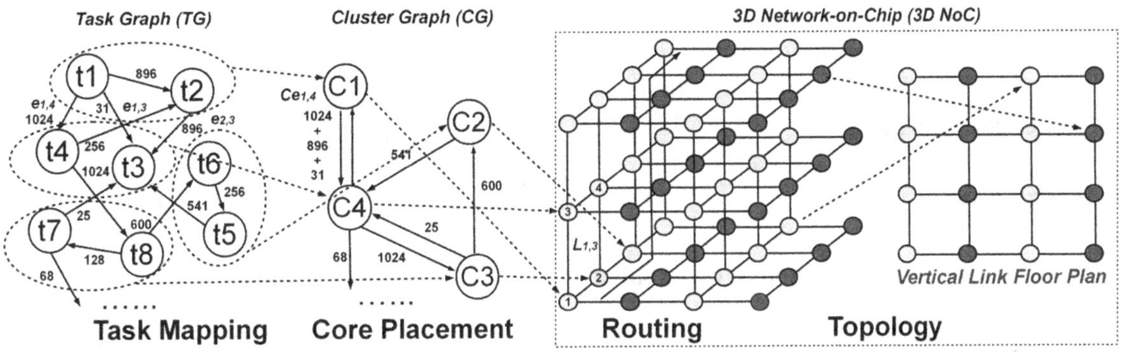

TG(t,e): Task graph, which includes the complete application execution and communication information.

ti: The single task i.

ei,j: The edge in the *TG*, connecting from *ti* to *tj*. It also indicates the communication transaction which initiated by *ti* and send data to the sink *tj*.

bwei,j: The bandwidth requirement number of the *ei,j*, which is normalized to the maximal channel bandwidth.

wei,j: The communication weight (data volume) of the *ei,j*, counted as NoC flits.

Nt: The number of tasks in the *TG*.

Ne: The number of edges in the *TG*.

C: The task cluster, which contains several mapped tasks and itself has not been placed onto the NoC.

CG(C,Ce): Cluster graph, which includes the *C* to *C* communication information and all the *Ce*s have not been mapped onto the NoC links.

Cei,j: The communication edge between *C*s, from *Ci* (initiator) to *Cj* (sink).

bwCei,j: The bandwidth requirement number of the *Cei,j*, which is normalized to maximal bandwidth capacity.

wCei,j: The communication weight (data volume) of the *Cei,j*, counted as NoC flits.

NC: The number of *C*s in the *CG*.

Node: A single network node in the NoC, which includes a locally placed *C* and fixed logical address (position information) in the NoC.

NN: The number *Node*s in the NoC.

Lk,m: The path from *Nodek* to *Nodem*. It is a two dimensional vector, in which $Lk,m[n]$ [0] indicates the routing path *Node*s index numbers (from *Nodek* to *Nodem*) and $Lk,m[n]$ [1] indicates the output direction at the *Node* as $Lk,m[n][0]$, assuming n is in the range of $[0, |L_{k,m}|]$ and a particular routing algorithm is applied. In this case study, the output direction can only be East, West, North, South, Up, Down and Local. It should be noted that by applying different routing algorithms for the same topology and application, the Lk,m can be different even when the source and destination *Node*s remains the same.

Lbwk,m: The bandwidth requirement number of the Lk,m, which is normalized to the maximal bandwidth capacity.

Lwk,m: The communication weight (data volume) of the Lk,m, counted as NoC flits.

$|L_{k,m}|$: The routing path length (counted as NoC hops) of the $L_{k,m}$.

direction: The possible routing directions in 3D NoC, as East, West, North, South, Up, Down and Local.

X, Y, Z: The logic scale of the 3D NoC in X, Y and Z (vertical) dimensions.

VL: The vertical link connection pillar.

NVL: The number of *VL* connected *XY Nodes* on each *Z* layer.

VD: The vertical link connection density number.

VF: The vertical link floor plan configuration (*VL* connection pattern).

Task Mapping

As shown in Figure 1, the task mapping (*M*) results in task 1 & 2 (*t1* & *t2*) being mapped in cluster 1 (*C1*) and task 3 & 4 (*t3* & *t4*) mapped in cluster 4 (*C4*). Hence, the communication edges between *t1*, *t2*, *t3* and t4 (*e1,3*, *e1,4* and *e2,3*) in *TG* can be transferred to the cluster communication edges between *C1* and *C4* in *CG*, as *Ce1,4*. *Ce1,4* must contain all of the information that *e1,3*, *e1,4* and *e2,3* hold, such as *w* and *bw*. For example, *we1,3*, *we1,4* and *we2,3* are equal to 31, 1024 and 896 flits, respectively. As the combination of them, the *wCe1,4* should be equal to the sum of 31, 1024 and 896. According to the description, it is clear to derive the formula of *M*, as,

$$
M\left(t_i\right) \to C_m, M\left(t_j\right) \to
$$
$$
C_n, \forall i,j \in \left[1, N_t\right], m,n \in \left[1, N_C\right] \Rightarrow
$$
$$
e_{i,j} \to Ce_{m,n}, w_{e_{i,j}} \to w_{Ce_{m,n}}, bw_{e_{i,j}} \to bw_{Ce_{m,n}};
$$
$$
(1)
$$

According to (1), after defining the *M*, all of the *t*s should be distributed to different *C*s. All *e*s are mapped on different *Ce*s. While the mapping, all *wCe*s and *bwCe*s in *CG* can obtain the numbers from the *we*s and *bwe*s in the *TG* accordingly.

Core Placement

The core placement (*P*) rules are that all of the *C*s should be placed on different NoC positions. Back to the example in Figure 1, *C1* and *C4* are placed on position 1 and 3. According to the placement, the *Ce1,4* in *CG* should be mapped

as *L1,3* in the NoC. Hence, it is clear to derive the formula of *P*, as,

$$
P\left(C_i\right) \to Node_k, P\left(C_j\right) \to
$$
$$
Node_m, \forall i,j \in \left[1, N_C\right], k,m \in \left[1, N_N\right] \Rightarrow
$$
$$
Ce_{i,j} \to L_{k,m}, w_{Ce_{i,j}} \to Lw_{k,m}, bw_{Ce_{i,j}} \to Lbw_{k,m};
$$
$$
(2)
$$

According to (2), after the *P* is defined, all of the *C*s are on different *Node*s (NoC positions) and all of the *Ce*s are placed on different *L*s. While the placement running, all of the *Lw*s and *Lbw*s in the NoC can obtain the numbers from the *wCe* and *bwCe* in the *CG* accordingly.

Topology (Vertical Link Floor Plan) and Routing

As we already declared in this chapter, the 3D NoC with irregular reduced *VL* connection topology configurations is utilized in the case study to demonstrate our system-level NoC design optimization methods. The topology (*T*) design configuration contains the information as *X*, *Y*, *Z* and *VF*. For the design configuration *T*, we assume that during the design optimization period only the *VF* can be changed and the scale of the NoC should be fixed.

Figure 2 shows the example of different *VF*s for 4x4xN 3D NoC. For each *VL*, we assume that it connects the NoC nodes between two neighborhood *Z* layers with the same *X* and *Y* coordinates (position). For example, if a *VL* connected *Node* is on position *(i, j, k)*, where *i*, *j* and *k* (*k>0* and *k<Z-1*) represent the coordinates values at *X*, *Y* and *Z* dimensions. The *Nodes* on *(i, j, k+1)* and *(i, j, k-1)* are connected to the *Node* at *(i, j, k)* through the *VL*. Also the *Nodes* from position *(i, j, 0)* to *(i, j, Z-1)* are *VL* connected *Nodes*, because the *VL*s are set as pillars from the bottom to the top *Z* layer in this case study configuration.

Figure 2. Demonstration of Four Different VFs on 4x4xN 3D NoC

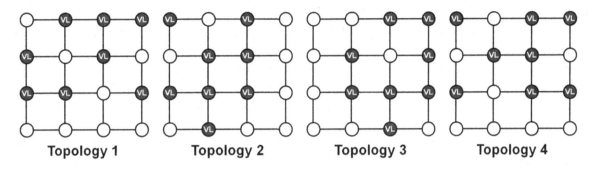

Each *VL* supports the communication in both Up and Down directions. Thus the *VL* connected *Node* should have different ports in Up and Down directions to support the vertical communication. For example, the router Down port of the *VL* connected *Node* on *(i, j, k)* connects the router Up port of the *Node* on *(i, j, k-1)* and the router Up port of this *Node* on *(i, j, k)* connects the router Down port of the *Node* on *(i, j, k+1)*.

According to the definitions, the *VD* can be calculated as,

$$VD = \frac{N_{VL}}{X \times Y}; \qquad (3)$$

In our previous work, according to the different irregular 3D NoC topologies, we developed a series of routing algorithms (as *R*) to efficiently route data from the transaction source to the destination *Node*s (Ying, 2013 a). However, for each different *R* the *VF* constraints are different. Once the *R* is fixed, the *VF* constraints have to be satisfied while the *T* is being optimized. In this case study, we collect our own *R*s from the work (Ying, 2013 a) and make a routing repository to support the system level optimization.

Simulated Annealing (SA)

We apply SA as the NoC design optimization algorithm, because SA is a generic probabilistic meta-heuristic algorithm for a global optimiza-

tion problem. It locates a good approximation to the global optimum of a given function in a large search space. SA is often used when the search space is discrete. For certain problems, it is more efficient than exhaustive enumeration – providing that the goal is merely to find an acceptably good solution in a fixed amount of time rather than the best possible solution (Kirkpatrick, Gelatt, & Vecchi, 1983).

Once SA is started, the algorithm checks that if the current temperature reaches the ending temperature threshold. If the current temperature is less or equal to the ending threshold, the SA should be terminated. If the current temperature is still at high number to be reduced, the SA process should continue. The current design solution cost function value should be saved. At each iteration in the current temperature, a new design solution is generated and the corresponding cost function value is calculated as well. Then, according to the old and new cost function values, the metropolis probability number can be calculated. Meanwhile, a pure random probability number is generated and the decision of accepting the new solution can be determined by comparing these two probability numbers. If the new solution is accepted and the iteration round has not yet been finished, the remaining iterations should continue until the limitation number of iterations in the temperature is reached. If the new generated solution is rejected, an internal counter will be increased by one. If the value of this internal counter reaches a certain number (stable iteration time), although the iteration limitation has not been reached, the temperature should be reduced directly and the SA should update itself to the next new iteration state. It should be noted that the determination of the stable iteration time number in each temperature is very important and has to be carefully considered. The potential optimization degree in each temperature can be lost if the number is too low. On the other hand, if the number is very close to the original iteration limitation number, the potential optimized solution might be visited, however, this increases the SA running time and the optimization might be not guaranteed. If assuming the current solution is up-to-now the best that can be found in the last temperature state and the SA is hard to find new better solutions after a number of temperature reductions, the algorithm should be terminated as well, although the ending temperature point has not been reached. There are several SA related terminologies to be clarified, as,

Temp: The temperature.

ETemp: The ending temperature. Once the temperature reaches this value, the SA should be terminated.

CS: The cooling step coefficient (in the range of 0 to 1), which helps the temperature to be reduced.

STT: The stable temperature times number. If the temperature has been reduced for continuously *STT* times and no new result is accepted, the SA should be terminated.

IT: The iteration times number. For each temperature, the SA must run *IT* times iteration to find a better result in the worst case.

SIT: The stable iteration times number. Once the SA cannot find a better result for continuous *SIT* times at the particular temperature, the SA should reduce the temperature directly and search the result in the new round (at new temperature).

Algorithm 1 demonstrates the SA algorithm procedure. It should be noted that the functions to regenerate M and P are purely random, which indicates if new M and P are requested, the functions simply generate and differentiate the new M and P *to* the current ones. The T regeneration function is also random, however the R must be valid for the new generated T. The T focus on the VF in irregular 3D NoCs and for different VFs the R might be different to avoid deadlock in NoCs. In our previous work (Ying, 2013 a), we demonstrated several routing algorithms for irregular 3D NoCs topologies with different VFs constraints. Therefore, the R generation function behaves like picking-up a routing algorithm from the repository. Before each time changing the T, the R must be fixed first and following the prerequisite VF constraints can vary the T.

Genetic Algorithm (GA)

In the computer science field of artificial intelligence, a genetic algorithm (GA) is a search heuristic that mimics the process of natural selection. This meta-heuristic is routinely used to generate useful solutions to optimize the searching problems (Mitchell, 1996).

In GA, all of the chromosomes have to be generated randomly in the first generation. Once the first generation is successfully constructed, the GA algorithm sorts all the chromosomes in an order of the cost function values from low to high. According to Algorithm 2, certain chromosomes with the best cost function values are directly passed to the next generation and the other chromosomes should go through the mutation and crossover operations. Once all of the remaining chromosomes are engaged mutation and crossover, the next generation is successfully constructed. If the generation number is already reached the limitation, the GA should be terminated. In the last generation, the chromosome with the best cost function value represents the final solution

Algorithm 1. SA algorithm flow

```
1 SA starts:
2 Input: TG, NoC configuration information and SA
parameters;
3 Output: TG with optimized M, P, T and R;
4 Begin:
5 STT_counter = 0; SIT_counter = 0; IT_counter = 0;
6 Calculate the heuristic cost value (H_cost);
7 Label: Temperature Check:
8 if Temp = ETemp then
9 goto SA Terminate;
10 else
11 while STT_counter < STT do
12 while IT_counter < IT do
13 IT_counter ++;
14 Re-generate the M, P, T and R;
15 Calculate the iteration cost value (I_cost) value;
16 Generate the random probability Pro;
17 Calculate the meta-stable probability value (Mpro):
MPro = exp[(-1) * (I_cost – H_cost) / Temp];
18 if Pro < MPro then
19 New design configuration solution accepted;
20 H_cost = I_cost;
21 SIT_counter = 0;
22 STT_counter = 0;
23 else
24 STT_counter ++;
25 if SIT value reached then
26 STT_counter++;
27 goto Cool the Temperature;
28 end if
29 end if
30 end while
31 Label: Cool the temperature:
32 Temp = CS * Temp;
33 end while
34 end if
35 Label: SA Terminate:
36 End the SA program;
37 End
```

of the optimization. There are some terminologies to declare GA process, as,

chromosome: The GA representation of a complete design configuration, as M, P, T and R, which can be expressed as *chromosome* = (M, P, T, R).

npop: The *chromosome*s number in each generation.

ngen: The number of generations in the GA algorithm.

nbest: The number of the *chromosome*s with better cost function values can be directly fetched to next generation.

Mutation: The function to vary the current *chromosome*. Each element in one *chromosome* can be differentiated through the mutation operation.

Crossover: In GA, *Crossover* function indicates to exchange two different elements between two *chromosomes*. However, because of the *VF* constraints for different *R*s, the T and R are considered together as one element.

As we already explained in the SA section, the T and R highly depend on each other, because the T must obey the *VF* constraints that are needed by different *R*s to avoid deadlock. Therefore, at each time *Mutation*, the R must be determined before generating the new T. Besides the *Mutation*, in the *Crossover* step, the design element exchange must take the T and R together into consideration as one element. Figure 3 demonstrates the *Crossover* process.

Similarly in the SA process, the M and P regeneration in the *Mutation* and the exchange in *Crossover* in GA are purely random without any important constraints.

Tabu Search (TS)

Tabu Search (TS) is a meta-heuristic search method used for mathematical optimization by employing the local search mechanism. Local (neighborhood) searches take a potential solution to a problem and check its immediate neighbors in the hope of finding an improved solution. Local search methods have a tendency to become stuck in suboptimal regions or on plateaus, where many solutions are equal. TS enhances the performance of these techniques, by using memory structures that describe the visited solutions or user-provided sets of rules (Glover, 1986, 1989). If a potential solution has been previously visited within a certain short-term period or if it has violated a rule, it is

Algorithm 2. GA algorithm flow

```
1 GA starts:
2 Input: TG, NoC configuration information and GA
parameters;
3 Output: TG with optimized M, P, T and R;
4 Begin:
5 m = 0; n = 0; g= 0;
6 while n < n_pop do
7 Randomly generate chromosome for the first generation;
8 n++;
9 end while
10 while m < n_gen do
11 Calculate cost function values of all the chromosomes;
12 Sort: all chromosomes are arranged in the order from low
(better) cost
13 function value to high (worse) cost function value;
14 Fetch first n_best chromosomes directly to the next generation;
15 while g < n_pop - n_best do
16 Crossover to generate new chromosomes;
17 Mutation of each generated chromosome;
18 Pass the new chromosome to next generation;
19 g++;
20 end while
21 g = 0;
22 m++;
23 end while
24 GA process done, terminate algorithm;
25 End
```

marked as forbidden so that the algorithm refuses that possibility repeatedly. We have included TS into our design methods as well, because TS has least memory demand for the calculation and can escape from suffering jumping back to the state where previously discarded after evaluation.

In TS, a dedicated list is constructed to store a number of the best visited neighborhood solutions of each current solution to avoid re-evaluating the abandoned solutions. The first step of TS in each search iteration is to create a new randomly gener-

ated solution. If the list still has free space and the new generated neighborhood solution has not been generated and with better cost function value, this solution can be stored in the list. If the list is full, certain number of solutions that have the worst cost function values should be removed from the list in order to release the free space for the new generated solutions. The algorithm should make a judgment if the new generated solution has been generated before and already stored in the list. If the new solution is as same as one of the stored solutions, it should be abandoned. After certain rounds of generating new solutions that cannot be accepted, the TS should terminate the current search iteration and start the next one. Once all of the search iterations are finished, the TS should be terminated. The solution that stored at the tail of the list with the best cost function values is the optimized solution. There are some parameters should be defined to describe TS algorithm, as,

List: The TS search list.

ListSize: The size of the TS list, counted as design solutions.

nexp: The expiring number of solutions in the *List* if it is full.

texit: The number of new generated solutions that cannot be accepted by TS. If this number is reached in the algorithm, the TS should jump out of the current search iteration.

nsearch: The total number of search iterations in TS.

Figure 3. Demonstration Example of Crossover Process in GA

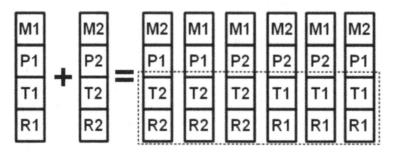

Similar to the *chromosome* GA, each design solution in TS contains the entire target NoC design configurations as *M*, *P*, *T* and *R*. The possible neighborhood solution of the current one can be generated through varying a single design configuration. Therefore, for each design solution in TS, there are four possible neighborhood solutions around in this case study.

Cost Functions for SA, GA, and TS

As declared above, for meta-heuristic algorithms such as SA, GA and TS, efficient cost functions are desired to guide the optimization to a correct direction. In this chapter, four different cost functions (system metrics) for optimizing the *M*, *P*, *R* and *T* are introduced, which are Link Utilization Distribution Degree (LUDD), NoC Communication Energy (ENG), Global NoC Routing Path Length (GRPL) and Guaranteed Bandwidth (GBW).

Link Utilization Distribution Degree (LUDD)

A two-dimensional matrix named *DMatrix* is created to store the communication weights and bandwidth requirements distribution. The row indicated all *Nodes* in the network and the column indicated all *directions*.

$$
DMatrix\left[L_{k,m}[n][0]\right]\left[L_{k,m}[n][1]\right] = \sum\nolimits_{k,m=1}^{N_N}\left(Lw_{k,m} \times Lbw_{k,m}\right), \forall n \in \left[1, |L_{k,m}|\right];
$$
(4)

Now the *DMatrix* contains the total communication weight and bandwidth distribution information. The parameter N_L is determined as the number of total used link slots in the NoC. The link slot means the point-to-point link between two neighborhood *Nodes*. Therefore, the average weight and bandwidth of one NoC link slot (wbw_{avg}) can be calculated as,

$$
wbw_{avg} = \frac{1}{N_N}\sum\nolimits_{a \in direction}\sum\nolimits_{b=1}^{N_N}DMatrix[b][a];
$$
(5)

Once the communication weights and bandwidth requirement distribution over the NoC and the wbw_{avg} are known, the deviation of the product of all links communication data volume and bandwidth requirement can be calculated as,

$$
Dev = \left[\frac{1}{N_L}\sum\nolimits_{a \in direction}\sum\nolimits_{b=1}^{N_N}\left(\frac{DMatrix[b][a]}{wbw_{avg}} - 1\right)^2\right]^{\frac{1}{2}};
$$
(6)

Finally, the cost function value of LUDD can be represented as,

$$
CF_{LUDD} = wbw_{avg} \times Dev;
$$
(7)

The idea of LUDD is to reduce the average product of the distributed communication data volume and the accumulated bandwidth requirement for each NoC link slot. Because by reducing the product, the probability of contention occurrence will be reduced consequently. Another point of LUDD is to distribute the communication (both data and bandwidth) as evenly as possible, which is the reason to take the deviation into consideration. Once the communication is evenly distributed to the NoC, the overheated problem of certain NoC links is solved.

NoC Communication Energy (ENG)

According to the *TG* described application communication profile and the NoC configuration information, it is possible to model the communication energy based on the hardware power

Algorithm 3. TS algorithm flow

```
1 TS starts:
2 Input: TG, NoC configuration information and TS
parameters;
3 Output: TG with optimized M, P, T and R;
4 Begin:
5 for i = 1 to nsearch do
6 m = 0;
7 Randomly generate new design solution far from the current
one;
8 while m < t_exit do
9 Generate all possible neighborhood solutions of the current
solution;
10 Try to pick up the solution with the best cost function value
and not in List;
11 if All neighborhood solutions are in List already then
12 Goto Next_Search;
13 end if
14 if The picked up solution has worse cost function value than
the current then
15 m++;
16 end if
17 if ListSize is reached (List is full) then
18 Delete nexp solutions in List with lowest cost function
values;
19 end if
20 Store the new generated design solution into List;
21 end while
22 Label: Next_Search;
23 end for
24 TS process done, terminate algorithm;
25 End
```

macros at system level. An energy model for NoC communication components (both of the NoC routers and interconnect wires) is introduced.

The total router energy consumption (E_{router}) can be represented as the sum of router dynamic energy ($E_{dynamic}$) and router static energy (E_{static}) consumption.

$$E_{router} = E_{dynamic} + E_{static};$$

(8)

For each transaction, the router energy ($E_{router-transaction}$) model can be calculated as,

$$E_{router-transaction} =$$
$$a \times \left(P_{dynamic} + P_{static} \right) \times D_{router} \times | L_{k,m} |, \forall k,m \in \left[1, N_N\right];$$

(9)

$P_{dynamic}$ and P_{static} are the dynamic and static power macro numbers of the router. If the target NoC router hardware implementation is available, it is simple to extract these two numbers from SYNOPSYS design compiler. D_{router} represents the router pipeline propagation delay and $| L_{k,m} |$ is the routing length of the current transaction. α is the coefficient that to estimate the contention effect. Because in (9), the calculation after α is the ideal communication energy consumption. Once the contention occurred, the energy consumption will be obviously more. Therefore, we put a factor here to let the designers estimate the contention effect. The value of α should be equal or greater than one and the NoC communication will be assumed contention and congestion free if the α is equal to one.

The wires can be divided into two wire classes, which are the normal XY planar interconnection wires ($E_{wire-XY-transation}$) and the VLs for inter-Z-layer communications ($E_{wire-TSV-transation}$). Certainly, a link can also be separated to two parts, the normal XY planar wires (LXY) and the VLs (LVL). Therefore, it is possible to calculate $E_{wire-XY-transation}$ as,

$$E_{wire-XY-transaction} =$$
$$\left(| L_{k,m_{XY}} | -1 \right) Lw_{k,m_{XY}} W_{L_{XY}} N_W V_{dd}^2 f \left(C + \frac{h_{opt}}{K_{opt}} C_0 \right),$$
$$\forall k,m \in \left[1, N_N\right];$$

(10)

and $E_{wire-VL-transaction}$ as,

$$E_{wire-VL-transaction} =$$
$$\left(| L_{k,m_{VL}} | -1 \right) Lw_{k,m_{VL}} W_{L_{VL}} N_W V_{dd_{VL}}^2 f C_{VL},$$
$$\forall k,m \in \left[1, N_N\right];$$

(11)

C_0 is the input capacitance of a repeater with minimum size; h_{opt} is the optimal size of the repeater; K_{opt} is the optimal length of the global interconnection wires; V_{dd} is the power supply and C is the capacitance of the single bit line with 1 mm length. These values can be directly extracted from the target technology library file.

WL is the physical channel wire length of a router-to-router connection; N_w is the number of single-bit wires in the router-to-router physical channel (bit-width). By multiplying $Lw_{k,m}$ in (11) is to determine the total time that the wires are on duty for this transaction. $|L_{k,m}|$-1 indicates the total routing length of the current transaction.

The *VL* can be validated through Through-Silicon Via (TSV) technology. Therefore, *CVL* can be recognized as the capacitance value of the single bit line with 1 μm length TSV and *VddVL* can be recognized as the voltage supply number for TSVs.

According to (8) to (11), the total NoC communication energy can be modeled as,

$$
CF_{ENG} = \sum_{i=1}^{N_e} \left(\begin{array}{l} E_{router-transaction_i} \\ +E_{wire-XY-transaction_i} \\ +E_{wire-VL-transaction_i} \end{array} \right);
$$

(12)

Global NoC Routing Path Length (GRPL)

Once the *TG* communication transaction profile, the NoC configuration information and the routing algorithm are known, it is straightforward to calculate the routing path length for all transactions in the NoC precisely as (13) shows.

$$
CF_{GRPL} = \sum_{k,m=1}^{N_N} | L_{k,m} |;
$$

(13)

Guarantee Bandwidth (GBW)

Since the bandwidth requirement of each transaction is known, after equipping the *M, P, R* and *T* configurations, the bandwidth requirement of each NoC link slot can be calculated. As discussed above, the *bw* value is normalized to the maximal bandwidth capacity of the NoC links. If the bandwidth requirement for any NoC link slot is exceeded over 100%, the contention situation might happen. Therefore, the number of NoC links that has more than 100% bandwidth requirement is tried to be minimized in this cost function.

A two-dimensional matrix named *bwMatrix* is created to store the bandwidth requirements distribution; row indicated all *Node*s in the network and column indicated all *directions*.

$$
bwMatrix\Big[L_{k,m}\big[n\big]\big[0\big]\Big]\Big[L_{k,m}\big[n\big]\big[1\big]\Big] =
\sum_{k,m=1}^{N_N} Lbw_{k,m}, \forall n \in \Big[1,|\mathrm{L}_{k,m}|\Big];
$$

(14)

And the cost function value of GBW (CF_{GBW}) is the total number of elements in *bwMatrix* that hold the values to be greater than 100%.

Hybrid Constructive Heuristics (HyCH)

Besides SA, GA and TS algorithms, a different algorithm that employs hybrid heuristic constructive (HyCH) algorithm is introduced in this chapter. Unlike iterative meta-heuristic algorithms, HyCH builds the whole system design configuration constructively and can escape from time consuming of long iterations.

If the entire NoC system is built from extremely abstract specifications (neither *M, P, T* nor *R* is determined), constructive heuristics algorithms might be difficult to find the acceptable global optimized solution. The NoC communication cost depends on the *M, P, T* and *R* and these NoC design configurations can affect the NoC communication cost individually. Hence, a problem by using constructive heuristics algorithm to optimize the entire NoC system in such a situation might occur. For example, without a predefined starting point of the NoC setup, the first step is to determine the starting point of the algorithm (in this NoC optimization application, it can be the initial *M*, *P*, *T* or *R*). After applying constructive heuristics algorithms, the 'optimized' solution should be found. But this solution is lack of the quality guarantee, because the starting point of this algorithm limits the optimization. According to the definition of constructive heuristics algorithms, it is impossible to change the starting point while running the algorithm, although much better solutions can be found by changing the starting point. This problem leads the optimization to an incorrect direction.

However, if certain design configurations of the NoC system are predefined and only one design configuration is floating and to be optimized, constructive heuristic algorithms can be easily applied as the meta-heuristic algorithms (SA, GA and TS). However constructive heuristics algorithms consumes much shorter computation time in comparison to meta-heuristic algorithms.

In this chapter, supposing a HyCH algorithm is applied to optimize the *P* configuration and the other three NoC design configurations *M*, *T* and *R* are fixed as constraints. For using HyCH to optimize *P*, it is necessary to place one *C* onto the NoC after another. The situation that one *C* has many candidate positions will occur. Hence, a proper cost function is desired as well to guide the algorithm to select the right positions for all *C*s among a number of available choices. Therefore, the cost function for HyCH is defined as,

$$CF_{HyCH} = \sum_{k,m=1}^{N_N} \left(Lw_{k,m} \times | L_{k,m} | \times Lbw_{k,m} \right); \tag{15}$$

Instead of placing different *C*s onto the NoC positions directly, the general idea of HyCH method is to allocate different *Ce*s in the *CG* on the *L*s in the NoC. The process of allocating *Ce*s is accomplished in two steps. The first step is to re-arrange all of the *Ce*s in the *CG* and to finally make an allocation order for them. Then, the second step is to place all the re-arranged ordered *Ce*s on the *L*s with the least accumulated *CF*_{HyCH}.

Two phases (phase 1 and phase 2) are needed to re-arrange all the *Ce*s in the *CG* to obtain a better allocation order. In phase 1, the allocation order of the *Ce*s will be re-arranged. Some terminologies are defined in order to present the process,

WtotC: The total communication weight that has the direct connection to the *C*. For example, the $Wtot_{Ci}$ should include all communication data volume received by the cluster C_i and all the communication data volume injected by the C_i.

ndep: The total number of *Ce*s that are connected to the *C*.

$$O_{C_i} = \frac{Wtot_{C_i}}{ndep_{C_i}}; \tag{16}$$

The order factors of *C*s (O_c) are calculated as (16). According to (16), the allocation orders of all *C*s are determined in the order from high to low O_cs numbers.

In phase 2, although the *C*s with higher number of communication connections are placed first, some potential optimization points can still be achieved. For example, if a *Ce* belongs to a *C* with higher O_C and the Cew_{Ce} is very low, this *Ce* can be placed in a low priority and release its high priority to another *Ce*, which has low O_C but high Cew_{Ce}. Therefore, in this phase, the order setup by in phase 1 is maintained and slightly modified according to the Cew_{Ce} numbers in phase 2.

The $wavg_{Ce}$ is defined as the average communication weight of all of the Ces in the CG as (17),

$$wavg_{Ce} = \frac{\sum_{i,j=1}^{N_N} Cew_{Ce_{i,j}}}{N_{Ce}} ; \qquad (17)$$

By modifying the order determined in phase 1, the $wavg_{Ce}$ is set as a threshold value. If the currently evaluated Cew_{Ce} is less than the threshold, it should be assigned to a lower priority and vice versa.

Figure 4 and 5 show the example of the Ce re-arranging phase 1 and 2. After phase 1, the Ces are arranged according to the value of O_cs. Then, after phase 2, the allocation order of Ces is re-arranged according to the previous order (phase 1) and the $wavg_{Ce}$ value. For example, the C_1 has the highest O_C, and in phase 1 the C_1 related Ces are arranged as the top priority to be placed. The Ce $C_1 \rightarrow C_8$; 97 has the small communication data volume and it should be assigned a lower placement order in phase 2.

Design Optimization Methods Utilization and Evaluation

Besides the NoC system design optimization methods, both of the corresponding utilization and evaluation methods are also demonstrated. According to the NoC system specifications and constraints, such as the NoC scale, target applications and so forth, the design flow can be started from optimizing the *M*, *P*, *T* and *R*. When the design optimization is finished, the optimized design configurations can be evaluated through the system level cycle-accurate simulation in our GSNoC simulator (Ying, 2013 b). After the simulation, the NoC system performance and cost metrics, such as flit latency, transaction throughput, NoC communication energy, NoC area and system efficiency factor are calculated and the quality of the optimization can be evaluated. If

the degree of the optimization is still hard to reach the expectation, the optimization process can be prolonged for re-doing the optimization and evaluation. Figure 6 demonstrates the entire flow.

System Performance and Cost Metrics

In order to verify the validity and efficiency of our design optimization methods, a system level cycle-accurate simulation is prefer to be utilized. To judge the overall performance and communication overhead of the NoC system, several key performance factors are important to be considered, which are latency, throughput, energy, area and the overall system efficiency.

Flit Latency

The performance of the optimized NoC system can be represented by the flit latency. The flit latency number is defined as the total number of clock cycles that the flit consumed from being injected into the NoC at the transaction source node to being ejected from the NoC at the transaction sink node. For some applications, such as automobile and real-time applications, the communication latency is the most important factor. It should be noted that the communication is more efficient in this NoC design configurations if the flit number is less. In case, the performance of these applications can be guaranteed if the flit latency can be limited in small numbers.

Flit Data Rate

The flit data rate represents the throughput of the NoC data communication transactions. For certain applications (e.g. video streaming, video recording, etc.), the data communication from one core to another needs very high data rate to guarantee the application throughput (as QoS in guaranteed throughput). The calculation of this number is to divide the communication data volume of

Figure 4. The example of the re-arrange process (Phase 1 and 2)

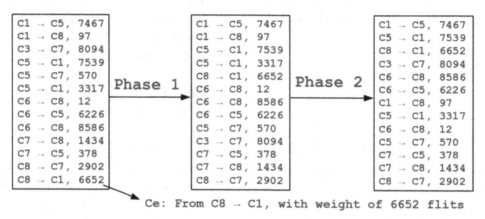

Ce: From C8 → C1, with weight of 6652 flits

Figure 5. The Ce re-arrange process flow

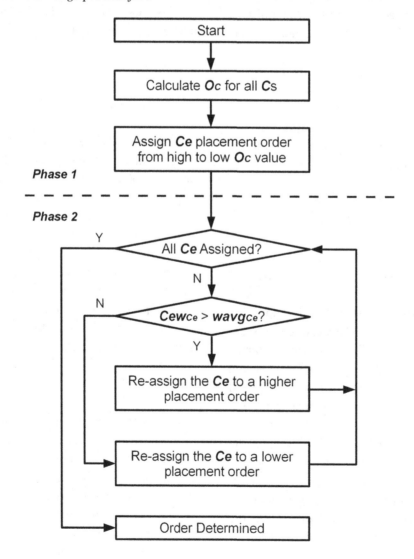

Algorithm 4. HyCH node placement algorithm flow

```
1 HyCH starts:
2 Input: CG and NoC Information;
3 Output: System Setup with Optimized Node Placement;
4 Begin:
5 m = 0;
6 Re-arrange the CG Ce Phase 1;
7 Re-arrange the CG Ce Phase 2;
8 while m < N_Ce do
9 Assuming: Ce_i is the Ce from C_j to C_k;
10 if C_j and C_k are neither placed then
11 Randomly Search the Free NoC Position for C_j;
12 Place C_k in another NoC Position with the Least CF_HyCH
value;
13 else if One of the C_j and C_k is not placed then
14 Place Cj (or C_k) in another NoC Position with the Least
CF_HyCH value;
15 else if C_j and C_k are both placed then
16 n = 0;
17 while n < NN do
18 if C_n is not placed then
19 Branch to Next_Ce;
20 end if
21 n++;
22 end while
23 end if
24 Label: Next_Ce:
25 m++;
26 end while
27 HyCH finished;
28 End
```

the transaction by the transaction latency. The transaction latency is the time from transmitting the first flit of this transaction at the source node to the last flit of this transaction received by the destination node.

NoC Communication Energy

The NoC communication energy contains two parts, the router hardware energy and the wire energy. The wire energy can be calculated from using equation (10) and (11), and related technology macros numbers can be found in our previous work (Ying, Jaiswal, Ghany, Hollstein, & Hofmann, 2012). To evaluate the router energy, the router hardware design is imported to SYNOPSYS Design Compiler by including the real technology library (using TSMC_65_nm_LP in this chapter)

to obtain the power and area numbers. Multiplying the power number with the NoC system running time for the target applications can derive the router energy number.

NoC Area

The NoC area number is the sum of all NoC routers and wires. In this 3D NoC case study, the area number should cover all of the routers, *XY* layer wires and the *VL* supporting hardware. In general, if a NoC node connects a *VL*, the router needs seven ports to support the communication (East, West, North, South, Up, Down and Local). However, if the router is isolated to *VL*, it only needs five ports (removing Up and Down ports). Assuming all of the ports in the same router are equivalent, it is simple to determine the area ratio between a *VL* connected router and a *VL* unconnected router as 0.714 (5/7). According to the definition of *VD*, the area number of the entire NoC can be calculated as,

$$
\begin{aligned}
Area = N_N \times \Big[VD + 0.714 \times \big(1 - VD\big)\Big] \\
\times Area_{router-7-port} + N_N \times VD \\
\times Area_{VL-pitch} + Area_{XY-wires};
\end{aligned}
$$

(18)

The *AreaVL-pitch* is the area number of TSV wires for a single *VL*. According to the ITRS road map, TSV diameter is in the range of 1.0 μm to 1.5 μm and the pitch of a single TSV is between 3 μm and 5 μm till 2015 (ITRS). Therefore, the single TSV area number is in the range of 25 μm² to 64 μm². If the bit-width of each *VL* is 32-bit, assuming the area of a single TSV to be 64 μm², the *AreaVL-pitch* is about 4096 (32*2*64, as Up and Down directions) μm².

Figure 6. Evaluation flow of design optimization methods

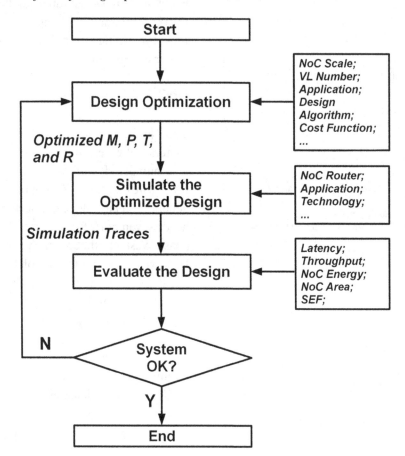

System Efficiency Factor

In order to determine the entire NoC system efficiency, all of the performance and cost factors must be considered. A System Efficiency Factor (*SEF*) which involves the latency, throughput, communication energy and area overhead is introduced to evaluate the overall design configuration

$$SEF = \frac{Transaction.Throughput}{Flit.Latency} ;$$
$$\times NoC.Communication.Energy$$
$$\times NoC.Area$$

(19)

The overall NoC system design configuration (*M*, *P*, *T* and *R*) achieves advanced trade-off point between the performance and cost when the *SEF* is high.

Simulation Setup

It is necessary to introduce the environment first in order to clearly demonstrate the simulation.

Generic Scalable Pseudo Application (GSPA) and Benchmark Applications

The Generic Scalable Pseudo Application (GSPA) is the extension to Task Graphs for Free (TGFF) (Dick, Rhodes, & Wolf, 1998) especially for NoCs. TGFF provides only simple application generation, for NoCs, throughput, latency and power need to be evaluated by employing more complex test scenarios. GSPA is a type of fully configurable task graphs and can perfectly fit the complexity requirement for evaluating NoC systems.

Table 1 shows the abbreviations of the GSPA task graph. The first row in Table 1 indicates the meanings of every column. *PEN* indicates the processing elements (cores) index number, *TSK* is the task index number and the *EXE* is the execution time (in clock cycles) of this task. *EDG, COM* and *BWR* indicate the index number, communication data volume (in flit) and bandwidth requirement (normalized tp the maximal bandwidth capacity) of the transaction that connected to the task in the same row. *FTK* and *TTK* indicate the index numbers of the source and sink tasks of the current transaction. *FPE* and *TPE* represent the index numbers of the initiating and sink cores of the transaction in this graph.

From the explanations in Table 1 and the example in Figure 7, two tasks *TSK* 1 and 19 are in *PEN* 1. For *TSK* 1, the execution time of this task is 83 clock cycles. Four transactions are connected to *TSK* 1, as *EDG* 17, 22, 25 and 28, with 348, 343, 340 and 810 flits communication volume and with

62%, 79% 71% and 81% bandwidth requirement, respectively. *TSK* 1 must completely receive the data carried by transaction *EDG* 14, 20 and 18 that initiated by *PEN* 3 and 4 first. Then, it can be executed and can initiate the *EDG* 28 to *TSK* 13 in *PEN* 6.

For *TSK* 19, it needs not to receive any transactions from other tasks and it can be directly executed and can initiate two transactions, as *EDG* 15 and 16 with 355 and 804 flits communication volume and with 24% and 37% bandwidth requirement to *TSK* 6 and 13, which located in *PEN* 6.

Not only the GSPA is applied to evaluate the design optimization methods and simulation, several state-of-art benchmark applications such as PARSEC (Bienia, 2011), SPLASH-2 (Woo, Ohara, Torrie, Singh, & Gupta, 1995), NU-Mine (Liao, Pisharath, Liu, & Choudhary, 2005) and ALPBench (Adve,, Li, Sasanja, & Chen, 2005) are also involved. Instead of executing the real applications, the application execution traces are extracted in advance with PinComm (Heirman, Stroonamdt, Miniskar, Wuyts, & Catthoor, 2010) and formulated to the format as Figure 7 shows.

NoC Router Model: 3D eXtendable Hierarchical Network-on-Chip (3D-XHiNoC)

XHiNoC is developed in TU Darmstadt, Germany (Samman, 2010). Due to the hierarchical architecture, it can be easily extended to different number of ports (each port as both input and output function blocks). In each port, four components as First In First Out (FIFO), Routing Engine (RE), Flit-by-Flit Round Robin Arbiter (ARB) and ID Management Unit (IDM). In XHiNoC, each packet consists of a head flit, several data body flits and a tail flit. XHiNoC uses a wormhole based ID switching technique. As shown in Figure 8, one packet with ID 0 enters the router from the local port. Once the head flit of this packet enters the RE at this local port, the RE determines that the packet should be routed to North direction. The

Table 1. Abbreviations explanation of GSPA

PEN	The processing element (cores) index number.
TSK	The task index number in the current PE.
EXE	The execution time for the task (counted as clock cycles).
EDG	The current transaction index number.
COM	The communication data volume for the current transaction (counted as flits).
FTK	The source task of the current transaction.
TTK	The destination task of the current transaction.
FPE	The source core of the current transaction in the NoC.
TPE	The destination core of the current transaction in the NoC.
BWR	The bandwidth requirement of the current transaction.

Figure 7. GSPA example

PEN	TSK	EXE	EDG	COM	FTK	TTK	FPE	TPE	BWR
1	1	83	17	348	14	1	4	1	62
1	1	83	22	343	20	1	3	1	79
1	1	83	25	340	18	1	4	1	71
1	1	83	28	810	1	13	1	6	81
1	19	72	15	355	19	6	1	6	24
1	19	72	16	804	19	13	1	6	37
2	2	86	8	786	10	2	6	2	26
2	2	86	11	542	11	2	4	2	8
2	2	86	20	828	2	20	2	3	52
2	2	86	21	299	2	13	2	6	99
2	17	40	18	611	14	17	4	2	24
2	17	40	19	622	17	5	2	5	36
3	3	77	6	139	8	3	8	3	36
3	15	63	1	772	12	15	6	3	61
3	15	63	29	605	6	15	6	3	30
3	20	36	2	725	12	20	6	3	30
3	20	36	20	828	2	20	2	3	52
3	20	36	22	343	20	1	3	1	79
...	...	...	...	...	...	...	...	...	...

ID Look-Up-Table (LUT) records the packet ID value and the routing out direction (for example here it is ID 0 for North direction). Once the data body flits and tail flit of the packet enters the RE, they check the LUT to which direction should be routed according to the ID number. It is because the head flit of the packet already records the ID and routing direction information in the LUT. If the tail flit enters the RE, the recorded ID information of the packet should be erased.

The ARBs of XHiNoC run a flit-by-flit round robin arbitration algorithm. If there are more than one input directions requesting the same output direction, the ARBs release the access permission of each requesting direction port one by one in a round. There is another kind of ID LUTs in XHiNoC located at IDMs. Once the ARBs have forwarded the granted accessed data to IDMs, the IDMs should check the type of the input flits. If the current flit is a head flit, it updates the ID number of the flit according to LUT situation (the IDM will look for a new unused ID for the coming packet). If the coming flits are either data body or tail, their IDs should be updated as well to the ID that the head flit has been updated to. Once the tail flits enters the IDMs, the ID updated information in the LUT should be erased for the current packet. The more ID slots in the LUT are

reserved, the more packets are currently interleaved at the same output port. If the ID number reaches the limitation of the ID LUT, the new incoming flits will be ejected out of the XHiNoC. Also, because of the flit-by-flit round robin arbitration, if at least two directions are requesting the same output port concurrently, the granted accessed flits belong to different packets at each different clock cycle. Therefore, XHiNoC supports flit interleaving stream communication.

Since XHiNoC supports the flit-by-flit interleaving traffic, where flits from different packet can be distinguished by the ID information, no virtual channels are needed in the router. Because the interleaving communication mode prevents the situation that one (or more) port is blocked for extremely long time. Also, if more than one FIFO is inserted on the input side of the port (as virtual channel), in XHiNoC it needs another level of arbitration. This creates more latency and area overhead. Therefore, the virtual channel technique is isolated to the target XHiNoC architecture. XHi-NoC is implemented in VHDL and according to SYNOPSYS design compiler with TSMC 65 nm low power technology, XHiNoC with 3D topology configuration reaches 1GHz maximal frequency.

Figure 8. XHiNoC architecture block diagram

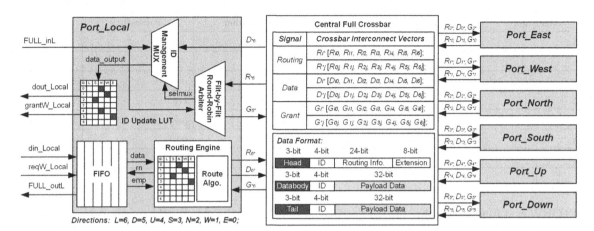

Experimental Results Analysis

The optimized design configurations (for all *M*, *P*, *T* and *R*) are evaluated on an 8x8x4 3D NoC with nine different *VD* number (from 10% to 90%) topologies. The target application is GSPA with 600 tasks and the assuming the target system runs at 1 GHz clock frequency. For each transaction, the traffic injection rate is fixed at 50% of the maximal bandwidth number.

According to Algorithm 1, 2 and 3, the design computation time lengths based on Table 2 for SA, GA and TS are close. In SA, if at every temperature running 30 iterations in average and cooling about 25 to 30 times temperature (because after 15 times cooling if no new solution updated, the SA will be terminated), about 800 iterations in total for SA should be calculated. In GA, the number of iterating calculations should be fixed at 800 times (as (50-10)*20). In TS, the *texit* directly indicates that after continuously 10 times of generated new solutions being rejected the algorithm should be terminated, which is quite close to the SA configuration. Also the total search iteration number is set as 50 in TS that is the same as GA generation number. Therefore, by referring the configuration parameters on Table 2, the optimization processes lengths for SA, GA and TS are equivalent.

As shown in Figure 9 (a) and (b), the reduction degree of flit latency number from 50% *VD* to 90% *VD* is extremely small. So does the increasing degree of flit rate number. Therefore, it is possible to judge that the system performance can hardly be further improved by increasing the *VD* number when the *VD* number reached 50%. Also, in Figure 9 (c), it is straight to derive the energy consumption number that is even worse, when the *VD* number is over 50%. In conclusion, the 50% *VD* number reaches the best trade-off point of the entire NoC system with the target applications. Figure 9 (d) proves the fact from the *SEF* perspective. In other words, by using this design methods, up to 50% *VL* can be saved while maintaining the system performance and reducing the system overhead.

Figure 10 shows the simulation results of the entire NoC system configuration that optimized by GA through LUDD, ENG, GRPL and GBW cost functions. From the results, the GA optimized NoC system achieves better optimization degree, since the 40% *VD* number configuration reaches the best SEF metric number. It is clear that maximal 60% *VL*s can be saved by using GA methods. Figure 10 (a) and 10 (b) explain that the system performance is improved dramatically by increasing the *VD* number up to 50%, which is quite similar to the SA optimized results. However, the GA algorithm

Table 2. SA, GA and TS configuration parameters comparison

Algorithm	Parameter	Value	Algorithm	Parameter	Value
SA	*Temp*	1000	GA	*npop*	50
SA	*ETemp*	10	GA	*ngen*	20
SA	*IT*	50	GA	*nbest*	10
SA	*CS*	0.9	TS	*ListSize*	100
SA	*SIT*	25	TS	*nexp*	25
SA	*STT*	15	TS	*texit*	10
--	--	--	TS	*nsearch*	50

with GBW cost function reaches the least energy consumption number at 40% *VD* configuration. Also, with higher *VD* numbers such as 80% and 90%, the GA optimized energy numbers are much better in comparison to SA.

Figure 11 shows the TS optimized system simulation results. In comparison to SA and GA optimized simulation results, the TS design optimization methods still keep the mean fact of what SA and GA achieve. According to Figure 11 (d), it is clear to see that up to 60% *VL*s can be saved while keeping the high system performance by using TS with LUDD configuration.

In general, while increasing the *VD* number, the system performance is improved. However, with high *VD* number configurations, the energy consumption overhead is critical. Therefore, finding the best trade-off point in the system configuration is the first-order task. The *SEF* metric is one of the most important evaluation standards. By applying the introduced system level design optimization methods, the best trade-off point can be found and up to 60% *VL* can be saved in the 3D NoC configurations according to the above presented experimental results (GA with GBW cost function configuration).

Figure 12 shows the average computation run time comparison between SA, GA and TS with different cost functions and different *VD* configurations. Figure 12 (a) shows the computation run time comparison among SA, GA and TS that averaged in applying four cost functions. Figure

12 (b) demonstrates the comparison among four cost functions that averaged in SA, GA and TS. The measurement is based on seconds and the machine is constructed with 24 Intel Xeon CPUs (2.4 GHz) and 64 GB RAM.

Generally, it is clear to observe that with the increment of the *VD* number, the run time for all of the three algorithms and four cost functions is increasing as well. With rising the *VD* number, the calculation time of each iteration in meta-heuristic algorithms is prolonged due to the complexity of NoC data communication transaction traffic.

For example, if the *VL* number is quite limited, the size of the traffic matrix model at each algorithmic iteration is tiny due to the limited routing path in 3D NoC. However, if the *VL* number is large, that leads to a number of available routing paths in the 3D NoC. The traffic is certainly distributed to the overall NoC more evenly and the size of the traffic matrix model gets larger. The larger the size of the matrix in computer is, the longer time for the program to assess it. Another reason is that more *T* configurations can be found if the *VL* number is high, which leads to the searching space enlargement. In case, the probability of finding a better solution is also raised. For meta-heuristic algorithms, if the algorithm can find better solution at more iteration, the best solution candidates must be updated. This operation costs more time than simply ignoring the newly found solution.

In order to demonstrate the efficiency of HyCH, another set of simulations with running

Figure 9. SA with Four Cost Functions Optimized NoC System Configuration (M, P, R and T) Simulation Result. (a). Average Flit Latency; (b). Average Flit Rate; (c). NoC Communication Energy; (d). NoC SEF Numbers.

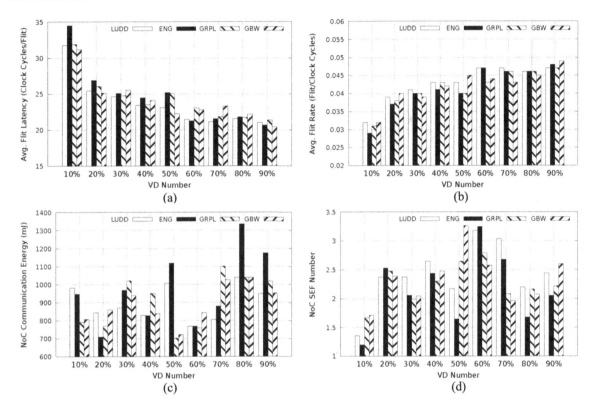

state-of-art benchmark applications are evaluated in this chapter. According to the conclusion of last experiment, more than 50% *VL* can be saved to maintain the best trade-off point in this case study. Therefore, in this set of experiments, the NoC scale is set as 4x4x4 with 50% *VD* topology and the traffic injection rate as 25% of the maximal bandwidth capacity. HyCH, SA, GA and TS (with LUDD cost function) are used to optimize *P* and the *M, T* and *R* are predetermined and cannot be changed during the optimization. All the other simulation configurations remain the same as in the last experiment.

The normalized NoC system performance and cost comparison results are shown from Table 3 to Table 6. It is clear to observe that HyCH can either achieve better or worse system design configurations for different applications (for

mpeg2enc HyCH achieves better *SEF*, however for plsa HyCH obtains 23.5% disadvantage in comparison to GA). In another word, the advantage of HyCH is application dependent. The reason is that once the current step of the overall solution has been fixed, it cannot be alternated although much better candidates can be found afterward. However, this drawback for meta-heuristic algorithms can be eliminated through a number of searching iterations.

There is one interesting point to discuss about the application categories that are suitable to be optimized by HyCH. The communication traffics in some applications are loose, such as blackscholes, mpeg2enc and x264 (according to Table 7, the design computation time numbers by applying SA, GA and TS are much less than fft and plsa). If only certain transactions in the ap-

Figure 10. GA with Four Cost Functions Optimized NoC System Configuration (M, P, R and T) Simulation Result. (a). Average Flit Latency; (b). Average Flit Rate; (c). NoC Communication Energy; (d). NoC SEF Numbers.

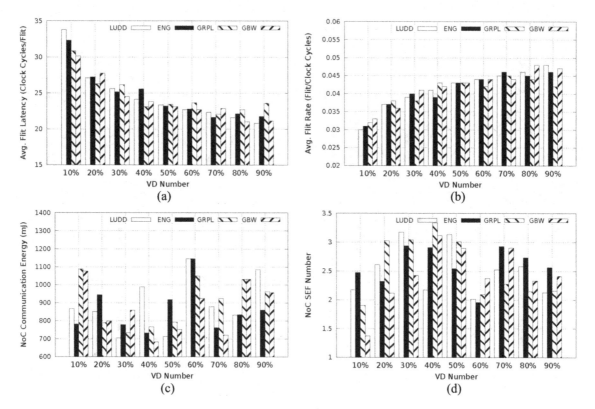

plication have very high data volume number and bandwidth requirement, such as the video (image) data frame stream in mpeg2enc and x264 applications, HyCH is directive to arrange the core placement pattern to guarantee the bandwidth of these transactions and to reduce the latency numbers. However, for some applications like fft, the communication traffics are dense, as quite a number of transactions need high bandwidths with high data volumes. Due to the algorithm description of HyCH, it might lose the direction to optimize the applications and difficult to find the best trade-off point in the optimization process. In this case, the design optimization quality is made more secure by employing meta-heuristic algorithms.

The advantage of HyCH is the extremely short computation time. Table 7 shows the normalized design computation time between HyCH, SA,

GA and TS for the selected five applications. In summary, HyCH is much faster than SA, GA and TS (maximal 1/266 in comparison to GA by optimizing fft application).

CONCLUSION AND FUTURE RESEARCH DIRECTIONS

In this chapter, the system level design optimization methods with respect to task mapping, core placement, topology and routing were demonstrated. The Simulated Annealing, Genetic Algorithm and Tabu Search with four cost functions, as Link Utilization Distribution Degree, NoC Communication Energy, Global Routing Path Length and Guaranteed Bandwidth are utilized to optimize the entire system. A fast core placement method

Figure 11. TS with Four Cost Functions Optimized NoC System Configuration (M, P, R and T) Simulation Result. (a). Average Flit Latency; (b). Average Flit Rate; (c). NoC Communication Energy; (d). NoC SEF Numbers.

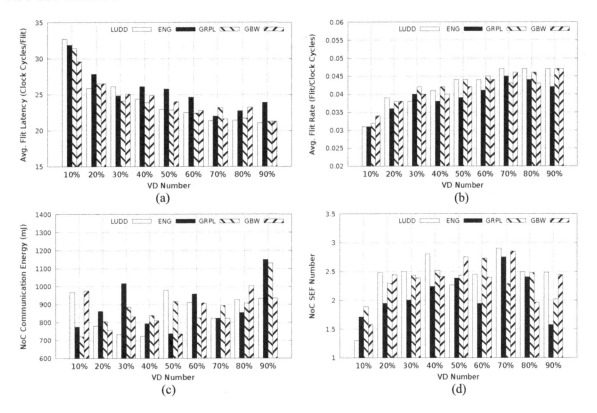

Figure 12. Design Optimization Methods Computation Run Time Comparison in Computer for Undertaking above Experiments. (a). Average Algorithm Computation Run Time Comparison; (b). Average Cost Function Computation Run Time Comparison.

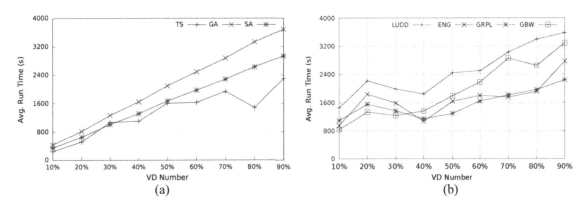

based on Hybrid Constructive Heuristic algorithm is introduced as well. Besides the optimization methods, the utilization and evaluation flow of these methods are given.

Table 4. Normalized flit rate comparison between HyCH, SA, GA and TS

Normalization	blackscholes	mpeg2enc	fft	plsa	x264
HyCH/SA-LUDD	0.963	0.968	1.014	0.956	0.953
HyCH/GA-LUDD	0.948	0.966	1.031	0.873	0.966
HyCH/TS-LUDD	0.981	0.966	1.019	0.977	0.945

Table 5. Normalized NoC communication energy comparison between HyCH, SA, GA and TS

Normalization	blackscholes	mpeg2enc	fft	plsa	x264
HyCH/SA-LUDD	0.999	0.982	1.021	0.981	0.992
HyCH/GA-LUDD	0.997	0.982	1.017	0.985	0.983
HyCH/TS-LUDD	1.000	0.997	1.008	0.983	0.995

Table 3. Normalized average flit latency comparison between HyCH, SA, GA and TS

Normalization	blackscholes	mpeg2enc	fft	plsa	x264
HyCH/SA-LUDD	0.955	0.960	1.144	1.152	1.086
HyCH/GA-LUDD	0.996	0.951	1.015	1.153	1.083
HyCH/TS-LUDD	1.001	0.950	1.100	1.126	1.073

Table 6. Normalized system efficiency factor comparison between HyCH, SA, GA and TS

Normalization	blackscholes	mpeg2enc	fft	plsa	x264
HyCH/SA-LUDD	0.955	1.025	0.868	0.844	0.887
HyCH/GA-LUDD	0.950	1.031	0.913	0.765	0.909
HyCH/TS-LUDD	0.976	1.020	0.914	0.878	0.886

Table 7. Normalized design computation time comparison between HyCH, SA, GA and TS

Normalization	blackscholes	mpeg2enc	fft	plsa	x264
SA-LUDD/HyCH	36.000	39.500	113.500	73.000	30.000
GA-LUDD/HyCH	52.500	61.000	266.125	205.500	73.500
TS-LUDD/HyCH	43.250	49.750	214.625	165.625	59.500

In this chapter, the design optimization methods are employed to a case study – 3D NoCs with reduced irregular vertical link connection topologies. Randomly generated task graphs (generic scalable pseudo applications) are applied to evaluate these design optimization methods. Up to 60% vertical link number can be saved while maintaining the system efficiency. Five benchmark applications are also used to evaluate these design optimization methods. According to the experimental results, HyCH can also achieve excellent

NoC design configurations in comparison to SA, GA and TS methods.

The possibility of leading these algorithms to achieve more advanced optimum system design configurations could be the improvement of cost functions. Currently in this chapter, four generalized cost functions are introduced. However, if the system performance optimization needs to be extremely guaranteed, a cost function with the strict straight and precise performance metric is desired (e.g. exact accurate estimated transaction latency).

In the future, we will extend our methods to optimize task scheduling and the extremely irregular customized topologies with the corresponding routing mechanisms.

REFERENCES

Abderazek, B., Akanda, M., Yoshinaga, T., & Sowa, M. (2007). Mathematical Model for Multi-objective Synthesis of NoC Architectures. In *Proceeding of the International Conference on Parallel Processing Workshops (ICPPW)*, (pp. 36). Xian, China: IEEE.

Addo-Quaye, C. (2005). Thermal-aware mapping and placement for 3-D NoC designs. In *Proceeding of the International SoC Conference*, (pp. 25-29). Herndon, VA: IEEE.

Adve, S., Li, M., Sasanja, R., & Chen, Y. (2005). The Alpbench Benchmark Suit for Complex Multimedia Applications. In *Proceeding of the International Symposium on Circuits and Systems*, (pp. 34-45). Austin, TX: IEEE.

Amory, A., Marcon, C., & Lubaszewski, M. (2011). Task mapping on NoC-based MPSoCs with faulty tiles: Evaluating the energy consumption and the application execution time. In *Proceeding of the International Symposium on Rapid System Prototyping*, (pp. 164-170). Karlsruhe, Germany: IEEE.

Bienia, G. (2011). *Benchmarking Modern Multiprocessors*. (Unpublished doctoral dissertation). Princeton University.

Chen, Y., Xie, L., & Li, J. (2009). An energy-aware heuristic constructive mapping algorithm for Network on Chip. In *Proceeding of the 8th International Conference on ASIC (ASICON)*, (pp. 101-104). Hunan, China: IEEE.

Chou, C., & Marculescu, R. (2008). Contention-aware application mapping for Network-on-Chip communication architectures. In *Proceeding of the International Conference on Computer Design*, (pp. 164-169). Lake Tahoe, CA: IEEE.

Choudhary, N., Gaur, M., Laxmi, V., & Singh, V. (2011). GA Based Congestion Aware Topology Generation for Application Specific NoC. In *Proceeding of the Electronic Design, Test and Application (DELTA)*, (pp. 93-98). Queenstown, New Zealand: IEEE.

Dick, R. P., Rhodes, D. L., & Wolf, W. (1998). TGFF: task graphs for free. In *Proceeding of the International Workshop Hardware/Software Co-Design*, (pp. 97-101). Seattle, WA: IEEE.

Duato, J., Yalamanchili, S., & Ni, L. (2003). *Interconnection Networks – An Engineering Approach*. San Francisco, CA: Morgan Kaufmann Publishers.

Glover, F. (1986). Future Paths for Integer Programming and Links to Artificial Intelligence. *Computers & Operations Research*, 5(13), 533–549. doi:10.1016/0305-0548(86)90048-1

Glover, F. (1989). Tabu Search - Part 1. *ORSA Journal on Computing*, 2(1), 190–206. doi:10.1287/ijoc.1.3.190

Heirman, W., Stroonamdt, D., Miniskar, N. R., Wuyts, R., & Catthoor, F. (2010). PinComm: Characterizing Intra-application Communication for the Many-Core Era. In *Proceeding of the International Conference in Parallel and Distributed Systems*, (pp. 500-507). Shanghai, China: IEEE.

Hredzak, B., & Diessel, O. (2011). Optimization of placement of dynamic network-on-chip cores using simulated annealing. In *Proceeding of the 37th Annual Conference on IEEE Industrial Electronics Society*, (pp. 2400-2405). Melbourne: IEEE.

Hu, J., & Marculescu, R. (2005). Energy- and performance-aware mapping for regular NoC architectures. *IEEE Transactions on Computer-Aided Design of Integrated Circuits and Systems*, *4*(24), 551–562.

Jin, X., & Watanabe, T. (2010). An Efficient 3D NoC Synthesis by Using Genetic Algorithms. In *Proceeding of the Region 10 Conference (TEN-CON)*, (pp. 1207-1212). Fukouka, Japan: IEEE.

Kirkpatrick, S., Gelatt, C. D., & Vecchi, M. P. (1983). Optimization by Simulated Annealing. *Science*, *4598*(220), 671–680. doi:10.1126/science.220.4598.671 PMID:17813860

Kwon, S., Pasricha, S., & Cho, J. (2011). POSEIDON: A Framework for Application-Specific Network-on-Chip Synthesis for Heterogeneous Chip Multiprocessors. In *Proceeding of the International Symposium on Quality Electronic Design*, (pp. 1-7). Santa Clara, CA: IEEE.

Liao, W., Pisharath, J., Liu, Y., Choudhary, A. (2005). Nu-MineBench 2.0. *Center for Ultra-Scale Computing and Information Security Technical Report*, CUCIS-2005-08-01.

Mitchell, M. (1996). *An Introduction to Genetic Algorithms*. Cambridge, MA: MIT press.

Motoyoshi, M. (2009). Through-Silicon Via (TSV). *Proceedings of the IEEE*, *1*(97), 43–48. doi:10.1109/JPROC.2008.2007462

Samman, F. (2010). *Microarchitecture and Implementation of Networks-on-Chip with a Flexible Concept for Communication Media Sharing*. (Unpublished doctoral dissertation). Technische Universitaet Darmstadt.

Shi, B., Srivastava, A., & Bar-Cohen, A. (2012). Hybrid 3D-IC Cooling System Using Micro-Fluidic Cooling and Thermal TSVs. In *Proceeding of the Computer Society Annual Symposium on VLSI*, (pp. 33-38). Amherst, MA: IEEE.

Tino, A., & Khan, G. (2011). Multi-Objective Tabu Search Based Topology Generation Technique For Application-Specific Network-on-Chip Architectures. In *Proceeding of the Design, Automation & Test in Europe Conference & Exhibition (DATE)*, (pp. 1-6). Grenoble, France: IEEE.

Todorov, V., Mueller-Gritschneder, D., Reinig, H., & Schlichtmann, U. (2013). A Spectral Clustering Approach to Application-Specific Network-on-Chip Synthesis. In *Proceeding of the Design, Automation & Test in Europe Conference & Exhibition (DATE)*, (pp. 1783-1788). Grenoble, France: IEEE.

Woo, S. C., Ohara, M., Torrie, E., Singh, J. P., & Gupta, A. (1995). The SPLASH-2 Programs: Characterizing and Methodological Considerations. In *Proceeding of the International Symposium on Computer Architecture*, (pp. 24-36). Santa Margherita Ligure, Italy: IEEE.

Xu, T., Liljeberg, P., & Tenhunen, H. (2011). Optimal Number and Placement of Through Silicon Vias in 3D Network-on-Chip. In *Proceeding of the Design and Diagnose of Electronic Circuits and Systems*, (pp. 105-110). Cottbus, Germany: IEEE.

Ying, H., Hollstein, T., & Hofmann, K. (2013). Deadlock-free generic routing algorithms for 3-dimensional Networks-on-Chip with reduced vertical link density topologies. *Journal of Systems Architecture*, *7*(59), 528–542. doi:10.1016/j.sysarc.2013.03.005

Ying, H., Hollstein, T., & Hofmann, K. (2013). GSNoC - The Comprehensive Design Platform for 3-Dimensional Networks-on-Chip based Many Core Embedded Systems. In *Proceeding of the International Conference on High Performance Computing and Simulation (HPCS)*, (pp. 217-223). Helsinki, Finland: IEEE.

Ying, H., Jaiswal, A., Abd El Ghany, M., Hollstein, T., & Hofmann, K. (2012). A Simulation Framework for 3-Dimension Networks-on-Chip with Different Vertical Channel Density Configurations. In *Proceeding of the conference on Design and Diagnose of Electronic Circuits and Systems*, (pp. 83-88). Tallinn, Estonia: IEEE.

Zhang, Y., Dembla, A., & Bakir, M. S. (2013). *Silicon Micropin-Fin Heat Sink With Integrated TSVs for 3-D ICs: Tradeoff Analysis and Experimental Testing. IEEE Trans. on Components, Packaging and Manufacturing Technology*.

Zhong, W., Chen, S., Ma, F., Yoshimura, T., & Goto, S. (2011). Floorplanning Driven Network-on-Chip Synthesis for 3-D SoCs. In *Proceedings of International Symposium on Circuits and Systems (ISCAS)*, (pp. 1203-1206). Rio de Janeiro, Brazil: IEEE.

Zhou, Y., Sheng, W., Liu, X., He, W., & Mao, Z. (2011). Efficient temporal task partition for coarse-grain reconfigurable systems based on Simulated Annealing Genetic Algorithm. In *Proceeding of the 9th International Conference on ASIC (ASICON)*, (pp. 941-944). Xiamen, China: IEEE.

KEY TERMS AND DEFINITIONS

3D NoC: 3-Dimensional Network-on-Chip.

Cost Function: A system level metric to represent the current state of the optimization. In this chapter, four cost functions that describe the NoC system status are introduced to guide the optimization to a correct direction.

Design Configurations: 3D NoC design configurations in this chapter include task mapping (M), core placement (P), topology (T) and routing (R).

GA: Genetic Algorithm.

HyCH: Hybrid Constructive Heuristic algorithm.

SA: Simulated Annealing algorithm.

TS: Tabu Search algorithm.

VL: The vertical link connection in 3D NoCs.

Section 2
Development Methodologies and Tool Suites

Chapter 8
MADES FP7 EU Project:
Effective High Level SysML/MARTE Methodology for Real-Time and Embedded Avionics Systems

Alessandra Bagnato
SOFTEAM, France

Imran Quadri
SOFTEAM, France

Etienne Brosse
SOFTEAM, France

Andrey Sadovykh
SOFTEAM, France

Leandro Soares Indrusiak
University of York, UK

Richard Paige
University of York, UK

Neil Audsley
University of York, UK

Ian Gray
University of York, UK

Dimitrios S. Kolovos
University of York, UK

Nicholas Matragkas
University of York, UK

Matteo Rossi
Politecnico di Milano, Italy

Luciano Baresi
Politecnico di Milano, Italy

Matteo Carlo Crippa
Txt e-Solutions, Italy

Stefano Genolini
Txt e-Solutions, Italy

Scott Hansen
The Open Group, UK

Gundula Meisel-Blohm
Airbus Defence and Space, Germany

ABSTRACT

This chapter presents the EU-funded MADES FP7 project that aims to develop an effective model-driven methodology to improve the current practices in the development of real-time embedded systems for avionics and surveillance industries. MADES developed an effective SysML/MARTE language subset, and a set of new tools and technologies that support high-level design specifications, validation, simulation, and automatic code generation, while integrating aspects such as component re-use. This chapter illustrates the MADES methodology by means of a car collision avoidance system case study; it presents the underlying MADES language, the design phases, and the set of tools supporting on one hand model verification and validation and, on the other hand, automatic code generation, which enables the implementation on execution platforms such as state-of-the-art FPGAs.

DOI: 10.4018/978-1-4666-6194-3.ch008

INTRODUCTION

In recent years, continuous technological advances in hardware/software along with rapid increase in targeted application domains have led to new challenges in the design specification and implementation of real-time embedded systems (RTES). These systems are now omnipresent, and it is difficult to find a domain where RTES have not made their mark. Thus, large complex RTES are becoming increasingly difficult to manage, resulting in critical issues and what has finally led to the notorious productivity gap. The design space, representing all technical decisions that need to be elaborated by the design team, is therefore becoming difficult to explore. Similarly, manipulation of these systems at low implementation levels such as Register Transfer Level (RTL) can be hindered by human interventions and the subsequent errors.

Henceforth, effective design methodologies and efficient design tools are needed to decrease overall development costs and time-to-market, while resolving issues such as those related to system complexity, verification and validation, etc. High-level system design approaches have been developed in this context such as Model-Driven Engineering (MDE) (OMG, 2007), in which the system is modeled through, for example, the Unified Modeling Language (UML), thus increasing the level of abstraction in the design phases.

In addition to fostering the introduction of better abstractions, MDE facilitates the partitioning of the system design by allowing for parallel independent specifications of the system hardware and software, their eventual allocation, and the possibility of integrating heterogeneous components into the system. Usage of UML models increases system comprehensibility as it allows designers to provide high-level descriptions of the system, easily illustrating its internal concepts (hierarchy, connections, dependencies etc.). The implementation-independent nature of these specifications also facilitates reuse, depending upon underlying tools and user requirements. MDE exploits different technologies and tools such as UML and related profiles for high-level system specifications. Model transformations (Sendall & Kozaczynski, 2003) can be used to automatically generate executable models or code from these abstract high-level design models.

This chapter provides an overview of the results of the MADES project (Bagnato et al., 2010; MADES, 2011). MADES aims to develop novel MDE techniques to improve the current practices in the development of real-time embedded systems for the avionics and surveillance domains. It proposes an effective subset of existing UML profiles for embedded systems modeling, in particular (OMG, 2012), and MARTE (OMG, 2011), while avoiding incompatibilities resulting from simultaneous usage of both profiles. The MADES methodology integrates new tools and technologies that support high-level SysML/ MARTE system design specification, their verification and validation (V&V), component re-use, and automatic code generation to enable execution platform implementation.

Whereas many works deal with embedded systems specifications using only either SysML or MARTE, the MADES approach combines them in a synergic way. This, by itself, is a significant contribution as while both these profiles provide numerous concepts and supporting tools, they are difficult to be mastered by system designers. The presented approach is based on the MADES language, which defines an effective subset of the SysML and MARTE profiles and proposes a specific set of diagrams for expressing different aspects related to a system. This chapter provides an overview of the diagrams comprising the MADES language, which enables rapid design and incremental composition of system specifications. MADES models are used by the underlying toolset to achieve component re-use, verification and validation of designs, or automatic code generation, as briefly described in this chapter.

We illustrate the various concepts of the MADES methodology, language and toolset by means of a realistic case study, a car collision avoidance system.

The rest of this chapter is organized as follows. Some related projects are presented initially. Afterwards a brief overview of the MADES project is given: its proposed methodology and integrated toolset. Subsequently we present the car collision avoidance case study and its design phases: modeling, verification and code generation. Finally, we provide the conclusion of the overall chapter.

BACKGROUND

A number of works exploit SysML or MARTE to provide high-level abstractions and Model-Driven Engineering techniques for RTES design and implementation.

The MoPCoM project (Koudri et al., 2008) uses the MARTE profile to target modeling and code generation of reconfigurable embedded systems. While the project takes inspiration from SysML concepts such as requirements and blocks, they are not fully integrated in the design flow. The project uses the IBM Harmony process coupled with the Rhapsody UML modeling tool. Additionally, MoPCoM proposes two distinct flows for system modeling and schedulability analysis that increase design efforts. Similarly, eDIANA (eDIANA, 2011) is an ARTEMIS project that uses the MARTE profile for RTES specification and validation. However, detailed specification of software and hardware aspects are not illustrated in the project. The TOPCASED project (TOPCASED, 2012) differs from MADES, as it focuses primarily on IDE infrastructure for real-time embedded systems and not on any particular implementations. SATURN (Mueller et al., 2010) is another EU FP7 project that aims to use a high-level co-modeling approach for RTES simulation and synthesis. However, the project only takes SysML into account and proposes multiple UML

profiles, for co-simulation, synthesis and code generation purposes, respectively. The goal is to carry out hardware/software modeling via these profiles and generate SystemC for eventual VHDL translation and FPGA implementation. Unfortunately, the project does not utilizes the MARTE standard for hardware/software co-design modeling and increases the learning curve due to the introduction of several new dedicated profiles.

In (Mura et al., 2008), the authors provide a mixed modeling approach based on the SysML and MARTE profiles to address design space exploration strategies. However, the shortcomings of this approach are that they only provide implementation results by means of mathematical expressions and no actual experimental results were illustrated. The OMEGA (European project Information Society Technologies, 2009) is also dedicated to the development of critical real-time systems. However it uses UML specifications for system modeling and proposes a UML profile (Ober et al., 2005), which is a subset of an earlier UML profile for Scheduling, Performance and Time (SPT), that has been integrated in MARTE. The MARTES project emphasizes the combined usage of UML and SystemC for systematic model-based development of RTES. The results from this project, in turn, have contributed to the creation of the MARTE profile. Finally, the EU FP7 INTERESTED project (INTERESTED, 2011) proposes a merged SysML/MARTE methodology where SysML is used for requirement specifications and MARTE for timing aspects; however, it does not define rules on the combined usage of both profiles. In (Faugere et al., 2007), the authors compared AADL to MARTE, which is an ongoing research at OMG (Object Management Group); and illustrate that MARTE and AADL are complementary in nature. However, tools supporting both profiles do not exist at the moment.

The MADES project aimed to resolve this issue and thus differs from the works mentioned above, as it focused on an effective language subset combining both the SysML and MARTE profiles for rapid design and specification of RTES. The two profiles have been chosen as they are both widely used in embedded systems design, and are complementary in nature (Espinoza et al., 2009). MADES proposed automatic generation of hardware descriptions and embedded software from high-level models, and integrated verification of functional and non-functional properties, as illustrated in the next section. Thus, as evidenced by the projects cited above, both SysML and MARTE are being widely used in both the academia and the real-time embedded systems industry. SysML is normally used for high-level system design specifications and requirement engineering, while MARTE enables the possibility to enrich a system specification with non-functional properties, hardware/software co-design along with timing,

performance and schedulability analysis aspects. Hence, a merge of both SysML and MARTE is a logical step, as it enables a designer to carry out SysML-based high-level requirements and functional system descriptions and then enrich these models with MARTE concepts.

AN OVERVIEW OF THE MADES PROJECT

In this section, we provide a brief overview of the MADES design methodology, as illustrated in Figure 1. Initially, the high-level system design models are carried out using the MADES language and associated diagrams, which are described later on. After the creation of the design models that

Figure 1. The global MADES methodology

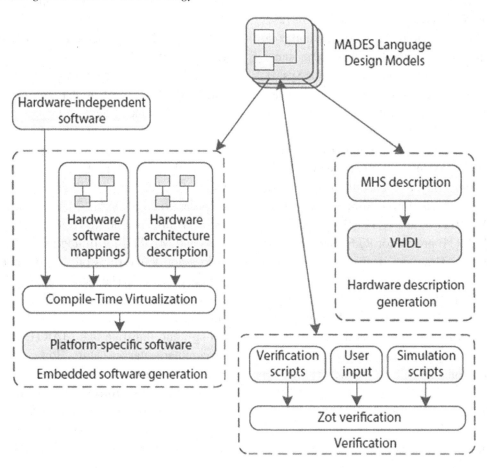

include user requirements, related hardware/software aspects and their eventual allocation, model transformations (*model-to-model* and *model-to-text*) are used to bridge the gap between these abstract design models and subsequent design phases, such as verification, hardware descriptions of modeled targeted architecture and generation of platform-specific embedded software from architecturally neutral software specifications. To realize the model transformations, MADES uses the Epsilon platform (Kolovos et al., 2006), which enables model transformations, code generation, model comparison, merging, refactoring and validation (Matragkas et al., 2010).

Verification and validation activities in MADES include verification of key properties of designed concepts (such as meeting deadlines, etc.) and simulation of closed-loop models, comprising both the system being designed and the physical environment with which it interacts (Baresi et al., 2010, 2011, 2012a). For verification and simulation purposes, MADES uses the Zot tool (Zot, 2012), which permits the verification of timed properties of models, including real-time ones. Closed-loop simulation on design models facilitates functional testing and early system validation.

Additionally, MADES employs the technique of *Compile-Time Virtualization* (CTV) (Gray & Audsley, 2009), for targeting of non-standard hardware architectures, without requiring development of new languages or compilers. Thus a programmer can write architecturally neutral code which is automatically distributed by CTV over complex target architectures. Finally, via model transformations, one can generate code (for example, VHDL for hardware, or Real-Time Java for software) that can be eventually executed on various architectures, such as modern state-of-the-art FPGAs (Xilinx, 2014). Currently. MADES model transformations target Xilinx FPGAs, however it is also possible for them to adapt to FPGAs provided by other vendors such as Altera or Atmel. A detailed description regarding the global MADES methodology can be found in (Gray et al., 2011).

MADES Language: Design Phases and Related Diagrams

We now provide an overview of the underlying MADES language that is used in the overall methodology for the initial model-based design specifications. The MADES language focuses on a subset of the SysML and MARTE profiles and proposes a specific set of diagrams for specifying different aspects of a system, such as requirements, hardware/software concepts, etc. Along with these specific diagrams, MADES also uses classic UML diagrams such as *State* and *Activity* diagrams to model internal behavior of system components, and *Sequence* and *Interaction Overview* diagrams to model interactions and cooperation between different system elements. Softeam's Modelio, UML Editor and MDE Workbench provides full support of MADES diagrams and associated language (Modelio, 2014). We now provide a brief description of the MADES language and its related diagrams.

In the initial specification phase, a designer needs to carry out system design at high abstraction levels. This design phase consists of the following steps:

- **System Requirements:** The user initially specifies the requirements related to the system. For this purpose, a MADES *Requirements Diagram* is utilized that integrates SysML requirements concepts.
- **Initial Behavioral Specification:** Afterwards, initial behavioral specification is carried out by means of UML use cases, interactions, state machines or activities during the preliminary analysis phase.
- **Functional Specification:** Once the behavioral specifications are completed, they are then linked to SysML blocks (or internal blocks) by means of MADES *Functional Block* (or *Internal Functional Block*) *Specification Diagram*, which contains SysML block (or internal block) concepts. This functionality is independent

of any underlying execution platform and software details. It thus determines 'what' is to be implemented, instead of 'how' it is to be carried out.

- **Refined Functional Specification:** This level refines SysML aspects into MARTE concepts: The *Refined Functional Specification Diagram* models MARTE components, each corresponding to a SysML block. Here, MARTE's *High level Application Modeling* package is used to differentiate between active and passive components of the system.

The refined functional specification phase links SysML and MARTE concepts but avoids conflicts arising due to parallel usage of both profiles (Espinoza et al., 2009). The conflicts are avoided as we do not mix SysML and MARTE concepts in the same design phase, except the allocation aspects, present in both profiles. While the allocation concept is present both in SysML and MARTE, MARTE enriches the basic SysML allocation aspects and is thus the one adopted for our methodology. SysML is used for initial requirements and functional description, while MARTE is utilized for the enriched modeling of the global functionality and execution platform/software modeling along with their allocations, creating a clear separation between the two profiles. Afterwards, the designer can move onto the hardware/software partitioning of the refined functional specifications. These following steps are elaborated by means of MARTE concepts.

Related to the MARTE modeling, an allocation between high-level and refined high-level specifications is carried out using a MADES *Allocation Diagram*. Afterwards, a Co-Design approach (Gajski & Khun, 1983) is used to model the hardware and software aspects of the system. The modeling is combined with MARTE *Non-Functional Properties* and *Timed Modeling* package to express aspects such as throughput, temporal constraints, etc.

We now describe the hardware and software modeling, which is as follows:

- **Hardware Specification:** The MADES *Hardware Specification Diagram* in combination with MARTE's *Generic Resource Modeling* package enables modeling of abstract hardware concepts such as computing, communication and storage resources. The design level enables a designer to describe the physical system, albeit at an abstraction level higher than the detailed hardware specification level. By making use of MARTE GRM concepts, a designer can describe a physical system such as a car, a transport system, flight management system, among others.

- **Detailed Hardware Specification:** Using the *Detailed Hardware Specification Diagram* with MARTE's *Hardware Resource Modeling* package allows extension and enrichment of concepts modeled at the hardware specification level. It also permits modeling of systems such as FPGA based System-on-Chips (SoCs), ASICs etc. A one-to-one correspondence usually follows here: for example, a computing resource typed as MARTE ComputingResource is converted into a hardware processor, such as a PowerPC or MicroBlaze, effectively stereotyped as MARTE HwProcessor. Afterwards, an *Allocation Diagram* is then utilized to map the modeled hardware concepts to detailed hardware ones.

- **Software Specification:** The MADES *Software Specification Diagram* along with MARTE's *Generic Resource Modeling* package permits modeling of software aspects of an execution platform such as schedulers and tasks; as well as their attributes and policies (e.g. priorities, possibility of preemption).

- **Detailed Software Specification:** The MADES *Detailed Software Specification Diagram* and related MARTE's *Software Resource Modeling* are used to express aspects of the underlying Operating System (OS). Once this model is completed, an *Allocation Diagram* is used to map the modeled software concepts to detailed software ones: for example, allocation of tasks onto OS processes and threads. This level can express standardized or designer based RTOS APIs. Thus multi-tasking libraries and multi-tasking framework APIs can be described here.
- **Clock Specification:** The MADES *Clock Specification Diagram* is used to express timing and clock constraints/aspects. It can be used to specify the physical clocks present in the hardware platform and the related constraints, or logical clocks related to the software functionalities. This diagram makes use of MARTE's *Time Modeling* concepts such as clock types, clocks and related constraints.

Iteratively, several allocations can be carried out in our design methodology: an initial software to hardware allocation may allow associating schedulers and schedulable resources to related computing resources in the execution platform, once the initial abstract hardware/software models are completed, in order to reduce *Design Space Exploration* (DSE).

Subsequently this initial allocation can be concretized by further mapping of the detailed software and hardware models (an allocation of OS to a hardware memory, for example), to fulfill designer requirements and underlying tools analysis results. An allocation can also specify if the execution of a software resource onto a hardware module is carried out in a sequential or parallel manner. Interestingly, each MADES diagram only contains commands related to that particular design phase, thus avoiding ambiguities

of utilization of the various concepts present in both SysML and MARTE, while helping designers to focus on their relative expertise. Additionally, UML behavioral diagrams in combination with MADES concepts (such as those related to verification) can be used for describing detailed behavior of system components or the system itself.

Finally, the MADES language also contains additional concepts used for the underlying model transformations for code generation and verification purposes, which are not present in either SysML or MARTE. A detailed description of these aspects can be found in (Bagnato et al., 2012).

Once the modeling aspects are completed, verification and code generation can be carried out, as explained next.

Verification and Validation of MADES Diagrams

Verification is carried out by transforming MADES diagrams into temporal logic formulae, using the semantics defined in (Baresi et al., 2012a). These are, in turn, fed to the Zot verification tool (Zot, 2012), which signals whether the stated property holds for the modeled system or not, and in the latter case returns a counterexample, i.e., a system trace violating the property.

In fact, once the temporal logic model is created from the diagrams describing the system, the Zot tool can be used in two ways: to check whether user-defined properties hold for the system; and to produce traces compatible with a formal model, in what amounts to a simulation of the system. The simulation capabilities of the Zot tool can be used, as described in (Baresi et al., 2011), in combination with a simulation tool such as OpenModelica (OpenModelica, 2012) to perform closed-loop simulations of the designed embedded system with its physical environment.

In this section we briefly present the mechanisms through which MADES diagrams are translated into temporal logic formulae. The interested reader can refer to (Baresi, L. et al.,

2012b, 2013) for a more thorough description of the technique and its application. A detailed description of the Zot verification tool, including an analysis of its performance, can be found in (Pradella et al., 2013).

To carry out formal verification and simulation, each MADES diagram is translated into a set of temporal logic predicates and axioms. The predicates correspond directly to the elements of the MADES models (e.g., a pair of predicates is introduced for each message of a sequence diagram, one to represent the sending of the message, the other to represent its reception). The axioms describe how different elements are related to each other (e.g., the sending of a message and its reception occur at the same time if the message is drawn horizontally), effectively representing the actual semantics of MADES models.

This temporal logic-based approach has a number of interesting characteristics. Firstly, the semantics is decoupled from the predicates that represent model elements: one can change the semantics (and experiment with different solutions and alternatives) whilst translation from UML to the predicates remains unaffected. In addition, the logic-based formalization is easily extensible: Adding a new diagram type only requires the definition of predicates that represent its elements and their associated axioms. Finally, to manage the possible complexity of the resulting formalization, the MADES approach supports analysis of partial models by translating only the diagrams of interest.

In the MADES approach, the temporal logic formulae capturing the semantics of diagrams are completely hidden from the modelers; they are specified in TRIO (Ciapessoni et al., 1999), a first-order linear temporal logic that supports a metric on time. TRIO defines a single basic modal operator, *Dist*, that relates the *current time* (left implicit in the formula) to another time instant. Given a time-dependent formula F (a term that maps the time domain to truth values) and a (arithmetic) term t (indicating a time distance (either positive or negative), the formula $Dist(F,t)$ specifies that F holds at a time instant whose distance is exactly t time units from the current instant. While TRIO can exploit both discrete and dense sets as time domains, MADES assumes the standard model of the non-negative integers $\mathbb{N}$ as a discrete time domain. For convenience, in specifying formulae, TRIO defines a number of *derived* temporal operators from the basic *Dist* through propositional composition and first-order logic quantification. For example, $Past(F,t)$ states that F held t instants in the past of the current one, and is defined as $t > 0 \land Dist(F,t)$; similarly, $Lasted(F,t)$ states that F held for the past t instants, and is defined as $\forall d \in (0,t]\ Dist(F,d)$. More details about the TRIO language can be found in (Bersani et al., 2010).

TRIO specifications can be analyzed through the Zot tool. Zot can deal with numeric domains such as integers or reals (Bersani et al., 2010), which can appear in MADES models. The input to the Zot tool is a script comprising a set of TRIO formulae expressed as Lisp statements, while its output is plain text. Given an input specification, Zot checks whether it is satisfiable or not. Using this basic mechanism, given a target model Zot can perform both verification of user-defined properties and simulation tasks.

We now briefly introduce the MADES formal semantics, starting with the predicates defined to encode UML models, and then hinting at the axioms that formalize the meaning of the different concepts. A more comprehensive presentation can be found in (Baresi, L. et al., 2012b).

We indicate by *idx* the identifier of a model element x, which is unique by UML rules. Then, for every clock c in a Clock diagram, a temporal logic predicate $Clock_{idc}Tick$, is declared, which holds every T time units, where T is the period of c. For every operation x belonging to an object y we declare Boolean predicate $OBJ_{idy}OP_{idx}$, which holds when operation x is invoked on object y.

Given a Sequence diagram x, predicates $SD_{idx}Start$, $SD_{idx}End$, and SD_{idx} are declared, which are true, respectively, at the beginning, at the end, and during the diagram execution. Also, predicate $SD_{idx}Stop$ holds if the diagram terminates before reaching its end (e.g., because it is interrupted). For every message m we declare predicates $Msg_{idx}Start$ and $Msg_{idx}End$ that hold at the beginning and at the end of the message. Similar predicates are introduced to describe other elements of Sequence diagrams (e.g., execution occurrences), and also the elements of other diagrams, and in particular State diagrams and Interaction Overview diagrams.

Let us now illustrate some of the formulae that are produced to capture the semantics of MADES diagrams.

For each clock c with period T the following axiom holds, which states that a clock ticks iff it did not tick during the last T-1 time units, which implies that it ticks at times $T, 2T, 3T, ...$[1]:

$$Lasted(\neg cTick, T\text{-}1) \leftrightarrow cTick \qquad (1)$$

Objects that are linked to a clock c either in the Class diagrams or in the Object diagrams run on a time base defined by c. All events that belong to these objects can only happen when c ticks. For example, suppose there is an object o linked to clock c, and a Sequence diagram where o sends a message m; then the following axiom holds, which states that event Msg_mStart can occur only in those instants in which clock c ticks:

$$Msg_mStart \rightarrow cTick \qquad (2)$$

The periods of clocks in a MADES specification are all expressed in relation to a uniform ideal discrete time that underlies the whole model. This abstract view of time is suitable for high-level specifications of timed systems, and it is not intended to capture implementation-level concepts such as the physical hardware clocks associated with computing devices. The notion of clock in MADES UML can be seen as an abstraction of such concepts, in that clocks can be used to introduce periodic behaviors in the specification. In fact,

the TRIO language and the Zot tool support also more sophisticated notions of time; for example, they can deal with zero-time transitions (Ferrucci et al., 2012), where a system can be in different states at the same time, and with models with an underlying continuous notion of time (Bersani et al., 2013), which can be used to capture fully asynchronous systems. These issues however have not been explored in MADES, and are left for future work.

Let us now consider a Sequence diagram. This is defined as a set of lifelines, where every lifeline is an ordered list of events (e.g., message start/end, execution occurrence start/end). For every ordered pair of events i,j that occur along a lifeline, if i holds at some instant, then j will follow in the future if the diagram is not stopped. This is formalized by the following axiom:

$$Ev_i \rightarrow Until(\neg Ev_i \wedge \neg Ev_j, SD_xStop) \vee Until(\neg Ev_i \wedge \neg SD_xStop, Ev_j) \qquad (3)$$

where Ev_i and Ev_j are the predicates corresponding to events i and j, respectively.

Sequence diagrams (as well as State diagrams) can include time constraints between pairs of events, as shown in Figure 10. A time constraint is an inequality between two events. For example, for the diagram of Figure 10 the following formula holds:

$$SD_{sendBreakCommand} \wedge SD_{sendBreakCommand}End \rightarrow Past(SD_{sendBreakCommand}Start, \qquad 2)$$

Code Generation with Compile Time Virtualization

The code generation activities of the MADES approach enable developers to write architecturally-neutral Java code, which can then be automatically refactored to target complex, heterogeneous, embedded architectures. This greatly simplifies embedded software development because:

- The developer can write Java code as if for a simple, a homogeneous architecture, and the MADES tool flow will refactor it to target complex, non-uniform architectures.
- Software threads and data can be moved throughout such complex architecture simply by redrawing the allocation model. The input software remains the same.
- Equally, the input software can be ported to totally new architectures without any rewriting.

The tool which achieves this is called AnvilJ (Gray & Audsley, 2012), an implementation of a research technique known as *Compile-Time Virtualization* (Gray & Audsley, 2009). Without a system like AnvilJ, Java programs are restricted to executing within a single Java Virtual Machine (JVM). This has the effect of limiting the architectures supported by Java to those architectures over which an existing JVM can execute.

To solve this problem, AnvilJ refactors a single input Java program into a set of output programs, each of which runs in its own JVM, and can make use of complex hardware features that are normally unavailable to the Java programmer. These include:

- Multiple, heterogeneous processors with differing capabilities and speeds.
- Complex memory hierarchies with regions of both shared and non-shared memory that may be different for each processor of the system.
- Non-standard communications topologies in which not every processor can directly communicate with each other processor, or in which some communication links may perform differently to others.

The user provides a file which describes how their code is deployed over the target architecture. This file describes the input architecture and maps elements of the input program over it. For example,

this file can be used to place particular system threads onto specific processors of the system, or to place instances of shared data structures in specific memory spaces of the system.

AnvilJ does not explicitly consider real-time constraints. Instead it focusses on ensuring that if the user's software is suitable for use in a real-time system then it will not degrade this. AnvilJ's runtime is written to have bounded execution times and memory use and it only changes the input code at well-defined points. However, if the input code is written without real-time concerns then AnvilJ cannot make such software into real-time Java.

The platforms that AnvilJ can handle are heterogeneous systems with non-uniform memory architectures, but as a Java-based tool, the processing elements of the target system must be able to support Java or software created by compiling Java, for example the JamaicaVM (Aicas GmbH, 2013) which translates real-time Java to C for execution. There is no requirement for cache coherency or shared memory between processing elements. The user has to provide drivers for the communication fabric of the platform which the AnvilJ runtime will automatically include and use.

The CTV Virtual Platform (VP) should not be confused with virtualization environments such as the CoWare Virtual Platform (CoWare Inc., 2013) which are software simulations of target hardware. These virtual platforms are simulators that provide introspection and observability to aid software design. Instead, CTV's VP is a compile-time technique for bridging the *programming model gap* - the observation that modern programming languages do not provide the programmer with the concepts required to target modern complex heterogeneous systems. CTV's VP simplifies the complex target platform so that the programmer only needs to develop simple software. Also, because the VP translates the input software at compile-time, so there is no virtualization present at run-time. The user's software executes natively on the real hardware.

AnvilJ and AnvilJ Shared Objects

AnvilJ needs to be told how to map parts of the input software to the architecture. This is done by providing a mapping file, called architecture. xml. This file can be hand-written (it is just normal XML) but in the MADES tool flow it is automatically generated from the system model. The architecture.xml file identifies Java threads and object instances in the input project that the designer wishes to place throughout the computing resources of the target architecture. When a thread is mapped in this way it is referred to as an *AnvilJ Thread*. When an object instance is mapped like this it is called an *AnvilJ Shared Object*. Together they are called *AnvilJ Objects*. This is important because restrictions are placed on the code of AnvilJ Objects, as described in the next section. So which object instances should be made into AnvilJ Objects? The following rule must be obeyed:

- If any thread in the system accesses a field or method of an object instance X, and that communication crosses from one processing node to another, then X must be an AnvilJ Object.

All other code need not be marked as an AnvilJ Object (but there is no harm in doing so).

Restrictions on the Input Code

Code passed through AnvilJ must be written according to a set of restrictions, detailed below. In all these examples, myThread is assumed to be an AnvilJ Thread.

AnvilJ Objects Must be Declared as Static Final Fields

```
//Correct
static final Thread myThread = new
Thread();
//Incorrect
int main(void) {
        Thread myThread;
}
```

It is permitted to use a static initializer to initialize myThread, but one statement may actually assign to myThread. For example:

```
//Incorrect
static final Thread myThread;
static {
        if(someCondition) {
                myThread = new
MyThread(10);
        } else {
                myThread = new
MyThread(5);
        }
}
```

Here the refactoring engine cannot determine offline which assignment will be used and it will report an error. Rewrite it as follows:

```
//Correct
static final Thread myThread;
static {
        myThread = new
MyThread(someCondition);
}
//MyThread checks someCondition in
its constructor
```

AnvilJ Objects Must be Accessed by Direct Static Reference

Whenever a field or method of an AnvilJ Object is accessed, the name of the AnvilJ Object should be fully-qualified. References to AnvilJ Objects cannot be copied (for example, by passing them into a method).

```
//Correct
MyDefinitions.myThread.start();
//Incorrect
Thread getThread() {
return MyDefinitions.myThread; //This
is not permitted
}
int main(void) {
        getThread.start();
}
```

Arguments and Return Values of Shared Methods Must be Serializable

The arguments and return values of methods that of AnvilJ Objects must implement the java.io.Serializable interface, or a descendent interface. The refactoring engine will warn about this if it is not the case.

Using the Code and Hardware Generation Transformations

In the MADES project, the AnvilJ code generation tools are implemented as plug-ins for the Eclipse development environment[2].

The code generation flow is as follows:

1. The developer starts with a Java project that they wish to implement in a complex architecture.
2. The developer models the target architecture and models the input software (as described previously).
3. The developer creates an allocation diagram which assigns elements of the software model to elements of the hardware model. They export this model as an architecture.xml file which is read by AnvilJ.
4. The developer runs the AnvilJ tools, creating the distributed output programs.

Figure 12 shows an example of a software model and allocation model as used in the MADES flow.

Bindings

In the MADES flow it is necessary to link the model elements of a software model to the Java source code elements to which they refer. This is done using *bindings*, and their use is facilitated by the MADES AnvilJ Eclipse plug-ins. The developer can point to a software element in the source code of their editor, and ask the plug-in for its *binding key*. This is a textual string which uniquely identifies the source code element and is added to the class instances of the software model to uniquely bind the model elements to their corresponding code. This process is shown in Figure 2.

Once the binding information is entered the developer can now execute the MADES code generation to automatically build the architecture.xml file which will control AnvilJ. Running the transformation simply involves selecting it from a menu. Figure 3 shows the resultant architecture.xml from the example model shown in Figure 12.

The developer can validate the generated architecture.xml because any mapped source code elements will now be highlighted and a tooltip shows to what hardware element the item is bound.

Running AnvilJ

Now that the developer has an architecture.xml file, the AnvilJ code generation process is launched from the Eclipse menus.

Figure 2. (a) Obtaining the binding key of a source code element, (b) The binding key, (c) Adding the binding key to the software model.

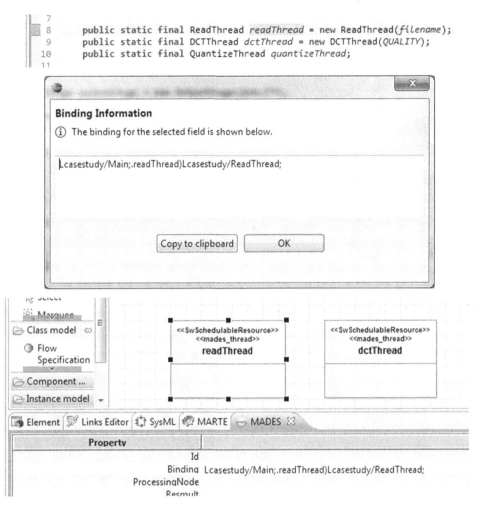

AnvilJ will refactor the example project into a set of output projects, one for each target CPU.

Testing the Output Projects

AnvilJ cannot automatically create the low-level driver code that is needed to handle on-chip communications in the real hardware; the Java developer will add this themselves. However the generated projects include a simple TCP-based communications driver that is intended for simulation and functional verification. As a result, the output projects can be built and executed in separate JVMs but they will still communicate over TCP to complete their work.

If, after testing, the developer determines that the allocation may need to change then only changes to the allocation model are required. The developer merely changes the model, regenerates the architecture.xml file and reruns AnvilJ. No code editing is required. Equally, to move code to a new architecture the developer only needs to create a new hardware model and allocation, they do not need to edit their software.

Figure 3. The generated architecture.xml

```
 1 <architecture name="Example Architecture" mainclass="example.Main" maincpuid="1">
 2     <cpu name="CPU1" id="1">
 3         <thread binding="Lexample/Main;.readThread)Lexample/ReadThread;"/>
 4     </cpu>
 5     <cpu name="CPU2" id="2">
 6         <thread binding="Lexample/Main;.quantizeThread)Lexample/QuantizeThread;"/>
 7         <thread binding="Lexample/Main;.dctThread)Lexample/DCTThread;"/>
 8     </cpu>
 9     <channel name="MainBus">
10         <endpoint cpu="CPU1"/>
11         <endpoint cpu="CPU2"/>
12     </channel>
13 </architecture>
14 |
```

Figure 4. Illustrating the different threads

```
 7
 8        public static final ReadThread readThread = new ReadThread(filename);
 9        public static final DCTThread dctThread = new DCTThread(QUALITY);
10    AnvilJ thread "quantizeThread" bound to CPU "CPU2" antizeThread;
11
12⊖        static {
```

Figure 5. AnvilJ performing code refactoring and generation

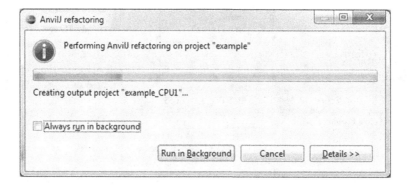

Model Transformations and Code Generation Features

The underlying MADES model transformations focus on the following areas:

- **Generation of Platform-Specific Software from Architecturally-Neutral Software Specifications:** Through the AnvilJ described previously, architecturally neutral code can be developed which is then ported to the real hardware. This enables hardware independence without redevelopment of the software functionality. Thus the software can be automatically refactored in case of change in details related to the underlying hardware. Additionally, software can be restructured throughout the target architecture: tasks can be moved from an overloaded processor without recoding the application. AnvilJ will generate the split output code appropriately, and handle all communications and shared memory use to ensure that the code still operates correctly.

- **Generation of Hardware Descriptions of the Modeled Target Architecture:** The MADES transformations allow for the generation of implementable hardware descriptions of the target architecture from the input system model. The input model is created by means of Modelio and the MADES language detailed previously. The generated hardware could be a complex, heterogeneous system with non-uniform memory architecture, but is supported and programmed by the software generated via the code generation transformations described earlier.

- **Verification of Functional/Non-Functional Properties:** Verification capabilities are provided in the MADES framework by the Zot tool, as described previously, which requires a verification script and a set of properties to carry out verification. The verification script is automatically generated from a combination of the behavioral diagrams of the MADES language, particularly State, Sequence and Interaction Overview diagrams. A specification of the structure of the system is also needed which is derived from the MADES structural diagrams. Moreover, timing/clock information is required, which can be extracted from the *Clock Specification Diagram* present in the MADES language. The properties to verify must be solicited from the user. Results from Zot are fed back into the modeling tool in order to give the user feedback on them and locate errors, if any are found. The code generation facilities are used to integrate the back-end of the verification tool, which is Zot, with the front-end, which are the models expressed using the MADES language.

- **Simulation of Embedded Systems:** In the case of simulation, the simulation tool requires an appropriate simulation script and a Modelica (Modelica, 2012) model. The simulation script will be automatically generated from a combination of the behavioral diagrams of the MADES Language, particularly State, Sequence and Interaction Overview diagrams. A specification of the structure of the system, and of its links to the environment is also needed which is derived from the MADES diagrams. Finally, information about the environment will be required, and this information can be modeled using the MADES language.

- **Traceability Aspects:** The capture/maintenance of traceability information is of paramount importance in order to ensure consistency between the various artifacts or tools present in the MADES tool chain. Traceability support is provided for tracing the results of the verification activity back to the models, for tracing the generated code back to its source models and finally for tracing requirements to model elements such as use cases or operations, as well as to implementation files and test cases.

Together, these assist with mapping the programmer's code to complex hardware architectures, describing that architecture for implementation (possibly as an ASIC or on an FPGA) and verifying the correctness of the final system. Detailed descriptions about these model transformations, along with their installation and usage guidelines have been provided in (Bagnato et al., 2012; Quadri, 2012a).

MADES Component Repository

The MADES Component Repository (CRP) is used to store, search and download MADES components created by the MADES developer with the Modelio UML Editor and MDE Workbench. It accesses a central MADES component database while offering various web services via a flexible graphical user interface to manage the components stored within the database, and the queries that have been performed on its contents. Thus the CRP enables *Intellectual Property* (IP) re-use, enabling designers to create, store or re-use IP blocks to build different applications, platforms or complete systems, while reducing design time. Complete details about the MADES CRP can be found in (Bagnato et al., 2012; Quadri, 2012a).

CAR COLLISION AVOIDANCE SYSTEM EXAMPLE

We now provide the car collision avoidance system (CCAS) case study that is modeled in Modelio using the MADES language and then carry out verification and code generation aspects using the MADES methodology. While the MADES project developed two real-life case studies provided by Cassidian Electronics and TXT e-solutions, focusing on a ground-based radar processing unit and an onboard radar control unit, respectively, the CCAS has been developed as a reference example to provide guidelines to the MADES partners as well as to the general embedded systems community for usage of the MADES language and the methodology. This is a generic case study, and the results and practices observed during development of this case study have led to the development of the actual TXT and Cassidian case studies related to avionics and surveillance systems.

The car collision avoidance system, or CCAS for short, when installed in a vehicle, detects and prevents collisions with incoming objects such as cars and pedestrians. The CCAS contains two types of detection modules. The first one is a radar detection module that emits continuous waves. A transmitted wave, when it collides with an incoming object, is reflected and received by the radar itself. The radar sends this data to an obstacle detection module, which in turn removes the noise from the incoming signal and performs other tasks such as a correlation algorithm. The distance of the in-coming object is then calculated and sent to a primary controller for appropriate actions.

The image-tracking module is the second detection module installed in the CCAS. It permits the system to determine the distance of the car from an object by means of image computation. The camera takes pictures of incoming objects and sends the data to a secondary controller, which executes a distance algorithm. If the results of the computation indicate that the object is closer to the car then a specified default value, that means a collision can occur. The result of this data is then sent to the primary controller. The primary controller, when receiving the data, acts accordingly to the situation at hand. In case of an imminent collision, it can carry out some emergency actions, such as stopping the engine, or applying emergency brakes; otherwise if the collision is not imminent, it can decrease the speed of the car and can apply normal brakes.

The CCAS has been exhaustively modeled using the MADES language in the open source Modelio UML Editor/MDE Workbench, as shown in Figure 6. We refer the reader to (Quadri et al., 2012b) for a detailed description related to the modeling of the CCAS.

In this chapter, we only focus on an extract of the CCAS and illustrate the associated modeling, verification, code generation, and implementation aspects.

Modeling of the CCAS Using the MADES Language

The CCAS design specifications start with SysML-based modeling, which involves the initial design decisions such as system requirements, behavioral specifications and functionality description. Using the SysML-inspired MADES Requirements Diagram, system requirements are described at the initial system conception phase, as illustrated in Figure 7. It should be mentioned that only the functional requirements of a system are described at this level. Afterwards, an initial behavioral specification phase is carried out, and in the particular case of CCAS, some

Figure 6. Open source Modelio UML editor/MDE workbench

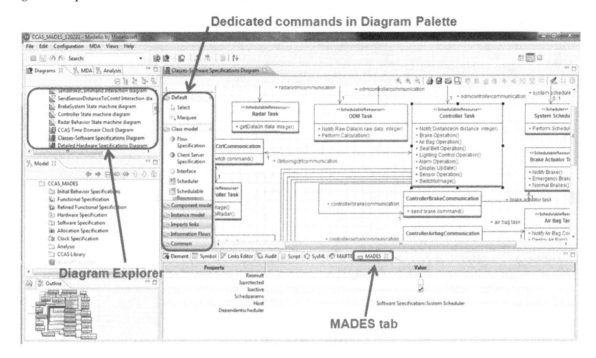

use cases are specified to describe the different system scenarios of the car containing the CCAS module. Subsequently, the designer describes the functional description of the CCAS system, using SysML-inspired Functional/Internal Functional Block diagrams. These behavioral and functional specifications are in turn used to complete the initial requirements, as shown in Figure 7. Here, the Car Collision Avoidance Module block and the Avoid Collisions use case help to complete the requirements.

Figure 8 illustrates several design phases, mainly the behavioral, functional and refined functional specifications and the mapping between them. The functional specification illustrates the whole architecture of the car, of which we are mainly interested in the Car Collision Avoidance Module of CCAS. A use case is mapped to this block to describe its behavior, and the block is then refined into an equivalent MARTE concept using the refined functional specification phase.

Afterwards, this refined MARTE component or the RH_Car Collision Avoidance Module is partitioned into hardware and software specifications using a Co-Design approach, as shown in parts (a) and (b) of Figure 9, each consisting of a large number of concepts. As viewed in Figure 7, the CCAS also has some strict timing constraints, an example of which is shown in Figure 10. For example, the timing constraint of Figure 10(a) states that the distance between the sending of message notifyDistance and the reception of message sendSensorDistance is exactly 2 time units (where a time unit in this case corresponds to 10ms), i.e., the transmission of the message through the CAN bus must take exactly 2 instants. In a similar way, the timing constraint of Figure 10(b) states that the duration of the depicted interaction (i.e., the distance between its termination and its beginning) must be exactly 2 time units. Both timing constraints are expressed using MARTE syntax.

From here on, we only focus on the image-tracking aspect of the CCAS, which determines the distance of the car from an object by means of image computation. The Image Processing Module and the Img Processing Task in parts (a) and (b) of

Figure 7. The global system requirements related to the CCAS

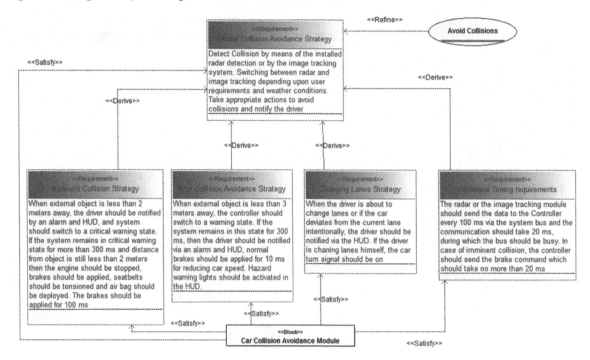

Figure 8. Extract of CCAS functional/refined functional specifications

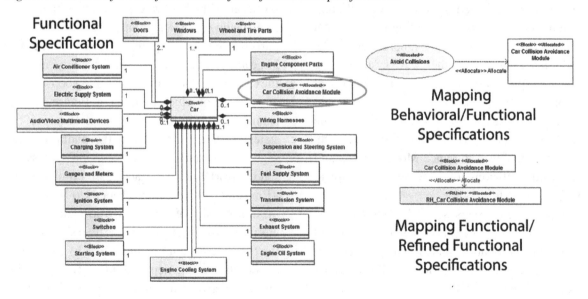

Figure 9, respectively, represent the generic hardware and software aspects of the image-tracking part of the CCAS, and are subsequently refined to detailed levels, corresponding to MADES detailed hardware and software specifications, shown in Figure 11 and part (a) of Figure 12, respectively.

Figure 11 depicts the refined structure of the Image Processing Module, consisting of three processors with distributed memory architecture, connected to a UART and a camera via PLB bus. The module also contains a system clock called clock of the type mainClk specified in the MADES

Figure 9. Extract of CCAS: (a) Hardware specification (b) Software specification

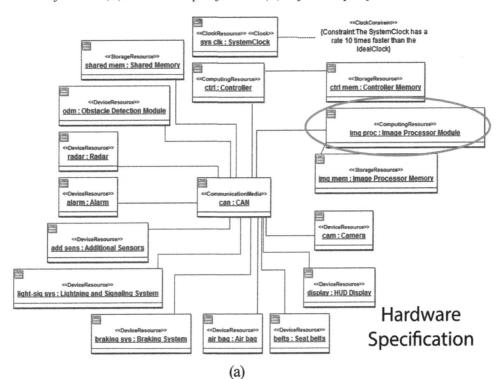

Hardware
Specification

(a)

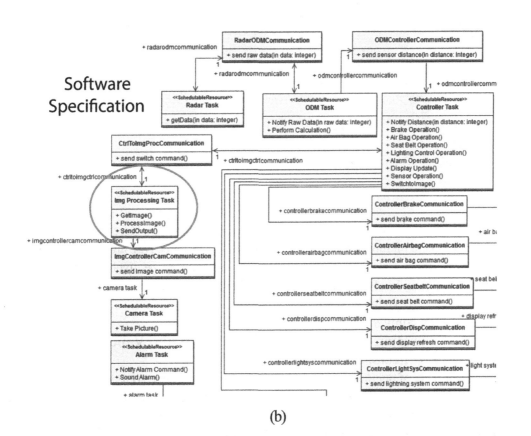

Software
Specification

(b)

Figure 10. Timing constraints in sequence diagrams

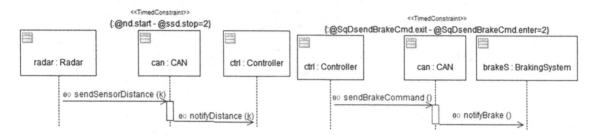

Figure 11. Detailed hardware specification of the image processing module

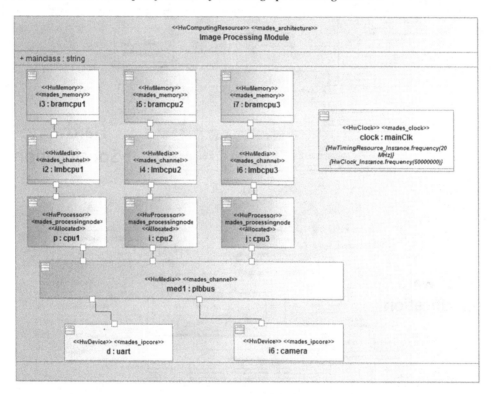

Clock Specification Diagram, but also shown here to represent a complete picture. The different classes/instances are annotated with MARTE concepts, but also with certain MADES concepts defined in (Bagnato et al., 2012) relative to verification and code generation. Similarly, part (a) of Figure 12 represents the refined internal structure of the Image Processing Task. It consists of several threads containing a number of operations, along with a shared object or mutex. Finally, part (b) of Figure 12 describes the allocation of the detailed software/hardware aspects related to the CCAS

image tracking part. Here, the readThread and dctThread instances are allocated to instances of cpu1 and cpu2, respectively, while the instances of quantizeThread and OutputStage are allocated to an instance of cpu3.

Verification and Validation

After creating the MADES diagrams describing the behavior of the components of the system and of their interactions, the user can use suitable forms to define what properties of interest are to

Figure 12. (a) Detailed software specification of the image processing task (b) Allocation of detailed software/hardware aspects

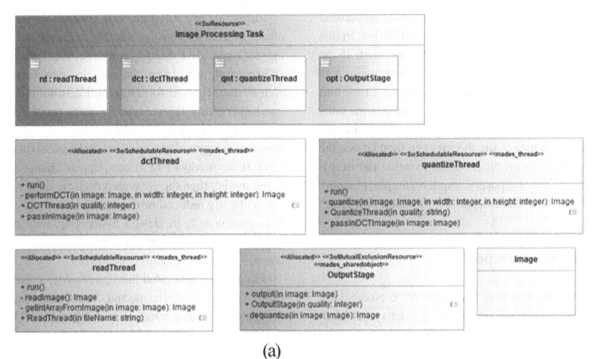

(a)

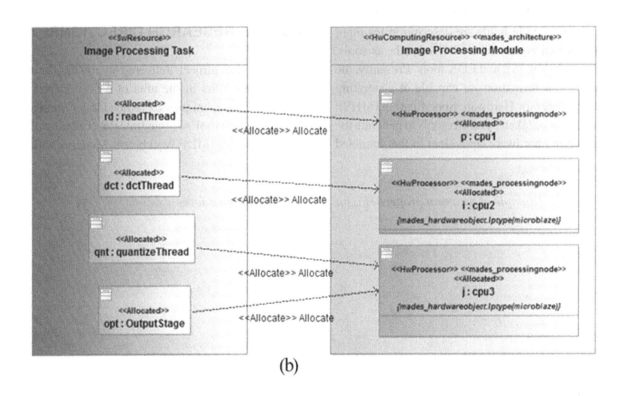

(b)

be checked on the model. For example, Figure 13 shows the dialog box of the MADES tool that allows the user to define properties to be verified and then to launch the actual verification. In this case, the property of interest states that, if the distance received by the controller remains less than 2 meters for 50 time units (where 1 time unit corresponds to 10ms), within those 50 time units the system must have started to brake. Using the MADES tool chain, the user can then launch the verification on the modeled system, and in this case the tool reports a counterexample, meaning the system does not satisfy the stated property.

Hardware and Software Code Generation

Once the modeling and verification phases have been completed, it is possible to carry out hardware/software code generation by means of the model transformations previously described in the chapter. The hardware related model transformations take the MADES allocation model of Figure 12, and generate hardware description for input to standard commercial FPGA synthesis tools, such as Xilinx ISE and EDK tools. Presently, the model transformation are capable of generating Microprocessor Hardware Specification (MHS), which can be taken by Xilinx tools to generate the underlying hardware equivalent to that modeled

using the MADES language, as seen in part (a) of Figure 14.

Regarding the software code generation, the model transformations are capable of transforming user-provided, hardware-independent code and rewriting it to target the modeled hardware architecture. The transformation builds a minimal-overhead runtime layer to implement the modeled system, as seen in part (b) of Figure 14; and translates the user-provided software to make use of this layer. If the hardware or allocations are changed in the model, then the generated runtime layer is automatically reduced or expanded accordingly. This greatly aids in Design Space Exploration (DSE) aspects. The details regarding these aspects can be found in (Bagnato et al., 2012).

Finally, the generated hardware/software are used to carry out synthesis, and then subsequent implementation is carried out on a Xilinx ML505 board containing a Virtex V series FPGA, as seen part (c) of Figure 14.

FUTURE RESEARCH DIRECTIONS

The MADES project delivered interesting and promising results in the area of Model Driven Engineering techniques for embedded systems. The MADES tool set integrates a commercial UML Editor and MDE Workbench, Modelio, with

Figure 13. Example of temporal properties input by the user through a form

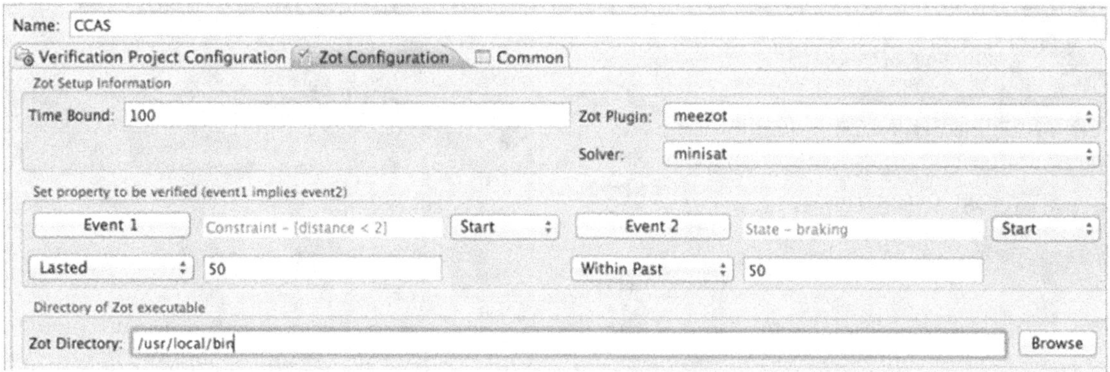

Figure 14. (a) MADES based hardware generation (b) Generating software code using Anvil J and CTV (c) Synthesis and implementation on a Virtex V FPGA

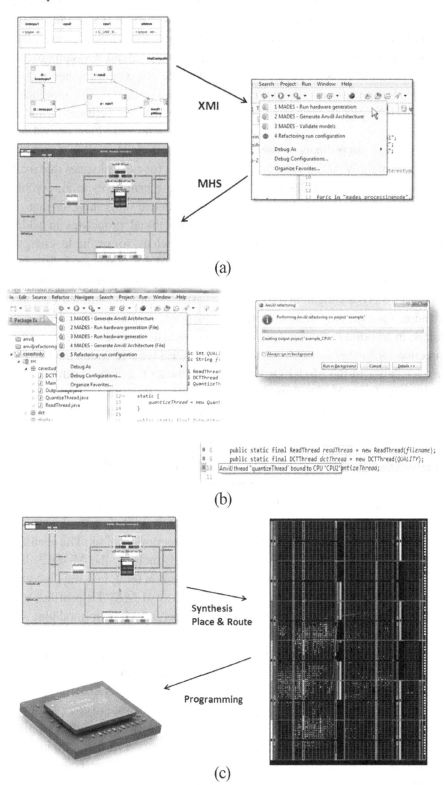

academic tools for formal verification and validation and for code manipulation and refactoring. It achieves this through a well-established model transformation platform that is available as plugin of the popular eclipse platform. MADES pursued a variety of lines of research in modeling, model transformation, formal verification and validation, code generation, which we plan to further extend in several ways.

Though avionics and surveillance systems were the target domain of the MADES project, its results can be applied to other domains, especially those where timing requirements are of paramount importance. This was already shown with the CCAS example earlier on in the chapter. In recent years, energy concerns have become more and more relevant, so, at the general level, we plan to extend the current MADES methodology to include also features for explicitly dealing with energy constraints, in addition to timing ones.

One key direction for further research relates to support for traceability in the Model-Driven Engineering workflow. From MADES models, analysis models and code can be generated, and trace-links are produced as a side-effect, particularly to support the reflection of counter-examples generated by analysis tools in the source models. A custom traceability editor was produced to assist in this process. This editor was useful for monitoring and managing trace-links between models produced by two tools, but more general support for multi-paradigm models (e.g., behavioral models, assurance models and performance analysis models) is needed. Thus, we are currently investigating ways of treating traceability as a multi-paradigm modeling problem, using MDE techniques to automate the production, querying and impact analysis of trace-links.

The Compile-Time Virtualization technique presented in this chapter was developed to target embedded architectures. Consequentially, it is primarily focused on applications that are largely static and known at compile time. An interesting area of research would be to extend this technique to add support for more dynamic systems, with correspondingly increasing overhead. For a fully-dynamic system CTV would offer no benefits over existing approaches. However, full dynamism is rarely required and so systems (or parts of systems) that are static would still benefit from the reduced overhead offered by the approach.

The MADES verification and validation tools can be improved along several directions. They can be extended to allow users to analyze richer models, for example ones that include additional modeling primitives (e.g., combined fragments of Sequence diagrams), or that deal with other nonfunctional properties in addition to timing ones such as, for example, energy consumption. The MADES V&V tools are currently capable of dealing with continuous variations of physical variables only in a limited way, through approximations; we plan to exploit some recent developments in the verification techniques underlying the MADES tools to widen the range of applications that the tools can deal with to include hybrid systems, i.e., those that mix discrete and continuous quantities, including time.

CONCLUSION

This chapter described the EU MADES FP7 project, its global methodology and the supporting integrated tool set. The results of the MADES project, include: the MADES language, which is based on (and, in a way, reconciles) the UML SysML and MARTE profiles; a plug-in for the commercial Modelio modeling workbench, that supports the aforementioned language; tools for the formal verification and validation of MADES models, that are based on a formal semantics of MADES diagrams; tools for automatically mapping software to complex architectures from an architecturally-neutral application. Model transformations are used to integrate the various tools in a consistent framework. The language and techniques defined during the project have been illustrated through a Car Collision Avoidance System (CCAS) case study. The results of the MADES project are a promising foundation for building innovative Model Driven Engineering techniques that can cover the whole lifecycle of the development of embedded systems, from early design to implementation across different platforms.

ACKNOWLEDGMENT

This research presented in this chapter is funded by the European Community's Seventh Framework Program (FP7/2007-2013) under grant agreement no. 248864 (MADES).

REFERENCES

Aicas Gmb, H. (2013). *JamaicaVM*. Retrieved from https://www.aicas.com/cms/en/JamaicaVM

Bagnato, A., et al. (2010). MADES: Embedded systems engineering approach in the avionics domain. In *Proceedings of First Workshop on Hands-on Platforms and tools for model-based engineering of Embedded Systems* (HoPES). HoPES.

Bagnato, A., et al. (2012). *D1.7: MADES Final Approach Guide*. Technical Report. Retrieved from http://www.mades-project.org/

Baresi, L., et al. (2010). *D3.1: Domain-specific and User-centred Verification*. Technical Report. Retrieved from http://www.mades-project.org/

Baresi, L., et al. (2011). *D3.2: Models and Methods for Systems Environment*. Technical Report. Retrieved from http://www.mades-project.org/

Baresi, L., et al. (2012a). *D3.3: Formal Dynamic Semantics of the Modeling Notation*. Technical Report. Retrieved from http://www.mades-project. org/

Baresi, L., et al. (2012b). A logic-based semantics for the verification of multi-diagram UML models. In *Proceedings of SIGSOFT Software Engineering Conference*. (pp. 1-8). ACM.

Baresi, L. et al. (2013). Formal verification and validation of embedded systems: The UML-based MADES approach. In *Proceedings of Software & Systems Modeling Conference*, (pp. 1-21). Academic Press.

Bersani, M. M., et al. (2010). Bounded reachability for temporal logic over constraint systems. In *Proceedings of the International Symposium on Temporal Representation and Reasoning* (TIME), (pp. 43-50). TIME.

Bersani, M. M., et al. (2013). A tool for deciding the satisfiability problem of continuous-time metric temporal logic. In *Proceedings of International Symposium on Temporal Representation and Reasoning* (TIME) (pp. 99-106). TIME.

Ciapessoni, E. et al. (1999). From formal models to formally-based methods: an industrial experience. *ACM Transactions on Software Engineering and Methodology*. doi:10.1145/295558.295566

CoWare Inc. (2013). *CoWare Virtual Platform - Hardware/Software integration and testing... without hardware*. Retrieved from http://www.coware.com/products/virtualplatform.php

eDIANA. (2011). *ARTEMIS project*. Retrieved from http://www.artemis-ediana.eu/

Espinoza, H., et al. (2009). Challenges in Combining SysML and MARTE for Model-Based Design of Embedded Systems. In *Proceedings of ECMDA-FA'09 Conference* (pp. 98–113). ECMDA-FA.

Faugere, M., et al. (2007). MARTE: Also an UML profile for modeling AADL applications. In *Proceedings of 12th IEEE International Conference on Engineering Complex Computer Systems*, (pp. 359–364). IEEE.

Ferrucci, L., et al. (2012). A Metric Temporal Logic for Dealing with Zero-Time Transitions. In *Proceedings of International Symposium on Temporal Representation and Reasoning* (TIME), (pp 81–88). TIME.

Gajski, D. D., & Khun, R. (1983). New VLSI Tools. IEEE Computer, 16, 11–14, 19.

Gray, I., et al. (2011). Model-based hardware generation and programming - the MADES approach. In *Proceedings of 14th International Symposium on Object and Component-Oriented Real-Time Distributed Computing Workshops*. Academic Press.

Gray, I., & Audsley, N. (2009). Exposing non-standard architectures to embedded software using compile-time virtualisation. In *Proceedings of International conference on Compilers, architecture, and synthesis for embedded systems* (CASES'09). CASES.

Gray, I., & Audsley, N. (2012). Developing Predictable Real-Time Embedded Systems Using AnvilJ. In *Proceedings of IEEE Real-Time and Embedded Technology and Applications Symposium*. IEEE Computer Society.

Information Society Technologies. (2009). *OMEGA: Correct Development of Real-Time Embedded Systems*. Retrieved from http://www-omega.imag.fr/

INTERESTED. (2011). *EU FP7 Project*. Retrieved from http://www.interested-ip.eu/index.html

Kolovos, D. S., et al. (2006). Eclipse development tools for Epsilon. In *Proceedings of Eclipse Summit Europe, Eclipse Modeling Symposium*. Academic Press.

Koudri, A., et al. (2008). Using MARTE in the MOPCOM SoC/SoPC Co-Methodology. In *Proceedings of MARTE Workshop at DATE'08*. Academic Press.

MADES. (2011). *EU FP7 Project*. Retrieved from http://www.mades-project.org/

Matragkas, N., et al. (2010). *D4.1: Model Transformation and Code Generation Tools Specification*. Technical Report. Retrieved from http://www.mades-project.org/

Modelica. (2012). *Modelica: An object-oriented equation based language*. Retrieved from https://modelica.org/

Modelio. (2014). *Open source UML Editor and MDE Workbench*. Retrieved from www.modelio.org

Mueller, W., et al. (2010). The SATURN Approach to SysML-based HW/SW Codesign. In *Proceedings of IEEE Computer Society Annual Symposium on VLSI* (ISVLSI). IEEE.

Mura, M., et al. (2008). Model-based Design Space Exploration for RTES with SysML and MARTE. In *Proceedings of Forum on Specification, Verification and Design Languages* (FDL 2008), (pp. 203–208). FDL.

Ober, L., et al. (2005). *Projet Omega: Un profil UML et un outil pour la modelisation et la validation de systemes temps reel*. Academic Press.

OMG. (2007). *Portal of the Model Driven Engineering Community*. Retrieved from http://www.planetmde.org

OMG. (2011). *Modeling and Analysis of Real-time and Embedded systems (MARTE)*. Retrieved from http://www.omg.org/spec/MARTE/1.1/PDF

OMG. (2012). *Final Adopted OMG SysML Specification*. Retrieved from http://www.omg.org/spec/SysML/1.3/

OpenModelica. (2012). *Open-source Modelica-based modeling and simulation environment*. Retrieved from http://www.openmodelica.org/

Pradella, M., et al. (2013). Bounded satisfiability checking of metric temporal logic specifications. ACM Transactions on Software Engineering and Methodology, 22(3).

Quadri, I. R., et al. (2012). *D1.6: MADES Tool Set - Final Version*. Technical Report. Retrieved from http://www.mades-project.org/

Quadri, I. R., et al. (2012). MADES: A SysML/-MARTE high level methodology for real-time and embedded systems. In *Proceedings of International Conference on Embedded Real Time Software and Systems* (ERTS2 2012). ERTS2.

Sendall, S., & Kozaczynski, W. (2003). Model Transformation: The Heart and Soul of Model-Driven Software Development. *IEEE Software, 20*(5), 42–45. doi:10.1109/MS.2003.1231150

TOPCASED. (2012). *The Open Source Toolkit for Critical Systems*. Retrieved from http://www.topcased.org/

Xilinx. (2014). *Virtex Series FPGAs*. Retrieved from http://www.xilinx.com/products/silicon-devices/fpga

Zot. (2012). *The Zot bounded model/satisfiability checker*. Retrieved from http://zot.googlecode.com

KEY TERMS AND DEFINITIONS

Model Driven Architecture: Model Driven Architecture or MDA is a software development methodology defined by the Object Management Group (OMG) in 2011. This latter starts with a very high level and independent model called CIM (for Computation Independent Model) which will be transformed in order to target instances of specific system from a specific machine, programming language, operating system, or other implementation technology. A developer designs at the Computation Independent Model (CIM) level which is then transformed to a platform-independent model (PIM) level which is then transformed to a platform-specific model (PSM). Designing at a platform independent level enables reuse of software system designs on many platforms.

Model Driven Development: Model Driven Development or MDD is the general term for MDA whether or not UML is used for modeling purpose.

Modeling and Analysis of Real Time and Embedded Systems Profile: Modeling and Analysis of Real Time and Embedded systems profile or MARTE profile in short is the OMG standard for modeling real-time and embedded applications with UML2. Currently, only two open-source tools are available for system modeling using the UML2 standard and MARTE profile: Modelio which provides an open source modeling environment for designing high level UML2 models extendable with its implementation of the MARTE profile specification, and also provides guidelines on the utilization of MARTE concepts; while an open-source implementation based on the EMF implementation of the MARTE profile is available with Papyrus.

OMG: OMG or Object Modeling Group is a standardization organization providing several standard specifications as UML for example.

Platform: Platform as defined in the MDA process is a particular environment that influences a concrete product: machine, operating system, component platform, or domain ontology.

SysML: The OMG systems Modeling Language (OMG SysML™) is a general-purpose graphical modeling language for specifying, analyzing, designing complex systems. In particular, the language provides graphical representations with a semantic foundation for modeling system requirements, behavior, structure, and equations, which is used to integrate with other engineering analysis models.

TOG: TOG or The Open Group is a nonprofit standards organization defining several IT standards as TOGAF for example.

UML: UML or Unified Modeling Language is a means of modeling object-oriented systems. The UML is standardized by the OMG.

UML Profile for Schedulability, Performance, and Time Specification: UML Profile for Schedulability, Performance, and Time Specification is OMG's profile for UML which influenced the definition of the OMG MARTE UML profile.

UML Profiles: UML profiles are a means of extending UML models with a vocabulary for a specific domain available as stereotypes and properties. Stereotypes can be defined in order to extend UML model elements, such as classes, associations, and attributes. They are used to give the ability to structure and categorize models and systems during different stages of the development process. The properties are used to set attributes with a specific value to each single element of the model extended by a given stereotype.

XMI: eXchange Model Interface is an XML format for exchanging metadata information like UML models.

ENDNOTES

[1] TRIO axioms are implicitly asserted for all time instants, hence formula (1) is implicitly interpreted as "$Alw(Lasted(\neg cTick, T\text{-}1) \leftrightarrow cTick)$", where $Alw(F)$ means that formula F always holds, i.e., in all instants.

[2] www.eclipse.org

Chapter 9
Requirements Refinement and Component Reuse:
The FoReVer Contract–Based Approach

Laura Baracchi
Intecs, Italy

Silvia Mazzini
Intecs, Italy

Alessandro Cimatti
FBK-Irst, Italy

Stefano Puri
Intecs, Italy

Gerald Garcia
Thales Alenia Space, France

Stefano Tonetta
FBK-Irst, Italy

ABSTRACT

The development of complex computer-based systems poses two fundamental challenges. On one side, the architectural decomposition must be complemented by a suitable refinement of the requirements. On the other side, it is fundamental to provide the means for component reuse in order to limit development costs. In this chapter, the authors discuss the approach taken in FoReVeR, a project funded by the European Space Agency (ESA), where these two issues are tackled in the setting of space systems. The approach taken in FoReVeR is based on the idea of contracts, which allow one to formally specify the requirements of components at different levels of abstraction and to formally prove the correctness of requirements decomposition. In particular, the authors show how system-level requirements can be progressively refined into software requirements and how the contract-based framework supports the reuse of the components of a reference architecture under development by ESA. The authors discuss how the proposed solution has been integrated in a space development process and present the results of case studies.

INTRODUCTION

The top-down design of complex critical system poses two fundamental challenges. The first one is the refinement of requirements, along with the progressive decomposition of the system architecture. In general, the quality and the traceability of requirements are fundamental for the whole design. Flaws in the requirements are in fact recognized as a major source of problems

DOI: 10.4018/978-1-4666-6194-3.ch009

in the development, and may require major revisions in the advanced phases of the development cycle (Lutz, 1993). The second challenge is to enable for a correct reuse of (previously certified) components, which can lead to huge savings in development and certification costs. Unfortunately, the composition of correct components does not necessarily result in a correct system.

In this chapter we report how these issues have been addressed, in the context of space systems, within the FoReVeR project (see https://es.fbk.eu/projects/forever/). FoReVer (Functional Requirements and Verification Techniques for the Software Reference Architecture) is a European Space Agency (ESA) study conducted by a consortium led by Intecs with partners Thales Alenia Space France (TAS-F) and Fondazione Bruno Kessler (FBK).

The goal of the FoReVer project was to define an integrated methodology to introduce the formal verification of system properties from the early stages of the development process. The methodology had to be complemented by supporting toolset, to rely on a model-based approach, to allow the designers to check the correctness of model refinements, and to enable full traceability of design choices along the whole development process. Moreover, the study had to cover the refinement of the avionics system-level properties down to the software level, in order to enable the reuse of software components implemented in the On-Board Software Reference Architecture (OBSW-RA). The OBSW-RA is a reference architecture defined by the SAVOIR-FAIRE working group, as part of a large ESA initiative on Space AVionics Open Interface aRchitecture (SAVOIR), and was recently consolidated by several studies, the most recent of which is the ESA TRP COrDeT2 project (see http://cordet.gmv.com/).

The FoReVer methodology builds upon the Model-Based Space System Engineering process (MBSSE) derived in the System and Software Functional Requirement Techniques study (SS-FRT) ESA study (Mazzini, Puri, Olive, Burte,

Paccagnini, & Tronci, 2009). MBSSE is focused on the application of model-based engineering technologies based on SysML to support the space system and software development processes, from mission level requirements to software implementation through model refinements and translations.

FoReVer enriches the MBSSE process with the introduction of contract-based formal verification of properties, at different stages from system to software level, through a step-wise refinement of components. The contract-based approach allows to combine the top-down process of MBSSE with the reuse of OBSW-RA components, which represent a bottom-up driver in the process to ensure convergence to a solution compatible with the OBSW-RA.

In FoReVer, contract-based reasoning relies on the formalism proposed in (Cimatti & Tonetta, 2012), where contracts are specified in a language that is natural and expressive to formalize requirements of embedded systems (Cimatti, Roveri, Susi, & Tonetta, 2012). The underlying temporal-logic formulas (Cimatti, Roveri, & Tonetta, 2009) represent assertions on the possible interaction of each component with its environment. Tool support for contract reasoning (e.g. checking the correctness of refimenents) is based on OCRA (Cimatti, Dorigatti, & Tonetta, 2013), a tool for the verification of logic-based contract refinement for embedded systems, able to prove the correctness of contract refinements by reduction to a set of entailments in temporal logic. The reasoning engines used for verification of logic-based contracts refinement are provided by NuSMV3 (https://es.fbk.eu/tools/nusmv3/), an extended version of the NuSMV symbolic model checker.

In order to support a model-driven component-based methodology, the tools support in FoReVer is based on an enhanced version of CHESS (Mazzini, Puri, Veran, Vardanega, Panunzio, Santamaria, & Zovi, 2011). The CHESS component model is fully compatible with the Space Component Model adopted by the OBSW-RA. With FoReVer, CHESS extended its concerns from concentrating only on the Software level to embracing also the System level design phase and SysML models. Integrated with OCRA, CHESS combines the support to component-based modeling and model-based traceability with the contract-based specification and refinement verification.

The FoReVer methodology was experimented with two use cases. The first one, lead by FBK, was based on the analysis of the Eagle Eye reference mission. The second one, lead by TAS-F, was based on the Thales Alenia Space Global Star2 mission. These case studies provided validation of the approach and positive feedback as well as useful hints and challenging guidelines for future work.

This chapter is structured as follows. First, we give account of the background for the project: model-based engineering in the space domain; component-based software engineering; the ESA OBSW-RA initiative; and contracts for system design. In the following section, we review the challenges posed by the project, present the proposed solutions, and discuss the tool chain and the case studies. Then, we present some directions for future work, and draw some conclusions.

BACKGROUND

Model-Based System Engineering in the Space Domain

The ECSS Process

Many engineering disciplines are involved in the space development, including electronics (power generation, avionics, microwave, etc.), mechanics (structural, thermal, material, etc.), software, communication, control, production and operation. Space system engineering is the overall process that integrates all the engineering disciplines in the effort to define, develop, integrate and maintain the whole system product.

ECSS (European Cooperation for Space Standardization) is a set of standards, developed as a cooperative effort between the European space agencies and space industries to provide a common and unambiguous framework to be applied for the management, engineering and product assurance in space projects and applications.

The ECSS M-10 Project Planning and Implementation (ECSS-M-ST-10C, 2009) defines the following phases of a space project lifecycle:

- **Phase 0:** Mission analysis/needs identification.
- **Phase A:** Feasibility.
- **Phase B:** Preliminary Definition.
- **Phase C:** Detailed Definition.
- **Phase D:** Qualification and Production.
- **Phase E:** Utilization.
- **Phase F:** Disposal.

Phase A is a feasibility phase which results in finalizing the expression of needs identified in phase 0 and proposing solutions to meet the perceived needs.

Phase B is a preliminary definition phase which results in the system technical specification and the demonstration that the selected solution meets the technical requirements. The following phases – C, D and E, are more and more detailed definition, implementation and exploitation phases.

It is important to notice that the system engineering process of a spacecraft is done step by step, by going deeper and deeper into detail at each step.

In terms of responsibility and process: phase 0 is mainly an activity conducted by the project prime, the top level customer and representatives of the end users. The outputs of this process consist of formally documented and approved mission requirements that will govern the project, including required system capabilities, functions and/ or services, quality standards, cost and schedule constraints, concept of operations and concept of support. Phase A is mainly conducted by the top level customer and one or several first level suppliers with the outcome being reported to the project initiator and representatives of the end users for consideration. This phase allows to obtain a function tree representing the system. A function tree is a method for functional decomposition and concept generation. Requirements can be attached to these functions. In terms of modeling, a first trade off could be done at this phase. Typically at the end of Phase A the logical architecture is defined with allocation of functionalities to be refined/detailed in Phase B. During phase B the Functional Analysis, i.e. the functions tree, defined in Phase A are further developed/refined, the Logical System Architecture initially defined in Phase A is further developed/refined, trade-offs are conducted for allocation of functions and related behavior to the Logical Architecture, and the Physical Architecture is finally defined, including the final hardware selection.

The MBSSE Methodology

The use of modeling techniques at the different stages of the development process is of crucial importance in order to successfully define the space systems. Model-based system engineering is the application of modeling to support system engineering activities starting from the initial development phases and continuing in manufacturing, operation and maintenance until the demission of the system. It aims at providing a common core modeling language and an integrated methodological framework for system engineering to provide consistency, integration and control over the engineering (and the related modeling) of the different involved disciplines, possibly adopting an adequate level of abstraction in modeling.

The Model-Based Space System Engineering (MBSSE) methodology, defined as a result of the SSFRT (System and Software Functional Requirements Techniques) ESA/ESTEC study (Mazzini et al., 2009), represents an application of model-based engineering technologies to support the

space system and software development processes, from the initial definition of mission needs to the elaboration of a feasible system definition through model refinements and translations. It is strongly related to the ECSS process and was conceived with reference to the technical processes and the principles defined in the ISO/IEC 15288 (ISO/IEC 15288, 2008), the major system engineering standard providing a common process framework that can be applied as a reference for any domain to cover the life cycle of man-made systems, and to the INCOSE Systems Engineering Handbook (Haskins, 2011), that provides a large guideline for system engineering with the application of the ISO/IEC 15288.

As several engineering areas and disciplines are involved in the ECSS development processes, SysML was identified as an expressive, yet simple and adaptable, modeling language, that may cover system engineering processes, from high–level requirements to architecture and verification, spanning over different domains.

The MBSSE methodology is based on a model-centric definition of the system using SysML which acts as a unifying modeling language to describe space systems and is easily related to UML, or any UML profile language, for the engineering of software components.

A SysML/UML generic profile for MBSSE was defined as a domain specific language that takes into account the modeling practices currently adopted in the space domain, as well as the ECSS standards. This profile is generic for the space domain and was conceived to be tailored on a project or industrial practice basis. Other complementary and domain specific modeling languages may be integrated in the MBSSE methodology according to a model-based engineering approach.

The MBSSE methodology, synthetized in Figure 1, was tailored on top of the three initial phases of a space project life cycle as defined in (ECSS-M-ST-10C, 2009) and describes the activities to be carried out during the project phases 0, A and B and their interrelation.

Figure 1. Overview of the MBSSE methodology

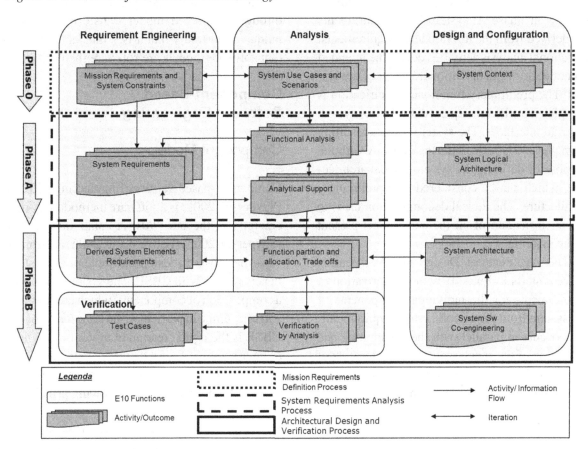

The MBSSE activities belong to the complementary engineering areas of Requirement Engineering, Analysis, Design and Configuration, and Verification: the different activities are strongly interrelated, providing feedback to each other and implementing an incremental overall process.

As showed in Figure 1, three main System Engineering Processes, derived from the technical processes defined in the ISO/IEC 15288, are identified in the MBSSE methodology:

- The *Mission Requirements Definition Process*, carried out during phase 0,
- The *System Requirements Analysis Process*, carried out during phase A, and
- The *Architectural Design and Verification Process* carried out during phase B.

According to MBSSE, during the Mission Requirements Definition Process that is activated in Phase 0, mission-level activities begin with mission requirements elaboration whereby use cases and scenarios support the elicitation of requirements. As soon as a base set of requirements is available to characterize the mission, the system context is defined. This context makes it possible to refine and better position the use cases and scenarios and to consolidate the mission level requirements. At mission level, requirements can be expressed by text (or SysML requirements), detailed by some diagrams (e.g. activity diagrams or use cases in SysML) which are used to document the operational scenarios. These requirements and scenarios contain most of the elements and actors of the system to design. No software requirements are considered yet at mission level.

With the System Requirements Analysis Process in Phase A, system level requirements are derived from the mission level requirements. Functional analysis activities define the intended functionalities and operational aspects of the system. The preliminary functional specification is completed by the subsequent definition of system external interfaces. The system context resulting from phase 0 is refined during Phase A with the purpose of defining the system logical architecture, which can be considered as a preliminary architecture. The logical decomposition leads to the identification of all the subsystems present in the system.

The Architectural Design and Verification Process starts in Phase B with the derivation of requirements for the individual components of the system from the overall system requirements. This occurs in parallel with the partitioning and allocation of the functionality to the elements of the logical architecture and the identification/consolidation of the architecture.

Model Driven Engineering

When dealing with software systems, the principle of model-based engineering can be extended in a very interesting way by exploiting the fact that the model and the "real thing" are both software artifacts, leading to the concept of "Model-Driven Engineering" (MDE) (Schmidt, 2006) (France & Rumpe, 2007) briefly illustrated hereafter.

In the quest for increased quality and productivity, Model Driven Engineering promotes:

1. The use of models at various levels of abstraction as a vehicle for system specification, in the place of source code artifacts and informal diagrams that do not qualify as models;
2. The use of automated transformations to progressively turn the user model into a software product ready for final compilation, binding and deployment.

The possibility to generate a software product through automated model transformation is a unique opportunity that arises thanks to the fact that software models are software themselves.

Component-Based Software Engineering

Component Models

Component-based Software Engineering (CBSE) (Szyperski, 2003) is a software methodology that emerged in the late '90s. A *component model* (Szyperski, 2003) (Lau & Wang, 2005) is a framework that is used to design and implement a system in accordance with CBSE. The system is built as a composition of components, which are reusable software units. In particular, the long-term goal of CBSE is the rapid creation of systems, designed as an assembly of reused components.

Two important concepts that are applicable in the CBSE approach are the following principles:

*   The principle of *composability*, that requires that properties of components are retained after the component is assembled with other components and deployed to the target system.
*   The principle of *compositionality*, instead, that requires that it is possible to derive the properties of the overall system by applying some system-specific function to the properties of the components the system is comprised of a Component Model Suitable for the Space Domain

ESA initiated in 2008 a joint initiative between space agencies and software prime contractors in order to establish a Space AVionics Open Interface aRchitecture (SAVOIR). As part of this initiative a specific subgroup on avionics and on-board software reference architectures, called SAVOIR Fair Architecture and Interface Reference Elaboration (SAVOIR-FAIRE), was established.

A particular component model, suited for the development of on-board software, was envisaged as a first result of the SAVOIR-FAIRE initiative of the European Space Agency and described by Marco Panunzio and Tullio Vardanega in (Panunzio, M. & Vardanega, T., 2010).

This component model, referred to in SAVOIR-FAIRE as the Space Component Model (SCM), explicitly separates functional from non-functional (real time and dependability) aspects of a system.

We can recognize three different entities that are essential elements of the SCM: *components*, *connectors* and c*ontainers*.

Components are reusable software units that encapsulate a distinct functional part of the system. Components can be accessed only through their exposed *interface*, which comprises: (i) a set of *provided services*, which are the services offered to the system, and (ii) a set of *required services*, which are the services that the component requires from other components or from the environment in order to discharge its own obligations towards its service users. The fundamental role of the *container* is to decouple the *functional concerns* of the component, from the *extra-functional concerns* that the realization of the component is required to exhibit at run time.

In particular, the container layer is in charge of the realization of tasking, timing behavior, fault containment and fault tolerance, security, configuration management, interface the components with the system in general and the execution platform in particular.

The connection or binding between two distinct components entails a notion of interaction between the two parties that is explicitly modeled as a *connector* (Bálek & Plasil, 2001). The use of an explicit notion of connector clearly separates the functional/computational part of the problem (which resides in the component) from the interaction part of the problem (Mehta, Medvidovic & Phadke, 2000), thus easing the reuse of the former independently of the latter.

Figure 2. Components, containers and connectors

CHESS

A specific support to CBSE comes from the CHESS (Composition with Guarantees for High-integrity Embedded Software Components Assembly) ARTEMIS JU Call 2008 project, aimed at developing solutions to property-preserving component assembly in real-time and dependable embedded systems.

The CHESS project promoted the adoption of Component-based Development and Model Driven Engineering for the development of High Integrity Systems (Mazzini et al., 2011), supporting the description, verification, and preservation of non-functional properties of software components at the abstract level of component design as well as at the execution level.

The CHESS Component Model is based on the same principles and provides a methodology and tool support for the realization of the SCM adopted for the Space Domain. Components are modeled in a dedicated view, in which the designer describes only the functional aspects. A distinct design view allows annotating the component with its desired non-functional attributes. Non-functional properties are analyzed and verified for individual components in isolation and are retained once the component is assembled with other components, and deployed to the target system. In this way the system can be built as an assembly of components, as usual, but where both functional and non-functional concerns are taken into consideration at design time.

The specification of non-functional attributes of components (for instance the real-time activation pattern of a given provided operation) is used in CHESS for the automated generation of the container of a component.

The CHESS component model specification, as defined at user level in terms of functional behavior and non-functional property specification, is therefore completely platform-independent (hence it represents a Platform Independent Model or PIM). However, the definition of containers and connectors is platform- and computational model-specific (it resides in the Platform Specific Model or PSM).

Operationally it is the CHESS tool-chain that guarantees the implementation of the correct by construction paradigm (Hall and Chapman (2002)) by supporting:

- Analysis and verification of non-functional properties (e.g. upon the target computational model);
- Propagation of the results back to the model;
- Consistent and property-preserving automated generation of code and deployment on the target execution platform.

Figure 3 illustrates the CHESS concept and process.

Here property preservation means that the non-functional properties statically assumed in the PIM and PSM models, and verified by the analysis, are preserved in the generated code and monitored at run-time. The monitoring at run-time allows the notification of any events that violate the guarantees proved at model level and their treatment in accordance with the applicable system level policies.

The consistency of the implementation is bound to the following principles:

- Semantic constraints of the specific computational model supported by the target platform;
- Adoption of a specific programming model;
- Specific run-time services offered by the execution platform.

Figure 3. The CHESS methodological approach

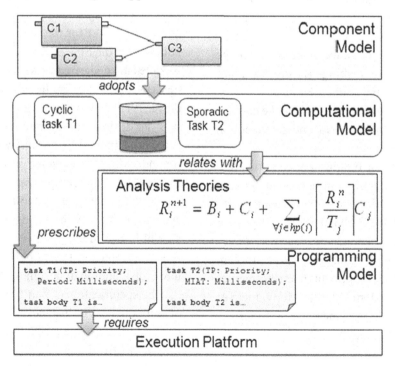

On-Board Software Reference Architecture

The OBSW-RA (also called COrDeT reference architecture) is a reference architecture for both avionics and on-board software that aims at solving the "faster, sooner, softer" challenge as described in [FSW2010]: critical and real-time software is exposed to the same challenges as traditional software, i.e. deliver it faster (shortening of development cycle), deliver intermediate versions (several increments of the software very early for reducing global system planning) and missions are more and more demanding on the software (autonomy, fault tolerance, image processing, …). The reference architecture is providing a set of architectural patterns and design solutions that are shared across European space industry and enable better reuse and interoperability of building blocks, shorter product life cycles. This effort is very similar to the AUTOSAR initiative in the automotive domain.

The reference architecture is based on the space component model presented in previous sections. Adopting this component model enforces the separation between an execution platform presenting a set of horizontal services and a set of interconnected components living on top of this execution platform.

This reference architecture describes also the representation of a certain number of domain oriented services in the component model. For example, many of the services used for building the failure detection, isolation and recovery (FDIR) function are defined as a set of components (called *pseudo-components*) that are then supported by dedicated services of the execution platform.

The component model and the related tooled-up process are being developed in the frame of ESA studies. Being the central repository for the software system design this component model will enable analysis, code generation, and test generation. These generative techniques will be applied during the development process and the phase of manual coding will be mostly reduced

to the functional part of the components: the communication between components (all the ground to space communication handling), the signalling of events and the real-time architecture will be deduced from the model and generated automatically.

To illustrate the concept of the reference architecture, one of the most stringent examples is the handling of parameter monitoring on-board and the reaction to violation of monitoring bounds. They are described by particular components (called pseudo components as they do not exist at run-time) having predefined patterns and constraints. For example the monitoring component will be a component requiring a port with an attribute to be monitored, configured by the type of monitoring (limits, delta between two acquisitions, …) and the associated bounds and finally an event to be raised once the thresholds are violated in order to eventually start the execution of a recovery sequence. The execution platform will be in charge of implementing the monitoring described by all the monitoring pseudo components at runtime. One traditional implementation is to use a standard PUS (packet utilisation service standard) service 12, which is providing such monitoring capabilities (see ECSS E-70 Telemetry and Telecommand Packet Utilization (ECSS-E-70-41A, 2003)).

The reference architecture is still an on-going effort of the European space software community and will be enhanced by many other patterns in the coming months and years. These patterns will be of great help for providing proved and homogeneous behaviour across different execution platforms in the space domain.

Contract-Based Design

Contracts and Components

Contract-Based Design (CBD) is an approach to the design of software systems that prescribes a formal specification of the interfaces of the system components in order to allow a compositional verification of the system and a correct reuse of components. CBD has been first conceived by Bertrand Meyer (Meyer, 1992) for object-oriented programming and is now applied also to embedded systems (cfr., e.g., (Benveniste, Caillaud, Ferrari, Mangeruca, Passerone, & Sofronis, 2007) and (Bauer, David, Hennicker, Larsen, Legay, Nyman, & Wasowski, 2012)). Contract-based design provides an ideal paradigm for a correct design of a system architecture, with a clear description of the expected interaction of each component with its environment. This enables compositional reasoning, independent refinement and a proper reuse of components.

The *interface* of a component S can be formally described by a set V_S of ports divided into input ports I_S and output ports O_S (i.e., $V_S = I_S \cup O_S$). The ports define the events E_S and data variables D_S with which the component interacts with its environment. We have therefore the following four sets of ports: input events $IE_S = I_S \cap E_S$, output events $OE_S = O_S \cap E_S$, input data $IO_S = I_S \cap D_S$, and output data $OD_S = O_S \cap D_S$.

When the component is seen as a black box, the interaction with the environment is described by a trace that shows a sequence of events in E_S and evaluation of the data variables D_S.

In formal terms, a trace is a sequence of events and assignments to the data variables. Traces may take into account also the time when events occur and the possible continuous evolution of the data variables between two events. In this case, we speak of hybrid traces (since they alternate discrete events with continuous evolution of data). Figure 4 shows an example of hybrid trace over three data variables ("temperature", "limit", and "warning") and an event ("alarm"). The temperature evolves continuously in time; the limit is constant; warning is a Boolean variable that is set to true when there is the alarm event, which happens after the temperature violated the limit (with a certain delay).

When we look into the internals of a component, we distinguish between *composite components*, which are decomposed into a set of interacting components, and *basic components*, which do not have subcomponents. The subcomponents of a composite component interact through *connections* and the ports of the parent component are *delegated* to the port of the children. Figure 5 shows an example of a composite component with two subcomponents, a sensor and an FDIR.

When instantiated into a system description, a component is given an implementation and an

Figure 4. Trace example

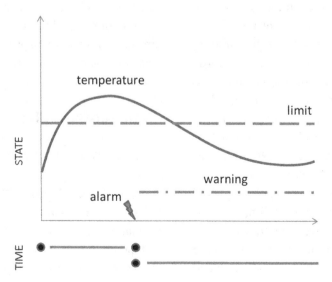

Figure 5. Components interaction in CHESS

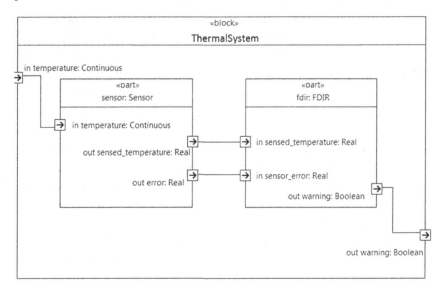

environment. These are set of traces over the ports of the component interface.

The implementation of a basic component is described by a behavioral model. Instead, the implementation of a composite component is given by the composition of the implementations of the subcomponents.

Similarly, the environment of the system is defined by a behavioral model, while the environment of a subcomponent is given by the composition of the environment of the parent component and the implementation of the sibling components.

Properties, Contracts, and Contracts Refinement

The properties of a component are structured into contracts, i.e. pairs of assumptions and guarantees. The assumptions are properties that the component environment should satisfy, while the guarantees are properties that the component implementation should satisfy when the assumptions hold. More formally, a component implementation Imp satisfies a contract $\langle A, G \rangle$ (denoted as $Imp \vDash \langle A, G \rangle$) if and only if the traces of the implementation restricted to the assumption are

included in the guarantee, i.e. $Imp \cap A \subseteq G$; a component environment Env satisfies a contract $\langle A, G \rangle$ if and only if it satisfies the assumption, i.e., $Env \subseteq A$. Finally, the semantics of a contract is given by all the implementations and all the environments that satisfy the contract.

If the component is constituted by sub-components, the correctness of the decomposition can be verified compositionally by exploiting the contract specification and the notion of *contract refinement*. A contract refinement links a contract $\langle A, G \rangle$ of a composite component S to the contracts of its subcomponents. The contract refinement of A, G is correct if and only if the following conditions hold:

1. If the implementations of the subcomponents satisfy their contracts, the composite implementation of S (i.e., their composition) satisfies the contract $\langle A, G \rangle$;

2. If the environment satisfies $\langle A, G \rangle$ and the implementations of the subcomponents satisfy their contracts, then the composite environment of each subcomponent satisfies its contracts.

Figure 6 shows the contracts attached to the components of Figure 5: the contract of the system is refined in the contracts of the subcomponents. The language used in the contracts is the one supported by OCRA (see the following section).

OCRA

OCRA (Othello Contract Refinement Analysis) is a command-line tool that allows to verify the correct refinement of contracts specified in a temporal logic, as first proposed in (Cimatti & Tonetta, 2012) and described in (Cimatti et al., 2013). It allows to define a component-based system architecture where every component is enriched with contracts. Assumptions and guarantees of contracts are specified in

Othello (Cimatti et al., 2012), a property specification language that allows to express discrete as well as real-time constraints. OCRA automatically checks if the refinement of contracts is correct. Checking the correctness of contracts refinement

is supported by generating a set of sufficient and necessary conditions. These proof obligations are temporal logic formulas obtained from assumptions and guarantees, so that they are valid if and only if the contracts refinement is correct.

A distinguishing feature of the tool is its high degree of expressiveness: the underlying temporal logic, HRELTL (Cimatti et al., 2009), is a variant of LTL (Pnueli, 1977) where formulas represent sets of hybrid traces, mixing discrete- and continuous-time steps, and is therefore amenable to model properties of timed and hybrid systems. When restricted to the propositional fragment, the proof obligations can be proved valid using BDD- or SAT-based model checking techniques for LTL. In the general case of HRELTL, reasoning relies on Satisfiability Modulo Theory (SMT, see (Barrett, Sebastiani, Seshia, & Tinelli, 2009)). Since logical entailment for HRELTL is undecidable, bounded model checking techniques are used to find counterexamples to the contract refinement (Cimatti et al., 2009), (Cimatti & Tonetta, 2012).

Figure 6. Components decomposition and contract refinement in CHESS

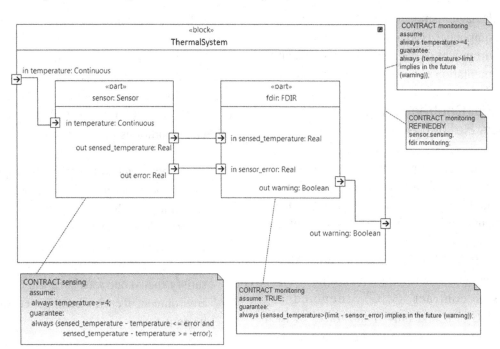

OCRA has been developed within the European project SafeCer, focusing on the compositional certification of embedded systems. The tool is publicly available (see https://es.fbk.eu/tools/ocra/).

The ultimate goal of the tool is to provide support to:

- **Composition Verification:** The system (or any component) satisfies its contracts if the refinement is correct and the subcomponents satisfy their own contracts; the method is compositional because the refinement checking is performed independently from the implementation of the subcomponents.
- **Reuse of Components:** If the refinement is correct, any implementation of the components can be used provided it satisfies the related component contracts; the method allows to reuse an already verified component implementation provided that the verified contracts match the ones in the new architecture.

The input language of OCRA is a textual description of the component interfaces, their contracts and refinement. For example, the above example on the monitoring of the temperature is described as in Figure 7.

CONTRACT-BASED REQUIREMENTS REFINEMENT AND COMPONENT REUSE

Domain Problems

From System Requirements to Software Requirements

One of the major problems in the application of formal verification to real complex systems in domains like space is that it is difficult to have some techniques that harmonize the modeling and verification of requirements along the different

Figure 7. OCRA example

```
COMPONENT ThermalSystem

INTERFACE
INPUT PORT temperature: continuous;
OUTPUT PORT warning: boolean;
PARAMETER limit: real;

CONTRACT monitoring
  assume:
  always temperature>=4;
  guarantee:
  always (temperature>limit implies in the future (warning));

REFINEMENT
SUB fdir: FDIR;
SUB sensor: Sensor;

CONNECTION sensor.temperature := temperature;
CONNECTION warning := fdir.warning;
CONNECTION fdir.limit := limit;
CONNECTION fdir.sensor_error := sensor.error;
CONNECTION fdir.sensed_temperature := sensor.sensed_temperature;

CONTRACT monitoring REFINEDBY sensor.sensing, fdir.monitoring;

COMPONENT Sensor

INTERFACE
INPUT PORT temperature: continuous;
OUTPUT PORT sensed_temperature: real;
OUTPUT PORT error: real;

CONTRACT sensing
  assume:
  always temperature>=4;
  guarantee:
  always (sensed_temperature - temperature <= error and
            sensed_temperature - temperature >= -error);

COMPONENT FDIR

INTERFACE
INPUT PORT sensed_temperature: real;
INPUT PORT sensor_error: real;
OUTPUT PORT warning: boolean;
PARAMETER limit: real;

CONTRACT monitoring
  assume: TRUE;
  guarantee:
  always (sensed_temperature>(limit - sensor_error) implies in the future (warning));
```

design phases. The rigorous system and software development process and the stringent verification and validation regimes that are required in the space domain demand for formal methods that are able to cover the different phases from system level to software level.

Requirements are usually specified first at system-level defining the system functionalities and the required level of safety and dependability, and second at software-level defining the functions that the software components must implement and the non-functional constraints such as real-time and resource constraints that these software components should respect. Different formal techniques can be applied in different phases of the design and traceability links trace the derivation of the software requirements from the system requirements. However, in most of cases there is no semantics-based derivation of software requirements from system requirements, and therefore there is no integration of the verification performed at system level with the verification performed at software level.

The introduction of MDE in the development of space systems enabled the verification of functional and non-functional requirements already early in the development life cycle. The properties of the system and software are expressed in this approach at model level in the appropriate formalisms, allowing the use of (formal) verification methods with the goal of "Correct by Construction" (see Section on Model-Based Software Engineering). However, in the standard practice, there is a fundamental gap between the system-level and the software-level worlds. The properties that are considered at software level are not formally derived from system-level requirements. This poses serious threats to the confidence and integrity of the developed systems.

Several ESA R&D studies (ASSERT/TASTE, OMEGA, COMPASS, SSFRT, SAVOIR-FAIRE) highlighted that the use of modeling techniques at the different stages of the development process is of crucial importance in order to successfully design complex space systems. However, they have also confirmed the need to connect the definition of system and software requirements to ensure a consistent trace between the verification at the different system design steps, down to the software level (ESA ITT AO6523, 2010).

OBSW-RA Awareness in System-Level Design

The OBSW-RA is a key asset on which ESA is investing. It provides a reference architecture with built-in services that may have a lot of benefits for the development of space systems. However, due to its complexity, it is not easy to exploit the OBSW-RA to ensure the correctness of new

system designs built on top of it. The properties of the provided services must be formalized and mechanisms to prove a correct reuse should be provided.

A certain number of guarantees are built-in into the reference architecture, here are two examples:

- On communication layers (I/O layers) a certain number of protocols are required by the reference architecture (use of ECSS standards for telemetry packets for example) and will provide a certain number of guarantees on the exchanges between the ground and the board (for example preservation of order and integrity of the messages).
- For implementing the FDIR, the reference architecture ensures that a standard behaviour will be implemented by the execution platform and a particular instance of the execution platform will be qualified for providing this behaviour providing assumptions that will simplify the correct by construction approach.

We can distinguish two different kinds of guarantees provided by the reference architecture: either the guarantees come from the reference architecture specification (which are true for all OBSW-RA implementations), or they come from a particular implementation of the OBSW-RA.

The adoption of the space component model will enable a model-based approach associated to generative approaches for on-board software code. Generative approach will be of great help to ensure properties preservations.

During the system design phase, the suitability of the reference architecture for this particular project will be assessed. Indeed the majority of projects will take benefits of this reference architecture, but some will have functional, or non-functional (timing, safety, ..) constraints that will not be compatible with the reference architecture. Once adopted as target execution platform, a library of proven design patterns having their implementation in the reference architecture instance will be available to the designer in order to map onto its functional analysis. This library will ease the design by providing design patterns that have already been assessed, thus limiting the remaining proof obligations to be performed during the system development. For each design choice that diverges from the patterns provided by the reference architecture, a trade-off must be performed in order to compare reduction of proof effort offered by the reference architecture pattern and benefits for the project to deviate from it.

Evolution of the Design along the Development Process

Most of formal methods, including those described in the Section on Contract-Based Design, tend to focus on a specific design, providing techniques to specify and verify models in a particular moment of the development process. A systematic approach is needed to embed these methods into the development process that is used at the state of the art in the space industry. In particular, the modelers' activities must be organized in standardized architectural levels: from the initial functional architecture, the logical architecture, down to the physical architecture comprising a HW and a SW architecture. As systems become more and more complex, their consolidated definition comes later and later in the project due also to a high number of revisions, thus system requirements and models are never stable and even when software engineering comes into play requirements may still be quite fluid.

Consistent integration and traceability between models of the system and software levels is crucial for achieving a clean and significant development process, providing common modeling techniques for system and software engineers to communicate the system and software specifications with each other and ensure to achieve a common understand-

ing across different organizations. Traceability along the whole development process allows also a precise evaluation of changes' effects.

The definition of clear guidelines together with specific language and tool support for modeling each of the architectural levels, based on an extension of MBSSE and related also to the ECSS lifecycle phases, would guarantee a neat and sound process.

It was therefore necessary to extend the MBSSE process to describe the system and software co-engineering activities at the end of phase B and to cover also phase C, which is related to the software engineering and starts with the software and hardware requirements derived at the end of phase B: in Phase C the software requirements composing the Technical Specification are derived from the Requirement Baseline defined in phase B.

Contract-Based FoReVer Solution

Contract-Based Requirements Formalization and Refinement with OCRA

Overview of the Approach

The FoReVer project addressed the problems of how to formalize requirements into formal properties at different levels (i.e. at system, sub-system, avionics and software level) and how to ensure that the properties at one level of abstraction are derived from properties at the higher level. In fact, performing a verification at one design stage will rely on assumptions and guarantees of lower levels and will only be valid if these contracts are then fulfilled by the component implementations. In consequence, the analysis of properties at higher level will generate an additional set of requirements for the lower levels to ensure that the properties for the higher level are holding. However, sometimes those assumptions for verifications are implicit or are stated implicit. This should not be the case, all assumptions need to be made explicit.

In the project, we adopted the OCRA framework to formalize requirements into contracts and to specify their refinement along the architecture decomposition. The stepwise refinement of the contracts for the different design stages – by a treewise contract relationship – allows for a traceability of a guarantee from higher to lower levels and, vice versa, the traceability of an assumption from the components up to the system. This enables a different kind of analysis, e.g. the early validation of a high-level architecture evaluating the impact of early design choices.

Note that, when combining the top-down refinement with the reuse of existing components, it may be necessary to revise the refinement to adjust the contracts to the ones provided by the reused components. This applies also to the last step of the refinement, when an existing implementation of components is chosen. In fact, this implementation satisfies the contracts with specific assumptions (e.g. on the value of parameters such as bounds on data, time, frequency, etc.). Therefore, also in this case, the refinement may be adjusted to satisfy such assumption (or the components cannot be reused).

In the following, we will describe the envisaged process of specifying the contracts and their refinement and the related issues that we encountered in the project.

Contracts Specification and Refinement

During the project, we defined a process for the contracts specification and refinement. The first step of the system specification is to define the system requirements and how the system communicates with the environment. The designer shall start drafting the system component and its ports. The system requirements are formalized with Othello properties. The designer shall specify a set of system contracts, structuring the mentioned properties into guarantees that the system must fulfill and assumptions that the environment

should satisfy. At the first step, assumptions on the environment may be not clear and may be simply ignored specifying "true".

Note that both assumptions and guarantees are expressions containing only references to the ports of the system component. So, it may be necessary to complete the set of ports initially drafted.

Starting from the top-level system component, the designer should follow iteratively the following steps:

1. Choose a component (let us call it S) without subcomponents and decompose it specifying the children subcomponents;

2. For each type of the defined subcomponents, declare the component and its ports;

3. Detail the decomposition of the component S chosen at step 1 defining the connections among the subcomponents and the delegation connections between S and the subcomponents;

4. For each type of the subcomponents, specify the contracts that are necessary to fulfill the contracts of S;

5. For each contract C of S specify the refinement relationship, i.e., which contracts of the subcomponents refine C;

6. Check the refinement with OCRA and adjust the contracts in order to remove all issues in the refinement; this requires a bottom-up iterative propagation that is described with the following inner loop, where S' is initialized with the component S:

    a. Try to fix the contracts of the subcomponents of S' in order to make the refinement correct; if successful, exit the inner loop (go to 7);

    b. Otherwise, try strengthening the assumption of S', and go to 6.a considering as a new S' the parent component of the current S';

c.   If it is not possible to fix the contract refinement, the current architecture is not correct, and the refinement loop terminates unsuccessfully and a new architectural solution must be found;

7.   If there are no more components to be refined, terminate successfully; otherwise, go to 1.

Assumptions vs. Guarded Guarantees

One of the issues emerged during the project is on the role of assumptions in contracts. In fact, the designer has often to specify that a property G on the output ports is guaranteed by a component only if a certain condition A on the input holds. In these cases, the designer has to decide if the condition must be specified as assumption (i.e., $\langle A, G \rangle$) or as the premise of an implication in the guarantee (i.e., $\langle true, A \to G \rangle$). The two contracts have a different semantics in terms of environment (while they are satisfied by the same implementations): in the first case, the environment of the component must satisfy A, while in the second case the environment is not obliged to (if A does not hold, then the component simply does not guarantee G). These different notions of assumptions are known in the literature as strong and weak assumptions respectively. In order to understand which one to choose, the designer has to ask the question: "Must the environment satisfy the assumption or can an execution in which A does not hold be accepted by the component?". Consider for example that a component takes in input a real variable "y", which is used internally as a denominator for a division. The designer can decide if it is responsibility of the component to trap the case in which "y=0" to avoid a division by zero or if it can assume that the environment will never feed "0" as value for "y". In principle, at software level, one may adopt a defensive programming approach, where the programmer is responsible to trap all cases writing as many checks as possible. Contract-based design instead proposes to split this responsibility between the implementation of the component

and its environment. The first approach is not even possible for hardware components of the system or for non-functional attributes such as time. Examples of strong assumptions at system level are the expected range of attributes such as time, temperature, or memory.

Bottom-Up Propagation of Assumptions

As described in the inner loop of the above procedure, the refinement of a component S performed at each iteration of the main loop may highlight the necessity of some assumptions on a subcomponent's environment (which consists of the sibling components and the environment of S). This assumption is either fulfilled by another subcomponent of S or must be propagated on the environment of S. In the second case, the assumption of the contract of S under refinement must be strengthened accordingly. This upward propagation of the assumption is controlled by the overall development process, which decides if and how the assumptions can be modified. If possible, this propagation may be iterated up to the assumption of the system component.

Contract-Based Reuse of OBSW-RA Components

Specification and Reuse of OBSW-RA Pseudo-Components

The FoReVer project delivered the specification of some OBSW-RA pseudo components (see Section on the On-Board Software Reference Architecture) in terms of component interfaces with contracts. These contracts are parameterized by a set of parameters. These parameters are used by the system top-down design to instantiate the components for specific purposes. For example, a monitoring component must monitor periodically a certain variable with a period that is lower than a certain "upper bound"; in this case, the upper bound is set by the refinement of the parent component.

An implementation of the pseudo-component satisfies its contracts for a region of parameters that is dependent on the implementation. This region is added as assumption to the contracts of the pseudo-component. For example, the mentioned monitoring component is able to fulfill its contract only with a period that is higher than a lower bound. Thus, the implementation satisfies the contract assuming that the parameter "upper bound" is greater than a certain constant. As for the other refinement steps, this new assumption must be propagated up as described in the previous section or the implementation cannot be reused.

OBSW-RA and Top-Down Refinement

One of the targets of the contract-based approach is the reuse of OBSW-RA components. This reuse is inherently a bottom-up process. The top-down refinement must be adapted to take into account such reuse at earlier levels of the refinement. In fact, the ideal situation in which one has a set of libraries and one of the existing components fits the contracts of the top-down design is unlikely.

To this purpose we distinguish between two levels of existing components:

- Reference components are specified in terms of ports and contracts and are kept as generic as possible (minimizing assumptions and maximizing the number of parameters);
- Implemented reference components are specified with the same interface of a reference component apart from having possibly additional assumptions on the values of the parameters; implemented components are associated to an implementation that satisfies the component contracts.

We identify three different levels of modeling in the refinement of the FoReVer model:

- The level that is purely top-down because it is only dependent on the mission (for example, the specification and refinement of the required functionalities of the mission itself whatever the implementation will be);
- The level that is dependent on the fact that we will execute on a physical and software platform that will conform to the OBSW-RA; therefore, the refinement uses some reference components; the contracts of such reference components are parameterized to take into account the different possible implementations;
- The level that is linked to a particular OBSW-RA implementation (containing particular OBSW-RA specificities), replacing the reference components with specific implemented components and instantiating the parameters in contracts with concrete values.

Embedding Contracts in the Development Process

The FoReVer Modeling Language

The definition of a FoReVer development methodology that would exploit the concepts of contracts and stepwise refinement, together with an innovative perspective on reusable OBSW-RA components, entailed the definition of a supporting modeling language. The FoReVer modeling language was envisaged to enable the modeler to describe an avionic system with its component structure, behavior, contracts and requirements. The language needed also to allow the modeler to express step wise refinement of the system architecture and contracts, as required by the approach.

This FoReVer language is fully formal although it contains some informal modeling elements such as textual requirements. It contains all of the elements and relationships required by the methodology but it does not contain any of the implementation details. A simple meta-model (depicted in Figure 8) was derived from it to provide a simplified overall picture of the involved entities. A FoReVer model has the following elements:

- **Requirements:** Which may be expressed in formal or natural language and are referred to system Blocks.
- **Blocks:** HW or SW elements in the System's architecture.
- **Ports:** Interaction points for the flow of data/commands between blocks.
- **Contracts:** Formal expression of requirements described in terms of an assumption and a guarantee property.
- **State Machines:** To describe the nominal behavior of blocks.
- **Properties:** Formal verifiable expressions used to represent assumption or guarantee parts of the contracts.

The following relationships are used in the FoReVer model to link the elements to each other:

- A Requirement is associated to a Block by means of a *satisfy* relationship.
- A Requirement is formalized into a Contract.
- A Block is decomposed into other Blocks (the sub-blocks). In the FoReVer terminology we refer to this decomposition as a "*refinement*".
- A Block can have one or more Ports for the flow of data/commands with other Blocks.
- A Port must be connected to one or more other Ports (by means of an *isConnectedTo* relationship).
- A Requirement is decomposed into other Requirements (by means of a *derive* relationship), called the derived requirements, and associated to the sub-blocks defined in the "refinement" process (again by means of a *satisfy* relationship).

Figure 8. FoReVer domain specific language meta-model

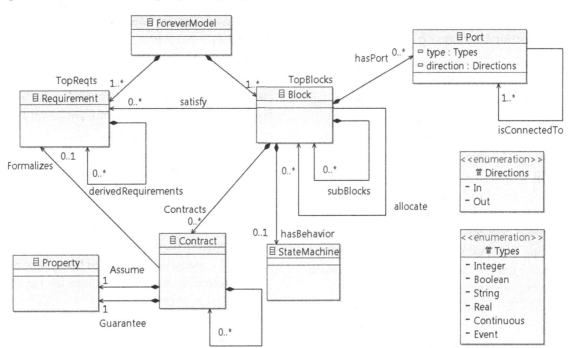

- A Contract is composed by two Properties (the assumption and the guarantee).
- A Block is associated to one or more Contracts.
- A Contract is decomposed into sub-contracts associated to the sub-blocks.
- A Block is optionally associated to one StateMachine.
- A Block can be mapped onto other Blocks by means of an *allocate* relationship.

The above relationships support different types of traceability:

- Traceability of Blocks to the Requirements that they satisfy.
- Traceability of Blocks to sub-blocks and Contracts to sub-contracts in the step wise refinement process.
- Traceability of Blocks modeled at different levels of abstraction (e.g. blocks in the functional architecture to blocks in the logical architecture or blocks in the logical architecture to blocks in the physical architecture).

The FoReVer Methodology

The FoReVer methodology was defined as an extension to the MBSSE, elaborated to address the FoReVer pivotal concepts of property formalization, formal verification and step-wise refinement with contract-based reasoning. The MBSSE process was also improved beyond the boundaries of the ECSS phases 0, A, B to better comprehend phase C, related to software engineering. Actually the System and SW co-engineering, which takes place between the end of phase B and the beginning of phase C, is the main focus of the FoReVer Methodology: it is the bridge between system engineering and SW engineering.

The FoReVer methodology relies at system level on a specific profile of SysML that implements the Domain Specific Language described

in the previous section and illustrated in Figure 9, offering modeling process support in Phases 0, A and B, according to the ECSS E-10 Space Engineering System engineering General Requirements standard (ECSS-E-ST-10C, 2009). At software level it relies on the CHESS Modeling Language (a profile of UML, SysML and MARTE), with specific support for system and software co-engineering and overall software development according to the ECSS E-40 Software Standard for Space Engineering (ECSS-E-ST-40C, 2009).

Specific support for system and software co-engineering enables the transition from the architectural and functional information available in the SysML model to the initial software and hardware (i.e. hardware related to the software deployment) architecture in the CHESS Modeling Language as a seamless process.

In the following we present an overview of the FoReVer methodology highlighting some of its most significant contributions.

The FoReVer approach is based on a *hierarchical decomposition* approach: during the whole modeling process, from the early phases - at a higher level of abstraction - down to the later phases - at a lower level of abstraction -, the system is described in terms of architectural components described formally with their well-defined interfaces and related properties. During each phase the components are considered as black boxes until they are refined into new lower level components in the next phase.

The FoReVer approach follows the *contract-based* approach of OCRA. Component's properties are formalized in terms of *contracts* and thus composed of an *assumption* and a *guarantee* modeled as formal properties. In particular from phase A system requirements must be expressed as formal contracts associated to the system and to the external interfaces representing interactions with the external environment.

The whole process runs through different *conceptual models*:

Figure 9. FoReVer V model development process

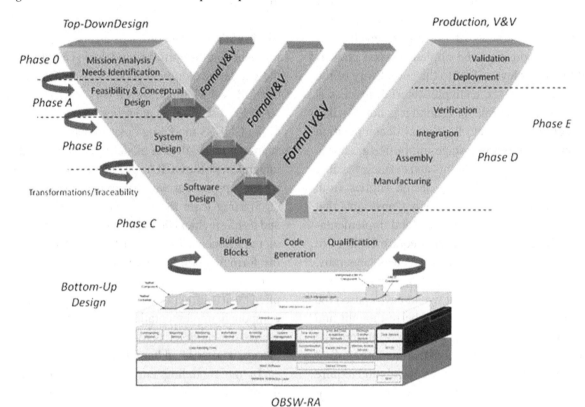

- From the higher level Functional architecture,
- To the Logical architecture,
- Down to the lower level Physical architecture with specification of Software and its allocation on Hardware.

At each conceptual level, the model describes a refinement with the decomposition of components into subcomponents and the refinement of contracts into a collection of contracts over subcomponents. Such refinement is subject to formal verification and is key-point in the overall verification process.

When stepping from one conceptual level to the next (e.g. from the Functional architecture to the Logical architecture), on the other hand, a new model is created and links are created to maintain the connection between corresponding entities in the two different architectures with different decomposition structure and contracts, mainly for the sake of traceability.

OBSW-RA components are used as a library of available standard components with associated contracts: different implementations for components can be selected during the modeling process according to the required contracts. In the top-down modeling process envisaged in FoReVer, the presence of such a library of OBSW-RA components represents a bottom-up driver to ensure convergence to a feasible solution based on the reuse of OBSW-RA components. At the end the availability of pseudo-components representing the feasible contracts for devices is a key element to enable the formal verification of the implementation.

The process envisaged in the FoReVer methodology is an *iterative top-down* process where requirements of the higher level guide the decomposition and implementation choices at the lower levels. Due to the complexity of the systems, however, a simple waterfall process is usually not possible: in general it is not possible to define a "perfect" functional decomposition right from the earliest stages of the design, nor to identify feasible constraints and define a feasible allocation of functions to design entities from the earliest stages of the design. Constraints that stem from later decomposition and implementation choices may sometimes require changes to higher level assumptions or guarantees. Generally, before looking at changes of higher levels, the lower level decisions that would have caused the need for these changes must be re-thought and a different decomposition or allocation must be pursued, if possible. Changes that cannot be solved by rearrangements at the lower levels and require to be propagated upwards must be negotiated for compatibility with the higher level requirements. If such changes are accepted, the refinement verification must be executed again from the stage where the contracts are changed onwards.

In synthesis the FoReVer methodology is a Model-Based incremental iterative process for the development of space avionics systems. The envisaged process is a mixed top-down and bottom-up process based on the early application of formal techniques and verification methods with step-wise refinement down to the implementation where a library of OBSW-RA components represents a bottom-up driver in the process to ensure convergence to a feasible solution based on the reuse of OBSW-RA components.

The FoReVer methodology implements an enhanced version of the traditional V-model development process as depicted in Figure 9.

Tool Support

The FoReVer toolset provides an integrated environment that supports the modeler in carrying out the whole development process as envisaged in the FoReVer Methodology. It was developed as a set of Eclipse plugins and relies on the extension of the CHESS modeling environment to provide support for the FoReVer modeling language, and to integrate with the OCRA verification environment, which supports formal refinement of contracts.

Starting from the description of the system and its hierarchical decomposition, the definition of requirements associated to components and the formalization of requirements as contracts, through a step wise refinement process with explicit verification of contract refinements and of component implementations, the FoReVer toolset assists the modeler across all the development phases, as described hereafter.

In the modeling environment the modeler designs an avionic system using the FoReVer profile to describe the system with its component structure, behavior, contracts and requirements as well as step wise refinement of the system architecture and contracts, as required by the FoReVer approach.

For example, Figure 10 shows how contracts are specified in CHESS.

Once the modeler has designed an architecture with its refinement hierarchy, the FoReVer toolset offers the functionality to validate the model (e.g. detecting unconnected required ports) and then to perform formal verification of the contract refinement.

The result of the formal verification of the refinement is delivered back to the modeler in the FoReVer editing environment: if the verification fails, the failing points are highlighted in terms of the model elements with their original naming, so the modeler can suitably adjust the refinement and continue with further process iterations.

Figure 10. Components and contracts in CHESS

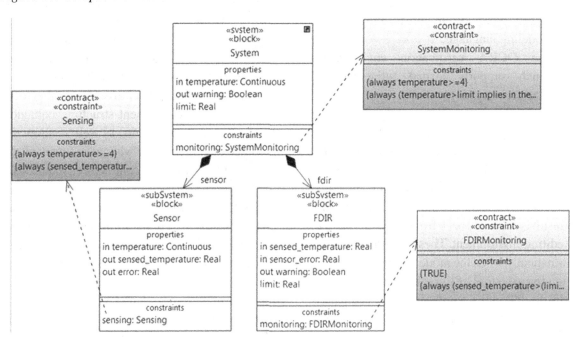

Figure 11. The FoReVer toolset

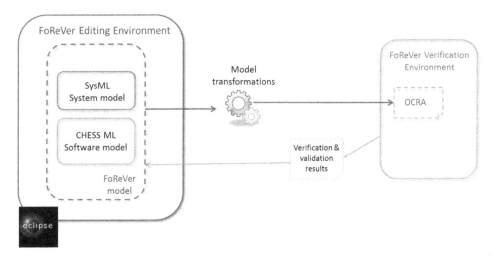

Once the refinement is proven correct, the toolset offers the functionality to formally verify the implementation of the leaf components (some leaf components may not need to undergo this verification, for instance if they are selected from a library of OBSW-RA components and therefore come with their own qualified contracts).

Once the whole verification process is successfully completed, and analysis results are satisfactory, automatic code generation provided by CHESS can be exploited for the definition of a feasible implementation of the system.

The toolset relies on the integration of two environments:

- The CHESS modeling environment, extended to provide support for the FoReVer modeling language;
- The OCRA verification environment, which supports formal refinement of contracts.

Formal verifications are carried out by the FoReVer toolset in the following steps: first a model transformation is performed into the OCRA input language, then the OCRA tool is in charge of executing the actual formal verification; finally the result is delivered back from the OCRA tool to the editing environment. These steps are executed automatically when the modeler invokes a verification from the toolset's graphical user interface.

In the following we describe the extensions to CHESS that were carried out for the FoReVer toolset integration.

The CHESS methodology, as originally defined, was devoted to support the development of software. With FoReVer, our space of interest was broadened to cover all the development process from the system level, down to the software level. We were thus facing the problem to define an integrated methodology that would lead the modeler across all the phases of development, from the initial definition of system level requirements and system level design, down to the definition of hardware and software modules and their modeling.

We adopted an integrated solution where the CHESS methodology extends its concerns from concentrating only on the software level to embracing also the System level design phase. A "System View" was introduced for this purpose in the CHESS editing environment where to model the System architecture with contracts, relying on a specific profile of SysML. System level design entities can be linked to corresponding software level entities by means of the SysML «allocate» dependency: this way system and software co-engineering is implemented as a seamless process enabling the modeler to design system and software using one tool (CHESS).

Moreover the CHESS modeling environment was extended to provide support for the FoReVer modeling language, a SysML/UML profile defined to allow the modeler to describe an avionic system with its component structure, behavior, contracts and requirements, as well as allow the modeler to express step wise refinement of the system architecture and contracts, as required by the FoReVer approach.

Linking together system and software model elements, designed in the same development environment allows to perform correct and fluent modeling at all levels, fully exploiting the expressiveness of SysML with the FoReVer profile for the system design and of CHESS-ML for the software, while maintaining a consistent vision of the system that can be shared among systems and software engineers and bridge the gap between Phase B and Phase C activities.

Checking the Contract Refinement with OCRA

The FoReVer tool allows to check if the contract refinement of a given architecture is correct interfacing with the OCRA tool. OCRA checks for each refined contract if the refinement is correct. If the refinement is not correct, the tool provides an execution of the involved composite component that violates the refinement. Otherwise, in case of propositional contracts (those involving only finite-domain variables), the tool proves that the refinement is correct; if instead the contracts involved in the refinement contain timing expressions or infinite-domain variables, OCRA proves that there are no counterexamples up to a certain bound. Although it is planned to integrate in OCRA algorithms to prove the absence of counterexamples also in infinite-state systems, the problem is undecidable and the proof method is not complete. The confidence of the designer in the correctness of the refinement depends on such bound. Note that the refinement is local to the decomposed component and therefore typically involves only few components. Since the length of the execution trace depends on the interaction of the components, we can argue that a small bound is sufficient to find counterexamples on most of cases. However, the user cannot consider it as an exhaustive check and at the moment there is no way to judge the confidence that the user can have in the result. An interesting direction of research would be to develop metrics to define the coverage of bounded model checking as they exist for testing.

CASE STUDIES

We now discuss two case studies that were tackled during the project. We first describe the activities oriented to the industrial validation, and then we present some specific verification activities on a satellite model.

Applicability to Industrial Case Studies

In order to demonstrate the applicability of the FoReVer methodology, Thales Alenia Space has applied the methodology on a concrete use-case derived from an existing low earth orbit telecom-munication mission. The proposed process was followed in order to verify the applicability of the method to industrial cases and its effectiveness.

The considered use-case is the functional chain related to the attitude and orbit control function of the avionics (the set of sensors, algorithms and actuators that ensure a proper orbit to the spacecraft and the proper "orientation"). This functional chain is highly critical (as a failure may lead to the loss of the spacecraft), the associated software will be developed according to ECSS E-40 and Q-80 European software development and quality standards equivalent to the DO-178C DAL B for the aeronautical domain (DO-178C, 2012).

The first level of modeling is the functional analysis, where we design a control algorithm that reads measurements from a rate sensor and from an optical device that gives the sun position w.r.t. the spacecraft frame and computes a torque to be applied by the thruster (see Figure 12). This particular control algorithm is often used for implementing safe mode which is the last and the lowest reconfiguration mode used as last chance which ensures proper thermal balance, electrical balance and communication with the ground.

On this functional model some properties to be guaranteed during implementation are expressed. For example, in Figure 13, the reaction of the system to a request to go to safe mode.

Figure 12. Example of high level functional decomposition of the system

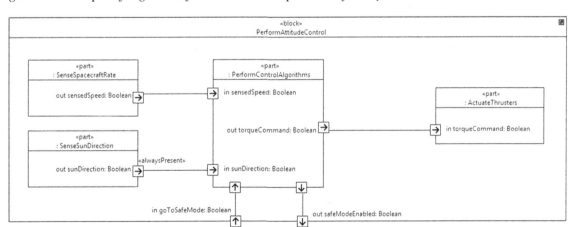

At each refinement level, the tool enables to check if the properties are correctly implemented by the modeled refinements providing counter examples if a contract is violated.

During the refinement, system details are introduced to fulfill refinement proof obligation. The example given in Figure 14 shows the handling of redundancy introduced by the fact that the rate sensor may fail. This will violate the higher level requirement on the fact that the safe mode is always available. To fulfill the obligation proof, the design has to be refined by adding two different rate sensor functions, the setup of the redundancy management and monitoring func-

tions to detect failures. Here the supposition is that we are tolerant to only one failure (only one sensor failure may occur).

The different properties may be expressed for each block as shown in Figure 15.

The subsequent steps of the process were also tested during the use case. For example the mapping onto the physical architecture (see for example Figure 16) to map functions and logical components onto hardware nodes. At this step, we introduce refinements that are linked to the timing characteristics of the hardware and the communication links in order to verify if the properties expressed at system level without taking into

Figure 13. Example of properties

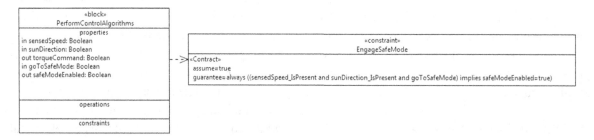

Figure 14. Refinement of a block

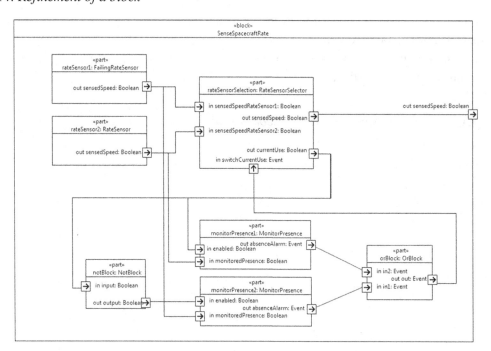

Figure 15. Example of properties for a functional block

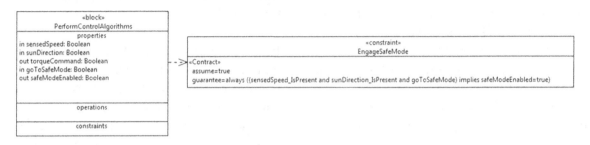

Figure 16. Hardware architecture

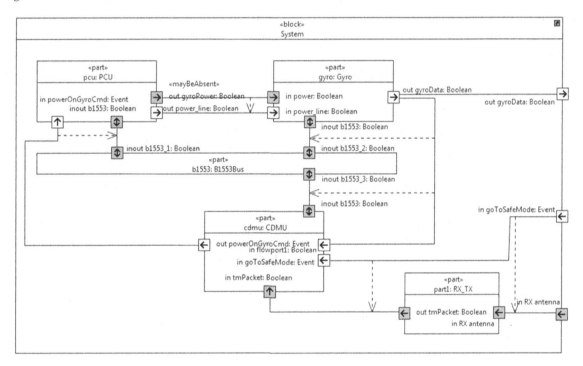

account hardware architecture are still valid or if to make them still valid we need either to choose another hardware architecture, or another function mapping or to change the system requirements.

In particular, Figure 16 shows the hardware architecture with the different hardware boxes and logical exchanges between those boxes (for example request for powering on the gyroscope) that will be mapped onto physical links (for example here this last request will be mapped to an exchange on the physical MIL-1553 buses). This mapping refinement will imply new properties like data latency or hardware link failures. The

introduction of this physical level will permit to demonstrate that the proposed hardware architecture will preserve system properties.

Contract-Based Refinement of the EagleEye Critical Values FDIR

The Eagle-Eye Case Study

Another case study that was considered during the FoReVer project concerned the EagleEye reference mission. This is a small virtual satellite for Earth observation, which carries a payload (called

"GoldenEye"), which consists in a high-resolution imaging camera. It has been developed in different ESA studies as workbench for evaluating new tools and techniques. Remarkably, the same case study was used by the CORDET-2 project to develop the Software Reference Architecture.

In FoReVer, we considered the refinement of FDIR requirements because of their clear link with the monitoring pseudo components of the OBSW-RA and a detailed documentation of the related PUS monitoring table capabilities (see Section on On-Board Software Reference Architecture).

A typical FDIR requirement at system level may require that "in case of unhandled anomalies, the system shall switch to Safe Hold Mode (SHM)". This means that whenever the system detects an anomaly that cannot be handled autonomously, the system shall switch to SHM, which is the mode in which the system waits for commands sent by the ground to solve the anomaly. This type of requirement is usually refined in requirements dedicated to specific anomalies. For example, an FDIR requirement at software level may require that, "when the health status of a thermal critical value is not OK (NOK), then the FDIR shall command a transition to SHM". In this informal refinement, there are many assumptions on the other components or on the environment that are implicit. For example, it is necessary that some other component makes the transition to SHM, while some other component provides the NOK signal in case of anomalies. This in turn must rely on some monitoring function that may require some assumption on the observability of the anomaly. This reasoning is lost in the informal traceability linkage that is usually performed from system to software-level requirements.

We describe in the following how we formalized this refinement with the proposed contract-based approach. In order to ease the readability of the description, we simplify the used components and their contracts.

Contract-Based Specification of OBSW-RA Pseudo-Component

In the refinement of the FDIR of critical values, we use two OBSW-RA pseudo-components.

The first is called Device_OBSW-RA_PseudoComponent, which takes in input a continuous variable and provides the operation GetValue to get the variable through a sensor and return the sensed value. Thus, the component provides a software interface and hides hardware components that are part of its implementation. The sensor is supposed to be connected to the onboard computer through a bus. The component's contract guarantees that the returned value does not differ from the input critical value more than a certain constant. Moreover, the bus creates a delay between the call of GetValue and its return and the contract of Device_OBSW-RA_PseudoComponent guarantees that such delay is bounded by another constant.

The second pseudo-component that we use is the Monitoring_OBSW-RA_PseudoComponent. Here, we use a simplified version with only the interface necessary to monitor the critical value, but in reality it provides different options (e.g., to monitor an expected value rather than a range) and a richer interface (e.g., to enable and disable the monitoring). In this context, Monitoring_OBSW-RA_PseudoComponent has just one parameter, the "critical_threshold", requires an operation to get the monitored value and outputs an alarm event to signal the exceeding of the limit. Its contract guarantees that the value is read periodically every "sensing_period" time units and that whenever the read value is above the "critical_threshold", the alarm is triggered.

Contract-Based Refinement of the EagleEye Critical Values FDIR

We now describe the top-down refinement of the FDIR requirement using the above OBSW-RA pseudo-components. First of all, the system-level requirement is refined into more detailed system-level requirements specifying the different anomalies that must be monitored. Let us consider for example the following requirement: "in case of a thermal critical value bigger than a threshold, the system shall switch to SHM". This can be formalized into an Othello property "always (critical_value>critical_threshold implies in the future SHM)", where "critical_value" is an input port, "critical_threshold" is a parameter, and "SHM" a Boolean output port of the system component. Since "critical_value" is a temperature sensed from the environment, it changes continuously in time and we declare the type of "critical_value" as continuous and the type of "critical_threshold" as real.

As second step, the system is decomposed into a sensor component, an FDIR SW component, and a SMGT (System mode Management), which manages the modes and mode transitions of the system.

For the sensor, we use the Device_OBSW-RA_PseudoComponent, whose provided Get-Value is connected to the analog operation required by the FDIR SW component. The FDIR and the SMGT are connected through the operation SwitchToSHM provided by the SMGT to set SH to true. Thus, the system input critical variable is delegated to the input variable of the sensor, while the output SHM is delegated to the homonymous port of the SMGT.

The FDIR SW calls periodically the sensor to get the value of the monitored variable and when this is greater than the threshold, it calls a function provided by the SMGT that performs the mode transition to SHM. The corresponding formal property is

"(always time_until(ProducerGetValue_call)<sensing_period) and (always ((ProducerGetValue_ret and ProducerGetValue_ret_value>=critical_threshold) implies in the future switch_to_SHM_call))".

The property of the SMGT instead is simply "always (switch_to_SHM_call implies in the future SHM)".

The FDIR is further decomposed into two sub-components, a monitor and a controller. The monitor is a Monitoring_OBSW-RA_Pseudo-Component, while the controller in this simple example just receives the alarm of the monitor and calls the SwitchToSHM operation.

So far, we only discussed guarantees leaving all assumptions as empty (equivalent to true). The contract refinement as it is, however, is not correct. A trace provided by OCRA shows that the temperature reaches the threshold and returns below the threshold so quickly that the FDIR (which has a sensing period) cannot detect it. Therefore, we added some assumptions on how the temperature can vary in time: first, we assume that cannot have discrete jumps (such as the reset of timer); second, we assume that the derivative is always in a certain concrete range. With these assumptions, the contract refinement is correct.

Notice that we weaken the initial property by adding explicit assumption on the input temperature. Such kind of modifications must be controlled by the development process and the assumptions must be validated. In fact, the risk is to strengthen at will the assumptions to make the refinement correct resulting into a non-realistic model.

CONCLUSION AND FUTURE RESEARCH DIRECTIONS

In this chapter we described a practical experience on applying a hot-topic design method, namely contract-based design, to solve concrete open points in the model-based engineering of space systems. After presenting some background material, we showed how to use contract-based design for the refinement of avionics system-level properties along the system architecture and for the reuse of the components of the OBSW-RA. The FoReVer methodology was implemented in a toolset, and experimented with by the FoReVer partners Thales Alenia Space and Fondazione Bruno Kessler, in order to validate the applicability of the approach in an industrial setting.

The project yielded interesting feedback, as well as useful hints and challenging guidelines for future work.

From an industrial point of view, the FoReVer methodology has been proved very useful and made an important step forward by splitting the modeling activities into several levels (functional, logical, physical). A key innovation is that these levels are not necessarily deduced from each other by a refinement from one level to the other. As a result, the methodology supports a flexible way of decomposing requirements and exploring various solutions: in fact, it is possible to keep the design consistent across different levels, reducing the impact of late design decisions and changes taken at one level on the other levels.

In terms of support for component reuse, the FoReVer study has demonstrated strong potential. It provided interesting and useful input for the OBSW-RA definition, and we believe that further experimentation of the FoReVer methodology and toolset will be an important driver towards an actual definition of the OBSW-RA. In particular, the use of contracts to specify the semantic interface of OBSW-RA components will be an enabling factor for proper and correct reuse. This can also leverage on the availability of different modeling views (e.g. functional, logical, physical) and the use of related contracts.

The proposed methodology and tools have been evaluated very positively in terms of applicability in an industrial setting. On the one side, contract-based refinement is simpler to be operationally used by industrial users if compared to more complex formal approaches. The properties are in the end quite simple to understand, and close to the natural thinking of system and software engineers.

In the course of the use-case, only a few trial-errors were necessary to build correct properties for an untrained user. The features of the property language were sufficient to express many conditions found during the modeling.

On the other side, the tool has always given results very quickly, which is a very good indicator of industrial applicable formal methods. The capabilities of the approach enable verification of non-trivial composition problems that are more realistic than problems claimed to be solved by many other formal-based methods.

Overall, the contract-based refinement was perceived as a very promising approach to introduce formal verification into industrial systems: it is easier and more natural to be understood by the user and seems to be quite well supported by the model checkers, compared with other formal approaches. The analysis resulted in a good ratio between modeling investment and proofs return on investment, and suggests that there are definitely good reasons to continue improving the Technology Readiness Level (TRL) of the proposed solutions.

From the point of view of future research, the FoReVer approach highlighted several interesting directions. In terms of integration within the development process, there are natural links between this kind of methods and the traditional integration, verification and validation activities that are performed in real-world projects. Given that contract refinement provides a formal specification of properties for the software components, a natural direction is to integrate the contract-based refinement with software verification and in particular with testing. Indeed at each decomposition level of the system, the assumptions and guaranties are a natural specification for manual test and verification, that can be directly translated into test scenario to be applied on the system. We could also imagine that due to the formal aspect of these assumptions and guaranties, test scenario may be automatically translated into test scripts to be executed.

A more ambitious goal is to combine the approach with code generation from detailed behavioral models. Once these models are verified against the component contracts and the code generations is proved correct, the code results "correct-by-construction" with regard to the refined system properties. The possibility to use the verified behavior to generate the implementation should be investigated, i.e. the open point is to see to what extent the behavior that can be formally checked can be detailed in order to make it usable/useful for the automatic generation of the implementation.

The project also highlighted several important research directions in terms of formal verification techniques. A first goal is to increase the deductive capabilities of the verification engines: although the class of problems they are confronted with is undecidable, it is possible to conceive techniques that will be able to derive definite conclusions in many more practical cases. Another interesting direction would be the development of metrics to estimate the coverage provided by incomplete techniques, such as the bounded analysis currently employed by OCRA for the real-time contracts. On the lines of coverage metrics for testing, the metrics can provide both confidence and means to increase the coverage.

Another important direction is the definition of analysis methods for the improvement of contract understanding. For example, the tool could provide the designer with information regarding which contracts are sufficient for (or prevent) correct refinement. The support of component reuse could be improved by exploiting the parameterized contracts to synthesize the weakest assumption under which the contract refinement would be correct.

Finally, some areas have been identified that need further investigation. Given that the study focused mainly on the refinement of functional and timing requirements, an open investigation area is to achieve a better integration of the CHESS real-time properties used for schedulability and the real-time contracts supported by OCRA.

Safety aspects have been addressed manually extending the component interfaces with ports such as faults. A possible extension to the FoReVer approach is to automatize the insertion of faulty behavior allowing to perform fault-tree analysis and more in general model-based safety analysis.

REFERENCES

Bálek, D., & Plasil, F. (2001). *Software Connectors and their Role in Component Deployment*. Paper presented at the Third International Conference on Distributed Applications and Interoperable Systems. New York, NY.

Barrett, C. W., Sebastiani, R., Seshia, S. A., & Tinelli, C. (2009). Satisfiability Modulo Theories. In Handbook of Satisfiability 2009 (pp. 825-885). Academic Press.

Bauer, S., David, A., Hennicker, R., Larsen, K., Legay, A., Nyman, U., & Wasowski, A. (2012). Moving from Specifications to Contracts in Component-Based Design. In *Proceedings of Fundamental Approaches to Software Engineering - 15th International Conference, FASE 2012* (pp. 43-58). FASE.

Benveniste, A., Caillaud, B., Ferrari, A., Mangeruca, L., Passerone, R., & Sofronis, C. (2007). Multiple Viewpoint Contract-Based Specification and Design. In *Proceedings of Formal Methods for Components and Objects, 6th International Symposium, FMCO 2007* (pp. 200-225). FMCO.

Cimatti, A., Dorigatti, M., & Tonetta, S. (2013). OCRA: A Tool for Checking the Refinement of Temporal Contracts. In *Proceedings of 28th IEEE/ACM International Conference on Automated Software Engineering, ASE 2013* (pp. 702-705). IEEE/ACM.

Cimatti, A., Roveri, M., Susi, A., & Tonetta, S. (2012). Validation of requirements for hybrid systems: A formal approach. *ACM Transactions on Software Engineering and Methodology*, *21*(4), 22. doi:10.1145/2377656.2377659

Cimatti, A., Roveri, M., & Tonetta, S. (2009). Requirements Validation for Hybrid Systems. In *Proceedings of Computer Aided Verification, 21st International Conference, CAV 2009* (pp. 188-203). CAV.

Cimatti, A., & Tonetta, S. (2012). A Property-Based Proof System for Contract-Based Design. In *Proceedings of 38th Euromicro Conference on Software Engineering and Advanced Applications, SEAA 2012* (pp. 21-28). SEAA.

Dijkstra, E. W. (1982). On the role of scientific thought. In *Selected writings on Computing: A Personal Perspective* (pp. 60–66). New York, NY: Springer-Verlag.

DO-178C. (2012). *Software Considerations in Airborne Systems and Equipment Certification – RCTA 2012*.

ECSS-E-70-41A. (2003). *Telemetry and Telecommand Packet Utilization*. First Issue, January 2003.

ECSS-E-ST-10C. (2009). *Space engineering - System Engineering General Requirements*. Issue 3, 6 March 2009.

ECSS-E-ST-40C. (2009). *Space engineering – Software*. Issue 3, 6 March 2009.

ECSS-M-ST-10C. (2009). *Space project management - Project planning and implementation*. Rev. 1, March 2009.

ESA ITT AO6523. (2010). *Functional Requirements and Verification Techniques for the Software Reference Architecture*.

France, R. & Rumpe, B. (2007). Model-driven Development of Complex Software: A Research Roadmap. In *Proceedings of Future of Software Engineering. FOSE '07*. IEEE Computer Society. http://dx.doi.org/10.1109/FOSE.2007.14

Hall, A., & Chapman, R. (2002, January-February). Correctness By Construction: Developing a Commercial Secure System. *IEEE Software*, *19*(1), 18–25. doi:10.1109/52.976937

Haskins, C. (Ed.). (2011). INCOSE Systems Engineering Handbook: A Guide for System Life Cycle Processes and Activities, (v. 3.2.2, INCOSE-TP-2003-002-03.2.2). International Council on Systems Engineering.

ISO/IEC 15288. (2008). *System engineering, System life cycle processes*. ISO/IEC 15288:2008(E) IEEE Std 15288-2008.

ISO/IEC/IEEE42010. (2011). *Systems and software engineering - Architecture description*. Author.

Kruchten, P. (1995). The 4+1 View Model of Architecture. *IEEE Software*, *12*(6), 45–50. doi:10.1109/52.469759

Lau, K., & Wang, Z. (2005). A Taxonomy of Software Component Models. In *Proceedings of the 31st Euromicro Conference on Software Engineering and Advanced Applications*. Euromicro.

Lutz, R. (1993). Analyzing software requirements errors in safety-critical, embedded systems. In *Proceedings of IEEE International Symposium on Requirements Engineering, RE 1993* (pp. 126-133). IEEE.

Mazzini, S., Favaro, J., & Vardanega, T. (2013, June). *Cross-Domain Reuse: Lessons Learned in A Multi-Project Trajectory*. Paper presented at The 13th International Conference on Software Reuse. Pisa, Italy.

Mazzini, S., Puri, S., Olive, X., Burte, G., Paccagnini, C., & Tronci, E. (2009, October). *SSFRT Report3: Guidelines for Model Based Space System Engineering*. Issue 1.2.

Mazzini, S., Puri, S., Veran, G., Vardanega, T., Panunzio, M., Santamaria, C., & Zovi, A. (2011, May). *Model-Driven and Component-Based Engineering with the CHESS Methodology*. Paper presented at The International Space System Engineering Conference, DASIA. La Valletta, Malta.

Mehta, N. R., Medvidovic, N., & Phadke, S. (2000). *Towards a Taxonomy of Soft-ware Connectors*. Paper presented at the 22nd International Conference on Software Engineering. New York, NY.

Panunzio, M., & Vardanega, T. (2010). A Component Model for On-board Software Applications. In *Proceedings of 36th Euromicro Conference on Software Engineering and Advanced Applications, SEAA 2010* (pp. 57-64). SEAA.

Pnueli, A. (1977). The Temporal Logic of Programs. In *Proceedings of 18th Annual Symposium on Foundations of Computer Science, FOCS 1977* (pp. 46-57). FOCS.

Schmidt, D.C. (2006). Guest Editor's Introduction: Model-Driven Engineering. *Computer*, *39*(2), 25–31. http://dx.doi.org/10.1109/MC.2006.58

Szyperski, C. (2003). *Component Software - Beyond Object-Oriented Programming* (2nd ed.). Addison-Wesley / ACM Press.

KEY TERMS AND DEFINITIONS

Contract: Property of a system or component composed of an assumption and a guarantee. A contract represents an agreement between the system/component and its environment: the environment must respect the assumption, and in response the implementation of the system/component respects the guarantee.

Environment: Context of a system or component determining the data and events in input to the system/component.

Functional Requirement: A requirement that define a function that a component or system must be able to perform.

Interface: The boundary of a component consisting of the declaration of a set of public features, data and/or events, used to interact with the environment.

Meta-Model: The set of frames, rules, constraints, models and theories applicable and useful for the modeling in a predefined class of problems.

Model Checker: A tool that automatically checks whether a model meets specific requirements.

Proof Obligation: A logical formula associated to a correctness claim for a given verification property. The formula is valid if and only if the property holds. The correctness of the property under verification is "delegated" to proving the correctness of the new formula.

Requirement: A condition that should be satisfied or capability that should be possessed by the system or component under definition.

Stepwise Refinement: A development technique in which the requirements and design of a system are first defined at a high-level of abstraction and then further define increasing the level of detail.

Chapter 10
Model–Based Analysis and Engineering of Automotive Architectures with EAST–ADL

Sara Tucci-Piergiovanni
CEA, LIST, 91191 Gif-sur-Yvette CEDEX , France

Mark-Oliver Reiser
Technische Universität Berlin, Germany

DeJiu Chen
KTH Royal Institute of Technology, Sweden

Ramin Tavakoli Kolagari
Nuremberg Institute of Technology G. S. Ohm, Germany

Chokri Mraidha
CEA, LIST, 91191 Gif-sur-Yvette CEDEX , France

Nataliya Yakymets
CEA, LIST, 91191 Gif-sur-Yvette CEDEX , France

Henrik Lönn
Volvo Technology, Sweden

Renato Librino
4S s.r.l., Italy

Nidhal Mahmud
University of Hull, UK

Sandra Torchiaro
Centro Ricerche Fiat, Italy

Agnes Lanusse
CEA, LIST, 91191 Gif-sur-Yvette CEDEX , France

ABSTRACT

Modern cars have turned into complex high-technology products, subject to strict safety and timing requirements, in a short time span. This evolution has translated into development processes that are not as efficient, flexible, and agile as they could or should be. Model-based design offers many potential solutions to this problem. This chapter presents the main aspects and capabilities of a rich model-based design framework, founded on EAST-ADL, and developed during the MAENAD project. EAST-ADL is an architecture description language specific to the automotive domain and complemented by a methodology compliant with the ISO26262 standard. The language and the methodology set the stage for a high-level of automation and integration of advanced analyses and optimization capabilities to effectively improve development processes of modern cars.

DOI: 10.4018/978-1-4666-6194-3.ch010

INTRODUCTION

Commercial automobiles have become complex high-technology products in a relatively short time span. Different factors contribute to this complexity. One of them is the increasing number of vehicle functionalities supported by software, electronics and mechatronic technologies; a trend that does not seem to slow down. The involvement of carmakers in the development of these functionalities differs from one vehicle domain to the other (chassis, body, powertrain), ranging from black box integration to white-box developments. Another factor is the way in which car manufacturers have evolved from their historical mechanical and manufacturing background to the intricate organizations that develop the automobile products of today. The advent of the electrical vehicle makes this last two factors even more evident, not only because of the "untraditional" technologies that carmakers need to master, but also because the arrival of new stakeholders, actors and interests around the electrical vehicle mean that the traditional scope of the automobile has changed.

Generally, this evolution has translated into development processes that are not as efficient, flexible and agile as they could or should be (Chale, Gaudre & Tucci-Piergiovanni, 2012). The need to master these different complexity-inducing factors and improve the efficiency of product development, plus the arrival of the ISO 26262 standard (which besides from safety-related aspects, also raises issues concerning development processes of automotive systems, currently under-formalized) have motivated the adoption of model-based system engineering. Model-based system engineering advocates the use of models, conforming to a common semantic meta-model, all along the system development process. The meta-model specifies a common unambiguous semantics formalizing system engineering terminology and then providing a common language for system descriptions, i.e. models. Models, produced along the development process, provide system descriptions at different abstraction levels. Abstraction levels help human reasoning and analysis capabilities allowing system specifications to be refined and incrementally validated as long as the comprehension of the system increases. The meta-model approach is also attractive for system development as meta-models and their related models can be easily extended to support an open ended evolution of domain specific concepts.

But model-based system engineering is not only about meta-models, with their possibility to provide unambiguous system descriptions at different abstraction levels. Indeed, models, when formalized through a meta-model, provide the sufficient level of precision to be computer-interpreted. This feature allows providing a computer assisted system engineering process that formalizes and automates system design activities.

Thanks to these capabilities, the adoption of model-based design has several benefits including an improvement of quality, through a more rigorous and costless traceability between requirements, design, analysis and testing. While the benefits of model-based design are widely understood, there is no COTS solution today providing a full-fledged model-based environment for automotive systems. The first problem is that many commercial solutions use proprietary meta-models that scarcely fit automotive design needs. Moreover, ideally, the meta-model should be shared in the entire automotive domain, and then proprietary languages should be avoided opting instead for standard languages. UML extensions as SysML, could be an option, but SysML, per se, does not support many concepts of vital importance for the automotive domain, as for instance, concepts for safety analysis, timing analysis and variability. To support these concepts UML needs to be specialized through specific profiles. Even though some efforts have been spent in that direction in literature – e.g. for safety (Cancila, Terrier, Belmonte, Dubois, Espinoza, Gerard, & Cuccuru, 2009), for timing (OMG MARTE, 2011) – we did not reach the stage in which these efforts are unified and integrated in SyML.

EAST-ADL2 (EAST-ADL, 2012) (Electronics Architecture and Software Technology - Architecture Description Language) is an architecture description language specially targeting automotive systems. EAST-ADL2, is a result of a series of consecutive projects: EAST-EEA (EAST-EEA, 2001), ATESST I and ATESST II (ATESST, 2006). In the MAENAD project (MAENAD, 2009) a further refinement of this language has been made. The main objective of EAST-ADL2 lies in encompassing all the relevant concepts to holistically support automotive engineering activities. To this end EAST-ADL2 aims at addressing: the upcoming ISO 26262 standard (ISO, 2011) – which provides a general framework for functional safety handling in automotive systems –, electrical vehicle specific concerns and related standards, as long as timing, variability, and feature modeling. We believe that EAST-ADL2 successfully supports automotive engineering by providing as well methodological guidance on models to produce at different abstraction levels. Moreover, the methodology defines separated design flows (called swimlanes) following a separation of concern principle. A core design flow, only dedicated to mainstream system activities, is complemented by other three design flows, one to handle safety related activities (in conformance with the ISO26262), one dedicated to timing-related activities, and one called FEV swimlane to manage all the activities specific to fully electric vehicle sub-systems (not included then in the core design flow).

The language and methodology provided by EAST-ADL form the basic building blocks for a complete automation of the system development process. The MAENAD project focused on employing and further developing model-driven engineering technologies to automate time-consuming and error-prone engineering activities prescribed by the methodology. These activities range from behavioral analysis of system functions to safety assessment, from power analysis to timing analysis. For safety and timing analysis

advanced algorithms have been conceived, in order to provide fine predictions on system properties. Moreover a model-based optimization framework completes the panorama, by adding the capability of optimizing the system under conflicting goals. A typical example comes when the safety assessment outcome suggests adding a software redundancy mechanism. The software redundancy mechanism, on the other hand, is time and resource consuming and can degrade system response time. Multi-objective optimization finds the right trade-off to not degrade too much system performance (or other safety conflicting goals as economic cost) and to assure the right level of safety.

This paper aims at presenting on one side the remarkable coverage of EAST-ADL of the broad range of relevant concepts in the automotive domain, and on the other side the high level of integration of novel sophisticated analyses, for safety and timing in particular, and optimization capabilities. To this end, we firstly present the EAST-ADL methodology, explaining in detail swimlanes and abstraction levels. We present all the models produced in the core swimlane using a case study running example. For the non-core swimlanes, we illustrate in the paper the safety and timing swimlane, in order to present the novel analyses developed during the MAENAD project. Principles for model-based optimization are also presented as the opportunity of dealing with conflicting goals.

The paper is organized as follows: Section 0 presents a literature review on modeling languages and related model-based design techniques. Section 0 presents the principles of the system development process depicting the abstraction levels EAST-ADL models conforms to. Section 0 presents the EAST-ADL methodology and swimlanes. Section 0 illustrates the core swimlane, presenting the models to be produced at each abstraction level and an example of verification activity based on model-checking. Section 0 presents main models to be produced in the safety swimlane and novel concepts for safety analysis. Section 0 presents main concepts for timing modeling and presents advanced analysis for system schedulability estimation. Section 0 presents the optimization framework, while Section 7 concludes the paper.

BACKGROUND

In this section we will evaluate modeling languages with regard to their capacity to support non-functional properties covering safety aspects, timing aspects and FEV aspects. We focus on standard modeling languages.

Table 1 lists some standard modeling languages and shows whether they provide support for safety, timing, and FEV non-functional aspects.

The table presents the abstraction level each language can be used. At system abstraction level, vehicle features are specified and logical functions realizing the features are identified. At design abstraction level the functional architecture, the hardware architecture, and an allocation of the functions to hardware resources are defined. On the implementation level, the design architecture is implemented on a concrete platform.

AADL (SAE, 2009) (Architecture Analysis and Design Language) is an architecture description language standardized by SAE. AADL was first developed in the field of avionics and derived from MetaH, made by Honeywell. AADL is a Domain Specific Modeling Language designed for the specification, analysis, and automated

integration of real-time performance-critical distributed systems. It allows analysis of designs prior to the implementation. AADL is adapted for systems architecture specification but lacks some standard support for requirements specification at system level.

UML (Unified Modeling Language) (OMG UML, 2011) is the most known modeling language. UML provides several views/diagrams for modeling structural and behavioral aspects of a system. UML is an object-oriented modeling language that is suitable for object-oriented software design. It is a general purpose modeling language, and while providing a basic support for timing specification (through timing observations and timing durations concepts), it lacks detailed modeling concepts for non-functional properties. For more specific modeling needs, UML provides a standard extension mechanism called profile. Examples of standard UML profile are SysML (OMG SYSML, 2012), MARTE (OMG MARTE, 2011) or QFTP (OMG QFTP, 2008).

SysML is a specialization of UML for system modeling. SysML provides support for requirements modeling, and a support for quantities and dimensions as the only support for non-functional aspects. MARTE is an extension of UML for real-time and embedded systems. It provides advanced concepts for the design and analysis of such systems, including modeling constructs for non-functional properties, time, resources. However, safety aspect is not addressed by the standard.

Table 1. Safety, timing, and FEV support of standard modeling languages

Modeling Language	Safety	Timing	FEV	Level
AADL	X	X		Design/Implem
UML		X		Design/Implem
SysML		X		System
MARTE		X	X	Design/Implem
QFTP	X			Design
AUTOSAR	X	X	X	Implem

QFTP is a UML profile for modeling quality of service and fault tolerance characteristics and mechanisms, but it is not especially conceived to support safety activities prescribed by the ISO26262 standard.

Except for AUTOSAR, none of the presented languages provide support for the whole set of non-functional properties of interest. However, AUTOSAR targets the implementation of software parts of automotive systems and does not provide concepts for requirements specification, refinement and traceability; hindering then its application at system level.

Mixing different languages to cover all levels (system, design and implementation) with a support for all non-functional properties modeling may be inappropriate. In fact, a joint usage of modeling languages can raise semantic and/or syntactic problems (Di Natale & Vincentelli, 2010). Transformations from one language to another can lead to a loss of semantics in the output model. This can be the case even between two UML profiles like SysML and MARTE (Espinoza, Cancila, Selic & Gerard, 2009).

PRINCIPLES OF THE OVERAL SYSTEM DEVELOPMENT PROCESS

This section is devoted to the presentation of the main EAST-ADL principles guiding the development process of automotive systems. To explain how EAST-ADL can be used, a classical V model is used as reference. According to the classical V model, design steps from top level requirements collection to component realizations are represented on the left in the V. Bottom-up test and integration is represented on the right side of the V.

Four development phases, corresponding to four abstraction levels of a system model, are identified. Error! Reference source not found. shows the EAST-ADL phases in a V model context. Vehicle phase corresponds to the early stages in the product life cycle, while implementation phase

corresponds to the final stages of development. The Operational phase corresponds to stages in which the concrete vehicle is operational.

The development phases can be detailed as follows:

- **Vehicle Phase:** During this phase the analysis of external requirements is carried out with the objective of constructing a top-level feature model. The top-level feature model provides the most abstract definition of expected functionalities by a vehicular embedded system. Through a vehicle feature model, the expected system functionalities in terms of features are configured and linked to the corresponding specifications of system level requirements, verification and validation cases.

- **(Functional) Analysis Phase:** Typically based on the inputs of automatic control engineering, system design at this level refines the vehicle level system feature specification by indentifying the individual functional units necessary for system boundary (e.g., sensing and actuating functions for the interaction with target physical plant) and internal computation (e.g. feedback control functions for regulating the dynamics of target physical plant). The design focuses on the abstract functional logic, while abstracting any SW/HW based implementation details. Through an analysis level system model, such abstract functional units are defined and linked to the corresponding specifications of requirements (which are either satisfied or emergent) as well as the corresponding verification and validation cases.

- **Design Phase:** System design at this level refines the analysis level model to obtain a logical representation of the system functional units that are now structured for their realizations through computer hardware and software. This representation is obtained by capturing the bindings of system functions to I/O devices, basic software, operating systems, communication systems, memories and processing units, and other hardware devices. Again, through a design level system model, the system functions, together with the expected software and hardware resources for their realizations, are defined and linked to the corresponding specifications of requirements (which are either satisfied or emergent) as well as the corresponding verification and validation cases. Moreover, the creation of an explicit design level system model promotes efficient and reusable architectures, i.e. sets of (structured) HW/SW components and their interfaces, hardware architecture for different functions. The architecture must satisfy the constraints of a particular development project in automotive series production.

- **Implementation Phase:** This phase focuses on the HW/SW implementation and configuration of the final solution. This part is mainly a reference to the concepts of AUTOSAR, which provides standardized specifications at this level of automotive

software development. However, the use of AUTOSAR concepts is not mandated by the methodology. Other, in particular more traditional implementation concepts can be used in this phase while leaving the other phases unchanged.

It is worth to notice that at the end of each phase, the main artifact to produce is a complete system definition in EAST-ADL. While being defined with the specific concepts used at each abstraction level (features, functions, etc.), each EAST-ADL model consists essentially of a set of abstract system constituent entities. Typically, "m-to-n" relationships (from n entities of a higher level to m entities of the lower level) allow refining models throughout the process for an incremental system concretization. In particular, the analysis architecture and its requirements is a refinement of the feature model. This results in "m-to-n" relationships between the vehicle feature model entities and analysis architecture entities. In its turn the design architecture is a refinement of the purely functional analysis architecture. Again "m-to-n" relationships between the analysis functional architecture entities and design architecture

Figure 1. EAST-ADL phases in a V-model context

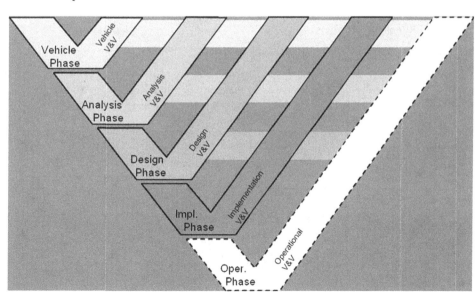

entities there exist. Error! Reference source not found.Figure 2 shows an example of 'm-to-n' relationships between features, analysis functions and design functions.

Summarizing EAST-ADL phases serve to explain the steps involved in engineering automotive systems, following a staged approach for integration, validation and verification. This staged approach not only allows addressing the requirements corresponding to the current abstraction level, but implicitly allows addressing, all the way back, top level requirements as the design evolves and gets more concrete.

Let us remark that, even if illustrated on a V cycle process, the involved engineering steps can be deployed in any overall framework, from waterfall to agile development. Together with the support of EAST-ADL language, this definition of development phases allows a common reasoning of engineering activities, related design artifacts, and thereby any need for traceability, reuse and safety lifecycle management.

EAST-ADL METHODOLOGY: SWIMLANES AND MAIN ACTIVITIES

In this section we aim at presenting the EAST-ADL methodology. The methodology elaborates system development process principles presented in Section 2, giving guidelines on the set of engineering activities that help in incrementally define and validate designs in compliance with relevant standards.

Interestingly, the EAST-ADL methodology defines and organizes development activities in so-called swimlanes (MAENAD Methodology, 2013) (TIMMO2USE, 2012). The structuring of swimlanes follows a separation-of-concerns principle, in which core system design activities are separated from activities related to specific aspects, as safety, timing and FEV. This structuring results in four separated lanes:

- Core lane, covering design core activities, i.e. activities aiming at (i) representing core system structure and behavior and (ii) verifying functional properties of the system;

Figure 2. EAST-ADL models and refinements

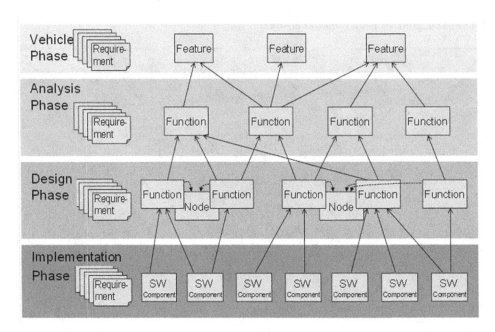

- Functional Safety lane, covering safety activities, i.e. activities aiming at representing and assessing system safety. The safety lane conforms to the ISO26262 standard;
- Timing lane, covering timing activities, i.e. activities aiming at representing and verifying timing properties of the system;
- FEV lane, covering FEV-related activities; i.e. activities aiming at representing and assessing system properties related to electric vehicles, in compliance with electric vehicle standards.

It is worth to notice that each lane covers all the EAST-ADL phases (feature, analysis, design, etc.). The possibility, however, to carry out some particular verification/assessment uniquely depends on the information available at each level of abstraction. For instance, timing activities related to schedulability estimation are not applicable until the design phase is reached, as information of hardware resources and allocation is needed. The same reasoning applies to most of the FEV related activities, which are mainly related to hardware properties. In the following, for each lane, assessment/verification activities are detailed for the Feature, Analysis and Design phases.

Safety Assessment Activities

The Functional Safety lane has been modeled by taking into account the ISO 26262 safety life-cycle. In the automotive domain, the ISO 26262 standard provides a complete set of process flow recommendations covering analysis, design and implementation of safety-critical systems and helping to respect the safety issues all along the life-cycle.

Following a top-down approach, the functional safety lane starts from the EAST-ADL Vehicle phase. The activities at this phase include Item definition in terms of target feature and the malfunction definition (feature flaws), as anomalies of the Item's outputs. On Vehicle phase, it is already possible to perform a Preliminary Hazard Analysis (PHA) and risk assessment, to estimate the level of risk associated with the Item (called Automotive Safety Integrity Level or ASIL), and to define a safety goal (and if it is possible the safe states) for each hazardous event identified, as well as, the set of essential safety requirements.

Once the functional safety concept (safety goals, ASILs, safety requirements, hazards and risks) is specified, the Item can be developed with a system perspective in the EAST-ADL Analysis Phase. The functional safety lane at the EAST-ADL Analysis Phase includes definition of the functional safety requirements and then their allocation to a preliminary architecture. At this phase, the System Hazard Analysis (SHA) can be conducted – in addition to the PHA and risk assessment – to study the propagation of failures across the system architecture. At this level the preliminary safety assessment can be conducted as well. Typical safety assessment at this phase employs Fault Tree generation and qualitative Analysis (FTA), Failure Mode and Effects Analysis (FMEA), Common Cause Analysis (CCA). FTA and FMEA are complementary methods to analyze propagation of faults through the system. Since there is no information on allocation to the hardware components available at the Analysis phase, only qualitative analysis can be performed. Expected results may include list of possible failure modes of analyzed system components, fault trees generated for the feared (or top) events corresponding to the priory defined hazards and risks, minimal cut sets, FMEA tables and a list of common cause failures (CCF).

During the Design phase, it is possible to define the technical safety requirements and allocate them to architectural elements. This allows performing quantitative analysis of system hardware components. Safety activities imply refining priory obtained FTA, FMEA and CCA results, performing quantitative FTA, and in particular, calculating probability of the top events and minimal cut sets, calculating Probability of Failure on Demand (PFD) and Probability of Failure per Hour (PFH), etc.

Table 2. Safety lane main activites

Phase	Verification Activities and Methods	Expected Results
Vehicle	Preliminary Hazard Analysis Risk Assessment	Hazards & Risks, Safety goals and ASILs, Safety Requirements
Analysis	Preliminary Hazard Analysis and Risk Assessment System Hazard Analysis using FTA&FMEA Preliminary Safety Assessment using FTA, FMEA, CCA	Hazards & Risks, Safety goals and ASILs, Safety Requirements (refined) Qualitative FTA, Minimal Cut Sets, Top Events, FMEA, CCF
Design	Safety Assessment using FTA, FMEA, CCA	Qualitative & Quantitative FTA and FMEA, Top Events probability, PFD, PFH, CCF

In Section 0 we present the main models prescribed by the EAST-ADL methodology in the safety swimlane along with advanced safety analyses developed during the MAENAD project.

Timing Assessment Activities

The Timing swimlane gives guidelines on timing related activities conducted on EAST-ADL phases. Timing activities start on the EAST-ADL Analysis phase where functions that realize the vehicle features are introduced. This functional model is enriched with timing properties (e.g. activation rates for chain of functions) and constraints (e.g. end-to-end deadlines). However, in the Analysis phase, functions worst case execution times (WCETs) are unknown. In fact these WCETs needed for timing properties verification are available only after the implementation phase, which is a quite late point in the process to detect design errors. As a workaround to the missing WCETs, an activity called Time Budgeting allows specifying so-called time budgets. A global budget that might come from end-to-end deadlines is decomposed and allocated to functions. The outcome of this time budgeting activity is to enrich each function with a budget for its execution time and a budget for its local deadline. These budgets represent the timing requirements used as input of the following Design phase.

On the EAST-ADL Design phase, two main timing activities might be conducted:

1. The first one uses the function decomposition made in the Design phase to perform time budgets refinement. The result of this time budgeting activity is to enrich each atomic design function with an execution time budget. These refined budgets represent the timing requirements used as input of the implementation phase.

2. The second timing activity makes use of the refined time budgets, the allocation model and the timing specification, to achieve a first estimation of system schedulability. Actually, schedulability analysis applies at implementation level, once the application has been mapped on execution tasks. Nevertheless, at design level, simulation and verification techniques can detect timing errors on functional models. In TIMMO (TIMMO, 2007) and TIMMO-2-USE (TIMMO2USE, 2012) projects, some methodologies for timing validation & verification of EAST-ADL models have been proposed. In this context (Arda, Suryadevara, Peraldi-Frati & Mallet, 2013) provide a formal validation & verification approach based on simulation and model checking for the design phase. In MAENAD we proposed another approach for schedulability estimation of EAST-ADL models, based on optimization techniques and schedulability analysis. Section 0 presents such an approach along with main EAST-ADL models enabling schedulability estimation.

Fully Electric Vehicle Assessment Activities

The Fully Electric Vehicle swimlane is a guideline to develop FEVs by addressing the systems that are specific of this kind of vehicles. In particular, the functions and the systems considered have been grouped as follows: Electric propulsion, Regenerative Energy Storage, Regenerative Braking, Recharging, Energy conversion, Insulation and Protection, Anti-theft system and Human Machine Interface (HMI). In order to provide an effective support to FEV development, for most of the activities of the process, the reference to the applicable standards and regulations, and some synthetic requirements of the norms are sufficient. The norm references include the relevant ISO, IEC, EN, SAE standards, and UNECE and FMVSS regulations. Table 4 illustrates specific analysis activities related to FEV development, such as energy flow analysis, vehicle performance and range analysis, insulation resistance compliance analysis, etc. In the model-based framework developed in the MAENAD project, FEV-related analyses have been applied thanks to the integration between EAST-ADL models/tools and simulation models/tools, but no research efforts have been conducted on the analyses themselves. For this reason activities of the FEV swimlane are not further detailed in this chapter.

Interdependencies Among Swimlanes

Swimlanes identify activities related to a specific concept (core, safety, timing, FEV), however, they cannot be considered as independent. In particular it is expected that core swimlane artifacts

Table 3. Timing lane main activities

Phase	Verification Activities and Methods	Expected Results
Vehicle	N/A	N/A
Analysis	Time budgeting (methods: constraints resolution)	Time budgets on functions
Design	Time budgeting, Schedulability estimation (model checking, schedulability analysis, simulation, optimization)	Time budgets on design functions, nodes and buses utilization, response-times

Table 4. Fev lane main activities

Phase	Verification Activities & Methods	Expected Results
Vehicle	N/A	N/A
Analysis	Analysis of vehicle performance, energy consumption and range through functional simulation	Verification of vehicle performance, energy consumption and range, according to test condition and test case requirements
Design	Insulation analysis through on-purpose analysis	Overall insulation resistance, voltage compliance
	Analysis of charging inlet voltage decrease through circuit simulation	Compliance with voltage-time requirements of charging inlet
	Analysis of the Regenerative Energy Storage System through multi-physics simulation	Current and thermal effects in the case of short circuit
	Matching analysis of power equipment through functional simulation	Matching verification of component current and voltage
	Power requirement analysis in key-off mode through power budgeting	Compliance with specification
	Analysis of the Braking System through functional simulation	Phasing correctness of braking sources, safe brake operation at battery depleted state of charge, compliance with battery limits

will be input for safety, timing, FEV-swimlanes and viceversa. Figure 3 shows a general process, formalized in SPEM, describing the interaction between the core swimlane and an X-swimlane (where X stands for Safety, or Timing or FEV) in any phase '*i*' (where *i* stands for Vehicle, Analysis, Design). This process is iterative: through activity 1 'manage core requirements', core requirements are defined (possibly refined from higher-level requirements and taking into account the outcome of the previous iteration, if any). Core requirements and the core model from the higher phase (if any) are the input of activity 2: "create and verify core model". Through this activity, a solution for the core model is defined. This core model is input for the X-swimlane. In the X-swimlane, X-related requirements are managed through activity 3 (possibly taking as input the X-requirements coming from the higher phase) and then an X-model is defined and verified through activity 4 'create and verify X-model'. The X-model captures all the information required to carry out verification activities/analyses prescribed for the

given swimlane at the given phase. This model is typically built on the core model, by adding annotations to capture the X-related information. Once these activities are performed the X model can be enriched with activities/analysis results. Finally activity 5 'elaborate outcome' provides a complete document representing the outcome of the swimlane for the given phase. This document could serve to refine/validate X-requirements (coming back to activity 3) and/or could contain recommendations for the core swimlane. In the core swimlane the X-swimlane outcome will be inspected through activity 6 'inspect X-swimlane outcome and decide for a new iteration'. Through this activity it will be decided if a new iteration is needed or it is possible to move down to the lower phase.

The methodology does not specify in detail how to proceed if the outcomes from different X-swimlanes are conflicting. For instance the safety swimlane can recommend adding a software redundancy mechanism to address a safety goal, whereas the timing swimlane will declare

Figure 3. Spem process describing interaction between Core and the other Swimlanes

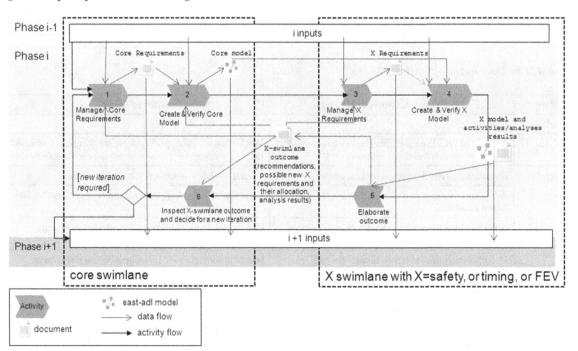

the software redundancy mechanism as exceeding the maximal CPU resource utilization. The resolution of this kind of conflicts is in general left to experienced system engineers. However, due to the increasing level of complexity of automotive architectures, system engineers cannot solve this kind of conflicts only relying on a manual approach. For this reason, automatic model-based optimization is going to play a central role in system development, helping system engineers to find appropriate trade-offs in case of conflicting goals. In the MAENAD project, a model-based optimization framework has been developed and will be presented in Section 0.

In the following we will detail modeling and verification support provided by the MAENAD model-based framework, focusing on the core, safety and timing swimlane.

MODELS AND VERIFICATION IN THE CORE LANE

The main aim of this section is to present the modeling concepts and their use to build artifacts in the core swim lane through a case-study, i.e. a power regenerative braking system. It shows how EAST-ADL covers design concepts throughout the design process, from high-level features to hardware/software functions identification, to capture key architectural concerns.

The Power Regenerative Braking System

The system combines conventional braking with power regeneration. The driver request is monitored through a brake pedal position sensor. A rotation speed sensor, an ABS (Anti-lock Braking System) controller, and an electromagnetic brake actuator are placed at each wheel. When requested, the ABS controller regulates the braking through the electromagnetic brake actuator. By collecting the measured wheel rotation speed, an ABS controller also detects the occurrence of wheel slip

by comparing the measured rotation speed with current vehicle speed. In the case of wheel slip, the controller adjusts the brake torque value for maximizing the traction and braking effectiveness. For the braking control of entire vehicle, a global brake controller receives the measured wheel rotation speeds and driver braking request and then sends an estimation of current vehicle speed and brake force request to each ABS controller. Instead of having the braking force completely realized by electromagnetic brake actuators, the regenerative braking allows a fraction or whole of kinetic energy of braking to be recovered and stored in battery. To support this, the global brake controller also receives the observed battery and motor status and estimates the maximum possible braking torque to be offered by an electrical motor. The controller then arbitrates the braking torques to be provided by the motor and brake discs.

The system implementation will be based on a distributed electrical architecture with 6 nodes: one central vehicle control node, four wheel brake control nodes, and one power electronic control node. The system has a communication network for distributing signals. For example, the estimated battery status information is fed from the battery observer to the power electronic control function for the torque estimation.

Core Models

Vehicle Feature Model

On Vehicle Level, the abstract system description is obtained by managing the features of an entire product line. In Figure 4, the feature tree of the braking system is shown. Each vehicle feature (VF) denotes a functional characteristic, such as the functional, non-functional, or even mechanical properties to be supported. As a child of the longitudinal control (LongitudinalCtrl) feature, the braking control feature (BrakingControl) is needed for the vehicle longitudinal control. The regenerative braking feature (PowerRegenerativeBraking) is a child feature of power control, allowing the kinetic energy produced by braking to be converted to electrical energy and stored in capacitor or/and battery. The interdependencies of vehicle features are supported by feature links (FeatureLink). In a feature link definition, the precise semantics of a feature relationship is given by the type attribute (Kind) and the direction attribute (isBidirectional).

In EAST-ADL, this feature model is the so-called core feature model, i.e., a technical feature model, describing on the topmost level the abstract boundaries of the system, although the architectural boundaries are, of course, not concretely defined, because the first architecture description happens on Analysis Level. This core feature model is connected via a Configuration Decision Model to the topmost feature models on Analysis Level and Design Level each. The Configuration Decision Model collects a set of configuration decisions. Each configuration decision expresses a connection between a specific (de)selection of features in the source feature model (here: the core feature model) and the

required (de)selection of features in the target feature model (here: either the topmost feature model on Analysis Level or the topmost feature model on Design Level). By that, a pre-selection of features in the core feature model requires a specific pre-selection of features in the respective target feature models, i.e., the core feature model is the main source for configuring the variability of the system. Let us note that feature modeling in EAST-ADL is an orthogonal concept, not only providing variability for Vehicle level then, but for the Analysis and Design levels as well. This capability is used for design space specification as explained in Section 0.

Functional Analysis Architecture Model

As the first step towards system realization, each vehicle feature (VF) of concern is refined into some functional design solutions, mainly from a control engineering perspective. Figure 5 shows an excerpt of the functional analysis architecture (FAA) for the vehicle feature ABS braking (ABSBraking).

Figure 4. Vehicle feature model of the regenerative braking system

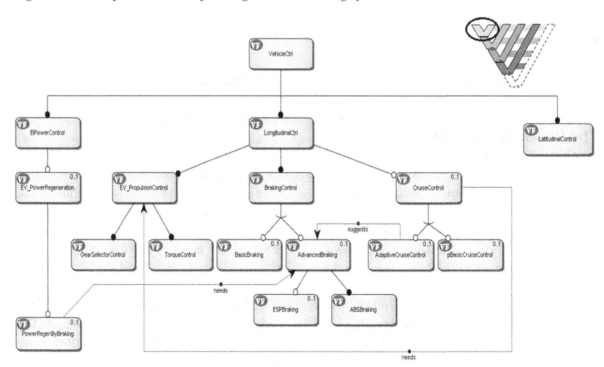

For design traceability, a realisation model is used to maintain the realisation mappings from vehicle features to the functional design solutions.

Compared to the vehicle feature models, a functional analysis architecture model provides additional information about the variables to be monitored and controlled, the internal computation blocks and their interactions. Here, the types of system internal computation blocks and the types of the system external I/O transformation blocks are classified by two different EAST-ADL constructs, i.e. AnalysisFunction and FunctionDevice, respectively. The composition description follows the basic *type-prototype* pattern of EAST-ADL, where a prototype represents a particular instantiation of a given type in a context. For example, the design shown in Figure 5 includes four prototypes (one for each wheel) of the same function device (WheelSpeedSensor).

In regard to execution, each function prototype runs according to a *run-to-completion* semantics (Chen, Feng, Qureshi, Lönn, & Hagl, 2013): when triggered, it reads all input parameters, executes the computation, and then writes the output parameters. If new data of the input parameters arrives during the execution or writing phase, it cannot be processed in the current executing cycle. Moreover, each port represents a one size buffer that does not block the sender when it is full or the receiver when it is empty. Each connector relates a pair of ports of the same type with a shared variable semantics.

Design Architecture Models

The design level architecture further details the analysis level design by taking the software and hardware resources into consideration. Again, the

Figure 5. Functional analysis architecture of the regenerative braking system (excerpt)

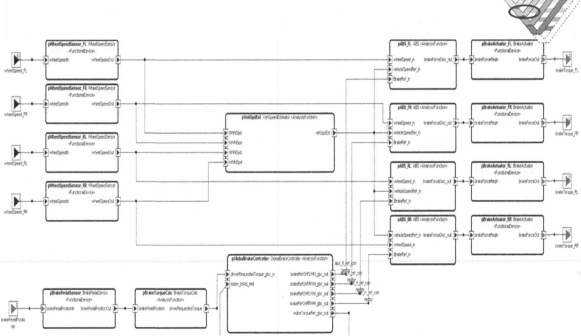

design traceability is maintained by a realisation model. Figure 6 shows an excerpt of the functional design architecture for the braking system. As it can be noted each wheel speed sensor analysis function (WheelSpeedSensor) in Figure 5 is here refined in two different design level functions: 1. one hardware transfer function for the encoder hardware (WhlRotationEncoder), of which the type is classified by the construct HardwareFunction; and 2. one design function for the encoder software (WhlSpeedSensorDevice), of which the type is classified by the construct DesignFunction. While a hardware transfer function is realized directly by hardware, a design function has instead a software based implementation. For example, the WhlSpeedSensorDevice function is further decomposed into a local device manager for application interactions and a basic software module for lower level hardware control. Each prototype with the corresponding type classified by design function has the same run-to-completion execu-

tion semantics as for the analysis level functions. The execution of a hardware transfer function is however given by the corresponding physical hardware. EAST-ADL allows additional behaviour constraints in regard to the physical dynamics to be annotated (see Section 4.3.).

One particular architectural design decision is related to the deployment of functions on hardware. To this end, EAST-ADL provides necessary language support for hardware modeling. The focus is on the specification of available electronic and electrical resources as well as the circuit design, such as communication network, I/O devices, ECUs (electronic control units) and power supplies. Being the allocation targets of design functions, these hardware resources are characterized by properties like memory size, clock frequency, bandwidth, etc. Figure 7 shows an excerpt of the hardware architecture model for the braking system, including the encoder device, the ECU, the brake actuator of a wheel,

Figure 6. Functional design architecture of the regenerative braking system (excerpt)

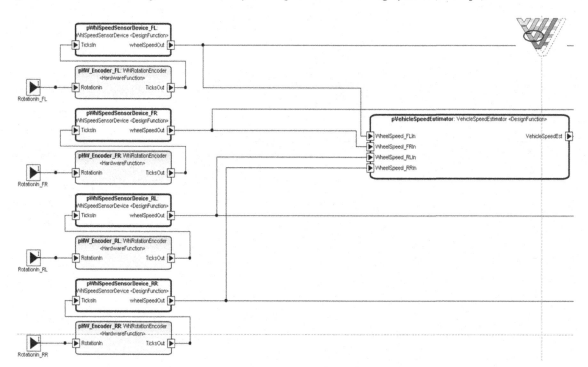

and the power supply unit. The connectors among these blocks represent the electrical wires, further characterized by physical circuit properties like length, resistance and insulation. Each wire connects a pair of hardware pins (HardwarePin) of the same type, representing the electronic or electrical connection points, such as the device power pins connected to the positive pole (v+) and minus pole (v-) of the 12V DC power supply (serviceBattery).

With EAST-ADL, dedicated allocation links (functionalAllocation) are introduced to specify the mapping from design functions to hardware resources. Figure 8 shows the EAST-ADL specification of allocations for some of the design functions with a matrix view and a textual view. Coming back to design functions shown in Figure 6, it can be noticed that the encoder device pEncoder_FL (with the column name checked in the matrix view) hosts now one prototype of the design function WhlRotationEncoder (pWhl-SpeedSensorDevice_FL) and one prototype of the hardware transfer function WhlRotationEncoder (pMW_EncoderFL).

Functional Verification via Model-Checking

EAST-ADL aims to obtain most of its analytical leverage through well established analysis methods and tools. To this end, the language package,

referred to as Behavior Constraint Description Annex (Chen et al., 2013), provides support for capturing and formalizing various behavioral concerns in the context of architectural design. On the basis of a formal semantics, several model transformations from EAST-ADL behavior constraint descriptions to several external tools (e.g. SPIN, UPPAAL, and Matlab/Simulink) have been developed. In the reminder of this section we introduce the basic EAST-ADL concepts for behavior descriptions through the ABS function.

Behavior Constraints for the ABS

In EAST-ADL, a behavior annotation, referred to as *behavior constraint*, can get different roles depending on the declared target associations. For example, such a behavior constraint can be used to capture the bounds of the acceptable behaviors of a system function. A behavior constraint can also be used to refine the textual statements of requirements including assumed system operational situations. Moreover, a behavior constraint can be introduced to provide a formalization of error annotations. The content of a behavior constraint is organized into the following three categories:

- **Attribute Quantification Constraint:** Relating to the declarations of value attributes and the related acausal quantifications (e.g., $U=I*R$).

Figure 7. Hardware architecture of the regenerative braking system

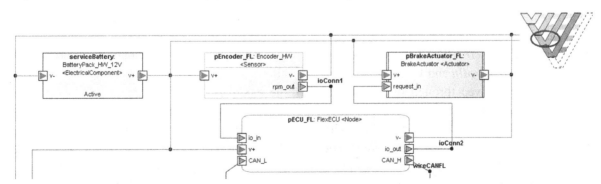

Figure 8. Allocation model for the regenerative braking system

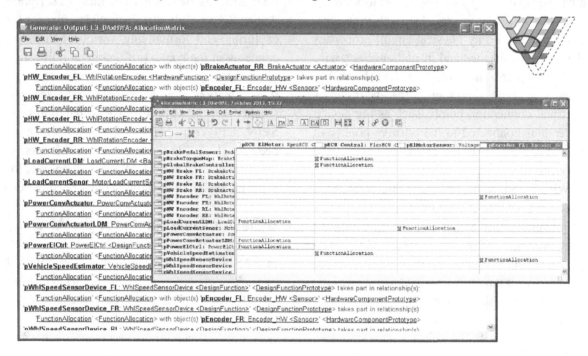

- **Temporal Constraint:** Relating to the declarations of behavior constraints where the history of behaviors on a timeline is taken into consideration.

- **Computation Constraint:** Relating to the declarations of cause-effect dependencies of data in terms of logical transformations (for data assignments) and logical paths.

For example, the quantification constraint in regard to the slip rate estimation by ABS function is given in Figure 9. According to the constraint description, the estimated slip rate (*SlipRate*) should follow the slip rate quantification (*SlipRateQuantification*) with the expression: *SlipRate=(VehicleSpeedIn-WheelSpeedIn*WheelRadius)/VehicleSpeedIn*. Here, the *VehicleSpeedIn* and *WheelSpeedIn* are two variables received through the functional ports vehicleSpeedRef_in and wheelSpeed_in respectively. The *WheelRadius* is a constant with the value of maximum allowed wheel radius. The EAST-ADL Behavior Constraint Description Annex uses an abstract notion of time, referred

to as logical time condition, as the time basis for quantifying physical dynamics by means of continuous- and discrete-time model, or for defining the timed guard conditions and invariants of state-machines or computations.

In Figure 10, the behavior constraint is further elaborated by a temporal constraint description in state machine (SM). The state invariants and transition guards are precisely defined by some attribute quantification specifications. In Figure 11, the specification of computation constraint declares two valid invocations to a transformation *Set_ABSBrakeTorqueOut* that calculates the ABS brake torque request.

As already mentioned, the EAST-ADL behavior constraint descriptions are transformed to external tools for the analysis support. This allows the engineers to exhaustively verifying the model against requirements. The verifiable requirements include assertion, freedom of deadlock, reachability of the desired state, avoidance of or compliance with given execution patterns, and linear temporal logic (LTL) statements. Figure 12 shows the PROMELA code section

Figure 9. The attribute quantification constraint description for an ABS function

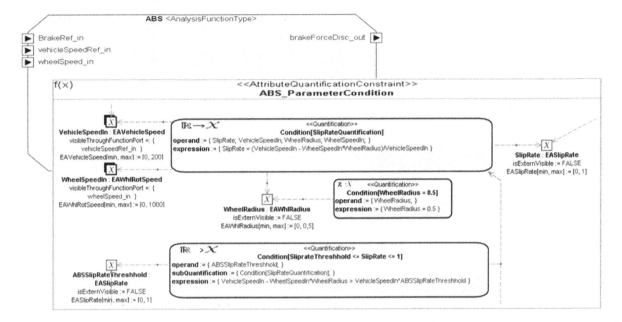

of the ABS function. Please note the assertion assert(0) is an added statement to guide the tool to search the execution path which indicates the locked condition of a wheel. In model checking terminology, the path is a counterexample, which gives the designer the hint on how the given state may be reached.

MODELS AND VERIFICATION IN THE SAFETY LANE

The safety swimlane focuses on the provision of methodology and modeling support allowing all safety related information according to ISO 26262 to be captured and managed seamlessly along with the core system design specification (Chen, Johansson, Lönn, Blom, Walker, Papadopoulos, Torchiaro, Tagliabo & Sandberg, 2011). In this section we present the main models prescribed by the EAST-ADL methodology in the safety swimlane. Advanced safety analyses – developed during the MAENAD project – are also briefly presented.

Dependability Models

Through its Dependability package, EAST-ADL allows a wide range of functional safety related concerns (e.g. hazards, faults/failures, safety requirements) to be declared and structured seamlessly along with the lifecycle of core system development as shown in Figure 13. One key role of EAST-ADL dependability model is to capture the related system requirements and design information from which the safety requirements are elicited.

Along with the modeling support for the elicitation of safety requirements, EAST-ADL also allows the engineers to precisely defining the related error behaviors for the purposes of safety analysis through explicit error models. These analytical models provide the support for associating the annotations of error descriptions (i.e., faults and error propagations) within the target system. See Figure 14 for a modeling example, where the connection links represent the error propagations due to communication links or allocation relations in the design.

Figure 10. The temporal constraint description for an ABS function

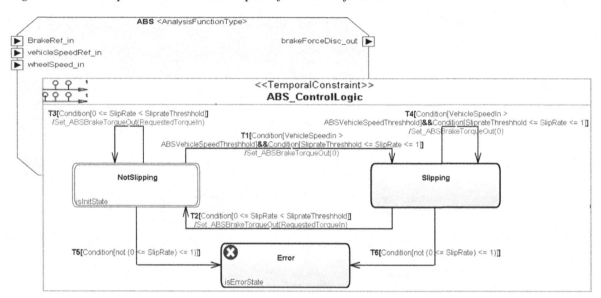

Figure 11. The computation constraint description for an ABS function

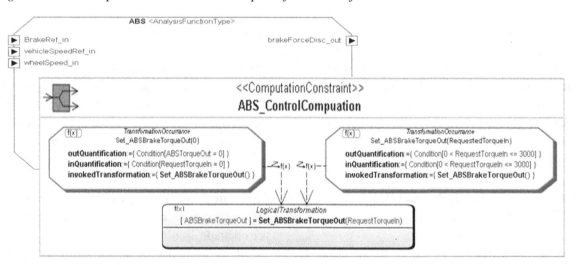

Each block in the error model contains the descriptions of plausible anomalies (*Anomaly*) in terms of faults and failures that a target system entity can have. The ports declare which faults the targeted system entity can receive from its environment and which failures the targeted system entity can propagate to the environment. Such ports are analytical and can be traced to the corresponding communication ports of functions or components.

Within each error model, there is a declaration of error behavior (ErrorBehavior) for relating the declared output failures to the declared faults. The exact formalism could be chosen according to the analysis methods of interest as well as the complexity of error logic. For example, the formalism can be directly based on Boolean logic expression as given in HiP-HOPS. For a state-machine (SM) based definition of error behaviors, the EAST-ADL temporal behavior constraint is used (Chen,

Figure 12. The PROMELA Code of the ABS Function

```
        /* The ABS function at each wheel satisfies the run-to-completion semantics */
proctype abs(byte id; chan RequestedTorqueIn, VehicleSpeedIn, WheelSpeedIn, ABSBrakeTorqueOut)
{
    byte reqTorq, vehSpd, whlSpd, ABSBrakeTorq; /* Local variables */

    do
    :: trig_abs[id] ? _ ->                      /* The execution trigger */
        read_Inport(RequestedTorqueIn, reqTorq);    /* Read all inports and save the values */
        read_Inport(VehicleSpeeddIn, vehSpd);       /* in local variables */
        read_Inport(WheelSpeedIn, whlSpd);
                /* Note: the vehSpd in this process is the estimate from the average */
                /* of the speeds of the 4 wheels. */
        if
        :: vehSpd > ABSVehicleSpeedThreshold &&
            vehSpd - whlSpd*WheelRadius > vehSpd*ABSSlipRateThreshold ->
                                            /* If locked, release the brake */
            ABSBrakeTorq = 0;                   /* Set_ABSBrakeTorqueOut(0) */
            assert(0)                           /* Flag an error when a wheel is locked */
        :: else ->      /* If not locked, apply the full torque demand */
            ABSBrakeTorq = reqTorq          /* Set_ABSBrakeTorqueOut(RequestedTorqueIn) */
        fi;

        write_Outport(ABSBrakeTorqueOut, ABSBrakeTorq)      /* Write the outports */
    od
}
```

Mahmud, Walker, Feng, Lönn, & Papadopoulos, 2013). This is shown in Figure 15, where the error model description targets a system control function with two internal parts func_a and func_b. The initial state is AB to indicate that the internal parts are both working and the failure of the system is sequence-dependent—i.e., func_a and func_b both need to fail in sequence for the whole system to fail (state FAILED). However, if func_b fails first or alone then the system enters a DEGRADED state. Such a sequence-dependent behavior is not uncommon in safety-critical systems; for example, in simple primary-standby architecture, if a sensor fails and the monitored component (the primary) fails afterwards, then the redundant component cannot be activated. But if the primary fails first or alone, then the system can still function in standby mode.

Safety Analysis

There are several well-known approaches to automated safety analysis. Some of these approaches infer the effects of component failures on the overall system by means of model-checking and simulation techniques, such as the approaches described (Bozzano & Villafiorita, 2003). These approaches can be computationally expensive due to their inductive nature (i.e. from causes to effects), especially when combinations of failures need to be considered. Instead, a deductive approach (i.e. from effects to causes) can often be more efficient. One example is the HiP-HOPS method, originally described in (Papadopoulos, & McDermid, 1999) for a static safety analysis, but recently extended in Walker & Papadopoulos (2009), and in Mahmud, Papadopoulos, & Walker (2010), Mahmud (2012) for a temporal analysis.

HiP-HOPS starts taking place early in the design lifecycle with exploratory FFA; but can be mainly used after a hierarchical model of the system has been developed. The failure behavior of components is analyzed using a modification of classical FMEA, called the Interface Focused FMEA (IF-FMEA). The application of this technique generates a model of the local failure behavior of the component which is represented as a table. The table provides a list of component failure modes observed at the component outputs. For each component output failure, the causes are determined as a logical combination of internal malfunctions or deviations of the component

Figure 13. Dependability model structuring information related to safety goals

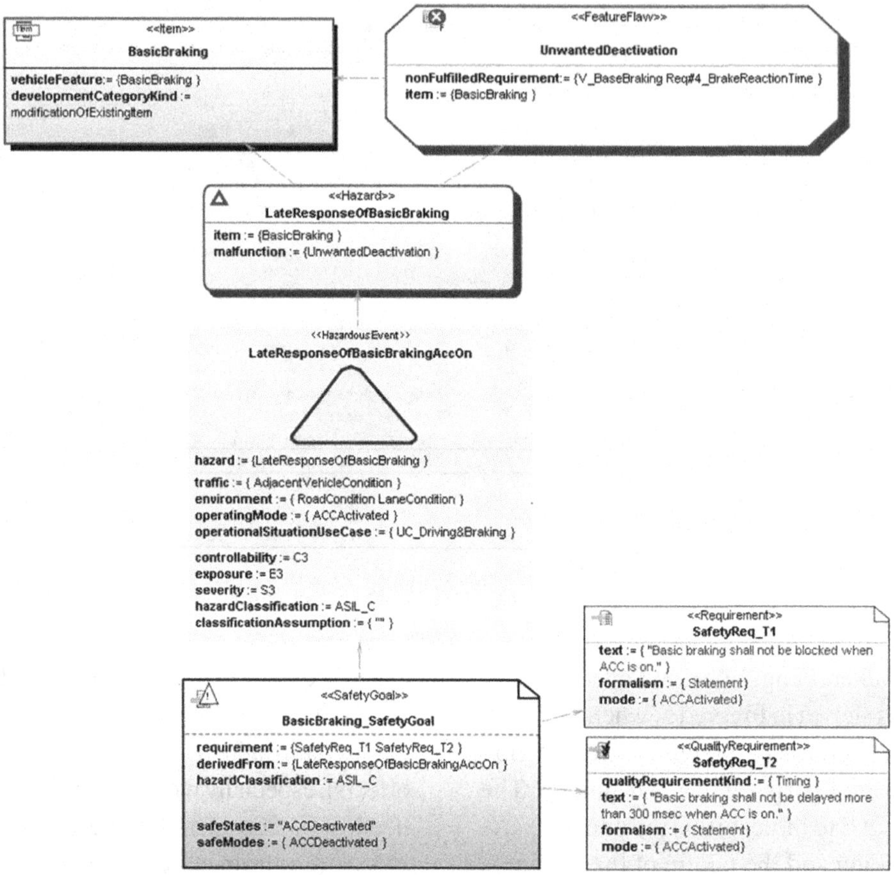

<<Item>>
BasicBraking
vehicleFeature:= {BasicBraking }
developmentCategoryKind := modificationOfExistingItem
<<FeatureFlaw>>
UnwantedDeactivation
nonFulfilledRequirement:= {V_BaseBraking Req#4_BrakeReactionTime }
item := {BasicBraking }
<<Hazard>>
LateResponseOfBasicBraking
item := {BasicBraking }
malfunction := {UnwantedDeactivation }
<<HazardousEvent>>
LateResponseOfBasicBrakingAccOn
hazard := {LateResponseOfBasicBraking }
traffic := { AdjacentVehicleCondition }
environment := { RoadCondition LaneCondition }
operatingMode := { ACCActivated }
operationalSituationUseCase := { UC_Driving&Braking }
controllability := C3
exposure := E3
severity := S3
hazardClassification := ASIL_C
classificationAssumption := { "" }
<<Requirement>>
SafetyReq_T1
text := { "Basic braking shall not be blocked when ACC is on." }
formalism := { Statement}
mode := { ACCActivated}
<<SafetyGoal>>
BasicBraking_SafetyGoal
requirement := {SafetyReq_T1 SafetyReq_T2 }
derivedFrom := {LateResponseOfBasicBrakingAccOn }
hazardClassification := ASIL_C
safeStates := "ACCDeactivated"
safeModes := { ACCDeactivated }
<<QualityRequirement>>
SafetyReq_T2
qualityRequirementKind := { Timing }
text := { "Basic braking shall not be delayed more than 300 msec when ACC is on." }
formalism := { Statement}
mode := { ACCActivated}

Figure 14. Error model defining the faults and error propagations of target system hardware and functions

dsw_DF: ErrM_BswDF
dsw_BSW: ErrM_DswBSW
dsw_TF: ErrM_DswTF
dsw1_hw: ErrM_Switch
dsw2_hw: ErrM_Switch
WiredConnection1_TF: ErrM_WiredConnectionTF
WiredConnection2_TF: ErrM_WiredConnectionTF
wiredConnection1_hw: ErrM_Wire
wiredConnection2_hw: ErrM_Wire
vehicleCtrlUnit_DF: ErrM_vehicleCtrlUnitDF
vehicleCtrlUnit_BSW: ErrM_VehicleCtrlUnitBSW
vehicleControlUnit_hw: ErrM_VehicleControlUnit
CANConnection_TF: ErrM_CANConnectionTF
CAN_hw: ErrM_CAN
powerInverter_DF: ErrM_powerInverterDF
powerInverter_BSW: ErrM_powerInverterBSW
powerInverter_hw: ErrM_PowerInverter
Potential Causes of Random Failure by Drive switches contacts: Contact stuck, open circuit, loss of power supply, short to GND, short to PS;
Potential Causes of Random Failure by Wired connections: Mechanical break;
Potential Causes of Random Failure by VehicleControlUnit: typical random faults related to an ecu (ram, I/O, etc).
Potential Causes of Random Failure by CAN: cable in SC to Vbat / to Gnd / interrupted, EMC, false contact on connectors, oxidation, cut wire, pin damage, loose fastened wire;
Potential Causes of Random Failure by Power Converter: Potential Causes of Random Failure: typical random faults related to an ecu (ram, I/O, etc).

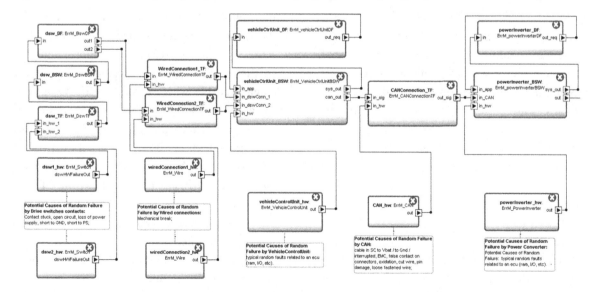

Figure 15. A state-machine based error logic description

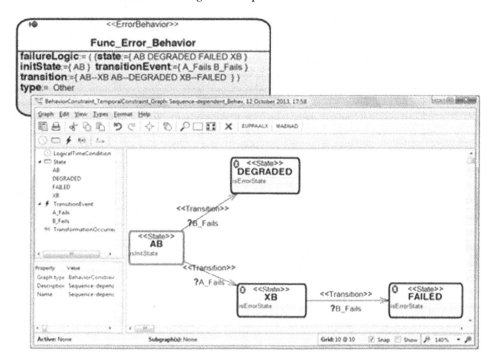

inputs. An IF-FMEA table records component reactions to failures that are generated by other components. Moreover, the table determines the failure modes that the component itself generates and may propagate to other components. Upon determination of local failure behavior of all components, HiP-HOPS can show how the functional failures (identified in the exploratory FFA) arise from combinations of the low-level component failure modes (identified in the IF-FMEAs). This is done by automatically synthesizing fault trees. A fault tree is generated incrementally by parsing the expressions, which are derived from the IF-FMEA, and encountered during a hierarchical traversal of the system model. The tool automatically performs minimal cut-set analysis and probabilistic calculations on the minimized fault trees to predict the reliability and availability of the system.

The failure annotations required by HiP-HOPS are originally Boolean-based. For example, with an error behavior of the vehicle speed estimator (see Regenerative Braking System in Figure 6)

such that omission of output is caused either by an internal failure or by omission of any front wheel speed input or combined omission of rear wheel speed inputs. Furthermore, omission of output from any wheel speed sensor is caused either by an Electro Magnetic Interference (EMI) or by omission of input; and similarly, omission of output from any wheel rotation encoder is caused either by an internal failure or by omission of input. Figure 16 shows some cut sets (calculated by the tool) of the synthesized fault trees shown in Figure 17.

Figure 18 represents an FMEA table produced by the tool to show each failure mode, its further effect and the contributing failure modes.

As for SM-based failure descriptions, these can be basically compiled into fault trees such that each state that represents a system failure becomes the top event of a fault tree. Each branch of that FT represents the conjunction of the events that label a full path (from the initial state to the failure state). A conjunction of events represents one cut set of the fault tree, and if it contains no redundancies,

Figure 16. Cut Sets displayed by HiP-HOPS for Omission of Vehicle Speed Estimator (excerpt)

Figure 17. The HiP-HOPS synthesized fault trees for Omission of Vehicle Speed Estimator

then it is a minimal cut set (MCS). If there is a path with a loop (like in the SM describing an ABS function in Figure 10), then the conjunction of the events which label that path is not minimal

and the loop needs to be removed. Therefore, the fault tree expression which corresponds to the error state of the SM of Figure 10 is as follows:

Error = SlipRateOverstep + SlipRateOverstep . [(VehicleSpeedInGreaterThanABSThreshold) . (SlipRateGreaterThanThreshold)]

where '+' and '.' represent the Boolean 'OR' and 'AND' respectively. The events 'Slip-RateOverstep' corresponds to the condition [not(0<=SlipRate <= 1)], 'VehicleSpeedIn-GreaterThanABSThreshold' corresponds to the condition [VehicleSpeedIn>ABSVehicleSpeed Threshold] and 'SlipRateGreaterThanThreshold' corresponds to the condition [SlipRateThreshold <=SlipRate <=1].

The failure expression of the corresponding fault tree can be simply minimized to:

Error = SlipRateOverstep

Figure 18. FMEA displayed by HiP-HOPS (excerpt)

Component: RotationIn_RL				
Failure Mode	Further Effect	Severity	Contributing Failure Modes	
○ RotationIn_RL.Failure	Omission-VehicleSpeedEstimator.VehicleSpeedEst	0	○ RotationIn_RR.Failure	
			○ WhlRotationEncoder_RR.Failure	
			○ WhlSpeedSensorDevice_RR.EMI	

Component: RotationIn_RR				
Failure Mode	Further Effect	Severity	Contributing Failure Modes	
○ RotationIn_RR.Failure	Omission-VehicleSpeedEstimator.VehicleSpeedEst	0	○ RotationIn_RL.Failure	
			○ WhlRotationEncoder_RL.Failure	
			○ WhlSpeedSensorDevice_RL.EMI	

Component: WhlRotationEncoder_RL				
Failure Mode	Further Effect	Severity	Contributing Failure Modes	
○ WhlRotationEncoder_RL.Failure	Omission-VehicleSpeedEstimator.VehicleSpeedEst	0	○ RotationIn_RR.Failure	
			○ WhlRotationEncoder_RR.Failure	
			○ WhlSpeedSensorDevice_RR.EMI	

Component: WhlRotationEncoder_RR				
Failure Mode	Further Effect	Severity	Contributing Failure Modes	
○ WhlRotationEncoder_RR.Failure	Omission-VehicleSpeedEstimator.VehicleSpeedEst	0	○ WhlRotationEncoder_RL.Failure	
			○ RotationIn_RL.Failure	
			○ WhlSpeedSensorDevice_RL.EMI	

Concerning sequence-dependent failures, however, Mahmud et al., (2010, 2012) proposed an approach which extends the HiP-HOPS method for dynamic analysis by generating and synthesizing Pandora Temporal Fault Trees (TFTs) from the state machines. On the one hand, Pandora is designed for temporal qualitative analysis (Walker et al., 2009); it is equipped with temporal laws which are very useful in enabling the minimization of the TFTs. On the other hand, the proposed conversion approach generates fault trees extended only with the necessary temporal information—i.e., it detects and preserves the significance of the sequencing of faults during the conversion and all along the logical analysis. Thus, the approach remains as close as possible within the flexibility and ease-of use of the conventional fault trees.

To correctly capture the sequence-dependent failures, the approach mainly uses the Pandora Priority-AND gate (PAND, symbol '<') and the Priority-OR gate (POR, symbol '|'). A PAND gate represents a sequence of events typically from left to right, while a POR gate models a priority situation where one event (leftmost) must occur first and other events may or may not occur subsequently. To support a qualitative analysis, Pandora defines a set of temporal laws for identifying and removing redundant sequences of events. For example, $(A|B)$. $B \Leftrightarrow A<B$, where the left hand side conjunction expression (A must occur first, but B must also occur) is equivalent to the right hand side expression (A occurs before B, both events have to occur).

The conversion algorithm which generates (temporal) FTs from the SMs performs backward traversals from each final state that represent a system (or a component) failure to the initial state. At each join state (a state at which paths diverge) during the traversal, if there is a common event with another divergent path, then the FT becomes temporal using POR. For example, the conversion of the SM of Figure 15 generates temporal rather conventional FTs since the two divergent paths at the join state (the initial state in this case) share a common event, and hence:

$$Degraded = B\_Fails | A\_Fails$$

$$Failed = B\_Fails \cdot A\_Fails | B\_Fails$$

The failure expression which corresponds to the Failed state is equivalent to A_Fails<B_Fails (using the temporal law described previously). The other expression specifies that only B_Fails needs to occurs, A_Fails may or may not occur afterwards.

The order in which failure events occur is captured in a probabilistically sound way, initially using POR only, then together with PAND, depending on the temporal law used. For example, in the case of exponential failure distribution for the basic events, the solution of the corresponding Markov model gives the same probabilistic results associated with the states FAILED and DE-GARDED as those given in Fussel, Aber & Rahl

(1976) and in Merle, Roussel, Lesage & Bobbio (2010) for the PAND and POR-like respectively, see Mahmud (2012) for a detailed comparison.

This conversion approach is used as part of a novel compositional method SAFORA1, which has been developed in Mahmud (2012) to increase scalability. Safora (Figure 19) is a top-down synthesis of (temporal) FTs generated during backward traversals of component SMs. The synthesis starts from a highly abstract SM describing the monolithic behavior of the system (top level SM in the hierarchy), and from which we generate preliminary fault trees. Then we start expanding these fault trees from the SMs local to the components. The fault trees get minimised

Figure 19. Overview of the Safora method

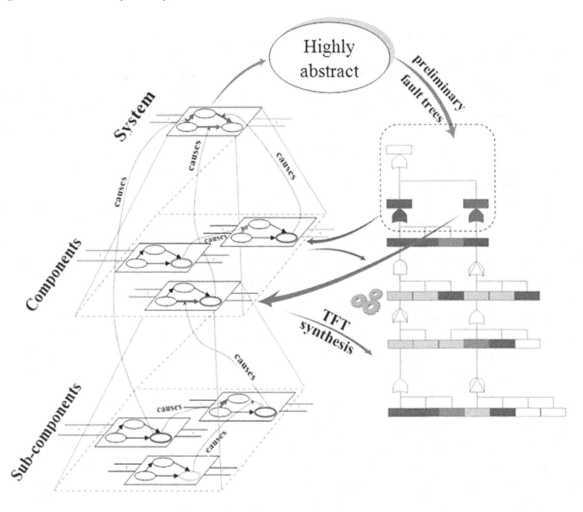

when appropriate during synthesis. A final analysis takes place for each system failure (temporal) FT which is completely synthesized— i.e., when no more expandable or non-atomic events remain in the fault tree.

MODELS AND VERIFICATION IN THE TIMING LANE

Timing Models

Timing modeling in EAST-ADL results from the work done in TIMMO project (TIMMO, 2007), which produced a dedicated language called TADL and from Timmo2Use, which produced a second version of the language called TADL2 (TIMMO2USE, 2012). TADL concepts were integrated in the course of the ATESST2 project in the EAST-ADL language. TADL2 concepts will be integrated in EAST-ADL during the third year of the MAENAD project, but in the current language version (2.1.10) TADL2 has not been integrated yet. For this reason we will refer to TADL in the reminder of the section.

EAST-ADL divides timing information into timing requirements and timing properties, where the actual timing properties of a solution must satisfy the specified timing requirements. EAST-ADL currently focuses on modeling of timing requirements on the functional abstraction levels of the architecture description language. The implementation level, i.e. AUTOSAR, is currently not explicitly considered, but it is expected that the information can be modelled in a similar way. The same holds for timing properties on both the functional abstraction levels and the implementation level.

Timing information on the functional abstraction levels is perceived as follows: timing requirements for a function can be captured on logical abstraction levels where no concrete hardware is yet available. This allows the specification of general timing requirements such as end-to-end delays from sensors to actuators regardless of how

the final solution is built. This reflects the notion that a purely logical functional specification is not concerned with its technical realisation, i.e. how many ECUs or bus systems are ultimately involved. What matters from the functional perspective are the recurring end-to-end delays of a control application, which need to keep pace with the real plant. Specifying timing requirements on the implementation level might be both too late in the development process and rather difficult because of language complexity (e.g. AUTOSAR) and the number of details on this level. However, it sounds more feasible to refine the timing requirements on the implementation level from the timing requirements of the design functional model. Indeed AUTOSAR Timing Extensions (TIMEX) (AUTOSAR, 2011) allows timing specifications in the AUTOSAR implementation level. It is important to note that the short semantic distance between TADL and TIMEX facilitates this refinement of timing requirements.

Timing properties are characteristics of a solution, e.g. actual response times, and should be reflected in the functional abstraction levels.

In EAST-ADL, timing requirements are divided into various kinds of delays (or latencies) for single time-consuming modeling entities as well as specific requirements for temporal synchronisation of input or output data. The delays are either end-to-end delays, which are subject to segmentation along the functional decomposition track (e.g. end-to-end delay for a top-level function), or the delays form part of an end-to-end timing chain, and thus constitute segments of such an end-to-end timing chain. More precisely, EAST-ADL Timing concepts are based on:

- **Events:** Relate to EAST-ADL entities and depict observables: e.g. data arriving on a port, triggering of function execution, etc.
- **Event Chains:** Bind together events to establish sequences/relations between events e.g. to capture a complete end-to-end flow requirement between data sent by a sensor to output by an actuator.

- **Constraints:** Put temporal constraints on sets of events or on event chains, e.g. deadlines to be met, expected delays, patterns of data arrival, synchronisation of outputs on a set of ports, etc. Note that these constraints represent measured/computed properties when attached to a VVactualOutcome, concept coming from Verification&Validation constructs of EAST-ADL.

One example is featured in Figure 20 in which an excerpt of the functional design architecture of the Regenerative braking is shown. The timing model here must capture maximal end-to-end delays that must hold from the instant of time in which data arrives at the pedal sensor to the instant of time in which the output is produced by brakes actuators. The figure shows how to model this maximal delay for the output produced at the brake actuator of the front left wheel. To identify the instants in which data is available at input/output ports, two events are here defined. The first event ('BrakePedalSensorInputPortEvent') represents the data arrival at the input port of the brakeSensor function, while the second one (BrakeActuatorFLOutputPortEvent') represents the data availability at the output port of the actuator. These two events represent respectively the stimulus and the response of the event chain. The event chain is subject to a reactionConstraint whose maximal tolerated value is 50ms.

Other common constraints/properties characterizing timing models are execution timing constraints. The difference between a reaction constraint and an execution timing constraint is appreciable at design level in which hardware allocation is specified. Execution time constraint concerns the time needed by the function to be executed in isolation. It can be considered as a minimal bound for the function to be executed. A reaction constraint is a requirement that set the upper bound for the function to complete its execution; it must be greater than the execution time.

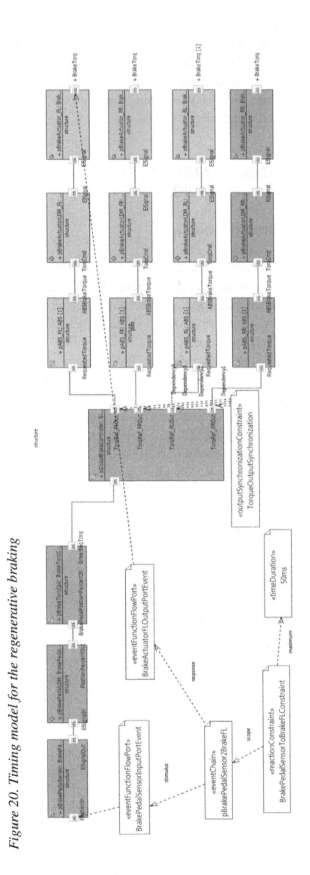

Figure 20. Timing model for the regenerative braking

Timing constraints on data availability can be specified as well. For instance, an output synchronization constraint expresses a timing constraint on the output synchronization among the set of response events. On Figure 20, for readability concern we have omitted to display flow port events and event chains that are constrained by the output synchronization constraint 'Torque-OutputSynchronization'.

The functional model of the design phase depicted in Figure 20 specifies a graph of functions. Activation semantics is added to that functional graph through events definition and timing constraints among these events. This gives a timed partial order of execution for functions which is needed to make timing analysis. The following subsection shows timing analysis made on this BBW timed functional architecture model.

Timing Analysis

As explained in Section 3, two timing verification activities can be conducted at design level: time budget refinement and schedulability estimation. In this section we focus only on schedulability estimation.

Schedulability estimation at design level is able to detect resources overload situations that will prevent the schedulability of the system, computing bus and processor utilization. Following formulas are used for the computation of processors utilization (on the left hand side) and buses utilization (on the right hand side). In these formulas:

- s_i is the ith signal of the system.
- f_i is the ith function of the system.
- β_i is the ith communication bus.
- c_i is the ith processor.
- The $\rightarrow$ relation indicates that the left term (function/signal) is allocated on the right term (processor/bus).

- $\omega_{i,j}$ represents the WCET/WCTT of the function/signal i on the processor/bus j.
- P_i is the activation period of the function/signal i.

$$U_{c_i} = \sum_{f_i \to c_i} \frac{\omega_{f_i, c_i}}{P_{f_i}}$$

$$U_{\beta_i} = \sum_{s_i \to \beta_i} \frac{\omega_{s_i, \beta_i}}{P_{s_i}}$$

Based on this formulation for the Regenerative Braking we obtained a bus utilization of 36%. For processor utilization we obtained the results shown in Figure 21 provided by the Qompass tool (MAENAD, 2013).

Even though, bus and processor utilization are key indicators for system schedulability, the respect of maximal resource utilization capacities does not imply that the system is schedulable. System schedulability can be verified only by computing end-to-end latency of each path from sensors to actuators and comparing latencies against end-to-end deadlines. So-called response-time analysis is usually employed to compute end-to-end latency. Response time analysis, however, considers tasks chains instead of function chains. Functions and tasks, however, are not the same thing: a task is the software resource that executes functions. Response time is very sensitive to the way in which functions are partitioned into tasks. For this reason response-time analysis is usually reserved to the implementation phase. During the MAENAD project, however, we investigated solutions to anticipate response-time analysis to the design phase. As a result of this investigation, three different advanced optimization approaches have been elaborated, in order to provide a prediction on latency of end-to-end chains at design level. The first approach lies in computing latency assuming the best partitioning of functions to tasks (from now on called simply partitioning) and best priority assignment to tasks (from now on called

Figure 21. Resources utilization for a manual allocation of functions to ECUs

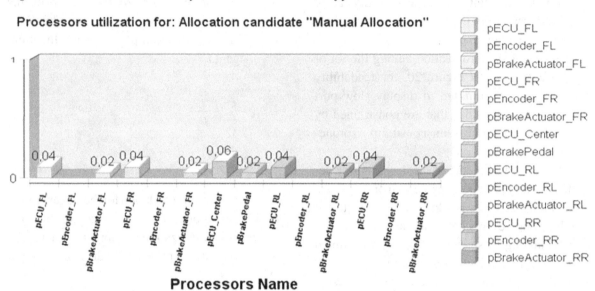

scheduling) with respect to latency minimization. Operationally, this means: to start from a manual allocation of functions to nodes (available at design level), to find a partitioning and scheduling that minimize latency via an optimization method, and then to output minimal latency as the latency for the initial manual allocation. The other two approaches aims at improving the first approach treating as well the allocation problem (functions to nodes) in the optimization loop. RTCSA (Mehiaoui, Tucci-Piergiovanni, Babau & Lemarchand, 2012) is a two-stage optimization approach. First stage of this approach deals with allocation optimization with respect to resource utilization. Allocation found in the first stage is given as input to the second stage that deals with partitioning and scheduling optimization with respect to latency. LCTES (Mehiaoui, Wozniak, Tucci-Piergiovanni, Mraidha, Di Natale, Zeng, Babau, Lemarchand & Gerard, 2013) is an improvement of RTCSA. Concretely, like RTCSA an optimized allocation is found and an optimized partitioning and scheduling is found for this allocation, but here the allocation is optimized with respect to latency already in the first stage, by combining two classical optimization strategies: divide and conquer and iterative improvement. Divided-and-conquer

consists in dividing the allocation, partitioning and scheduling (PPS) problem in two sub-problems solved in cascade, in which allocation is solved first (PP stage), and then partitioning and scheduling (PS stage). In both sub-problems, we minimize the latency. Iterative improvement is used to move towards the optimum. Figure 22 shows the main algorithmic steps of the approach.

Each iteration starts from a PP optimization with an initial (valid) configuration for PPS as an input. PP provides the allocation of functions/signals to nodes/buses in an implicit manner. Namely, during this stage, tasks and messages are allocated on nodes/buses; however, knowing the partitioning of functions/signals at this stage, their allocation can be derived. Next, the PS stage tries to find a new partitioning and scheduling solution that improves the solution found in the PP stage.

The inner loop tries to find an optimal system configuration by applying iteratively an optimization sequence until convergence (two successive solutions are the same). Depending on the selection of the initial configuration, the PP+PS solution may be a local optimum. To move away from local minima, the outer loop selects random initial configurations for expanding the exploration space.

Figure 22. Overview of the LCTES optimization approach

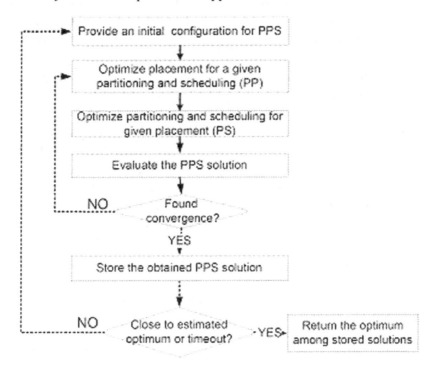

Figure 23. Formulation of functions response time computation

$$R_{f_i} = J_{f_i} + W_{f_i}$$

$$J_{f_i} = \max_{\substack{f_j \in F: \\ \tau_{f_i} = \tau_{f_j}}} \left[\max_{\substack{s_i \in \Phi: \\ f_j \in rec(s_i)}} [R_{s_i}] \right]$$

$$W_{f_i} = \omega_{f_i, c_j} + \sum_{\substack{f_k \in \{F \setminus f_i\}: \\ \tau_{f_i} = \tau_{f_k}}} \omega_{f_k, c_j} + \sum_{f_k \in hp(f_i)} \left\lceil \frac{W_{f_i} + J_{f_k}}{P_{f_k}} \right\rceil \cdot \omega_{f_k, c_j}$$

Figure 24. Formulation of the response time computation for signals

$$R_{s_i} = J_{s_i} + \omega_{s_i, \beta_j} + \sum_{\substack{s_k \in \{\Phi \setminus s_i\}: \\ \mu_{s_i} = \mu_{s_k}}} \omega_{s_k, \beta_j} + W_{s_i}$$

$$J_{s_i} = \begin{cases} \max_{\substack{s_j \in \Phi: \\ \mu_{s_i} = \mu_{s_j}}} [R_{snd_{s_i}}] & s_i \text{ is transmitted between processors} \\ R_{snd_{s_i}} & s_i \text{ is transmitted between tasks} \\ J_{snd_{s_i}} & s_i \text{ is transmitted within a task} \end{cases}$$

$$W_{s_i} = B_{s_i} + \sum_{s_k \in hp(s_i)} \left\lceil \frac{W_{s_i} + J_{s_k}}{P_{s_k}} \right\rceil \omega_{s_k, \beta_j}$$

Based on an MILP (Mixed Integer Linear Programming) formulation of these stages this algorithm has been implemented in Qompass tool (MAENAD, 2013). Figure 23 and Figure 24 give formulas for response time, *computed on chains of functions and signals*. These formulas are an adaptation of traditional formulas for chains of tasks and messages, assuming pre-emptive tasks and non-preemptive messages. These formulas are used to set the objective function and the latency constraint of the MILP formulation (not shown here for space reasons).

Within these formulas in addition to the previously described terms the following ones mean:

- R_i is the Worst-Case Response Time (WCRT) of function/signal i.
- J_i is the jitter of the activation of function/signal i.
- W_i is the completion time of function/signal i.

- $hp(i)$ is the set of functions/signals with a priority greater than the priority of function/signal i that are allocated on the same processor/bus.
- B_i is the blocking time of function/signal i.
- Φ is the set of signals of the system.
- F is the set of functions of the system.
- τ_{fi} is the task on which function f_i is allocated.
- μ_{si} is the message transmitting signal s_i.
- snd_{si} is the function sending the signal i.
- $rec(s_i)$ is the set of functions that receives the signal i.

The global WCRT for a function f_i (Figure 23) is computed as the sum of the jitter (representing the delay between the instant of the external event arrival, the instant of function activation) and the function completion time (representing the delay between the instant of its activation and the instant of its termination).

The global WCRT of a signal (Figure 24) is equal to the sum of its jitter, its worst-case transmission time, the worst-case transmission time of all signals that are allocated to the same message, and the longest duration of waiting in the queue before its election for a transmission on the bus.

Figure 25 gives end-to-end chains latencies for the three approaches and allows their comparison. We can notice that latencies of the manual allocation have been improved by the two other approaches (LCTES 2013, and RTCSA 2012). We can also notice that LCTES 2013 approach has improved latencies of RTCSA 2012 approach.

Figure 26 gives processors and bus utilizations obtained with the three approaches. We can observe that in terms of utilization 'Manual Allocation' and 'RTCSA 2012' are comparable, whereas 'LCTES 2013' improves bus utilization which is the cause of the global latencies improvement observed in Figure 23. This is due to the fact that distant communications are source of a large latencies value.

As can be seen results of these advanced analyses give hints on how to improve core models (allocation in particular). In the regenerative brake example, the new allocation found with the LCTES method can be part of the recommendations for the core swimlane in order to improve global latency.

Figure 25. Comparison of end-to-end chains latencies for the three approaches

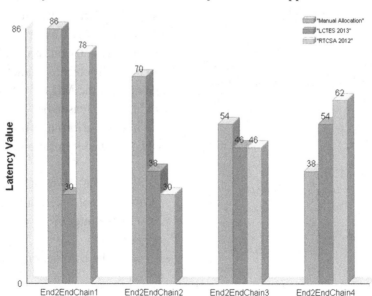

Figure 26. Comparison of processors and bus utilization for the three approaches

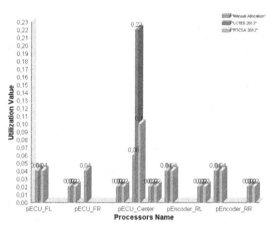

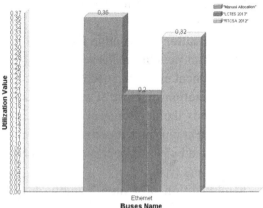

BEYOND ISOLATED LANE ACTIVITIES: MULTI-OBJECTIVE OPTIMISATION

Swimlanes are an effective means for organizing a methodology that allows separating activities that come from different concerns, for example safety or timing concerns. However, architectural choices cannot be conducted and evaluated using a completely independent validation approach for each swimlane. In particular, these concerns may lead to a conflict of goals. Typically a safety mechanism can be introduced to satisfy a safety goal, but the timing cost of this mechanism not only must be evaluated but if different mechanisms lead to different timing costs, then the timing cost becomes the discriminating factor for the choice of the safety mechanism. If the safety mechanisms have different levels of dependability, then there is a complex trade-off to make between dependability and timing cost in order to choose the most appropriate mechanism. The process of finding the "best" solution by making trade-offs between conflicting goals is called multi-objective optimization.

In this chapter we show how EAST-ADL can be used as a basis for design space exploration through multi-objective optimization. There are two main factors that make EAST-ADL a suitable basis for this: as a comprehensive modeling language it integrates many different aspects of software engineering (introduced by the different swimlanes presented in earlier sections) and, on the other hand, with its extensive variability modeling support it provides means for defining the optimization space, i.e. the set of system design alternatives to be considered during optimization.

An Optimization Scenario

An EAST-ADL model comprises a wide range of different information relevant to the automotive engineer. As this information is available in one place in a coherent format and since the information can be organized in variants (i.e., the design space variants, see section 7.1), the following scenario becomes possible. An automotive engineer develops an EAST-ADL model with design space variants. This leads to a huge design space from which non-optimal design candidates should be removed. The surviving design space is a model of a product line (a model range) with no other design space candidate being dominant in *any* relevant optimization objective. The concrete objectives to take into account depend on the use case; typical optimization objectives include:

- **Minimization of Latency:** Response time along an end-to-end flow made of functions.
- **Maximization of Function Extensibility:** Maximum possible increase of execution time without exceeding node capacity.
- **Minimization of Cost:** The total cost is defined as the development cost for each component type plus the sum of piece cost multiplied by piece count summed over all component types.
- **Minimization of Cable Length:** Cable length is a static measure.
- **Minimization of Power Consumption Peak Values:** The different power consumption levels in each mode are investigated.
- **Averaging Power Supply:** The power distribution is a critical service in an all-electrical vehicle. Each feature is realised by functions allocated to nodes in the HardwareDesignArchitecture. Nodes have HardwarePins that may be used for power. There is a PowerSupply component.

The identification of this ideal candidate is possible because of the comprehensive nature of EAST-ADL: the engineer modeled timing constraints with the respective EAST-ADL stereotypes that in turn can be analyzed according the optimization objectives: *Minimization of latency* and *Maximization of function extensibility*; the model of the components to be produced can be analyzed to find solutions with good price and performance for high volume products as opposed to solutions that only benefit low volume products, i.e. optimization objective: *Minimization of cost*; the modeled genericConstraintValue over all GenericConstraints with the genericConstraintType cableLength can be analyzed according the optimization objective: *Minimization of cable length*; the modeled genericConstraintValue over all GenericConstraints with genericConstraintType powerConsumption can be analyzed according

the optimization objective: *Minimization of power consumption peak values*; and functions together with their allocation to nodes, sensors and actuators can be analyzed according the optimization objective: *Averaging power supply*.

In short, the modeled EAST-ADL constraints are the basis for the optimization analysis, which performs a comparison of the different design candidates according to relevant objectives.

The engineer could even perform more optimization analyses because EAST-ADL is extensible by so-called User Attributes, where additional information can be captured when needed by specific optimization analyses (e.g., Markov Chain analysis may need a *FailureProbability* attribute for DesignFunctions).

Multi-Objective Optimization

As illustrated in the previous section, EAST-ADL models shall be optimized according to a variety of objectives to enable better designs to be rapidly evaluated and evolved (Walker et al 2013). To achieve these optimization objectives, there are three main steps that must be fulfilled:

- It must be possible to define the design space. The design space is the name given to the set of all possible solutions that can be derived from modifying the original starting point. It is called *design* space because it is the set of all possible designs that can be obtained via the variability inherent in the original model. This is primarily a language issue and means ensuring that EAST-ADL and its variability mechanisms can be used to define optimization-based variability (design space variants) as well as normal product line variability.
- It must be possible to evaluate the design candidates according to optimization objectives. An optimization objective is the goal of the optimization process and typically takes the form of an evaluation cri-

terion and a direction, e.g. to maximize safety, or minimize cost. Some optimization approaches combine multiple objectives into a single objective via some kind of weighted formula, but the goal is still to minimize or maximize the result of the formula. In order to evaluate the design candidates a close link with both existing and developing analysis tools is required.

- The multi-objective optimization heuristics must allow for an efficient exploration of the design space. Multi-objective optimization is the optimization of more than one objective simultaneously. This means that multiple evaluation methods are required (to evaluate each objective) and it also requires some kind of heuristic for resolving the inevitable trade-offs between multiple, possibly conflicting objectives.

In a multi-objective optimization, there is no global "best" solution because everything is a trade-off between the various objectives. However, it is possible for one solution to dominate another if it is evaluated to be at least as good in all objectives. Thus the dominating solution would always be chosen over the dominated solution (it is the optimal design for those particular objective values).

The set of all dominating solutions that have been found is called Pareto frontier (none of the Pareto solutions dominate one another). Essen-

tially, it is the set of current "optimal" solutions, representing the best trade-offs between the various objectives that have been found so far.

The first step is the variability support. If it is not possible to define the design space, then no optimization can take place. The central principle here is substitutability: the language has to allow the designer to specify alternative versions of model elements while ensuring that the alternatives are sufficiently constrained such that they can readily be substituted for one another by the optimization algorithm. If swapping one alternative for another results in an invalid model, then they are not substitutable. To give an impression of how such variations are defined in EAST-ADL, we provide the definition of one FunctionType from our brake-by-wire case study in the Figure 27. Long dashed lines indicate explicit optionality, which means that an element shown with a long dashed line was marked optional by the modeler. In the example, this is the case for elements "pWheelSensorSecondary", "pWheelSensorAND", and the connector from port "WheelSpeed" of FunctionPrototype "pWheelSensorPrimary" to port "WheelSpeed" of the containing FunctionType "WheelSensorWheel". Short dashed lines denote implicit optionality, i.e. the element was not declared optional by the modeler but is still optional because it depends on some other element that is (either explicitly or implicitly) optional. The connectors to/from FunctionPrototypes "pWheelSensorSecondary"

Figure 27. Design space specification for wheel

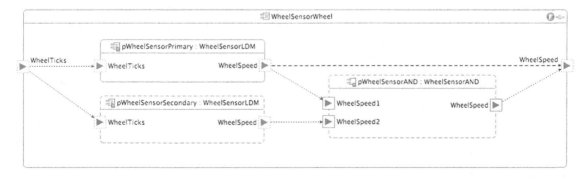

and "pWheelSensorAND" are examples of implicit optional elements. Having defined which elements are optional, the modeler will then add so-called *internal bindings* to the model. These define how optional architectural elements, e.g. an optional FunctionType like "pWheelSensorAND" in the figure, will be selected or deselected depending of the configuration of the core feature model on vehicle level. For example, it could be defined that "pWheelSensorSecondary" and "pWheelSensorAND" will be selected if feature "USA" is selected on vehicle level and deselected in all other configurations. In summary, the EAST-ADL variability modeling concepts used here to define the optimization space are: optionality of structural elements (e.g. optional sub functions, ports, connectors), internal bindings that define when to select or deselect the optional elements, and feature models as a context to define the internal bindings (see "Vehicle Feature Model" in Section 0).

Of particular difficulty here is ensuring a consistent interface; some variants may have more ports or connections than other variants, and so it has to be possible to ensure that those connections remain valid regardless of which variant is chosen. For example, if a variant with more connections to other components is chosen, then failure propagation should be possible along those connections. Similarly, constraints defined in the EAST-ADL model in form of GenericConstraints or its more specific subtypes of constraints may apply to all variants or only some variants. EAST-ADL provides modeling means to deal with these cases.

This leads on to the second step—evaluation of design variants. The notion of substitutability is encapsulated in practice by the process of variability resolution wherein a model containing variability is resolved to produce a new model in which all the variability has been fixed to choose a particular configuration. Based on a model defined in this way, it is then possible to produce models with resolved variability that can be subsequently evaluated. These resolved models will then include all information from the base model that is relevant to a particular form of evaluation and analysis, including the basic system architecture and any relevant meta-information (for example a timing constraint or any form of GenericConstraint). The third step, multi-objective optimization, is then realized as several individual analyses – one per objective – and an integration of the individual analysis results. The coming section will explain this in more detail.

Architecture of the Optimization Framework

In the MAENAD project, an entire work task was dedicated to an investigation of how to conduct such a multi-objective optimization in the context of EAST-ADL modeling. First, a reference architecture for an optimization framework was defined that is capable of integrating diverse analysis engines and combining the results of their analyses within a single embracing multi-objective optimization. In a second step, this abstract optimization architecture was implemented as a Java-based plugin for the Eclipse platform and evaluated in a series of extended examples and a case study. This led to several refinements of the optimization architecture.

A detailed account of this optimization architecture and the related implementation and evaluation effort is not in the scope of this chapter. To complement the presentation of the methodology above, we just provide a brief overview of our approach for multi-objective optimization to give the reader an impression how this can support the swimlane-based structuring and organization of the EAST-ADL methodology.

Figure 28 shows the architecture for a framework for multi-objective optimization as proposed by the MAENAD project.

It consists of several major elements:

- **Optimization Space Definition Module (OSDM):** This module takes a variant-rich EAST-ADL model and generates a 'master encoding hierarchy', which is a hierar-

Figure 28. The architecture of the optimization framework

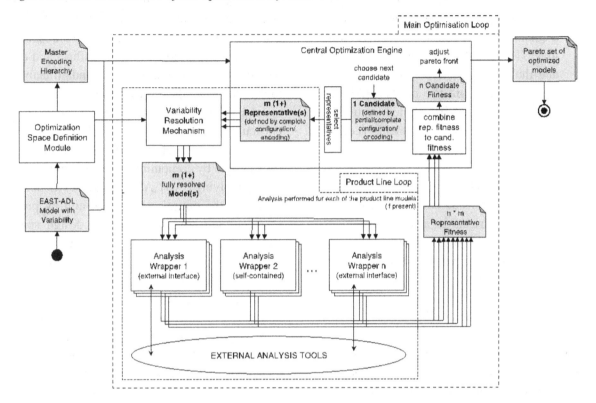

chical key to the design space represented by the model variability. In practice, this takes the form of a cardinality-based feature model as defined by Czarnecki et al. (2005) (with slight modifications).

- **Central Optimization Engine (COE):** The COE is the driver of the optimization process. It is responsible for exploring the optimization design space on the basis of heuristic algorithms such as genetic algorithms. It generates an encoding for a particular design candidate, which is then resolved by the VRM (see below) and evaluated by analysis plugins to determine its relative score in each of the objectives being optimized (e.g. reliability, performance, cost, energy consumption etc.). Pareto-optimal candidates are preserved while dominated designs are discarded. Once the process is complete, the COE will generate a report containing the set of pareto-optimal design candidates.

- **Variability Resolution Mechanism (VRM):** The COE does not manipulate the EAST-ADL model directly. Instead, it modifies encodings (essentially configurations of feature models), and then passes each encoding to the VRM, which is responsible for resolving the variability in the original model according to the encoding in order to produce a new model — a design candidate — that can then be analyzed and evaluated.

- **Analysis Modules:** For each objective being analyzed, there needs to be a corresponding analysis module. The intention is that these analysis modules can be either external tools (such as dependability analysis tools like HiP-HOPS or timing analysis tools like Qompass) or plugins written for the modeling/analysis environment (e.g. Papyrus, MetaEdit+, EPM etc.). The optimization architecture does not necessarily interact with them directly; instead there is a common approach, implemented by 'wrapper' objects if necessary, to present a consistent interface to the analysis modules. This will allow new analysis modules and thus new objective types to be added (or removed) from the optimization process without requiring modification of the main optimization elements (i.e., the OSDM, COE and the VRM).

So far, this description of the optimization architecture only considered design space variants, i.e. system variants defined by the engineer to indicate alternative viable designs among which the optimal design is to be found. Ultimately, only a single design space variant will be selected and built. However, as indicated above, there exists a second form of variation in EAST-ADL: product line variation. This refers to system variants that do not constitute alternative designs but different models and configurations that will all be built and shipped in parallel (to different customers). Typical examples of such variation include low-end vs. high-end models, optional equipment, trucks with two vs. three axles, an optional stability control. Performing an optimization across product line variants does not make sense: if we were performing a cost optimization across all models and optional equipment variants a car manufacturer has on offer, then always the low-end model without any optional equipment would turn out to be the "optimal" variant.

Obviously, we have to clearly distinguish between product line and design space variation during optimization. This is difficult because in a large system model the two forms of variation are mixed and tightly coupled. In the EAST-ADL optimization architecture proposed in the MAENAD project, this is handled by distinguishing between optimization candidates and representatives. A candidate is a system model with all design-space variability resolved but all product line variability unresolved. For each such candidate, one or more representatives are generated: system models where also the product line variability is resolved.

During optimization, we are primarily interested in the fitness of the candidates, but the candidate system models still contain unresolved variability (the product line variability) and can therefore not be analyzed by most standard analysis tools. Therefore, the representatives are analyzed instead. In order to then obtain the fitness of a particular candidate the individual fitness values of its one or more representatives are combined, for example by computing the arithmetic mean.

By applying EAST-ADL variability modeling to define the optimization space and by properly distinguishing EAST-ADL's design space and product line variability, the optimization architecture presented here is closely tailored to EAST-ADL and makes extensive use of its specific capabilities. However, the approach could be applied to other modeling languages as well, if missing modeling constructs were added to the target language (e.g. feature models, internal bindings, constructs to define architecture variants).

An initial prototype tool, OptiPAL, was developed within the MAENAD project. Analysis is provided by a simple cost analysis plugin and a bridge to the HiP-HOPS safety analysis tool for dependability analysis via FTA. OptiPAL is primarily intended as a proof of concept and as a way of testing out the optimization concepts on test models, to provide feedback to facilitate further development of the optimization architecture concept. It will be made publicly available at the end of the MAENAD project.

CONCLUSION AND FUTURE WORK

This chapter presented model-based analysis and engineering capabilities offered by the MAENAD modeling and analysis framework. Thanks to the omni-comprehensive nature of the EAST-ADL language, a wide range of advanced analyses have been seamlessly integrated in the framework, providing fine predictions of system properties at different abstraction levels. These predictions allow front-ending verification activities at early stages of the system development process. Beside functional properties, verified by well-known model-checkers, the chapter presented as well novel analysis methods for safety and timing analysis. Power analysis capabilities, even if not shown in the chapter, could be easily provided thanks to available transformations towards simulation tools. The possibility of encompassing in one single framework different analyses has the further advantage of making possible optimization activities, where different analyses results are gathered by a centralized optimization framework able to rank analyzed model candidates in Pareto-optimal configurations.

While we think that model-based optimization is an emerging trend in both industry and research domains, multi-layered design flows pose several challenges from an optimization perspective (Broy, Chakraborty, Goswami, Ramesh, & Satpathy, 2011). It is not clear, in particular, how front-end optimization activities impact lower level designs, where new design elements (not taken into account in the higher-level optimization) emerge.

REFERENCES

Arda, G., Suryadevara, J., Peraldi-Frati, M.-A., & Mallet, F. (2013). Analysis Support for TADL2 Timing Constraints on EAST-ADL Models. In *Proceedings of the 7th European Conference on Software Architecture,* (pp 89-105). Academic Press.

ATESST. (2006). *FP7 ATESST 1 & ATESST 2 Projects.* Retrieved from http://www.atesst.org

AUTOSAR. (2011). *AUTOSAR Specification of Timing Extensions, Release 4.0.* Retrieved from http://www.autosar.org/download/R4.0/AUTOSAR_TPS_TimingExtensions.pdf

Bozzano, M., & Villafiorita, A. (2003). Improving System Reliability via Model Checking: the FSAP /NuSMV-SA Safety Analysis Platform. In *Proceedings of 22nd International Conference on Computer Safety, Reliability, and Security, SAFECOMP,* (pp. 49-62). Academic Press.

Broy, M., Chakraborty, S., Goswami, D., Ramesh, S., & Satpathy, M. (2011). Cross-layer analysis, testing and verification of automotive control software. In *Proceedings of the 11th International Conference on Embedded Software,* (pp 263-272). Academic Press.

Cancila, D., Terrier, F., Belmonte, F., Dubois, H., Espinoza, H., Gerard, S., & Cuccuru, A. (2009). SOPHIA: a Modeling Language for Model-Based Safety Engineering. In *Proceedings of 2nd International Workshop On Model Based Architecting and Construction Of Embedded Systems,* (pp 11-26). Academic Press.

Chale, G., Gaudré, T., & Tucci-Piergiovanni, S. (2012). Towards an Architectural Design Framework for Automotive Systems Development. In *Proceedings of the Third International Conference on Complex Systems Design & Management, CSD&M,* (pp 241-258). Academic Press.

Chen, D., Feng, L., Qureshi, T. N., Lönn, H., & Hagl, F. (2013). An Architectural Approach to the Analysis, Verification and Validation of Software Intensive Embedded Systems. *Computing, 95*(8), 649–688. doi:10.1007/s00607-013-0314-4

Chen, D., Johansson, R., Lönn, H., Blom, H., Walker, M., Papadopoulos, Y., Torchiaro, S., Tagliabo F., & Sandberg, A. (2011). Integrated Safety and Architecture Modeling for Automotive Embedded Systems. *E&I - Elektrotechnik und Informationstechnik, 128*(6).

Chen, D., Mahmud, N., Walker, M., Feng, L., Lönn, H., & Papadopoulos, Y. (2013). Systems Modeling with EAST-ADL for Fault Tree Analysis through HiP-HOPS. In *Proceedings of 4th IFAC Workshop on Dependable Control of Discrete Systems*. IFAC.

Czarnecki, K., Helsen, S., & Eisenecker, U. (2005). Formalizing Cardinality-based Feature Models and their Specialization. In *Software Process* (pp. 7–29). Improvement and Practices. doi:10.1002/spip.213

Di Natale, M., & Sangiovanni-Vincentelli, A. L. (2010). Moving From Federated to Integrated Architectures in Automotive: The Role of Standards, Methods and Tools. *Journal of the IEEE*, *98*(4), 603–620. doi:10.1109/JPROC.2009.2039550

EAST-ADL. (2012). *EAST-ADL*. Retrieved from http://www.east-adl.info/

EAST EEA. (2001). EAST EEA ITEA Project. Retrieved from https://itea3.org/project/east-eea.html

Espinoza, H., Cancila, D., & Selic, B. Gerard, & S. (2009). Challenges in Combining SysML and MARTE for Model-Based Design of Embedded Systems. In *Proceedings of the 5th European Conference on Model Driven Architecture - Foundations and Applications,* (pp 98-113). Academic Press.

Fussel, J. B., Aber, E. F., & Rahl, R. G. (1976). On the quantitative analysis of priority-and failure logic. *IEEE Transactions on Reliability*, *25*(5), 324–326. doi:10.1109/TR.1976.5220025

ISO. (2011). *ISO 26262, Road vehicles – Functional safety*. Author.

MAENAD. (2009). *MAENAD FP7 Project*. Retrieved from http://www.maenad.eu/

MAENAD. (2013). *MAENAD Analysis Workbench, D5.2.1*. Retrieved from http://www.maenad.eu/public_pw/MAENAD_Deliverable_D5.2.1_V3.0.pdf

Mahmud, N. (2012). *Dynamic Model-based Safety Analysis: From State Machines to Temporal Fault Trees*. (Ph.D. dissertation). Department of Computer Science, University of Hull, Hull, UK.

Mahmud, N., Papadopoulos, Y., & Walker, M. (2010). A Translation of State Machines to Temporal Fault Trees. In *Proceedings of the 40th IEEE/IFIP International Conference on Dependable Systems and Networks,* (pp. 45-51). IEEE.

Mahmud, N., Papadopoulos, Y., & Walker, M. (2012). Compositional synthesis of Temporal Fault Trees from State Machines. *ACM SIGMETRICS Performance Evaluation Review*, *39*(4), 79–88.

Mehiaoui, A., Tucci-Piergiovanni, S., Babau, J. P., & Lemarchand, L. (2012). Optimizing the Deployment of Distributed Real-Time Embedded Applications. In *Proceedings of International Conference on Embedded and Real-Time Computing Systems and Applications,* (pp. 400-403). Academic Press.

Mehiaoui, A., Wozniak, E., Tucci-Piergiovanni, S., Mraidha, C., Di Natale, M., Zeng, H., et al. (2013). A Two-step Optimization Technique for Functions Placement, Partitioning, and Priority Assignment in Distributed Systems. In *Proceedings of 4th ACM SIGPLAN/SIGBED Conference on Languages, Compilers and Tools for Embedded Systems,* (pp. 121-132). ACM.

Merle, G., Roussel, J.-M., Lesage, J., & Bobbio, A. (2010). Probabilistic Algebraic Analysis of Fault Trees With Priority Dynamic Gates and Repeated Events. *IEEE Transactions on Reliability*, *59*(1), 250–261. doi:10.1109/TR.2009.2035793

MAENAD Methodology. (2013). *MAENAD Design Methodology, D2.2.1*. Retrieved from http://www.maenad.eu/public_pw/MAENAD_Deliverable_D2.2.1_V2.0.pdf

OMG MARTE. (2011). *UML Profile for Modeling and Analysis of Real-Time and Embedded system*. formal/2011-06-02, Version 1.1.

OMG QFTP. (2008). *UML Profile for QoS and Fault Tolerance*. formal/2008-04-05, Version 1.1.

OMG SYML. (2012). *System Modeling Language, formal specification*. 2012-06-01, Version 1.3.

OMG UML. (2011). *Unified Modeling Language*. formal/2011-08-06, Version 2.4.1.

Papadopoulos, Y., & McDermid, J. (1999). Hierarchically performed hazard origin and propagation studies. In *Proceedings of 18th International Conference on Computer Safety, Reliability, and Security, SAFECOMP*, (pp. 139-152). Academic Press.

SAE. (2009). *Architecture Analysis and Design Language* (AS-5506A). The Engineering Society for Advancing Mobility Land Sea Air and Space, Aerospace Information Report, Version 2.0.

TIMMO2USE. (2012). *Timing Model – Tools, algorithms, languages, methodology, USE cases, D13*. Retrieved from http://www.timmo-2-use.org/deliverables/TIMMO-2-USE_D13.pdf

TIMMO. (2007). *ITEA2 Project*. Retrieved from http://www.timmo-2-use.org/timmo/index.htm

Walker, M., & Papadopoulos, Y. (2009). Qualitative temporal analysis: Towards a full implementation of the Fault Tree Handbook. *Control Engineering Practice*, *17*(10), 1115–1125. doi:10.1016/j.conengprac.2008.10.003

Walker, R. M-O., Tucci-Piergiovanni, S. M., Lönn, H., Mraidha, C., Parker, D., Chen, D., & Servat, D. (2013). Automatic optimisation of system architectures using EAST-ADL. *Journal of Systems and Software*, *86*(10), 2467–2487. doi:10.1016/j.jss.2013.04.001

KEY TERMS AND DEFINITIONS

AUTOSAR: AUTOSAR (AUTomotive Open System ARchitecture) is an open and standardized automotive software architecture, jointly developed by automobile manufacturers, suppliers and tool developers. It is a partnership of automotive OEMs, suppliers and tool vendors whose objective is to create and establish open standards for automotive E/E (Electrics/Electronics) architectures that will provide a basic infrastructure to assist with developing vehicular software, user interfaces and management for all application domains.

EAST-ADL: EAST-ADL is an Architecture Description Language (ADL) for automotive embedded systems, developed in several European research projects. It is designed to complement AUTOSAR with descriptions at higher level of abstractions. Aspects covered by EAST-ADL include vehicle features, functions, requirements, variability, software components, hardware components and communication. Currently, it is maintained by the EAST-ADL Association in cooperation with the European FP7 MAENAD project.

Failure Mode and Effects Analysis: Failure mode and effects analysis (FMEA) is an inductive reasoning (forward logic) single point of failure analysis and is a core task in reliability engineering, safety engineering and quality engineering. A successful FMEA activity helps to identify potential failure modes based on experience with similar products and processes. FMEAs can be performed at the system, subsystem, assembly, subassembly or part level.

Fault Tree Analysis: Fault tree analysis (FTA) is a top down, deductive failure analysis in which an undesired state of a system is analyzed using Boolean logic to combine a series of lower-level events. This analysis method is mainly used in the fields of safety engineering and reliability engineering to understand how systems can fail, to identify the best ways to reduce risk or to determine (or get a feeling for) event rates of a safety accident or a particular system level (functional) failure. FTA is used in the aerospace, nuclear power, chemical and processpharmaceutical, petrochemical and other high-hazard industries; but is also used in fields as diverse as risk factor identification relating to social service system failure.

Model-Based Systems Engineering: Model-based systems engineering (MBSE) is the formalized application of modeling to support system requirements, design, analysis, verification and validation activities beginning in the conceptual design phase and continuing throughout development and later life cycle phases. A model usually offers different views in order to serve different purposes. A view is a representation of a system from the perspective of related concerns or issues.

Model Checking: model checking aka property checking refers to the following problem: Given a model of a system, exhaustively and automatically check whether this model meets a given specification. Typically, one has hardware or software systems in mind, whereas the specification contains safety requirements such as the absence of deadlocks and similar critical states that can cause the system to crash. Model checking is a technique for automatically verifying correctness properties of finite-state systems.

Modeling and Analysis of Real Time and Embedded Systems Profile: Modeling and Analysis of Real Time and Embedded systems profile or MARTE profile in short is the OMG standard for modeling real-time and embedded applications with UML2.

Schedulability Analysis: Schedulability analysis for a real time system consists of checking whether all tasks can be finished within their deadlines.

SysML: The OMG systems Modeling Language (OMG SysML™) is a general-purpose graphical modeling language for specifying, analyzing, designing complex systems. In particular, the language provides graphical representations with a semantic foundation for modeling system requirements, behavior, structure, and equations, which is used to integrate with other engineering analysis models.

UML Profile: UML profile provides a generic extension mechanism to customizing UML models for particular domains and platforms. Extension mechanisms allow refining standard semantics in strictly additive manner, preventing them from contradicting standard UML semantics.

UML: UML or Unified Modeling Language is a general-purpose modeling language in the field of software engineering, which is designed to provide a standard way to visualize the design of a system.

ENDNOTES

[1] State Automata to Fault-trees extended (if necessary) with temporal information (ORA in Greek).

Chapter 11
Fostering Analysis from Industrial Embedded Systems Modeling

Michel Bourdellès
Thales Communications and Security, France

Shuai Li
Thales Communications and Security, France

Imran Quadri
Softeam, France

Etienne Brosse
Softeam, France

Andrey Sadovykh
Softeam, France

Emmanuel Gaudin
PragmaDev, France

Frédéric Mallet
INRIA, France

Arda Goknil
University of Luxembourg, Luxembourg

David George
Rapita Systems Ltd., UK

Jari Kreku
VTT Technical Research Centre, Finland

ABSTRACT

In most industrial embedded systems development projects, the software and the hardware development parts are separated, and the constraint requirements/capabilities are informally exchanged in the system development phase of the process. To prevent failures due to the violation of timing constraints, hardware components of the platform are typically over dimensioned for the capabilities needed. This increases both cost and power consumption. Performance analysis is not done sufficiently at early stages of the development process to optimize the system. This chapter presents results of the integration of tools and extra modeling to offer new performance analysis capabilities in the early stages of the development process. These results are based on trace generation from code instrumentation. A number of enhancements were made, spanning the system modeling stage down to the execution stage (based on an ARM dual core Cortex A9-based target board). Final results taken from a software-based radio case study (including the analysis and validation stages) are presented.

DOI: 10.4018/978-1-4666-6194-3.ch011

INTRODUCTION

An industrial embedded systems development project comes within a global context including the respect of quality requirements, configuration management requirements and strong reporting and communications efforts with the system team, other parts of the system equipment development teams, and customers. A precise development process is defined to respect all these aspects. This process is, in the industrial domains concerned, driven by tests and based on system requirements validation.

Due to increases in system complexity, requirements validation has also become more complex. For example, the radio protocol domain faces new challenges and requirements due to increased execution platform component complexity. With the lack of proper tool support it is the responsibility of skilled architects to perform the complex and tedious task of validation. Consequently, the use of hardware platform modeling and enhanced performance verification is an identified issue in embedded system design environments.

The overall concept developed in this chapter is the ability to validate non-functional properties (such as performance) at an early stage in the development process. If an improvement in this area is achievable, a better fit of the software components to the execution platform is expected. To achieve this goal, new tools are introduced to existing ones. In this chapter, the project tools are defined, combined and integrated to create new design-space exploration techniques in the existing validation process. This allows the developer to better evaluate and test different allocation strategies of software components to the execution platform.

The addition of new tools to the development process must conform to the validation done by manual tests derived from requirements. It must not take too much extra development team effort in terms of time and the need for expertise.

The analysis must make the best use of existing validation environments. The methodology presented here will be based on traces already collected by test harnesses. These traces will be used to feed both functional and non-functional analysis tools. By reusing an existing validation environment, new tools and methods can be easily integrated into the current development process. As a complement, performance simulation is also studied.

We present in this chapter the results of the ARTEMIS collaborative project PRESTO (PRESTO, 2013). We illustrate how custom solutions from PRESTO (implemented in tools such as Modelio) were used to achieve trace generation and a verification flow that explores:

- Modeling of a TDMA radio protocol.
- Annotation of elements in a high level model for instrumented wrapper code generation.
- Functional and non-functional properties specification.
- Verification of properties based on traces coming from the generated instrumented code.
- Performance simulation and evaluation with respect to execution on the target platform.

BACKGROUND

The PRESTO project aims to improve the software tools used in the recovery of information and extended specification data during the software development life cycle. The main information recovered from the software development process is a description of the software application as a set of interconnected components with their interface specified as input of the MARTE profile (OMG, 2013), or specific domain-specific languages supporting software/hardware allocation. Also recovered are test traces from "classical" software test integrations on functional behaviors.

- **Software Modeling:** E.g. part of the MARTE profile, or any other similar language extension, supporting software and hardware allocation: the software component modeling specification will be done at the same time as the software design specification (Software Requirements Specification, Interface Requirements Specification). The definition of the components and their interface should be sufficient for performance modeling. This will require in particular a correlation between inputs and outputs on a trace-by-trace basis. Particular constraints, for example well-known timing constraints on components communication could be defined at this stage, to eliminate hardware platform candidates at the software/hardware allocation step. These constraints can also be specified outside of the software components modeling using test traces. Apart from the OMG MARTE profile, Domain specific languages such as SDL (SDL, 2013), EAST-ADL2 (ATESST, 2013) and AADL (AADL, 2013) give a more precise semantic to timing constraints applied to components and communication between them. Specific modeling elements have been defined for timing requirements expression and their relationships with the system modeling elements.

- **Position with Respect to the Background:** The design process adaptation presented hereafter is based on the MARTE modeling specification, but may be adapted to any other Software/Hardware allocation modeling notation.

- **Formal Modeling of Properties:** Requirements are specified on system specification documents, but they are described in natural language (functional or timing constraints requirements) and validated only in platform execution. We propose to specify the timing constraints formally to be used by the timing analysis tools in addition to the model of the software/hardware allocation modeling and of a model of the application, more precisely execution scenarios describing the application actions on the platform components. The format and expressiveness of these timing properties are defined in the project jointly with timing tools analysis providers. Since timing constraints are closely related to sequences of actions defined in the functional requirements and behavioral models, formal models of properties will link both functional and non-functional properties. This is consistent with the MARTE approach to modeling.

- **Position with Respect to the Background:** The notation for the modeling of properties leads to find the better trade-off between the power of properties expressiveness from analysis tools, and industrial requirements in the variety of notations and easiness of understanding.

- **Timing Constraints:** The timing constraints will be present in the scenarios description specification, and be formally described in the test scenarios as timing constraints between two or more actions of the scenarios. These constraints will be specified in a correct formal notation and may include constraints on rate, latency, jitter, synchronization etc. A mixed notation of timing and temporal logic will be studied in the project. This may include the derivation of timing constraints from temporal logic.

- **Position with Respect to the Background:** Full exploitation of the accurate information that may be cached in the traces is expected to be potentially used for the analysis.

- **Test Trace Generation:** Different levels of expressiveness can be generated depending of the kind of properties to be verified: Message exchange, Function calls, Host timing results, Variables assignments, Time tags *etcetera*. A set of information will be defined in respect with the kind of property being analyzed and the capabilities of the analysis tools. Open Trace Format (PARATOOLS, 2013) is a trace definition format for high-performance computing platforms. OTF addresses three objectives: openness, flexibility and performance. From the traces, specific libraries and tools (e.g. VAMPIR, VITE, etc…) allows for visualizing or searching through the traces, with OTF file generated after code instrumentation. The Program Database Toolkit (PDT) (University of Oregon, 2013) may be used to analyze the code for automatic instrumentation by the Tuning and Analysis Utilities (TAU) tools.
- **Position with Respect to the Background:** The process flow adaptation presented hereafter presents results with the PragmaTracer and RapiTrace tools, but is independent of a specific code instrumentation and trace generation toolset.

In a similar manner, the main information recovery of the hardware development flow process includes:

- **Hardware Modeling:** The description of the hardware platform and its modeling using the DRM (Detailed Resource Modeling) sub-profile of the MARTE profile. This modeling should be smoothly integrated to the hardware design flow. At this stage several architectures may be specified and modeled by the prototyping tool and compared with software components and architecture.

- **Comparison between Timings Analysis and Execution:** To validate the timing analysis results, they have to be compared with real platform execution analysis. To this aim the proposed solution is to compare timing results with the execution (or simulation) of the application on the platform at different levels of granularity (e.g.: single function, full trace…).

The results will allow the adaptation of the parameters needed for predicting performance using timing analysis. The transition between functional simulation and execution is typically gradual; the verification of those parts where design has proceeded further should be possible quickly. Therefore, mixed situations have to be taken into account.

- **Fast Platform Prototyping Tool Definition:** To this aim, we propose in this project to define a -as- fast -as possible- platform prototyping tool, based on the MARTE UML profile for embedded systems, or using existing hardware and software architecture modeling languages. This will be used to describe the allocation of the software components on the annotated platform to provide performance verification, such as timing analysis in respect with specific software/hardware allocation, scheduling analysis, performance dependence on hardware parameters and the best proportion of the hardware components to respect the performance constraints given.
- **Use of the Test Traces as Entry Point of the Property and Performance Analysis Environment to Design:** The sequences of actions in traces are exploited as the behavioral representation of the system. The objective of this project is to benefit from these sequences of actions and to use them as an entry point to performance analysis tools. Actually, test scenario specifications

consist of a first level of sequences of actions that are validated in the integration phase from message receipts of the external interface of the whole system to verify. The test framework may generate more accurate information, such as message passing between components, function calls, host execution timing information and variables assignments. This information is generally used to help the debug of the system but is not fully interpreted. As these traces contain huge functional information, we propose in the project to exploit them for functional as well as non-functional property verification through two directions: from explicit property specification, as available from the formal modeling of requirements and by inferring properties or sequence patterns from traces.

- **Simulation Results Confrontation with the Real Platform Execution:** As the modeling of the platform is not supposed to be designed by a hardware expert and should be as fast as possible, one key of top-down analysis from the application to the platform execution is the level of confidence in the fast prototyping tool performance predictions. The solution to validate this modeling is to compare the predicted performance with the real execution on the platform for different classes of systems used as benchmarks, in order to identify the dominant parameters for suitable platform modeling.

RATIONALE OF THE APPROACH

New Analysis Needed

Evolutions in industrial Real Time Embedded Systems (RTES) led to new challenges in their design process. By nature, RTES are constrained by the limited amount of resources available (e.g. computing time, power, and memory size). These constraints need to be taken into account in the engineering process. Requirements on such systems led to the need to adapt the current design process in order to analyze both functional and non-functional (F&NF) properties in the mapping of an application to a specific platform.

Status of Industrial Flow in the Verification of RTES

Current analysis applied in the industry is mostly based on intensive testing of the system. Much development time is allocated to design of test scenarios and implementation of such tests. On the other hand, although wrapper code is currently generated from component based modeling of the application, abundant analysis techniques based on a Model-Driven Engineering approaches are usually not used in the design process. In the current situation, functional assessment is processed on host, and performance evaluation is processed only at the real integration on the hardware platform.

Requirements on Industrial Integration of Analysis Tools

Among the common objectives and requirements the integration of these new tools face, let us mention:

1. **No Change in the Methodology (Waterfall Cycle, Iterative Development):** Regarding the global requirements of a project, due to technical, management, quality and customer requirements, a development methodology is defined for the development process. The new tools have to fit these methodology choices.

2. **No Design Environment, Test Tools, and Specific Languages Required by the Tools:** The choice of the design and test environment is also the result of a trade-off and can't be imposed due to purely technical aspects (formalization capability in regards with the license cost of a design environment,

habits of a development team or a specific embedded systems design environment). It may also be imposed by the customer. The tools developed in PRESTO must refer to standards and be modular, with no impact on the global development environment.

3. **Easy Use of the New Tools to Formalize, Press Button Usage, Weak Need of Experts to Specify the Platform:** The complexity of the analysis tools reduces their use by the product development team. Particular attention must be paid to the smooth use of the tools to formally specify requirements at the specification phase and in the detailed conception phase. Extra analysis of test trace exploitation must be done with a simple and effective interface.

4. **No Loss of Time, Gain and Loss Evaluation by the Use of the New Design Framework:** Time is one of the most critical criteria in industrial development projects when guiding choices in which design environment and analysis tools to use. The time for extra specification must be as small as possible.

5. **No Specification Effort without Being Analyzed:** Precedent use of UML profiles for embedded systems failed in industrial development because the analysis capability was considered weak in comparison to the modeling effort. We propose to specify in MARTE only what is needed for the non-functional requirements analysis and can be analyzed by the available or to-be-developed tools.

6. **Gain and Loss Evaluation, in Particular Result Analysis Evaluation with Real Platform Execution:** To be accepted, new tools in the development process must have the impact of their use evaluated. These tools will be compared to the current process of software integration. The specific time to specify the hardware architecture and the efficiency of performance optimization and verification will be evaluated.

Fostering Analysis Based on Traces: the PRESTO Approach

To foster analysis for functional & non-functional analysis based on a smooth adaptation of the current flow, code instrumentation, execution trace generation and extra modeling are added. For modeling, structural models of systems, platform models (e.g. operating system, hardware), properties specification and behavior information as sequence diagrams are integrated into existing models used by engineers. Instrumented code is then generated from the model. Existing test scenarios are run with the instrumented code so execution traces can be generated. Execution traces and models are finally checked by the analysis.

SOLUTIONS AND RECOMMENDATIONS

The PRESTO Method

The PRESTO method can be summarized by the flows in Figure 1.

The general idea behind this method is to re-use existing elements in a product's development cycle, while appending analysis possibilities coming from the project. The goal is to integrate the new possibilities into the development cycle without breaking existing engineering processes. For example the software and platform (e.g. hardware and OS) design flows are ones that are already part of the development cycle, while the project adds the ability to explore designs at system level and exploit execution traces that are obtained by using existing software and platform elements. The PRESTO method is thus applicable to an industrial development cycle, if it follows the software and platform design flows described in Figure 1.

Figure 1. PRESTO method

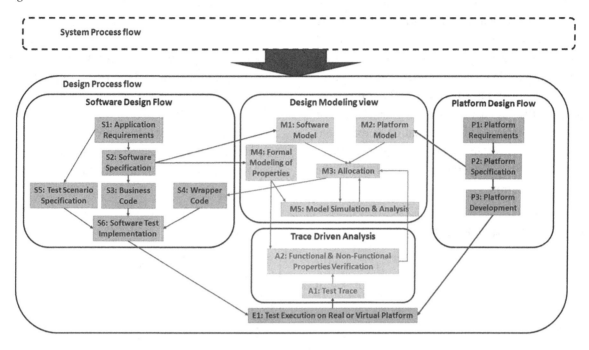

Software Design Flow

The software design flow is the process used to develop the specific software (or application) for the system (i.e. business code). In this process, the application's requirements are first defined (S1). From the requirements, software specification documents are created (S2). These specifications lead to the development of the business code (S3) which is specific to the application. Parallel to the process leading to the business code development, software test scenarios are specified (S5) according to the application's requirements. The test scenarios are then implemented (S6) using the business code (S3) and wrapper code (S4), which is generated separately.

Platform Design Flow

Much like the software design flow, the platform design flow is the process of developing a specific platform for the system. In this process, the platform's requirements (P1) are defined at first. This

leads to platform specification (P2) documents being elaborated, from which a new hardware platform is developed (P3) or an existing one is chosen (which conforms to the specification).

System Design Modeling

The system design modeling parts (M1) and (M2) are, in the PRESTO process, the place in which the allocation (M3) of software application components to platform modeling is captured. This information is mandatory for any early stage performance analysis of the application. This modeling does not prerequisite deep modeling of the application as full behavior specification. The exploitation of this modeling is mainly used for wrapper code generation on different target platforms. The advantages of this code generation are manifold: ease of portability and full exploitation of the structural view information in the model in addition with software/hardware allocation information.

The system design modeling phase is also the place in which behavioral information from the system level design may be captured and mixed with performance information as sequence diagrams with timing constraints to express requirements (M4). This information uses the component interfaces access actions as atomic elements of this specification. This information is exploited to verify the requirements in the final implementation from trace generation as expressed in the following section.

Test Execution and Trace Driven Analysis

Capturing a system's behavior through traces and analyzing the traces to verify properties are the heart of the PRESTO project. Once software tests have been implemented on a platform (that can be virtual at first), they are executed (E1), outputting execution traces (A1). These traces are used to analyze both functional and non-function

Table 1. Tools used in the PRESTO method

Tool Name	Type	Used in step
Description		
Modelio	Modeler	Software Model, Platform Model, Wrapper Code Generation, Properties formal modeling
Modelio is a CASE tool including a UML modeler. Modelio has the capacity to create viewpoints with specific meta-models created using MARTE sub-profiles. A viewpoint corresponds to a diagram where commands only allow specific elements to be created (e.g. hardware components in a hardware model diagram). The goal behind this is to filter MARTE and help the designer use the profile.		
TimeSquare & CCSL	Formal modeling of properties and analysis tool	Formal modeling of properties and early stage analysis
TimeSquare is an MDK (Model Development Kit) provided as a set of Eclipse plugins that can be downloaded or installed into an existing Eclipse installation. TimeSquare is based on the formal Clock Constraint Specification Language (CCSL), which allows the manipulation of logical time. Logical time is a relaxed form of time where any events can be taken as a reference for counting (e.g. do something every 30 openings of the door). It can be used for specifying classical and multiform real-time requirements as well as formally specifying constraints on the behavior of a model (either UML-based or a DSL model). These constraints are solved and a simulation is conducted at the model level.		
PragmaDev Tracer	Properties specification, trace generation and analysis tool	Functional and non-function analysis and test trace generation
PragmaDev Tracer is a tool for requirements, properties, and traces specification, using a graphical Message-Sequence Chart (MSC) representation. Requirements and properties can be expressed in MSC and traces can be obtained online or offline with the tool. Analysis is done by exploiting both the properties expressed in MSC and the traces.		
RVS	Timing analysis, constraints checking and execution tracing tools	Functional/non-functional analysis and performance evaluation
RVS (Rapita Verification Suite) consists of a suite of tools supporting instrumentation, tracing and analysis of time constrained embedded software. RVS analyses traces taken from *on-target* execution, based on instrumentation points inserted into software at the source code level (supporting C, C++ and Ada). Traces are then collected from an on-target execution, allowing analysis of multiple execution properties. Timing constraints can be checked using RapiTime, while code coverage and execution tracing can be covered using the RapiCover and RapiTrace tools respectively. In the PRESTO project, Rapita have also developed a constraints checking tool called RapiCheck, allowing developers to verify high level constraints (such as function ordering and execution times) against an execution trace performed on target.		
ABSOLUT	Early-phase performance estimation tool	Software Model, Platform Model, Allocation, Model simulation and analysis
ABSOLUT is a system-level performance and power consumption simulation approach which follows the Y-chart model. It is based on the virtual system approach, where abstract models of both applications and platforms are used and thus it is intended for early evaluation. Applications are modeled as workload models consisting of processes, functions, basic blocks and, ultimately, abstract instructions read, write, and execute. The workload models are allocated on a platform model, which consists of computation, communication and storage resources organized as subsystems. The allocated system model is simulated using transaction-level SystemC and performance and power data is extracted using probes incorporated into the workload and/or platform models. The probes are able to extract information about e.g. resource utilization, execution time, latencies, etc.		

properties (A2) that have been modeled formally previously.

The following section will show some examples of tools in the PRESTO project that are used in the system level exploration and trace driven analysis.

Tools Used in the PRESTO Method

The different steps in the PRESTO flow uses tools from the project's partners. Let us describe here some examples of these tools, focusing on the ones that we used for a THALES case-study that will be presented later in this chapter.

EXPERIMENTS ON APPLYING THE PRESTO METHOD

The PRESTO method was applied on an industrial case-study from THALES. The following sections describe this experiment's case-study, the experimental results and lessons learnt from applying the PRESTO method.

Radio Protocol Case Study

Pieces of Application Description

The case-study used for the experiment is a TDMA radio protocol. A radio protocol is embedded in communicating stations as part of a mobile ad-hoc wireless network. The use case proposed for the PRESTO validation features is a static TDMA application, implementing generic services, as initialization, emission, reception and synchronization provided by a TDMA service.

The TDMA service handles protocol specific functionalities while the control of its state (transmission, reception, idle) or its configuration is managed by a dedicated Network Controller (NC). The latter orders the TDMA service to send or receive data through the physical layer, which is managed by another specific component. Data gathered by the NC is transmitted to applicative layers if necessary.

Pieces of Platform Description

Figure 2 shows the system's architecture from a software point of view.

The application is divided into several modules. Each module is implemented as a thread and a buffer. Threads communicate with each other by sending messages to each other. The messages are stored in the buffers when they arrive.

All the tools took this application as a case study, except for performance simulation (AB-SOLUT tools set) on which an inner component's (Medium Access Control) single task processes were simulated with performance requirements within an order of a few milliseconds (around 5 milliseconds).

Figure 2. TDMA radio protocol case-study

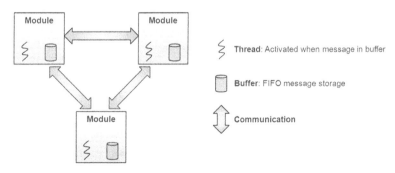

APPLICATION OF THE PRESTO METHOD

Modeling

The PRESTO method was applied on this application to verify its properties. To apply the method's concept, we developed a specific solution. First the application had to be modeled; then instrumented code was generated from the model. Afterwards instrumented code was executed and execution traces were generated. Traces were finally exploited by analysis tools to verify properties.

The radio protocol case-study is well suited for a component-based modeling. Indeed each module can be modeled as a component. Modeling was done in Modelio using specific viewpoints developed for the PRESTO project. Some examples of the viewpoints are the following:

- **Application Diagram:** Component-based model with functional components connected by ports.
- **Interface Definition Diagram:** Definition of interfaces and operations implemented by the functional components' ports.

- **Type Definition Diagram:** Definition of data types, enumerations typing a interface's operation's parameters.
- **Hardware Diagram:** Hardware components, e.g. processors and cores.
- **Allocation Diagram:** Shows how components in the application are allocated onto components in the hardware.

Figure 3 shows an example of an Application Diagram in Modelio. In this figure, we see how the radio protocol's modules have been modeled as UML components inter-connected through ports.

Instrumentation Code Selection and Generation

To generate instrumented code from the model, a new UML profile was created. This profile is shown in Figure 4.

The **<<InstrumentedElement>>** stereotype is applied to a class, a property or an operation. It can thus be applied to a component, port and an interface's operation. When applied to a component, the user can choose if instrumented code will be generated for the whole component. When

Figure 3. Application diagram

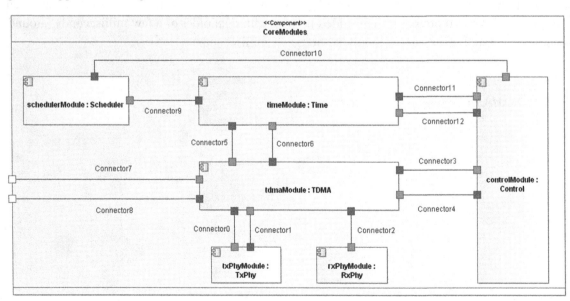

Figure 4. Instrumentation UML Profile

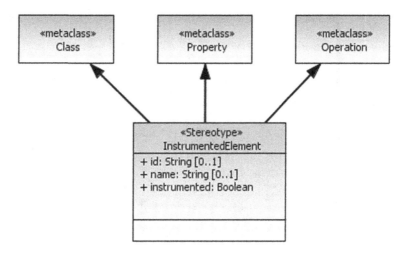

applied to a port, the user can choose if instrumented code will be generated for all operations of the port. Finally when applied to an operation, the user is able to choose if a specific operation is instrumented.

The **<<InstrumentedElement>>** stereotype has three attributes:

- **ID:** Indicates the element's real identifier in the real application (if model names differ from the real application).
- **Name:** Indicates a user-friendly name different from the element's name in the model. This can be displayed during trace visualization.
- **Instrumented**: Boolean that indicates if the element is instrumented or not.

A Modelio plug-in was developed to explore the model and generate instrumented code from elements stereotyped <<InstrumentedElement>>. The plug-in generates wrapper code for the application's modules (components). Generated instrumentation points were PragmaDev Tracer macros.

Trace Generation and Analysis

Once the instrumented wrapper code had been generated, along with the business code, the application was run. During execution, whenever an instrumentation points is hit, data is sent to the PragmaDev Tracer, which can then display the application's execution trace.

Once the application has finished, PragmaDev Tracer can export the trace and then analyze it by comparing it with message sequence charts specified in the tool. The specified MSCs represent properties to be verified. Figure 5 shows an example of comparing an MSC specified in the tool and an MSC generated from an execution trace. The initial scenario to be validated from preliminary design specification is presented in the left part of the figure, with its translation as a property in the PragmaTracer tool in the middle of the figure. Trace generation of message sequences are presented in the right part of the figure. Property matching analysis helped to validate the initial scenario is verified. (The Services and NC initial lifelines are groups in the Control lifeline (activator). Timing accesses of the services are separated.

Figure 5. PragmaDev Tracer MSC Comparison

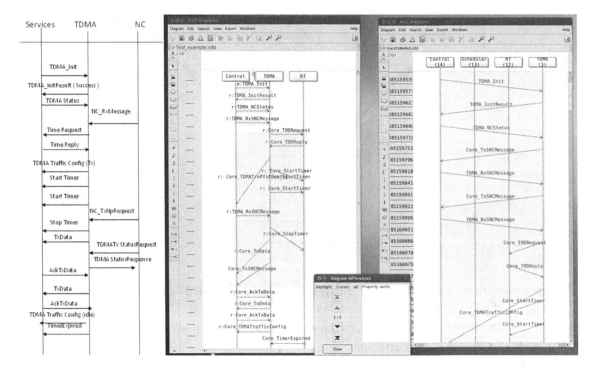

Instrumentation is also a critical part of analyzing code using Rapita's RVS toolkit. However, the RVS instrumentation approach utilizes source code which has previously been written or generated, rather than attempting to add instrumentation at code generation time.

To facilitate this, RVS is *integrated* with the users build system and existing code base. This involves running the RVS instrumentation and structural analysis tools as part of the build process for the user's application. This allows calls to an instrumentation library to be added to the source code of the application. These calls will generate a trace when the instrumented code is built and executed on the intended target. Instrumentation libraries often differ based on the specific platform they are targeting, as the method for generating a trace is often platform specific and may use memory, IO ports or writes to disk depending on available hardware resources. Structural information is also generated to give context to the trace at analysis time.

Once RVS has been integrated into the user's build system, binaries can be generated containing calls to the instrumentation library. When these binaries are run on the target platform, traces are collected. The method of trace collection varies based on the specifics of the integration library, but may involve simply copying trace files or, for more resource constrained targets, collecting trace files from a debugger or logic analyzer.

The generated trace is then analyzed using a suite of GUI tools. In the PRESTO project, much of the analysis of traces has been performed using RapiTrace, a new prototype developed for the PRESTO project. RapiTrace allows the user to visualize the on-target execution of their code at function and task level, providing detailed information on observed timings and task/function execution patterns.

Figure 6 shows RapiTrace displaying an on-target execution of the TDMA radio case study. In this instance, two threads are displayed in 'thread view', showing only when two high level tasks were executing and when they were idle.

Figure 6. RapiTrace viewer showing 'task view' in the TDMA radio case study

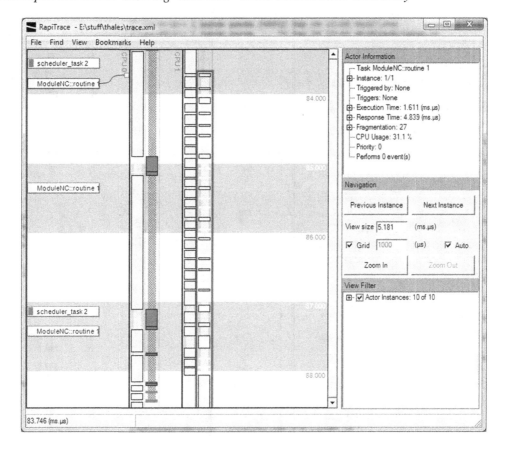

Figure 7 illustrates the same execution but in 'function view', showing all functions which executed on the target and the amount of time they were observed to execute for. Rather than segregating functions into their respective tasks, all functions are shown in this view, allowing for detailed analysis of execution on-target as it occurred. Detailed information on execution timings and patterns taken from real execution on-target allows developers to better troubleshoot execution timing issues and verify performance criteria from high-level models.

Functional and Non-Functional Analysis

PRESTO methodology combines several technologies and tools. For instance, it combines UML/MARTE models with MSC diagrams. It also supports several formats of traces. This interoperability is achieved through the use of standards (MSC, UML/MARTE) and through the use of common notations. Only a subset of UML/MARTE has been selected to ensure that analyses are possible. Aside the component model (shown in Figure 4), UML interactions and activities can be used to capture functional and non-functional properties to be checked. These models are adorned with MARTE stereotypes when temporal references are needed.

Figure 8 gives a simple example of functional and non-functional properties to be checked.

The functional property part concerns the component Time and demands that no SlotTick be received between the reception of a request (TimeOfDay Request) and the emission of the corresponding reply. This functional property is captured through a negative combined fragment denoted Neg.

Figure 7. RapiTrace Viewer showing 'function view' in the TDMA radio case study

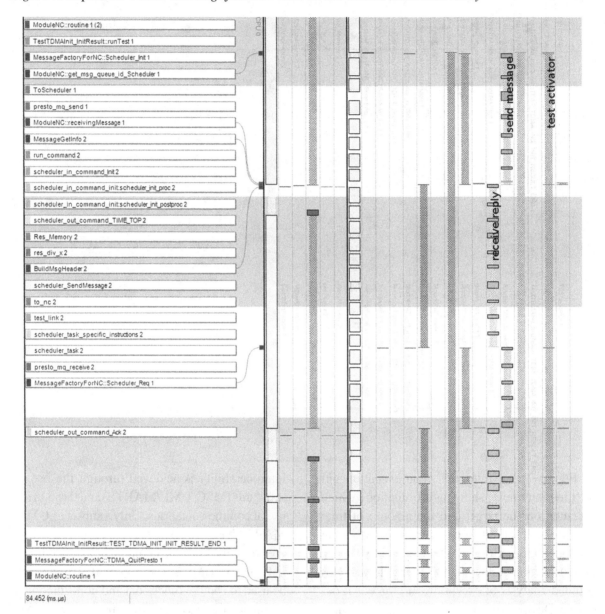

The non-functional property part focuses on what happens on component TDMA. It requires that there is a maximum duration of 50 ms between the sending of a TODRequest message and the reception of the reply message. This is captured through a duration constraint. Note that, the unit (here ms) is one of the important construct provided by MARTE in its Non-Functional Property sub-profile and that was not supported by the standard UML notation.

TimeSquare can be used to verify that a given trace satisfies these two properties. Within PRESTO, on this particular case study, around 29 properties (functional or non-functional) have been identified, which may be merged or split on diagrams using the property notation defined within the project.

The process is complementary from the verification performed in 2.c. It can support uniformly both functional and non-functional properties.

Figure 8. PRESTO property notation: example validated on traces

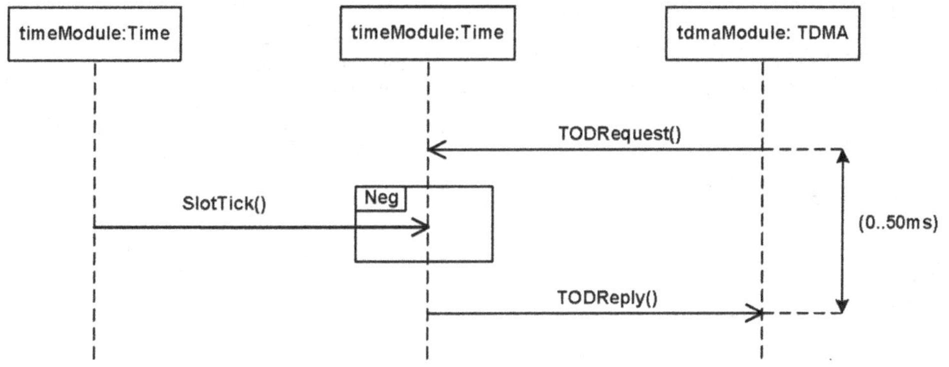

TimeSquare transforms through a high-order transformation the UML/MARTE interaction into a CCSL specification. The Clock Constraint Specification Language (CCSL) (André et al., 2007) has been defined in an annex of MARTE as a language dedicated to the specification of functional and non-functional properties and is designed around the notion of logical clock (André et al., 2010) borrowed from synchronous languages (Benveniste et al., 2003). A CCSL specification can be used to generate Java observers (Mallet F., 2013). An observer (Halbwachs N et al., 1994) is a simple automaton usually generated to perform model-checking but it can also be used in simulation.

In our case, the observer browses the trace and emits a violation message when the trace violates the property. Here, there are two cases of violations. Either a SlotTick is received between a request and a reply, or the reply is received from TDMA more than 50 ms after the request was sent.

In PRESTO, several trace formats are supported. The observer can used PragmaDev traces, but can also use other formats. This can prove handy when running the code on targets with only limited resources, in which cases, specific target-specific formats should be used. To be agnostic of the trace format actually used, PRESTO methodology recommends using a common Trace API. The observers generated by TimeSquare uses this common API rather that depending on a specific trace format.

Performance Estimation

During this step, the performance of the application on an OMAP4-based target platform was estimated using the ABSOLUT approach (Kreku J., 2012). A capacity model of the OMAP4 platform model was created utilizing the publicly available information about the platform. The model contains component models of the two ARM Cortex A9 processors, crossbar interconnect and SDRAM memory. These component models were instantiated from the ABSOLUT model library. The hardware accelerators of the OMAP4 platform were not included in the models since the aforementioned documentation did not cover the capabilities of those components in enough detail. Thus, the application was utilizing only the ARM processors of the platform and was not hardware accelerated.

ABSOLUT uses abstract workload models of applications during simulation. For this case study, the workload models were automatically generated from the application source code using ABSINTH2 (Saastamoinen J & Kreku J, 2011), a GCC-based workload model generator, on an Intel x86_64 workstation. Since ABSINTH2 does not yet support code optimizations, the effect of optimizations was taken into account by scaling the workload models down with a correction factor $C = I_{opt}/I$, where I_{opt} and I are the number of instructions in the optimized and un-optimized application, respectively. The capacity model of the platform in ABSOLUT uses statistical models of instruction and data caches. The values for the hit probability parameters of the caches were obtained with Cachegrind (Valgrind user manual, 2013).

RESULTS AND DISCUSSION

After conducting the experiment, several lessons were learnt. The following section evaluates the described solution.

Integration in the Development Cycle

The developed solution integrates well into the THALES development cycle. First of all the model uses a component-based approach which is common practice in radio protocol development. The UML profile for instrumentation adds stereotypes to be applied on existing elements in the model so it does not ask for model structural or behavioral modification. Finally the strategy to instrument only the wrapper code does not interfere with business code development.

Instrumentation Overhead Evaluation

Experiments have been applied on a Pandaboard ES target with an ARM Cortex A9 (700 MHz, L1: 32K instruction 32K data, L2: 1M) and 8G DDR2 800MHz using Linux 3.2.14 with gcc 4.5.3. The analysis strategy using code instrumentation and execution trace generation is only valid if real-time constraints are not violated by the instrumentation overhead. Table 2 shows results on measured instrumentation overhead.

The instrumented execution does not result in any missed deadlines when they are equal to 100ms, the smallest deadline in the application. On the other hand in other radio protocols, deadlines are on the scale of 1ms. A maximum of 30 points would then be allowed. In the experimental execution, deadlines would have been missed.

Table 2. Instrumentation Overhead

Number of message types	21		
Instrumentation points hit during execution	38		
Single instrumentation point overhead (μs)	Min	Max	Avg
	31.00	40.00	33.09
Ratio (single overhead) / (total time)	0.03%		
Ratio (total overhead) / (total time)	1.07%		

With the instrumentation method developed, the overhead can be limited by choosing the number of instrumentation points at the model level.

ANALYSIS RESULTS

The analysis by PragmaDev Tracer gave several results. First of all it was observed that certain test scenarios had more messages exchanged than expected, although the scenario's general steps were followed. In other scenarios, bugs were solved by comparing specified message sequence charts with the execution traces.

Performance Simulation Results

The performance simulation has been demonstrated on a specific Medium Access Control (MAC) radio resource allocation processes. The one called TCHAllocation particularly dimensioning in terms of time consumption of the MAC processing on TDMA frames.

The system model in ABSOLUT consists of the workload models of applications allocated on the components of the capacity model of the platform. The system model was simulated to estimate the execution time of the application and individual functions on the target platform. The longest time was spent on TCHAllocation function, one iteration of which took 4067 μs according to the simulation run. For comparison purposes, the real application was measured to execute in

4814 μs in the real target platform, resulting to an error percentage of -15%. This is in line with the accuracy level expected from virtual system simulation approaches in the evaluation metrics provided at the beginning of the project.

Conclusion on the Experiment

Among the advantages of applying the PRESTO method in our experiment, we can mention that bugs were found, and unexpected behaviors were detected. The developed solution to apply the PRESTO method also integrates well into the development cycle. On the other hand instrumentation overhead can break application deadlines and this is a real issue since the PRESTO method is heavily based on execution trace generation. However, experiments on a real application have shown for F&NF properties verification the number of instrumented points is limited with a small impact on performance overhead. Experiments on performance simulation met the overhead ratio targeted with respect to the on board execution.

FUTURE RESEARCH DIRECTIONS

In the future research directions, we plan to work on a more important exploitation of the information modeled in the specification, in particular the platform, in order to tune them at application level from automatic code generation. One other research direction is to use traces as an input to performance analysis tools, as model level simulators, or performance estimates from one target execution to another, in order to realize as accurate as possible an estimate of design space exploration at a high level of platform modeling. Moreover, efforts are also focused on a more integrated toolset with an optimized exploitation of properties specification at modeling level (as in Modelio) by trace analysis tools (as PragmaTracer analysis tools), by property code generation.

CONCLUSION

This chapter presents the results of the addition of extra specification in order to offer performance capabilities at the early stage of the embedded software development life cycle. This flow adaptation is mainly based on trace instrumentation and generation. Enhancements are applied to the specification with new annotation capabilities and instrumentation of the wrapper code generated. Analysis of properties from trace generation has been validated. The known issue of timing overhead due to code instrumentation has been proved as limited for the instrumentation points needed for the properties verification defined at modeling level.

REFERENCES

AADL. (2013). Architecture Analysis & Design Language. Retrieved from.http://www.aadl.info

André, C., DeAntoni, J., Mallet, F., & Simone, R. D. (2010). The Time Model of Logical Clocks Available in the OMG MARTE Profile. In Synthesis of Embedded Software: Frameworks and Methodologies for Correctness by Construction (pp. 201-227). Springer.

André, C., Mallet, F., & Simone, R. D. (2007). Modeling Time(s). In *Proceedings of ACM/IEEE International Conference On Model Driven Engineering Languages and Systems* (MoDELS/UML'07), (pp. 559-573). ACM/IEEE.

ATESST Project. (2014, March 15). Retrieved from http://www.atesst.org

Benveniste, A., Caspi, P., Edwards, S. A., & Halbwachs, N. L., Guernic, P., & Simone, R.D. (2003). The synchronous languages 12 years later. *Proceedings of the IEEE, 91*(1), 64–83.

Halbwachs, N., Lagnier, F., & Raymond, P. (1994). Synchronous observers and the verification of reactive systems. In *Proceedings of Third International Conference on Methodology and Software Technology* (AMAST '93), (pp. 83–96). AMAST.

Kreku, J. (2012). Early-phase performance evaluation of computer systems using workload models and SystemC. Acta Universitatis Ouluensis. Series C. *Technica, 435,* 106.

Mallet, F. (2013). Automatic generation of observers from MARTE/CCSL. In *Proceedings of 23rd International Symposium on Rapid System Prototyping* (RSP'12), (pp. 86-92). RSP.

OMG MARTE. (2013). MARTE profile. Retrieved from http://www.omgmarte.org

PARATOOLS. (2014, March 15). Retrieved from http://www.paratools.com/otf.php

PRESTO ARTEMIS Project. (2014, March 15). Retrieved from http://www.presto-embedded.eu

Saastamoinen, J., & Kreku, J. (2011). Application workload model generation methodologies for system-level design exploration. In *Proceedings of Design and Architectures for Signal and Image Processing Conference* (DASIP 2011). DASIP.

SDL. (2013). Specification and Description Language. Retrieved from http://www.sdl-forum.org

University of Oregon. (2014, March 15). Retrieved from http://www.cs.uoregon.edu/Research/pdt/home.php

Valgrind User Manual. (2013). Cachegrind. Retrieved from http://valgrind.org/docs/manual/cg-manual.html

KEY TERMS AND DEFINITIONS

AADL: That has its origins in the avionic domain, is a SAE standard for the development of real-time embedded systems. In AADL, the design can be represented in the forms of processes and threads which can interact via port connections, program calls and shared data access.

EAST-ADL: An Architecture Description Language (ADL) for automotive embedded systems, designed to be utilized as a complement to AUTOSAR. Aspects covered by EAST-ADL include vehicle features, functions, requirements, variability, software components, hardware components and communication.

Model-Driven Engineering: MDA is a software development methodology defined by the Object Management Group (OMG) in 2011. It allows designers to develop systems from a computation independent model to a platform dependent model, and incorporates technologies such as model transformations and model based repositories for artifact reuse.

Modeling and Analysis of Real Time and Embedded Systems Profile: MARTE profile is the OMG profile for modeling complex embedded systems and their software/hardware characteristics along with allocation, performance and quantitative analysis aspects.

OTF: Open Trace Format is a trace monoid definition and representation for use with large-scale parallel platforms, developed by ParaTools and the Center for High Performance Computing, University of Dresden, Germany

SDL: Specification and Description Language is a language that has been developed to specify and describe the behavior of reactive and distributed systems.

TDMA: Time division multiple access is a channel access method for shared medium networks. It enables multiple users to share the same frequency channel. This is done by dividing the signal into different time slots.

UML: Unified Modeling Language is a means of modeling complex systems. The UML is standardized by the OMG.

UML Profiles: A means of extending UML models with additional notations and concepts, termed as stereotypes.

Chapter 12
A Model–Driven Engineering Method for DRE Defense Systems Performance Analysis and Prediction

Katrina Falkner
The University of Adelaide, Australia

Nickolas Falkner
The University of Adelaide, Australia

Vanea Chiprianov
The University of Adelaide, Australia

Claudia Szabo
The University of Adelaide, Australia

Gavin Puddy
The University of Adelaide, Australia

ABSTRACT

Autonomous, Distributed Real-Time Embedded (DRE) defence systems are typically characterized by hard constraints on space, weight, and power. These constraints have a strong impact on the non-functional properties of the final system, especially its performance. System execution modeling tools permit early prediction of the performance of model-driven systems; however, the focus to date has been on the practical aspects and creating tools that work in specific cases, rather than on the process and methodology applied. In this chapter, the authors present an integrated method to performance analysis and prediction of model-driven DRE defense systems. They present both the tools to support the process and a method to define these tools. The authors explore these tools and processes within an industry case study from a defense context.

BACKGROUND

Mission-critical Distributed Real-time and Embedded (DRE) systems, such as naval combat systems or mission-systems, can have life-cycles that can be counted in the decades (Falkner, 2013). The design complexity and cost of such long-lived large systems continue to grow while

business owners continue to seek improvements in the return on investments for such projects. While an understanding of both functional and non-functional aspects of the system design is important, issues associated with the non-functional aspect of the design are of greater concern for resource-constrained platforms, such as submarines or autonomous vehicles. With strict budget

DOI: 10.4018/978-1-4666-6194-3.ch012

allocations for space, weight and power for various systems installed in such platforms, any early insight into the performance of these systems, and their corresponding deployment and budget considerations, becomes crucial.

Prediction of software performance has developed from early approaches based on abstract models to *Model-Driven Engineering* (MDE) based approaches (Woodside, 2007a). MDE operates through the definition of *Domain Specific Modeling Languages* (DSMLs), which are used to develop *models* that encapsulate the essential requirements of the problem space at a high level of abstraction, using abstractions that fit the domain of the problem space, and are hence more understandable to domain experts. MDE follows a process by which these models are transformed, either manually or automatically, through stages of increased specificity and detail, eventually resulting in the provision of an executable software system.

MDE techniques are typically applied to the development of application software components, but may also be used to model and solve the configuration and deployment phases, as well as system execution emulation, testing and analysis. *System Execution Modeling* (SEM) (Hill, 2010), a recent development from research into measurement-based performance prediction, provides detailed early insight into the non-functional characteristics of a DRE system design. A SEM-based approach supports the evaluation of overall (software) system performance, incorporating component interactions and the performance impact of 3rd party software such as middleware. These approaches are based upon simple models of resource consumption from the component's "business logic" (Hill, 2010; Paunov, 2006) and support detailed performance modeling of software systems, enabling predictions of performance through execution of representative source code of behavior and workload models deployed on realistic hardware test-beds.

SEM and MDE may be used in combination to support the emulation of system components and performance models, enabling performance data to be used to redesign and reconfigure the system, prior to any construction of the corresponding real system (Falkner, 2013). This is becoming increasingly important with the trend towards the development of *open* DRE systems, which must support frequent and rapid evolution, changes in component integration, communication partners and respond to run-time changes (Trombetti, 2005). The use of MDE, DSMLs, automatic code generation and utilisation of off-the-shelf technologies has enabled the SEM approach to abstract the development complexities of DRE systems, while still ensuring detailed performance insight to the level required to provide performance evaluation of mission-critical systems.

RELATED WORK

There are numerous works on model-based performance engineering, including comprehensive surveys (Balsamo, 2004; Smith, 2007; Koziolek, 2010; Isa, 2011) that explore the many individual systems, approaches and methodologies and case studies. (Koziolek, 2010) presents a survey of both model- and measurement-based approaches performance prediction and evaluation for component-based systems, classifying the main prediction approaches in five categories: based on UML (among which those based on the UML profiles SPT and MARTE (Espinoza, 2006)), based on proprietary meta-models, focused on middleware, formal approaches, and measurement approaches. In this categorisation, our method would most likely be part of the category of approaches based on proprietary meta-models. (Balsamo, 2004) presents a survey of model-based performance prediction approaches, while (Becker, 2006) provides an overview of performance modeling and measurement methods for component-based systems

UML MARTE (Modeling and Analysis of Real-Time and Embedded Systems) (Espinoza, 2006; OMG, 2011) defines a UML profile, which provides for the inclusion of non-functional requirements (i.e. performance, reliability, scalability) as UML models, which can then be analysed as part of the software development process. MARTE provides functionality for quantitative analysis techniques used to verify and validate temporal characteristics in MDE systems. This work forms the next stage in inclusion of non-functional requirements as standardised by the OMG, extending and replacing previous standard profiles, UML-SPT (Schedulability, Performance and Tim Specification) and UML-QoS&FT (Modeling Quality of Service and Fault Tolerance Characteristics and Mechanisms). MARTE defines annotations to selected UML model elements, both structural and behavioural, to represent basic quantitative and qualitative non-functional properties (such as sequences of values, and simple functions) as well as more complex compositions. MARTE provides support for the modeling of both application level components, as well as the potential to model middleware and hardware to provide support for full system performance modeling and simulation. Performance Analysis is performed using well-established existing theories of schedulability and performance analysis, using model transformation to extract the relevant information from the MARTE models for use by the appropriate tools (Woodside, 2007b).

Our approach is complementary to that provided by MARTE, in that we provide support for emulation of performance models above existing middleware and hardware to support early performance evaluation within multiple realistic deployment scenarios, in addition to integrated analysis and visualisation. Further, emulation of performance models within a domain-specific performance prediction framework provides a more specialised and easier to adopt methodology for parameterising performance models according to different usage and resource environments.

Several researchers explore the potential for modeling performance based on an understanding of the system architecture; we highlight several examples of interest here. (Hemer, 2009) adopt an Architecture Description Language (ADL)-based approach for modeling non-functional properties, which may include performance or timing concerns. (Edwards, 2007) utilises a dynamic analysis approach for exploring performance scenarios, within a blended ADL/MDE framework. Their focus on scenario-driven experimentation matches our approach, however, they utilise more advanced and specialised simulators to model behaviour, presenting a more complicated approach with the concomitant requirement for greater modeling effort. (Wu, 2003) exploits the reusability of components in component-based software engineering, introducing a hierarchical model of performance prediction based on the reuse of previously extracted performance profiles of existing components. They adopt a component assembly model that supports the integration of existing performance profiles for sub-components, which may be parameterised with workload information to provide more accurate prediction. Crucial to this approach is the existence of a component library containing both components and performance profiles.

(Groenda, 2012) and (Trubiani, 2013) address performance prediction with the aim of exploring the impact of different deployment scenarios. However, both of these approaches adopt statistical modeling approaches. (Groenda, 2012) explores the specification of multiple scenarios of usage patterns, deployment and hardware environment using minimum and maximum deviation scenarios, while (Trubiani, 2013) differs by considering the statistical distribution of uncertain parameters.

(Denaro, 2004) (Paunov, 2006) and (Hill, 2010), define initial approaches to System Execution Modeling, employing the use of prototyping to gain a detailed understanding of system design performance. (Denaro, 2004) constructs component-level temporal performance models outside of internal business-logic, while (Paunov, 2006) and (Hill, 2010) exploit the construction of workload models based on internal business-logic to provide more detailed and complete insight into overall system performance. We build upon this work by applying SEM techniques within a broader performance prediction framework, employing scenario-based performance prediction, multi-modeling and evolution to explore early indications of system performance.

Among this large corpus of works, we focus here on the methods, i.e. processes and associated tools. A survey of such processes and tools is presented for example in (Smith, 2007). This reference also proposes a generic process for Software Performance Engineering. However, this process is designed to be abstract and generally applicable, while the process we propose in this chapter is specific to DRE systems and the requirements of the domain. Fritzsche and Johannes (Fritzsche, 2008) introduce a process, Model-Driven Performance Engineering (MDPE) which combines MDE and performance engineering principles, based on Software Performance Engineering. In this approach, performance engineering is introduced through two models, the Software Execution Model and the System Execution Model, and is applied throughout all phases of the software development life-cycle. The execution models are represented as flow graphs annotated with resource demands and contention constraints. This approach is integrated directly with MDE, with performance analysis integrated with each stage of model transformation. It is not the intention for developers to directly annotate their models with performance-related information but for this information to be either generated from development models or automatically generated performance data. This may limit the practicality of this approach.

(Isa, 2011) compares four methods for performance assessment and modeling: Performance Assessment of Software Architecture (PASA) (Williams, 2002), Continuous Performance Assessment of Software Architecture (CPASA)

(Pooley, 2010), Performance Refinement and Evolution Model (PREM) (Ho, 2007), Performance by Unified Model Analysis (PUMA) (Woodside, 2005). According to this comparison, most methods score low or at most average (for CPASA) for the implementation level of the development life-cycle process. Our method focuses on design and implementation, thus being very strong in these levels of the life-cycle and complementing the existing methods.

PROPOSED APPROACH

A *software development method* can be loosely defined (Ramsin, 2008) as consisting of two main parts, namely, a set of modeling conventions (i.e., a modeling language) and a process. In accordance with this definition, we provide two software development methods:

- A *performance analysis and prediction method* for DRE defence systems, defining tools specific to this activity and a process for using these tools.
- A *tool definition method* for the description and development of the tools used in the performance analysis and prediction method, defining a set of (meta-)tools used in the method and a process for using these (meta-)tools.

We present these two methods, along with their processes and associated tools.

Performance Analysis and Prediction Method

Process

The performance analysis and prediction *process* has five main steps, presented in Figure 1: Model; Execute; Predict; Evaluate; and Evolve. The DRE system is first modelled from different points of view. The modeling step includes the modeling of the DRE system's performance constraints together with scenarios of exercising the system in different conditions. From these models, distributed code is generated for different platforms of interest. The generated code is executed in the second step and information about its execution on various platforms is captured and aggregated into performance metrics. In the evaluation step, the metrics are shown to the expert through context-specific visualisations, such that (s)he can decide if the model fulfils the performance requirements. Depending on the expert's decision, modifications may be proposed to the initial models. These modifications may explore several alternatives, and each may result in a new generation of alternatives in the evolution step. The process continues from the modeling step and stops only when the expert decides to do so.

In the modeling phase of the process shown in Figure 2, the DRE system is modelled from various perspectives, including *Architectural structure* and *Behaviour*. As discussed above, these models form an initial modeling perspective, which can be then iteratively evolved by the system expert in the *Evolve* phase as shown in Figure 6. These model facets are weaved in a composed model, forming the *System model*. The system model will be deployed on a hardware test-bed. The *Deployment* model describes the way in which the software components, part of the System model, are mapped to the hardware.

The performance constraints and system workload are specified in parallel with the system model, resulting in a *Performance model* as shown in Figure 2. Weaved together with the *System model*, it describes the *System execution*

Figure 1. Overview of the performance analysis and prediction process

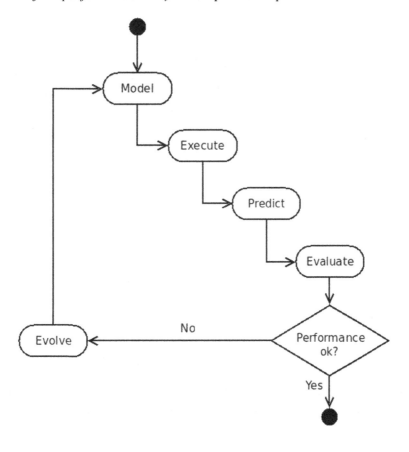

Figure 2. The model phase of the performance analysis and prediction process

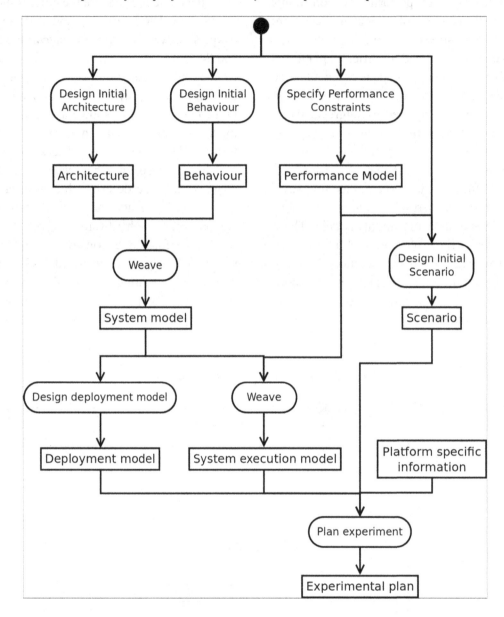

model (SEM). The SEM models how the system is predicted to execute in a generic situation. We propose the use of *Scenarios* to analyse the system performance under various constraints. Scenarios describe data flow into the system from external sources. The SEM, Deployment model, Scenarios and information specific to the platforms on which the SEM will be deployed can be combined in various possible experiments.

An *Experimental plan* chooses from the different available alternatives for deploying the SEM on available hardware, together with a specified scenario. The purpose of the experimental plan is to address a specific performance question that may be asked within the combination of an individual deployment, and a scenario designed to simulate the necessary system interactions to produce relevant performance data.

Using the *Experimental plan*, the modeller selects the platform on which the SEM will be deployed, the *Deployment model,* and the *Scenario*. Distributed code is generated automatically from the SEM for that platform, as shown in Figure 3. It is then deployed automatically according to the *Deployment model*. In a similar manner, code for the scenario is generated to simulate system interactions. This code injects data simulating sensors into the distributed code of the SEM, which introduces distributed data flows as indicated by the scenario. Executing the SEM code

Figure 3. The Execute phase of the Performance analysis and prediction process

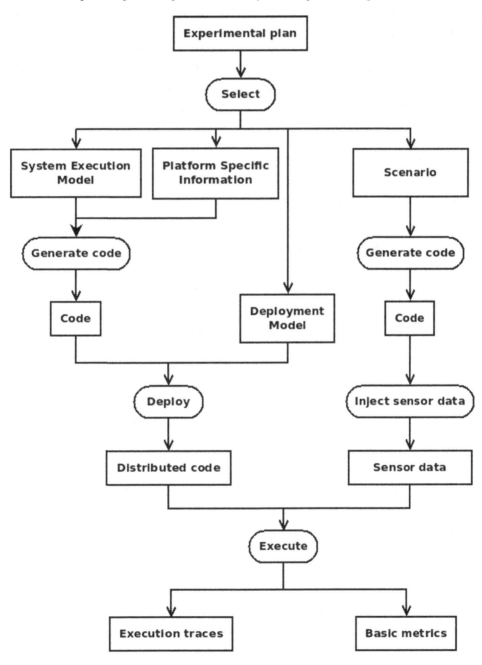

within its indicated deployment, and as driven by the scenario produces *Execution traces* and *Basic metrics* about the system performance.

To predict the system performance, basic metrics are gathered together with execution traces, and combined into more complex metrics, Figure 4. These offer quantitative estimations of how the system will perform in real-world situations simulated by the scenarios.

The aggregated metrics indicating the predicting performance of the modelled system can now be visualised and compared against the performance requirements as shown in Figure 5. If the predictions do not meet the requirements, the issues can be traced to their sources, for example simulated data source or component interaction, with the help of the maintained traceability links. Traceability links are maintained from the *Model* phase and in all phases. They describe relations *between* different facets of models, thus creating a

multi-model. The user can interact with the system to visualise, query, identify, and analyse the functional paths that generated specific performance measurements. After identifying the causes of the performance issues, the system expert may adjust the models of the system. When the system model is judged as meeting the performance requirements, the performance prediction and analysis process ends.

Based on the analysis in the *Evaluate* phase, the decision to change particular aspects of the system, e.g., structure, behaviour, deployment, may have been taken. In this case, the changes may affect the architecture or behaviour of the modelled system, the scenarios, the deployment model, the deployment platform choice, or combinations of these, as defined in the experimental plan. These changes are captured in the *Evolve* phase, Figure 6.

Model Tools: DSMLs and Multi-Modeling

In the following, we discuss the *tools* used in each phase of the performance analysis and prediction process. In the *Model* phase, we employ the following tools: for modeling the architecture: the Platform Independent Component Modeling Language (PICML) (Hill, 2008); for modeling behaviour: the Component Behavior Modeling Language (CBML) (Hill, 2010); for modeling workload: the Workload Modeling Language (WML) (Hill, 2010); for multi-modeling and

Figure 4. The Predict phase of the Performance analysis and prediction process

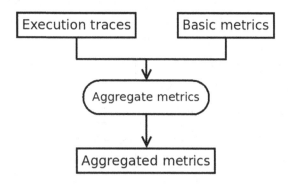

Figure 5. The Evaluate phase of the Performance analysis and prediction process

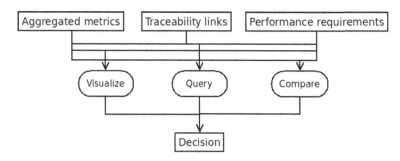

Figure 6. The Evolve phase of the Performance analysis and prediction process

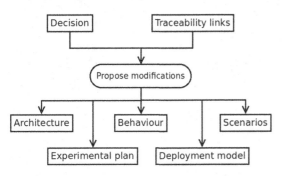

traceability: the Semantic Multi-Modeling (SeMM) (Szabo, 2013); for modeling scenarios: Scenario DSML (Falkner, 2013) (Falkner, 2013b). In the *Execute* phase, we discuss the use of DRE middleware (OMG, 2007; OMG, 2008). Metric AGgregation modulE (MAGE) (Falkner, 2013) is our *Prediction and evaluation* tool. We also develop a visualisation tool (Falkner, 2013). Lastly, Component Evolution Modeling Language (CEML) and its associated tool captures model *Evolution*. The use of these tools is exemplified in the section *Industry Case Study*, therefore we use the figures presented in that section to show the GUIs and syntax of the tools and languages.

The SEM is a middleware and platform-independent model composed of several aspects: the systemic structure of the System Under Study (SUS) into main software components and their connections, a high-level description of the functional behaviour of each of these components, a workload model of the resources consumed by the functional behaviour of each of these components, and a model of how the software components are deployed on the distributed hardware test-bed. These aspect models are woven together by domain-specific aspect model weavers (Gokhale, 2008).

The tools that we use to create these models are the DSMLs provided by Component workload emulator Utilization Test Suite (CUTS) (Hill, 2006): PICML for modeling compositions, deploy-

ments, and configurations of SEM components; CBML to model component behaviour, and WML to model component workload. CBML attempts to model the behaviour of components through formal specification using the I/O Automata formalism (Lynch, 1989); CBML extends the I/O Automata formalism with several domain-specific constructs. An example of PICML syntax is presented in Figure 9, in which components like *UAV1_GPS*, *UAV1_CTRL* and *UAV1_COMMS* are connected through input and output ports and signals like *rxGP* and *txGP*. Figure 10 presents examples of CBML and WML. Described in CBML is the behaviour of the *UAV1_CTRL* component, consisting in a sequence of activities like *logger* and *cpu*. Each activity is followed by a state; a special type of state is that of *branch*. WML describes workloads as attributes of activities. For example, in Figure 10, what appears as a figure annotation *WORKLOAD AIR = 10 msec*, is actually an attribute of the *cpu* activity that is set to the value of 10 msec.

Once a developer defines the behaviour of the component as a CBML model, model interpreters can then be used to generate configuration information for emulation and simulation tools. WML is used to characterise individual component assemblies with workload behaviour information, through the specification of profiles for processor and memory behaviours; WML interpreters are then used to produce, using generative programming techniques, executable operations in the target platform. PICML represents the structural DSML that integrates CBML and WML. In this integration, an explicit mapping from components and connectors in the structural model is performed to equivalent behaviours and connections in the behavioural model.

Scenarios capture the interactions of the system under study with other systems and are used to analyse the performance of the SEM across these interactions. To describe scenarios, we introduce a *Scenario DSML* (Falkner, 2013b), whose meta-model is defined by leveraging the existing concep-

Figure 7. The visualisation tool

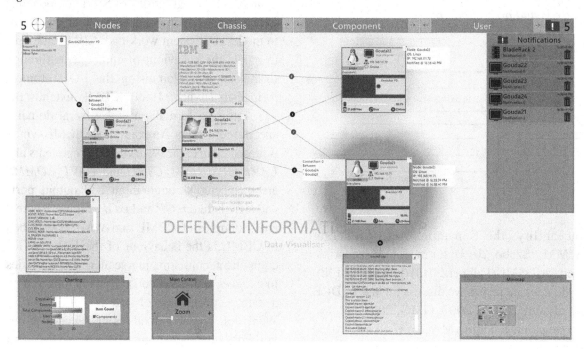

tual model and authoritative domain information of the SISO standard Military Scenario Definition Language (MSDL) (SISO, 2008). The *Synthetic Environment* that models these interactions injects data into the SEM, simulating different situations and thus enabling the analysis of the SEM and whether it meets its performance requirements.

The concepts from MSDL relevant to us are: *Scenario*, which contains several *Organisations* that model the actors, each of them containing several *Units* (e.g. UAV, ship), each with a *Disposition* modelled by a *GCC*-Geocentric coordinate in the *Environment*. The most important addition we made to these concepts is related to an event mechanism. This mechanism was chosen to model the behaviour of *Units* and their response to the actions of other *Units*. The concepts related to the event mechanism are: *Event*, which has several *Conditions* that have to be met in order for the event to be triggered. *Conditions* can be of different types, either on the data that is exchanged between events - *ExchangedDataTypeCondition*, or on the time when an event is triggered - *Time-Condition*. Once the event has been triggered, it performs *Actions*. These can be one-shot actions, or *IterativeActions*, in which case a *frequency* with which the repetition is happening and an *offCondition* need to be indicated. An example of a model described using the *Scenario DSML* is presented in Figure 12, showing the UAV as the system under study and its interactions with other systems such as the Combat Management System (CMS).

We have defined a tool for constructing the deployment model (Falkner, 2013), which enables the system expert to construct a model of how the software components are to be distributed across the available hardware. The *Deployment Tool*, also shown in Figure 11, has three divisions: a palette with all the software components at the left, a palette with the available hardware nodes at the right and a deployment window in the middle, in which the expert decides which component is deployed on which node. The deployment tool employs generative programming techniques to complete the final stages of code generation, and generation of necessary configuration information for the specified experimental plan.

Figure 8. Overview of the tool definition method

```
                              ●
                              │
        ┌─────────────────────┼──────────────────────────────────────┐
        │        ┌────────────┤                                       │
        ▼        ▼            │                                       │
   ┌─────────────────────┐    │                                       │
   │ Define metamodel of DSLᵢ │                                       │
   └─────────────────────┘    │                                       │
             │                │                                       │
             ▼                │                                       │
   ┌──────────────────┐  ┌─────────────────────┐                      │
   │ Metamodel of DSLᵢ │  │ Distributed specificity │                 │
   └──────────────────┘  └─────────────────────┘                      │
        │      │              │                                       │
        │      └──────────┐   │                                       │
        ▼                 ▼   ▼                          ▼
 ┌────────────────────┐ ┌──────────────────────┐ ┌──────────────────────────────┐
 │ Define concrete syntax of DSLᵢ │ Define compiler for DSLᵢ │ Provide time mangement mechanism │
 └────────────────────┘ └──────────────────────┘ └──────────────────────────────┘
          │                    │                          │
          ▼                    ▼                          ▼
 ┌──────────────────┐  ┌─────────────────┐     ┌───────────────────────────┐
 │ Concrete Syntax of DSLᵢ │ Compiler of DSLᵢ │     │ Time management mechanism │
 └──────────────────┘  └─────────────────┘     └───────────────────────────┘
```

Figure 9. The systemic structural architectural model of UAV1

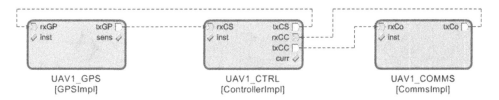

With the large number of models contained in the system under study, a challenge remains in capturing the dependencies between them and in enabling change management through traceability. Towards this, we propose a multi-modeling paradigm that facilitates the semantic alignment between entities in different domains. Multi-modeling aims to bring together different aspects of the same system in a consistent manner through the integration of models developed in various modeling environments. This approach promises to facilitate system analysis on many aspects, through the ability to capture multi-model interdependencies, and maintain multi-model consistency across various environments by tracing changes and analysing their impact. This ability is

Figure 10. The workload and behaviour models of UAV1

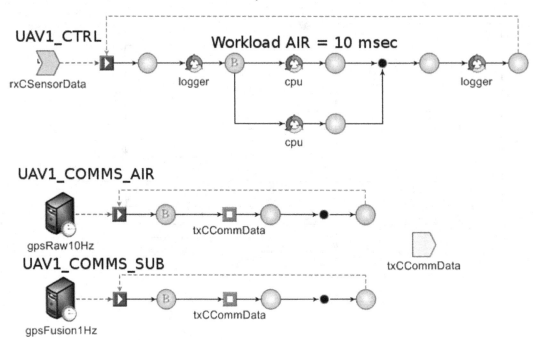

Figure 11. The deployment graphical editor with the deployment model of UAV1

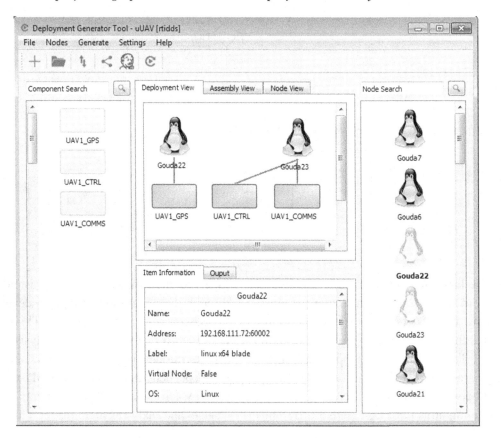

crucial when considering both the development, and evolution, of mission-critical systems in response to early performance prediction analysis.

Our approach captures relationships between entities in a relationship meta-model that is used for change traceability. The relationships defined in the correspondence meta-model can be classified as direct, one-to-one mappings, or indirect, in which some entities in both models are affected by a change in a single entity. Based on this classification, the change traceability module alerts registered stakeholders and logs models affected by change.

These modules are implemented in the Semantic Multi-Modeling (SeMM) tool (Szabo, 2013), which employs the Jenkins1 continuous integration framework to monitor models of interest. Models of interest are added to a SeMM project by the system expert, and relationships, together with their type, importance, and stakeholder, are defined. Once a change happens to a model, the change traceability module traverses the relationship tree and highlights important change effects

to the registered stakeholders that can then resolve relationship warnings. The SeMM tool permits the addition of new modeling languages either through the definition of Query-View-Transformations (OMG, 2007a) from the model DSML to SeMM entities, or through the implementation of parsers.

Execute Tools: DRE Middleware

As we are interested in predicting the performance of systems, and not only software, we prototype system architectures. These include four levels of abstraction: application, middleware, operating system and hardware. At the application level, the SEM and scenarios are defined. For middleware, we support the selection of appropriate middleware as dictated by the system of interest, enabling experimentation and performance prediction above multiple middleware deployments. To support experimentation within the DRE system domain, we support the use of both OMG CORBA (OMG, 2008) and the OMG standard Data Distribution Service (DDS) (OMG, 2007), due to their ex-

Figure 12. BlueOcean scenario

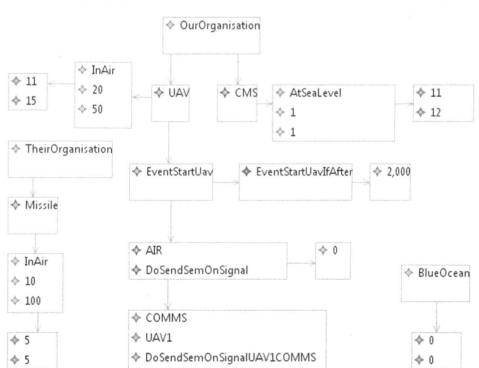

tensive use in DRE systems and their extensive support of non-functional properties through QoS policies that support various time and data management mechanisms.

The selection of operating systems and hardware is again driven by Defence needs. In order to evaluate the performance of the modelled system, different configurations of all levels of abstraction have to be analysed. MDE simplifies this task by automating the generation of code specific for each configuration from platform-specific models.

The platform-independent models produced in the *Modeling* step are further enriched with information about the platform they will be executing on through middleware and platform-dependent models. For example, information specific to middleware, such as DDS topics for subscriptions or CORBA Naming bindings, is added. From these platform-specific models, code for those middleware and platforms is generated. An example of the C++ code generated from the *System execution model* and the *Corba middleware platform specific information* is presented in Figure 13.

Predict Tools: MAGE

Our performance evaluation engine permits the definition of unit tests to analyse non-functional concerns such as the system throughput and resource utilization among others. An example of using MAGE to define a complex aggregation

metrics – *utilization*, as a combination of simpler metrics such as SUM and *runtime* - is presented in Figure 16. As the execution engine is executing the SEM based on the specified scenario, several performance metrics are recorded and passed to the evaluation engine for performance prediction and evaluation. Our execution engine records a large amount of information related to the execution of the SEM. This includes all data passed between the components of the SEM, out-of- band data within the SEM, as well as the data exchanged between the SEM and the Synthetic Environment.

MAGE (Falkner, 2013) transforms the raw data into aggregated information, according to the procedures specified by the performance requirements. Based on the performance constraints and the aggregated metrics, the evaluation module determines if performance constraints have been met. This information, together with the collected data, is passed to the visualisation component. The visualisation component completes the performance study by offering the user a more informed overview on the causes of particular performance metric values.

Evaluate Tools: Visualisation

Visualisation, Figure 7, is designed to show relationships, activities and alert or error conditions to indicate where the model is working correctly and where constraints are not being met (Falkner,

Figure 13. Snippet of distributed generated code from the SEM

```
Controller::Controller (void)
: gpsTransmit_ (false),
  gpsData_ ("                                "),
  gpsUID_ (0)
{
  this->rxCSensorData_event_handler_.init (this, &Controller::push_rxCSensorData_i);
}
//
// sink: rxCSensorData
//
void Controller::push_rxCSensorData (::sensorDataEvent * ev)
{
  this->rxCSensorData_event_handler_.handle_event (ev);
}
```

Figure 14. Snippet of generated code from the scenario – creating and waiting for threads

```
void Organisation::Execute(){
  vector<std::thread> executedThreads;

  //Start threads
  for(int i = 0; i < this->units.size(); i++){
    Unit currentUnit = this->units.at(i);
    executedThreads.push_back(std::thread(currentUnit));
  }

  //Wait for threads to finish.
  for(int i = 0; i < executedThreads.size(); i++){
    executedThreads.at(i).join();
  }
}
```

Figure 15. Execution traces of the SEM

	lid	timeofday	se	hostn	thread id	message	
41	41	2013-02-20 12:19:42	4	gouda·	1688213760	Start state AIR processing event 1973521009 at 33270582.038085	
42	42	2013-02-20 12:19:42	4	gouda·	1688213760	Stopped state AIR processing event 1973521009 at 33270582.048307	
43	43	2013-02-20 12:19:42	4	gouda·	1688213760	Start state AIR processing event 1973521010 at 33270582.332725	
44	44	2013-02-20 12:19:42	4	gouda·	1688213760	Stopped state AIR processing event 1973521010 at 33270582.342895	
45	45	2013-02-20 12:19:42	4	gouda·	1688213760	Component state AIR stop 4202431877 at 33270582.360349	
46	46	2013-02-20 12:19:42	4	gouda·	1688213760	Component state SUB start 4202431878 at 33270582.360484	
47	47	2013-02-20 12:19:42	4	gouda·	1688213760	Start state SUB processing event 1973521011 at 33270582.583316	
48	48	2013-02-20 12:19:43	4	gouda·	1688213760	Stopped state SUB processing event 1973521011 at 33270583.084886	
49	49	2013-02-20 12:19:43	4	gouda·	1688213760	Start state SUB processing event 1973521012 at 33270583.085224	
50	50	2013-02-20 12:19:43	4	gouda·	1688213760	Stopped state SUB processing event 1973521012 at 33270583.586865	

2013). It is possible to show physical relationships between components and entities (for example, how servers are grouped in a rack, or executing processes are associated with a given server) as well as the connections between them. A set of inspectors can be placed over elements of the visualisation to provide additional information. This information ranges from simple configuration information, such as node OS or IP address, up to the information flowing across the DDS layer between elements. The visualisation also has a notification system that provides a focal point to the user when specific events, constraint violations or items of interest, occur within the model. Combined with the ability to scale up and down to be able to see all of a large model from a high level, while still being able to see all details for an individual component, this approach makes the visualisation system a very powerful tool in understanding how and if the system is working correctly.

Evolve Tools: CEML

We introduce a framework that provides insight into the potential evolution paths for the DRE system architecture, the deployment of those evolved architectures within a constrained computing resource environment, and their expected performances. At the centre of this framework is a new DSML, the Component Evolution Modeling Language (CEML). This DSML acts as a guide to extract information about system evolution to drive the construction of potential evolved sys-

Figure 16. Definition of complex aggregation metrics

```
<metric id="runtime">
    <name> runtime </name>
    <evaluation>LF4.stop - LF3.start</evaluation>
    <aggregation> EVAL </aggregation>
</metric>

<metric id="compute_time">
    <name> compute_time </name>
    <evaluation>LF2.stop - LF1.start</evaluation>
    <aggregation> EVAL </aggregation>
</metric>

<metric id="utlization">
    <name> utilization </name>
    <aggregation> compute_time / runtime</aggregation>
</metric>
```

tem architecture options, deployment within the resource constrained environment, and the testing against evolved system operational requirements. With the use of a DSML-based model and the architecture exploration capability in combination with deploy, test and analysis capabilities, the framework proposes to deliver a 'what-if' capability for system evolution design choices and their resultant performance. An important aspect of this approach is that all evolved architecture avenues are anchored to the original system design model. This allows for easy normalisation of changes to the architecture by the system architect visually and resultant performances gain or loss from the transition to the evolved architecture.

CEML is a DSML developed to capture the key characteristics of the evolution of system architecture and its deployment behaviour within the constrained computing resource environment. Using the Generic Modeling Environment (GME) and Meta-DSML (Ledeczi, 2001) as a DSML development environment, the CEML model forms the foundation for the system evolution performance evaluation framework and dictates the manner in which the system can evolve. More specifically, CEML articulates how the components making up the architecture should change, what changes may occur within components,

the resource constraints present, the architecture deployment, and what operational requirements are to be satisfied.

Tool Definition Method

The *process* for tool definition, presented in Figure 8, consists of (1) defining a series of domain specific modeling languages (DSMLs), involving the definition of the DSML *abstract syntax*, *concrete syntax*, and *compiler*; (2) defining specific tools for the DRE context, including the integration of distributed management of the SEMs and their execution, time management systems to support real-time constraints, and support for hardware deployment to facilitate the gathering of realistic performance information. This process involves several (meta-)tools, and includes the use of appropriate toolkits that support the development of DSMLs (e.g., Eclipse DSL toolkit, Xpand), and the use of appropriate distribution mechanisms, such as middleware (e.g. OMG DDS libraries).

Several DSMLs need to be defined to support the performance analysis and prediction process described above. These include: the DSMLs for describing the structural architecture and behaviour of the system, the DSML for creating deployment models, the scenario DSML, and the DSMLs for performance modeling, and traceability and multi-modeling. To define these DSMLs we employ a model-driven engineering approach, in which we first define the DSMLs *abstract syntax*, followed by its *concrete syntax* and the generation of a *compiler* to interpret DSML files. The abstract syntax is specified as a meta-model (Kurtev, 2006). Based on the meta-model, the concrete syntax is defined as a model. The meta-model is also used as input for defining the DSML compiler. As this process is dedicated to DRE systems, the compiler produces code that is dedicated to distributed platforms, and thus such information needs to be included in the compiler generator.

The generated code is deployed on a distributed platform. However, as the systems under study are distributed and *real-time*, the minimum requirements that the distributed platform will need to fulfil are related to time constraints and thus a time management mechanism needs to be provided. Furthermore, the distributed software platform will run on top of a hardware test-bed. Because the hardware has a major influence on the performance of the system, it is essential that it be selected and configured properly. Next, a means to collect the execution traces and analyse them is necessary to perform performance prediction and analysis. This implies that meta-models of the respective DSMLs need to be defined for each of these aspects.

Whenever the meta-models of the DSMLs, the distributed platform, the time management requirements, or the hardware test-bed change, the tools that employ them have to evolve as well. Model-driven engineering is especially well-suited for supporting this iterative process, as many transitions between artefacts are described as model transformations, which increases the degree to which the entire process can be automated.

For defining DSMLs, it is necessary to utilise (meta-)tools for defining the abstract and concrete syntax of the language, such as GMF and EMF (Eclipse DSL Toolkit), and for defining the compiler for the language, in this case Xpand. Ad-

ditional tools are necessary for the DRE context, specifically the use of middleware libraries (DDS) to aid event-based communication and distribution, the Makefile, Project, and Workspace Creator (MPC) to generate make files for the different platforms included within the specified deployment in an experimental plan, and appropriate language support for real-time communications (C++). Meta-tools required to support the gathering and storage of performance information – i.e. *Provide execution trace collector and Database -*, and build the time management mechanism, are again language specific (e.g. C++).

The tool definition method influences mainly the tools used to analyse and predict the performance of the system under study; it influences only indirectly the analysis of the system under study itself. Using meta-tools and model driven engineering approaches, our tool definition method has the advantage of enabling rapid building and low cost of defined tools, and a simple changing process of the defined tools, that consists in updating mainly their specification, i.e. meta-models. Our method also has the advantages of offering a clear separation between abstract syntax, concrete syntax and semantics, easy evolution of both language design and tools, easy composition of several languages and partial generation of language-associated tools from meta-models. These benefits influence the analysis of the system under study itself by enabling more rapid and less expensive adaptation of the analysis tools to new analysis use cases and requirements.

INDUSTRY CASE STUDY

We explore the use of our performance analysis and prediction method with a case study for the DRE defence domain. Within this case study, we illustrate how the tools and methods presented previously can be combined and applied in the modeling and performance analysis of two modelled systems, namely, a *reference combat management system* and an *unmanned aerial vehicle*.

We analyse the performance of a hypothetical Unmanned Aerial Vehicle (UAV) that is able to communicate within both air and underwater environments. The UAV communicates with a Combat Management System (CMS) located on a submarine that could be located on the ocean surface or submersed, leading to a significant and abrupt change in available network. The CMS uses a communication link to send to the UAV the coordinates of targets to investigate, whereas the UAV sends back its position and images of the targets of interest. The environment is represented by the air and ocean. The main event that impacts the performance is when the UAV is transmitting to the submerged submarine. This impacts the communication link and therefore the performance of the UAV: when transmitting underwater, the communication link has less bandwidth, which implies that the UAV will do more processing, e.g., compressing the data it is sending, and thus consume more resources. The workload model captures these situations. In our scenario, the CMS detects the presence of a third party, i.e. a threat, and indicates to the UAV to change its activities in response.

The outputs of the *Performance analysis and prediction process* for the UAV are presented in what follows. As part of the *Modeling* phase in Figure 2, we describe the initial structural architectural model of the UAV, presented in Figure 9, and written using PICML. It is made up of three components: a *Controller* (UAV1_CTRL), a *GPS* (UAV_GPS), and a *Communication* (UAV1_COMMS). The *Controller* component does the main processing of the UAV. The data that is processed by the *Controller* is sent to the UAV by the *GPS* component, in the form of GPS coordinates. The *Communication* component exchanges control signals with the CMS and its performance is influenced by the available bandwidth.

The main functional behaviour of the UAV is described in the *Controller* component, as a behavioural model, written in CBML, as shown in Figure 10. The *Controller* exhibits two types of behaviour corresponding to the two states of transmitting through the air and water, as shown by the upper and lower branches of the workload model respectively. The *cpu* activities of both branches describe the workload the *Controller* has to perform in the two states. This workload is written in WML and indicated as an annotation in the figure and consists of setting the service time of the *cpu* to 10 msec and 500 msec, corresponding to the UAV conducting air and underwater communication respectively, and to the increased workload with underwater communication. As it can be seen, the workload model, part of the performance model, is closely weaved with the behaviour model. The behaviour model also describes the transmission of data between the UAV and the CMS, shown in the lower part of Figure 10, also corresponding to the two states of communicating in the air and underwater. The first sequence of actions models a bandwidth of 10Hz, corresponding to the UAV transmitting GPS data via the air. The second sequence models a smaller bandwidth of 1 Hz, corresponding to the UAV transmitting to the submerged submarine CMS.

Next, the system expert constructs a model of the deployment of the software components on the distributed hardware, using the *Deployment Tool*, as shown in Figure 11. In the deployment tool's middle window, the expert decides which component is deployed on which node.

From the deployment model, configuration files are generated. The building and deployment activities are automated through the use of Python scripts in the continuous integration framework Jenkins. Continuous integration frameworks such as Jenkins perform automated system builds, execute suites of unit tests to validate basic system functionality, evaluate source code to ensure it meets coding standards, and execute code coverage analysis.

An abridged version of the Scenario model described by the system expert / script writer, using the *Scenario DSML*, is presented in Figure 12. It consists of two organisations, *OurOrganisation* and *TheirOrganisation*, and a *BlueOcean* environment. The *BlueOcean* has no detail modelled, only a Geocentric Coordinate (GCC) of *0,0*. *OurOrganisation* has two units: a *CMS*, with an *AtSeaLevel* disposition, at a certain GCC *11,12*, and an *UAV* with an *InAir* disposition, at a certain GCC *11,15*. *TheirOrganisation* has only one unit, a *Missile*, with an *InAir* disposition, at a certain GCC *5,5*.

In this scenario, the UAV has four events, from which only the first one is shown in Figure 12. The first event starts the UAV in air - *EventStartUav*. The event has a triggering time condition – *EventStartUavAfter* – with a time value of *2000* msec. The *DoSendSemOnSignal* action associated with this event tells the UAV SEM to start in the *AIR* communication state. The communication with the UAV SEM is controlled through the use of a *DoSendSemOnSignalUAV1COMMS SemComponentPolicy*, which indicates the name of the SEM model – *UAV1* – and the name of the SEM component inside it – *COMMS* – to which the communication is to be relayed. The second event starts sending GPS data from the UAV to the CMS. The CMS may discover a threat and submerge, leading to underwater communication between the UAV and CMS – the third event. Finally the UAV is sent a signal to stop – the fourth event.

These are the main models produced in the *Modeling* phase. They now will be executed as discussed above. The *System execution model* of the UAV, comprising the structural architectural, behavioural and workload models weaved together, is used as input for the code generation process. The generated code is specific to a certain platform and middleware, e.g., CORBA (OMG 2008) or DDS (OMG 2007). A snippet of the C++ code generated from the *System execution model* for the CORBA middleware is presented in Figure 13. It is a class implementing the *Con-troller* component that registers an event handler for the data coming in from the *Communication* component.

Code is generated from the Scenario model as well. The *Units* in a Scenario are distributed entities, corresponding to a SEM. Therefore, the *Organisation* containing the *Units* creates Threads for each *Unit* as shown in Figure 14. The generated code is written in Java.

After execution, traces are saved in a database as shown in Figure 15. Traces are collected in the form of log messages, containing a timestamp, the hardware node name on which the component was deployed, a message indicating the Unit's state, and information about the event it currently processes. One can see for example two events happening while the UAV is in the AIR communication state (lines 41-44), then the UAV stops being in the AIR communication state (line 45) and starts the SUB communication state (line 46), after which two more events are shown while the UAV is in the SUB communication state.

The component receives a message to start, and sends another message once it has fully completed execution, in the format:

LF1: Component state {STRING state} start {INT evid} at {INT startTime}.

LF2: Component state {STRING state} stop {INT evid} at {INT startTime}.

The fact that a component processes a message is signified by the component receiving and logging a *start processing* message, and the ending of the processing is signified by an *end processing message* as:

LF3: Start state {STRING state} processing event {INT evid} at {INT startTime}.

LF4: Stopped state {STRING state} processing event {INT evid} at {INT startTime}.

The data format file specifies the four formats described above, namely, LF1 to LF4.

Current aggregation metrics supported by our framework include simple aggregation such as MIN, MAX, SUM, and AVG, but also more complex aggregators such as ABS_MEAN (absolute value of mean), CI (confidence interval) and VAR (variance estimate), as well as CSV, which permits the output of the raw data to a Comma Separated Value (CSV) file for later use.

To facilitate the calculation of performance measurements we propose more complex aggregations defined as sequences of simple aggregation metrics. For example, consider the *utilisation* of a particular component that could be defined as:

u = service_time / runtime

that is, the fraction of the total component runtime that the component is in service.

For the calculation of utilization, the specification defines the complex aggregation as a series of simple operations, using MAGE, as shown in Figure 16. A complex aggregation metric such as *division* is defined as a combination of simpler aggregation metrics such as SUM, and other performance metrics defined in the system, such as *runtime*. Our metric aggregation module selects from the logs of all messages only the messages that match the formats described above, and, for this particular example, extracts the starting and ending time stamp. Then, following the definitions of the aggregation metrics, calculates the desired performance metric. The current implementation of this module permits the definition and implementation of a rich palette of unit tests that analyse various performance metrics. However, the process relies on component messages that are stored in various logs and databases. Our future work will look at extending this process with a performance model defined in a DSMLs inspired by MARTE (OMG, 2011), which would facilitate performance definitions tuned to component attributes and behaviours.

CONCLUSION

The non-functional design aspects of mission-critical distributed real-time embedded defence systems such as naval combat management systems need to be understood early in the design process, before these systems are built and deployed. To better understand the performance of a system, our work describes the use of model-driven engineering techniques to facilitate performance prediction and analysis at design-time, using models of the system components, their interactions, and the system execution on 3rd party middleware and hardware environments, called System Execution Modeling (SEM). A SEM-based approach supports the evaluation of overall system performance. In this chapter, we describe our extensions to SEM that support the integration of realistic data sources, the visualisation of the causes of performance issues, as well as the understanding of models and relationships affected by various performance constraints, towards a complete performance prediction system.

Our performance prediction system is able to identify the performance issues of a SEM that is executed under a variety of conditions, using data obtained from real, emulated, or simulated sources. The performance study of a SEM is divided into five main steps, namely *model, execute, predict, evaluate* and *evolve*. In this chapter, we describe each of these processes, including the tools and methods adopted in each. In the *modeling* step, the performance model and the scenario model describing the interaction of the SEM with other systems are defined, while multi-modeling tools are utilised to trace the impact of modeling changes. Our Synthetic Environment executes the SEM according to the scenario model in the *execution* step. The design of the Synthetic Environment permits the periodic injection of data into the SEM but also allows for more complex data-generating components. Based on the information defined in the scenario to support the assessment of specific *predictions* and using our deployment configuration tool, various components of the SEM can be deployed on different virtual and hardware environment, operating system, and middleware configurations. Data in the form of messages is collected into a database. In the *evaluate* step, data is aggregated and various simple and complex metrics are calculated. A visualisation module offers the user additional insight into the performance of the SEM, supporting context-specific visualisations that support the expert in determining if the model fulfils the performance requirements. Depending on the expert's decision, modifications may be proposed to the initial models. These modifications may explore several alternatives, and each may result in a new generation of alternatives in the evolution step.

Our case study analyses the performance of a hypothetical Unmanned Air Vehicle (UAV). The UAV communicates with a Combat Management System (CMS) through a communication link, on which it sends its GPS coordinates and images captured from the targets of interest communicated by the CMS. When the CMS is submerged, the communication bandwidth of its link with the UAV is reduced. This impacts the amount of processing the UAV performs, as images need to be compressed further to cater for the reduced bandwidth. The Synthetic Environment executes the UAV SEM according to the described scenarios and experimental plan. Data is collected and aggregated, and complex metrics such as utilisation are computed. The visualisation module highlights the increase in utilisation but also shows the state of the communication links, additional notifications and node status among others.

In this chapter, we describe the tools, languages and processes adopted in our approach. We utilise existing modeling tools and approaches for modeling SEM workload, while we introduce new Domain Specific Modeling Languages for modeling scenarios and model evolution, in addition to domain-specific tools for visualisation, metric aggregation and analysis, multi-modeling and evolution. We explore not only those tools, languages and processes adopted in our approach

to performance prediction, but also those (meta-) tools that are needed in the definition of such a system.

Our system enables the analysis not only of one system, but also of a system of systems. Each system can be represented by a SEM, connections can be modelled in the Synthetic Environment, and metric aggregations can be defined to analyse these connections on top of SEM analysis. This permits the definition of more complex and comprehensive studies to increase insight into the performance of the system. Of course, this requires the definition of a specific architecture that enables loose coupling between SEMs, and enrichment of the Scenario DSML with concepts that enable expression of more complex interactions between systems.

REFERENCES

Avison, D. E., & Fitzgerald, G. (2003). Where now for development methodologies? *Communications of the ACM, 46*, 78–82. doi:10.1145/602421.602423

Becker, S., Grunske, L., Mirandola, R., & Overhage, S. (2006). Performance Prediction of Component-based Systems: A Survey from an Engineering Perspective. In R. H. Reussne, J. A. Stafford & C. A. Szyperski (Eds.), *Architecting Systems with Trustworthy Components: Proceedings of International Seminar* (LNCS) (vol. 3938, pp. 169-192). Berlin: Springer.

Denaro, G., Polini, A., & Emmerich, W. (2004). Early performance testing of distributed software applications. *SIGSOFT Software Engineering Notes, 29*, 94–103. doi:10.1145/974043.974059

Edwards, G., Malek, S., & Medvidovic, N. (2007). Scenario-driven dynamic analysis of distributed architectures. In *Proceedings of the 10th International Conference on Fundamental Approaches to Software Engineering*, (pp. 125-139). Academic Press.

Espinoza, H., Dubois, H., Gerard, S., Medina, J., Petriu, D. C., & Woodside, M. (2005). Annotating UML Models with Non-functional Properties for Quantitative Analysis. In J. Bruel (Ed.), *Satellite Events at the MoDELS 2005 Conference: Proceedings of MoDELS 2005 International Workshops Doctoral Symposium, Educators Symposium* (LNCS) (vol. 3844, pp. 79-90). Berlin: Springer.

Falkner, K., Chiprianov, V., Falkner, N., Szabo, C., Hill, J., Puddy, G., et al. (2013). Model-driven performance prediction of distributed real-time embedded defence systems. In *Proceedings of the 18th International Conference on Engineering of Complex Computer Systems (ICECCS)*. Singapore: ICECCS.

Falkner, K., Chiprianov, V., Falkner, N., Szabo, C., & Puddy, G. (2013). Modeling scenarios for the performance prediction of distributed real-time embedded systems. In Proceedings of MilCIS 2013: Military Communications and Information Systems Conference. Canberra, Australia: MilCIS.

Fritzsche, M., & Johannes, J. (2008). Putting performance engineering into model-driven engineering: Model driven performance engineering. In Proceedings of Models in Software Engineering. Academic Press.

Gokhale, A., Balasubramanian, K., Krishna, A. S., Balasubramanian, J., Edwards, G., & Deng, G. et al. (2008). Model driven middleware: A new paradigm for developing distributed real-time and embedded systems. *Science of Computer Programming, 73*(1), 39–58. doi:10.1016/j.scico.2008.05.005

Groenda, H. (2012). Improving performance predictions by accounting for the accuracy of composed performance models. In *Proceedings of the International Conference on the Quality of Software Architectures (QoSA)*, (pp. 111-116). QoSA.

Hemer, D., & Ding, Y. (2009). Modeling Software Architectures using CRADLE. In *Proceedings of the 18th World IMACS/MODSIM Congress*, (pp. 404-410). IMACS/MODSIM.

Hill, J., Schmidt, D., Edmondson, J., & Gokhale, A. (2010). Tools for continuously evaluating distributed system qualities. *IEEE Software, 27*(4), 65–71. doi:10.1109/MS.2009.197

Hill, J., Schmidt, D., Porter, A., & Slaby, J. (2008). CiCUTS: Combining System Execution Modeling Tools with Continuous Integration Environments. In *Proceedings of Engineering Applying System Execution Modeling Tools to Evaluate Enterprise Distributed Real-time and Embedded System QoS of Computer Based Systems*, (pp. 66 –75). IEEE.

Hill, J., Slaby, J., Baker, S., & Schmidt, D. (2006). Applying System Execution Modeling Tools to Evaluate Enterprise Distributed Real-time and Embedded System QoS. In *Proceedings of RTCSA 06: The 12th IEEE International Conference on Embedded and Real-Time Computing Systems and Applications*. Sydney, Australia: IEEE.

Ho, C. W., & Williams, L. (2007). Developing software performance with the performance refinement and evolution model. In *Proceedings of the 6th international workshop on Software and performance WOSP*, (pp. 133 – 136). WOSP.

Isa, M. A., & Jawawi, D. N. A. (2011). Comparative Evaluation of Performance Assessment and Modeling Method for Software Architecture. In *Proceedings of Second International Conference, ICSECS*. Kuantan, Malaysia: ICSECS.

Koziolek, H. (2010). Performance evaluation of component-based software systems: A survey. *Performance Evaluation, 67*(8), 634–658. doi:10.1016/j.peva.2009.07.007

Kurtev, I., Bezivin, J., Jouault, F., & Valduriez, P. (2006). Model-based DSL frameworks. In *Proceedings of 21st ACM SIGPLAN symposium on Object-oriented programming systems, languages, and applications*. Portland, OR: ACM.

Ledeczi, A., Maroti, M., Bakay, A., Karsai, G., Garrett, J., Thomason, G., et al. (2001). The Generic Modeling Environment. In *Proceedings of WISP'2001: IEEE International Workshop on Intelligent Signal Processing*. Budapest, Hungary: IEEE.

Lynch, N., & Tuttle, M. (1989). An Introduction to I/O Automata. *CWI-Quarterly*, *2*(3), 219–246.

Object Management Group. (2007). *Data Distribution Service for Real-time Systems Version 1.2*. OMG Std. Retrieved from http://www.omg.org/spec/DDS/1.2/

Object Management Group. (2007). *MOF QVT Final Adopted Specification*. OMG document ptc/07-07-07. Retrieved from http://www.omg.org/spec/QVT/

Object Management Group. (2008). *Common Object Request Broker Architecture Version 3.1*. OMG Std. Retrieved from http://www.omg.org/spec/CORBA/

Object Management Group. (2011). *UML Profile for MARTE: Modeling and analysis of Real-Time Embedded Systems V1.1*. OMG Std. Retrieved from http://www.omg.org/spec/MARTE/1.1/

Paunov, S., Hill, J., Schmidt, D., Baker, S., & Slaby, J. (2006). Domain-specific modeling languages for configuring and evaluating enterprise DRE system Quality of Service. In *Proceedings of the 13th Annual IEEE International Symposium and Workshop on Engineering of Computer Based Systems*. IEEE.

Pooley, R. J., & Abdullatif, A. A. L. (2010). CSAPA: Continuous Performance Assessment of Software Architecture. In *Proceedings of 17th IEEE International conference and Workshops on Engineering of Computer Based Systems*, (pp. 79-87). IEEE.

Ramsin, R., & Paige, R. F. (2008). Process-centered review of object oriented software development methodologies. *ACM Computing Surveys*, *40*(3), 1–89. doi:10.1145/1322432.1322435

SISO. (2008). *Military Scenario Definition Language (MSDL)*. SISO-STD-007-2008.

Smith, C. U. (2007). Introduction to software performance engineering: origins and outstanding problems. In *Proceedings of the 7th International Conference on Formal Methods for Performance Evaluation*, (pp. 395-428). Bertinoro, Italy: Springer.

Smith, C. U., & Williams, L. G. (2002). *Performance solutions: a practical guide to creating responsive, scalable software*. Reading, MA: Addison-Wesley.

Szabo, C., & Chen, Y. (2013). A Model-driven Change Traceability Method in System Modeling Execution. In *Proceedings of the 22nd Australasian Software Engineering Conference*. Academic Press.

Trombetti, G., Gokhale, A., & Schmidt, D. C. (2005). A Model-driven Development Environment for Composing and Validating Distributed Real-time and Embedded Systems: A Case Study. In S. Beydeda & V. Gruhn (Eds.), Model-driven Software Development. Springer.

Trubiani, C., Meedeniya, I., Cortellessa, V., Aleti, A., & Grunske, L. (2013). Model-based Performance Analysis of Software Architectures under Uncertainty. In *Proceedings of the International Conference on the Quality of Software Architectures (QoSA)*, (pp. 69-78). QoSA.

Williams, L. G., Lane, R., & Smith, C. U. (2002). PASA SM: A Method for the Performance Assessment of Software Architectures. *Architecture (Washington, D.C.)*, 179–189.

Woodside, M. (2007). From Annotated Software Designs (UML SPT/MARTE) to Model Formalisms. In *Proceedings of the 7th International School on Formal Methods (SFM'07) for the Design of Computer, Communication and Software Systems*. Academic Press.

Woodside, M., Franks, G., & Petriu, D. C. (2007). The Future of Software Performance Engineering. In *Proceedings of Future of Software Engineering FOSE*, (pp. 171 – 187). FOSE.

Woodside, M., Petriu, D. C., Petriu, D. B., Shen, H., Israr, T., & Merseguer, J. (2005). Performance by unified model analysis (PUMA). In *Proceedings of the 5th International Workshop on Software and Performance – WOSP*. ACM Press.

Wu, X., McMullen, D., & Woodside, M. (2003). Component-based performance prediction. In *Proceedings of the 6th ICSE Workshop on Component-Based Software Engineering*. ICSE.

ADDITIONAL READING

Aldrich, J., Garcua, D., Hahenberg, M., Mohr, M., Naden, K., Saini, D., et al. (2011). "Permission-based Programming Languages". In *Proceedings of the International Conference on Software Engineering*, pages 828-831, May.

Androutsopoulos, K., & Binkly, D. D., D. Clark, D., N. Gold, N., M. Harman, M., K. Lano, K, & and Z. Li, Z. (2011), "Model Projection: Simplifying Models in Response to Restricting the Environment". In *Proceedings of the International Conference on Software Engineering*, pages 291-300, May 2011.

Balasubramanian, K., Gokhale, A., Karsai, G., Sztipanovits, J., & Neema, S. (2006). Developing Applications Using Model- Driven Design Environments. *IEEE Computer, 39(2)*.

Balasubramanian, K., & Schmidt, D. C. D. C., Z. Molnár, Z., & A. Lédeczi, A. (2008), "System Integration via Model-Driven Engineering". In Pierre F. Tiako (Ed.), Designing Software-Intensive Systems: Methods and Principles. Hershey, PA: IGI Global.

Balek, D., & Plasil, F. (2001). Software Connectors and their Role in Component Deployment, In *Proceedings of the IFIP TC6 / WG6.1 Third International Working Conference on New Developments in Distributed Applications and Interoperable System*.

Beydeda, S., & Book, M. (2010). M., and& V. In V. Gruhn (Ed.), *Model Driven Software Development*. Springer.

Cassou, D., & Balland, E. E., C. Consel, C., & and J. Lawall, J., (2011). "Leveraging Software Architectures to Guide and Verify the Development of Sense/Compute/Control Applications". In *Proceedings of the International Conference on Software Engineering*, pages 431-440, May 2011.

Cicchetti, A. and d.& D. Ruscio, D. (2007). Decoupling Web Application Concerns Through Weaving Operations. *Science of Computer Programming, 70*, 62–86. doi:10.1016/j.scico.2007.10.002

Dam, K., Winikoff, M., & Padgham, L. (2006). An Agent-Oriented Approach to Change Propagation. In *Software Evolution. Australia Software Engineering Conference*, 309–318.

Denton, T., Jones, E., Srinivasan, S., Owens, K., & Buskens, R. W. (2008). NAOMI - an experimental platform for multi-modeling. *International Conference on Model Driven Engineering Languages and Systems*, 143–157.

Fontoura, M., Pree, W., & Rumpe, B. (2000). UML-F: A Modeling Language for Object-Oriented Frameworks. In *Proceedings of ECOOP 2000 - Object Oriented Programming*, 63-82.

Garlan, D., and& M. Shaw, M. (1993),. "An Introduction to Software Architecture". In *Advances in Software Engineering and Knowledge Engineering*, Volume *1*, World Scientific Publishing Company, New Jersey, 1993ny.

Greenfield, J., & Short, K. (2003). Software factories Assembling Applications with Patterns, Models, Frameworks and Tools. In *Proceedings of OOPSLA'03*.

Han, J. (1997). Supporting Impact Analysis and Change Propagation in Software Engineering Environments. *International Workshop on Software Technology And Engineering Practice*, 172–182.

Hassan, A. E., & Holt, R. C. (2004). Predicting Change Propagation in Software Systems. *International Conference on Software Maintenance*, 284–293.

Hill, J., Schmidt, D. C., & Slaby, J. (2008). System Execution Modeling Tools for Evaluating the Quality of Service of Enterprise Distributed Real-Time and Embedded Systems. In P. F. Tiako (Ed.), *Designing Software-Intensive Systems: Methods and Principles*. Hershey, PA: IGI Global. doi:10.4018/978-1-59904-699-0.ch011

Hill, J., Sutherland, H., Stodinger, P., Silveria, T., Schmidt, D. C., Slaby, J., & Visnevski, N. (2011). OASIS: An Architecture for Dynamic Instrumentation of Enterprise Distributed Real-time and Embedded Systems. In the *International Journal of Computer Systems Science and Engineering*, Special Issue on Real-time Systems, 2011.

Hill, J., Turner, H., Edmondson, J., & Schmidt, D. C. (2009). Unit Testing Non-Functional Concerns of Component-based Distributed Systems. In *Proceedings of the International Conference on Software Testing, Verification and Validation*.

Holmes, R., & Notkin, D. (2011). Identifying Opaque Behavioural Changes. In *Proceedings of the International Conference on Software Engineering*, pages 995-997, May 2011.

Holmes, R., & Notkin, D. (2011). Identifying Program, Test and Environmental Changes that Affect Behaviour. In *Proceedings of the International Conference on Software Engineering*, pages 371-380, May 2011.

Nuseibeh, B. J. K Kramer, J., and& A. F Finkelstein, A. (1993). Expressing the Relationships between Multiple Views in Requirements Specification. *International Conference on Software Engineering*, pages 181– 196, 1993.

Shirabad, J., & Lethbridge, T. C. T. C., &and S. Matwin, S. (2001). Supporting Software Maintenance by Mining Software Update Records. *International Conference on Software Maintenance*, pages 22–31, 2001.

Yie, A., Casallas, R., Deridder, D., & Wagelaar, D. (2009). A Practical Approach to Multi-Modeling Views Composition. *International Workshop On Multi-Paradigm Modeling*, 1–10.

KEY TERMS AND DEFINITIONS

Distributed Real-Time Embedded DRE System: Is a computer system with a dedicated function, embedded as part of a larger device, whose components are located in a network and that must guarantee response within strict time constraints.

Domain Specific Modeling Language (DSML): Is a computer language for creating models that are specific to a certain domain. It offers expressive power focused on a particular problem domain through appropriate notation and abstractions.

Model Based (Software) Performance Prediction: Is the process of predicting (at early phases of the life cycle) and evaluating (at the end) based on performance models, whether the software system satisfies the user performance goals.

Model Driven Engineering (MDE): Is a field of software engineering, that uses models for documenting, executing, visualising and analysing software and systems.

Software Development Method: Consists of a set of modeling conventions (i.e., a modeling language) and a process.

System Execution Modeling (SEM): Offers detailed early insight into the non-functional characteristics of a DRE system design. A SEM-based approach supports the evaluation of overall (software) system performance, incorporating component interactions and the performance impact of 3rd party software such as middleware. These approaches are based upon simple models of resource consumption from the component's "business logic", and support detailed performance modeling of software systems.

ENDNOTES

[1]   http://jenkins-ci.org/

Section 3
Industry Perspective and Applications

Chapter 13
Industrial Applications of Emulation Techniques for the Early Evaluation of Secure Low-Power Embedded Systems

Norbert Druml
Graz University of Technology, Austria

Manuel Menghin
Graz University of Technology, Austria

Christian Steger
Graz University of Technology, Austria

Armin Krieg
Infineon Technologies Austria, Austria

Andreas Genser
Infineon Technologies Austria, Austria

Josef Haid
Infineon Technologies Austria, Austria

Holger Bock
Infineon Technologies Austria, Austria

Johannes Grinschgl
Independent Researcher, Austria

ABSTRACT

Embedded systems that follow a secure and low-power design methodology are, besides keeping strict design constraints, heavily dependent on comprehensive test and verification procedures. The large set of possible test vectors and the increasing density of System-on-Chip designs call for the introduction of hardware-accelerated techniques to solve the verification time problem. As already described earlier, emulation-based methodologies based on FPGA evaluation platforms prove capable of providing a solution compared to traditional system simulation. This chapter gives an introduction into a multi-disciplinary emulation-based design evaluation and verification methodology that is based on various techniques that have been presented in chapter 5. Test and verification capabilities are enhanced by the augmentation of this approach using model-based analysis units: gate-level-based power consumption models, power supply network models, event-based performance monitors, and high-level fault modes. The feasible usage of this verification methodology in the field of contactlessly powered smart cards is finally demonstrated using several industrial case studies.

DOI: 10.4018/978-1-4666-6194-3.ch013

INTRODUCTION

Semiconductor industry advances have led to technology capabilities permitting the integration of an increasing number of features on the same chip size. This comes along with a number of challenges, first, the increasing susceptibility of these systems to power and supply voltage variations translating to higher demands in system reliability. Second, a growing number of these highly integrated systems are deployed in security applications (electronic passports, electronic payment, etc.), yielding higher requirements in system security.

In recent years, however, the industry has faced a multitude of design challenges. First, the lack of rich design tools and effective design methodologies has caused an emerging productivity gap between the potential of presently available technology and the exploitation of its potential (ITRS Working Group, 2012, ITRS). Second, the late design phase applicability of many tools has blocked designers from investigating the potential design issues and introducing countermeasures early in the design phase. Early design phase monitoring of the following physical parameters such as, system performance, power and supply voltage, and security-relevant system behavior,

is essential in order to reduce the productivity gap and to further push semiconductor advances.

Figure 1 illustrates a typical industrial near-field communication (NFC) system giving a prime example of contemporary power-constrained embedded systems. A smart-phone, a multi-feature and inherently power-constrained device, must provide power to the contactless smart card system (through a wireless air interface, e.g., ISO-14443 standard) by electromagnetic induction. This way of powering a device is described as a loosely power-coupled system. On the smart card end, power management is a critical issue due to the varying nature of its power supply and power consumption. While the strength of the electromagnetic field is set by the reader, the consumption is directly dependent on the smart card functions: it rises according to an increase in activity in its arithmetic and logic units and vice-versa. If power consumption is higher than power supply for a duration that cannot be compensated by draining the capacitor of its charge, then hazardous supply voltage drops can occur, which lead to operational failures. Contrarily, if power supplied is higher than power consumed for a duration that cannot be compensated by charging the capacitor up to its maximum voltage, then the excess energy is bled out of the system

Figure 1. Reader/smart card system and dedicated smart card power/voltage trends. Peak power consumption provokes hazardous supply voltage drops which may compromise the smart card's operational stability.

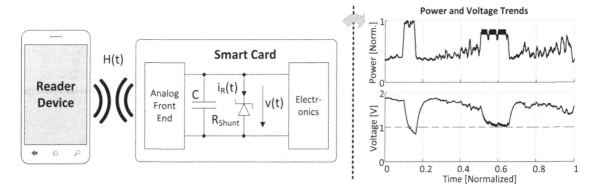

via the shunt resistor R_{Shunt}, which is depicted by a Zener diode in a simplified way. Its purpose is to protect the smart card electronics against power surges and to reduce side-channel information leakage.

In addition, smart card systems may be the target of security attacks. Such attacks must be countered by the smart card and, at the same time, it has to perform its normal functions in a reliable fashion and, whenever it is possible, with the best possible performance.

OBJECTIVES

Figure 2 shows our proposed comprehensive early design phase evaluation platform. It enables functional, power consumption and supply voltage, as well as performance and fault-attack investigations of power-constrained embedded systems.

A characterization process is required initially in order to model power consumption and supply voltage as well as performance and fault-attacks. The design-under-test is then synthesized on an FPGA prototyping platform incorporating all models. The functional emulation of the design-under-test coupled with all established models on the prototyping platform delivers much informa-

tion (i.e., power, supply voltage, performance information, etc.) about all system parameters, as discussed previously.

The objectives are to gain insights by using early evaluation based on emulation techniques and to integrate the effective feedback of this information into the development process. They are essential in order to reach truly secure and power-aware embedded systems.

BACKGROUND

Smart Card Applications in Power-Constrained Insecure and Secure Environments

Security controllers embedded in smart cards are deployed in many today's markets in order to secure sensitive data and to protect our privacy. Smart card systems are used in government applications such as national IDs, e-passports, or e-health insurance cards. Moreover, they are used in mobile phones (subscriber identification module), in mobile payments (credit cards, NFC applications, public transport systems) or secure platforms such as personal computers or pay-TV applications.

Figure 2. Principle of the early design phase evaluation flow

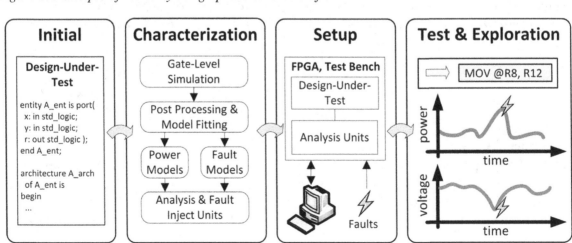

Critical Infrastructure

New markets for smart cards are evolving in critical infrastructure. Efficiency enhancements and a sustainable energy supply are crucial to our society. Future smart-grids must cope with highly heterogeneous energy supply networks incorporating many decentralized energy producers. A highly automated smart-grid together with smart-metering is required in order to automate the network's load control and the customer billing system. Moreover, the customer can remotely control their home's energy consumers. Hence, these systems can be vulnerable to hacker attacks. Smart card systems can act as security anchors that control data integrity and prevent unauthorized manipulations.

Industrial Control

The German government coined an initiative Industrie4.0. One focus is 'smart factories' to connect decentralized fully automated production sites. In addition, the initiative targets 'smart production' having a logistics network of multiple companies.

Supervisory Control and Data Acquisition (SCADA) has been introduced to control and monitor industrial processes that can range over multiple sites and long distances.

Data integrity of all involved components, remote terminals, or deployed sensors must be ensured. Smart cards are the device of choice in order to sustain hacker attacks and maintain secure system operation in Industrie4.0 applications.

The impact of failures in industrial environments on the safety of humans and the environment requires highly reliable and secure data processing and transactions, while these systems are often deployed in power-constrained environments. These smart cards must fulfill highest security requirements, hence they are complex System-on-Chips holding analog components as well as

a multitude of peripherals (I2C, SPI, USB, etc.). Not to mention that these systems are loosely powered via their contactless power interface.

In order to fulfill the security requirements for a broad range of industrial application fields, Infineon has released a new security concept called Integrity Guard. Integrity Guard stores and processes on-chip data (including computations in the CPU itself) entirely encrypted. Moreover, to allow comprehensive error detection, the concept of two redundant on-chip CPUs checking each other's results is utilized.

The increasing complexity of these systems renders the maintenance of high test coverage a challenge, not only from a functional perspective, but also from the system's power and supply voltage behavior, as well as fault attack resistance.

Increasingly long redesign cycles emerge if potential failures are not detected in an early design phase before the first prototype is available.

We believe that emulation techniques provide early design phase investigation tools to fulfill comprehensive verification of complex System-on-Chips, while maintaining high test coverage. This early design phase approach avoids long redesign cycles and moreover decreases time-to-market.

EMULATION TECHNIQUES FOR THE EARLY DESIGN EVALUATIONS

In this section, we will present a comprehensive emulation methodology that is used in industry for design evaluations early in a product's development cycle. This methodology comprises power consumption analysis, supply voltage analysis, performance and activity analyses, as well as fault injection techniques for security and reliability analyses. The presented methodology uses hardware emulation techniques. It is performed by hardware-accelerated calculations, design-under-test evaluations are carried out in real time, and results are delivered for each clock cycle. Thus, engineers are supported with accurate and fast tools to explore and evaluate novel hardware/ software designs.

Power Emulation

Power emulation, first introduced by Coburn et al. (2005) as a variant of estimation-based power profiling techniques, derives power information from evaluating power models. In principle, these power models can be implemented on various levels of abstraction, which influences their accuracy and complexity. Power emulation is operated on a relatively high level of abstraction in order to limit the model complexity and in turn hardware costs, which is a key requirement for low-power implementations of contactless smart cards. Models on this level of abstraction are often based on linear regression methods as depicted in (1).

$$\hat{P}(\mathbf{x}) = c_0 + \sum_{i=1}^{m} c_i \cdot x_i \qquad (1)$$

$x = \begin{bmatrix} x_1, x_2, \ldots x_n \end{bmatrix}$ gives the vector of model parameters and $c = \begin{bmatrix} c_1, c_2, \ldots c_n \end{bmatrix}$ represents the model's coefficients. In its simplest form, model parameters are mapped to system states such as smart card's low-power modes (e.g., sleep / halt) or memory read / write accesses. The vector of model coefficients c_i contains power information that is dissipated during the active phase of a certain system state x_i. The linear combination of the model coefficients c_i and the model parameters x_i form the power estimate $\hat{P}(\mathbf{x})$. Model coefficients c_i are determined in a power characterization process (Krieg et al., 2011), which is explained in further detail below.

Apart from performing pure power profiling on an embedded system (e.g., contactless smart cards), the hardware's power consumption gives

important information for security evaluation methodologies as well. Simple Power Analysis (SPA) and Differential Power Analysis (DPA) are representatives of this group. Moreover, faults injected by such security evaluation techniques can induce significant power consumption changes. If these are detectable by power estimation methods, security relevant countermeasures can be exploited (e.g., security traps or hardware resets).

The proposed system-level fault analysis concept extends the power emulation approach based on linear regression models explained above. Security relevant power information leakage can be extracted and evaluated, which gives room for design corrections before tape-out. The concept is illustrated by Krieg et al. (2012). The power model stated in (1) is extended according to (2).

$$\hat{P}(\mathbf{x}) = \hat{P}_{Static} + \hat{P}_{StateDynamic}(\mathbf{x}) + \hat{P}_{DataDynamic}(\mathbf{x}) \qquad (2)$$

The model distinguishes between static power consumption $\hat{P}_{Static}$ and dynamic power consumption $\hat{P}_{Dynamic}$. Moreover, it allows for the separation of state-dependent $\hat{P}_{StateDynamic}$ and data-dependent power consumption information $\hat{P}_{DataDynamic}$. State-dependent power consumption information is covered by the simple power model in (1). The power estimates' data dependency is introduced in order to support security relevant power analysis, such as SPA and DPA as shown in (2).

$$\hat{P}(\mathbf{x}) = c_0 + \sum_{i=1}^{m} c_{si} \cdot x_i + \sum_{i=1}^{n} c_{di} \cdot x_i \qquad (3)$$

Relevant signal states x_{si} and x_{di} and corresponding model coefficients c_{si} and c_{di}, respectively, are determined during a power characterization process (Krieg et al., 2011). A vector-based representation of the power model is given in (4).

The difference between the real power consumption and the estimates given by the developed model is described by ε as depicted in (5). The average estimation error ε can be reduced by considering more system information in the form of additional states and their corresponding model coefficients. Finally, power sensors map state-dependent (SD) and data-dependent (DD) system states of the system-under-test to corresponding power value estimates. Estimation accuracies of greater than 90% compared to physical measurements can be achieved.

$$\hat{P}(\mathbf{x}) = c_0 + \mathbf{c}_s \mathbf{x} + \mathbf{c}_d \mathbf{x} \qquad (4)$$

$$P(\mathbf{x}) = \hat{P}(\mathbf{x}) + \varepsilon \qquad (5)$$

Power Characterization

The established power model highly influences power-profiling quality. The choice of model parameters that represent most power-relevant system states are of great importance. Model parameters and their corresponding model coefficients are determined during the power characterization process as illustrated in Figure 3. The proper number and the right choice of these model parameters impacts on the model's complexity and accuracy.

First, an exhaustive benchmarking suite is executed on the design-under-test on a gate-level basis. These benchmarks should be designed in a way that they cause system activity across the entire system in order to reach representative results in terms of power consumption.

These simulations uncover activity information for any signal of interest within the system. Once acquired, they form the basis for power simulations resulting in corresponding power values.

Activity and power information is processed in the model-parameter selection process. A relevancy analysis using statistical methods must be performed in order to select the most relevant power parameters. Finally, a linear regression model fitting process is performed determining relevant power model coefficients c_0, $\mathbf{c}_s$, and $\mathbf{c}_d$.

Supply voltage estimation techniques form another important field of research. Supply voltage information of a system can shed light on its susceptibility to supply voltage variations and,

Figure 3. Power characterization flow

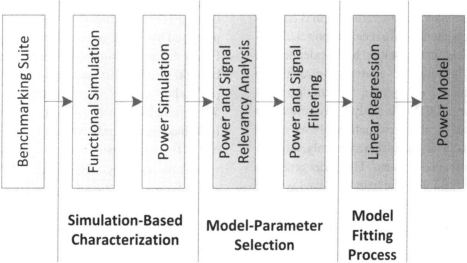

in turns, to its reliability. This is of particular importance for contactless smart card systems.

Because of the mathematical relationship between power and voltage, power information is a key prerequisite in order to gain insights into supply voltage behavior. Hence, power emulation provides a good basis for supply voltage analysis emulation techniques.

Supply Voltage Characterization and Emulation

A smart card system's contactless power transfer is very limited. As a consequence, a smart card is prone to supply voltage drops caused for example by high power consuming computations or an insufficient magnetic field strength. A smart card hardware/software engineer must be aware of these power supply issues. Therefore, it is of high importance to support engineers with accurate and fast supply voltage and power consumption estimation tools early during the design phase. Here we present a methodology featuring the evaluation of a contactlessly powered smart card's supply voltage behavior early during its hardware/software design time. This methodology comprises the following three phases: power network model characterization and model creation, augmentation, and emulation.

During the first phase, the power supply network of the reader / smart card system is characterized. A contactless smart card is powered by a magnetic field that is emitted by a reader device. Figure 4 illustrates the equivalent circuit of a reader / smart card system, as introduced by Finkenzeller (2003). It is analytically defined by (6). This analytical approximation is based on the law of Biot-Savat and is therefore only valid for rectangular shaped antennas. The reader generates a magnetic field with the help of a fixed voltage v_1, the resonance circuit C_R, L_R, and R_R, and an alterable resistor $R_{\mathrm{Rel}}(t)$. By means of induc-

tive coupling, electrical power is transferred contactlessly to the smart card. The coupling factor between smart card and reader is defined by the parameter k. After rectification, electrical energy is buffered within the capacitor C_B. The capacitor's charge level $Q_c(t)$ sets the crucial voltage $v(t)$, which is supplied to the electronics. The shunt resistor R_{Shunt}, which is depicted in a simplified form of a Zener diode, prevents the adjacent electronics from power surges and reduces security related side-channel information leakage. The changing resistor of the smart card's CPU is given by $R_{CPU}(t)$. $R_L(t)$ comprises the smart card electronics' total changing resistance. Depending on the smart card CPU's power consumption and the power provided by the magnetic field, capacitor C_B charges or discharges. It is crucial to provide a proper voltage level $v(t)$ to the electronics. If this voltage $v(t)$ drops below a certain threshold, the electronics' operational stability is lost.

However, in order to develop an appropriate model of a smart card's power network which can be feasibly calculated by dedicated Arithmetic and Logic Units (ALUs) within an FPGA prototyping board, further simplifications need to be performed. Therefore, the electrical current and voltage characteristics of the reader / smart card system are measured. Based on these characteristics, a Thévenin voltage source is introduced, as proposed by Wendt et al. (2008) and depicted by Figure 4. The resulting equivalent circuit can now be expressed by a first order differential equation (if the shunt resistor's functionality is simplified). With the help of a charge-based approach, which is defined by (7), the behavior of the supply voltage $v(t)$ can be easily computed in hardware. It should be noted that the voltage level of $v_i(t)$ depends on physically related parameters such as antenna characteristics, distance between reader and smart card, orientation of the smart card

Figure 4. Equivalent circuits of a reader/smart card system's power supply network

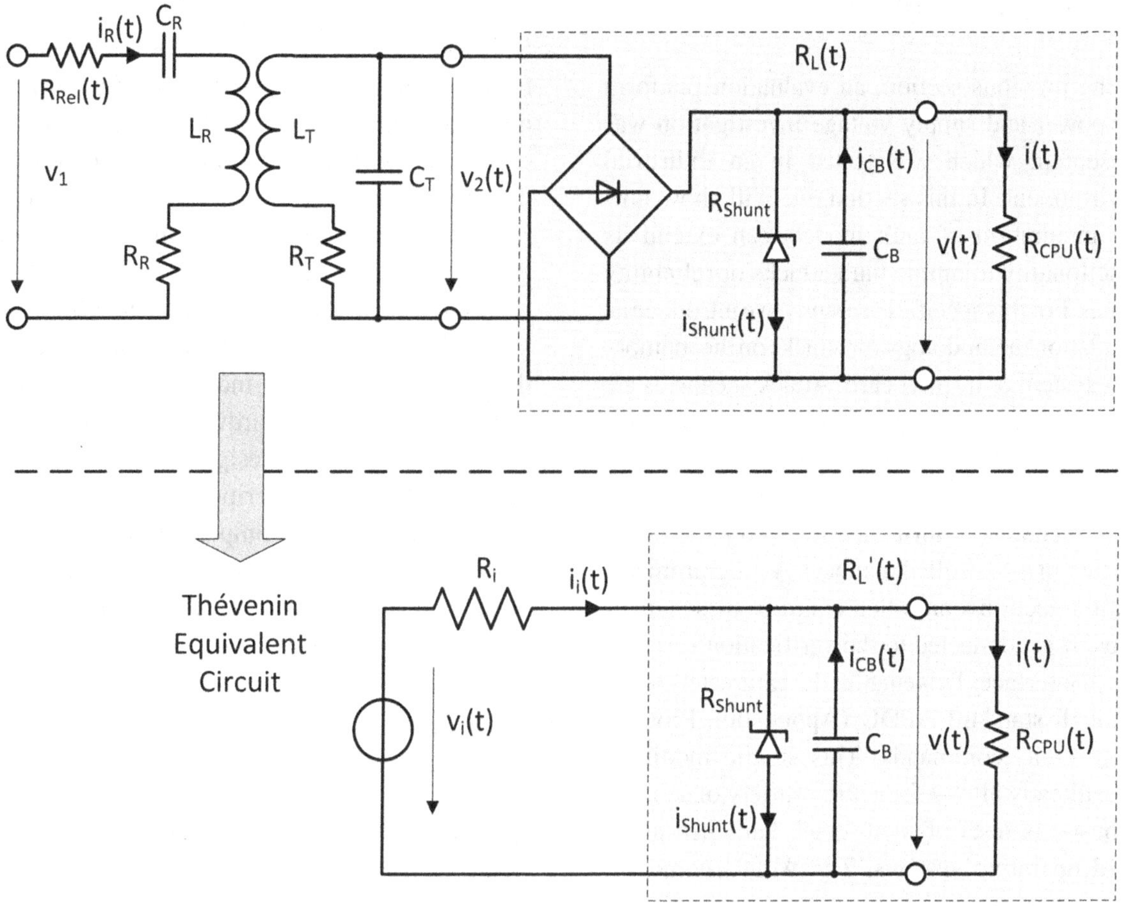

within the magnetic field, etc. The amount of electrical current $i(t)$ that is consumed by the smart card's CPU is estimated by the dedicated power estimation unit, which was introduced in the previous section. The presented model-based supply voltage analysis technique accounts for a maximum estimation error of only 2%, according to Wendt et al. (2008) and Druml et al. (2012).

$$v_2(t) = \frac{\omega k \sqrt{L_R L_T}\, i_R}{\sqrt{\left(\frac{\omega L_T}{R_L} + \omega R_T C_T\right)^2 + \left(1 - \omega^2 L_T C_T + \frac{R_T}{R_L}\right)^2}} \tag{6}$$

$$v(t+1) = \frac{Q_C(t) + \dfrac{v_i(t) - v(t)}{R_i}\Delta t - i(t)\Delta t}{C} \quad \text{if}$$
$$v(t) < V_Z \tag{7}$$

During the augmentation phase, a smart card design-under-test is enhanced with the presented power supply network model and the dedicated power emulation unit. All components, which are available in a hardware description language, are then synthesized in an FPGA prototyping board. Now, the design-under-test is ready and can be emulated. Supply voltage and power consumption estimates are gathered in real-time and for each clock cycle.

Emulation-Based Fault-Attack and Bit-Flip Emulation

In the previous section, an evaluation platform for power and supply voltage investigation was presented, which was tested in an industrial environment. In this section, we will show how the integration of fault models can extend its functionality to mimic fault attacks or reliability issues. For this specific case study, we introduce an emulation methodology for attacks on the memory sub-system of a smart card. Attack scenarios are mapped on the cache data bus of the target, which can be a LEON3 processor or security controller, using integrated saboteur modules (specific hardware elements to influence selected parts of the system in a controlled manner). A programmable fault injection controller controls these attack runs. It is connected to the verification system's serial interface. This enables the parameterization through standard APDU (Application Protocol Data Unit) commands. This simple modification already allows for a wide variety of security robustness tests of fault-attack hardened smart card operating systems. The APDU command integration permits the seamless integration of the platform into a standard software verification system. For more details on this emulation system please refer to the work shown in Grinschgl et al. (2013).

The high performance of the FPGA-based emulation platform allows high fault attack coverage of real-world applications using a multitude of attack vectors. On the other hand, as described in Krieg et al. (2013), a saboteur-based implementation for dependability evaluation has to be created in a completely different way. The random nature of these fault effects comes with the need of the integration of a large number of saboteurs. For this type of fault-injection testing, zones in the target implementation have to be defined, where faults would most likely directly result in disturbed operation.

Performance Emulation

If a design-under-test is given which needs to fulfill certain real-time or performance constraints, it is of high importance to carry out performance evaluations during early design stages in order to detect hardware/software design flaws as soon as possible. For this performance analysis purpose, the use of Hardware Performance Counters (HPC) represents a common technique. An HPC represents a small circuit that is integrated into the design-under-test and monitors performance events e of signals or hardware units of interest. Given the fact that the design-under-test is available in a hardware description language, HPCs can be added to any component easily without changing the component's original functionality. A performance event e is triggered if a logical function f over a set of input signals s_n is satisfied, according to (8). These trigger events are captured by incrementing their dedicated performance counters. For example, if a processor system is being evaluated regarding its performance, performance events of interest can be memory accesses, cache misses, pipeline stalls, etc. within a certain period of time. The HPC data is gathered and can then be evaluated online by the design-under-test's software or hardware components. If HPCs are used in an early design phase prototyping board, as presented in this paper, all HPC data is transferred to a host PC in order to perform offline analysis and verification tasks. The presented performance analysis technique helps detect and correct hardware and software problems, which would otherwise violate worst-case execution time or real-time requirements.

$$e(s) = f(s_0, s_1, s_2, \ldots s_n) \tag{8}$$

Activity Emulation

The first task includes the analysis of the LEON3 processor implementation in order to collect all relevant control signals of the system. A set of general benchmark applications is then executed to retrieve global control signal activity values. For this purpose, we relied on an adapted version (for the SPARC architecture) of the benchmark programs described in the following work (Bachmann et al., 2010). These applications are partially based on widely used benchmark suites like MiBench, Dhrystone, and Coremark. Furthermore, standard algorithms such as the quick-sort and AES encryption implementations have been added to better cover the application used on our embedded system.

The generated temporal tracing results are, for example, extracted from the Coremark benchmark by evaluating three system modules of the LEON3 processor. Detailed activity information can be extracted from such traces to be used in accurate fault injection models. Such an investigation for the Coremark benchmark shows a high even activity in the integer unit and MMU, but quite low control activity in the cache management modules. Fault injection into these cache management modules would therefore not be successful for targeted attack runs.

Also power estimation models are in need for such activity evaluations as, for example, large data buses have an impact on power consumption of System-on-Chip designs, which cannot be ignored. Hence, a characterization process also needs to include data signals to reduce the estimation error. However, bus line capacitances, which are the cause for this kind of power consumption, are only available after at least a preliminary physical implementation has been prepared.

The following metrics have been defined as a base for activity emulation evaluations:

N_{max} = number of observed signal lines (9)

N_{cycles} = number of observed clock cycles (10)

$$N_{bc}[t] = \sum_{i=1}^{N\max} is\_changed(bit(i))[t] \dots \text{ number}$$
of changed signals (11)

$$A[t] = \frac{N_{bc}[t]}{N_{max}} \dots \text{ cycle activity at a certain point}$$
of time (12)

$$A = \frac{\sum_{i=0}^{N_{cycles}} A[i]}{N_{cycles}} \dots \text{ global activity over the ob-}$$
served time frame (13)

INDUSTRIAL CASE STUDIES

In the following two sections, we outline evaluation results of our emulation methodology which was applied to an industrial smart card design and a freely available LEON3 processor design. We evaluated power and supply voltage behaviors, and we evaluated the design's resistance against fault attack test runs.

Case Study: Smart Card Power and Supply Voltage Evaluations

Figure 5 depicts the basic setup of the early design phase emulation platform. It consists of an FPGA prototyping board and a host PC. The FPGA board implements the design-under-test, which must be available in a hardware description language (e.g., VHDL, Verilog). Power consumption sensors, supply voltage sensors, activity sensors, and fault injectors are added to any component of interest. The data of each individual sensor is gathered by dedicated control units in real-time and for each clock cycle. The fault injection controller's task is to inject faults into specified components at specified points in time by means of saboteur

Figure 5. This figure depicts the basic emulation platform setup consisting of the FPGA prototyping board and a host PC for offline analysis tasks

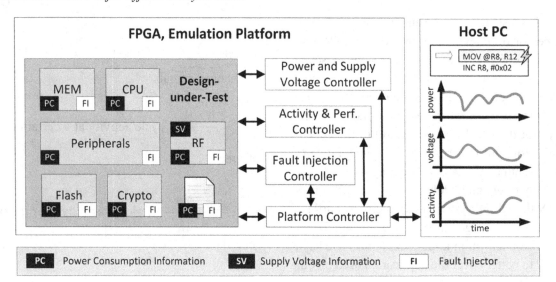

or mutant techniques. Trigger units are used for this decision process, which monitors specified signals (providing trigger information of the selected target application or hardware module). If the monitored signals match a specified pattern, a fault is triggered to be injected into the predefined target component. A platform controller is used to configure and control all units of the emulation platform. Furthermore, it temporarily buffers all gathered analysis data into the FPGA board's memory. At the same time, the analysis data is transmitted to the host PC by means of a high-data-rate interface. On the host PC, the data is archived and offline analyses can be carried out.

The presented early design phase emulation platform was set up for an industrial RF-powered contactless smart card design, which was used as design-under-test; cf. Druml et al. (2013). The aim of this test was the evaluation of the question whether an AES encryption application can be feasibly implemented. The left subplot of Figure 6 illustrates the smart card's power consumption and supply voltage behavior when operating the smart card with a maximum clock frequency of 31 MHz. The monitored power consumption pro-

file reveals a low power consuming initialization phase and high power consuming cryptographic operations. During these cryptographic operations, the smart card's supply voltage drops below the crucial threshold of 1 V. As a consequence, the operational stability of the smart card would be compromised. Because of these early design phase evaluation capabilities, an engineer is able to detect power and supply voltage issues caused by hardware and software implementations before the tape-out or before software is released.

Thanks to dynamic voltage and frequency capabilities of the smart card, the detected instability can be resolved, for example by reducing the hardware's clock frequency. The right subplot of Figure 6 depicts this approach. After the low power consuming initialization phase, the hardware's clock frequency is reduced to 25 MHz programmatically. As a consequence, the AES encryptions dissipate less electrical power and hazardous supply voltage drops can be omitted. The smart card's operational stability is maintained. However, due to the clock frequency reduction, the total execution of this test case is prolonged by 17%.

Figure 6. Power, supply voltage, and clock frequency trends of a smart card performing AES encryptions

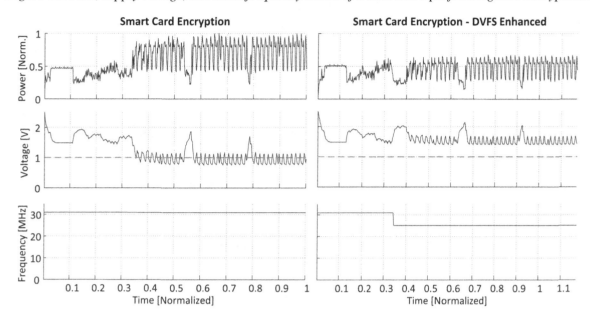

Case Study: LEON3 Fault Attacks

As described in previous sections, an industrial fault injection platform has been created that permitted the automated long-term testing of smart card systems. The combination of a high-security operating system and controller implementation resulted in strongly secured system that could not be successfully attacked. For the documentation of these results, please refer to the work presented in Grinschgl et al. (2013). For demonstration purposes, a more general approach based on the LEON3 System-on-Chip will be presented. Please note that this configuration cannot be directly transferred to a smart card system (e.g., there is no Ethernet interface in smart cards) but the same principles apply. For a general dependability evaluation, saboteurs have been placed at various positions of the design such as the integer pipeline and an Ethernet interface controller. The injection architecture for these tests and the injection results is depicted in Figure 7.

The following conclusions can be drawn from these tests:

- Fault injection into the communication channel itself results in lost data packages, meaning data failures are correctly detected and the packets are not accepted. The larger benchmark results in more lost packages because of the longer turn-around time.
- The second set of tests shows that if faults do not happen in the communication channel but within the controller memory, fault detection in the communication protocol fails and corrupted packets are transmitted.
- The same characteristics can be observed if faults happen in the processor memory itself, again the communication protocol provides no protection.
- Self-test routines provide very high fault coverage by design, which could also be verified using fault injection into the processor hardware.

In conclusion, our saboteur-based approach allows simplified automated fault evaluation at various levels of communication abstractions.

Figure 7. Long-time fault injection implementation

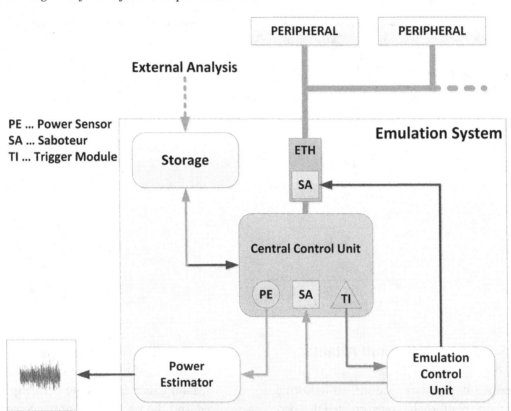

Fault Injection into Ethernet Communication					
Benchmark	Injected Faults	CRC Fails	Sent Packages	Received Packages	Lost [%]
Basicmath_small (client)	>255000	0	13860	9761	29,6
Basicmath_small (server)	>255000	0	9761	9761	-
Basicmath_large (client)	>162000	0	1900	302	84,1
Basicmath_large (server)	>162000	0	302	302	-

Fault Injection into Ethernet Controller Memory					
Benchmark	Injected Faults	CRC Faults	Sent Packages	Received Packages	Lost [%]
Basicmath_small (client)	>260000	10	7929	7019	11,5
Basicmath_small (server)	>260000	835	7094	7929	-
Basicmath_large (client)	>248000	3	1608	1361	15,4
Basicmath_large (server)	>248000	157	1451	1608	-

Fault Injection into Embedded Processor Memory				
Benchmark	Injected Faults	Calculations	Corrupted	Corrupted [%]
Basicmath_small (client)	>1460000	5637182	590432	10,47
Basicmath_large (client)	>791000	3048202	264451	8,68

Evaluation of Processor Self-Test Routines				
Self-Test	Injection Type	Injected Faults	Detected Faults	Fault Coverage
Multiplier	Stuck-At 1	1000	1000	100%
Multiplier	Transient 1	1000	1000	100%
ALU	Stuck-At	1000	1000	100%
ALU	Transient	1000	1000	100%
Shifter	Stuck-At	1000	1000	100%
Shifter	Transient	1000	1000	100%

Case Study: Improving Fault Injection Evaluation and Power Characterization

As described in Section "Power Characterization", benchmark characterization tasks have to be executed, after which an existing power modeling flow can be evaluated. To achieve optimal characterization applications, the generated activity information can be used in a further process.

Another important field of application for fault injection testing is self-test routines as they are used in the safety domain. Such software-based self-tests for processor cores need to have a deterministic behavior while providing high stuck-at fault coverage. Such deterministic applications and their evaluation have been shown in the work of Paschalis et al. (2001) introducing tests with a high fault coverage. We extended these test applications after a first exhaustive investigation to provide testing of all investigated sub-modules. For such simple self-tests, a very evenly distributed and high activity could be identified for both control and data signals.

To enable a comparison of a benchmark-based power characterization processes using traditional test applications and an emulation-supported activity analysis approach, we retrieved the application sets from the work shown in Bachmann et al. (2010). We applied power and signal correlation filters to select model coefficients, the same way it has been done in previous work. For the hardware implementation and application behavior characterization both approaches have been integrated into a LEON3-based FPGA system. By using a new application selection based on our activity emulation approach, we achieved similar power emulation accuracy while reducing the size of the power macro model by up to 20%. This allows for less complicated characterization and simpler hardware implementation, simplifying the testing of large multi-processor systems.

Recommendation: Application-Specific Benchmarks

The following conclusions can be drawn from such application investigations. First, as expected the automotive application of the MiBench suite shows similar signal activity. Further temporal evaluations of the associated signal traces also show that their temporal performance is similar, as expected from a domain-specific benchmark. Second, MiBench, quick-sort, most memory test and AES cryptography applications did not make use of any specialized arithmetic hardware like multipliers and dividers. Therefore, these and the remaining test candidates that also only resulted in little impact on arithmetic hardware activity were not well suited for an accurate power characterization process.

Figure 8. Benchmark characterization

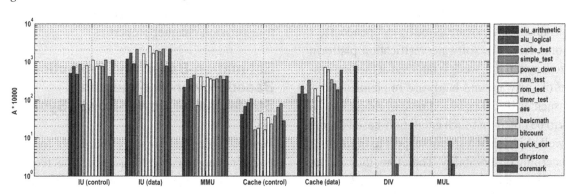

Data from exhaustive activity evaluations suggests the selection of less domain-specific characterization benchmark applications. Hence, applications with an evenly distributed high activity spectrum have been chosen. In the end, a final selection consisted of generic arithmetic; logical, cache, and RAM test applications. The control set contained benchmarks from the widely used Coremark and Dhrystone suites.

As described earlier, although the coefficient set shrunk by about one fifth because of the better activity mix, comparison showed similar or even better emulation results. This results in a strong call for more specific testing suites, and evaluation systems that allow a detailed look into the target system.

FUTURE RESEARCH DIRECTIONS

Static and Formal Analysis for High-Level Power and Security Properties

A major challenge during and after the design of a novel implementation is the provision of trust between the manufacturer and a customer of high security products. In order to enable a defined level of trust between all participants, system certification aims at securing the supply chain of security critical products. Common Criteria, for example, defines such assurance levels to describe how well documented the design process (besides other processes) of such a product needs to be. High assurance levels, as applied to certain types of smart cards, include the necessity that certain fault attack scenarios are tested by independent test laboratories. The software verification platform introduced in this work is targeted at the preparation of software and hardware implementations for such artificial tests and real-world attacks. It has to be noted that such emulation-based testing as well as physical tests are suspect to limitations concerning observability. Therefore, they cannot provide a guarantee that the investigated system covers all possible attack scenarios.

Another point that has to be taken care of is the increasing complexity of smart card systems, which also causes a widened evaluation space. The verification problem that is also known from functional verification creates a strong need for an extended use of formal methods during the design and verification phases of the implementation. Recently published literature shown in academia and industry tried to solve these problems, but so far, it has not been possible to find comprehensive solutions responding to the specific needs of this industry sector (secure embedded systems).

System-Level Power and Security Evaluations of Mobile Systems

Payment and personal ID sectors have seen a massive introduction of smart cards in recent years that have come with an increasing introduction of mobile reader systems that are needed to communicate with these devices. Smart card and reader systems are closely examined for the power and security related challenges they are facing. Unfortunately, research has concentrated on the resolution of issues for only these isolated problem domains. Challenges resulting from the wireless connection and interaction between a contactless smart card and the reader system have not been sufficiently investigated. Therefore, possible security problems could have been missed and power consumption issues on the reader side could emerge, as the transmission power is kept at a maximum level at all time. The latter results from the fact that currently neither smart card nor reader system have detailed information about transmission channel properties.

Estimation-Based and Prediction-Based Power-Management Strategies for Lower-Power Systems

Power emulation can serve the needs for novel power management techniques, without requiring analog components. In traditional approaches, analog measurements provide information to power management algorithms. Instead, power information from emulation techniques enables power management with low hardware overhead in a purely digital manner. This reduces the power management complexity and eases on-chip integration.

This approach can directly steer dynamic voltage and frequency scaling (DVFS) approaches that vary system frequency and supply voltage in order to optimize the system's power consumption.

Next generation embedded systems that harvest energy from the environment require even more sophisticated power management techniques. High load changes can severely harm these systems and compromise reliable system operation. Power and supply voltage emulation techniques extended with prediction techniques can help to tackle these challenges. Monitoring internal system information in order to estimate power and supply voltage information could be complemented with observing pipeline information in order to predict future load changes and supply voltage drops.

CONCLUSION

In this chapter we presented a multi-disciplinary early design evaluation methodology that is capable of evaluating a design-under-test's functionality, power and supply voltage behavior, performance, temporal activity of components, and fault robustness. The design-under-test was integrated into an FPGA prototyping board along with model-based analysis and fault-injection units. Results were gathered hardware accelerated in real-time and for each clock cycle.

Smart cards are enabler products for new industrial applications in critical infrastructures such as smart-grids or cloud-controlled industrial fabrication sites.

We demonstrated the applicability of our approach on a number of case studies executed on our evaluation platform. The reliability of a

smart card system was investigated by power and supply voltage profiling in order to detect harmful supply voltage drops. Security strength was illustrated in a fault-attack scenario carried out on the emulation-based evaluation platform. A benchmarking characterization study showed how to improve power and fault injection characterization by means of emulation techniques.

ACKNOWLEDGMENT

The authors would like thank the Austrian Federal Ministry for Transport, Innovation, and Technology, which funded the POWERHOUSE, POWERMODES, and META[:SEC:] projects under the corresponding FIT-IT contracts FFG 815193, 825749, and 829586.

REFERENCES

Bachmann, C., Genser, A., Haid, J., Steger, C., & Weiss, R. (2010, September). Automated Power Characterization for Run-Time Power Emulation of SoC Designs. In *Proceedings of 13th Euromicro Conference on Digital System Design* (pp. 587-594). IEEE.

Coburn, J., Ravi, S., & Raghunathan, A. (2005, June). Power emulation: A new paradigm for power estimation. In *Proceedings of the 42nd annual Design Automation Conference* (pp. 700-705). ACM.

Druml, N., Menghin, M., Steger, C., Weiss, R., Genser, A., Bock, H., & Haid, J. (2013, February). Emulation-Based Test and Verification of a Design's Functional, Performance, Power, and Supply Voltage Behavior. In *Proceedings of 21st Euromicro International Conference on Parallel, Distributed, and Network-Based Processing* (pp. 328-335). IEEE.

Druml, N., Steger, C., Weiss, R., Genser, A., & Haid, J. (2012, March). Estimation Based Power and Supply Voltage Management for Future RF-Powered Multi-Core Smart Cards. In *Proceedings of Design Automation and Test in Europe Conference and Exhibition* (pp. 358-363). IEEE.

Finkenzeller, K. (2003). *RFID Handbook: Fundamentals and Applications in Contactless Smart Cards and Identification* (2nd ed.). New York, NY: John Wiley & Sons, Inc. doi:10.1002/0470868023

Grinschgl, J., Krieg, A., Steger, C., Wei, R., Bock, H., & Haid, J. et al. (2013, March). Case study on multiple fault dependability and security evaluations. *Elsevier. Microprocessors and Microsystems, 37*(2), 218–227. doi:10.1016/j.micpro.2012.05.016

Krieg, A., Bachmann, C., Grinschgl, J., Steger, C., Weiss, R., & Haid, J. (2011, June). Accelerating early design phase differential power analysis using power emulation techniques. In *Proceedings of Hardware-Oriented Security and Trust (HOST)*, (pp. 81-86). IEEE.

Krieg, A., Grinschgl, J., Steger, C., Wei, R., Bock, H., & Haid, J. (2012, April). System side-channel leakage emulation for HW/SW security coverification of MPSoCs. In *Proceedings of Design and Diagnostics of Electronic Circuits & Systems (DDECS)*, (pp.139-144). IEEE.

Krieg, A., Preschern, C., Grinschgl, J., Kreiner, C., Steger, C., Weiss, R., Bock, H., & Haid, J. (2013, May). Power And Fault Emulation For Software Verification and System Stability Testing in Safety Critical Environments. *IEEE Transactions on Industrial Informatics, 9*(2), 1199-1206.

Paschalis, A., Gizopoulos, D., Kranitis, N., Psarakis, M., & Zorian, Y. (2001, March). Deterministic software-based self-testing of embedded processor cores. In *Proceedings of the Conference on Design, Automation and Test in Europe* (pp. 92-96). IEEE Press.

Wendt, M., Grumer, C., Steger, C., Weiss, R., Neffe, U., & Muehlberger, A. (2008, November). System Level Power Profile Analysis and Optimization for Smart Cards and Mobile Devices. In *Proceedings of ACM Symposium on Applied Computing*, November (pp. 118–121). ACM.

ADDITIONAL READING

Abke, J., Böhl, E., & Henno, C. (1998, July). Emulation based real time testing of automotive applications. *4th IEEE International On-Line Testing workshop* (pp. 28-31).

Antoni, L., Leveugle, R., & Fehér, B. (2003, October). Using run-time reconfiguration for fault injection applications. *Instrumentation and Measurement. IEEE Transactions on, 52*(5), 1468–1473.

Armengaud, E., Steininger, A., & Horauer, M. (2008, August). Towards a systematic test for embedded automotive communication systems. *Industrial Informatics. IEEE Transactions on, 4*(3), 146–155.

Baraza, J., Gracia, J., Blanc, S., Gil, D., & Gil, P. (2008, June). Enhancement of fault injection techniques based on the modification of VHDL code, *Very Large Scale Integration Systems. IEEE Transactions on, 16*(6), 693–706.

Baraza, J. C., Gracia, J., Gil, D., & Gil, P. J. (2005, November). Improvement of fault injection techniques based on VHDL code modification. *High-Level Design Validation and Test Workshop, 2005. Tenth IEEE International* (pp. 19-26). IEEE.

Baronti, F., Petri, E., Saponara, S., Fanucci, L., Roncella, R., & Saletti, R. et al. (2011, March). Design and verification of hardware building blocks for high-speed and fault-tolerant in-vehicle networks. *Industrial Electronics. IEEE Transactions on, 58*(3), 792–801.

Conte, T. M., & Hwu, W. M. (1991, January). Benchmark characterization. *Computer*, *24*(1), 48–56. doi:10.1109/2.67193

Corno, F., Esposito, F., Sonza Reorda, M., & Tosato, S. (2004, October). Evaluating the effects of transient faults on vehicle dynamic performance in automotive systems. *Test Conference, 2004. Proceedings. ITC 2004. International* (pp. 1332-1339). IEEE.

Daveau, J. M., Blampey, A., Gasiot, G., Bulone, J., & Roche, P. (2009, April). An industrial fault injection platform for soft-error dependability analysis and hardening of complex system-on-a-chip. *Reliability Physics Symposium, 2009 IEEE International* (pp. 212-220). IEEE.

Genser, A., Bachmann, C., Haid, J., Steger, C., & Weiss, R. (2009, July). An Emulation-Based Real-Time Power Profiling Unit for Embedded Software. *International Conference on Embedded Computer Systems: Architectures, Modeling and Simulation* (pp. 67-73), IEEE.

Genser, A., Bachmann, C., Steger, C., Weiss, R., & Haid, J. (2010, October). Power emulation based DVFS efficiency investigations for embedded systems. *International Symposium on System on Chip* (pp. 173-178). IEEE.

Grießnig, G., Mader, R., Steger, C., & Weiß, R. (2009, April). Fault insertion testing of a novel CPLD-based fail-safe system. *Proceedings of the Conference on Design, Automation and Test in Europe* (pp. 214-219). European Design and Automation Association.

Guthaus, M. R., Ringenberg, J. S., Ernst, D., Austin, T. M., Mudge, T., & Brown, R. B. (2001, December). MiBench: A free, commercially representative embedded benchmark suite. *Workload Characterization, 2001. WWC-4. 2001 IEEE International Workshop on* (pp. 3-14). IEEE.

Guzman-Miranda, H., Aguirre, M. A., & Tombs, J. (2009, May). Noninvasive fault classification, robustness and recovery time measurement in microprocessor-type architectures subjected to radiation-induced errors. *Instrumentation and Measurement. IEEE Transactions on*, *58*(5), 1514–1524.

Jenn, E., Arlat, J., Rimen, M., Ohlsson, J., & Karlsson, J. (1994, June). Fault injection into VHDL models: the MEFISTO tool. *Fault-Tolerant Computing, 1994. FTCS-24. Digest of Papers., Twenty-Fourth International Symposium on* (pp. 66-75). IEEE.

John, L. K., Vasudevan, P., & Sabarinathan, J. (1999). Workload characterization: Motivation, goals and methodology. [IEEE.]. *Workload Characterization: Methodology and Case Studies*, *1998*, 3–14.

Kocher, P., Jaffe, J., & Jun, B. (1999, January). Differential power analysis. *Advances in Cryptology - CRYPTO'99* (pp. 388-397). Springer Berlin Heidelberg.

Leveugle, R. (2000, October). Fault injection in VHDL descriptions and emulation. *Defect and Fault Tolerance in VLSI Systems, 2000. Proceedings. IEEE International Symposium on* (pp. 414-419). IEEE.

Leveugle, R. (2007, October). Early analysis of fault-based attack effects in secure circuits. *Computers. IEEE Transactions on*, *56*(10), 1431–1434.

Mangard, S., Oswald, E., & Popp, T. (2007). *Power analysis attacks: Revealing the secrets of smart cards* (Vol. 31). Springer.

Myaing, A., & Dinavahi, V. (2011, January). FPGA-based real-time emulation of power electronic systems with detailed representation of device characteristics. *Industrial Electronics. IEEE Transactions on*, *58*(1), 358–368.

Poovey, J. A., Conte, T. M., Levy, M., & Gal-On, S. (2009, August). A benchmark characterization of the eembc benchmark suite. *Micro, IEEE, 29*(5), 18–29. doi:10.1109/MM.2009.74

Valderas, M. G., Garcia, M. P., Cardenal, R. F., Lopez Ongil, C., & Entrena, L. (2007, June). Advanced simulation and emulation techniques for fault injection. *Industrial Electronics, 2007. ISIE 2007. IEEE International Symposium on* (pp. 3339-3344). IEEE.

Zheng, H., Fan, L., & Yue, S. (2008, December). FITVS: A fpga-based emulation tool for high-efficiency hardness evaluation. *Parallel and Distributed Processing with Applications, 2008. ISPA'08. International Symposium on* (pp. 525-531). IEEE.

KEY TERMS AND DEFINITIONS

Error: An error describes a deviation from the expected system behavior caused by a fault. Therefore, an error is a final consequence after a fault was activated and the result is stored by internal or external resources.

Fault Attack: A fault attack is an intentional manipulation of the integrated circuit or its state, with the aim to provoke an error within the integrated circuit in order to move the device into an unintended state. The goal is to access security critical information or to disable internal protection mechanisms.

Fault: A fault constitutes a deviation of normal internal system states or signals. Such deviation could lead to the generation of wrong results, but it could also be masked by the current system state.

Hardware Emulation: Hardware emulation is a technique that integrates a hardware design into a reconfigurable (e.g. FPGA-based) prototyping platform in order to allow the functional testing of a design-under-test including its firmware. This way both hardware and software can be evaluated in a realistic performance setting.

Power Emulation: Power emulation extends the hardware emulation technique with power sensors and corresponding power models in order to gather estimated power analysis data of the design-under-test.

Smart Card: A smart card is a device with an integrated circuit including its own memory and central processing unit. Besides a standard contact-based interface, it can also be powered contactlessly by means of an alternating and modulated magnetic field, through which contactless communication is also enabled.

System-on-Chip: A System-on-Chip (SoC) is an integrated circuit integrating all circuits and electronics (such as analog, digital, mixed-signal, or RF components) necessary for a system on a single chip.

Vulnerability: Vulnerability describes a certain inability of a system to withstand the effects of an attack in a hostile environment.

Chapter 14
Dynamically Reconfigurable Embedded Architectures for Safe Transportation Systems

Naim Harb
Polytechnic Faculty of Mons, Belgium

Smail Niar
LAMIH-University of Valenciennes Le Mont Houy, France

Mazen A. R. Saghir
Texas A&M University at Qatar, Qatar

ABSTRACT

Embedded system designers are increasingly relying on Field Programmable Gate Arrays (FPGAs) as target design platforms. Today's FPGAs provide high levels of logic density and rich sets of embedded hardware components. They are also inherently flexible and can be easily and quickly modified to meet changing applications or system requirements. On the other hand, FPGAs are generally slower and consume more power than Application-Specific Integrated Circuits (ASICs). However, advances in FPGA architectures, such as Dynamic Partial Reconfiguration (DPR), are helping bridge this gap. DPR enables a portion of an FPGA device to be reconfigured while the device is still operating. This chapter explores the advantage of using the DPR feature in an automotive system. The authors implement a Driver Assistant System (DAS) based on a Multiple Target Tracking (MTT) algorithm as the automotive base system. They show how the DAS architecture can be adjusted dynamically to different scenario situations to provide interesting functionalities to the driver.

INTRODUCTION

Embedded applications in transportation systems are becoming increasingly complex, and new applications have emerged to respond to people and societal needs and to ensure driver and passenger safety. Applications such as Vehicle-to-Vehicle (V2V), Vehicle-to-Infrastructure (V2I) communications, in-vehicle infotainment, and assistance for elderly and disabled drivers require powerful

DOI: 10.4018/978-1-4666-6194-3.ch014

processing and communication capabilities. Moreover, modern transport tools play the leading role in strategically worldwide projects such as green and sustainable mobility in future smart cities. To fulfill these tasks, the number and types of sensors in next generation of transport systems will continually increase. This requires significant computing power, low energy consumption and high reliability.

At the technological level, advances in microelectronic fabrication technologies have resulted in a proliferation of electronic and micro-electronic devices in automotive systems. While early electronic control units (ECUs) were mainly used for engine and transmission control or simple cabin control functions, contemporary ECUs are used in a wide range of applications including audio and video entertainment, navigation and trip planning, communications and networking, passenger safety, and driver assistance.

Driver assistance systems (DAS) are an increasingly important class of automotive applications, particularly in commercial vehicles where they can greatly reduce a driver's workload and improve road safety in stressful driving conditions such as at night or in bad weather. Driver assistance systems commonly require real-time monitoring of the driving environment and other vehicles on the road. The availability of low-power automotive radar systems makes it possible to track the speed, distance, and relative position of multiple obstacles, called targets through the chapter, in the radar's field of view. Such Multiple-Target Tracking (MTT) functions are crucial for driver assistance applications such as collision avoidance, intelligent cruise control, or automatic parking.

As the driving conditions and environment change, the type of processing required for MTT also changes. In this chapter, we show how the functionality and accuracy of Driver Assistant Systems (DAS) can be automatically tuned to match the dynamics of moving obstacles on the road. We show how dynamic partial reconfiguration (DPR) can be used to free hardware resources for other uses, such as tracking more obstacles, accelerating other computational functions, or reducing power consumption.

We also demonstrate how the accuracy of the filtering blocks can be dynamically and automatically tuned to match the characteristics of the operational environment. This contrasts with prevailing approaches to dynamic reconfiguration, which are mainly demand-driven.

In this chapter, DPR is used to adapt the MTT embedded system architecture according to driving conditions in the two following scenarios:

1. **Obstacle Density:** The computational needs of a MTT system increase with the *number of targets* that must be tracked. When the environment changes from, say, open highway to narrow city street, higher levels of accuracy in the obstacle position calculation are needed to track multiple, potentially closer targets. Conversely, when the driving environment changes from dense to sparse, the accuracy of the filter can be reduced to minimize resource utilization and energy consumption. We also demonstrate the ease with which we can switch between hardware implementations automatically using a simple heuristic.

2. **Obstacle Positions:** When targets move *closer to the radar*, they should be tracked at higher levels of accuracy since they can potentially become more hazardous. On the other hand, when targets move further away, less accurate tracking (filters) can be used. The functionality and accuracy of an MTT system can be automatically tuned to match the dynamics of moving obstacles on the road. To support efficiently obstacles at *different distances*, three filters are used in different configurations to support different driving scenarios (Far, Medium and Close). These filters include a Kalman filter for angle estimation (KFA), a Kalman Filter for distance estimation (KFD) and an extended

α-β filter. This last filter is used over KFA and KFD and provides better distance and angle estimation. The extended α-β is used for tracking obstacles with high hazard level to offer a better position prediction. These three filters offer different resource/accuracy trade-offs.

The different situations in terms of number and distance of obstacles offer six different MTT implementations that correspond to different contexts and scenarios. We present a smart heuristic to switch between the different hardware implementations with no reconfiguration overhead because the system can still function with the original configuration.

DYNAMIC AND PARTIAL RECONFIGURATION IN FPGAS FOR AUTOMOTIVE ELECTRONIC SYSTEMS

As automobiles integrate with smart infrastructure and evolve to support driverless operations, enhanced safety, and vehicle-to-vehicle communications and control, more powerful data processing and computing platforms will be needed. While multi-core processors and highly integrated systems-on-chip (SoC) will be more prevalent in new automotive systems, Field Programmable Gate Arrays (FPGAs) will also play an increasingly important role (Parnell, 2005).

With their high logic densities, inherent support for spatial parallelism, and rich sets of soft IP cores and embedded hardware components, FPGAs are very well suited for implementing computationally demanding applications. Some FPGAs even include embedded processor cores that can run real-time operating systems. Their flexibility, programmability, and fast design turnaround times also enable system designers to quickly introduce new features or update existing ones in response to changing requirements or new standards. Some

FPGAs also support dynamic partial reconfiguration, which enables the functionality of a device to be modified while it is still running.

Reconfigurability is a major advantage of using FPGAs. The functionality of the device can be modified by loading a new bit-stream into the FPGA configuration-memory. This flexibility is obtained using a dedicated hardware controller. FPGAs are typically configured at system start-up time. The entire configuration memory is loaded with a new bit stream, a process that can take tens to hundreds of milliseconds depending on the size and logic density of the corresponding device. These delays are tolerable for many applications where FPGA functionality seldom needs to change. However, for some real-time applications that require frequent changes to FPGA functionality, the overhead can be unacceptably high. One solution to this problem is to implement all the required functionality in the FPGA, and select the required functions at run-time. While this ensures fast context switching, it results in increased area, resource utilization, and power consumption.

Another solution is device support for dynamic partial reconfiguration (DPR). Most contemporary FPGAs support DPR, which enables modifying part of the device's functionality at run time. This is achieved by loading a partial bit stream into the configuration memory, which modifies the functionality of a specific region within the device called a frame. While DPR still incurs some reconfiguration overhead, it is usually significantly smaller than the overhead associated with reconfiguring the entire device. This makes DPR suitable for applications that require modifications to FPGA functionality and can tolerate a small amount of overhead. However, the biggest advantages of DPR are the large savings in area, resource utilization, and power consumption, which are achieved by time-multiplexing hardware logic into a shared FPGA frame. These in turn can reduce system costs by enabling the use of smaller devices with sufficient logic capacities for the required application.

DPR is typically supported by the FPGA vendor design tools. Designers use the tools to define a partially reconfigurable region (PRR) within the device to host the required logic. The logic capacity and embedded hardware resources of the PRR must be chosen to accommodate the largest expected logic block. Appropriate interfaces that are common to the different logic blocks must also be defined between the static portions of the FPGA device and the PRR. When a PRR is not being used, a blank partial bit stream can be used to effectively disable the PRR and ensure it does not consume unnecessary power. In the remainder of this chapter, we describe the design of multiple-target tracking systems that use DPR to reduce FPGA resource utilization.

DRIVER ASSISTANT SYSTEM APPLICATION AND THEIR REAL-TIME CONSTRAINTS

Driver Assistant Systems: Related Work

DASs are an increasingly important class of automotive applications in today's commercial vehicles. For this reason, different types of DAS systems have been proposed in the last few years. Among the most popular DAS functionalities, we can cite: adaptive cruise control, lane keep assistance, parking assistance systems and obstacle detection/avoidance systems (Vahidi, 2003). In the past, most programmable platforms were based on 8-bit or 16-bit micro-controllers, named ECU for *Electronic Control Unit*. These platforms are however unable to efficiently support new processing intensive automotive applications.

Recent research activities have concentrated on the use of DAS in complex environments and scenarios, such as detecting vulnerable road users, such as pedestrians and children. The proposed systems in these projects are implemented by different hardware and/or software architectures. From the hardware point of view, dedicated hardwired ASIC to pure programmable processors were used. To offer a good performance/flexibility/cost trade-off, researchers designed multi-processor system-on-chips (MPSoC) and/or fixed FPGA-based circuits that are widely used in DAS systems.

Different types of DAS systems have been proposed in the last few years. Most of the existing DAS systems have either limited functionalities or are too costly for a large-scale automotive utilization. The detection functionality is, generally realized by one or more sensors set around the host vehicle.

The embedded in-vehicle application consistently receives and analyzes the detection data delivered by sensors. In case of danger, the driver is alerted in real time by an audio or visual alarms.

Existing DAS systems can be classified following two criteria:

According to the Used Sensor(s) and the Provided Driver Assistant Functions

Different types of sensors and data sources may be used such as Lidar, Camera, Radar, Vehicle-to-Vehicle (V2V) and/or Vehicle-to-Infrastructure (V2I) communications. The European Project PREVENT (http://www.prevent-ip.org/) was aimed at developing preventive and corrective safety systems for automotive applications. INTERSAFE (Intersafe, 2005), another project, was established to support the vision of IP PReVENT to create electronic safety zones around vehicles by developing and demonstrating a set of complementary safety functions. It is based on laser scanners, video cameras and bidirectional vehicle-to-infrastructure (V2I) communications.

The LKAS system (Figure 1), proposed by HONDA, is based on camera utilization to control the speed of the vehicle relative to the vehicle ahead. This camera helps also the driver to position the vehicle in the middle of the road. This approach was also used by Valeo in the *Guideo* system.

Figure 1. Architecture and functions provided by LKAS

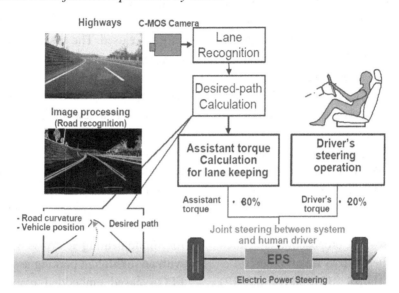

In Murphy-Chutorian (2008) an automotive head pose estimation and tracking is proposed. The authors consider head pose as a strong indicator of a driver's field-of-view and current focus of attention. The driver is then alerted only in situations where he appears to be unaware of the possible hazard in front of the vehicles. Their algorithms for head pose estimation and tracking uses only one camera and Graphical Processing Unit (GPU).

Our group at university of Valenciennes also proposed several DAS systems for obstacle recognition and tracking (Khan, 2008) (Khan, 2009) (Harb, 2011) (Harb, 2012) (Liu, 2011). In these papers, the proposed architecture uses a radar sensor and enables the DAS, in addition to detecting obstacles, to recognize and categorize these obstacles by using their radar signatures. Thanks to its large Field of View (FoV), radar sensors are more interesting as they allow to detect obstacles at longer distances and consequently ensures longer reaction time for vehicle drivers. Moreover, the radar system behaves better in bad visibility conditions (foggy weather, rain and snow etc.) and has lower computational requirements when compared to camera-based DAS.

According to Their Embedded System Hardware Architectures

ImapCAR (ImpCar, 2006) and EyeQ2 (EyeQ2, 2010) systems are two examples of full programmable processors MPSoC that are dedicated to automotive security applications using vision system. The ImapCar adopts an Single Instruction Multiple Data (SIMD) architecture of 128 processing elements and a 4-way Very Long Instruction Word (VLIW) control processor.

The EyeQ2, a single chip with mono-scopic embedded vision system, consists of two 64-bit floating-point RISC 34KMIPS processors for scheduling and controlling the concurrent tasks, five vision computing engines and three vector microcode processors and eight processors for vision and vector processing.

These two architectures provide support for a specific set of real time data intensive applications. Therefore, these systems are unable either to accommodate new applications or to adapt the hardware to different scenarios. The AutoVision processor (Claus, 2007) is a dynamically reconfigurable MPSoC (Multiple-Processor System On Chip) prototype for video-specific pixel processing. Pixel processing engines offer functions such as object edge detection or luminance segmentation, and are implemented as dedicated hardware accelerators to ensure real time processing.

In Khan (2008), Khan (2009) and Khan (2010) we designed multiple-target tracking DAS that detects and monitors the dynamic behavior of one or more obstacles in the way of the host vehicle. The embedded system is based on an MPSoC architecture on FPGA. The role of the MTT (Multiple Target Track), in all these designs and the present work, is to balance the inaccuracy of the low-cost radars by the utilization of data tracking and filtering processes. The proposed architectures contain up to 23 Altera NIOS II soft cores.

In Harb (2009), Harb (2012) and Harb (2012) we extended the previous architectures along two dimensions. We first used HW accelerator for the Kalman Filters to reduce the complexity of the design by about 80% and secondly we proposed the utilization of the dynamic and partial reconfiguration feature of Xilinx FPGA to adapt the DAS architecture to adapt the architecture to changing driving scenarios (e.g. from urban to suburban to rural).

Partial dynamic reconfiguration for automotive application has been proposed by (Claus; 2007). In this project, three different situations are considered: highway, tunnel entrance, and Inside tunnel. For each situation a given hardwired co-processor

must be loaded and mapped on the FPGA. Two PowerPc (PPC) hard cores, in the FPGA static part, were used. The first PPC realizes high-level image processing while the second is in charge of control and management functions. Consequently, when this PPC detects a modification of the car environment, a new image-processing algorithm must be executed and thus new co-processor is defined. The system is especially designed to detect taillights of ahead moving vehicles in dark environments.

In Shreejith (2013), the authors propose the utilization of dynamic partial reconfiguration for implementing a cruise control application with an intelligent parking assistant system. The FPGA-based embedded platform can also be programed to act as custom FlexRay communication controller. At the opposite of the DAS for the MTT application that we proposed in this paper, in Shreejith (2013) mode switch is triggered by user commands.

Multiple Target Tracking System

Driver Assistance Systems (DASs) have become a widespread class of automotive applications in today's commercial vehicles. They lend even more confidence to driving and improve road safety in stressful driving conditions (e.g. at night or in bad weather).

Figure 2. Autovision architecture with the reconfigurable coprocessors (Claus, 2007)

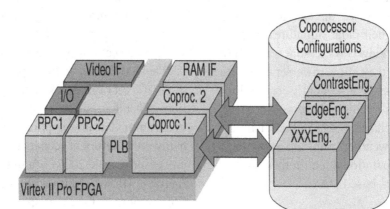

DAS system is usually composed of three stages: The capturing stage, the treatment stage and the restitution stage (Figure 3). In the capturing stage, sensor(s) is/are mounted on the user's car to capture inputs to the DAS system. Such sensors can be a camera or radar. In the treatment stage, the data are taken from the capturing phase and applied a set of algorithms that defines the functionality of the DAS system. Some algorithms are image processing based, like when using a camera sensor. In the restitution phase, the output from the treatment stage is treated before delivering them in voice, image, or mechanical action to the user.

A MTT algorithm implements the treatment component is figure 3 and uses an on board sensor(s) to keep track of the speed, distance, and relative position of all vehicles within its field of view (Figure 4). Such information is crucial in applications such as collision avoidance or intelligent cruise control. The computational needs of a MTT system increase with the number of targets that must be tracked. It is therefore very difficult for a single processor to handle these computational requirements alone. In this section, we present a general overview of the DAS system and the MTT utilization in automotive applications as a DAS application.

The basic elements of a MTT system are shown in Figure 4. It is composed of three basic building blocks:

1. The *Measurement Data Processing* block responsible for the data processing before sending it into the MTT functional blocks. This block includes all signal processing blocks including the radar sensor device.
2. The *Data Association* block, which plays an important role in the tracking of multiple obstacles and assigning each to a specific track.
3. The *Filtering&Prediction* block, which incorporates the assigned observations into a set of updated track estimates.

Figure 3. Functional three stages of a typical DAS system

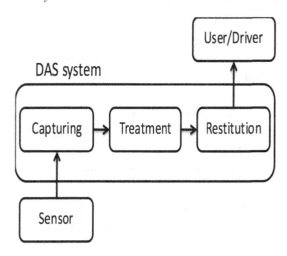

Figure 4. MTT functional architecture

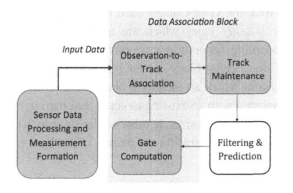

A MTT system functions, as shown in Figure 5, in the following manner: when an observation is received from the sensor device, specific signal processing is performed before sending the information into the Data Association Block. First, incoming observations are considered for existing tracks from previous scans. Gate Computation tests which of the possible observation-to-track assignment is more "reasonable" at the beginning before a more refined algorithm is used to determine the final pairing. In this case, certain observations without associated tracks can generate new tracks. A track is instantiated and confirmed only when the number and quality of observations satisfy a certain criteria. In a similar manner, low quality tracks, over time are deleted. Finally, a gate is set around each track and the cycle repeats itself (Blackmann, 1999).

In Figure 6, we show a more detailed architecture of the MTT system and its inner blocks. Starting from the first stage of the input data, in our system, we use an AC20 TRW (www.trw.com) radar based sensor device mounted in front of our car, realizing a scan every 25 msec The data sent to the MTT system includes: targets' distance measured away from the radar, positional angle, linear velocity and angular velocity.

The *Gate Computation block* is the first step in the data association process. This block receives targets' predicted states and predicted errors covariance from the *Filtering&Prediction* blocks. Using these two values, the predicted states and errors, the Gate Computation block defines the *probability gates* which are used to associate incoming observations to existing targets. The *Gate Checker* block carries inside of it the criteria in which an incoming observation is to be assigned with an existing target or the creation of a new detected target. In other words, this block is mainly responsible for the pairing of predictions

to observations according to a certain criteria. The cost of every pairing inside a gate is sent to the *Cost Matrix Generator* block. This block, as the name implies, is responsible for the generation of a set of cost matrices including the cost of assigning certain measurements to existing targets. Based on these matrices, the *Assignment Solver* block is responsible for the final pairing between measurements and the existing targets. The output will be a one-to-one assignment of one measurement to one existing target.

The *Track Maintenance* block is made up of three sub-blocks: Obs-less Gate Identifier, New Target Identifier and Track Initialize/Delete. In real situations, some targets might leave the FOV of the radar. In other cases, a new target might enter the FOV of the radar. When a target leaves the FOV of the radar, the Obs-less Gate Identifier identifies this target and triggers the Track Initialize/Delete block to remove this specific target from the calculations and predictions since it left the detection area of the radar. However when a new target is detected, the New Target Identifier identifies that a new target has entered the FOV of the radar and hence a new track must be ini-

Figure 5. Measurement and Prediction states in the MTT

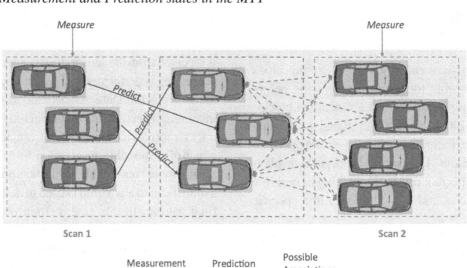

Figure 6. MTT system's detailed building blocks. The Observation-to-Track Association and Track Maintenance blocks are shown as detailed inner blocks in the figure.

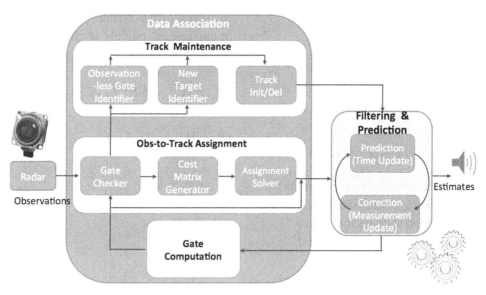

tialized. This block triggers the Track Initialize/Delete block in order to establish a new track for the new detected target.

The Filtering&Prediction block is particularly important as the number of filters implemented inside this block is the same as the maximum number of targets to be tracked. In the earlier work of Khan (2008), 20 Kalman filters were implemented in order to support the tracking of a maximum number of 20 targets.

Filtering and Prediction Block in Tracking Systems

The MTT application can be implemented using a variety of adaptive algorithms including *α-β filter, mean-shift* algorithm, and *Kalman* filter (Backmann, 1999). In our system, we have chosen to implement both the Kalman and the α-β filters. The Kalman filter is used because it is an important block in the whole MTT system. It behaves properly and effectively with the other MTT blocks. A Kalman filter is designed to track a moving object having a constant velocity. The

process and measurement models presented above for target dynamics can be classified as linear models with Additive White Gaussian Noise (AWGN). For this reason we use the Kalman filter because it is a recursive Least Square Estimator (LSE) considered to be the optimal estimator for linear systems with AWGN probability distribution (Blackmann,1999).

Due to the importance of the Kalman filter in our implementation, it is important to cite the mathematical computations inside this filter. The Kalman filter mathematical computations are shown in equations (1) to (8).

$$Z_k = Distance; Angle \qquad (1)$$

$$Y_{k\,pred} = A * Y_{k-1} \qquad (2)$$

$$P_{k\,pred} = A * P_{k-1} * A' + Q \qquad (3)$$

$$K = P_{k\,pred} * H' * \left(H * P_{k\,pred} * H' + R \right)^{-1} \qquad (4)$$

$$Y_{k\,estim} = Y_{k\,pred} + K * \left(Z_k - H * Y_{k\,pred} \right) \qquad (5)$$

$$P_{k\,estim} = \left(I - K * H \right) * P_{k\,pred} \qquad (6)$$

$$Y_{k-1} = Y_{k\,estim} \qquad (7)$$

$$P_{k-1} = P_{k\,estim} \qquad (8)$$

Z$_k$: Is the measured input distance and angle.
A: Is the assumed known state transition matrix.
Y$_{k\,pred}$: Is the predicted state vector.
Y$_{k-1}$: Is the previous estimated state vector.
Y$_{k\,estim}$: Is the estimated state vector.
P$_{k\,pred}$: Is the predicted error covariance matrix.
P$_{k-1}$: Is the previous estimated error covariance matrix.
P$_{k\,estim}$: Is the *estimation error covariance matrix*.
Q: Is the AWGN assumed known covariance matrix.
H: An observation matrix that relates the current state to the Z$_k$.
K: Is the Kalman *gain matrix*.
I: Is an identity matrix.
R: Is the measurement noise covariance matrix.

In summary, the Kalman filter takes as inputs: The vector Z_k representing the measured distance and the measured angle as in equation (1). As for matrixes *A*, *Q*, *H*, *R* and *I*, they are considered input matrixes from other MTT functional blocks respectively. Y_{kestim} is the filter's only output matrix, sent to the driver or restitution phase, that includes the predicted and filtered distance and angle.

However, real objects actually tend to move with variable accelerations and therefore different velocities. The choice of the α-β filter is due to its simple implementation and its consideration of target velocities in decision-making. In general, an α-β filter is a simplified estimation filter for data smoothing and control applications. When an α-β filter is applied to motion systems, it takes as inputs, the measured distance and velocity. Since we used this filter to enhance our results as will be shown in chapter 4, hence, we present the mathematical module of this filter in equations (9) to (15).

$$X_k = X_{k-1} + \Delta T * V_{k-1} \qquad (9)$$

$$V_k = V \qquad (10)$$

$$R_k = X - X_k \qquad (11)$$

$$X_k = X_k + á * R_k \qquad (12)$$

$$V_k = V_k + \left(\frac{\hat{a}}{\Delta T} \right) * R_k \qquad (13)$$

$$X_{k-1} = X_k \qquad (14)$$

$$V_{k-1} = V_k \qquad (15)$$

X: Is the input distance to the filter.
V: Is the input velocity to the filter.
ΔT: Is the time interval between measurements (e.g. the sensor's scans interval).
R$_k$: Is the input distance difference between the current and the preceding distance.
X$_{k-1}$: Is the previous predicted distance value.
V$_{k-1}$: Is the previous predicted velocity value.
α and β: Are constants correction gains of values between 0 and 1.

In conclusion, this straight forward filter takes selected α and β constants (adjusted experimentally), uses α times the deviation R_k to correct the position estimate, and uses β times the deviation R_k to correct the velocity estimate. The result of $\beta \times R_k$ is used in a consecutive iteration to further more enhance the target position.

DYNAMIC PARTIAL RECONFIGURATION FOR MULTIPLE TARGET TRACKING IN DRIVER ASSISTANT SYSTEM

In this section, we describe two implementations of a dynamically partial reconfigurable MTT module for our DAS system. Our modules leverage Dynamic Partial Reconfiguration (DPR) to implement a dynamically reconfigurable filtering block that changes with changing driving conditions. We provide experimental results that demonstrate the feasibility of our systems and its resilience against reconfiguration overhead, which enhances reliability and driver safety.

One of the disadvantages of static implementations of MTT system on FPGA is that the hardware blocks may become obsolete if the application around which they are based change. For example, different types of filters may be needed for tracking targets in different driving environments (e.g. urban, suburban, rural, etc.). A common solution to this problem is to implement a system with all the necessary hardware blocks, and use the appropriate blocks at run-time. However, this is not a very area-efficient solution, and it does not safeguard against hardware block obsolescence. Another solution, particularly for systems implemented in FPGAs, is to reconfigure the entire FPGA to implement a new system with new hardware blocks. However, this also is not very efficient since only a small portion of the hardware implementation typically needs to be reconfigured.

A better solution would be to build a dynamically reconfigurable system that enables an application to replace obsolete or inadequate hardware blocks with new ones on the fly. Xilinx provides devices and tools that support partial dynamic reconfiguration. This technology allows designers to map pre-synthesized, implemented, and routed blocks onto specific regions of an FPGA device. The bit streams needed to reconfigure a portion of an FPGA can be stored either on- or off-chip.

An internal configuration access port (ICAP) controller can be added to a system to manage the reconfiguration process, and dedicated bus macros can be used to interface the reconfigurable portions of the architecture with the rest of the system.

In this section, we describe a dynamically reconfigurable implementation of our MTT system. We also show how our system can automatically adapt its hardware configuration in response to changing driving conditions. We investigate two utilizations of DPR that can be used in order to support multiple driving environments and obstacle behaviors. In the first implementation, we explore the use of DPR to modify the physical structure of the Kalman filtering subsystem in a MTT application. We also demonstrate how the accuracy of the filter block can be dynamically and automatically tuned to match the characteristics of the operational environment. This can be very useful when the environment changes from, say, open highway to narrow city street where higher levels of accuracy are needed to track multiple, potentially closer targets. Conversely, when the driving environment changes from dense to sparse, the accuracy of the filter can be reduced to minimize resource utilization and energy consumption. We provide experimental results that demonstrate the feasibility of this approach and its low overhead. We also demonstrate the ease with which we can switch between hardware implementations automatically using a simple heuristic. This contrasts with prevailing approaches to dynamic reconfiguration, which are mainly demand-driven.

As for the second implementation, we explore the use of DPR according to targets proximity to the radar sensor. As targets move closer to the radar, they should be tracked at higher levels of accuracy since they can potentially become more hazardous. On the other hand, as targets move further away, less accurate tracking can be used. We show how the functionality and accuracy of an MTT system can be automatically tuned to match the dynamics of moving obstacles on the road. Since lower levels of accuracy generally require fewer hardware resources, DPR can be leveraged to release hardware resources for other uses, such as tracking more obstacles, accelerating other computational functions, or reducing power consumption. In our work, free hardware resources are used to enhance the radar detection unit, which improves the detection of targets at different distances. Our design is based on using three modular filters that can be dynamically combined in three configurations to match different driving scenarios. Our design also includes an enhanced detection unit module for post-processing acquired radar signals and pre-filtering them before they are delivered to our MTT system. Our system is also designed to continue operating even when being reconfigured, and this enhances the system's reliability. Our experimental results demonstrate the feasibility and low overhead of our dynamically reconfigurable design.

Figure 7 shows the high-level view of our proposed system architecture. It includes a number of soft processor cores for executing the control-intensive portions of the MTT application. It also includes a number of slots that can be configured with pre-designed hardware blocks for accelerating the performance-critical portions of the application. The soft processors and hardware blocks would be able to exchange data through interconnected FIFO buffers. The system also includes an ICAP controller for managing the configuration of hardware blocks on the fly. The configuration bit streams could be stored on-chip or off-chip memories, while the loading, removal, and swapping of hardware blocks would be controlled by the main MTT application software using various performance-enhancing heuristics.

In Figure 8, we show the architecture of our dynamically reconfigurable MTT system. The basic blocks and their respective functionalities of the prototype design are the following:

- PowerPC processor used to implement all the blocks of the MTT application except the Kalman filtering block, which we implement as a dynamically reconfigurable hardware block. This mapping has been

Figure 7. The proposed dynamically partial reconfigurable MTT based system architecture

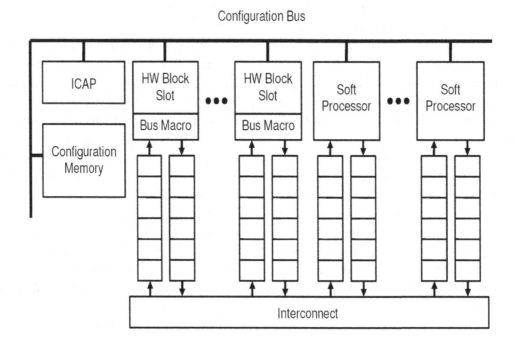

Figure 8. Validation architecture basic IP cores. The MTT system runs on the PowerPC except the Filtering&Prediction Kalman block that runs on the "Filter" hardware block

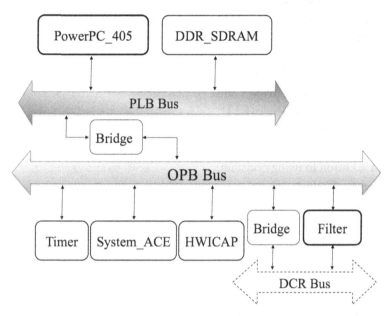

chosen to respect the application real-time constraint and to proof the feasibility of DPR in a MTT system. However the utilization of several micro-blaze soft-cores is possible but requires a more complex architecture.

- Processor Local Bus (PLB), used to provide fast communication between the processor and the external Double Data Rate Synchronous Dynamic Random Access Memory (DDR SDRAM).
- DDR SDRAM memory used to store the instruction and data files used by the MTT algorithm.
- On-Chip Peripheral Bus (OPB), used to connect various peripheral components and enable data transfers between the peripherals and the processor.
- "Timer" block, used to measure the latency of the hardware filter block and the time needed to transfer data and results between the processor (software) and the filter block.

- Advanced Configuration Environment (ACE) controller, used to load the configuration bit stream files of different filter block implementations from the compact flash drive. It is also used to configure the static portion of the system architecture and the MTT application code on system startup.
- HWICAP controller used for configuring reconfigurable regions in the FPGA. It is initialized and operated under software control.

Dynamically Adaptive MTT Based on Obstacle Density

We implemented the Kalman filter as a hardware block and we studied the ability of implementing different types of filters in a reconfigurable region in the FPGA. The main advantage of such an implementation is its ability to implement different filter architectures having different characteristics in response to changing operating conditions. Such change is very common in driving scenarios where environments are constantly changing from urban to suburban to rural. To that end we have designed two Kalman filter implementations with different levels of tracking accuracy to match the needs of different road environments. We use 2 filters: a lower accuracy Kalman Filter for Open (KFO) road environments such as highways and a higher accuracy Kalman Filter for Dense (KFD) road environments such as those inside cities.

1. **KFO Filter:** In addition to using constant, fixed-point filter coefficients, some coefficients are rounded to 2^x while others are restricted to 18 bits. Such restrictions reduce the complexity of the hardware block and the number of 18×18 hardware multipliers needed to implement the filter. They also reduce the accuracy of the filter, which is an acceptable trade-off in open driving environments where fewer cars are typically within range of the radar.

2. **KFD Filter:** This filter is based on the same architecture as the KFO filter but uses wider coefficients that result in a larger, more complex implementation. On the other hand, these also result in a more accurate filter that is better suited for dense driving environments (e.g. city streets) where more cars are within range of the radar.

Figure 9 shows the 2 scenarios where the filters KFD and KFO are used.

Our field studies had shown that, on average, in open environments the number of targets within range of the radar were fewer than six, while in dense environments this number increased to more than seven. Using these observations, we developed a simple heuristic that tracks the number of targets in range of the radar over the last five radar sweeps, and uses the appropriate filter implementation accordingly. The number of prior radar sweeps we track is arbitrary, but is done to ensure that the filter is not reconfigured unless

the observed conditions favor one configuration over another. Figure 4.5 shows the pseudo code for the filter reconfiguration heuristic.

```
while (true) {
        //Track number of
targets in last 5 sweeps
        for (i=0 ; i <= 3 ;
i++) {
                targets
[i+1] = targets [i];
        }
        //Check threshold
and use appropriate configuration
        if (targets [0] <= 6
&& targets [1] <= 6 &&
        targets [2] <= 6 &&
targets [3] <= 6 &&
        targets [4] <= 6) {
                Use KFO;
        }
        else if (targets [0]
>= 7 && targets [1] >= 7 &&
        targets [2] >= 7 &&
targets [3] >= 7 &&
        targets [4] >= 7) {
                Use KFD;
        }
    }
```

Table 1 summarizes the resource utilization for both hardware filter implementations (KFO and KFD). It is also important to note that the resources consumed by either implementation are allocated as part of the reconfigurable region. This is due to the current technology for implementing reconfigurable regions. In general, a reconfigurable region can be specified as a rectangular area in the FPGA fabric.

This region must contain all the hardware resources required by the most complex reconfigurable module implemented inside of it. As can be seen in Table 4.1, the dimensions of the RR region

Figure 9. KFD and KFO utilization in the MTT

were set to accommodate the slices required by KFD. Although the overall utilization of slices for both filters with respect to the reconfigurable region shows high efficiency (97%), the utilization of other resources within the region (DSPs, RAMB16s, etc.) is not as high due to the rectangular design constrain of a reconfigurable region.

Table 2 summarizes and compares both implementations in terms of hardware resources consumed and the resource reduction percentage of using the new MTT implementation. This table also shows the trade off in area of using a reconfigurable system compared to a software only implementation. As a conclusion of this table, a reduction of around 80% of hardware resources can be achieved by implementing the reconfigurable system. Note that this table compares the resources utilized by only the *Filtering&Prediction* blocks in both the original MTT system and the new DPR system.

Dynamically Adaptive MTT Based on Obstacle Positions

In this section, we present another utilization of DPR for an MTT system. The important issue about this system is that partial reconfiguration is triggered based on the targets positions. Closer targets that have higher probability to be more dangerous will be tracked more accurately than further targets. We first show the blocks of an MTT system alongside extra blocks from the captur-

ing and treatment phase. This step is important to show how free reconfigurable regions can be used as enhancement units as well. We then present a hybrid MTT system with new DPR based Kalman Filtering&Prediction block. The major difference in this implementation compared to the implementation in the previous section, is in the Filtering&Prediction block.

The MTT application can be implemented using a variety of adaptive algorithms such as α-β filter, mean-shift algorithm, and Kalman filter, etc (Blackmann, 1999). Each chosen filter has interesting features and could be used in specific situation. In our system, we have chosen to implement not only the Kalman filter but rather both the Kalman and the α-β filters. The Kalman filter is used because it is an important block in the whole MTT system. A Kalman filter is designed to track a moving object having a constant velocity. However, real objects actually tend to move variable accelerations and therefore different velocities. The choice of the α-β filter is due to its simple hardware implementation and its consideration of target velocities in decision makings.

Radar Signal Processing and Enhancement Block

The *radar signal processing* blocks in figure 10 are responsible for analyzing captured signals and delivering them to the MTT system for decision making. There are four main blocks that be can

Table 1. Hardware resources used by the different Kalman implementations. This table also shows the hardware resource utilization of an implemented filter with respect to a reconfigurable region (RR).

HW Resources	KFO	KFD	RR	Utilization
Slices	2837	3555	3646	97%
Slice Flip Flop	306	568	8352	7%
4 input LUT	5285	6897	8352	80%
DSP48s	6	14	28	50%
RAMBs	0	0	42	0%

Table 2. Base and new DPR Filtering&Prediction hardware resource utilization comparison

HW Resources	Base SW Filter	DPR HW Filter	Resource Reduction
Slices	37660	5679	85%
Slice Flip Flop	39080	11104	72%
4 input LUT	59780	11683	81%
DSP48s	140	28	80%
RAMBs	160	42	74%

be seen in Figure 10. The *Delay Estimation* block is based on correlation and *High Order Statistics* (HOS) algorithms related to noisy radar signals or a Fast Fourier Transform (FFT) algorithm for continuous wave radars such as the one used in our system. The *Detection Unit* is an adaptive threshold based signal detector that is responsible for target identification and tracking. The *Detection Unit Enhancement* block is used to amplify and filter weak signals detected from distant targets and obstacles. The *Sensor Data Processing* block realizes data translation and interpretation in order to be delivered to the MTT MPSoC based system.

Figure 11 shows the architecture of our dynamically reconfigurable MTT system. We implemented the system on a ML410 Xilinx board with an XC4VFX60 Virtex-4 FPGA. This system is used for validating the MTT's functionality and measuring data such as the reconfiguration overhead. Depending on the radar connected to the MTT and the number of obstacles to track, one or several hardware and software cores may be used. Here, as we focus on the dynamically reconfigurable

hardware realization of the *Filtering&Prediction* block, we use only one PowerPC processor to implement the data association block.

Different Filter Implementations

We have designed two Kalman filter implementations having different tracking characteristics and an α-β extension filter. These three filters have different characteristics and can be used in different driving environments. They are used in three different configurations to support three different driving scenarios. Namely, the filter set includes a Kalman filter for angle estimation only (KFA), a Kalman filter for distance estimation only (KFD) and an α-β extension filter for both angle and distance estimations (ABF). This filter is a simple filter mainly used for data smoothing and control applications. It realizes the prediction of both the distance and angle with the help of linear and angular input velocities.

The two Kalman filters differ in their building blocks due to the different behavior of the input

Figure 10. MTT and radar signal processing blocks

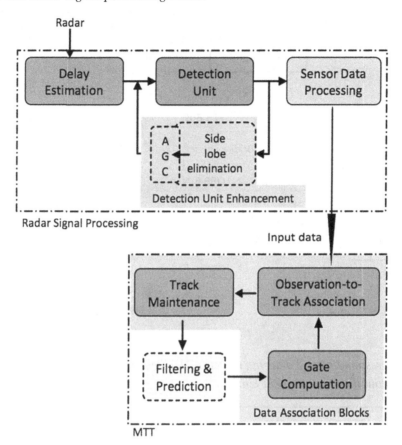

data. The tuning matrices, P_K and K matrices as mentioned in section 5.c, used to store different values for a distance input or an angle input are one of the major differences between these two filters. We also designed an extended α-β filter to provide even more accurate predictions for certain driving conditions. Three reconfigurable regions, RR1, RR2 and RR3 are respectively mapped to three designed filters as shown in Figure 11.

Filtering&Prediction Configurations

The Filtering&Prediction Block configurations used in figure 10 are directly related to a set of different combinations among the filters KFA, KFD and ABF. These configurations are associated with three regions: *Zone 1* between 160 meters and the maximum radar range, *Zone 2* between

100 meters and 160 meters and *Zone 3* between 100 meters and 0 meters as shown in Figure 12.

These regions are defined according to their proximity to the radar and are be mapped to 3 configurations simultaneously:

- **Configuration 1 (C1):** This configuration uses only the filter KFA. C1 is implemented when there are only targets tracked far away from the radar or those in Zone 1. These obstacles are considered to have a negligible hazard level. Also the distance estimation for such far away obstacles is considered to have a very low priority. Estimating just the angle for such obstacles is considered as an initiation step in the detection system. This means that when there are targets only in that region, then RR1

Figure 11. Validation architecture basic IP cores. The MTT system runs on the PowerPC except the Filtering & Prediction Kalman block that runs on the "RR1, RR2 and RR3" reconfigurable hardware blocks.

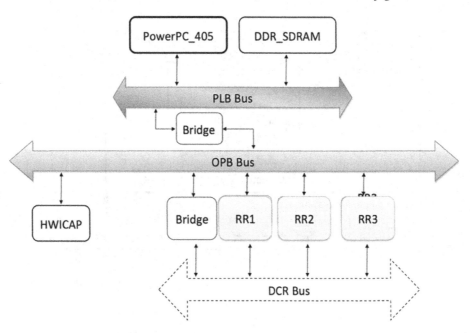

Figure 12. Data corresponding to 3 detected targets in the Detection Unit. The 2 targets in Z1 are hidden by target in Z2 without the Enhancement Unit.

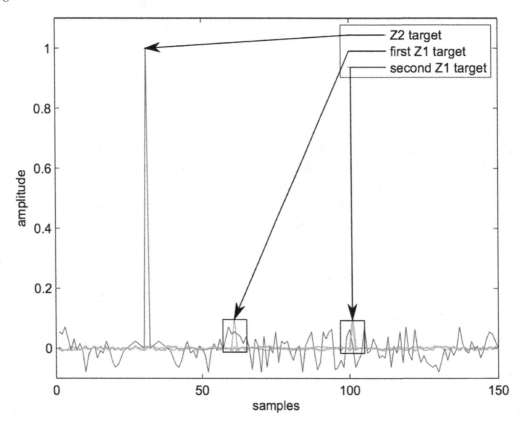

will be configured to KFA while RR2 and RR3 will just forward their inputs to the outputs. In addition to this, these regions (RR2 and RR3) will use different inputs for an enhancement block in the system. Only the signals related to the filtering block will be forwarded without any treatment.

- **Configuration 2 (C2):** This configuration uses both KFA and KFD. C2 will be used when targets are observed in Zone 2. Targets in that region can potentially be more hazardous than those in Zone 1. Thus, a better estimation will be computed for such targets by using estimated of both their distance and angle. Hence, RR1 and RR2 will be configured to KFA and KFD, respectively.

- **Configuration 3 (C3):** C3 includes the implementation of all KFA, KFD and ABF at the same time. If a target is spotted in Zone 3, it will be considered to have a high hazard level and a better prediction of its position is needed. This is why we consider ABF an enhancement over KFA and KFD that provides better distance and angle estimation of a target's data. In this configuration, RR1 will be configured as KFA, RR2 will be configured as KFD, and RR3 will be configured as ABF.

In configurations C1 and C2, the free reconfigurable regions are used as an enhancement unit related to the radar signal processing part as mentioned in the following subsection.

Detection Unit Enhancement Block

The Detection Unit Enhancement (DUE) block is used to improve the detection of weak target signals captured from far away targets. As mentioned earlier, in section 6.B.i, closer target signals tend to hide farther target signals. In potentially hazardous situations where targets are spotted in Zone 3, the signals from these targets are the most important and are strong enough for analyzing and

delivering to the MTT system. Other signals are not considered very important since they are not within the hazardous zone (Zone 3).

In situations where targets are only in Zone 2 and Zone 1, and with the free resources liberated from other reconfigurable regions, a better utilization of these resources can be achieved by implementing the DUE block in those regions. As an illustration, Figure 4.9 shows three detected signals, one from a target in Zone 2 and two other signals detected from targets in Zone 1. It is noticed that the signals detected from two targets in Zone 1 are hidden by the side lobes from the signal detected from the target in Zone 2.

Figure 11 shows the motivation for supporting a DUE hardware block whenever free reconfigurable regions are available. The DUE block consists of two basic functional blocks:

- Side lobe elimination unit and an automatic gain control (AGC) (Richard, 2005) for amplifying the weak signals as shown in Figure 12.
- After the side lobes are eliminated by the first unit, the AGC will amplify the signals after so that they will become ready for delivery to the MTT system.

Filters Output, Accuracy, and Resource Utilizations

In Figure 12 we give the measured distance of a target captured by the radar (system's input), its actual position, the output when implementing C2 (KFA+KFD output) and that when implementing C3 (KFA+KFD+ABF output).

When implementing C1, the output distance from the filtering block is identical to the measured distance so there is no error. On the other hand, our results show that the angle estimation error can reach a maximum of 1.8 degrees (15%), Table 4.5. This is similar to the angle estimation error achieved when implementing C2. However, since C2 filters the measured distance, it results in a distance estimation error that reaches a maximum

Figure 13. Our DPR system distance output of a target moving across all different configurations

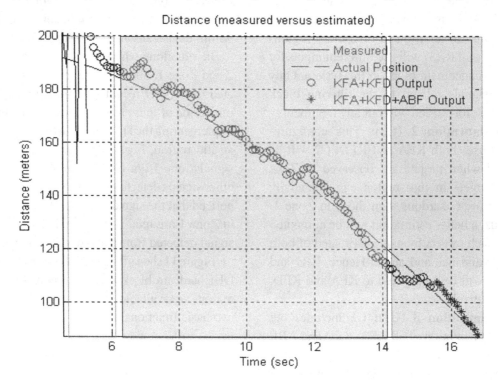

of 6 meters (6%). Implementing C3, results in the lowest distance and angle estimation errors, which reach a maximum of 3.2 meters (3%) and 0.7 degrees (7%), respectively. These results show that the extended ABF reduces distance and angle estimation errors by 50%.

Figure 14 summarizes the resource utilization for different hardware filter implementations (KFA, KFD and ABF). As it can be seen in figure 14, the dimensions of the RR region were set to accommodate the slices required by each filter according to its respective reconfigurable region. Although the overall utilization of slices for both filters shows very high efficiency (99%), the utilization of other resources within the region (DSPs, etc.) is not as high.

Tables 3 and 4 summarize the resources used by the reconfigurable regions RR1, RR2 and RR3. In addition to the resources required by the reconfigurable regions, we must also take into consideration the resources used by the HWICAP block, CF System ACE, and the DCR socket and

its bus. These components constitute the static part of our new system and are also shown in Table 4. Table 3 also shows the system's total hardware resource usage.

One of the main contributions of the work presented in this section is the possibility of using some hardware resources in other blocks other than those in the MTT application. When the system is in C1 or C2, the reconfigurable regions not used in the filtering block can be exploited for different uses. Our experiments showed that the free resources can be used in the detection unit enhancement of the radar. This block is only an enhancement and is used to detect weak signals from farther detected targets.

Reconfiguration Heuristics

The MTT application can reconfigure the filtering block automatically. The measured distance of any obstacle forms the basis for our reconfiguration heuristic. This information, along with the zone

Figure 14: A summary of the filters used in each respective configuration. The error obtained from each configuration is also mentioned.

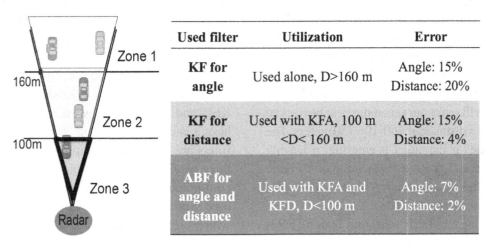

Used filter	Utilization	Error
KF for angle	Used alone, D>160 m	Angle: 15% Distance: 20%
KF for distance	Used with KFA, 100 m <D< 160 m	Angle: 15% Distance: 4%
ABF for angle and distance	Used with KFA and KFD, D<100 m	Angle: 7% Distance: 2%

Table 3. Hardware resources used by the different Kalman and α-β implementations. This table also shows the hardware resource utilization of an implemented filter with respect to the respective reconfigurable regions.

HW Resources	KFA	RR1	Util.	KFD	RR2	Util.	ABF	RR3	Util.
Slices	756	756	100%	936	931	99%	1319	1332	99%
4 input LUT	2477	3024	82%	3051	3744	82%	4323	5328	82%
DSP48s	7	10	70%	7	10	70%	2	18	12%

Table 4. Static and reconfigurable regions hardware resource utilization and total utilization by the new MTT system

HW Resources	Static	RR1	RR2	RR3	Total
Slices	1415	756	931	1332	4434
4 input LUT	2611	3024	3744	5328	14707
DSP48s	0	10	10	18	38

definitions will provide the decision to switch among the three configurations. For our experimental results we consider a real scenario where a target is traveling at 33.3 meters/sec (120 Km/hr) speed towards the radar. Since the reaction time of the driver should be around 2.7 secs, a distance of around 90 meters is considered safe and thus defining Zone 3.

To verify the presence of an obstacle in a given zone, we rely on a window of 12, consecutive 25-msec-radar sweeps. This number is obtained

through experimental testing. The value 12 is directly related to the user's relative linear velocity and the driver's reaction time and is therefore calculated frequently. 12 sweeps provide an additional margin of 10 meters around each zone threshold; 12 sweeps × 25 msec/sweep × 33.3 meters/sec = 9.99 meters.

For example if a target is initially spotted in Zone 1, 12 consecutive radar sweeps will be monitored to ensure that this target remains in Zone 1, upon which C1 will be instantiated. If the target moves closer and enters Zone 2, 12 consecutive radar sweeps will also be considered to ensure the target's position as well. These sweeps will be triggered for counting after the target crosses the 160 meters distance measured. Considering that the target is traveling at a speed of 33.3 meters/sec (Ma, 2006) and that each radar scan is 25 msec long, this will make our target ready to be tracked using C2 at a distance of 160-10=150 meters. The same applies if the target is entering or leaving Zone 1, Zone 2 or Zone 3. In summary, Figure 14 shows the reconfiguration triggering process based on measured distance.

Regarding the DUE unit, one region (RR3) out of the 2 free regions (RR2 and RR3) in configuration C1 will be implemented to as a DUE hardware unit. The same region will remain a DUE unit when the system changes into configuration C2 since RR3 will not change its configuration but only RR2. In configuration C3, the DUE unit will be replaced by the ABF filter.

Latencies and Reconfiguration Overheads

Latency analysis in driver assistant systems is very important to improve safety and ensure that drivers have adequate time to react to changing conditions. Starting from this point, we base our analysis on scenarios where targets travel towards the radar at 33.3 meters/sec (120 km/hr). Since the reaction time of the driver should be approximately 2.7 seconds, this results in a 33.3×2.7 = 90 meter safety buffer that we use to define Zone 3.

Regarding the implementation of the KFA, KFD and ABF filters, we note that they each have a latency of less than 50 nsec. Since these filters are in turn used to implement each of the three configurations, we note that the latency of configuration C1, which only uses KFA, is 50 nsec. Similarly, the latency of configuration C2, which uses filters KFA and KFD in parallel, is also 50 nsec. On the other hand, the latency of configuration C3, which uses the ABF to process the outputs of the KFA and KFD filters is 100 nsec.

The three reconfigurable regions can be reconfigured to KFA, KFD and ABF respectively as mentioned earlier. The time needed to reconfigure RR1 to KFA is 87.3 msec; RR2 to KFD is 82.8 msec; and RR3 to ABF is 130.1 msec. These are used in Table 5, which shows the reconfiguration time for the different scenarios that might occur.

When a target is detected in Zone 1 at a distance of 200 meters traveling at 33.3 meters/sec (120 Km/hr), four radar sweeps (100 msec) will be skipped due to the reconfiguration process. This

Figure 15. Reconfiguration triggering distances supposing a target travelling at a speed of 120 km/hr

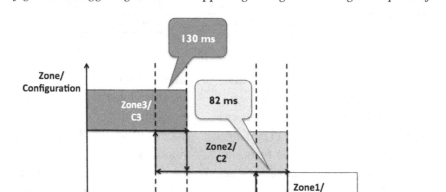

Table 5. Reconfiguration times needed for the switching among different configurations

	Reconfiguration Time
0-C1 / C1-0	87.3 msec
C1-C2 / C2-C1	82.8 msec
C2-C3 / C3-C2	130.1 msec

still enables configuration C1 to be ready while the target is at 200-3.33=196.67 meters. When the target passes through the 150 meters boundary, configuration C2 will be triggered. In turn, four radar sweeps (100 msec) within Zone 2 will maintain configuration C1 until configuration C2 is ready to be used. Hence configuration C2 will be enabled while the target is still at a distance of 150-3.33=146.67 meters.

Finally, when the target passes through the 90-meter boundary, configuration C3 will be triggered. In turn, six radar sweeps (150 msec) within Zone 3 will maintain configuration C2 until configuration C3 is ready. Hence the target will be tracked using configuration C3 when it is at a safe distance of 90-3.33-1.665=85.005 meters. Note that even when being reconfigured, our system is designed to continue operating and detecting obstacles using the previous configuration (Figure 5).

CONCLUSION AND FUTURE RESEARCH DIRECTIONS

In this chapter, an exploration of the DPR feature in FPGAs is studied for the benefit of a DAS system. We first demonstrated in this approach how the accuracy of the filtering block can be dynamically and automatically tuned to match the characteristics of the driving environment. This was very useful when the environment changes like from rush hours on highways or narrow city streets with more obstacles to track to calm open roads and less obstacles to track. In this case a high accurate filter used in order to track more targets in dense environments and hence, ease some stress off the driver and another less accurate, less resource-utilized filter, used in relaxing environments.

We then explored another possibility to benefit from DPR. We investigated, unlike the previous target density driven reconfigurable system, the possibility to automatically tune the accuracy of our filter to match the dynamics of moving obstacles on the road. Since lower levels of accuracy generally require fewer hardware resources, DPR can be leveraged to release hardware resources for other uses, such as tracking more obstacles, accelerating other computational functions, or reducing power consumption. Our design was based on using three modular filters that can be dynamically combined in three configurations to match different driving scenarios. Our design also included an enhanced detection unit module for post-processing acquired radar signals and pre-filtering them before they are delivered to our system.

Several extensions of the presented work are possible:

- We used in our approach only one radar sensor and applied DPR to the decision making system using this sensor. One room for investigation is to apply the same DAS system to support multiple radars (one in the front, one in the rear and two side radars for example).
- In our DAS DPR based system implementation, an enhancement block was implemented when RRs are free and not needed. One room for enhancement is to investigate more units from not only the capturing phase but also from the restitution phase. Such units can be sound amplification for sound based restitution DAS systems, or image-rendering enhancements for image base restitution DAS systems.

- Although our work was mainly focused on the treatment phase in a DAS system, other phases can be investigated for their implementations on a DPR basis separately as well. Once this is achieved, a whole system can be built with joined RRs that can support computational units from different DAS phases. A more detailed investigation can include hardware reuse whenever one phase is in no need for its hardware unit. Hence, regions reserved for this unit can be built as reconfigurable regions and can be reconfigured to become hardware accelerators used in other DAS phases.

REFERENCES

Becker, J., Hubner, M., Hettich, G., Constapel, R., Eisenmann, J., & Luka, J. (2007). Dynamic and Partial FPGA Exploitation. *Proceedings of the IEEE*, 95(2), 438–452. doi:10.1109/JPROC.2006.888404

Blackman, S. (1999). *Design and analysis of modern tracking systems*. Boston: Artech House.

Claus, C., Zeppenfeld, J., Müller, F., & Stechele, W. (2007). *Using Partial-Run-Time Reconfigurable Hardware to Accelerate Video Processing in Driver Assistance System*. Design, Automation & Test in Europe. doi:10.1109/DATE.2007.364642

EyeQ2. (2010). *The MobilEye safety project 2010*. Available: http://www.mobileye.com/node/69

Harb, N., Niar, S., Khan, J., & Saghir, M. (2009). A Reconfigurable Platform Architecture for an Automotive Multiple-Target Tracking System. *ACM SIGBED Review. Special Interest Group on Embedded Systems*, 6(3), 1–4.

Harb, N., Niar, S., Saghir, M., ElHillali, Y., & Ben-Atitallah, R. (2011). Dynamically Reconfigurable Architecture for a Driver Assistant System. In *Proceedings of IEEE Symposium on Application Specific Processors (SASP 2011)*. San Diego, CA: IEEE.

Harb, N., Saghir, M., & Niar, S. (2012). A Dynamically Reconfigurable Kalman Filtering Block for an Automotive Multiple Target Tracking System. In *Proceedings of 6th HiPEAC Workshop on Reconfigurable Computing*. Academic Press.

ImapCar. (2006). *Nec Electronics 2006, Nec introduces Imapcar image processor with advanced parallel processing capabilities*. Available from http://www.nec.co.jp/press/en/0608/2501.html

Intersafe. (2005). *The European FP7, Prevent-Intersafe project*. Retrieved from http://www.prevent- ip.org/en/prevent subprojects/intersection safety/intersafe/

Khan, J., Niar, S., Elhillali, Y., Rivenq-menhaj, A., & Dekeyser, J. (2008). An MPSoC Architecture for the Multiple Target Tracking Application in Driver Assistant System. In *Proceedings of IEEE International Conference Application-Specific Systems, Architectures and Processors (ASAP)*. IEEE.

Khan, J., Niar, S., Saghir, M., Elhillali, Y., & Rivenq-menhaj, A. (2009). Driver Assistance System Design and its Optimization for FPGA Based MPSoC. In *Proceedings of IEEE Symposium on Application Specific Processors*. SASP.

Khan, J., Niar, S., Saghir, M., Elhillali, Y., & Rivenq-menhaj, A. (2010). Trade-off Exploration for Target Tracking Application in a Customized Multiprocessor Architecture. *Journal on Embedded Systems*, 175043, 1-21.

Le Beux, S. (2006). FPGA Implementation of Embedded Cruise Control and Anti-Collision Radar. In *Proc. 9th Euromicro Conference on Digital System Design (DSD'2006)*, (pp. 280-287). DSD.

Liu, H., Niar, S., Elhillali, Y. & Rivenq-Menhaj, A. (2011). Embedded Architecture with Hardware Accelerator for Target Recognition in Driver Assistance Systems. *ACM SIGARCH Computer Architecture News*.

Liu, H., Niar, S., Elhillali, Y., & Rivenq-menhaj, A. (2011). Heterogeneous Embedded Architecture for Target Recognition in a Driver Assistant System. In *Proceedings of 2nd International Workshop on Highly Efficient Accelerators and Reconfigurable Technologies (HEART)*. HEART.

Ma, X., & Andreeasson, I. (2006). Driver reaction time estimation from real car following data and application in GM-type model evaluation. In *Proceedings of the 85th TRB Annual Meeting*. TRB.

Murphy-Chutorian, E., & Trivedi, M. (2008). HyHOPE: Hybrid Head Orientation and Position Estimation for Vision-based Driver Head Tracking. In *Proceedings of IEEE Intelligent Vehicles Symposium*. IEEE.

Parnell, K. (2005, 2nd quarter). The Changing Face of Automotive ECU Design. XCell Journal.

Richardsi, M. A. (2005). *Fundamentals of Radar Signal Processing*. New York, NY: McGraw-Hill.

Shreejith, S., Fahmy, S. A., & Lukasiewycz, M. (2013). Reconfigurable Computing in Next-Generation Automotive Networks. IEEE Embedded Systems Letters, 5(1).

Vahidi, A., & Eskandarian, A. (2003, September). Research advances in intelligent collision avoidance and adaptive cruise control. *IEEE Transactions on Intelligent Transportation Systems*, (3), 143–153. doi:10.1109/TITS.2003.821292

KEY TERMS AND DEFINITIONS

Detection Unit Enhancement (DUE): A block in the radar used to improve the detection of weak target signals captured from far away targets.

Driver Assistance Systems (DAS): A electronic mechanism for warning the driver of an approaching danger.

Dynamic Partial Reconfiguration (DPR): A feature in the FPGA where a a portion of an FPGA device can be reconfigured while the device is still operating.

Field Programmable Gate Arrays (FPGA): Integrated circuits designed to be reconfigured by customer demands after manufacturing.

Intellectual Property Core (IP core): A reusable unit of logic, cell, or chip layout design that is the intellectual property of one party. IP cores can be used as building blocks within an FPGA.

Kalman Filter (KF): A processing block within the MTT designed to track a moving object.

Multiple-Target Tracking (MTT): A DAS for the monitoring the dynamic behavior and trajectory evolution of several objects in front of the vehicle.

Chapter 15
Embedded Virtualization Techniques for Automotive Infotainment Applications

Massimo Violante
Politecnico di Torino, Italy

Gianpaolo Macario
Mentor Graphics Embedded Software Division, Italy

Salvatore Campagna
Politecnico di Torino, Italy

ABSTRACT

Automotive infotainment applications are examples of embedded systems in which a heterogeneous software stack is used, which most likely comprises a real-time operating system, an automotive-grade Linux, and possibly Android. Thanks to the availability of modern systems-on-a-chip providing multicore computing platforms, architects have the possibility of integrating the entire software stack in a single chip. Embedded virtualization appears an interesting technology to achieve this goal, while providing the different operating systems the capability of exchanging data as well as optimizing resource usage. Although very well known in server-class systems, virtualization is rather new to the embedded domain; in order to leverage its benefits, it is therefore mandatory to understand its peculiarities and shortcomings. In this chapter, the authors illustrate the virtualization technologies with particular emphasis on hypervisors and Linux Containers. Moreover, they illustrate how those technologies can cooperate to fulfill the requirements on automotive infotainment applications. Finally, the authors report some experimental evidence of the performance overheads introduced when using embedded virtualization.

INTRODUCTION

High-performance systems-on-a-chip (SoCs) are paving the way for new classes of embedded systems that promise lower cost, higher integration,

DOI: 10.4018/978-1-4666-6194-3.ch015

low power consumption and higher performance. Many applications exist where heterogeneous software components cooperate for reaching a common goal, which may benefit from the integration into SoCs, possibly based on multi-core technology. As an example, we can consider the architecture of two embedded systems belonging to different application scenarios:

- **Industrial Machines:** Embedded systems used for controlling industrial machines are typically running two types of software: a graphical front-end responsible for implementing the human machine interface (HMI), and a real-time backend responsible for executing the control loop of the machine. The two software components have different requirements in terms of dependability (HMI is typically not responsible for safety-critical operations, while the real-time backend is likely to be safety critical), and performance (the real-time backend has stringent timing requirements, while the HMI does not). HMI and real-time backend can be implemented resorting to different operating systems (e.g., Windows/Linux for HMI, and a real-time operating system like VxWorks, QNX, etc., for the real-time backend), and may be mapped on different processor-based systems.

- **Infotainment Systems:** Embedded systems employed in infotainment systems combine safety-relevant software components (for example for managing communications with the vehicle network), automotive-grade operating systems compliant with reference architectures like GENIVI (GENIVI, 2014) to provide all the services required by automotive applications (e.g., localization services, navigation services, etc.), as well as commodity software components for implementing other services, like Android for HMI and Android market access. Safety-relevant software components are normally delegated to specialized microcontrollers, while the other components are executed by a general-purpose microprocessor.

Analyzing the above-mentioned application scenarios we can see the benefit of high performance SoCs. SoCs (possibly equipped with multicore processors) can integrate on single devices all the software components, thus reducing the size of the resulting embedded systems, their power consumption, and costs. The benefits of SoCs are fully exploitable only if a proper infrastructure is available for allowing the coexistence of heterogeneous software components with conflicting requirements. As an example, running on the same device a software component that is safety-relevant along with a non-safety-relevant one poses new challenges to designers. Designers must indeed guarantee that the non-safety-relevant software never interferes with the safety-relevant one, no matter what it is doing. Similar considerations apply to the coexistence of real-time and non-real-time software components.

To facilitate the coexistence of heterogeneous software components, more than 40 years ago researchers developed the concept of virtual machines and hardware virtualization. Through virtual machines, designers can create a self-contained abstraction of the underlying hardware. As a result, any software component running on the virtual machine executes as if running on a dedicated hardware. Any misbehavior of a software component is confined inside the virtual machine running it; the virtual machine monitor, which orchestrates the operations of all the virtual machines, blocks any interference between different software components. For several years the concept of virtual machine remained relegated to high-end computing systems, which were the only ones capable of providing adequate computing power to run multiple virtual machines; only recently virtualization started becoming interesting also for embedded systems thanks to the availability of high-performance SoCs, and a number of products specifically designed for embedded systems started to appear on the market.

Being a relatively new technology for embedded systems, hardware virtualization needs to be understood before being deployed in real-life applications. On the one hand, designers must understand the effort needed to deploy this technology in real applications; on the other hand, quantitative evaluations are needed to understand the overhead hardware virtualization introduce.

In this chapter we provide an overview of two different hardware virtualization technologies: hypervisor, and Linux Containers. In our analysis we considered the automotive application scenario and in particular infotainment embedded systems, and we reported qualitative comparisons of hardware virtualization technologies, as well as quantitative comparisons gained on representative hardware.

The main contribution of this chapter is the comparison of two leading edge virtualization techniques, namely para-virtualization-based hypervisor and Linux Containers, from both a theoretical and quantitative point of view. To the best of our knowledge no work has provided this analysis so far.

VIRTUALIZATION TECHNIQUES

The purpose of this section is to present an overview of virtualization techniques (Popek & Goldberg, 1974) (Goldberg, 1974). The following terms are used:

- **Host Machine:** A computer, e.g., a multicore-based embedded system, providing the hardware needed for executing a software stack.
- **Host Operating System:** The operating systems running on the host machine.
- **Virtual Machine:** A software implementation of a computer that maps to a subset of the resources available in the host machine. Each virtual machine can access a portion of the host machine main memory, can use a certain amount of the host machine CPU time, and can access a subset

of the host machine I/O resources. As an example, a host machine equipped with 2 GBytes of RAM, one Ethernet port and one Controller Area Network (CAN) supports two virtual machines each having available 1 GBytes of RAM, one of the two running Linux and being able to access the Ethernet and the CAN ports, and one running Android without the permission to access to any of the communication ports.

- **Guest Operating System:** The operating system running on the virtual machine.
- **Userland:** A program execution environment, which looks and feels like a host machine for the applications that run inside it. The userland has its own set of processes, a dedicated file system, dedicated users, dedicated set of network interfaces with IP addresses, routing tables, firewall rules.

This section covers hypervisor solutions, which allow creating virtual machines on top of a host machine, and operating systems-level virtualization, which allows creating multiple userlands on the host machine.

HYPERVISORS

There are two main kinds of hypervisors: hosted hypervisors, and native or bare-metal hypervisors. Hosted hypervisors, also referred to as type 2 hypervisors, run inside a host operating system, while native hypervisors do not need any host operating system. A schematic representation of the two hypervisor solutions is reported in Figure 1.

In hosted virtualization the hypervisor is a special software running inside an operating system, and it can use all the primitives given by the host operating system. Since it does not have access to the bare hardware directly, the hypervisor could interfere with the guest operating system, but cannot compromise the host operating system. However, since the hypervisor does not have any

Figure 1. Hypervisor solutions. Type 1 hypervisor (a). Type 2 hypervisor (b).

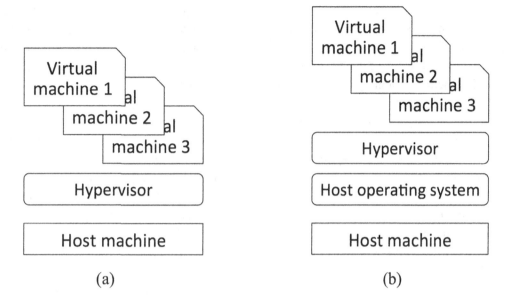

(a)   (b)

direct access to the hardware it can seldom make optimized use of the host computer resources, and all accesses the guest operating system require to the virtual machine hardware must be translated into accesses to the host computer hardware. As a result, big performance overheads are expected.

Some examples of this kind of hypervisors are:

- Virtualbox;
- VMWare;
- Parallels;
- KVM.

Bare-metal (or native) hypervisors (also known as Type 1 hypervisors) run directly on the guest machine hardware and do not need any host operating system. Two types of implementations are possible: full virtualization or para-virtualization that, although similar, use different approaches to allocate host machine hardware to the virtual machines.

- **Full Virtualization:** The hypervisor interacts directly with the host machine hardware resources (CPU, memory, mass stor-

age), and it serves as a virtual hardware platform for the guest operating systems. The hypervisor keeps each virtual machine completely independent and unaware of the other virtual machines running on the same host machine; each virtual machine runs its own operating system independently. The hypervisor monitors the host machine hardware resources. As virtual machines run applications, the hypervisor relays resources from the host machine to the appropriate virtual machine. This result can be achieved by classifying the instructions executed by the virtual machine code into two broad categories: instructions that do not change the state of the host computer (i.e., instructions that manipulate the memory area allocated to the virtual machine), and instructions that do change the state of host hardware (i.e., instructions that modify the configuration of the interrupt controller, of the memory management unit, or in general resources that the host computer shares among virtual machines). Instructions belonging to the

375

first category are allowed to run unmodified, as they do not have any impact on the other virtual machines running on the host. Conversely, instructions belonging to the second category are not allowed to execute, as the instructions running on one guest will produce an effect on the host machine visible to the other guests. Hypervisors address this issue using *virtual hardware* and the technique known as *trap and map*. For each of the host computer shared resources (e.g., interrupt controller) the hypervisor emulates a virtual hardware. As a result each virtual machine has its own set of virtual hardware resources and any modification the guest may request is done on the virtual hardware instead of the host machine hardware. To block the access to host machine hardware, the hypervisor implements the trap and map technique: each time an instruction trying to modify the host machine state is encountered, a trap to the hypervisor code is performed. The hypervisor then modifies the virtual hardware associated with the virtual machine. As a result, only the virtual hardware component is modified locally to the virtual machine, while the other virtual machines running on the host are not affected. As hypervisors implementing full virtualization emulate virtual hardware, they have their own processing needs, which means that the host machine must reserve some processing power and resources to run the hypervisor application. This can impact overall performance and slow down applications.

- **Para-Virtualization:** Unlike the full virtualization technique, guest operating systems are aware of each other. The hypervisor still maintains virtual hardware for each virtual machine, which runs modified guest operating systems. The source code of the guest operating system is modified

so that each instruction accessing the host computer shared resources is replaced with hypercalls, i.e., calls to the hypervisor. Each hypercall operates on virtual hardware in response to guest operating system requests.

No matter which technique is considered, a hypervisor provides Inter Process Communication mechanisms for allowing data exchange among virtual machines. The IPC allows establishing a flavor of connection spanning from simple serial one-to-one links, to more complex network-based links.

Full virtualization may require a significant amount of computing power to be available in the host machine. Each time an instruction accessing shared hardware resources is to be executed, a trap must be invoked, and the corresponding virtual hardware emulation software must be executed. Moreover, some critical instructions may not be associated with traps, which will make trap and map impossible. In this case, the binary code of the guest operating system must be scanned before starting its execution, and modified by replacing non-trappable critical instructions with trappable ones. As a result, the host computer should also set available a mass memory cache for storing hypervisor-ready guest binary code.

In case of embedded systems, full virtualization is not feasible as the host machine normally has limited computing power and very limited mass storage space, if any, therefore para-virtualization is likely the best option as guests are prepared for virtualization at compile time.

The main issue with para-virtualization is likely the management of the host computer hardware resources. For understating the adopted approaches, we can consider the following two scenarios, depicted in Figure 2.

- **Scenario 1:** Virtual machine VM1 that needs to access to the hardware resource

Figure 2. Pass-through hardware access (a) and client-server hardware access (b)

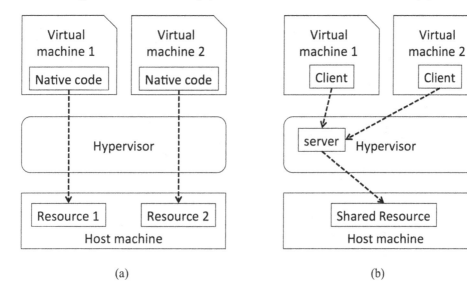

(a)   (b)

R1, and virtual machine VM2 that needs to access to the hardware resource R2.

- **Scenario 2:** Virtual machines VM1 and VM2 that need to access to the shared hardware resource R.

In scenario 1, although the host hardware resources R1 and R2 are needed by VM1 and VM2, they are not shared as VM1 will make use of R1 only and VM2 will make use of R2 only; therefore, each virtual machine is allowed to modify the resource directly. In this case, which is known as *pass-through*, the virtual machine can use its unmodified native code for accessing the resource without the intervention of the hypervisor (e.g., a native Linux driver can be used without the need for para-virtualization).

In scenario 2, both virtual machines need to access the same shared resource, and therefore the hypervisor must provide a mechanism to synchronize the accesses. The solution normally used is based on a *client-server* approach. The hypervisor runs the code for accessing the shared hardware (e.g., the Graphical Processing Unit device driver) that behaves as a server that queues requests coming from clients, and dispatches them

to the hardware. The guest operating system runs para-virtualized code for the shared resource. This code works as a client that issues requests to the server inside the hypervisor.

The challenge in implementing efficient hypervisor lies in the management of shared resources; in case of complex hardware devices, like for example Graphical Processing Units, custom device drivers must be implemented inside the hypervisor at high development and maintenance costs. Moreover, only hardware devices whose details are publicly known can be supported. In case of devices whose driver source code is not provided by the device manufacturers, efficient para-virtualization is nearly impossible unless the host machine processor provides special features (e.g, Input/Output Memory Management Unit).

OPERATING SYSTEM-LEVEL VIRTUALIZATION

Operating system-level virtualization is implemented by the host operating system itself, which is capable of running multiple userlands concurrently, as shown in Figure 3.

Figure 3. Operating system-level virtualization

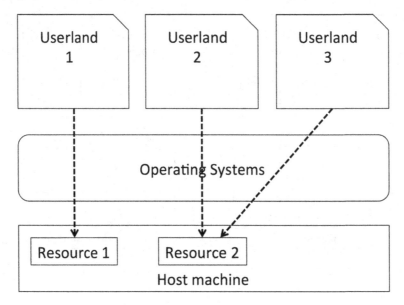

Some of the host machine resources can be dedicated to userlands, while others can be shared among several userlands. Multiple userlands co-exist within a host computer, they can even run on different operating system distributions, but all userlands operate under the same operating system kernel.

Since this form of virtualization is executing only one kernel on the host machine, it usually imposes little or no overhead in the execution with respect to hypervisors.

On the other hand, operating system-level virtualization is not capable of running on the host different guest operating systems, which is conversely possible when using hypervisors.

Another drawback of operating system-level virtualization is security. Being run on the same kernel, it is possible that wrong operations in one guest can affect the others. This situation is not possible with hypervisors as guests do not share any kernel code.

Several implementations of operating system-level virtualizations are available, such as:

- FreeBSD Jail.

- Solaris Zones/Containers.
- Linux Vserver.
- OpenVZ.
- Virtuozzo.
- Linux Containers (LXC).

In the following we will focus on Linux Containers.

Linux Containers

Linux Containers provide a lightweight virtual system mechanism for Linux, able to implement resource management, process management and isolation, exploiting Linux kernel features such as process control groups or root directory change.

Aiming at efficiency, Linux Containers follow an opposite approach if compared to many other virtualization tools. In fact, rather than starting from an emulated hardware (completely isolated) and then trying to reduce overhead and improve performances, it uses already efficient mechanisms and builds up isolation.

Each container provides a reduced view of the actual kernel that has created the container itself.

As a result, multiple containers may run on the same hardware and will share resources through the single kernel that created them.

Linux Containers rely upon a combination of a few features that have progressively been developed and integrated inside the Linux kernel codebase (The Linux Kernel Archives, 2014), more specifically: resource management via "process control groups", and resource isolation via new flags to the clone system call.

Resource Management

Resource management is obtained by means of *control groups* (cgroups), which is a Linux kernel feature to limit, account and isolate resource usage (CPU, memory, disk I/O, etc.) of process groups. This work was started by engineers at Google (primarily Paul Menage and Rohit Seth) in 2006 under the name "process containers" (Corbet, 2007). It was then renamed to Control Groups in late 2007 due to the confusion caused by multiple meanings of the term "container" in the Linux kernel and merged with kernel version 2.6.24. Since then, many new features and controllers have been added.

One of the design goals of cgroups was to provide a unified interface to many different use cases, from controlling single processes to whole operating system-level virtualization. Cgroups provide:

- Resource limiting: groups can be set to not exceed a set memory limit — this also includes file system cache;
- Prioritization: some groups may get a larger share of CPU or disk I/O throughput;
- Accounting: to measure how much resources certain systems use for e.g. billing purposes;
- Isolation: separate namespaces for groups, so they do not see each other's processes, network connections or files;

- Control: freezing groups or check pointing and restarting;

Resource Isolation

Resource isolation is obtained by using the Linux namespaces. In general, a namespace makes it possible for a process and all its descendants to have their own private view of shared resources in the kernel, such as the network stack, processes, and the mount table. As an example, inside a pid namespace, the first process created has pid 1, and only processes created inside the namespace are visible to each other. Linux Kernel implements six namespaces:

- **Mnt:** To separate mountpoints and filesystems. Processes can have separate root partitions and mounts.
- **Pid:** To separate process trees and environments. Each pid namespace has its own init process, which is associated with pid 1. A single process can reside in only one pid namespace at a time.
- **Net:** To separate network stack. The default net namespace contains the loopback device and all physical cards present in the system while newly created net namespaces contain only a single loopback device. In order to allow one namespace to reach other networks or utilize physical devices, a virtual ethernet (veth) device can be setup.
- **Ipc:** That consists in an isolated System V IPC namespace with isolated objects and POSIX message queues.
- **Uts:** Which is the hostname namespace, where each uts namespace provides different values for the uname() call: domain name, host name, os release, etc.
- **User:** To have separate users, groups and capabilities lists. Each namespace holds a mapping of host system user ids to user ids

in the namespace. This is the most recent addition to the Linux Kernel (since 3.8).

Resource isolation is obtained through new flags added to the clone system call that is now capable of creating several types of new namespaces. More specifically:

- **CLONE_NEWIPC (since Linux 2.6.19):** If set, create the process in a new ipc namespace
- **CLONE_NEWNET (since Linux 2.6.24):** If set, create the process in a new network namespace
- **CLONE_NEWNS (since Linux 2.4.19):** Start the child in a new mount namespace
- **CLONE_NEWPID (since Linux 2.6.24):** If set, create the process in a new pid namespace
- **CLONE_NEWUTS (since Linux 2.6.19):** If set, create the process in a new uts namespace

User Space Control Package

As previously described Linux Containers rely on several kernel features to achieve a kind of lightweight virtualization. The LXC project at SourceForge (LXC - Linux Containers, 2014) is the user space control package for Linux Containers that makes those features available and easier to be used for application programs.

The LXC package combines these Linux kernel mechanisms to provide a user-space container object, a lightweight virtual system with full resource isolation and resource control for an application or a system.

Since Linux Containers is a technology still under development, the LXC user-space package follows suit. At the time of this writing lxc-0.9.0 is the last official release. The Application Programming Interface will become stable together with the release of lxc-1.0.0 (currently alpha1).

The LXC project is released under the GNU Lesser General Public License v2.1 – which allows its usage inside both open and non-open source programs.

VIRTUALIZATION AND AUTOMOTIVE INFOTAINMENT APPLICATIONS

The purpose of this section is to analyze the application of virtualization techniques to evaluate benefits and shortcomings of the available technologies. For this purpose, let us assume the hypothetical infotainment system has to provide support for the following features:

- It must run a real time operating system to manage the communication between the infotainment embedded system and the rest of the vehicle over an automotive network (e.g., the Controller Area Network, CAN bus).
- It must run an automotive-grade Linux distribution compliant with the GENIVI specification to provide basic services such as navigation, phone connectivity, music playback, etc.
- It must run Android to provide users the capability of extending the features of the infotainment system through apps.

Let us suppose that a suitable hardware, based on a multicore SoC, is available providing adequate resources for the above software stack.

The system architect may deploy the three different operating systems on the SoC using an unstructured approach by dedicating each core of the adopted SoC to a different operating system. For example, if we assume a Texas Instruments Jacinto 6 automotive OMAP SoC is used, we have the following possible mapping:

- One of the two ARM Cortex M4 the SoC makes available can map the real time op-

Figure 4. Mapping of the architecture without virtualization

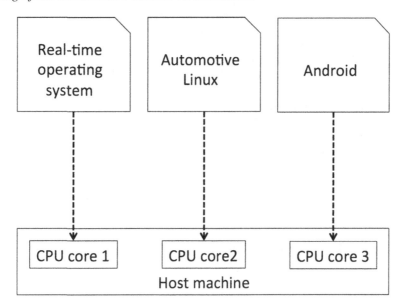

erating system, using the CAN serial interface available on the SoC for communications with the automotive network.

- One of the two ARM Cortex A15 the SoC includes can map the automotive-grade Linux.
- The other ARM Cortex A15 in the SoC can map Android.

With this solution, shown in Figure 4, two problems arise.

As the mapping is implemented without any specific virtualization solution, the different operating systems do not have communication methods for data exchange. As such, in case the real time operating system receives data that the automotive Linux or Android needs, it lacks methods to transfer the data. It is therefore up to the system architect to devise a method for implementing data exchange between different operating systems running on different cores.

In case the infotainment system has only one display unit, a suitable mechanism has to be implemented for allowing automotive Linux and Android to display information concurrently, for example for showing the navigation application (based on Linux) and the telemetry data (based on an Android app) at the same time. As the two operating systems are deployed on different cores, without specific synchronization mechanisms, it is up to the architect to devise suitable methods for accessing concurrently the shared resource.

To address these problems, virtualization can be very effective by leveraging its built-in communication and resource-sharing features.

The infotainment system we considered is based on a heterogeneous mix of operating systems and therefore a hypervisor-based solution as that show in Figure 5 appears suitable: three virtual machines can run on top of the hypervisor, which is responsible for running the real time operating system, automotive Linux, and Android concurrently (most likely still mapping the former on the ARM Cortex M4, and the latters on the ARM Cortex A15s), while providing a suitable communication channel among them. Although interesting, and provided that the hypervisor offers a suitable mechanism for graphics sharing between Linux and Android, this alternative solution still has one shortcoming. The RAM

Figure 5. Mapping of the architecture using hypervisors

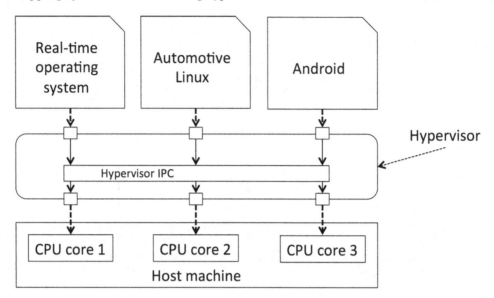

memory must be statically divided among the three virtual machines: some memory is likely to be wasted because the same code may be stored twice (e.g., the libraries that Linux and Android share are stored twice, one in the automotive Linux virtual machine, and one in the Android virtual machine). This issue, which may seem trivial, can have significant impact as it can mandate duplicating the amount of memory employed in the infotainment system. Being infotainment an automotive application, and being automotive very sensitive to cost issues, this hypervisor-only solution appears not to be optimal.

As a further enhancement of the architecture, we can leverage the fact that the Linux kernel can be enriched with the features Android needs. Therefore a single suitably instrumented Linux kernel can be used for running both Android and automotive Linux user lands, by exploiting operating system-level virtualization such as Linux Containers. Thanks to this approach, a more efficient usage of the system RAM memory is possible, thus allowing reducing the overall hardware cost.

The final architecture shown in Figure 6 can thus be the following: a hypervisor runs two virtual machines, one running the real-time operating system, one running an Android-friendly Linux kernel. The Android-friendly Linux kernel implements operating system-level virtualization and hosts Android userland and automotive Linux userland.

QUANTITATIVE COMPARISON OF VIRTUALIZATION SOLUTIONS

The purpose of this section is to provide quantitative performance assessments of a system using virtualization technology. We set-up our experimental environment according to the following rationale.

Hardware Set-Up

We selected two evaluation boards representative of actual infotainment electronic control units now in production. In particular, we selected the Freescale i.MX53 Quick Start Board, which features an ARM Cortex-A8 processor with 1GB of DDR RAM at 400 MHz, and the Pandaboard that features a Texas Instruments OMAP4430 based on 1 GHz dual core ARM Cortex-A9 processor.

Figure 6. Mapping of the architecture using hypervisors and Linux Containers

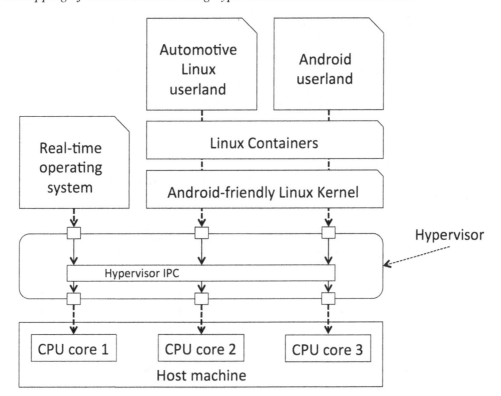

Software Set-Up

We selected a benchmark mix where well-known tests coming from the Phoronix Test Suite (Phoronix Test Suite, 2014) are used to mimic the behavior of infotainment software, which is typically the combination of applications with different characteristics. In infotainment software we can find *memory-intensive applications,* where cache and main memory are accessed frequently such in the navigation use case; *mass-memory intensive applications*, where the file system is heavily solicited, for example for building the catalog of MP3 songs on a USB stick; *mixed mass-memory and CPU-intensive applications*, where burst accesses to the mass-memory are interleaved with computations, such as in the case of MP3 playback.

As an example of memory-intensive applications we selected Cachebench and Stream. *Cachebench* is meant to evaluate the memory hierarchy throughput (cache and main memory, results are expressed in MB/s). *Stream* is meant to evaluate the system memory (RAM) performance. The result of this benchmark is the memory bandwidth (in MB/s) for performing a predefined set of memory accesses. As an example of mass-memory intensive applications we selected *Dbench*: this benchmark is designed to test the disk performance by performing a number of file-system calls. The result of this benchmark is the disk bandwidth (in MB/s) for performing a predefined set of disk accesses. As an example of mixed mass-memory and CPU-intensive applications we selected *Encode-mp3*: this benchmark computes the time (in seconds) required to encode a wave file in the MP3 format.

Table 1. Performance of native and virtualized set-ups

Benchmark	Native Performance		Virtualized Performance	
	i.MX53	Pandaboard	i.MX53	Pandaboard
Encode-mp3	995,2 sec	145,7 sec	986,7 sec	144,6 sec
Cachebench	85,1 MB/s	1.691,1 MB/s	85,1 MB/s	1691.1 MB/s
Stream	460,1 MB/s	617,9 MB/s	458,1 MB/s	615,9 MB/s
Dbench	9.45 MB/s	10.0 MB/s	8,57 MB/s	10.0 MB/s

Experimental Results and Discussion

As far as Linux Containers technology is considered, we adopted the following experimental procedure:

1. We executed the selected benchmarks under Linux operating systems on the two hardware set-ups. We recorded the achieved performance, which we will refer to as *native performance*.
2. We prepared a virtualization environment based on Linux Containers, configured to run one container. Using the virtualization environment, we repeated the execution of the selected benchmarks, recording the achieved performance, which we will refer to as *virtualized performance*.

Table 1 reports the attained results. When executing benchmarks in the virtualized set-up, the container runs the benchmarks, while the operating system does not run any particular task.

As the reader can observe, the impact of virtualization is negligible on all benchmarks for both the considered hardware platforms. For the benchmarks that involve I/O operations for accessing the mass memory, performance degradation is observed in the virtualized set-up with respect to the native set-up. We expect that this degradation is due the amount of checks the Linux kernel has to perform to grant the container access to the mass memory.

As the Pandaboard is equipped with a dual core processor, it is relevant to analyze the benchmark results when two containers are active, each mapped on one processor core. For this purpose we configured the virtualized set-up to implement two containers, and we collected the results in Table 2, where the benchmark running in Container 1 is reported in the row, and the benchmark running concurrently in Container 2 is reported in the column. Each cell contains the performance of the benchmark running in Container 1, when another benchmark is running in Container 2. As an example, Encode-mp3 takes 181,0 seconds to complete in Container 1, while Container 2 runs Dbench. Similarly, Dbench reaches 9,5 MB/s when running in Container 1, while Container 2 runs Encode-mp3. As the examples suggest, the table is not symmetric.

As the reader can observe, the benchmark results in Container 1 show some dependency with the benchmark running in Container 2, and in particular:

• When the two containers run benchmarks that do not require accessing the mass memory concurrently, no particular effect is observed. As an example we can consider the combination (Container 1/Container 2): Encode-mp3/Stream, Encode-mp3/Cachebench, Cachebench/Stream, and Cachebench/Encode-mp3. In all these cases, the benchmarks are using mostly the processor cores allocated to the containers, the memory subsystem, and one of the two

Table 2. Performance of the benchmark executed in Container 1 while Container 2 runs a second benchmark

		Container 2			
	Benchmark	Encode-mp3	Cachebench	Stream	Dbench
Container 1	Encode-mp3	145,8 s	149,9 s	146,2 s	181,0 s
	Cachebench	1.688,7 MB/s	1.687,6 MB/s	1.687,1 MB/s	1.683,2 MB/s
	Stream	594,1 MB/s	618,5 MB/s	611,1 MB/s	616,3 MB/s
	Dbench	9,5 MB/s	12,2 MB/s	10,1 MB/s	2,9 MB/s

makes use of the mass memory (Encode-mp3). As a result, the only shared resource is the main memory, where the L2 cache helps resolving contentions due to concurrent memory access.

- When the two containers run benchmarks that require accessing the mass memory concurrently, significant overheads are observed. As an example, we can consider (Container 1/Container 2): Encode-mp3/Dbench, Dbench/Dbench. In the former case, Encode-mp3 interleaves mass memory access with data processing, while Dbench performs burst accesses to the mass memory. As a result, whenever Encode-mp3 processes data, Dbench can access the mass memory undisturbed; conversely, when both Encode-mp3 and Dbench need accessing the mass memory, a contention takes place, and one of the two benchmarks is blocked waiting for the other to complete the access. The result is a moderate performance hit. In the latter case, both Containers are running benchmarks performing burst accesses to mass memory. As a result, numbers of resource contentions take place with significant performance hits.

Putting together the results of Table 1 and Table 2, we can claim that virtualization through Linux Containers is very effective in allowing multiple userlands to coexist on the same kernel. The recorded performance overheads when multiple containers run different applications are likely due to the application nature rather than the Linux Containers virtualization technique.

As far as hypervisor technology, we could not execute an experimental campaign due to the lack of a suitable solution for the considered hardware platforms. For comparing hypervisors with Linux Containers, we report data presented in (Campagna & Violante, 2012) which show the following scenario:

- Embedded hypervisor overhead in memory-intensive applications: < 5%.
- Embedded hypervisor overhead in CPU-bound applications: <10%.
- Embedded hypervisor overhead in I/O-bound applications: about 35%.

The results presented in (Campagna & Violante, 2012) highlight significant time overheads introduced by embedded virtualization with respect to Linux Containers. The explanation is likely to be found in the interrupt virtualization needed to implement I/O virtualization in absence of specific hardware support from the processor. Interrupt virtualization introduces additional latency due to the overhead required for the interrupt to be routed to the right virtual machine. Conversely, memory and CPU-bound applications show lower overheads, closer to that achieved in our experiments using Linux Containers. We could explain these results by considering that when accessing memory, or processing, the virtual machine in an hypervisor is likely not to perform any critical instructions; therefore, there is no need for invoking (either through traps or via hypercalls) the hypervisor.

CONCLUSION

We presented a comparative analysis of two virtualization technologies: hypervisor and Linux Containers.

From the qualitative comparison of the two technologies it appears that hypervisors are best suited when strong isolation is mandatory to fulfill some use cases, such as safety, while it can be problematic when complex devices (e.g., Graphical Processing Units) have to be shared efficiently among different guest operating systems. Conversely, Linux Containers technology is attractive when the use case allows lighter separation based on different user spaces, and requires sharing of complex device drivers. In this case, being based on a single Linux kernel, virtualization can be achieved at nearly no additional cost.

In terms of development efforts, hypervisors and virtualized operating systems should be provided by a tool vendor to minimize risks. Configuring and tuning the hypervisor, implementing the needed device drivers, and modifying the operating system to make it hypervisor-aware are critical operations that are too risky to be demanded to end users. Conversely, Linux Containers require essentially the definition of few system scripts, and therefore this activity can be demanded to skilled embedded system architects.

From the quantitative evaluation of the two technologies, it is evident that a hypervisor introduces additional latency to interrupt routing due to the need for interrupt virtualization in the hardware set-up we adopted. Conversely, negligible overhead has been considered in the case of I/O-bound benchmark for the Linux containers. The experiments also showed that negligible overhead is recorded when considering memory-bound benchmark for both hypervisor and Linux containers technology.

When applied to automotive infotainment applications, both technologies can coexist to solve multiple problems: hypervisors can be used for running real-time operating systems on the same SoC used for running Linux-based guests. Linux Containers appears the best solution for hosting in the Linux-based guest both automotive Linux and Android userlands.

ACKNOWLEDGMENT

We would like to acknowledge the contribution of Francesco Castagnotto, who prepared the experimental environment and executed the tests for the Linux Containers technology.

REFERENCES

Campagna, S., & Violante, M. (2012). On the Evaluation of the Performance Overhead of a Commercial Embedded Hypervisor. In *Proc. of the First Workshop on Manufacturable and Dependable Multicore Architectures at Nanoscale* (pp. 59-63). Academic Press.

Corbet, J. (2007). Process containers. Linux Weekly News, (5). Retrieved from http://lwn.net/Articles/236038/

GENIVI. (2014). About GENIVI. Retrieved from www.genivi.org

Goldberg, R.P. (1974). Survey of virtual machine research. *IEEE Computer*, 34-35.

LXC - Linux Containers. (2014). Retrieved from http://lxc.sourceforge.net

Phoronix Test Suite. (2014). Retrieved from www.phoronix-test-suite.com

Popek, G. J., & Goldberg, R. P. (1974). Formal requirements for virtualizable third generation architectures. *Communications of the ACM*, 17(7), 412–421. doi:10.1145/361011.361073 doi:10.1145/361011.361073

The Linux Kernel Archives. (2014). Retrieved from www.kernel.org

KEY TERMS AND DEFINITIONS

Embedded System: A special-purpose computer crafted to implement a limited set of operations in the context of a complex system (e.g., an engine, a vehicle, etc.).

Embedded Virtualization: A technique to create virtual machine in embedded systems.

Hypervisors: A software, firmware or hardware that creates and runs virtual machines.

Infotainment System: In-vehicle system that provides information and entertainment services such as navigation, and media player.

Linux Containers: An operating system-level virtualization method for running multiple isolated Linux systems (called containers) on a single computer.

Phoronix Test Suite: A free, open-source benchmark software for Linux and other operating systems.

Virtual Machine: A software implementation of a computer that executes programs like a physical machine.

Chapter 16
Studying Individualized Transit Indicators Using a New Low-Cost Information System

P. A. Castillo
University of Granada, Spain

A. M. Mora
University of Granada, Spain

A. Fernández-Ares
University of Granada, Spain

V. M. Rivas
University of Jaén, Spain

P. García-Fernández
University of Granada, Spain

J. J. Asensio
University of Granada, Spain

P. García-Sánchez
University of Granada, Spain

G. Romero
University of Granada, Spain

M. G. Arenas
University of Granada, Spain

J. J. Merelo
University of Granada, Spain

ABSTRACT

Current information systems used for data collection and to generate information on the state of the roads have two drawbacks: the first is that they have no ability to identify target-detected vehicles; the second is their high cost, which makes them expensive to cover the secondary road network, so they are usually located just on main routes. Thus, a new low-cost information system to monitor the traffic in real-time is proposed in this chapter. This system is based on scanning Bluetooth devices that are near the detection node. A large amount of data from passes of Bluetooth devices by different nodes (movements or displacements) have been collected. From this data, the frequency of appearance, average speed, or the number of devices that pass a certain site each day (on both working or non-working days) can be determined. The analysis of collected data has given statistics and indicators about the use of vehicles by the population of the monitored area. Specifically, the authors have obtained information about the total number of vehicles that each node has detected, on weekdays or holidays, information on traffic density by time range, on individual movements, the average speed on a section delimited by two consecutive nodes, and what demonstrates the power and features of the developed system.

DOI: 10.4018/978-1-4666-6194-3.ch016

INTRODUCTION

Nowadays, having a system of information on traffic conditions and the use of roads is very important, not only to obtain information about traffic density, but also about repetitions of passing vehicles. This kind of information about traffic flows that occur in a certain area could allow people to optimally manage their motion decisions.

Current technologies used in traffic monitoring include pneumatic tubes, loop detectors, floating vehicles or automatic recognition systems, among others. The main disadvantage of these systems is that they are unable to identify detected vehicles, in order to obtain origin/destination matrixes. Just the number of vehicles and their type can be obtained, but they do not allow to obtain traffic flow, nor to determine whether a certain vehicle passes repeatedly. In addition, their high cost makes it unprofitable covering secondary roads with them, so they are often located on major roads. Moreover, technologies based on video image detection are very costly compared to the previous and can be sensitive to meteorological conditions.

In this work, several individualized transit indicators are studied using a new low-cost system information, with a fast deployment and highly reliable. This system provides real-time information about the traffic status on different road types and in real time (available as web services), not only to the official organisms and agencies in charge of the traffic controlling, but also to any person who requests it.

Our aim is having information about traffic using a new system based on the Bluetooth (BT) devices detection using several collecting nodes. Thus, we are able to monitor the traffic density and car journeys, identifying the vehicles when they move from one node to another inside the monitored zone. Therefore, various needs have been found:

- A versatile and autonomous data collection and monitoring device is needed.
- It is also necessary to collect traffic data in real time.
- Once the data has been collected, it has to be processed properly.
- And finally, a system that allows sharing data and information with those who make decisions about mobility is needed, both from the institutional and personal points of view.

As stated, the proposed system is based on BT device discovery. Specifically, it detects waves emitted by different technological components incorporated on vehicles (hands-free phone sets, GPS) or accessories that the users incorporate to their vehicles, as well as their mobile phones. Although not all vehicles carry a BT transmitter, nowadays increasingly more and more vehicles are equipped with them. In addition, in a very high percentage of vehicles the driver might carry a mobile with BT. In any case, as stated in (Blobject, 2013) an a priori error estimation of 8.5% of detections was obtained.

The system collects the MAC address of the device BT card as well as the exact time at which it has been detected. The MAC is an unique identifier for each device, allowing us to identify passing vehicles. Additionally, analyzing the MAC allows us to determine the manufacturer and even distinguish what type of device it is (i.e. handsfree, PC, mobile phone, etc), as detailed in (IEEE BT, 2013) and (Wikipedia OUI, 2013).

From the point of view of data privacy, it is noteworthy that the data collected cannot be associated, at least without recurring to other methods, to any vehicle since there is no information collected that enables the association of the information we collect with a specific person. Unidirectional encryption technology is used, using nonstandard characters that preclude identifying the MAC of the wireless device.

Proposed system is part of a future prediction system that helps to make decisions, and able to apply knowledge in applications related to mobility. It is expected that the development and deployment of these systems will offer a set of information services with added value that are not achieved with current technologies.

The rest of the chapter is organized as follows: Following section reviews current technologies to monitor the traffic that passes through a certain area, as well as similar commercial products. Section "Objectives and expected results" details the goals of this chapter. In Section "Data-collecting hardware device", the Intelify device is presented. In Section "Data analysis" several analysis and statistics are reported from the data obtained. Finally, we present some conclusions and future work.

CURRENT TECHNOLOGIES

Nowadays, several technologies are used to data collection and generation of information on the state of the roads and traffic monitoring. Those systems can be classified according to the immediacy of data, completeness in the collection and intrusiveness (Martin et al., 2003).

According to the immediacy of data collection, systems are classified into direct data collection (the source obtains data experimentally), and indirect data collection (the data is obtained by further processing algorithms).

Taking into account the completeness of data collection, systems can be making nearly exhaustive (the number of measurements taken match the number of users), or non-exhaustive data collection (measurements related to a limited number of users are taken).

Finally, current monitoring technologies can be classified as intrusive technologies (installed in the pavement), not-intrusive technologies (no contact with the road, causing minimal effect on traffic flow), and floating vehicle technologies.

Figure 1 shows a classification of information systems according to the intrusiveness of the technology.

Main technologies currently used in traffic monitoring include pneumatic tubes, loop detectors, floating vehicles or automatic recognition systems, among others (Rodrigue et al., 2013).

Pneumatic tubes are placed on top of the lane to detect vehicles by the change in pressure generated when a vehicle passes over the tube. A device at the roadside counts vehicles. The main drawback is that its efficiency is subject to weather, temperature and traffic conditions.

A loop detector is a wire embedded into the roadway in a square configuration. A device at the roadside records the number of detected vehicles as they induce an electrical current when passing over the wire. Both the implementation and maintenance costs can be expensive.

The use of so-called floating vehicles consists on a vehicle provided with sensors to collect information while driving on a predefined route. This active device data collection is one of the most popular among operators of roads, used especially for the collection of travel time and for loop detector calibration. Depending on the level of automation in the data collection, the cost can vary.

The main disadvantage of these systems is that they are unable to identify detected vehicles, in order to obtain origin/destination matrixes. Just the number of vehicles and their type can be calculated, but does not allow to obtain traffic flow, nor to determine whether a certain vehicle passes repeatedly. In addition, their high cost makes it unprofitable covering secondary roads with them, so they are often located on major roads.

Finally, the automatic recognition technology has experienced an increase in recent years due to its ability to detect individual vehicles without relying on in-vehicle systems. Video image detection is a good example; in this case trip line and/ or tracking are used to record traffic data. Furthermore, they are used for automatic detection of

Figure 1. Information systems classification, according to the intrusiveness of the technology

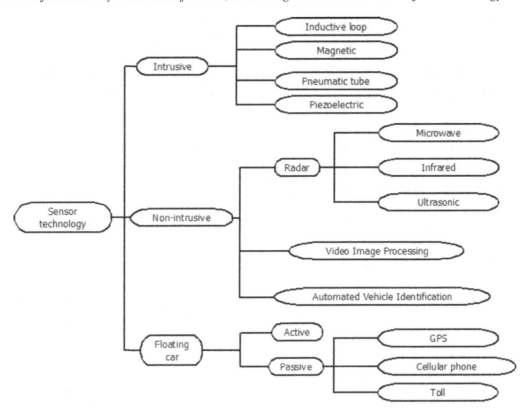

incidents on the road. That is the main advantage over previous information systems. However, system reliability might not be the best, as weather may limit accuracy. Moreover, these systems are very costly compared to the previous (Skszek et al., 2001). Finally, from a privacy point of view, the Spanish Data Protection Agency (*Agencia de Protección de Datos*) considers the car license plate as a personal data, so that it would require the user consent.

Commercial Products

There are different companies working in the traffic information area using approaches similar to the presented in this work:

- **Bit Carrier (Mendez, 2013; BitCarrier, 2013):** It offers a traffic management system based in BT to count people and commercial routes (pathsolver). Its technology

was deployed in highways managed by Abertis for traffic control and monitoring. Actually it has a 150 devices network in Catalonia, so it allows count the traffic times of 200.000 persons each day.

- **Trafficnow (Trafficnow, 2013):** Another BT system product. A pilot experience has been deployed in Vigo.
- **Traffax Inc (TraffaxInc, 2013):** It is a company that also has used BT for calculating origin-destination and transport time matrixes.
- **Savari Networks (SavariNetworks, 2013):** It offers the commercial product StreetWAVE for traffic monitoring to know in real time the traffic status.
- **TrafficCast (TrafficCast, 2013):** They have developed prediction models in different cities based on different technologies, such as cameras, BT and RFID included in the vehicles.

The proposal presented in this work has some common features with the previous approaches, offering similar functionalities with reduced cost.

OBJECTIVES AND EXPECTED RESULTS

The main objective was building a low-cost system to provide real-time information about the traffic status and flows that occur in a certain area, allowing to optimally manage motion decisions by citizens.

Thus, several features have been developed:

- **Data Collection Component:** It includes several sensors to continuously scanning and identifying BT devices. It uses a 3G connection to send data to the storage server. It is enclosed in hermetic boxes and uses a 220volt power line.
- **Data Processing Component:** It stores the obtained data, and offers some tools to serve them (through web services).
- **Information Service:** It provides the users the requested information related to the traffic status.

Six devices were installed for data collection. They send obtained data to servers for further data processing. Node locations are shown in the map on Figure 2. Locations were set according to the suggestions of DGT staff, looking for an adequate place, with a continuous flow of vehicles, and also taking into account the assembly difficulty of the monitoring devices.

A large amount of data corresponding to passing BT devices are collected, to populate a big database and to compute different statistics and indicators on the use of vehicles on the monitored area, driving habits and even the effect of important factors or events (key dates, nonworking days, etc).

Specifically, following statistics will be reported:

- Total amount of detected vehicles by every node.
- Total amount of detected vehicles in working days.
- Total amount of detected vehicles in non-working days.
- Number of times each vehicle is detected.
- Type of path the vehicles follow.
- Traffic density by time range and road type.
- Average speed in the road where two devices where set.

Data-Collecting Hardware Device

The first step of this study was to choose between several hardware devices to scan for BT devices. First tests were conducted on a PC with Linux and a BT module. This solution was quickly discarded because of its high size and power consumption (see Table 2).

Another possible solution studied was using Android cell phones. These are low power consumption devices, with high connectivity, highly available development tools and powerful processors.

A prototype application was developed for Android. The application was limited to three tasks: BT device discovery, BT identification and data sending to a server through its 3G connection. The server finally stored that information in a database. Both the Android application and its source code are available at:

- http://sipesca.ugr.es/download/descargas/sipesca_bt.apk.
- http://sipesca.ugr.es/download/descargas/com.pacv.bt.sipesca1__SRC.zip.

Despite the advantages of the cell phone, they include small and low power BT antennas. Because of that, their detection capability is very limited; thus, using cell phones was discarded.

Figure 2. Geographical node locations in the metropolitan area of Granada. Source http://bit.ly/SQdQkH

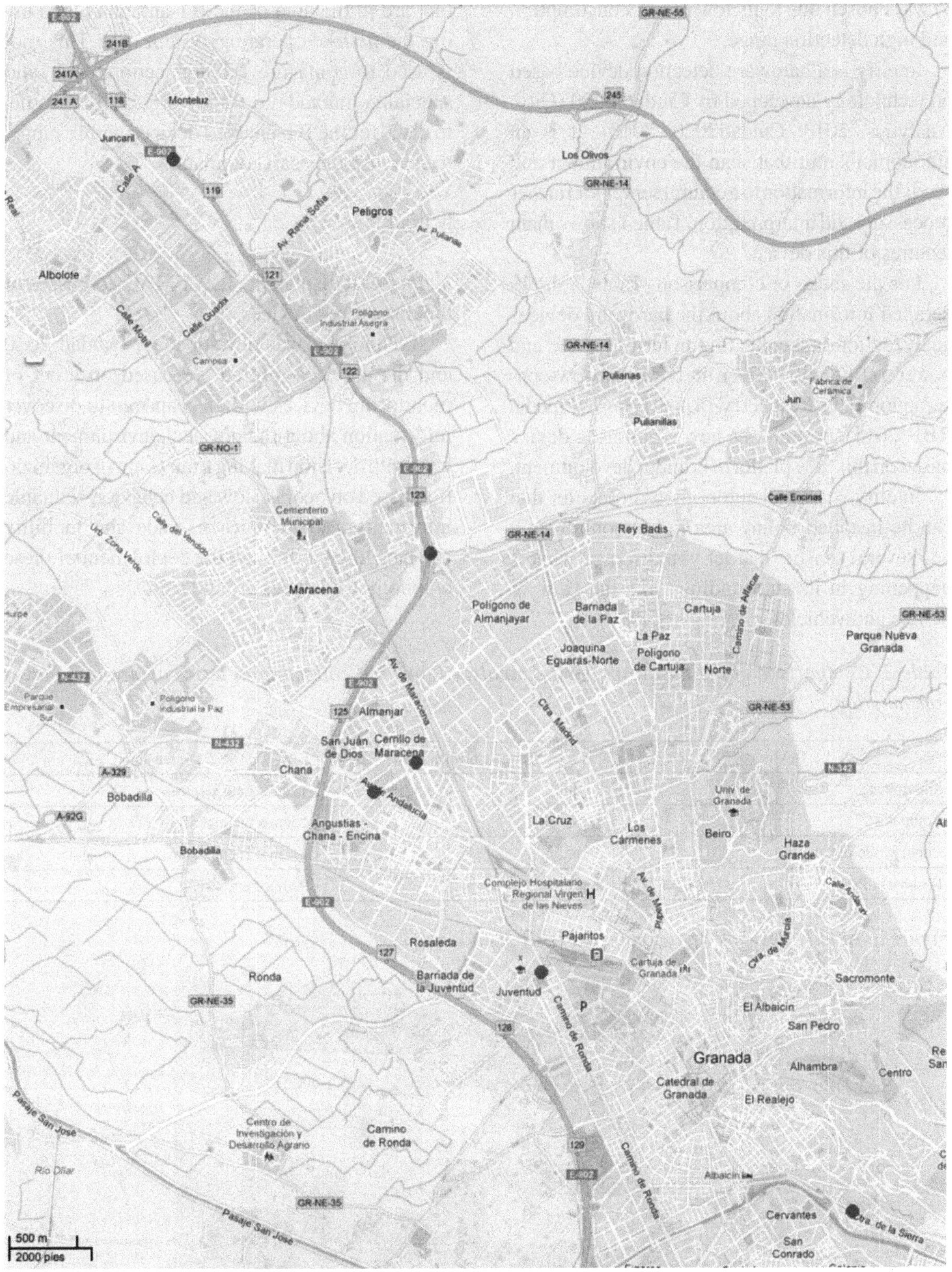

Finally the Intelify (Intelify, 2013) (see Figure 3) was chosen due to its low power consumption and high detection range.

Intelify is a hardware detection device based on technology developed by Ciudad 2020 (City-Analytics, 2013; Ciudad2020, 2013). It is an autonomous unit that scan the environment and sends the information to a central server for further processing and interpretation. Table 1 shows main features of this device.

For the shake of comparison, Table 2 shows detailed information about the hardware devices analyzed for data collecting in terms of size and power consumption. Given the power and low-consumption of the Raspberry-Pi platform (Wikipedia RBP, 2013), nowadays a new monitoring device based on this new platform is under development.

Intelify is a small autonomous computer that can be installed in any area to be monitored. It has several sensors that let you discover what is happening in its surroundings like the flow of people and vehicles.

Device operation is based on scanning devices that are in the area of the BT antenna range using the *hcitool* operating system tool. This tool is used to configure BT connections and send special commands to BT devices. For example, to discover the BT-enabled devices within range, we can use the scan command:

hcitool scan

hcitool will display the list of MAC addresses of the discovered devices.

Technology was developed by Ciudad 2020 and the services offered are based on a net of monitoring devices with the capacity to discover information about the physical environment and help with decision making to any kind of organization based on people flow and behavior. Valuable information about tourism, trade and mobility can be gathered through the deployment of these autonomous devices around a city.

Table 2. Comparison of the hardware devices analyzed for data collecting in terms of size and power consumption

Device	Power Consumption	Dimensions
Smartphone	6 watts	12cm x 6cm x 1cm
Computer	120 watts	25cm x 60cm x 57cm
Intelify (microPC-based)	8 watts	11cm x 16cm x 3cm
Raspberry-Pi	5 watts	9cm × 5cm x 1cm

Figure 3. Intelify device with a connected USB 3G dongle

Table 1. Main features of the Intelify device

Dimensions	113x163x30mm
LEDs	Power; 3G activity; Ethernet activity
Networking	Ethernet; Wireless; Bluetooth; 3G
USB ports	City Analytics Antenna; 3G dongle
Other ports	RS-232; VGA
Power	18v - 1200mA; external jack - 5.5mm; internal jack - 2.1mm
Network connections	Ethernet RJ45; 3G USB Modem
Antennas	City Analytics USB antenna; wireless antenna
Microphone	noise sensor
Temperature	main board temperature sensor with extrapolation
Box	1.5mm aluminum box; external use possible
Operating System	Debian 6.0 Squeeze

The cost of this solution is under $ 1000 per device, including remote maintenance, communications using a 3G service, storage and data management.

Data accuracy is very representative, as stated previously, having obtained an a priori error estimation of 8.5% of detections (Blobject, 2013).

Sharing Data and Information Using Web Services

To allow the integration with other systems, the Service Oriented Paradigm (Papazoglou et al., 2007; García-Sánchez et al., 2010) has been used. This paradigm allows the usage of available "service interfaces" (usually over Internet) to access to required information.

These interfaces allow the "service consumers" to interact "service implementations" with independence of the programming language or operating systems (Arsanjani et al., 2008; Castillo et al., 2012). Implementations can be changed and updated, allowing the interoperability and integration with other systems.

Whatever the technology used to deploy web services, they provide several advantages, like language independence and distribution mechanisms; it also increases the interoperability between different software elements (for example, it is possible to add communication libraries without modifying existing code), and facilitates code distribution (it is not required the use of a concrete implementation or library) among geographically distributed work teams (Castillo et al., 2013).

In this case, our platform uses Representational State Transfer (REST) web services (Fielding, 2000; Fielding et al., 2002; Vinoski, 2008), as this paradigm adheres much more closely to a web-based design. REST is an alternative method for building web services. This technology was proposed and defined by Roy Fielding (Fielding, 2000; Fielding et al., 2002). In a REST-style architecture, a client sends requests to the server who process them and return responses to the client. Requests and responses represent resources that can be addressed by an Uniform resource identifier (URI). Usually, resources are documents or programs the client need to access to.

REST web services are simple and lightweight (as no extra XML markup is needed), their message format is readable by humans, they are easy to build, and finally, developments achieve a high performance (Daigneau, 2011).

Developed services have been designed to extract/insert information in the database taking into account security and availability requirements. The implementation of this part of the system is being performed using Google web services, specifically Google Fusion Tables (Gonzalez et al., 2010; Gonzalez et al., 2010; Gonzalez et al., 2010) to serve information to end users. Thus, we ensure the availability of information to users, and at the same time we reduce our server load. This way, users can access our database with an extra layer of security and management (instead accessing the database directly).

This mechanism, and therefore allowing the usage of our system data by third parties, will facilitate the easy creation of web pages and mobile apps to serve useful information to the users.

In this sense, a cross-platform mobile application to allow users access any kind of data using computers, mobile phones and tablets is under development. Figure 4 shows several screenshots of this application. Both the application and its source code are available at:

- http://sipesca.ugr.es/download/descargas/sipesca_info.apk
- http://sipesca.ugr.es/download/descargas/com.pacv.info.sipesca1__SRC.zip

DATA ANALISYS

In this section the analysis of collected data during the monitoring period (November 8 to December 9, 2012) to obtain statistics and so study the use of vehicles is carried out.

Specifically, the following subsections report information about the total number of detected vehicles by each node, on weekdays or holidays, information on traffic density by time range and the average speed on a section delimited by two consecutive nodes.

Figure 4. Screenshots of the Android application developed to serve information to the users

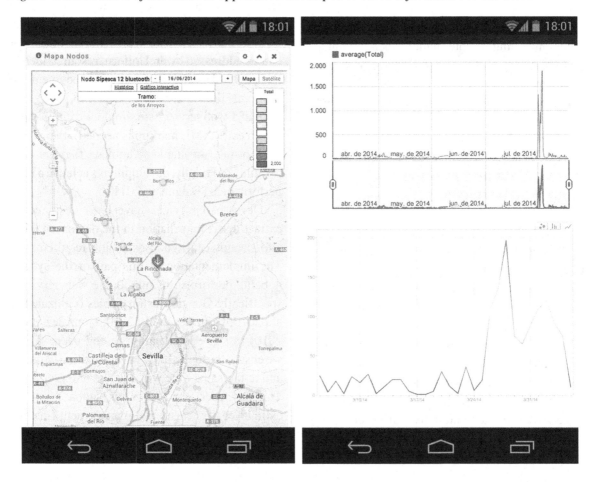

Total Number of Detected Vehicles (in Weekdays and Holidays)

The first analysis consisted in calculating the number of detected devices per node.

About 773845 BT devices have been detected in total. As shown in Table 3, nodes located in the Sierra Nevada Highway (A44, nodes 4 and 5) have collected a higher amount of data, while the node located in a side street (node 6) has detected the smallest amount of devices.

Total Detected Vehicles in Non-Working Days

To compare the traffic intensity between working and non-working days, the number of passes in holidays and non-working days have been obtained.

Table 4 shows how the number of detected devices is reduced in all nodes in non-working days, compared to the number of detections in

Table 3. Number of BT detected devices per node

Node Id.	Number of Detected Devices
1	31408
2	45032
3	33165
4	358494
5	297874
6	7872

Table 4. Total number of BT detected devices per node (only in non-working days)

Node Id.	Number of Detected Devices
1	2149
2	2804
3	2832
4	32182
5	24166
6	1269

weekdays. Nodes located in the Sierra Nevada Highway still collected much more data than the remainder, due to the traffic this road supports on holidays.

Traffic Density on the Road by Time Range

Traffic density can be calculated taking into account the total number of detected devices by time range.

Figure 5 shows the number of individual detected devices in each node along the day and taking into account six time-ranges.

As can be seen, a high density on all nodes is reached at peak times (7:00 to 10:00 and 16:00 to 20:00).

This might be due to the people going/returning to/from work and school, and those who are in leisure time.

This figure shows individual devices, eliminating repeated appearances of vehicles.

Total Detections by Time Range

Additionally we can calculate for each node the number of detected devices by time range, without differentiating whether the device is the same or not (repeated passes). In this case, repeated appearances of vehicles have been taken into account (Figure 6).

Figure 6 shows the total number of detected devices in each node along the day and taking into account six time-ranges. As in previous analysis (Figure 5), a high density on all nodes is reached at peak times (7:00 to 10:00 and 16:00 to 20:00).

Number of Individual Vehicle Detections

We can take advantage of the proposed system's ability to identify BT devices. Thus, it can detect and report whether a vehicle pass by different nodes.

Figure 5. For each node, the total number of different detected devices by time range is shown. Figure is shown in logarithmic scale.

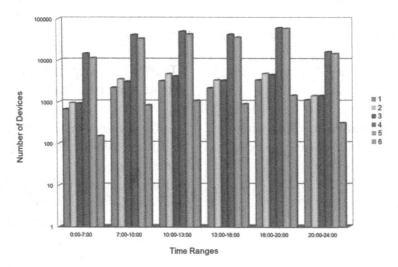

Figure 6. For each of the six nodes, the total number of detected devices by time range is shown. Figure is shown in logarithmic scale.

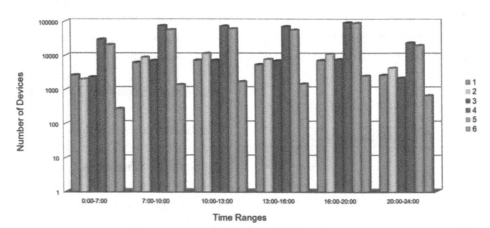

This figure displays how many times an individual device has been detected in each node, i.e., if device A has been detected three times in node 4, then A is shown into the range ">0 & <=5" for node 4.

Figure 7 shows a large number of vehicles that pass repeated times (up to 10 times) by some of the nodes (mainly those located in the A44). Even, it can be seen that nodes 4 and 5 detect about 1,000 vehicles passing more than 25 times repeatedly, what means that many vehicles repeat their pass over and over again. Paying attention to the remainder nodes, over 25 repetitions of the same device have been detected only around 120 times.

Finally, as most of the devices have been detected only one time, then the first range (">0 & <=5") includes the largest number of detected devices.

Complexity of Displacements

To study the complexity of displacements, the number of vehicles that have sequentially visited several nodes were calculated. Table 5 also shows the average number of times that vehicles have visited 2, 3, 4, 5 or 6 nodes.

Information in Table 5 is shown in Figure 8.

As expected, most of the BT devices rarely visited all nodes sequentially, while most of devices pass only by one or two of nodes (their displacements are focused on a small part of the monitored area).

Average Speed on a Section Delimited by Two Consecutive Nodes

Finally, taking two consecutive nodes located on the A44 highway, average speeds in the section bounded by nodes 4 (located at km 119.550) and 5 (located at km 123.250) can be calculated. This highway section where the study takes place is 3700 meters long. Actually, we can calculate the average speed in the global section, but not the instant vehicle speed within that section (shown in Table 6).

Figure 7. For each of the six nodes, the total number of detected devices N times (repeated occurrences of the same device) are shown. Figure is shown in logarithmic scale.

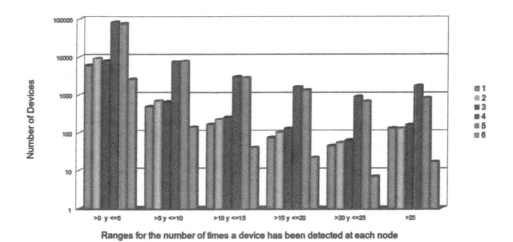

Figure 8. Complexity of displacements as the number of vehicles that have visited several nodes. Figure is shown in logarithmic scale.

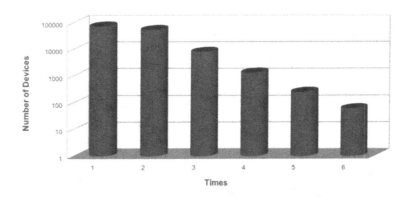

Table 5. Total number of vehicles that have visited two nodes, 3 nodes and up to 6 nodes, and average number of times that vehicles have passed through 2, 3, 4, 5 or 6 nodes. In some cases the deviations are high due to the fact that some devices have a very high number of occurrences for some nodes.

Number of Nodes	Number of Devices	Total Number of Passes	Mean ± Std. Dev.
1	72989	165033	2.26 ±31.16
2	53947	425667	7.89 ± 11.48
3	8125	131570	16.19 ± 24.71
4	1359	39241	28.88 ± 140.82
5	254	8603	33.87 ± 59.51
6	61	3731	61.16 ± 94.78

In that section, the speed is limited to 100 km/h. As can be seen, although most of the vehicles respect this limit, a lot of them exceed this limitation.

In the other hand, this analysis has allowed us to detect slow traffic and even jams. In a near future, mobile application users could receive alerts in case of traffic events. Additionally, the information system is configured to store the exact time when a device is first detected and the exact time when it is no longer detectable. Thus, if a device is detected for a time longer than a specified number of seconds, that means slow traffic.

FUTURE RESEARCH DIRECTIONS

Among future improvements to the system, as hardware device, one based on the architecture of Raspberry-Pi will be used, as it is more energy efficient and cheaper. Thus, reducing costs installing new nodes is expected. The hardware team may perform this hardware device evolution and migration to the new model with minimal effort and independently of the software development team.

Additionally, the mobile application to serve information will be improved, allowing users to receive, not only numeric and graphic data, but also alerts on traffic events, such as slow traffic.

Several future research lines have been opened. They are mainly focused on processing the collected data using data mining algorithms (Hastie

Table 6. Average speeds (globally) in the section bounded by nodes 4 and 5

Speed Range (km/h)	Number of Passes
v≤60	1495
60<v≤70	2585
70<v≤80	7421
80<v≤90	16339
90<v≤100	20144
100<v≤120	14384
120<v≤140	5434
v≥140	1326

et al., 2009), evolutionary computation methods (Eiben et al., 2003; Michalewicz et al., 2004; Yang et al., 2010), artificial neural networks (Castillo et al., 2001; Rivas et al., 2003; Castillo et al., 2007), machine learning models (Arenas et al., 2005) and statistical methods (Jiawei et al., 2006; Hill et al., 2007; Nisbet et al., 2009), which will be included and integrated as web services (Papazoglou et al., 2007; Garcia-Sanchez et al., 2007) in the system.

A critical task that any new intelligent transportation system should face is short-term traffic flow prediction. Thus, our purpose is to develop in the future a prediction system that helps to make decisions, and able to apply knowledge in applications related to mobility. In this sense, different time series prediction methods will be used in order to estimate the vehicle passing. Time series forecasting is usually tackled trying to find out an underlying model that describes the series behaviour. Our system will test a variety of methods and include some of them to perform forecast, using both linear and nonlinear models (Brown, 1959; Winters, 1960; Box et al., 1976; Tong et al., 1978; Qiu et al., 2011; Wang, 2011; Rivas et al., 2004).

It is expected that the development and deployment of these systems will offer a set of information services with added value that can not be achieved with current technologies.

CONCLUSION

The information systems currently used for collecting data about the road conditions are not able to identify detected vehicles, and if they do, these information systems have a high cost.

In this chapter a new low-cost information system to monitor traffic on different road types and in real time has been presented.

The main goal was getting exposure indicators using a new system based on the BT devices detection using several collecting nodes. This way, both the traffic density and car journeys have been monitored, identifying the vehicles when they move from one node to another inside the monitored zone.

Moreover, different hardware solutions have been studied to carry out device detection; some of them have been rejected due to their high prices,

due to their energy inefficiency or due to their short-range for detection.

In this study, different road types, with different traffic type have been taken into account. Statistical data have also been obtained grouped by days of the week and hours of day.

Several statistics of the collected data have been calculated during the monitoring period (November 8th to December 9th, 2012). Specifically, the total number of BT detected devices by each node has been analyzed, on holidays or working days. We also have analyzed the traffic density by time range, and the journeys in the monitored zone. As a final analysis, the average speed on a highway section delimited by two consecutive nodes has been obtained, allowing us to detect slow traffic.

Finally, the power and features of the system have been demonstrated. This has been complemented by developing a set of web services based on Google Fusion Tables for easy access to the data in real time, including different statistics.

ACKNOWLEDGMENT

This work is supported in part by the 0100DGT21285 project of the Spanish Dirección General de Tráfico, and the FEDER of European Union project *"Sistema de Información y Predicción de bajo coste y autónomo para conocer el Estado de las Carreteras en tiempo real mediante dispositivos distribuidos – SIPEsCa – G-GI3000/IDIF"* (*Programa Operativo FEDER de Andalucía*

Figure 9. Research supporters

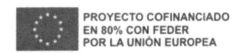

2007-2013). We also thank all Agency of Public Works of Andalusia Regional Government staff and researchers for their dedication and professionalism. The authors are very grateful to the anonymous referees whose comments and suggestions have contributed to improve this chapter.

REFERENCES

Arenas, M. G., Castillo, P. A., Romero, G., Rateb, F., & Merelo, J. J. (2005). Coevolving multilayer perceptrons along training sets. In Proceedings of Advances in Soft Computing: 8th Fuzzy Days, (pp. 503-513). Academic Press.

Arsanjani, A., Ghosh, S., Allam, A., Abdollah, T., Ganapathy, S., & Holley, K. (2008). SOMA: A method for developing service-oriented solutions. *IBM Systems Journal*, *47*(3), 377–396. doi:10.1147/sj.473.0377

BitCarrier. (2013). *BitCarrier*. Retrieved Dec 30, 2013, from http://www.bitcarrier.com/

Blobject. (2013). *CityAnalytics: Statistical Study*. Retrieved Nov 20, 2013, from http://bit.ly/TtnmLn

Box, G., & Jenkins, G. (1976). *Time series analysis: forecasting and control*. San Francisco: Holden Day.

Brown, R. (1959). *Statistical forecasting for inventory control*. New York: McGraw-Hill.

Castillo, P. A., Arenas, M. G., Castellano, J. G., Cillero, M., Merelo, J. J., & Prieto, A. et al. (2001). Function approximation with evolved multilayer perceptrons. In N. E. Mastorakis (Ed.), *Advances in Neural Networks and Applications. Artificial Intelligence Series* (pp. 195–200). Tenerife, Spain: Published by World Scientific and Engineering Society Press.

Castillo, P. A., Arenas, M. G., García-Sánchez, P., Merelo, J. J., & Bernier, J. L. (2012). Distributed Evolutionary Computation using SOAP and REST Web Services. Advances in Intelligent Modeling and Simulation. In J. Kolodziej, S. U. Khan, & T. Burczynski (Eds.), Artificial Intelligence-Based Models and Techniques in Scalable Computing. Series: Studies in Computational Intelligence (Vol. 422, pp. 89–112). Academic Press.

Castillo, P. A., García-Sánchez, P., Arenas, M. G., Mora, A. M., Romero, G., & Merelo, J. J. (2013). Using SOAP and REST web services as communication protocol for distributed evolutionary computation. *International Journal of Computers & Technology*, *10*(6), 1659-1677.

Castillo, P. A., Merelo, J. J., Arenas, M. G., & Romero, G. (2007). Comparing evolutionary hybrid systems for design and optimization of multilayer perceptron structure along training parameters. *Information Sciences*, *177*, 2884–2905. doi:10.1016/j.ins.2007.02.021

CityAnalytics. (2013). *CityAnalytics*. Retrieved Nov 20, 2013, from http://www.cityanalytics.net/?act=faq

Ciudad2020. (2013). *Ciudad2020: Blobject S.L.* Retrieved Nov 20, 2013, from http://www.cityanalytics.net/?act=nosotros

Daigneau, R. (2011). *Service Design Patterns: Fundamental Design Solutions for SOAP/WSDL and RESTful Web Services*. Westford, MA: Addison-Wesley Professional.

Eiben, A. E., & Smith, J. E. (2003). *Introduction to Evolutionary Computing*. Berlin, Heidelberg: Springer-Verlag. doi:10.1007/978-3-662-05094-1

Fielding, R. T. (2000). *Architectural Styles and the Design of Network-based Software Architectures*. (Doctoral dissertation). University of California, Irvine, CA.

Fielding, R. T., & Taylor, R. N. (2002). Principled Design of the Modern Web Architecture. *ACM Transactions on Internet Technology, 2* (2), 115-150.

García-Sánchez, P., González, J., Castillo, P. A., Merelo, J. J., Mora, A. M., Laredo, J. L. J., & Arenas, M. G. (2010). A distributed service oriented framework for metaheuristics using a public standard. *Studies in Computational Intelligence, 284,* 211–222.

García-Sánchez, P., Merelo, J. J., Sevilla, J. P., Castillo, P. A., Martín, M., & López, M. (2007). Plataforma de integración de servicios para la administración basada en BPEL y SOA. In *Actas de las III Jornadas en Servicios Web Y Soa (JSWEB 2007),* (pp. 111-118). Thomsom Editores Spain S. A.

Gonzalez, H., Halevy, A. Y., Jensen, C. S., Madhavan, J., Langen, A., Shapley, R., & Shen, W. (2010) Google Fusion Tables: Data Management, Integration and Collaboration in the Cloud. In *Proceedings of the First ACM Symposium on Cloud Computing, Industrial Track, SoCC2010,* (pp. 175-180). ACM.

Gonzalez, H., Halevy, A. Y., Langen, A., Madhavan, J., McChesney, R., & Shapley, R. et al. (2010). Socialising Data with Google Fusion Tables. *IEEE Data Eng. Bull., 33*(3), 25–32.

Han, J., & Kamber, M. (2006). *Data Mining: Concepts and Techniques* (2nd ed.). San Francisco, CA: Morgan Kaufmann.

Hastie, T., Tibshirani, R., & Friedman, J. (2009). *The Elements of Statistical Learning: Data Mining, Inference, and Prediction* (2nd ed.). Stanford, CA: Springer Series in Statistics. doi:10.1007/978-0-387-84858-7

Hill, T., & Lewick, P. (2007). *STATISTICS Methods and Applications.* StatSoft.

IEEE BT. (2013). *The IEEE public BT OUI listing.* Retrieved Dec 30, 2013, from http://standards. ieee.org/develop/regauth/oui/oui.txt

Intelify. (2013). *Intelify: Do it social: CityAnalytics.* Retrieved Nov 20, 2013, from http://www. intelify.net

Martin, P. T., Feng, Y., & Wang, X. (2003). *Detector Technology Evaluation. Technical Report.* Utah Transportation Centre.

Mendez, F. (2013). *System and method for monitoring people and/or vehicles in urban environments.* US Patent Application No: 2011/0128,127. Serial no 13/56,068. Retrieved Nov 30, 2013, from http://www.google.com/patents/US20110128127

Michalewicz, Z., & Fogel, D. B. (2004). *How to Solve It: Modern Heuristics. 2 Edition.* Berlin, Heidelberg: Springer-Verlag. doi:10.1007/978-3-662-07807-5

Nisbet, R., Elder, J., & Miner, G. (2009). *Handbook of Statistical Analysis and Data Mining Applications.* Waltham, MA: Academic Press.

Papazoglou, M., & van den Heuvel, W. (2007). Service oriented architectures: approaches, technologies and research issues. *The VLDB Journal, 16,* 389–415. doi:10.1007/s00778-007-0044-3

Papazoglou, M. P., & Van Den Heuvel, W. (2007). Service oriented architectures: Approaches, technologies and research issues. *The VLDB Journal, 16*(3), 389–415. doi:10.1007/s00778-007-0044-3

Qiu, W., Liu, X., & Li, H. (2011). A generalized method for forecasting based on fuzzy time series. *Expert Systems with Applications, 38*(8), 10446–10453. doi:10.1016/j.eswa.2011.02.096

Rivas, V., Merelo, J., Castillo, P., Arenas, M., & Castellano, J. (2004). Evolving RBF neural networks for time-series forecasting with EvRBF. *Information Sciences, 165*(3-4), 207–220. doi:10.1016/j.ins.2003.09.025

Rivas, V. M., Merelo, J. J., Rojas, I., Romero, G., Castillo, P. A., & Carpio, J. (2003). Evolving 2-dimensional fuzzy systems. *Fuzzy Sets and Systems*, *138*(1), 381–398. doi:10.1016/S0165-0114(02)00483-9

Rodrigue, J. P., Comtois, C., & Slack, B. (2013). *The Geography of Transport Systems* (3rd ed.). New York: Routledge.

SavariNetworks. (2013). *SavariNetworks*. Retrieved Dec 30, 2013, from http://www.savari-networks.com/index.html

Skszek, S. L. (2001). *State-of-the-Art Report on Non-traditional Traffic Counting Methods*. Report FHWA-AZ-01-503. Phoenix, AZ: Arizona Department of Transportation.

Tong, H. (1978). On a threshold model. In C. Chen (Ed.), *Pattern Recognition and Signal Processing: NATO ASI Series E: Applied Sc.(29)* (pp. 575–586). Netherlands: Sijthoff & Noordhoff. doi:10.1007/978-94-009-9941-1_24

TraffaxInc. (2013). *TraffaxInc*. Retrieved Dec 30, 2013, from http://www.traffaxinc.com/

TrafficCast. (2013). *TrafficCast*. Retrieved Dec 30, 2013, from http://trafficcast.com/products/

Trafficnow (2013). *Trafficnow*. Retrieved Dec 30, 2013, from http://www.trafficnow.eu/es

Vinoski, S. (2008). Serendipitous reuse. *IEEE Internet Computing*, *12*(1), 84–87. doi:10.1109/MIC.2008.20

Wang, C. (2011). A comparison study between fuzzy time series model and arima model for forecasting Taiwan export. *Expert Systems with Applications*, *38*(8), 9296–9304. doi:10.1016/j.eswa.2011.01.015

Organizationally Unique Identifier. (2013). In *Wikipedia*. Retrieved Dec 30, 2013, from http://en.wikipedia.org/wiki/Organizationally_unique_identifier

Raspberry Pi. (2013). In *Wikipedia*. Retrieved Dec 30, 2013, from http://en.wikipedia.org/wiki/Raspberry_Pi

Winters, P. (1960). Forecasting sales by exponentially weighted moving averages. *Management Science*, *6*(3), 324–342. doi:10.1287/mnsc.6.3.324

Yang, X. S. (2010). *Nature-Inspired Metaheuristic Algorithms* (2nd ed.). Frome, UK: Luniver Press.

ADDITIONAL READING

Ahas, R. (2010). Mobile positioning in mobility studies. In M. Büscher, J. Urry, & K. Witchger (Eds.), *Mobile Methods* (pp. 183–199). London: Routledge.

Ahas, R., & Mark, Ü. (2005). Location based services - new challenges for planning and public administration? *Futures*, *37*, 547–561. doi:10.1016/j.futures.2004.10.012

Ahas, R., Silm, S., Järv, O., Saluveer, E., & Tiru, M. (2010). Using Mobile Positioning Data to Model Locations Meaningful to Users of Mobile Phones. *Journal of Urban Technology*, *17*(1), 3–27. doi:10.1080/10630731003597306

Arnott, R., Rave, T., & Schöb, R. (2005). *Alleviating urban traffic congestion* (p. 250). Cambridge: MIT Press.

Astarita, V., Bertini, R. L., d'Elia, S., & Guido, G. (2006). Motorway traffic parameter estimation from mobile phone counts. *European Journal of Operational Research*, *175*, 1435–1446. doi:10.1016/j.ejor.2005.02.020

Brian, M. (2013). *Smart trash can knows how fast you walk and which smartphone you use*. The Verge. Retrieved August 9, 2013 http://www.theverge.com/2013/8/9/4604980/smart-uk-trash-cans-smartphone-speed-proximity-wifi

Cabeio, C. R. (2013). *Smart Cities, un sector con gran potencial de crecimiento. Magazine ActiBva.* Retrieved 14 de agosto de 2013. http://www.actibva.com/magazine/mas-que-economia/smart-cities-un-sector-con-gran-potencial-de-crecimiento

Calabrese, F., Colonna, M., Lovisolo, P., Parata, D., & Ratti, C. (2011). Real-Time Urban Monitoring Using Cell Phones: A Case Study in Rome. *IEEE Transactions on Intelligent Transportation Systems, 12*(1), 141–151. doi:10.1109/TITS.2010.2074196

Friedrich, M., Immisch, K., Jehlicka, P., Otterstätter, T., & Schlaich, J. (2010). Generating Origin-Destination Matrices from Mobile Phone Trajectories. *Transportation Research Record, 2196*(1), 93–101. doi:10.3141/2196-10

Gonzalez, H., Halevy, A. Y., Langen, A., Madhavan, J., McChesney, R., Shapley, R., et al. (2010). Google Fusion Tables: Web-Centered Data Management and Collaboration. In *Proceedings of the 2010 ACM SIGMOD International Conference on Management of data, SIGMOD2010,* pages 1061-1066, ACM New York, NY, USA, ISBN: 978-1-4503-0032-2

Göppert, J., & Rosenstiel, W. (1997). The continuous interpolating self-organizing map. *Neural Processing Letters, 5,* 185–192. doi:10.1023/A:1009694727439

Groth, D., & Skandier, T. (2005). *Network+ Study Guide* (4th ed.). Alameda, CA: Sybex, Inc.

HCITOOL man page. (2014). *Linux System Administration.* Retrieved Jan 7 2014. http://linux-command.org/man_pages/hcitool1.html

Järv, O., Ahas, R., Saluveer, E., Derudder, B., & Witlox, F. (2012). *Mobile Phones in a Traffic Flow: A Geographical Perspective to Evening Rush Hour Traffic Analysis Using Call Detail Records. PLoS ONE 7(11): e49171* (R. Lambiotte, Ed.). Belgium: University of Namur.

Kumapley, R. (2002). Updating Procedures to Estimate and Forecast Vehicle-Miles Traveled, *Final Report,* FHWA/IN/JTRP-2002/10, Purdue University, December 2002. http://docs.lib.purdue.edu/jtrp/214

Kwan, M. P. (2002). Time, Information Technologies, and the Geographies of Everyday Life. *Urban Geography, 23*(1), 471–482. doi:10.2747/0272-3638.23.5.471

Leduc, G. (2008). Road Traffic Data: Collection Methods and Applications. *Working Papers on Energy, Transport and Climate Change.* Available: ftp.jrc.es/EURdoc/JRC47967.TN.pdf

Luque-Baena, R. M., López-Rubio, E., Domínguez, E., Palomo, E. J., & Jerez, J. M. (2013). *A Self-organizing Map for Traffic Flow Monitoring. In 12th International Work-Conference on Artificial Neural Networks* (pp. 458–466). Berlin, Heidelberg: Springer-Verlag.

OECD. (2007). Managing urban traffic congestion. OECD, European Conference of Ministers of Transport, Transport Research Centre. Paris: OECD. pp. 294

Parras, E., Arenas, M. G., Rivas, V. M., & del Jesus, M. J. (2012). Coevolution of lags and RBFNs for time series forecasting: L-Co-R algorithm. *Soft Computing, 16*(6), 919–942. doi:10.1007/s00500-011-0784-2

Parras, E., del Jesus, M. J., Merelo, J. J., & Rivas, V. M. (2008). A Symbiotic CHC Co-evolutionary Algorithm for Automatic RBF Neural Networks Design. In *Proceedings of International Symposium on Distributed Computing and Artificial Intelligence 2008 (DCAI 2008). Advances in Soft Computing* Volume 50, 2009, pp 663-671

Parras, E., Rivas, V., & del Jesus, M. J. (2009). E-tsRBF: Preliminary Results on the Simultaneous Determination of Time-Lags and Parameters of Radial Basis Function Neural Networks for Time Series Forecasting. In *Proceedings of International Conference on Intelligent Systems Design and Applications* (pp.1445-1449). Los Alamitos, CA, USA: IEEE Computer Society.

Parras, E., & Rivas, V. M. (2010). Time series forecasting: Automatic determination of lags and radial basis neural networks for a changing horizon environment. *Proceedings of, IJCNN2010*, 1–7. doi: doi:10.1109/IJCNN.2010.5596797

Parry, I. W. H. (2002). Comparing the efficiency of alternative policies for reducing traffic congestion. *Journal of Public Economics*, 85(1), 333–362. doi:10.1016/S0047-2727(00)00163-8

Shastry, A. C. Gen. Electr. Global Res., Bangalore, India; Schowengerdt, R.A. (2005). Airborne video registration and traffic-flow parameter estimation. *IEEE Transactions on Intelligent Transportation Systems Volume:6*, Issue:4, pp. 391-405 ISSN 1524-9050. DOI 10.1109/TITS.2005.858621

STMicroelectronics. (2014). *STLinux*. Retrieved Jan 7 2014. http://www.stlinux.com/kernel/bluetooth/how-to-run-BlueZ

Stolfi, D. H., & Alba, E. (2013). Red Swarm: smart mobility in cities with EAS. In *Proceeding of the fifteenth annual conference on Genetic and evolutionary computation conference (GECCO13)*, Christian Blum (Ed.). ACM, New York, NY, USA, 1373-1380. DOI= doi:10.1145/2463372.2463540

Van Nuffel, N. (2007). Determination of the Number of Significant Flows in Origin–Destination Specific Analysis: The Case of Commuting in Flanders. *Regional Studies*, 41(1), 509–524. doi:10.1080/00343400701281808

Walter, J., & Ritter, H. (1996). Rapid learning with parametrized self-organizing maps. *Neurocomputing*, 12, 131–153. doi:10.1016/0925-2312(95)00117-4

Wikipedia Traffic Count. (2014). *Traffic Count*. Retrieved May 20, 2014, from http://en.wikipedia.org/wiki/Traffic_count

KEY TERMS AND DEFINITIONS

3G Connection: Or 3G, short for third Generation, is the third generation of mobile telecommunications technology.

Android: Operating system based on the Linux kernel and designed primarily for touchscreen mobile devices such as smartphones and tablet computers.

Artificial Neural Networks: Computational models inspired by the brain that are capable of machine learning and pattern recognition.

Bluetooth (BT): wireless technology standard for exchanging data over short distances (using short-wavelength microwave transmissions in the band from 2400–2480 MHz).

Data Mining: Interdisciplinary subfield of computer science. It is the computational process of discovering patterns in large data sets

Database: Organized collection of data.

DGT: Spanish Dirección General de Tráfico (Spanish Traffic Agency).

Encryption: The process of encoding messages (or information) in such a way that only authorized parties can read it.

Evolutionary Computation: Subfield of artificial intelligence (more particularly computational intelligence) that involves continuous optimization and combinatorial optimization problems.

Floating Vehicles: Technology to determine the traffic speed on the road network.

Google Fusion Tables: Web service provided by Google for data management. Data is stored in multiple tables that Internet users can view and download.

Hcitool: operating system tool used to configure BT connections and send special commands to BT devices.

Intelify: Bluetooth and wireless detection technology, developed by Bloject.

Loop Detectors: Electromagnetic communication or detection system which uses a moving magnet to induce an electrical current in a nearby wire. Inductive-loop traffic detectors, can detect vehicles passing or arriving at a certain point

MAC Address: Unique identifier assigned to network interfaces for communications on the physical network segment.

Machine Learning: Branch of artificial intelligence, concerns the construction and study of systems that can learn from data.

Monitoring: Using a monitor or measuring device to be aware of the state of a system (in this work, the traffic).

Pneumatic Tubes: Detection system placed on top of the lane to detect vehicles by the change in pressure generated when a vehicle passes over the tube.

Prediction System: Estimation of some variable of interest at some specified future date. Usually it is based on statistical and time series forecasting methods.

Raspberry-Pi: Small single-board computer developed in the UK by the Raspberry Pi Foundation with the intention of promoting the teaching of basic computer science in schools.

Representational State Transfer (REST) Web Services: Architectural style applied to the development of web services.

Storage Server: Shared storage of computer files that can be accessed by the computers that are attached to the network.

Time Series Forecasting: The use of a model to predict future values based on previously observed values.

Traffic Density: Concentration as the number of vehicles over a stretch of roadway (in units of vehicles per kilometer).

Traffic Flow: The study of the movement of individual drivers and vehicles and the interactions they make with one another.

Transit Indicators: Statistics and figures about the use of vehicles by the population of the monitored area.

URI (Uniform Resource Identifier): String of characters used to identify a name of a web resource.

Web Service: Method of communications between two electronic devices over the World Wide Web.

Wireless Device: Some kind of device that are not connected by an electrical conductor to another.

XML: Extensible Markup Language is a markup language that defines a set of rules for encoding documents in a format that is both human-readable and machine-readable.

Chapter 17
Mission Critical Embedded System Development Process:
An Industry Perspective

Stefano Genolini
TXT e-solutions, Italy

Matteo Crippa
TXT e-solutions, Italy

ABSTRACT

While analyzing currently available international research about embedded system development, it seems that as the complexity of embedded systems is continuously increasing, the major problems regarding their development remain always the same: vague requirements, insufficient time to develop, lack of resources, and complexity management. With the focus on the development process, it is shown, with examples coming from 20 years of experience, the industry perspective of a company managing such problems by adopting a consolidated set of good practices.

INTRODUCTION

Whilst a general-purpose computer, such as a personal computer (PC), is designed to be flexible and to meet a wide range of end-user needs, an embedded system is a computer system designed for specific control functions within a larger system, often with real-time computing constraints. Development of embedded software applications is becoming more and more complicated due to the increasing richness of features that are required to be managed.

An international on-line research[1] about embedded systems development conducted a periodic survey in 2012 by contacting industry developers; and presented a periodic report summarizing the major topics in embedded development industry. According to this research the most critical issues perceived by embedded software developers are:

- Incomplete or vague requirements (63%).
- Insufficient time for development (45%).
- Insufficient resources (41%).
- Design complexity (41%).

DOI: 10.4018/978-1-4666-6194-3.ch017

What is interesting to note is that, during the last several years, the major problems always remain the same: vague requirements, insufficient time to develop, lack of resources, management of system complexity, among others.

It is thus possible to argue that:

- Vague and incomplete requirements and design complexity are the consequence of increasing complexity of targeted applications;
- Insufficient time is the consequence of reduced time to market;
- Insufficient resources are the consequence of reduced budgets.

Complexity, time to market and costs issues together with development process are analyzed in the sections below:

COMPLEXITY

In recent years, complexity of embedded systems has continuously increased and is foreseen to augment more exponentially, as our lives are becoming integrated to a vast and complex ecosystem of embedded devices and part of an interconnected world. For example in the automotive domain, in a car, the number of communicating on-board computers or Engine Control Units (ECU), according to the car model, may be more than 100 in number. Maintaining connectivity between present ECUs is thus becoming an essential aspect in automotive domain, and this has led to more complex applications being developed, new user experiences for UI being created and new protocols being managed.

Of course, the overall design strategy has to also take into account issues such as related to quality, security, safety and, overall design costs.

TIME TO MARKET

Time to market for car model manufacturers (but this applies also to majority of application domains) forces them to stress reusability across cars variant. Reusability equally implies modularity in the solutions (both hardware and software), software portability on different platforms, adoption of Customized of the Shelf Components (COTS), customization of features, configurability, etc.

COSTS

Budget constraints also force to implement the same features with less effort. This can be managed by adopting a more structured way to operate, such as: enforcing reusability, adopting all-inclusive process development tools, adopting process development models in order to obtain better processes and better product quality and training personnel to better achieve their objectives.

All of these critical factors need to be managed together. Solving only one does not bring sensible advantages, but surely a structured (formalized) way to behave during the development can enforce a proper way to proceed. This is the reason that we introduce, subsequently in this chapter, the development process as the key factor to support a cost effective and quality based approach to development of embedded systems.

DEVELOPMENT PROCESS

In software production the process has been analyzed many times leading to different solutions and specific best practices. This is part of the history and the intent of this chapter is not to choose which is the best or create new process ideas.

In embedded systems the development process has always had a special role: what are the reasons for this? It is certain that certification constraints for safety critical systems are one of the possible reasons, but also because there is a need to coordinate hardware and software interdependence, a problem that leads to SysML (OMG, 2012), as well as the need to categorize, address and satisfy non-functional requirements. That at the end is one of the intentions of the MARTE profile (OMG, 2011b).

It is not purpose of the chapter to introduce the better process to be adopted for embedded development. The idea is to focus on a "canonic" process and to provide indications coming from the experience of more than 20 years of development in embedded systems: in particular onboard avionics developed with a RTCA DO-178B compliant process.

The intention is to show some examples about what is important to take into account setting up an embedded system development process, having already a precise idea of what is a software development process. The main concept is to demonstrate that embedded systems are like house of cards in which there is not a single unique important card: software and hardware cooperate to the fulfillment of requirements both functional and non-functional; if either the software or the hardware has a problem, the whole system will fail; the process is the glue that finds the point of balance.

Furthermore what will be discussed is the observability of the system: are the system designers doing a good job? Is the work in line with the schedule? Are any changes needed to meet the goals? Setting up a process has a meaning if it is measurable; thus useful metrics shall be evaluated according to proper thresholds and such threshold shall be refined according to previous projects history, application domains, project criticality, etc.. Examples of adopted metrics will be provided to understand how they can help to be aware of the development activities progress, and how they can warn about critical situations in earlier stage of development in order to have time to put in place corrective actions.

Finally, examples on how correlation of outputs from different process development phases can help improving software reusability, reducing risks and hardware dependencies. It will be illustrate that sometime what is considered a useless waste of effort due to certification constraints, can in fact be used as an advantage.

As explained in the introduction, this is not a methodological paper: we do not introduce any new methodology or any results of research (even if we quote some of them); our goal is to draw on the basis of our experience, a picture of system development process emphasizing good practices and common weaknesses, knowing that system complexity is growing year after year, making it more and more difficult to catch future opportunities.

With this aim, in the very first part of this chapter, we describe who we are and what we do, to tell where our experience came from initially. After this quick introduction, we analyze key points of the development process, and then from section *System Specification Phase*, we put the focus on the most critical phases of development, from system specification up to verification. At the end we point out some conclusions with an industry perspective.

TXT E-SOLUTIONS

TXT is an international software product and solutions vendor that has an extensive capability to implement autonomously highly critical systems for large customers that operate in critical domains, such as Aerospace & Defense industry.

Follows a brief, not comprehensive, summary of the most significant capabilities:

- For a large number of years, TXT has been developing for its customers important parts of aircraft on board flight management and mission systems. Based on Ada language and UML methodology, the full development life cycle is supported, starting from customer requirements until verification and validation (functional and structural testing). A complete model based approach is adopted supporting complex de-facto standards such as RTCA-DO178B/C.

- For the automotive domain, TXT implements the vehicle functions for on-board body computers and executes V&V activities adopting the Model Based Engineering approach.

- TXT is also involved in development of ground systems tools like training systems (from CBT to full flight simulators) and Flight and Mission Planning and Maintenance stations (ARINC 424, RTCA-DO200) (RTCA, 2013).

- TXT implements Digital Manufacturing support systems: a rich set of tools to support the management, planning, scheduling and execution of activity related to manufacturing of complex systems, such as aircraft production.

TXT leverages on thirty-years of experience in the development of mission critical projects in Aerospace & Defense and High Tech Industries, such as Avionics, Automotive, Telco, Industry and Medical domains. This kind of expertise and the continuous improvement attitude, allows TXT to take advantage of modern and consolidated methods and technologies in order to be more efficient and effective, while being able to stay profitable.

MANAGING CRITICAL FACTORS DURING DEVELOPMENT

From the statements above, it is possible to argue that the most critical factors software development may encounter can be summarized as: managing complexity, respect timing and satisfy budget constraints.

Figure 1. Company logo

Figure 2: Activities, resources, methods

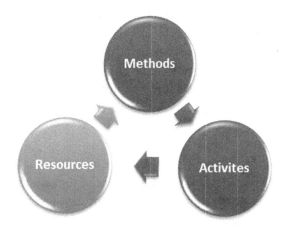

Development Process: Activities, Resources, Methods

The development process consists of a set of steps to be conducted for the realization of a product or software system, within predefined time and with the required levels of quality. The process consists of tasks (activities) executed by persons belonging to the organization using appropriated tools (resources) by respecting certain rules (methods).

Methods: Are the rules the organization selects in order to structure and monitor the development process with the objective to make it more efficient and with monitored levels of quality.

Activities: Are the set of tasks that shall be executed in order to develop the product.

Resources: Are the participants in the organization and the set of tools the organization adopted to support the execution of tasks.

If an organization runs several projects per year, then to be able to guarantee their correct accomplishment, a suitable *software factory* shall be put in place. The software factory can be defined as "a software product line" that configures extensive tools, processes, and content using a software factory template based on a software factory schema, in order to automate the development and maintenance of variants of an archetypical product by adapting, assembling, and configuring framework-based components. Such a software factory shall be tailored according to the project needs (such as: project size, project criticality, application domain, etc.).

Standards

Many models are available to measure the maturity of the organization in terms of software development process. By adopting a well-defined model and deriving a structured and managed development process, an organization may improve the quality of its products and execute its activities on time and on budget.

There are models which are quite general, such as ISO 9001:2008, that apply to many organizational processes (production, HR, purchasing, sales, etc.); others are well suited to software development such as CMMI.

Specific industries have their own models, for example:

- ISO15504 (SPICE), ISO 26262 for automotive.
- MIL-STD-498 (or J-STD-016 or ISO/IEC 12207), RTCA-DO-178B/C, EN9100 for avionics.
- CEI EN 62304, Part 11 for medical devices.
- IEC 61508, EN50128 for transportation.

Development vs. Critical Factors

For the development process the appropriate software development lifecycle model shall be selected. Many selection criteria can be adopted according to: project criticalities, skills, company organization, customer needs, etc. In the following text, no specific development lifecycle is considered, to be most generic as possible. All considerations can be applied when using a plain old Waterfall model or a more effective Agile model.

The major development phases to achieve this are considered:

- **System Specification:** Definition of the requirements, (both hardware and software). The system to be developed shall satisfy these requirements.
- **Solution Definition:** Establish the decomposition of the application (defining the architecture) the system under development shall support in order to handle the defined requirements.
- **Coding:** Implementation of the defined design using the selected programming language.
- **Verification and Validation:** Demonstrating that developed system conforms to specified requirements. In this phase testing is particularly stressed, additional verification activities are not taken into consideration in this context.

The development critical factors are therefore matched with the above development phases that can be considered part of a hypothetical development lifecycle.

For each process phase the following questions arise: How to monitor the development process? How to understand if operations are proceeding correctly? Are the organization objectives properly matched? Which tools can be adopted in order to evaluate how proceeding?

A common way to answer these questions is to establish a way to objectively evaluate the ongoing process. This is typically achieved by the adoption of indicators (metrics) that allow the analysis of the current situation and the understanding of the behavior in the near future (trend) in order to prevent erroneous conditions and to be able to take corrective actions in time.

In this chapter the minimal set of metrics that allow taking in control the complexity and ongoing activities are considered for each specific development phase. Metrics shall be defined according to the business objectives that the organization or project requires. Typical goals may be: to be able to respect timing in delivery of results, to match the budget forecast, to provide robust products, to maximize customer satisfaction, reduce time to market, etc.

According to the major goals the organization intends to satisfy, projects shall be monitored stressing specific issues, such as: cost expenditure, defect rate, delivery date, etc. In the same time, according to the customers and market, the appropriate life cycle shall be selected accordingly. For example if requirements are well specified, known and approved, then a waterfall like model could be easier to manage; however if requirements are not specified or customer often changes his mind, then an incremental approach is suggested; if requirements are in evolution, timing is strict, delivery is mandatory, then an Agile approach could be ideal.

In the next sections, for each specific development phase, a limited amount of metrics is suggested in order to take the work under control and be able to prevent wrong conditions.

System Specification Phase

This phase deals with requirement definition & management. Requirement definition analyzes user needs and develops user requirements, and consists of the following steps:

1. Elicitation: it consists of the most creative phase where user needs are collected and evaluated with the end users in order to detect all features to be implemented. This phase is quite critical for the success of the whole project and shall be led by domain experts. The main steps to be followed are:

a. Detection of actors and their roles within the operation of the application under definition. Actors may be humans or computer based system to interact with, or a set of services to be used.

b. Decomposition in parts of the system under definition (this can be considered as a very high level architecture), each part contains a set of capabilities that the system shall support.

c. Definition of the workflow among detected parts, understanding the data exchange.

d. Definition of the main purposes of each part in terms of major features to be supported.

All these steps shall be conducted by means of interviews, questionnaires, meetings, etc.; sketching high level hypothesis about system decomposition.

2. Definition: after the initial brainstorming with end users, things need to be slightly formalized. Use case scenarios are a useful mean to draw down in a comprehensible way the decomposition and behavior of the system. The end user is required to participate, at least in reviewing the use cases.

The two steps above need to be iterated until the required knowledge about the system under development is reached. Unfortunately there is not a clear defined statement that can decide that, the experience of the participants and their ability to extract all needed information, plays a fundamental role. There are two ways to continue:

- Adopt the scenarios as the base requirements (taking into account that scenarios normally cover only the major/critical cases) and start to develop the system based on these scenarios.

413

- Refine the scenarios into a more formal requirement document, detailing deeply all features.

3. Management: during the project lifetime, requirements drive the development (overall during the initial phases). Management aims to be able, at each instant in the development process, to know the status of requirements, for example: which are under development, by whom, their status (under development, completed, suspended, deleted, etc.). A requirement, to be further processed (developed) shall be accepted. This means it shall satisfy at least the following:

   a. A requirement shall be: readable, complete, consistent, not ambiguous, identified, traceable, implementable and verifiable.

   b. A useful tool to manage requirement is the traceability matrix: Traceability is the degree to which a relationship can be established between two or more products of the development process. The minimal trace supports where a requirement has been implemented (subsystem, module, procedure, the granularity depending on the importance of the information) and tested (test sequence, test case, etc.) and vice versa (bidirectional matrix).

4. Approval: what has been defined in terms of requirements is recommended to be approved by the stakeholders (customer key figures). Even if this may seem obvious, it is not always so simple because this implies a direct take of responsibility by the customer. A way to mitigate this point is to adopt an incremental approach to process development, in order to reduce the impact

of decisions: having decomposed the system under development in smaller parts. Each one can be developed in continuous refinements, reducing the risk of erroneous interpretations and making the development more under control. As consequence, the four identified steps need to be iterated at each refinement and this lead to the conclusion that requirement definition is not an activity that is done only at the beginning of the project development but it is conducted incrementally until the whole system is completely specified.

Beside user needs, it is useful to also describe interface and hardware requirements. This is particularly true for embedded systems where the hardware aspects are fundamental for the correct behavior of the final application. Aspects related to accessing to devices can introduce aspect related to timing, (mutual) usage of resources, concurrency, portability, etc. Furthermore, the adoption of multicore CPUs, which more and more used in embedded systems, can introduce other aspects like real parallelism, data exchange and multitasking/multiprocessing.

Last but not least, it is important to consider non-functional requirements. If the correct implementation of functional requirements is surely important, it is the proper implementation of non-functional requirements that makes the project successful. For example if the application perfectly handles a button click on a user interface but the response takes much more than expected, such application will be hard to be accepted by the end users.

It is very important to take into account non-functional requirements from the early stage of the project. They shall be considered and referenced in the requirement document as well, in order to be taken into account during implementation and to be evaluated during the V&V activities. A set of non-functional requirements is described in the ISO-9127, such as related to robustness, portability, performance, maintainability, reliability, etc. Of course the most important requirements for the application under development shall be considered.

If UML is the notation used to model the system under development, it is suggested to consider a global UML based approach by adopting SysML for the description of the system. SysML stands for System Modeling Language, a general purpose modeling notation for systems engineering applications (OMG SysML v1.3 issued in June 2012).

One of the criticisms of the UML notation is its software-centric view: UML is a well suited notation that describes precisely the software point of view of the system; UML is thus a very nice representation of the design view of a system but lacks to capture the essential "engineering" concepts.

SysML introduces two new diagrams with respect to UML, to capture the information: requirements and parameters. These are exactly what has been described previously in the chapter: the first one captures the requirements with all their relationships (refinements, details), allowing to define the functional and interface aspects. The second one is related to the non-functional requirements adding quantitative constraint, like performance, timing, etc.; to be taken into account also during the test phase.

The adoption of SysML enables to model the system architecture based on "Model-Based Systems Engineering" approach. Its notation is simpler than UML (having reduced the number of diagrams involved), but nevertheless maintain coherence among diagrams in a unique and clear notation that can be shared and understood by engineers, and not only software engineers.

A further construct provided by SysML is the allocation table. It allows correlating of various kinds of relationships between model elements. This is useful for V&V activities to follow elements in order to check completeness of activities. SysML also visualizes both hardware and software

components by means of the block diagram and this can be very important for developing an embedded system. Blocks can furthermore be decomposed by means of Internal Block diagrams. This allows a decomposition of the system from an engineering perspective.

SysML and UML can be used together. System engineers use SysML for requirements and system analysis, and the software engineers use UML for Software Design. This allows a unique notation and a graceful transition from the engineering to software views.

There are few essential metrics that can be useful when managing requirements:

- **Requirement Weight:** Assigning a weight – a number from 1(easy) to N (critical) – to detect complexity of each requirement is useful to understand where the process currently is. Common sense criteria can be defined to assign the weight, for example based on requirement size (description number of lines), involved actors, involved requirements, implicit not functional requirement, etc. It is important to adopt the same ranking mechanism within the project in order to make values really comparable. For this reason, it is suggested to appoint a requirement that is able to assign properly weights in a uniform way within the project.
- **Requirement Volatility:** Counting the number of changes a requirement has been modified is a useful metric to understand how good is the system specification phase. If the number of changes is too high, then a particular attention shall be paid on this phase and needs to be evaluated: consider involved persons (training needs?), analyze customer attitude on changes (need to involve higher level stakeholders?), the process is appropriated? (Change formalism, include specific reviews, formal or peer reviews), etc.

Solution Definition

In the embedded systems development, a particular attention shall be paid to the design phase: it is difficult, sometimes impossible, to describe with two separate levels: hardware and software, the system under development. The embedded system is a house of cards made of two cards, if you take out a card the building will not stay up anymore and will fall.

Divide et impera strategy could be a way to take under control the complexity of the system, but no indication is provided about how to divide the system: it seems natural to make a first cut at the separation between software and hardware. However, this is not always possible or convenient for embedded systems.

An example is the management of power consumption: hardware (with technologies as Intel SpeedStep and AMD Cool'n'Quiet) and software may cooperate to achieve optimal performance and consumption: but the system level requirements should be allocated to both.

Another classic example concerns the opportunity to delay allocation of specific functions to software or hardware, with the intent to choose the better strategy later on when the coding activities are almost completed. Let us think about an image acquisition system requiring MPEG compression: the designer can choose to compress the video stream by means of a hardware implemented codec, or in software writing the code or integrating a specific library.

The possibility to delay such decisions could be a good way for designers to catch opportunities not available at design time, that will have great effects on costs and time to market.

SysML is, in our opinion, a way to manage the peculiarities of embedded systems. The hardware/software holistic approach of MADES, described within the research perspective section of this book, confirms this, allowing one unique description approach and unique language for both hardware and software, modeling system and design requirements, with the capability of linking each item with relations like "refine", "satisfy" and "allocate" at any level of system description.

The difference emerging from the two examples above is the type of implemented requirements; the distinction between functional and non-functional requirements. MARTE extends SysML in this direction.

This distinction, often very subtle, underlies a set of non-functional properties such as:

- Maximum weight (for portable systems),
- Battery stand-by time,
- Battery use time,
- Electromagnetic compatibility (EMC),
- Robustness,
- Ingress Protection Rating (IP),
- Temperature range of operations.

SysML provides notations to describe the system and defines requirements, along with hardware and software decomposition, and gives the possibility to model items and trace relations between items, becoming the unique repository for most of process items.

It is important and central to our discussion to emphasize that SysML is a language and not a methodology, and the latter cannot be ignored: even by using SysML diagrams and views, it is not assured that the model will be correct and detailed enough to describe the system.

The aim of this chapter is not to embrace a specific method but to provide hints that can be tailored to the proper method. We firmly believe it is important to detail the software development process according to the peculiarity of the organization having in charge the development, the customer attitude, the external rules mandatory to follow (certification steps). It is also appreciated that the development process is well documented and agreed by all the actors of the whole process.

We assume the design standard should always be defined by an organization in order to describe how to operate, even when not explicitly required by a specific regulation. This document shall detail how the design will be made and the limits and constraints on it; for an extensible language like UML and SysML, the usage of all stereotypes shall be detailed.

A design standard should not be a simple list of all the allowed and denied features but, usually, shall contain all the methodological aspects related to the use of features: *when*, *what* and *how*. For example, it shall say that relations between classes are modeled inside class diagrams but it shall also detail where class diagrams will be used inside the design and which relations they will represent.

In fact, when projects are particularly large, class diagrams are overcrowded with relations, enclosing all the possible links between classes giving information is sometimes confusing or unusable. A trivial rule is to impose to detail, with a textual description, what will be represented inside the diagram and what is the intent of this view, before beginning to insert classes inside and draw relationships. This description is part of the documentation as well. This rule of common sense is valid not only for class diagrams, but has a general value for all the overall structure of the design.

A good description should:

- Make specific what is the aim of the diagram,
- Adopt in the diagram only the relationships (hierarchy, inclusion, dependency) that are meaningful for the purpose of the diagram,
- Create several views if different relationships shall be described; allow, by means of hyperlinks, to relate the views to each other, providing a full figure of the design.

Last but not least, the textual description for each item (diagram, class, method, etc.) is always needed and this should also be pointed out in the design standard.

The design standard remains the most important means to impose the process to follow the methodology adapted to the organization needs. By using a jurisprudential metaphor, if the methodology is the law, the design standard is the implementing rule.

Coding

Model based development, model-driven approach and automatic code generation leads to a new point of view on the coding phase where code is generated automatically from a design notation. But, where the manual coding phase is still present, and nowadays this is the general case, it is important to impose the correct use of the programming language construct.

In case there is a separation of roles between programmers and designers; the design decisions shall be shared with programmers, so that the programmer will not try to force the design to his understanding, but he will let the architecture guide him, finalizing what has already being drawn in design.

In this context, a good way to assure a smooth transition is to require participation of programmers to design review, which is a good rule as it being placed before the coding phase, so that programmers could participate in the critical analysis of the design and in the mean time they will agree and find the explanation of all choices determining the architecture.

A design review is suggested to be better placed before the beginning of the coding phase, even when not explicitly required for certification aspects. It shall be executed and a report should indicate corrective actions to be carried out as soon as possible, according to project timescale.

The coding phase is probably the most critical because it builds the product. Therefore, several aspects have to be considered defining the coding rules in order to adopt: structured programming languages (C++, Ada, Java, etc.), compilers, strict coding rules (MISRA C, SPARK), use of static analyzer, etc. All these considerations shall be placed in a specific Coding Standard. This document shall detail:

- The programming language and the constraints for its usage;
- All the allowed and prohibited statements;
- Naming convention regarding classes, attributes, methods, parameters and types;
- The style, and the language of the remarks;

To us, it is also important to introduce some constraints to avoid a bad programming style:

- A limit to the maximum number of SLOC for each method;
- A limit to the complexity of each method;
- Maximum number of methods for each class.

In order to make the coding phase efficient, specific training shall be put in place to share coding standard rules.

Verification

The verification phase? Managers see it as a useless extra effort, developer as a boring activity, project manager as a task to be shortened when the development is late. In the verification phase, all work products and outputs of all phases of the development life cycle are analyzed in order to check their correctness. Peer and/or formal reviews are normally used; however, when the work product is the source code additional verification steps should include static code analysis, functional testing and structural testing.

The Verification phase is one of the most important as it is needed to demonstrate the system maturity and quality. If executed correctly it can be useful to get information on future improvements of the system as well. Many quotes of Barry Boehm (Boehm, 1986) are aimed at underlining the exponentially rising cost of a bug; according to in which phase of the development life cycle is raised: the later the bug is detected, the more effort is required to correct it.

Technology has improved the way testing can be done: software (SIL) or hardware (HIL) in the loop, virtual target environments, simulators/emulators, model based testing, automatic scaffolding creation, etc.; all of these are just examples, more critical is the system under test more testing strategies could be put in place, even combining some of these available techniques.

Each test result indicating a possible defect should be evaluated carefully; all the information shall be collected, organized and saved as history base. Information related to a test result may include at least the following:

- Requirements baseline,
- Version of the software, version of the hardware,
- Actions performed, expected results, observed results,
- System impact (severity),
- Defect type classification (wrong specification, software bug, hardware problem, interface problem, wrong test, etc.).

To have an indication about how testing activity is proceeding, it is necessary to surely collect the number of defects. It is the basic ingredient for more complex metrics such as: defect density (with respect to SLOC) and defect impact (with respect to effort spent in correct it). No engineering tool can indicate how many test sequences need to be defined to completely verify your system; the structural test and code coverage may provide indications: test until all statements are executed; anyway, if the system is not critical you should at least test all the decisions expressed, explicitly or implicitly, in requirements.

A simple rule of thumb, pointed out by Capers Jones and Christof Ebert (Ebert & Jones 2009), says that the potential number of defects for an embedded application can be computed based on its size. If you find a particular lower number of defects, probably it will not be due to an excellent coding but to a poor verification phase.

In the same publication, the authors agreed that the complexity of embedded systems is continuously growing, indicating a grow rate between 10% and 30% per year: in a brutal oversimplification considering function points growing linearly with complexity of the system and assuming a 20% average trend of growth of complexity, industry should increase its budget for verification by 25% each year. Please note that the budget allocated to verification phase is 30% to 40% of the complete project costs; hence you can imagine how big this effort is for industry.

A chance to avoid costs increase is to invest on reusable scaffolding, automatic testing and verification technology. In any case, industry has to think about investing on verification phase.

Development Monitoring

During the development several questions arise: How can we force developers to pay attention carefully to the selected methodology? How to understand the trend and the progress of the development?

For all these questions, it is possible to answer with actions, tools and, especially, with a continuous monitoring of the process. All these questions can be summarized in "how can I verify that the work is proceeding in the good way, with the right timing and effort expenditure?"

Management of the process is not easy and, as previously explained, a bad monitoring of the process can yield unsuccessful results. Monitoring shall be performed based on objectives and measurable information; this leads to the ability to measure your process by means of metrics and how to analyze them. If the selected metrics are complicated to collect, it may happen that the obtained values are altered by errors introduced during their computation (clumsy metrics produce misunderstanding), collection and evaluation.

A motto from tools vendors saying: "the easiest manner to enforce a policy is to make it the most comfortable way to do things".

It means metrics shall be computed as part of the normal activity, there should not be a point of verification nor it should be urged by a request. Tools can greatly help in metric computation; the right development tool chain can make metric collection and computation really straightforward.

Finally the set of metrics can be enriched progressively. It is suggested to initially define very few metrics, but be able to measure progress of your activities, and start to adopt them. Having gained experience on initial set of metrics, it is possible to refine it adding further indicators. But, it should be remembered that the important thing is: metrics shall "describe" your process; metrics shall characterize your product.

We will mention some metrics in this chapter that can be used for assessment of the design and coding phases; this set is just a proposal of the most common and trivial metrics taken to explain their usage: more complex (and more specific for your lifecycle) metrics should be arranged relating, where possible, items/work products coming from different phases.

There are different ways to read and evaluate metrics; two opposite methods are: historical comparison and incremental interpretation. The former is the classic way of using metrics, compute the value of the metric and compare it with the historical data referred to the average of the same metric coming from similar projects; the latter is based on a continuous monitoring of the process through the computation of metrics and evaluation of the trend: where the curve has an inflection point or it changes the trend. It is thus necessary to understand what is happening to the process.

Taking as an example the coding phase and simply monitoring the daily production of SLOC: the average SLOC/days of all developers is supposed to grow (thanks to learning and familiarization at the beginning), up to a value that more or less becomes stable (average production); when this value decrease you have to suppose something not right is happening:

- Your team have a problem understanding requirements;
- Your programmers have difficulties with the given design;
- Your programmers have an issue with the interfaces;
- Your team has reached a good level of completion of the implementation.

Figure 3 shows the trend of the SLOC/day with respect to the completion in percentage of the development. Figure 4 shows details of the Figure 3 showing a possible problem between week 55 and 65 to be taken under consideration.

Intercepting problem allows taking immediate actions to understand and correct them. Of course SLOC/days is a quite simple metric that tells nothing about the quality of code; it is just a matter of productivity. For large development teams, it can be used to understand progress of activity. The metric is really easy to manage daily and does not introduce any overhead to the team for its computation and evaluation.

Figure 3. SLOC/day diagram and its trend

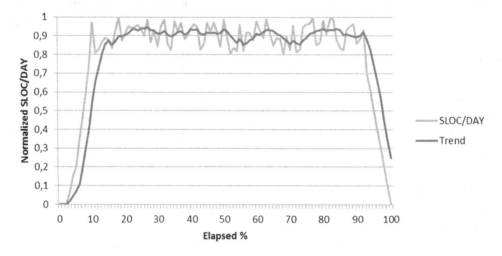

Figure 4. SLOC/day diagram detail

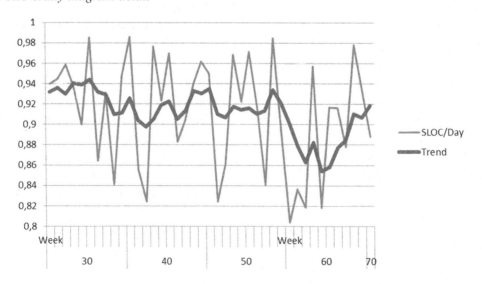

Metrics act through the whole process and are valid tools trying to detect, as earlier as possible, problems and errors; this fact has important implications concerning development duration and costs as frequently stressed by Barry Boehm's works. Other well-known metrics that allow evaluating code and design are conditional complexity of methods, number of methods for each class and number of SLOC for each method. This metric is related to the code quality and respect of coding standards.

With reference to these quantitative measures, a useful suggestion is to perform a code review on all the items belonging to the top 5-10% of their statistical distribution: if a class has a method with too many lines of code it may indicate a poor design or implementation of too much functionality which leads to difficulties during testing. In any case these are the parts of the system that require attention.

According to the Verification phase the followings are indicators of system maturity:

- The number of SLOC per defect (the mean value of SLOC for each one),
- The number of problems related to requirements or design or coding,
- The absolute number of defects for each software components.

These are just initial indications that need to be tailored according to the selected development life cycle, application domain, organization policies about quality, etc. Finally monitoring has to be related to the whole development process and should also consider requirements, traceability and documentation. A metric to be useful shall have an associated threshold. Overcoming the threshold requires attention from process owner and forces the owner to take corrective actions.

A basic metric like SLOC or number of defect is not a proper metric. It is difficult to put threshold on a SLOC value. But SLOC per module or per procedure can be a valid metric and meaningful threshold can be put in place. Establishing the right threshold is difficult and can be a long process, starting initially from vague values and then tuning the values while gaining knowledge of the process.

CONCLUSION

Purpose of this chapter is to outline the major development phases to be taken under control in order to accomplish successful projects. Adoption of a suitable methodology for the development is absolutely important, but after the selection it shall be customized by the organization and described in proper design/code of practices. For project management it is useful to collect indicators that can contribute to objectively understand the current development status, having as major purpose to estimate near future trends. If metrics give you the indication you are in trouble, then it is too late: you have to correct the situation and this could cost a lot because you may not at all have the possibility to carry out the modifications. If the metric foresees a negative trend you should have still time to correct and manage the situation in time. Of course, collecting data for metrics computation could introduce additional efforts in the process. The suggestion is to start with few indicators from each phase. The important thing is that they shall be:

- Representative of the process you have put in place,
- Able to provide useful indications to manage the process,
- Easy to compute, at least integrating your factory with tools that compute the metric values with a minimal effort from developers,
- Easy to understand and do not require many effort to combine them to obtain high level representation (such as graphical indication of trends),

- Having this information available it is easier to take the right decision because of better monitoring of the development cycle.

This is useful not only to correct possible problems but also to understand if and where lacks in specific development phases are present, if persons and tools involved in the development are really working in the proper way. This is the base for establishing a continuous process improvement activity within normal operations which is the standard for modern and successful organizations. The results of the survey indicated at the beginning of this chapter show how problems in development still remain the same, moreover, embedded system are becoming more and more complex: the challenge for industry is to look back for lessons learned (some of them detailed in this book chapter) and to look at the future investing in new methodologies and technologies. In fact, in one of the chapters of this book, the MADES approach is presented; which intends to provide the proper answers to the problems highlighted in terms of methodology and tools.

REFERENCES

ARINC. (2011) *ARINC Specification for Navigation System Database (ARINC 424-20)*. Retrieved from https://www.arinc.com/cf/store/documentlist.cfm

AUTOSAR. (2013). *Autosar Automotive 4.1*. Retrieved from http://www.autosar.org

Boehm, B. (1986). *Understanding and controlling software costs*. Center for Systems and Software Engineering, University of Southern California. Retrieved from http://csse.usc.edu/csse/TECHRPTS/1986/usccse86-501/usccse86-501.pdf

Brooks, F. P. (1975). The mythical man-month. In Essays on Software Engineering. Reading, MA: Addison-Wesley Publishing Company.

Ebert, C., & Jones, C. (2009, April). Embedded software: Facts, figures and futurE. *Computer Magazine, 42*(4), 42–52. doi:10.1109/MC.2009.118

ISO. (2008). *System and software engineering (ISO/IEC 12207)*. Retrieved from http://www.iso.org

ISO. (2012). *Road Vehicles Functional Safety (ISO 26262)*. Retrieved from http://www.iso.org

OMG. (2011a). *Unified Modeling Language (UML)*. Retrieved from http://www.omg.org/spec/UML/2.4.1/PDF

OMG. (2011b). *Modeling and Analysis of Real-time and Embedded system (MARTE)*. Retrieved from http://www.omg.org/spec/MARTE/1.1/PDF

OMG. (2012). *System Modeling Language (SysML)*. Retrieved from http://www.omg.org/spec/SysML/1.3/PDF

RTCA. (2013). *Software Considerations in Airborne System and Equipment Certification (DO178C)*. Retrieved from http://www.rtca.org http://www.rtca.org/documents

KEY TERMS AND DEFINITIONS

ARINC 424-20: ARINC Specification of Navigation System Database for avionics.

Autosar: AUTomotive Open System ARchitecture is a worldwide development partnership of car manufacturers, suppliers and other companies from the electronics, semiconductor and software industry.

HIL: Hardware in the loop is a specific technique used to develop and test embedded system by using the complete plant simulated or real.

IEC 61508: It is an international safety standard document adopted by industry; it is titled "Functional Safety of Electrical/Electronic/Programmable Electronic Safety-related Systems"

ISO 26262: Is a standard definition document with the title "Road Vehicles – Functional Safety" defining functional safety standard to be adopted in Automotive.

ISO/IEC 12207: is an international standard definition document "Systems and software engineering -- Software life cycle processes" that define different tasks needed to develop and maintain software.

MADES: Is a Specific Targeted Research Project (STREP) of the Seventh Framework Program for research and technological development of the European Community that aims to develop a holistic, model-driven approach to improve the current practice in the development of embedded systems.

MARTE: The OMG Modeling and Analysis of Real-Time and Embedded Systems™ is a specification of a UML® profile that adds capabilities to UML for model-driven development of Real Time and Embedded Systems (RTES).

MIL-STD-498: It is a military standard adopted by the Department of Defense to standardize software development and its documentation.

RTCA DO-178B(C); EUROCAE ED-12B(C): Are equivalent standard definition documents (edited in issue B and C) with the title "Software Considerations in Airborne Systems and Equipment" Certification issued from RTCA (for U.S.) and EUROCAE (for European Community) that are the most common means of compliancy for civil avionic systems.

SIL: Software in the loop is a specific technique used to develop and test embedded system by inserting the software in the complete control loop.

SysML: The OMG systems Modeling Language™ is a general-purpose graphical modeling language for specifying, analyzing, designing, and verifying complex systems that may include hardware, software, information, personnel, procedures, and facilities.

UML: The Unified Modeling Language™ is OMG's most-used specification, and the way the world models not only application structure, behavior, and architecture, but also business process and data structure.

ENDNOTES

[1]   Editor American Technology International, Inc. 2012

Chapter 18
Framework–Based Debugging for Embedded Systems

Gokhan Tanyeri
Clarinox Technologies Pty Ltd

Trish Messiter
Clarinox Technologies Pty Ltd

Paul Beckett
RMIT University, Australia

ABSTRACT

Debugging embedded systems is almost guaranteed to cause headaches. Embedded systems, and especially portable embedded systems, are becoming increasingly complex and have unique constraints that make them hard to debug. Traditional static debugging tools provided by the embedded development tool chains are important but are only part of the story. Time-dependant issues cannot be debugged by such tools. Embedded environments have to provide efficient mechanisms for managing a range of issues such as thread interaction, control of timers, semaphores and mutexes, IPC message passing, event handling, and finite-state machine organizations. This chapter looks at issues of escalating complexity in modern heterogeneous embedded systems and their impact on debugging techniques and advocates a framework approach to manage this complexity. Using the ClarinoxSoftFrame® Suite framework as an illustrative example, this chapter describes how a modular and open approach to debugging can aid the rapid development of robust wireless-enabled embedded systems that employ a variety of operating systems and platforms. The overall objective in this type of approach is to leverage prebuilt code infrastructure plus existing development skills as much as possible, thereby avoiding the need for engineering staff to learn and re-learn a range of compilers, operating systems, and the like. Overall, debug time can be greatly reduced by improved visibility into the complex interactions between cooperating processes within the code. Collateral benefits can include a reduction in the size of the necessary development team with a reduction in skills specialization.

DOI: 10.4018/978-1-4666-6194-3.ch018

INTRODUCTION

A recent industry survey of embedded systems designers (UBM Tech, 2013) found that more than half the respondents were involved in debugging hardware and/or software and they spent nearly a quarter of their development time on test and debug (see also: (Cadene, 2013)). When the survey asked the question: "If you could improve one thing about your embedded design activities, what would it be?", debugging tools came out on top as one of the most important – equal to compilers and/or assemblers. This is hardly a surprise. Tools for test and debug have been the single most requested area of improvement in embedded design support for many years (Nass, Sept 2, 2007).

Of course, the scope of the debugging process is much more wide-spread than just embedded systems software. However, embedded systems and particularly portable systems are becoming increasingly complex and more often than not have unique constraints which make them hard to debug. In contrast to general purpose computer software design, a primary characteristic of embedded environments is the sheer number of different platforms available to the developers, encompassing CPU architectures, vendors, operating systems and their variants. Embedded systems are, by definition, not general-purpose designs. They are traditionally developed for a single task or small range of tasks and the platform is chosen specifically to optimize that application. Not only does this make life tough for embedded system developers, it also makes the debugging and testing of these systems harder, since different debugging tools are needed for each unique platform (Yagi et al., 2009).

Trends such as the "Internet of Things" are driving explosive growth in the embedded market so that companies that are working in areas such as the *smart watch*, *smart glass* and the various examples of flying gadgets that are proliferating have to look for much more integrated solutions. These systems will tend to encompass a variety of CPUs, Real Time Operating Systems (RTOS) and wired/wireless interface technologies that can cause their code sizes to grow exponentially. There is clearly a need for tools and libraries to be able to cope with these demands.

While the ultimate goal may be to develop code that has zero issues, software engineers must live in the real and imperfect world where system complexity is such that invariably issues will occur. The fact that debugging remains the problematic and costly indicates that they must absorb the idea of ever increasing complexity, prepare for the challenge from day one and acquire more and better debugging tools to keep pace with the increasing demands on new developments. To do this, they need all the help they can get to close the so-called "complexity gap" (Raccoon, 1995). Embedded designers can choose to either loathe the frustration of what can easily become a lengthy and tiresome task or otherwise see it as a challenging game to be fought and won.

This chapter advocates a "framework" approach to debugging complex embedded systems by "plugging" the debugging tools into the framework thereby leveraging an appropriate level of prebuilt code infrastructure without incurring excessive overheads. An approach to debug built around this plug-in framework will encompasses the use both high and low level (static and dynamic) debugging tools and built-in unit testing based on an integrated debugging architecture, the seamless movement of run-time code between desktop and target system, the use flexible memory management tools, profilers and code coverage tools and the reuse of proven and well-tested software components.

Using a commercial tool, the ClarinoxSoft-Frame® (Farokhzad, Tanyeri, Messiter, & Beckett, 2010), as an illustrative example we emphasize how a modular and open approach such as this can aid the rapid development of robust, wireless-enabled embedded systems by providing a means to encapsulate and hide any underlying platform differences, both hardware and adjacent software layers and hence provides a common interface to the higher-layer applications. The objective is to offer a simple and common interface and avoid the need to provide special interfaces between proprietary debug tools.

COMPLEXITY IN EMBEDDED SYSTEMS

Debugging is twice as hard as writing the code in the first place. Therefore, if you write the code as cleverly as possible, you are, by definition, not smart enough to debug it. - Brian Kernighan

Brian Kernighan's oft-quoted aphorism could be paraphrased as "debugging is the hardest thing you'll ever do". Simply put, Embedded Systems Engineers are the victims of their own success. Technologies they have helped develop are feeding a growing interconnectedness of everything: from devices through to economies on to entire societies. As a result, a "complexity gap", first identified some 20 years ago (Raccoon, 1995), is increasingly impacting on our ability to comprehend and manage the systems of our own making. In this respect, we could equally (but perhaps unkindly) paraphrase Kernighan's maxim as "our systems are getting smarter, but we're not". The gap describes the difference between our comprehension of the application and our ability to use appropriate tools and methodologies to solve it. It represents the ambiguous and potentially chaotic region that separates the high level description from low-level implementation. Avoiding such system complexity is not an option and neither is simply increasing the scope and complexity of the tools.

Design complexity is already a major concern for embedded systems developers and is spreading inexorably across all markets. This is particularly true for wireless equipment companies as they deal with multiple standards, increasingly convoluted protocols, more demanding user interfaces, higher audio quality requirements, increased security and

so forth. Developers have responded with both hardware and software solutions. However, while hardware will always be important to achieve extreme performance and/or precise timing, or to manage and transform interface signals, there is a trend away from hardware-driven designs to a point where the majority of spending on embedded project development is focused on software (Cadene, 2013). A good example here is the medium access control (MAC) layer of most communication protocols that is responsible for establishing connections, paging remote devices, encoding and decoding data. This layer is now usually implemented in software, despite the fact that these protocols require precise timing information. On the hardware side, increased capability at lower prices is driving the uptake of more complex hardware such as heterogeneous multi-processor organizations.

Complexity has also been dealt with through an increasing percentage of projects using formal operating systems and middleware. As hardware capabilities increase, even operating system cores that were originally designed for PCs can now be used within embedded environments with little modification. Common examples here include the various "flavors" of embedded Linux. However, an operating system that might be a perfect fit for one application could equally be utterly useless for another. Traditionally, this has led to embedded code being written and optimized for a specific operating system, microprocessor and embedded environment. However, with this approach only a small proportion of code can be re-used in subsequent projects without major modifications, which tends to drive up project costs.

To circumvent the intrinsic complexity of embedded designs, some engineers have started using virtual embedded environments. These provide programming and debugging tools that are designed to be independent from the actual physical system to which they will eventually be mapped. A key advantage in this case is we no longer need to know the actual physical system as this has been "virtualized" away. The disadvantage is that the approach almost certainly mandates a more powerful embedded processor, thereby increasing cost. It is also impossible in this case to exploit software features which exclusively target the underlying physical system.

The resulting additional hardware costs may be justified by lower design complexity and shorter design lifecycle. However this needs to be considered on a project to project basis. An alternative approach, which has been adopted by many companies, is to build the application software on top of a common middleware framework. Informal market estimates of purpose-built middleware (Krasner, 2009) indicate their use in more than 50% of real-world applications, notwithstanding their lack of scalability, the large cost of managing and supporting deployed systems and their obvious performance overheads. It also appears that, just as in early days of embedded operating systems, the majority of companies that use middleware currently develop their own.

Middleware is a means of masking the differences between operating systems and processors and providing a single environment for all applications. It achieves this goal by encapsulating operating system API interfaces and services and providing its own API to the software developer. A typical example in the wireless industry is the use of middleware for embedded communications. Although the middleware-based approach suffers from the same problems as those encountered in virtual-machine-based designs, albeit to a much less degree, it tends less processor-intensive than a virtual machine.

To overcome the limitations forced on them by this approach, developers divide their code into two parts. The first is the middleware-based code incorporating a portion of the logic, which is independent from the underlying OS and processor and can therefore be reused with little modification in similar projects. The second represents the application specific part i.e., code that is solely developed and optimized for the current project and that therefore might be dependent on the processor,

peripherals and communication interfaces or that uses a specific feature of the operating system on which it runs. In this way, the middleware approach offers similar advantages to running under either the real or a virtual environment, without many of the disadvantages.

The trend these days, however, is towards more complete solutions. Development is often not viewed in isolation but as one part of the product life cycle. To cover the entire product life-cycle mandates a unified approach to embedded tools, middleware and life-cycle management. In this way, the embedded development system can be viewed as a cohesive solution, rather than as a loose group of isolated elements.

DEBUGGING PORTABLE EMBEDDED SYSTEMS

Embedded development environments differ from other IT developments in that it is usual for hardware and software to be developed simultaneously, something that automatically makes debugging embedded systems special and challenging. When things go wrong the first step has to be to identify whether the error is from software or hardware, or from their interaction (e.g. timing errors). Further, generalist IT systems typically have ample resources available. Embedded systems, on the other hand are more often deliberately resource limited (e.g., CPU capacity and memory). They often have restricted or no user interface so special tools and connections are required just to gain visibility into the system. Finally, many embedded systems operate in real time. In a real time system, a late answer is just as wrong as a wrong answer.

Embedded Prototype Debugging: An Example

The process of rapid prototyping is often performed by the integration of several main system components from various vendors. Components may include both software and hardware items such as an off-the-shelf 32 bit processor board, a real time operating system (RTOS), board support package, and protocol stack/s. It is not uncommon that at the end of a lengthy period of integration and application development that the final testing phase reveals a number of obscure failures.

Tracing the source is difficult as each individual component vendor can claim correct function out-of-box and there is no doubt that debugging is harder when various subsystems are tightly coupled, as changes in one subsystem may cause bugs to emerge in another. In this case, the subsystems are largely invisible as they are the product of external suppliers. This is a classic nightmare debugging scenario: software vendors claim that the problem is a hardware fault, and hardware vendors claim software errors, and none of your standard tests or tools have conclusively tied the error to one or the other.

Let us assume in this example that part of the function requires an interface to an external hardware device. The application software uses the device driver provided by an RTOS vendor. The issue seen is that, on rare occasions, the correct data is not received by the application. There are several elements to this,

1. The transmit side of the application.
2. The RTOS provided device driver on transmit side.
3. The external hardware.
4. The device driver on receive side.
5. The receive side of the application.

To determine which element has the issue, an attempt can be made to rewrite code to isolate the problem to a particular code segment by just including that particular code concerned with data transfer and eliminating other sections irrelevant to the issue. Of course, this immediately assumes that the issue is not due to timing or a corruption caused within the seemingly irrelevant code portions. Figure 1 depicts this hypothetical scenario.

To make sure that the application is sending and receiving the correct data, the most obvious solution is to print all data sent to, and received from, the device driver. However, the actual print mechanism available depends on the debugging ports on the hardware. It could be a spare serial port, a flash file system on the device itself, or as simple as a LED or a hardware port that could be monitored by a Logic Analyzer or storage oscilloscope. If the printing proves that the data is as per the specifications then the application transmit side has been proven to be working correctly and we have halved the problem scope.

If the data sent by the application is correct but the received data is not then it appears that we need to look deeper for a device driver or hardware issue. It is now time to use a protocol or logic analyzer to analyze bytes coming out of the processor board. If the data monitored at the hardware port of the board matches the data printed by the application, then we are running out of suspects. However, if the application sends the correct data (proven by printing) but the device driver does not generate the same data coming from application on the hardware port then we have found the error - in the device driver/Board Support Package. On the other hand, if correct data is transferred from the device driver and the external device generates data back to the board then the error can be assumed to be in the external hardware device.

But life is not likely to be that simple. We may see the expected sequence of data received at the input port of the hardware, thus clearing the external device. We then look at the possibility of the device driver receive side/Board Support Package receive issues versus an even more likely issue that we (the designers) have used the device driver incorrectly. How do we decide whether we have set it up correctly and the device driver is occasionally missing bytes or our receiving thread does not have high enough priority and while processing the previous packet we are causing a hardware receive buffer overrun. Now, is a good

Figure 1. Hypothetical embedded systems example

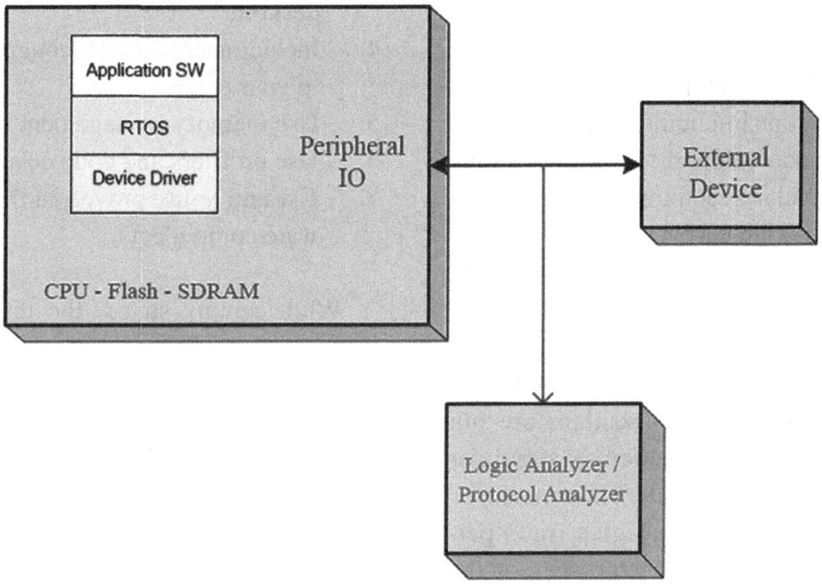

time to add error checking after each API call. By reading the hardware status register we may be able to *detect the unexpected*. Unfortunately, more often than not we will find the issue in our interpretation of the device driver APIs and its operation.

Finally, the most likely culprit has been found and the decision is in fact that there is an error within the RTOS supplied device driver. This needs to be forwarded to the real-time operating system vendor to obtain a fix (unless it is open source, or course). Presenting all the facts gained during testing is the key factor to get this required technical support in a timely manner. The documentation and restatement of every step taken and every result observed is a time consuming effort. Writing even what seem obvious or trivial steps such as "power on the unit, wait until the green LED is on, etc." will enable the correct flow to be tracked through third party code. In our example here, the RTOS vendor needs to know which elements of the device driver code have failed to be able to rectify the issue. Given the problem is intermittent it will be a portion of code only

reached by satisfying specific, infrequently met, criteria, which (by definition) will be difficult to reproduce.

It is clear even from this simple example that the key to ensuring that an embedded application operates robustly for long periods of time is a debug system with high visibility and good control capabilities. By this we mean that the debug environment must provide easy and efficient "hooks" into the code to both see what is happening and to control and evaluate its behavior. While all debug frameworks provide these basic functions, the actual mechanism will depend entirely on the specific target. The process itself almost invariably involves the following steps: remote tracing of the program execution, watching variables and transferring data of interest to a host. The differences between them often come down to a matter of focus and context.

Good debugger and profiler tools will make an embedded system controllable and observable at a number of levels, including assembly and source-level, syntax level and in-circuit. A traditional debugging process (Schneider &

Fraleigh, 2004) commences on a host machine using emulation and moves increasingly closer to the hardware until a final level involves special purpose test hardware incorporated into the target device. However, this In-circuit Emulation (ICE) approach offers poor support for hardware/software co-design and is becoming less viable with vastly shorter development cycles. Software-only approaches (e.g., (Kraemer et al., 2007)) offer at least a partial solution to the co-design problem, In this case, the platform-independent components of an application execute natively on the host while the platform dependent sections are run using a tightly coupled instruction set simulator for the target processor. As modern host machines typically exhibit significantly higher (raw) performance than an embedded target processor, the overheads of this approach might be relatively small. Future debug systems will need to become better at balancing this tension between software and hardware approaches.

A Structured Approach to Debug

We have already identified why there are many reasons why debugging can be considered to be the most problematic and costly issue within a development cycle. These can include exponentially increasing complexity, the need to balance conflicting constraints, increasingly inaccessible silicon, lack of bug reproducibility and greater pressure to meet shorter development schedule cycles.

Industry trends strongly predict that these driving forces will continue, so more tightly integrated approaches to debugging will be required into the future. The underlying principle is simple: use all available tools, low level and high level, to isolate and identify the core issue. Some simple suggestions include:

1. Bring both low-level and high-level debugging tools into the debug mix;
2. Include built-in unit testing in your code;

3. Make sure that your code can also run on a desktop;
4. Include an integrated debugging architecture in your code;
5. Use memory management tools;
6. Use profilers and code coverage tools;
7. Use and re-use proven and well-tested software components.

While simply stated, the difficulty will be managing all of these within a single environment. Obviously, many of these ideas have arisen from conventional software debugging processes. However, the objective in this case is to counteract the tendency for embedded systems to become more "opaque" as their overall level of functional integration increases.

High and Low Level Debugging Tools

To gain complete knowledge of a system at all levels it is important to make effective use of both high and low level tools. Low level tools are particularly useful during hardware debugging and in the early stages of a project, e.g. device driver development. On the other hand, while the use of tools such as the IDE, JTAG and logic analyzers for low level and hardware debugging is common, the increase in code size and complexity of an average project has already outstripped the growth in computer hardware. Most of the development time now tends to be spent integrating these drivers to the overall framework, which requires more than just simple breakpoints and CPU register analysis.

High level (dynamic) debugging tools are used to explore the protocol level to understand the characteristics of a system. In the ideal case, an integrated debugger would provide information about real-time events such as thread switching, memory use, inter-process communication and status of timers, while helping to integrate protocol tracing for I/O interfaces that are synchronized with the function level tracing and real-time events. Such tools provide dynamic (i.e., run-time) information about the system being debugged, whereas traditional static debuggers are intrusive in nature and they usually stop the execution and provide a snapshot about the system.

The key idea here is flexibility. Ideally, an Integrated Development Environment (IDE) would support an ability to flexibly integrate hardware and operating system specific support into what is otherwise a generic debugger framework. This has been a typical approach in when providing extensions to a standard IDE such as Eclipse, for example to support debugging remote applications. In a typical setup, a workstation might be connected to the debugger via a network interface while the debugger is connected to its remote target via JTAG. Plug-in modules provide specific software language support as well as the relevant background debug mode interface.

A number of IDEs extend this idea to provide RTOS awareness and information, which serves to improve visibility into real-time behavior. As well as the usual C/C++ compiler and debugger tools, the IAR Embedded workbench (IAR Systems, 2013) provides extensions into µC/OS-III RTOS internal details that display information regarding system threads, thread stack usage etc. A snapshot of some µC/OS-III threads within the IAR debugger can be seen in Figure 2. Plug-in modules specific to a particular RTOS extend the control and visibility of individual task and processes invoked under that system. These modules are typically sourced from the RTOS vendor and include specific low-level support for the relevant hardware boards and devices.

Tools such as the ClarinoxSoftFrame (Clarinox Technologies Pty. Ltd., 2010), which will be described in more detail below, also use a plug-in

approach to provide a common interface to the hardware and to shield the development team from the complexities of different CPU architectures, operating systems, debugging processes. In a similar way, the component-based debugger architecture described in (Murillo, Harnath, Leupers, & Ascheid, 2012) that targets heterogeneous multiprocessor systems on chip (MPSoCs), abstracts away the complex inner details of their hardware and software stacks. The various components communicate through well-defined interfaces and can be swapped or modified as required to target different hardware and software configurations. An event-based intermediate data representation abstracts away low-level processor activity and supports the analysis of inter-processor interactions. Scalability and performance is maintained by the use of a centralized tree-like organization that allows debug information to be aggregated from different sources. In a similar way, the Graphical Model Debugger Framework (GMDF) of (Kebin, Yu, & Angelov, 2010) has been designed to support model-driven development such that developers can focus on the high-level behavior of the system (i.e., at the model level, rather than the code level). In this case, a debug model is derived from the input meta-model and application model and a runtime engine interacts with the operating embedded code.

In summary, we maintain that visibility in the debugging process is greatly enhanced by the flexible integration of high and low level tools within a unified framework. This approach can offer the simplicity of a combined tool for faster debugging plus a formal framework targeting a variety of operating systems and platforms, thereby allowing for smaller development teams. Large

Figure 2. RTOS aware debugging

# Task Name	Priority	State	Pending On Object	Pending On	CPU Usage	Bar Graph	Context Switches	Stack Pointer	Stack Size	Stack Free	Stack Used	Stack Used %	Bar Graph
3 App Task Start	3	Pending	Semaphore	App Sem	0.00%		50	0x10002C00	2400	1955	445	18%	
7 uC/OS-III Idle Task	63	Ready			95.83%		15704	0x10006990	128	113	15	11%	
5 uC/OS-III Stat Task	62	Delayed			1.40%		314	0x10006B58	128	95	33	25%	
6 uC/OS-III Tick Task	1	Pending	Task Semaphore	Task Sem	2.71%		15865	0x10006D68	128	101	27	21%	
4 uC/OS-III Timer Task	62	Pending	Task Semaphore	Task Sem	0.03%		159	0x10006F60	128	99	29	22%	
2 SoftFrameDebugThread	9	Pending	Semaphore	Serial Rx Wait	0.00%		0	0x2000F5C8	500	400	100	20%	
1 SoftFrameTimerThread	3	Pending with Timeout	Semaphore	App Sem	0.00%		23	0x20011F18	1000	814	186	18%	
0 ClxUIEngine InputThread	3	Pending	Semaphore	App Sem	0.00%		3	0x20012EC0	1000	867	133	13%	

companies tend to have the resources to custom-build tools that specifically suit their development environment. In contrast, small teams generally do not have the resources to do the same.

Built-In Unit Testing

Divide and conquer, to eliminate bugs in a stepwise bottom-up manner, is one of the most fundamental approaches to debugging. The term unit test (IEEE Standards Board, 1999) describes an important part of the classical Software Development Life Cycle and most commonly represents a short program fragment that exercises some narrow part of the source code and checks the results (Kolawa & Huizinga, 2007), Other terms such as "developer testing" are sometimes used (Agile Alliance, 2013) but these mean essentially the same thing. Typically, only a "pass/fail" result is recorded. Various formal frameworks have been proposed to reduce the overheads associated with unit testing, although these tend more to be aimed at the general programming environment such as those under the .NET and Ruby frameworks (Britt & The Neurogami Group, 2013; Poole, Terrell, & Busoli, 2007; Wilson, 2013) or for the Java language (Xie, Taneja, Kale, & Marinov, 2007).

As the size of an application grows, automatic unit testing becomes an increasingly useful approach. Code testing is important enough that covering even just a small part of an application should be expected to take substantial time (Myers, 2004). The fact that it is potentially very error-prone serves to increase this further. Manually testing and verifying an entire application can take hours or even weeks. On the other hand, preparing useful unit test cases can be a time consuming activity in itself as it necessarily includes items such as the initialization of all dependent variables, creating stubs/drivers for irrelevant functions, intelligent post condition checking, report generation and so on. However, it has been shown (Bacchelli, Ciancarini, & Rossi, 2008) that while automatic test generation tools are able to produce a large number of test cases in a short time, the tests they generate must still be closely analyzed, validated and fine-tuned. Further, the rigor imposed by manual test generation tends to increase the accuracy and relevance of the tests. At present, it appears that an optimal approach combines automatic and manual tests in an integrated form.

Although by definition only the functionality of the units themselves are tested, taking out the individual unit errors first will tend to leave only those due to overall co-ordination, inter-process communication and timing issues. Spending the time up front to create a unit-test architecture will ensure that these work against the design criteria while automated unit testing will allow easy regression testing before each major release. Again, early bug finding is one of the basic *truisms* of debugging but its power can be forgotten in the struggle to get a product out the door.

Running Embedded Code on a Desktop

For a number of reasons, there appears to be general resistance to this idea within the embedded computing industry. Various strong counter arguments are raised, such as:

- "It is a waste of effort, we can't run most of our code anyway."
- "It is very hard to rewrite all our code for another platform."
- "System timings won't be the same, as the PC runs 100 times faster than our target."
- "It won't save much time anyway."

We can address these objections by looking at a simple example. Assume that the project is to integrate something like a GPRS module onto a target system. In this case an evaluation module, which can be connected to PC via serial port, will facilitate the majority of the development on the PC. The exception here will be the UART device driver. However, eliminating this item from the initial debugger framework can be an advantage as any specific issues here can be identified more quickly if the other modules are already correct. The key idea here is the use of a *middleware* framework that enables the code to be run on both a standard PC platform and on the target.

While it is undoubtedly true that after the code has been written it is difficult to port it to another platform. However, if an *intention* to use multiple platforms drives the overall system design from the very beginning, again through the use of middleware, then most of the code will be valid and will not need to be rewritten. As an additional benefit, the code is now more readily portable to other platforms, enhancing its security against obsolescence and even simplifying upgrades to future processor architectures that may offer higher performance and/or lower cost. Since a PC typically runs many times faster than the target, it is again undoubtedly true the timing behavior will not be the same, especially if the code depends on operating system calls such as *sleep()* to manage its timing relationships with external events or other threads. However, if the design uses mechanisms such as interrupt, messaging, semaphore or conditional variable concepts then this issue can be largely avoided, along with the cost of debugging complex synchronization and race conditions.

Heterogeneous, distributed and resource constrained systems present additional difficulties. The complex interactions between concurrent software (i.e., the application, operating system and any middleware support) and the hardware platform and its interconnecting networks can lead to obscure and unpredictable errors. (Ho, Hand, & Harris, 2004) addresses this issue by porting the operating system to a virtual machine monitor (VMM). By running each component of an application in its own virtual machine, a number of useful hardware and software abstractions can be represented within the debug system and the designer can be given greater control over the application and its environment. The Movidius Environment (moviTest) (Tite, Vig, Olteanu, &

Cuna, 2011) uses a script-based approach as a means to provide improved visibility into heterogeneous multi-core and parallel systems. The scripts are used to generate and manage sequences of automatic tests run on specific targets such as simulators, ASIC, FPGA, and heterogeneous multi-core VLIW SoC architectures. These test scripts may be compiled using different toolchains appropriate to the particular target. The environment then collects the resulting debug information during compile and execution time, enabling support for a range of the usual software debugging features.

The Marionette tool suite (Whitehouse et al., 2006) addresses the lack of visibility and control during execution via an embedded remote procedure call (ERPC) mechanism which tightly couples the running program on the PC and the target (typically, a small wireless sensor node). Parts of the application are executed on the PC client and remotely access function results and variables on the target when necessary. This approach trades off communication bandwidth against increased visibility and control during execution. The approach is similar to that taken by the *EmStar* environment (Elson, Girod, & Estrin, 2004; Girod et al., 2007), in which an interface to the hardware is defined that can be used over a wired channel by an application running centrally on a PC. The environment uses a multi-process service model that trades off performance against visibility by supporting a range of execution modes, from within pure simulation through to fully distributed operation on the target devices. In this way, the tool sacrifices some level of performance in return for increased robustness when debugging heterogeneous embedded sensor-actuator networks.

However, given that embedded systems tend to operate very close to their maximum resource limits, this type of virtualization or remote invocation mechanisms will have a significant but largely indeterminate effect on the very interactions it is trying to reveal. In the worst case, they may case a system to fail even if the code itself is correct. For example, the multi-hop, resource-constrained, and timing dependent nature of distributed wireless sensor networks make them very sensitive to input-output latency. The interaction between multiple virtual machines adds stochastic overheads that can interfere with such sensitive timing characteristics, introducing artifacts into the debug process.

Various alternatives have been proposed that try to address these overhead issues. The Esto NS (non-stop) Debugger (Chun, Choon-oh, & Duk-Kyun, 2007) employs a *tracepoint* method that triggers debug data collection at various points in the program without stopping its execution. In this respect, a tracepoint is simply a breakpoint with an associated action so that the debugger performs the specified action instead of (or, as well as) breaking program execution. Actions can include the saving of variables, registers, memory, stack, etc. which are then examined after that particular debugging run. However, it can be readily seen that this sort of scheme, while minimizing the timing overheads, does not completely remove them. There will have to additional resources allocated within the target to store the traced variables, and these are likely to be limited. The concept offers a small advance beyond the conventional *"break-and-dump"* of the kind exploited by many conventional debugging tools (including logic analyzers), as it allows a small number of disparate points to be traced in one run.

In a similar fashion, the *Clairvoyant* tool (Yang, Soffa, Selavo, & Whitehouse, 2007) uses a technique called *dynamic binary instrumentation* that attempts to maintain high performance by embedding debugging commands into the target binary. This approach succeeds in running the program at native speed directly on the target machine without requiring either additional hardware or source code changes. However, similar issues such as limited memory and flash lifetime severely restrict the resources available for debugging on the actual sensor nodes.

The JavaES framework (Holgado-Terriza & Viúdez-Aivar, 2012) consists of a set of tools targeting JAVA applications that allow the internal state of the JRE to be monitored including digital and analog input-output values, free memory, number of active threads, timers, etc. In addition, the framework supports the remote modifications of input-output (I/O) values and redirection of the standard outputs for remote reading. Similarly, the Java based Avrora framework (Titzer & Palsberg, 2005) includes a model that emulates each target device and supports interaction with the application code.

All of these software emulation approaches rely on the speed of the host processor to preserve the timing and synchronization behavior of the target application.

Finally, to address the idea that it won't save much time, consider the time required to connect a JTAG to the target and downloading an example 500KB application every time a test is run. Even though the sequential process of compile, link, connect, download and run might only take in the order of 1-3 minutes, repetitive cycles will add up quickly (30 re-runs will take up least a half an hour just for the compile/run operation itself). On a PC the test will run in 10 seconds, so the time for 30 runs will fall to five minutes, a time saving of over 80%. Multiply this out over an intensive test period of two weeks and extrapolate out to a larger project of, say, ten people, the savings become significant. The increased speed and visibility available in a desktop computing environment clearly argues for doing as much debugging within this environment as possible via the use of an IDE, virtualization, simulation and use of middleware tools.

Integrated Debugging Architectures

Integrated debugging is especially useful when running a desktop version of the code. Integrated function tracing that includes threading information will clarify the execution of the various application functions and their relationship to real-time events. It is also possible to use a remote debugger to extract information out of an embedded target device in a way that supports the analysis and display of debug information along with the visualization of the code flow, regardless of its complexity.

Code blocks that are initially set up to output debug information can be later harnessed to output the information to a serial UART port, Ethernet, console or even a simple LCD display. For the production code you can turn the debugging off by using the same code blocks to reduce the overhead and the code size, once you are confident with the product. However, it has to be noted that using an external debugger still creates timing overhead on the target device as an agent component of the debugger is required to send and receive debug information. As the amount of debug information grows, so will its effect on the timing characteristics of the system possibly leading to real-time over-runs. Taking this into account requires the code to be tolerant of these additional timing changes.

A strongly unified framework approach removes the need for developers to re-learn a range of different CPU architectures, operating systems and debugging tools. Instead of requiring more engineering staff and tools, the aim is to minimize infrastructure, to shrink the team size and to unify the development tool environment so that developers can concentrate their efforts on the problem to be solving instead of chasing integration problems between the various system elements. Note that there are many open source frameworks and tools, although they tend to focus specifically on the Linux operating system. A small number of open source real-time operating systems exist (e.g. eCos), but then the maintainers of those provide commercial tools instead of open source tools. Even where a vendor offers a closed-source architecture, it is important for users to have the ability to customize, add more components to improve visibility and port to other environments.

Memory Management Tools

Dynamic memory allocation has been fundamental to the operation of programs since the early days of computer systems. For a good historical review, see (Wilson, Johnstone, Neely, & Boles, 1995). However, the overall effect of allocating and de-allocating memory dynamically from a pool is intimately tied to the run-time behavior of the program and is therefore difficult or impossible to determine *a priori*. Memory management has become even harder in the multi-processor domain as it is also impacted by issues such as process communication, task migration, load balancing and the like (Almeida et al., 2010).

Memory management problems have always been the enemy of robust code as they invariably lead to inconsistent behavior that is hard to reproduce and therefore extremely difficult to diagnose. Further, tools that try to automatically detect memory management and threading errors tend to severely degrade the program's performance and fundamentally change its timing behavior, making them less suited to critical real-time systems. For example, the *Valgrind* suite (Valgrind Developers, 2013), aimed at the embedded Linux environment, operates by translating the program to a processor independent form and running that code under a virtual machine. In a similar way, the Hobbes suite (Burrows, Freund, & Wiener, 2003) includes an interpreter and a type checker analysis tool that is added to the target code and which is called by the interpreter when anything of interest occur in the target. As a result, the run-time performance of these systems can be a fraction of its native (un-instrumented) value.

It could be argued that dynamic memory allocation/de-allocation constructs can actually be a hindrance to safe code, as memory fragmentation can often cause a slow but eventually fatal ending. One solution here is to rely on fixed size buffer pools to eliminate memory fragmentation, although the optimal pool size is something that can only be determined after the code is written. It seems that this tension between flexibility and reliability in memory systems will always exist in stored program architectures.

Profilers and Code Coverage Tools

The profiling process aims to measure important aspects of a programs behavior such as its memory or run-time complexity, instruction usage, and the frequency and duration of function calls. Its overall objective is to allow the overall performance of a program to be analyzed with a view to optimizing individual code blocks that are found to be sub-optimal. Profiling is achieved by instrumenting either the program source code or its binary executable form using a tool called a profiler (or code profiler). A number of different techniques may be used by profilers, such as event-based, statistical, instrumented, and simulation methods.

The profiling system proposed in (Nagpurkar, Mousa, Krintz, & Sherwood, 2006) employs a hybrid hardware and software approach to sample the executing instruction stream and is based on the dynamic instruction stream editing (DISE) system of (Corliss, Lewis, & Roth, 2003). In turn, DISE is built around a hardware mechanism that extends the decode stage of a hardware pipeline so that it is able to dynamically insert instructions into the execution stream. The profiler combines the Hybrid Profiling Support (HPS) of (Mousa & Krintz, 2005) with a so-called Phase-Aware Sampling mechanism that exploits the cyclic behavior of typical programs to sample profile information with low overheads. Instructions of interest to the debug process are identified in software and replaced with a specific stream of instructions at run time that gather the profiling information.

The early identification and remediation of performance issues results in a greatly reduced likelihood of random system crashes due to real-time processor overload. Interestingly, it is often the case that eliminating unused code will uncover hidden design problems simply because such code is more often than not a result of early design errors which can remain dormant until uncovered by this step.

Use of Proven and Well-Tested Software Components

It is the nature of engineers to prefer to start with a clean slate rather than reuse or adapt an existing (i.e., somebody else's) design. However, engineers also have to remember that their primary objective is the development of products rather than the development of their own fundamental knowledge and skills. The latter is (usually) a by-product of the former. Too often this comes to represent a fundamental conflict between the engineering drive for what is best and the economic drive to be first.

As development time frames reduce, it is essential that product developers make best use of whatever tools and reusable code is at their disposal to gain extra efficiencies and hence faster time to market. This necessarily means re-using code that is proven from previous projects. It also means making a conscious effort to avoid re-inventing the wheel for every component to ensure that the focus is maintained on the product application. In this way, the introduction of new and different bugs can be minimized along with the requirement to maintain novel code.

The various tools and techniques already in common use exhibit drawbacks that can make them less useful in particular contexts. For example, debug tools tend to be platform specific and can require significant effort to port the design to a new platform with its dedicated environment and user interface. Some of these tools require specific debug-related code to be inserted into the application code, potentially complicating the porting process. Further, all debug tools necessarily produce huge amounts of data that will be difficult and error prone to analyze by hand. However, any attempt to filter and categorize the data may serve to hide valuable information, especially when the analysis is spread across a number of separate tools. Tools that operate separately and independently may not effectively capture important time-related and synchronization information.

Finally, developers may be forced to write their own debugging tools that suite their well-established design and development environment (e.g. a proprietary event-based debugger, or protocol analyzer etc.). However, apart from the obvious difficulties with writing a new tool from scratch, the time needed to develop a new debugging tool may be not justifiable if the tool is disposable in nature (i.e., when it is needed for one design only). The temptation is strong in this case to stay with existing design techniques and environment, even if it is marginally appropriate and can increase debug costs in the longer term.

One solution that addresses most of these issues is a debugging architecture based on plug-in modules. This so-called *middleware* based architecture is described in the following section.

An Example Debugging Framework: The ClarinoxSoftFrame® Middleware

As identified in the previous section, a unified framework approach will be able to support a variety of operating systems and platforms which can in turn lead to a need for smaller, less specialized development teams. Whereas large companies are able to custom build tools directly suited to their development environment, small companies generally do not have such a luxury. Using an integrated framework approach can abstract away the fine details of different CPU architectures, operating systems and debugging tools, allowing embedded developers to concentrate on the specific problem to be solved. In this section we look at the details of one example of a unified debugger framework, the ClarinoxSoftFrame (Clarinox Technologies Pty. Ltd., 2010), and show

how a middleware structure of this type can fit into, and support a complete debugger environment for portable embedded systems.

The key features of this environment are:

- It is built as a C++ interface class that is independent of the physical layer. In fact, the physical layer can be a network, a serial connection (e.g., RS232), or even a file on hard disk or flash memory;
- A robust DLL-based plug-in interface for the debugger enables developers to add their own debugging functionality to the base environment. A plug-in can receive and parse special messages sent by the debug target and can maintain its own window and thread context.

The overall structure of the framework shown in Figure 3 is an integrated tool suite that provides the base functionality to which plug-in modules are attached to provide specific capabilities. The architecture includes a channel that handles all of the underlying communications required between the debugger and system being debugged, including any signal or protocol translation. As the debugger typically runs on a PC, these two are generally located within different operating environments.

The channel infrastructure supports any form of physical communication (e.g. UART, wired or wireless TCP/IP network, embedded busses, etc.) and any form of logical communication (e.g. full-duplex, binary data transmission, packet-based data transmission). The architecture also provides for both online and offline debugging. In the offline debugging scenario, data are stored locally (e.g. in hard disk or flash memory), and then transferred to the debugger machine for analysis. This facility is particularly useful for small embedded systems with no means of external communication.

The overall framework is based on middleware code that encapsulates and hides the underlying

Figure 3. Plug-in based debugging framework (© 2013 Clarinox Technologies Pty Ltd Used with permission)

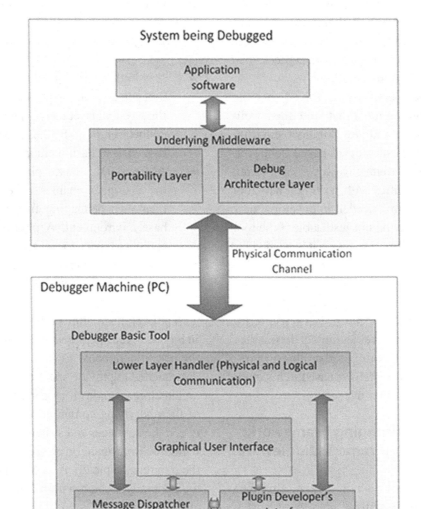

platform differences, and provides a common interface to the higher-layer application developers. This approach ensures that the architecture can operate in different platforms without a need for modification. The debug architecture receives and analyzes debug data from the target and dispatches them to the appropriate plug-in tool. The plug-in developer does not need to know anything about

how the underlying architecture works. The plug-in modules install handlers which are called when the related data are received. They have the job of analyzing the data, and returning a report to the main tool, if necessary.

The architecture provides a common interface to the plug-in modules. Modules are able to communicate with the central platform, with other modules or with the embedded system being debugged, thereby avoiding the need to provide special interfaces between proprietary debug tools. The interface must be very simple to the extent that it will justify any attempt to develop a special plug-in tool, even a disposable one.

Because all data come from the same communication channel and are then dispatched to the different plug-in modules, the data generation order is preserved. This order provides extremely important information on the effectiveness of parallelism in the code and can reveal synchronization issues. The underlying architecture provides means for the user to take advantage of information hidden in the order. Furthermore, the architecture provides categorization and filtering facilities to the plug-in developers, allowing developers to filter the data based on order.

As a substantial part of the Graphical User Interface is completely handled by the architecture, there is no need for the plug-in developer to become involved with GUI design tasks. On the other hand, this type of architecture automatically permits the development of special-purpose user interfaces and their connection to the tools interface, thereby providing additional methods of instrumenting the analysis and thus decreasing overall debugging time. The debug code will be automatically compiled into the application as part of the middleware used. Although this frees the developer from having to insert it manually there may still be a need to define the debugging configuration parameters (e.g., what communication hardware to use, and other related parameters).

It can be seen that this middleware technique is not really applicable to source-level and assembly level debugging. In that case, the debugger(s) must reside outside of, and run in parallel with the application, so they can completely control the execution path of the code. However, source-level debuggers are always tightly coupled with the CPU and the operating system on which the application runs and even the compiler used to

generate the code. It is therefore difficult to see how source-level debugging tools would fit into a framework that is intended to be independent from the platform and be portable to any embedded environment.

The Debug Architecture Layer depicted in Figure 4 comprises the Communication Channel Adaptation Layer (CCAL) and an associated message buffer. The CCAL is a layer of software which provides a common logic communication interface to the upper layer and communicates with the related hardware driver on behalf of the application. The interface must be flexible enough to encapsulate and integrate different type of communication channels (e.g., there is a concept of "connection" and "disconnection" in some communication technologies, while absent in others technologies).

The Applications Programmer's Interface (API, Figure 5) includes a GUI tool used to remotely debug ClarinoxSoftFrame based embedded applications. The operating system (OS) wrapper includes functions such as threading, timers, semaphores, mutexes, dynamic memory management, inter-process message passing, event/message handling, finite state machine templates, serial device driver encapsulation, USB device driver and TCP/UDP Socket encapsulation. The framework extends the debugging tools and Board Support Package or Hardware Adaptation Layer provided by RTOS manufactures and offers debugging tools that can handle multi-threaded applications that are not specific to just one environment.

In the debugging framework as implemented, the basic tool is a Windows GUI application which is able to dynamically attach to plug-in DLLs, thus avoiding the need to recompile the tool for each new plug-in. The debugger is able to receive messages sent by an application and to analyze and format the messages in real time. The user can also send command messages to the application to control the debug process. In general, messages can be categorized as:

Figure 4. Debug architecture layer (© 2013 Clarinox Technologies Pty Ltd Used with permission)

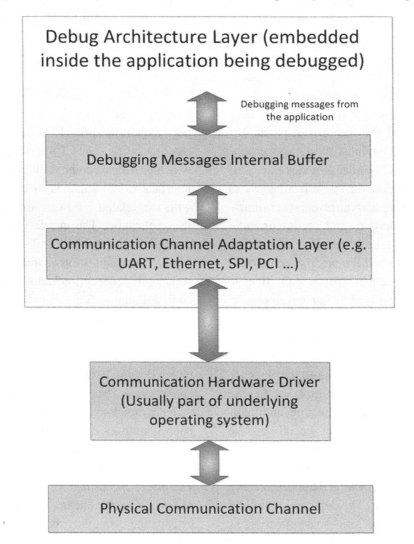

1. Thread related messages, including thread control.
2. Profiling and stack trace messages describing the call and return history and profiling information.
3. Informative (text) messages, including logs, warning and fatal events.
4. Memory messages providing information on allocations, and de-allocations in the code.
5. Protocol Stack Monitoring messages, including monitors for Bluetooth, RFID, and GPRS. These messages identify all stack activity, revealing all low-level protocol data and messages in real time.

The "Plug-In" Approach

This section explains how a plug-in DLL can be developed for the debugger software. The debugger receives text and binary debugging messages sent by any program written using the framework while in its debug configuration. Text messages simply provide logging information or specify errors which take place during the program execution. In contrast, binary messages cannot be directly displayed inside the debugger environment and so need to be analyzed first. Analysis is performed by plug-ins attached to the debugger software.

Figure 5. The ClarinoxSoftFrame® API (© 2013 Clarinox Technologies Pty. Ltd. Used with permission)

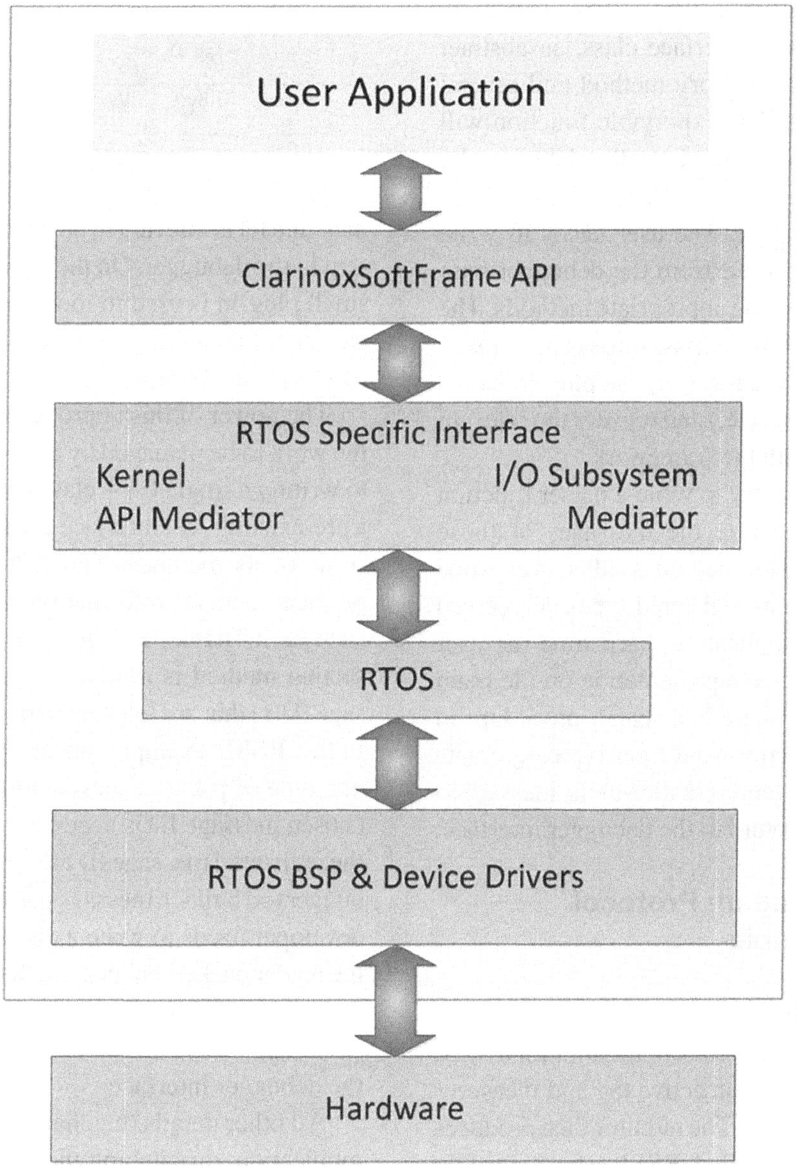

One or more DLL files (called "plug-ins") may be attached to debugger framework to provide further services. A plug-in needs to do any or all of the following:

- Analyze a user-defined message type;
- Provide services to other installed plug-in modules;

- Provide one or more items in context pop-up menus (e.g. that might be opened using a right click function on the debuggers main screen to offer additional status and/ or context information).

A plug-in DLL comprises only one export-able function. This function creates an instance of the main C++ class, and passes a pointer to the instance, to the debugger. Therefore, the main part of a plug-in is a C++ class. This class must inherit from a basic interface class, an abstract class with one compulsory method and several optional methods. The exportable function will identify the object methods to the debugger by passing the address of an instance of the plug-in class to the debugger. The user needs to write a C++ class (inherited from the debugger base class) and overload the appropriate methods. The overloaded function must pass some general information about the plug-in (i.e., the plug-in name, general description, etc.) and register the relevant message types with the framework.

It is then necessary to write a parser function to receive and analyze the messages of those registered types. This method is called every time a message of one of registered types is received from the target application, each time the user triggers the message representation on the main screen and when there is a search procedure in progress. The function would then typically create a human readable representation of the message to display, store or return to the debugger interface.

Building a Plug-in: Protocol Monitor Example

We will now illustrate an example of a simple plug-in, in this case a protocol monitor for a RSSI tag reader that reads an active tag and measures its signal power level. The monitor then produces a one-byte value called RSSI (approximately inversely proportional to the distance of the tag from the reader), encodes this byte into a packet and sends it to a computer or an embedded system via RS232 (Figure 6). This example shows how a protocol monitor for a proprietary RFID protocol can be quickly designed and deployed.

These packets are captured by the target software and also moved to the debugger machine for processing. Using a simple pre-defined macro, a header containing information such as an arbitrary

Figure 6. A simple RS232 packet structure

Delimiter	Length of Tag ID	Tag ID	Reader ID	RSSI
1 Byte	1 Byte	Variable	2 Byte	2 Bytes

message ID is inserted to the packets before being sent to the debugger. On the debugger machine, a small plug-in is used to monitor and analyze the packets of the chosen message ID and show the results on its main screen.

The power of this approach is now evident as the work to be managed by the developer reduces to writing a single C++ class which derives from a pre-existing API interface class, and to overload some of its methods. The API method already provides general information about the plug-in such as its name, a general description, etc. A second method is available to register the message ID(s) that are relevant to this particular plug. In this RSSD example, we can assume that only one type of packet exists so only one arbitrarily chosen message ID is necessary. All messages of the registered message ID are delivered by the debugger to a built-in message passing function. The developer needs to write a class method to parse the reader packets encoded in the format shown in Figure 6 and then to return human-readable text about the packet, which can then be displayed at the debugger interface.

All other details (e.g. handling physical communication, dispatching the messages to the appropriate plug-in, handling user interface details, loading and initializing the DLL plug-ins etc.) are handled by the debugging framework. Since the packets are redirected by the target system (rather than being captured directly from the reader), the plug-in demonstrates whether or not the target system is able to receive and properly separate the incoming data stream into independent packets. Furthermore, the result can be used to find the state of the target system when other errors happen and are captured by the debugger (e.g. what packet was being parsed by the remote system at the time the error happened). It can be seen that the DLL plug-in represents the point at which the physical layer is separated from the debugger, thereby simplifying the debugging process by offering a natural point of system partitioning.

Using a Plug-in: Memory Analysis Example

Memory management is extremely important in any resource limited environment such as that found in mobile platform development. Although the memory capacity of mobile devices has been increasing with successive technology generations, so have the demands of mobile applications. Tools such as the Eclipse Memory Analyzer (MAT) (The Eclipse Foundation, 2014) are widely available and support heap analysis of Java-based mobile applications by static analysis of a heap dump that can be triggered by an *Out-Of-Memory* exception thrown by the processor.

Of course, an *Out-of-Memory* error is a poor way to discover a memory leak, and will be impossible to differentiate from cases where the developer has simply allocated beyond the

capacity of the platform. Good memory analysis is therefore a critical development aid. The following example illustrates a few benefits of a applying memory analysis to a running program. The data memory usage for a sample application is shown in Figure 7. This view helps with the information of memory chunk sizes used by the application. If this information is obtained from the system at the end of the execution (or after completing a task) then the information is used as an indication of potential memory leakage. For a resource sensitive implementation, memory tuning is extremely valuable. It may be possible to choose a smaller memory architecture and in the case of mass production this could lead to a reduction in manufacturing costs.

As outlined above, another good use for the memory analyzer is detecting possible memory leaks. A memory leak is defined as a memory segment dynamically allocated but not released ("freed") back to the system. This area of memory will not be re-usable until is freed. The following code segment demonstrates use of memory leak detection. The code starts three threads and the implementation of each thread is almost identical. Each makes a call to a function that allocates a block of memory then converts the incoming

Figure 7. Data memory usage for a sample application

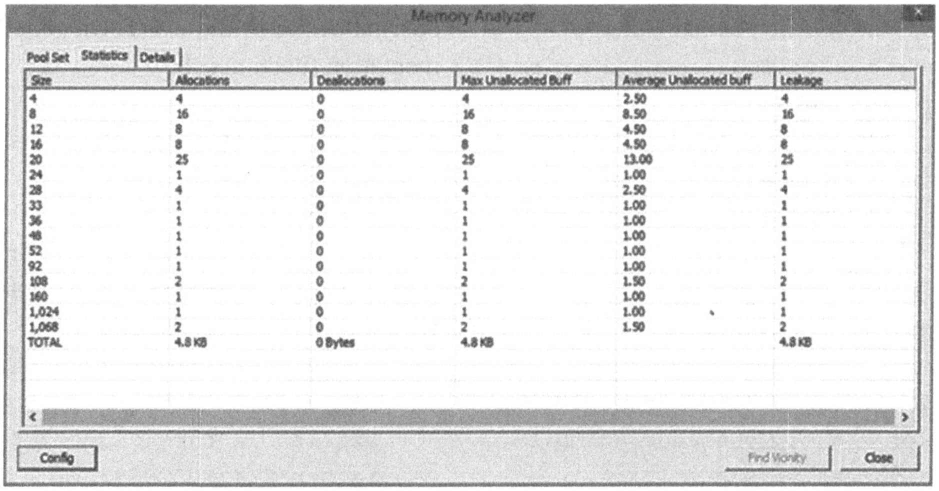

string to Unicode and returns back to the caller. The first two threads correctly delete the allocated memory, but the third thread mistakenly does not delete the allocated memory thereby causing a potential memory leak.

```
clxBeginThread(threadFunc_1, NULL,
"leakTest_thread_1", 0);
clxBeginThread(threadFunc_2, NULL,
"leakTest_thread_2", 0);
clxBeginThread(threadFunc_3, NULL,
"leakTest_thread_3", 0);
static u2* asciiToUnicodeBadImplement
ation(const s1* str)
{
    eee(4, 4, (ooo, "asciiToUnico-
deBadImplementation"));
    u4 len = clxStrLen(str) + 1;
    u2* ret = NEW u2[ len ];
    u4 i = 0;
    for(i = 0; i < len; i++)
    {
        ret[ i ] = str[ i ];
    }
    xxx((ooo, "asciiToUnicodeBadIm-
plementation "));
    return ret;
}
static ClxResult CLX_CALLBACK
threadFunc_1(void* data)
{
    eee(4, 4, (ooo, "threadFunc_1"));
    u2* str = asciiToUnicodeBadImplem
entation("test thread 1");
    delete str;
    xxx((ooo, "threadFunc_1 "));
    return CLX_SUCCESS;
}
static ClxResult CLX_CALLBACK
threadFunc_2(void* data)
{
    eee(4, 4, (ooo, "threadFunc_2"));
    u2* str = asciiToUnicodeBadImple-
mentation(" test thread 2");
    delete str;
```

```
    xxx((ooo, "threadFunc_2 "));
    return CLX_SUCCESS;
}
static ClxResult CLX_CALLBACK
threadFunc_3(void* data)
{
    eee(4, 4, (ooo, "threadFunc_3"));
    u2* str = asciiToUnicodeBadImple-
mentation(" test thread 3");
    // delete str; // oops forgotten
to delete...
    xxx((ooo, "threadFunc_3 "));
    return CLX_SUCCESS;
}
```

The screen capture in Figure 8 illustrates the position of the memory which is not freed including the file name and line number of the offending code. If this check is done after completing the execution of complete application or a particular functionality, the relevant threads and files can be searched for possible memory problems. Of course, identifying these problems can assist in finding more complex issues than just the missing memory *free* operation illustrated here. Additional examples of problems that might be uncovered include things like where a destructor of a class is not invoked correctly because of a class inheritance.

Investigating the code based on the log shows the missing code for releasing the memory previously allocated by the asciiToUnicodeBadImplementation function call.

```
static ClxResult CLX_CALLBACK
threadFunc_3(void* data)
{
    eee(4, 4, (ooo, "threadFunc_3"));
    u2* str = asciiToUnicodeBadImple-
mentation(" test thread 3");
    // delete str; // oops forgotten
to delete...
    xxx((ooo, "threadFunc_3 "));
    return CLX_SUCCESS;
}
```

While debugging with multiple communication protocols, associating various events to each other will improve the visibility of the overall implementation. Traditionally, a single dimension log file is kept and printed in order to analyze a problem or behavior within the code. Changing this architecture and keeping multi-dimensional log files and presenting them as multiple windows may improve the comprehension of the underlying system. This approach could be further improved by separating the communication protocol related data as a simplified protocol analyzer. As an example, Figure 9 shows a typical Bluetooth communication protocol messaging between the upper layer (AVDTP) and the Transport layer

(USB, UART or SDIO interface). The code execution corresponding to a protocol event can be monitored easily to associate these different views (communication protocol view and code execution view). Figure 10 shows a code execution view in which the highlighted line corresponds to the same event similarly highlighted in Figure 9 at 2:27.192 (i.e., 2 minutes, 27 seconds and 191 milliseconds from the start of execution).

In addition to these views, a co-operative tasking log (Figure 11) captured for the same scenario may be useful, particularly for complex applications using state machine based code. This view will allow an analysis of the logic of the code execution for debugging

Figure 8. Identification of memory with status not freed (line 46, thread 3)

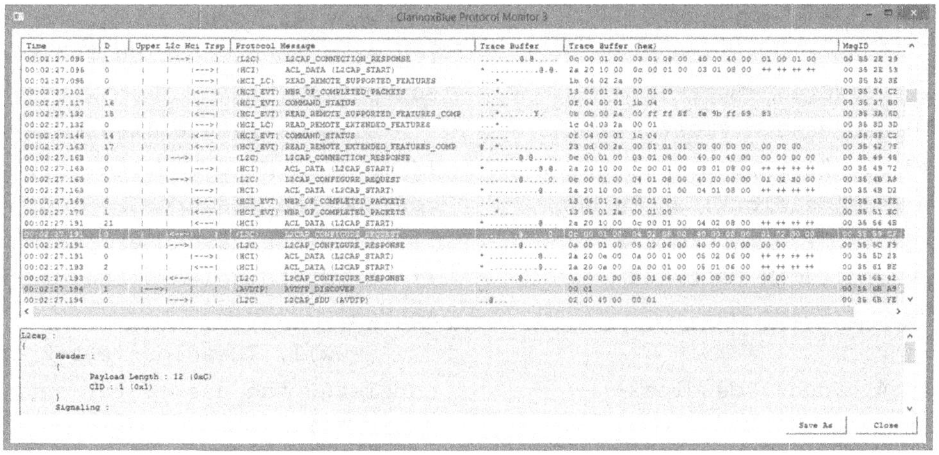

Figure 9. Example of Bluetooth communication protocol messaging between the upper layer (AVDTP) and the transport layer

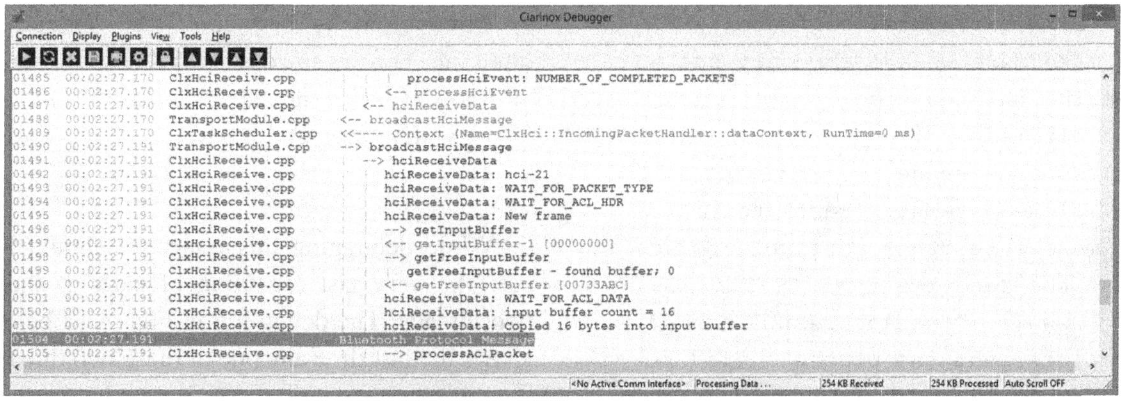

One of the most difficult and hard-to-catch issues is that of deadlocks. A deadlock can occur when two or more threads simultaneously enter a state where they are waiting for a resource from the other and are thus unable to, themselves, terminate. This situation can arise in any system requiring shared resources and/or process synchronization and is therefore a potential problem across a range of multiprocessing systems, parallel computing and distributed systems. Both software and hardware lock techniques are used to manage the interaction between processes and resources to avoid these types of synchronization problem.

One of the easiest ways to detect a deadlock point is to trace back the dysfunctional threads and detect their final activities before becoming dysfunctional. The following code fragment shows two interacting threads with a potential deadlock condition:

```
testMutex = clxCreateMutex();
clxBeginThread(deadlockTest_1, NULL,
"deadlockTest_1", 0);
clxBeginThread(deadlockTest_2, NULL,
"deadlockTest_2", 0);
static ClxResult CLX_CALLBACK
deadlockTest_1(void* data)
{
    eee(4, 4, (ooo, "deadlock-
Test_1"));
    clxSleep(1);
    wwww(1, "deadlockTest_1 thread
requires to use the shared re-
source");
    clxAcquireMutex(testMutex);
// make sure we are the only one ac-
cessing the resource
    clxSleep(1);
// resource usage
    clxReleaseMutex(testMutex);
// make sure others are able to ac-
cess the resource
    wwww(1, "deadlockTest_1 thread
completed the use of the shared re-
```

```
source");
    clxSleep(2);
// resource usage
    wwww(1, "deadlockTest_1 thread
requires to use the shared resource a
second time");
    clxAcquireMutex(testMutex);
// make sure we are the only one ac-
cessing the resource
    xxx((ooo, "deadlockTest_1 "));
    return CLX_SUCCESS;
}
static ClxResult CLX_CALLBACK
deadlockTest_2(void* data)
{
    eee(4, 4, (ooo, "deadlock-
Test_2"));
    clxSleep(1);
    wwww(1, "deadlockTest_2 thread
requires to use the shared re-
source");
    clxAcquireMutex(testMutex);
// make sure we are the only one ac-
cessing the resource
    // clxReleaseMutex(testMutex);
// forgot to release the shared re-
source
    wwww(1, "deadlockTest_2 thread
completed the use of the shared re-
source");
    wwww(1, "deadlockTest_2 thread
requires to use the shared resource a
second time");
    clxAcquireMutex(testMutex);
// make sure we are the only one ac-
cessing the resource
    xxx((ooo, "deadlockTest_2 "));
    return CLX_SUCCESS;
}
```

While debugging this issue, we should locate the very last execution of each of these two threads. The debug log in Figure 12 below shows the last time any one of these two threads

Figure 10. Code execution view of Bluetooth communication protocol messaging

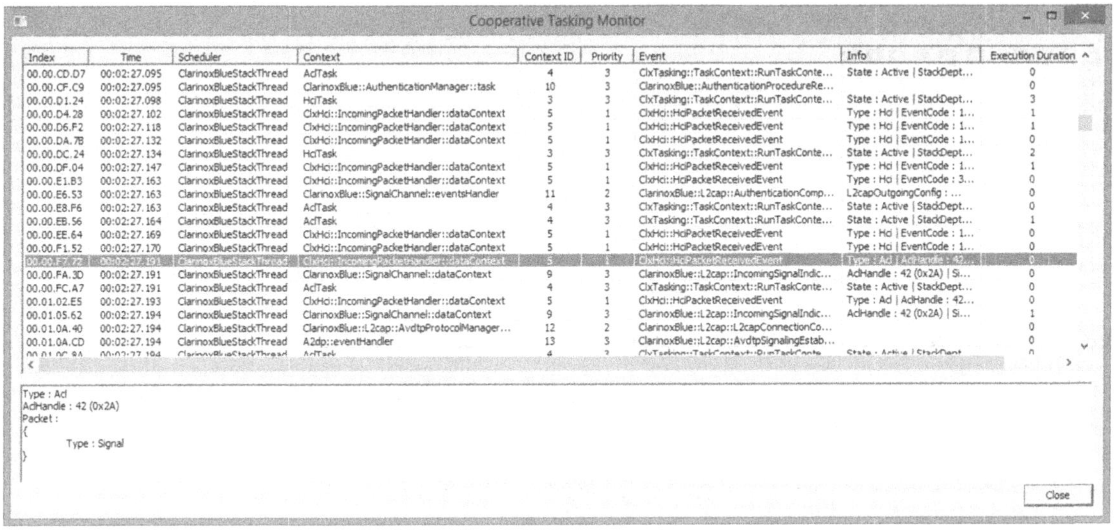

Figure 11. Co-operative tasking log view

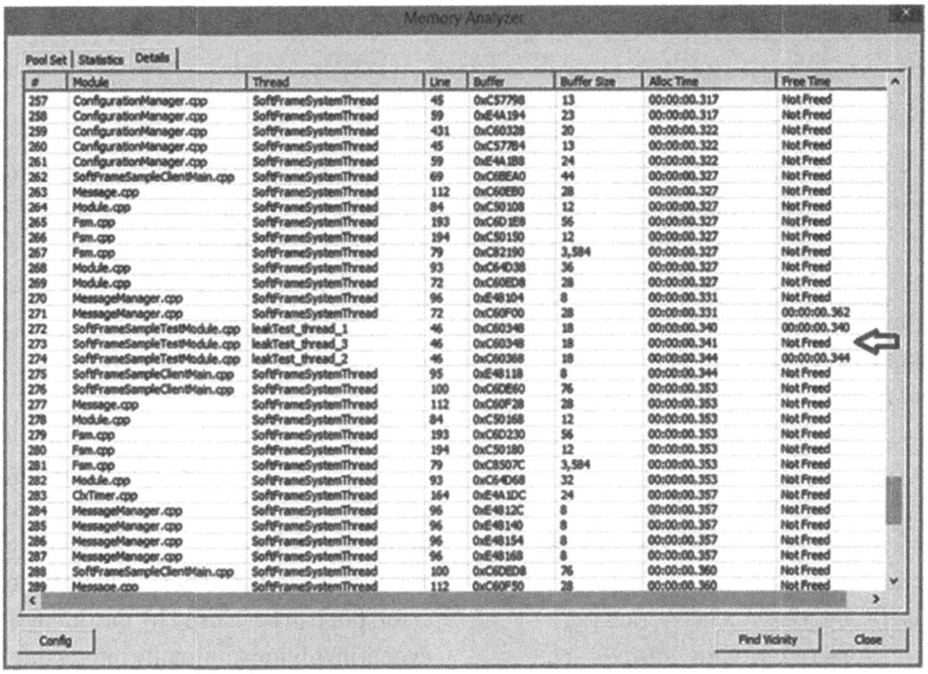

has been recorded. From this log we detect that the first thread is not able to access the resource for a second time. This indicates that a potential deadlock exists. The next part is to locate the previous traces of these two threads. The log in Figure 13 shows the last execution of the second thread. As the second thread was able to complete

the use of the shared resource, hence proving that the first thread successfully released the resource, the problem must be within the second thread. A closer look at the code fragment for the second thread (below) shows the missing release of the resource.

Figure 12. Debug log showing thread time

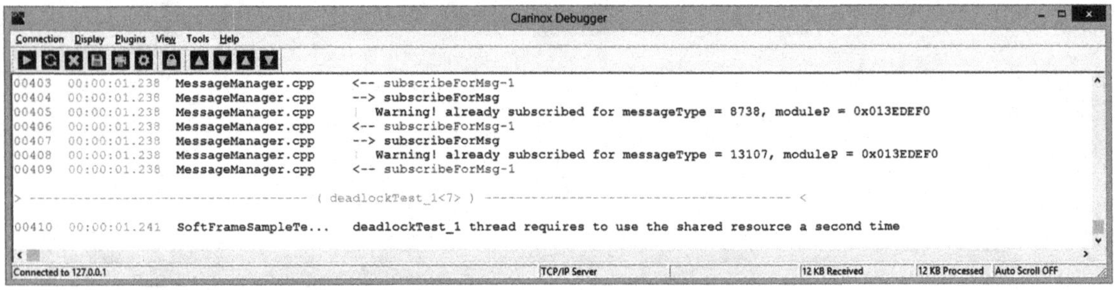

Figure 13. Log revealing the presence of a deadlock in the second thread

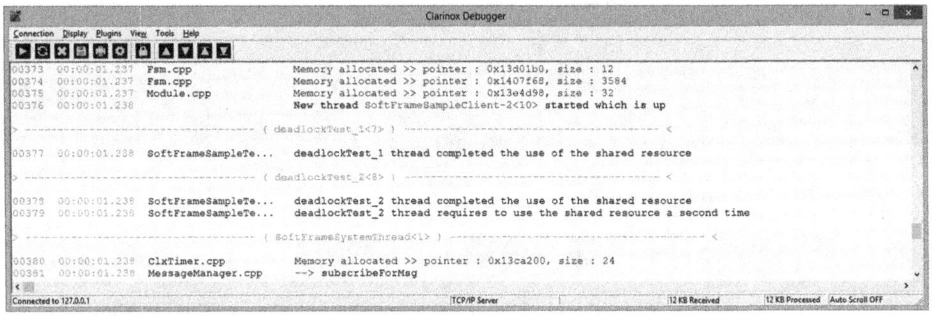

```
static ClxResult CLX_CALLBACK
deadlockTest_2(void* data)
{
    eee(4, 4, (ooo, "deadlock-
Test_2"));
    clxSleep(1);
    wwww(1, "deadlockTest_2 thread
requires to use the shared re-
source");
    clxAcquireMutex(testMutex);
// make sure we are the only one ac-
cessing the resource
    // clxReleaseMutex(testMutex);
// forgot to release the shared re-
source
    wwww(1, "deadlockTest_2 thread
completed the use of the shared re-
source");
    wwww(1, "deadlockTest_2 thread
requires to use the shared resource a
second time");
    clxAcquireMutex(testMutex);
// make sure we are the only one ac-
cessing the resource
    xxx((ooo, "deadlockTest_2 "));
    return CLX_SUCCESS;
}
```

It can be seen from even this simple example, that deadlocks can be a challenging and time consuming problem to fix. An interesting aspect of the problem is that they are not necessarily the result of what would normally be called a coding error, but can be caused by the order of a series of events involving minimally interacting processes. Running the same set of processes again with the same data might not result in the same sequence and thus deadlock might not occur. Achieving simultaneous multiple views of the same code threads is a useful way of detecting the presence of a deadlock condition.

FUTURE RESEARCH DIRECTIONS

The research issues in the debugging domain are usually cast in terms of a need to reduce the human skill level and the effort required in diagnosing and fixing defects through the use of computer-assisted techniques. However, this emphasis might be misleading. The key idea of the framework approach put forward in this chapter is to *increase* the average skill level being applied to the debug problem. This is done by capturing, distilling and encapsulating skills developed by generations of embedded engineers. Future debug tools will need to bring together a range of techniques, leveraging research in software debugging, high level specification, automated verification, repository mining, extreme visualization and other novel human interface methodologies.

The benefit of any new tool can be simplistically defined as its *usefulness* minus its *overhead*. It is clear that the law of diminishing returns applies here: unless a new debug tool saves more time than it costs to use, it does little more than to move the problem to somewhere else in the complexity gap that is a characteristic of all embedded systems. Earlier, we defined this gap as the difference between understanding and ability. The key idea is not so much to close the complexity gap but to bridge it with prior knowledge. For example, (Chandra & Orso, 2013) suggest a range of topics within the software debugging domain that might achieve this result. These are, of course, universal problems of clear relevance to hardware/software co-design and include the extensive use of large-scale data mining techniques, perhaps to discover otherwise hidden insights into the expected behavior of a system, or even to mine project repositories to identify and tap into relevant past experiences in order to identify and validate program debug options. Certainly, *artificial* intelligence will play an increasing role in replacing the real article, notwithstanding the slow progress over its previous 30—40 year existence.

A recurring theme in any discussion of future debugging relates to Embedded Instrumentation (EI) techniques. Although the concept been around since the emergence of built in self-test (BIST), it is gaining new impetus as a way of maintaining visibility into the increasingly complex operation of embedded chips. For example, advances in functional density such as stacked die packaging techniques, where several silicon die are stacked on top of one another in the same package, are exacerbating the issue of debug access (Collander, Katzko, & Gaborieau, 2010). On chip validation is made much more difficult if there is simply no physical place to probe. Further, signal integrity issues associated with high speed paths will often not allow the placement of a probe or jig, in any case. It seems clear that these trends in multi-die chip packages and even complete systems-in-package (Bolanos, 2010) will continue as new tightly coupled sensor-rich heterogeneous multi-processor systems increasingly emerge.

The concept of EI is moving away from an ad-hoc, special purpose applications used only during development, towards a formal set of design specifications supporting *whole of life* activities (e.g., including field upgrades). Emerging embedded instrumentation technologies include IEEE1149.7 and the IEEE P1687 Internal JTAG standard are designed to add architectural features for testing complicated System on Chip and other new device packages such as multi-die 3D chips. The objective is to specify an open instrument interface and access mechanism in a way that encourages the development of third party tools. As a result, the future of embedded tools will certainly involve some enhanced combinations of existing and new design-for-debug (DfD) hardware, for example (Park, Xu, Kim, & Park, 2012), (ARM Ltd., December 1995), (Leatherman & Stollon, 2005), within a framework of tools that capture the combined expertise of hardware, software and application engineers.

CONCLUSION

Embedded systems do not look like computer systems to the everyday user. They are the hidden systems, lurking behind anything from toys to trucks, from mobile phones to medical devices. It has long been the case that more microprocessors are used in embedded systems than in PCs and those already large numbers are increasing at a phenomenal rate as the devices that surround us in our everyday lives become smarter, a part of the era of the *Internet of Things*. One consequence is an inexorable drive towards devices that are connected – wired or wirelessly – that can access data anywhere, anytime.

Because embedded systems are in general designed to accomplish a very specific task or group of tasks the requirements placed upon them are quite different to those for desktop computing. While there can be no single set of design criteria that applies to the whole spectrum of embedded systems, they will tend to be characterized by a combination of robustness, small size and weight, real-time requirements, long life cycle and low price.

These constraints, although difficult, were entirely manageable in the days when applications were simple and small enough to and run without the need of an underlying operating system. This was no longer the case once the need arose to manage many simultaneous processes such as serial, USB, TCP/IP, Bluetooth, Wireless LAN, trunk radio, multiple channels, data and voice, enhanced graphics, along with complex system issues such as multiple states, multiple threads, numerous wait states and so on. At some point it becomes inefficient *not* to have an operating system to handle this plethora of tasks on behalf of the application. However, while a particular operating system might be a perfect fit for one application it might be utterly useless for another. This has traditionally led to embedded code being written and optimized for a specific operating system, microprocessor and embedded environment.

The dilemma is clear. An operating system platform must be selected for highly complex systems prior to starting the application development process. Thus the embedded operating system will be necessarily chosen on the basis of some combination of past experience and a "best-guess" of future requirement. What happens if these requirements change in a way that the chosen platform cannot support? What happens if a major client requests you change to another hardware platform? One way to deal with a requirement for multiple platforms is to deploy multiple teams of personnel experienced on a particular platform. Often developers are very familiar and experienced in one environment or one group of related environments only. For example, if there is a need to offer the application embedded under Linux, WindowsCE® and a proprietary RTOS, then three teams and three parallel developments may be required. Alternatively, the development may occur sequentially with an experienced team being required to port to each of the various platforms in turn. Or this problem is largely eliminated by the same framework approach that also provides assistance with debugging.

This chapter has advocated a "framework" approach to debugging complex embedded systems, using a commercial tool, the ClarinoxSoftFrame®, as an illustrative example. The objective of the approach is to achieve a modular and open approach to debugging that can minimize the work necessary by the development team and present a unified view of the system, regardless of its underlying hardware or operating system. In a *plug-in* environment, the development task reduces to preparing the application specific interfaces by inheriting C++ class information from a standard API and overlaying a small number of methods with special purpose code. Thus, its overall structure encapsulates and hides the underlying hardware and software differences and provides a common interface to the higher-layer applications that avoids the need to provide special interfaces between proprietary debug tools.

To achieve these objectives, the framework must provide the entire infrastructure necessary to allow an embedded software engineer to develop without the need to be aware of the detailed operation of the underlying hardware or real-time operating system. Ideally, prototyping and simulation would be undertaken on a PC, without the need for the target hardware. This is usually possible as modern PC systems typically run at least an order of magnitude (and often two orders or more) faster than the target processor. The middleware approach is intended to mask the differences between operating systems and processors and providing a single environment for all applications. The framework approach confers the ability for the application to be readily deployed to multiple target platforms. It achieves its goal by encapsulating operating system API and services and providing its own API to the software developer.

The middleware-based approach suffers from the same problems encountered in virtual-machine-based designs, but to a much smaller degree. Experience has shown that it imposes fewer overheads on the processor than does a virtual machine. To be effective at providing support for a comprehensive debugging environment, an operating system "wrapper" will have to include functions such as:

- Threading;
- Timers;
- Semaphores;
- Mutexes;
- Dynamic memory management without fragmentation;
- Inter-process message passing;
- Event/Message handling;
- Finite state machine;
- Serial device driver encapsulation;
- USB device driver encapsulation;
- TCP/UDP Socket encapsulation.

The middleware represents an extension to the debugging tools and Board Support Package or Hardware Adaptation Layer provided by RTOS manufactures so that the debugging tools can handle complex multi-threaded applications that are not specific to only one environment. As a side benefit, encapsulating the major functions of an operating system within a standardized API call structure can completely eliminate the effort of porting the application between platforms.

There is no doubt that isolating and correcting faults can be a tedious process, especially when working with program execution across multiple interacting processors. It could be said that the vast increase in hardware performance has been both the genesis of the problem and its solution. It has allowed complex embedded systems to be developed while at the same time, providing the necessary computing power to support extensive debugging capabilities. The sheer size of the gap between the complexity of the problem and our ability to control and observe the problem can be daunting. This chapter has provided some straightforward recommendations for systematically tracking problems via a stepped approach to debug and a framework that exploits the additional available computing power to simplify the development of commonly needed components for embedded systems.

REFERENCES

Agile Alliance. (2013). *Unit Testing*. Retrieved January 2014, from http://guide.agilealliance.org/guide/unittest.html

Almeida, G. M., Varyani, S., Busseuil, R., Sassatelli, G., Benoit, P., Torres, L., et al. (2010). *Evaluating the impact of task migration in multiprocessor systems-on-chip*. Paper presented at the 23rd symposium on Integrated circuits and system design. Sao Paulo, Brazil.

Bacchelli, A., Ciancarini, P., & Rossi, D. (2008). *On the Effectiveness of Manual and Automatic Unit Test Generation.* Paper presented at the Third International Conference on Software Engineering Advances. New York, NY.

Bolanos, M. A. (2010). *3D Packaging Technology: Enabling the next wave of applications.* Paper presented at the 34th IEEE/CPMT International Electronic Manufacturing Technology Symposium (IEMT). New York, NY.

Britt, J., & The Neurogami Group. (2013). *Test: Unit.* Retrieved January 2014, from http://ruby-doc.org/stdlib-2.1.0/libdoc/test/unit/rdoc/Test/Unit.html

Burrows, M., Freund, S., & Wiener, J. (2003). Run-Time Type Checking for Binary Programs. In G. Hedin (Ed.), *Compiler Construction* (Vol. 2622, pp. 90–105). Springer. doi:10.1007/3-540-36579-6_7

Cadene, S. (2013). *Embedded Market March 2013.* Retrieved August 2013, from http://www.slide-share.net/StephanCadene/embedded-mar1913

Chandra, S., & Orso, A. (2013). *International Workshop on the Future of Debugging.* Retrieved August 2013, from https://sites.google.com/site/futdeb2013/

Chun, I.-G., Choon-oh, L., & Duk-Kyun, W. (2007). *Esto NS-Debugger: The Non-stop Debugger for Embedded Systems.* Paper presented at the 9th International Conference on Advanced Communication Technology. New York, NY.

Clarinox Technologies Pty. Ltd. (2010). *The Clarinox Softframe.* Retrieved August 2013, from www.clarinox.com

Collander, P., Katzko, C., & Gaborieau, O. (2010). *Packaging technologies for 3D integration.* Paper presented at the 5th International Microsystems Packaging Assembly and Circuits Technology Conference (IMPACT). New York, NY.

Corliss, M. L., Lewis, E. C., & Roth, A. (2003). DISE: A Programmable Macro Engine for Customizing Applications. *International Symposium on Computer Architecture (ISCA), 31*(2), 362-373. http://doi.acm.org/10.1145/871656.859660

Eclipse Foundation. (2014). *Memory Analyzer (MAT).* Retrieved January 2014, from http://www.eclipse.org/mat/

Elson, J., Girod, L., & Estrin, D. (2004). EmStar: Development with high system visibility. *IEEE Wireless Communications, 11*(6), 70–77. doi:10.1109/MWC.2004.1368899

Farokhzad, S., Tanyeri, G., Messiter, T., & Beckett, P. (2010). *Plug-in Based Debugging For Embedded Systems.* Paper presented at the International Conference on Real-Time & Embedded Systems. New York, NY.

Girod, L., Ramanathan, N., Elson, J., Stathopoulos, T., Lukac, M., & Estrin, D. (2007). Emstar: A Software Environment for Developing and Deploying Heterogeneous Sensor-Actuator Networks. *ACM Transactions Sensor Networks, 3*(3), 13. http://doi.acm.org/10.1145/1267060.1267061

Ho, A., Hand, S., & Harris, T. (2004). *PDB: Pervasive Debugging with Xen.* Paper presented at the the Fifth IEEE/ACM International Workshop on Grid Computing. New York, NY.

Holgado-Terriza, J. A., & Viúdez-Aivar, J. (2012). JavaES, a Flexible Java Framework for Embedded Systems. In M. T. Higuera-Toledano, & A. J. Wellings (Eds.), *Distributed* (pp. 323–355). Springer. doi:10.1007/978-1-4419-8158-5_13

IEEE Standards Board. (1999). IEEE Standard for Software Unit Testing: An American National Standard, ANSI/IEEE Std 1008-1987. In IEEE Standards: Software Engineering, Volume Two: Process Standards, 1999 Edition. The Institute of Electrical and Electronics Engineers, Inc.

Kebin, Z., Yu, G., & Angelov, C. K. (2010). *Graphical Model Debugger Framework for embedded systems*. Paper presented at the Design, Automation & Test in Europe Conference & Exhibition (DATE). New York, NY.

Kolawa, A., & Huizinga, D. (2007). *Automated Defect Prevention: Best Practices in Software Management*. Wiley-IEEE Computer Society Press.

Kraemer, S., Gao, L., Weinstock, J., Leupers, R., Ascheid, G., & Meyr, H. (2007). *HySim: a Fast Simulation Framework for Embedded Software Development*. Paper presented at the 5th IEEE/ACM international conference on Hardware/software codesign and system synthesis. Salzburg, Austria.

Krasner, J. (2009). *Forecast 2010: What Is in Store for Embedded Developers*. Retrieved August 2013, from http://www.embeddedmarketintelligence. com/2009/12/02/forecast-2010-what-is-in-store-for-embedded-developers/

Leatherman, R., & Stollon, N. (2005). An embedding debugging architecture for SOCs. *IEEE Potentials*, 24(1), 12–16. doi:10.1109/MP.2005.1405795

ARM Ltd. (1995). Application Note 28: The ARM7TDMI Debug Architecture. *ARM DAI 0028A*. Retrieved January 2014, from http://infocenter. arm.com/help/topic/com.arm.doc.dai0028a/

Mousa, H., & Krintz, C. (2005). *HPS: Hybrid profiling support*. Paper presented at the 14th International Conference on Parallel Architectures and Compilation Techniques. New York, NY.

Murillo, L. G., Harnath, J., Leupers, R., & Ascheid, G. (2012). *Scalable and retargetable debugger architecture for heterogeneous MPSoCs*. Paper presented at the System, Software, SoC and Silicon Debug Conference (S4D). New York, NY.

Myers, G. J. (2004). *The Art of Software Testing*. Wiley & Sons.

Nagpurkar, P., Mousa, H., Krintz, C., & Sherwood, T. (2006). Efficient Remote Profiling for Resource-Constrained Devices. *ACM Transactions Architecture Code Optimization, 3*(1), 35-66. http://doi.acm.org/10.1145/1132462.1132465

Nass, R. (2007). Annual study uncovers the embedded market. *Embedded.com*. Retrieved from http://www.eetimes.com/design/other/4007166/Annual-study-uncovers-the-embedded-market

Park, H., Xu, J.-Z., Kim, K. H., & Park, J. S. (2012). On-Chip Debug Architecture for Multicore Processor. *ETRI Journal, 34*(1), 44-54. http://dx.doi.org/10.4218/etrij.12.0111.0172

Poole, C., Terrell, J., & Busoli, S. (2007). *NUnit*. Retrieved January 2014, from http://www.nunit. org/

Raccoon, L. B. S. (1995). The complexity gap. *SIGSOFT Software Engineering Notes, 20*(3), 37–44. doi:10.1145/219308.219315

Schneider, S., & Fraleigh, L. (2004). *The Ten Secrets of Embedded Debugging*. Retrieved January 2014, from http://www.eetimes.com/design/other/4025015/The-ten-secrets-of-embedded-debugging

IAR Systems. (2013). Retrieved January 2014, from http://www.iar.com/

UBM Tech. (2013). *Embedded Market Study*. Retrieved August 2013, from http://e.ubmelectronics. com/2013EmbeddedStudy/index.html

Tite, T., Vig, A., Olteanu, N., & Cuna, C. (2011). *moviTest: A Test Environment dedicated to multicore embedded architectures*. Paper presented at the 2011 International Symposium on System on Chip (SoC). New York, NY.

Titzer, B. L., & Palsberg, J. (2005). *Nonintrusive Precision Instrumentation of Microcontroller Software*. Paper presented at the 2005 ACM SIGPLAN/SIGBED conference on Languages, compilers, and tools for embedded systems. Chicago, IL.

Valgrind Developers. (2013). *Valgrind.* Retrieved January 2014, from http://valgrind.org/

Whitehouse, K., Tolle, G., Taneja, J., Sharp, C., Sukun, K., Jeong, J., et al. (2006). *Marionette: Using RPC for interactive development and debugging of wireless embedded networks.* Paper presented at the Fifth International Conference on Information Processing in Sensor Networks, IPSN 2006. New York, NY.

Wilson, B. (2013). *xUnit.net - Unit testing framework for C# and .NET.* Retrieved January 2014, from http://xunit.codeplex.com/

Wilson, P. R., Johnstone, M., Neely, M., & Boles, D. (1995). Dynamic storage allocation: A survey and critical review. In H. G. Baler (Ed.), *Memory Management* (Vol. 986, pp. 1–116). Springer. doi:10.1007/3-540-60368-9_19

Xie, T., Taneja, K., Kale, S., & Marinov, D. (2007). *Towards a Framework for Differential Unit Testing of Object-Oriented Programs.* Paper presented at the Second International Workshop on Automation of Software Test. New York, NY.

Yagi, H., Rosenstiel, W., Engblom, J., Andrews, J., Vissers, K., & Serughetti, M. (2009). *The Wild West: Conquest of complex hardware-dependent software design.* Paper presented at the 46th ACM/IEEE Design Automation Conference, DAC '09. New York, NY.

Yang, J., Soffa, M. L., Selavo, L., & Whitehouse, K. (2007). *Clairvoyant: A Comprehensive Source-Level Debugger for Wireless Sensor Networks.* Paper presented at the 5th international conference on Embedded networked sensor systems. Sydney, Australia.

KEY TERMS AND DEFINITIONS

Dynamic Debugging: Debugging of a computer system while it is executing. Optionally a dynamic debugger provides a console to interact with the system.

Embedded Framework: Software layers sit between the operating system and the user applications to provide OS agnostic and platform agnostic services for embedded developments.

Embedded System: An application specific microcomputer system that is a key part of a larger system.

Heterogeneous Embedded System: A computing system that includes a range of computational units with different instruction set architectures, each targeting specific parts of the overall task. Computational units could include general-purpose processors, digital signal processors, graphics processing units or application-specific integrated circuits.

Middleware: Software that extends the services provided to an application by the operating system, often related to special-purpose communication and input/output tasks.

Plug-In: A small DLL-based module by which developers can add their own debugging functionality to a base environment.

Real-Time Operating System: An operating system (OS) specifically set up to provide deterministic consistency when responding to application requests for services.

Wireless: Connection and communication over electromagnetic waves (e.g. radio frequency, infrared, light), rather than over a physical cable connection.

Chapter 19
Industrial Experiments in IMS, ATC, and SDR Projects of Property Verification Techniques

Emmanuel Gaudin
PragmaDev, France

ABSTRACT

The increasing complexity of embedded systems calls for verification techniques to make sure the systems behave properly. When it comes to safety-critical systems, this aspect is even more relevant and is now taken into consideration by certification authorities. For that matter, property verification is accepted to be done not only on the system itself but also on a representative model of the system. This chapter first introduces the different properties and how they could be expressed. Then associated modeling languages characteristics are discussed to describe the systems on which the properties can be verified. Finally, different technologies to verify the properties are presented, including some practical examples and existing tools. This last part is illustrated by several research projects such as the PRESTO ARTEMIS European project and the exoTICus System@tic Paris Region competitiveness cluster project.

PROPERTY DEFINITION

Properties of a system are difficult to define because they either seem obvious, like a plane should fly, or very tricky to explain, like the minimum speed of the plane is relative to its height and weather condition. Generally speaking the properties can be expressed as a set of relations on the inputs and the outputs of the system, or as an evaluation of some internal data in the system. For example a property such as "the speed of the plane should not exceed 900km/h" could be expressed

by a mathematical expression such as "system. speed<900" which can be verified automatically by a computer. Usually speaking properties are categorized to be functional or non-functional, and black box or white box.

Functional Property

A functionality is a given scenario of what a system should do; one of the expected behavior. If the system behaves differently it would not mean the functionality is not fulfilled, because all alterna-

DOI: 10.4018/978-1-4666-6194-3.ch019

tive scenarios are not meant to be described for a given functionality. But a functional property describes a mandatory relation between several events. It can be seen as an extension of a function of the system, a piece of scenario that should be verified in any case.

Non Functional Property

A non functional property is generally speaking about the quality level of a property. For example a basic functional property might be that when the button is pressed the light shall lit. A non functional requirement could be that the light should lit within 10mS after pressing the button. Or it could be that the light bulb should have a 10,000 hours lifetime. In a sense a functional property is very straightforward and can be mathematically verified where a non-functional property is more about the quality of a property and is difficult to evaluate. Still one of the verifiable non-functional properties is performance because it is easy to measure, and it can even be estimated with detailed models of the system.

Black Box Property

A black box property is a property that looks at the system as a black box and that only considers what happens on its interfaces. The interest of this type of property is that it can be verified on a real system or a simulated model of the system. The problem is that since the internal information is not visible, to make sure the property is always verified requires all possible surrounding situations to be generated. Without any knowledge of the internal design of the system, the number of possible scenarios might be so large that it might not be possible to explore them all.

White Box Property

A white box property will use the internal information of the system. It is therefore dependent on the system implementation. Verification of a white box property is by construction easier and more efficient but is not always applicable on a real system because the internal information might not be accessible.

TECHNOLOGIES

We will focus on event driven technologies regarding property verification. These technologies apply to communicating system where the possible number of values for the inputs in the system, and the possible sequences of events can create a huge number of different cases for the system. It is therefore interesting to use a model of the system so that the property can be verified on a simulated model.

Executable Model

A model is an abstract representation of the real system. A model is very useful for the different stakeholders to communicate, to document what is the system about, to ease maintenance and evolution of the system. A model can be very abstract or quite detailed depending on the goals to achieve.

In order to be able to verify properties which are essentially dynamic, the model must be somehow executable. That requires a semantic of execution and an action language in the modeling language. In the domain of communicating systems, a semantic of execution is about how the information is sent and received, how time is handled, and how concurrent processing is organized. An action language is a way to formally write precise instructions. To do so the modeling language requires data types and some basic operators. This is necessary even to express a simple behavior such as: the system, in case of no reply within 1s, sends again the same message three times. In the absence of a proper response the system goes to a special error state. These types of languages are called formal because they are complete and unambiguous. For the description of event driven systems the most mature language is certainly SDL

(International Telecommunication Union, 2014), an ITU-T recommendation originally designed to describe telecommunication protocols. For the purpose of verifying the model, more generic languages such as UML (Object Management Group, 2014a) or AADL (Society of Automotive Engineers, 2014) are also trying to make their model more formal with extensions such as fUML (Object Management Group, 2014b) to make UML formal and a Behavior annex for AADL.

A typical SDL state machine is showed in figure 1. In the connecting state, if the tConReq timer goes off, the ConReq is sent again 4 times and then fails if no reply is received. If the Con-Conf message is received the state machine goes to the connected state. One of the key element in that state machine is the SDL action language that allows in that example to increment a counter and more generally speaking that allows to design executable specification.

Message Sequence Chart

MSC (International Telecommunication Union, 2010) is an ITU-T recommendation. Its purpose is to provide a language for the specification and description of the communication behavior of system components and their environment by means of message interchange. Since in MSCs the communication behavior is presented in a very intuitive and transparent manner, particularly in the graphical representation, the MSC language is easy to learn, use and interpret. In connection with other languages it can be used to support

Figure 1. A typical SDL state machine

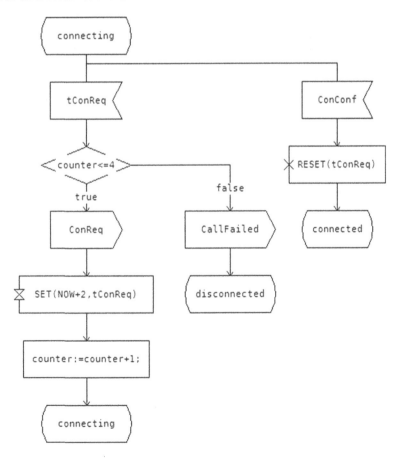

methodologies for system specification, design, simulation, testing, and documentation.

Special semantics can be added to MSC diagrams by the means of *inline expressions*. These can enclose one or several parts of the diagram and specify:

- If they are optional (*opt*);
- If one or the other part can happen (*alt*);
- If the part can be repeated (*loop*);
- If the parts happens in parallel (*par*);
- If the ordering within the part is significant (*seq*).

An example of an alternative inline expression is given in Figure 2.

MSC diagram can also define relative or absolute time constraints on a scenario such as in Figure 3.

MSC is a good candidate to describe basic functional or non-functional scenarios. But it does not really describe a property. A property requires a way to describe causality between events which is not possible with the MSC.

Figure 2. Inline alternative expression in MSC

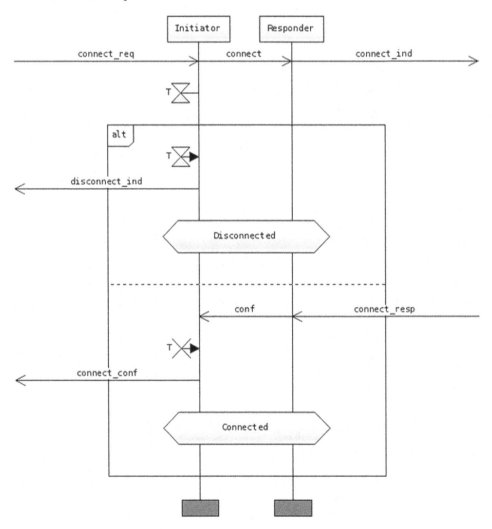

Figure 3. A relative time constraint on the exchange of messages

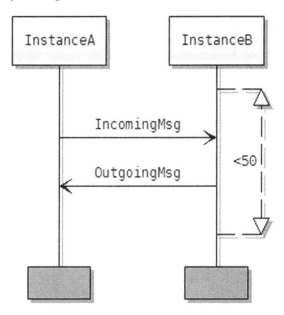

Property Sequence Chart

Property Sequence Chart (Autili, M., Inveradi, P. & Pelliccione P, 2007) (PSC) is a simple but expressive formalism that has been proposed to specify temporal properties without expertise in temporal logic. PSC is a language that extends a subset of the ITU-T Message Sequence Chart or the UML 2.0 Interaction Sequence Diagrams.

Within the PSC language, a property is seen as a relation on a set of exchanged system messages, with zero or more constraints. PSC may be used to describe both positive scenarios (i.e., the "desired" ones) and negative scenarios (i.e., the "unwanted" ones) for specifying interactions among the components of a system. For positive scenarios, PSC allows to specify both mandatory and provisional behaviours. In other words, it is possible to specify that the run of the system must or may continue to complete the described interaction.

The available symbols in PSC diagrams are displayed in Figure 4.

Instances are represented as in MSC diagrams. The parallel, alternative and loop operators are represented the same way as the par, alt and loop inline expressions in MSC diagrams respectively. The relative time constraint has the same representation and semantics as in MSCs.

Messages in PSCs have two representations:

- An arrow going from the sender to the receiver, just as in MSC diagrams;
- A textual representation, with the format "<sender instance name>.<message name>.<receiver instance name>". This representation is used in constraints, explained below.

Unlike messages in MSC diagrams, message arrows in PSC diagram can have 3 kinds:

- **Regular Message:** Identified by the prefix "e:" for the message text, is a precondition for what follows.
- **Required Message:** Identified by the prefix "r:" for the message text, is a message that must occur if the preconditions are met. Required messages must always appear after all regular messages.
- **Fail Message:** Identified by the prefix "f:" for the message text, is a message that must not occur if the preconditions are met. Fail messages must also always appear after all regular messages.

When describing a property, the default ordering is the loose ordering: anything can happen between a message specified in the PSC and the one following it. For cases where a strict ordering is necessary, i.e when a message in the PSC must be directly followed by the one following, the *strict operator* can be used, either on a message send or a receive. Examples are given in Figure 5.

Figure 4. PSC graphical notation

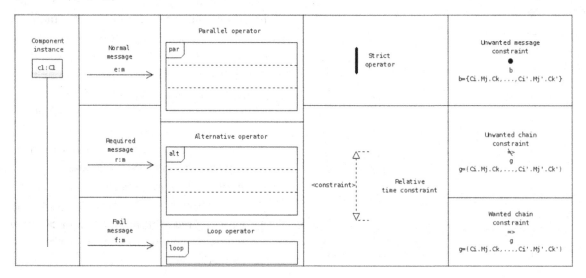

Figure 5. PSC strict operator

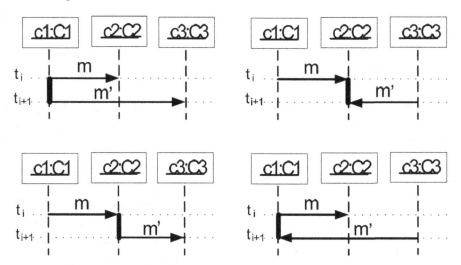

The PSC diagrams also allows to set *constraints* on the messages. These constraints are shown as symbols at the beginning or end of message arrows with an associated text. These constraints can have 3 types:

- **Unwanted Message Constraint:** Denotes a set of messages where none should happen before or after the message it is attached too, depending on whether it appears at the beginning or the end of the arrow.

- **Unwanted Chain Constraint:** Denotes a sequence of messages that should not appear as a whole before or after the message it is attached to.

- **Wanted Message Constraint:** Denotes a sequence of messages that must appear as a whole before or after the message it is attached to.

Figure 6 provides a simple example of a PSC diagram.

Figure 6. Example of a property expressed in PSC

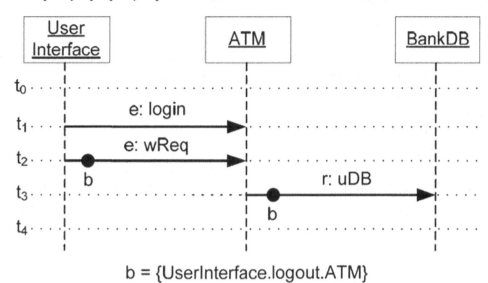

b = {UserInterface.logout.ATM}

According to the semantics described above, the property can be read as follows:

- *If* a message "login" is sent from UserInterface to ATM (normal message "e:login"),
- *And if* a message "wReq" is sent from UserInterface to ATM after the login, without a "logout" message sent from UserInterface to ATM in between (normal message "e:wReq" with the unwanted message constraint "UserInterface.logout. ATM");
- *Then* a message "uDB" must be sent from ATM to BankDB, unless a message "logout" has been sent from UserInterface to ATM before (required message "r:uDB" with unwanted message constraint "UserInterface.logout.ATM").

PSC representation is very close to the MSC representation. Since MSCs can be used by designers and testers of embedded systems to visualize the flow of control of a system. The benefit of the enhancements is to be able to express a property at the same level as the trace that will be generated by the execution or the simulation of a system.

PSC enables the user of the software to write non-functional properties and functional properties at a high level using well known MSC standard.

VERIFYING THE PROPERTIES WITH EXHAUSTIVE SIMULATION

Principles of Exhaustive Simulation

One of the key interests of having a model based on strong semantics is the possibility to execute it independently from a real target. Based on the interface of the system, it is possible to try any possible inputs. Once all inputs have been tried in every possible order with all possible parameter values, it means all possible cases have been tested. This is called exhaustive simulation. The basic principles of this popular model checking technique will be further described.

Global System State

It is important to first introduce the concept of global system state: that is a complete picture of the overall system. It combines the states of all finite state machines, the values of their local variables, the values of the object attributes, and the values of all global variables. For a given global system state, a given input will always produce the same result. In the simple example showed Figure 7, a state machine has four states: *disconnected*, *connecting*, *connected*, and *disconnecting*. The global system state is the state of the finite state machine and the value of the only local variable: counter. The combination of these two values fully describes the system state.

When an input is applied to the system, its global system state will change to a new one (Figure 8). Executing all possible inputs on the

system builds what is called a reachability graph or a behavioral tree. One path in the tree is a standard scenario.

Considering embedded applications are usually multi-threaded, a path from one global system state to the next might be defined by a full transition (from one state to the next of a finite state machine) or by an atomic instruction (because blocks of instructions can be pre-empted by the RTOS). Of course, if a branch of the reachability graph is an atomic instruction, that makes it much larger than if based on full transition.

Figure 7. Global system state combines the state and the variable values

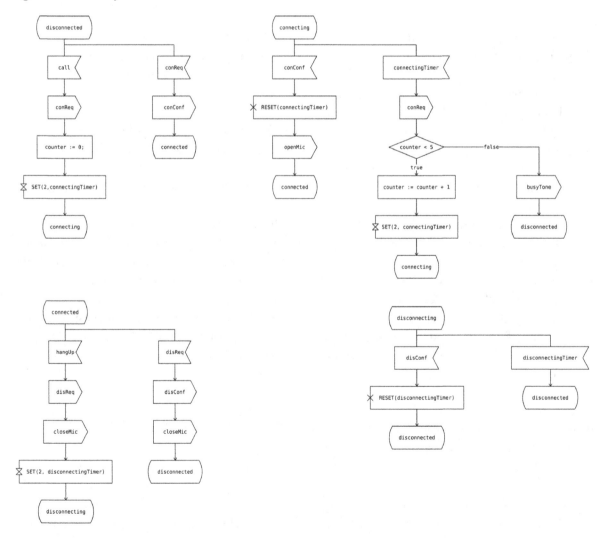

Figure 8. Each incoming event leads the system to a new global system state

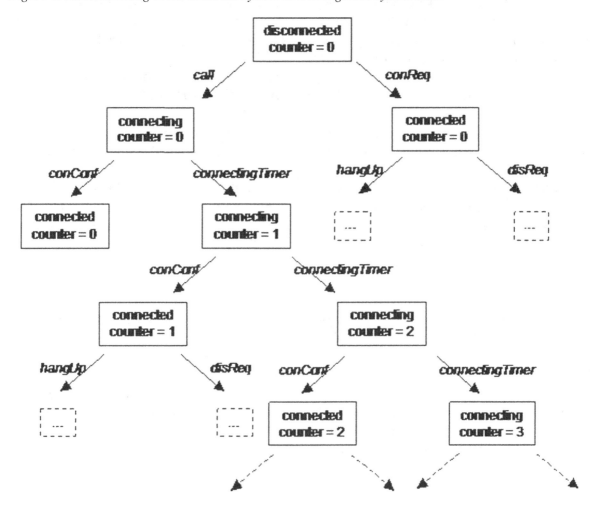

It is also important to notice that even a very simple state machine might lead to a very large graph. For example a one state automaton with one possible input and a simple *int* on 16 bits as a parameter will generate 2^{16} global system states with full transition branches. That means it will not be possible to explore all possible states on a real system because of the combinatorial explosion.

In order not to execute several times the same branches, all visited states must be remembered during an exploration. To do so, mathematical tools are used such as hash tables that compresses the system information to set a bit in a table. Whenever the same bit is set there is a probability related to the size of the table that it is the same state.

Another way to reduce the reachability graph is to cut branches in the tree. A simple way to do so for example is to reduce the possible values for some variables (for example instead of trying all possible values for an integer, try 1, 5, 10, and 256). That technique requires an internal expertise of the system to be checked in order to set the right values.

Dynamic and Static Rules

Each time a node in the graph is reached, static and dynamic rules can be verified. A static rule is based on the system state itself, for example the value of a state combined with the value of a variable. A dynamic rule is based on the evolution of the system states, so it can be a piece of a scenario: for example it is not possible for one of the state machine in the system to go directly from the disconnected state to the connected state.

The static rules, the dynamic rules, and the rules to restrict the graph are described in an automaton that is evaluated every time a new state is reached. It has access to all internal information (states, variables and others) and decides if one of the rules has been violated, if the branch should be cut, or if the exploration should go on.

The same technique can be used to generate test suites. In that case, the observer defines the test objectives and the exhaustive simulation will find all possible scenarios to get to the objectives.

Since it is a model simulation with access to all internal information, this technique can verify black box as well as white box properties. Verifying functional properties is what this technique does best. When it comes to non functional properties things get a bit more complex. For example to verify a time constraint, the model must also contain some relevant timing information associated to the execution, and the exhaustive simulation

must be able to handle this information. Exhaustive simulation can verify functional and non-functional, white box and black box properties.

Verifying the Properties with Symbolic Resolution

Exhaustive simulation executes the system for real and tries all possible inputs of the system. That creates an enormous amount of cases and even with advanced optimization techniques it is actually difficult to run on a real system. This is particularly true if the system receives a lot of data that does not have any impact on its execution. The exhaustive simulator will try all possible inputs even though it is not relevant. Another approach based on symbolic execution is to store all the events and instructions combined with the property and to try to solve it like one would solve a mathematical equation. In that case the solver can detect if the input parameters have any impact on the execution of the system, and the resulting output can actually be a range of possible values. This type of technology is very efficient on systems transmitting a lot of data, and also particularly

Figure 9. Dynamic and static rules

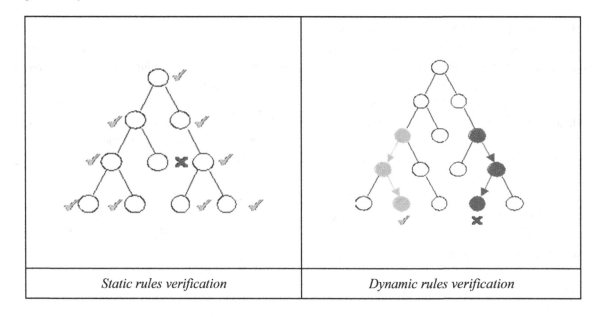

| Static rules verification | Dynamic rules verification |

Figure 10. A simple transition with a parameter in the input

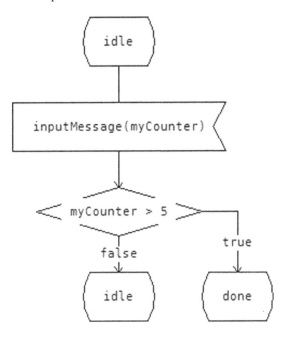

efficient when the goal is to generate inputs that trigger a maximum of the possible transitions. This is ideal for model based testing approach in order to generate test cases that will test all possible inputs in the system efficiently.

In the simple example Figure 10 there are two possible paths: one where the input parameter myCounter is strictly greater than 5, and the other one where the input parameter is lower than 5. These two symbolic equations lead to generate two test cases to cover all transitions. The first one will send the inputMessage with myCounter strictly greater than 5, and the second one will send the inputMessage with myCounter lower than 5.

This type of verification technique is based on a model of the system. The solver has access to all internal information and can verify black box as well as white box properties. When it comes to verifying time constraint it could even be possible to mathematically demonstrate a timing constraint can or cannot be verified. As a conclusion symbolic resolution can verify functional and non-functional, white box and black box properties.

USE CASES

IMS: IP Multimedia Subsystem in exoTICus Project

The first use case on property verification is an outcome of the exoTICus (Systematic Paris competitiveness cluster, 2014) collaborative project realized in the framework of the Systematic Paris Region competitiveness cluster. The goal of the project was to verify the compatibility and interoperability of the services using formal methods and model checking technology. The IP Multimedia Subsystem or IP Multimedia Core Network Subsystem (IMS) is an architectural framework for delivering IP multimedia services. The service used in the project was the PoC Push to Talk over Cellular service. It is a service option for a cellular phone network which permits subscribers to use their phone as a walkie-talkie with unlimited range. A significant advantage of PoC / PTT is the ability for a single person to reach an active talk group with a single button press instantly.

The service has been modeled with SDL. The architecture of the service in Figure 11 is quite simple and the different state machines have short transitions.

The full SDL model has been exported to IF (Queille, J. P. & Sifakis, J, 1982) pivot language and some properties have been defined in a separate file. The Verimag tool IFx have been used on the IF files to run an exhaustive simulation of the model with property verification at each execution of a transition. With such a configuration, with two users and four actions from the environment, the exhaustive simulation created around 40,000 states. The number of states reached 200,000 with five actions. This simple example proved that there could not be two clients in the Talking state at the same time, but it could be that a client is talking while all the others have left the conversation.

Figure 11. Push to talk over cellular architecture

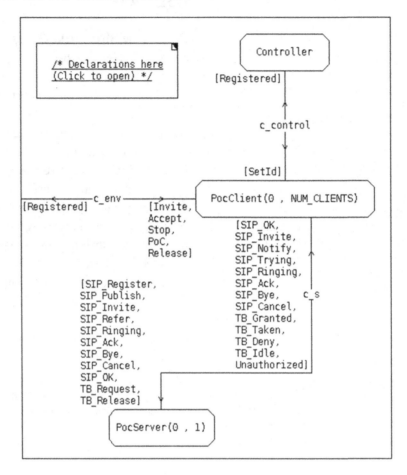

ATC Air Traffic Control in Industrial Development

This is an interesting case because it is based on a real industrial model of an Air Traffic Control software. The SDL model of the ATC is quite massive: an architecture of around 60 blocks containing 100 state machines defining in total 1,500 states. The model has been translated to IF (DUMAS X, 2011) and a few properties have been defined. It appeared the number of generated cases was so large that the results could not even been stored. As a first analysis it is probably because the input messages come with large parameters that actually do not have any impact on the system execution. Unfortunately the tool does not detect this and tries all possible inputs in the system generating a massive number of useless states. This is a typical case in which symbolic execution should give better results. This is currently under investigation with Diversity (Bahrami, D., Faivre, A. & Lapitre, A, 2012) tool from CEA.

SDR Software Defined Radio in EU FP7 PRESTO Project

The PRESTO project started on April 2011 for a duration of 36 months. It is co-funded by the European Commission under the ARTEMIS Joint Undertaking Programme. PRESTO stands for imProvement of industrial Real time Embedded SysTems development process. It aims at improving test-based embedded systems development and validation, while considering the constraints of industrial development processes. This project is based on the integration of test traces exploitation along with platform models and design space exploration techniques

The expected result of the project is to establish functional and performance analysis and platform optimisation at early stage of the design development. The approach of PRESTO is to model the software/hardware allocation, by the use of modeling frameworks, such as the UML profile for model-driven development of Real Time and Embedded Systems (MARTE). The analysis tools, among them timing analysis including Worst Case Execution Time (WCET) analysis, scheduling analysis and possibly more abstract system-level timing analysis techniques will receive as inputs on the one hand information from the performance modeling of the HW/SW-platform, and on the other hand behavioural information of the software design from tests results of the integration test execution.

Of particular novelty in PRESTO is the exploitation of traces for the exclusion of over-pessimistic assumptions during timing analysis: instead of taking all possible inputs and states into account for a worst-case analysis, a set of relevant traces is analyzed separately to reduce the set of possible inputs and states for each trace.

The partners involved in this project are Teletel (Greece), Thales Communications (France), Rapita Systems (UK), VTT (Finland), Softeam (France), Thales (Italy), MetaCase (Finland), INRIA (France), University of L'Aquila (Italy), Miltech Hellas (Greece), PragmaDev (France), Prismtech (UK), Sarokal Solutions (Finland).

In the context of that project, PragmaDev has developed a new Tracer (PragmaDev, 2014) that support both MSC (Message Sequence Chart) and PSC (Property Sequence Chart). The user can define its own property, trace execution, and verify the properties on the traces with the same tool.

The use case was the auxiliary Mobile Ad Hoc Network (MANET) in support of the Ultra-Wideband (UWB) positioning system, and in particular the OLSR (Optimized Link State Routing) level 3 network protocol. The existing code has been instrumented to gather a set of execution traces from the target. All the traces are using the MSC format, and three functional properties and one non-functional property, defined as PSCs have been actually verified on a real execution trace with PragmaDev Tracer.

CONCLUSION

In the domain of event driven systems, the PRESTO project demonstrated a functional property can be expressed with the Property Sequence Chart diagram, an extension to the Message Sequence Chart international standard. A PSC can be verified on a real or a simulated execution trace of the system with tools such as the PragmaDev Tracer.

The IMS and the ATC projects demonstrated that exhaustive simulation technologies can verify properties on a representative formal model but state space explosion is a major limitation to that approach. Symbolic resolution looks like an interesting option to verify properties on a model. Upcoming experiments will demonstrate its efficiency on real industrial models.

REFERENCES

Autili, M., Inveradi, P., & Pelliccione, P. (2007). Graphical scenarios for specifying temporal properties: an automated approach. *Automated Software Engineering*, *14*(3), 293–340. doi:10.1007/s10515-007-0012-6

Bahrami, D., Faivre, A., & Lapitre, A. (2012). DIVERSITY–TG: Automatic Test Case Generation from Matlab/Simulink models. In *Proceedings of ERTS2 Conference*. ERTS2.

Dumas, X. (2011). *Application des méthodes par ordres-partiels à la vérification formelle de systèmes asynchrones clos par un contexte: application à SDL.* (Doctoral thesis). Université de Rennes 1, Institut Mines-Télécom-Télécom Bretagne-UEB, France.

International Telecommunication Union. (2010). ITU-T - Message Sequence Chart. Z.120 recommendation. Retrieved from http://www.itu.int/rec/T-REC-Z.120/en

International Telecommunication Union. (2014). ITU-T - Specification and Description Language. Z.100 recommendation. Retrieved from http://www.itu.int/rec/T-REC-Z.100/en

Object Management Group. (2014a). OMG - Unified Modeling Language. UML recommendation. Retrieved from http://www.omg.org/spec/UML/

Object Management Group. (2014b). Foundational UML. fUML recommendation. Retrieved from http://www.omg.org/spec/FUML/

PragmaDev. (2014). PragmaDev Tracer. Retrieved from http://www.pragmadev.com/product/tracing.html

Queille, J. P., & Sifakis, J. (1982). Specification and verification of concurrent systems in CESAR. In *Proceedings of the 5th Colloquium on International Symposium on Programming* (pp. 337–351). Academic Press.

Society of Automotive Engineers. (2014). Architecture and Analysis Description Language. AADL recommendation. Retrieved from http://standards.sae.org/as5506b/

Systematic Paris Competitiveness Cluster. (2014). Retrieved from http://www.systematic-paris-region.org/en/projets/exoticus

KEY TERMS AND DEFINITIONS

AADL: Architecture Analysis and Description Language is an SAE specification to describe the hardware and software architecture of a system.

ATC: Air Traffic Control is an application to manage airplane traffic from the ground. Part of the application is running in the airplane and its counterpart is running on the ground.

Formal Model: A model which description is complete and non-ambiguous.

IMS: IP Multimedia Subsystem is a 3GPP framework designed to deliver multimedia services over mobile networks.

MSC: Message Sequence Chart is an ITU standard to describe interactions between entities.

PSC: Property Sequence Chart is a notation to express temporal properties in an MSC or a Sequence Diagrams that is defined by the University of l'Aquila.

SDL: Specification and Description Language is an ITU standard used to describe communicating systems.

SDR: Software Defined Radio is a technology in which software handles the modulation that was historically handled by hardware.

Compilation of References

AADL. (2013). Architecture Analysis & Design Language. Retrieved from.http://www.aadl.info

Abderazek, B., Akanda, M., Yoshinaga, T., & Sowa, M. (2007). Mathematical Model for Multi-objective Synthesis of NoC Architectures. In *Proceeding of the International Conference on Parallel Processing Workshops (ICPPW)*, (pp. 36). Xian, China: IEEE.

Abke, J., Böhl, E., & Henno, C. (1998, July). Emulation based real time testing of automotive applications. In *Proceedings of 4th IEEE International On-Line Testing workshop* (pp. 28-31). IEEE.

Addo-Quaye, C. (2005). Thermal-aware mapping and placement for 3-D NoC designs. In *Proceeding of the International SoC Conference*, (pp. 25-29). Herndon, VA: IEEE.

Adve, S., Li, M., Sasanja, R., & Chen, Y. (2005). The Alpbench Benchmark Suit for Complex Multimedia Applications. In *Proceeding of the International Symposium on Circuits and Systems*, (pp. 34-45). Austin, TX: IEEE.

Agarwal, M., Paul, B., Zhang, M., & Mitra, S. (2007). Circuit failure prediction and its application to transistor aging. In *Proceedings of the 25th IEEE VLSI Test Symposium*, (pp. 277-286). IEEE.

Agile Alliance. (2013). *Unit Testing*. Retrieved January 2014, from http://guide.agilealliance.org/guide/unittest.html

Aicas Gmb, H. (2013). *JamaicaVM*. Retrieved from https://www.aicas.com/cms/en/JamaicaVM

Alcalde, B., Cavalli, A.R., Chen, D., Khuu, D., & Lee, D. (2004). Network Protocol System Passive Testing for Fault Management: A Backward Checking Approach. In *Formal Techniques for Networked and Distributed Systems* (pp. 150-166). Academic Press.

Alexandersson, R., & Öhman, P. (2010). On Hardware Resource Consumption for Aspect-Oriented Implementation of Fault Tolerance. In *Proceedings of European Dependable Computing Conference* (pp. 61-66). Valencia, Spain: IEEE Conference Publishing Services.

Almeida, G. M., Varyani, S., Busseuil, R., Sassatelli, G., Benoit, P., Torres, L., et al. (2010). *Evaluating the impact of task migration in multi-processor systems-on-chip*. Paper presented at the 23rd symposium on Integrated circuits and system design. Sao Paulo, Brazil.

Alur, R., Courcoubetis, C., Halbwachs, N., Henzinger, T. A., Ho, P.-H., & Nicollin, X. et al. (1995). The algorithmic analysis of hybrid systems. *Theoretical Computer Science*, *138*, 3–34. doi:10.1016/0304-3975(94)00202-T

Amory, A., Marcon, C., & Lubaszewski, M. (2011). Task mapping on NoC-based MPSoCs with faulty tiles: Evaluating the energy consumption and the application execution time. In *Proceeding of the International Symposium on Rapid System Prototyping*, (pp. 164-170). Karlsruhe, Germany: IEEE.

André, C. (2009). *Syntax and Semantics of the Clock Constraint Specification Language (CCSL)* (Research Report RR-6925). INRIA.

André, C., DeAntoni, J., Mallet, F., & Simone, R. D. (2010). The Time Model of Logical Clocks Available in the OMG MARTE Profile. In Synthesis of Embedded Software: Frameworks and Methodologies for Correctness by Construction (pp. 201-227). Springer.

André, C., Mallet, F., & Simone, R. D. (2007). Modeling Time(s). In *Proceedings of ACM/IEEE International Conference On Model Driven Engineering Languages and Systems* (MoDELS/UML'07), (pp. 559-573). ACM/IEEE.

Antoni, L., Leveugle, R., & Fehér, B. (2003, October). Using run-time reconfiguration for fault injection applications. *IEEE Transactions on Instrumentation and Measurement*, *52*(5), 1468–1473.

Arda, G., Suryadevara, J., Peraldi-Frati, M.-A., & Mallet, F. (2013). Analysis Support for TADL2 Timing Constraints on EAST-ADL Models. In *Proceedings of the 7th European Conference on Software Architecture*, (pp 89-105). Academic Press.

Arenas, M. G., Castillo, P. A., Romero, G., Rateb, F., & Merelo, J. J. (2005). Coevolving multilayer perceptrons along training sets. In Proceedings of Advances in Soft Computing: 8th Fuzzy Days, (pp. 503-513). Academic Press.

ARINC. (2011) *ARINC Specification for Navigation System Database (ARINC 424-20)*. Retrieved from https://www.arinc.com/cf/store/documentlist.cfm

ARM Ltd. (1995). Application Note 28: The ARM7TDMI Debug Architecture. *ARM DAI 0028A*. Retrieved January 2014, from http://infocenter.arm.com/help/topic/com.arm.doc.dai0028a/

Armengaud, E., Steininger, A., & Horauer, M. (2008, August). Towards a systematic test for embedded automotive communication systems. *IEEE Transactions on Industrial Informatics*, *4*(3), 146–155.

Arsanjani, A., Ghosh, S., Allam, A., Abdollah, T., Ganapathy, S., & Holley, K. (2008). SOMA: A method for developing service-oriented solutions. *IBM Systems Journal*, *47*(3), 377–396. doi:10.1147/sj.473.0377

ATESST Consortium, ATESST Deliverable D3.1. (2007). The Modelling Approach: Overview of the EAST-ADL2. *ITEA, Tech. Rep., 2007, deliverable D.3.1*. Available from http://www.atesst.org

ATESST Project. (2014, March 15). Retrieved from http://www.atesst.org

ATESST. (2006). *FP7 ATESST 1 & ATESST 2 Projects*. Retrieved from http://www.atesst.org

Autili, M., Inveradi, P., & Pelliccione, P. (2007). Graphical scenarios for specifying temporal properties: an automated approach. *Automated Software Engineering*, *14*(3), 293–340. doi:10.1007/s10515-007-0012-6

AUTOSAR AUTomotive Open System Architecture. (2013). Retrieved from http://www.autosar.org/download/R4.1/Main.zip

AUTOSAR Specification of Timing Extensions, 1.1.0. (n.d.). *AUTOSAR Release 4.0.2, 2010-11-03*. AUTOSAR Development Cooperation.

AUTOSAR. (2011). *AUTOSAR Specification of Timing Extensions, Release 4.0*. Retrieved from http://www.autosar.org/download/R4.0/AUTOSAR_TPS_TimingExtensions.pdf

AUTOSAR. (2013). *Autosar Automotive 4.1*. Retrieved from http://www.autosar.org

AUTOSAR. (2014). *AUTOSAR specifications 4.1*. Available from http://www.autosar.org/index.php?p=3&up=0&uup=0&uuup=0

Avgustinov, P., Tibble, J., & de Moor, O. (2007). Making trace monitoring feasible. In R. P. Gabriel (Ed.), *ACM Conference on Object-Oriented Programming, Systems and Languages* (pp. 589-608). ACM Press.

Avison, D. E., & Fitzgerald, G. (2003). Where now for development methodologies? *Communications of the ACM*, *46*, 78–82. doi:10.1145/602421.602423

Avizienis, A. (1969). *Design Methods for Fault-Tolerant Navigation Computers*. Pasadena, CA: Jet Propulsion Laboratory.

Bacchelli, A., Ciancarini, P., & Rossi, D. (2008). *On the Effectiveness of Manual and Automatic Unit Test Generation*. Paper presented at the Third International Conference on Software Engineering Advances. New York, NY.

Bachmann, C., Genser, A., Haid, J., Steger, C., & Weiss, R. (2010, September). Automated Power Characterization for Run-Time Power Emulation of SoC Designs. In *Proceedings of 13th Euromicro Conference on Digital System Design* (pp. 587-594). IEEE.

Bae, K., Öleczky, P. C., Feng, T. H., & Tripakis, S. (2009). Verifying Ptolemy II Discrete-Event Models Using Real-Time Maude. In *Proceedings of the 11th International Conference on Formal Engineering Methods: Formal Methods and Software Engineering* (ICFEM'09) (LNCS) (vol. 5885, pp. 717-736). Rio de Janeiro, Brazil: Springer.

Bagnato, A., et al. (2010). MADES: Embedded systems engineering approach in the avionics domain. In *Proceedings of First Workshop on Hands-on Platforms and tools for model-based engineering of Embedded Systems* (HoPES). HoPES.

Bagnato, A., et al. (2012). *D1.7: MADES Final Approach Guide*. Technical Report. Retrieved from http://www.mades-project.org/

Bahrami, D., Faivre, A., & Lapitre, A. (2012). DIVERSITY–TG: Automatic Test Case Generation from Matlab/Simulink models. In *Proceedings of ERTS2 Conference.* ERTS2.

Bai, G., Bobba, S., & Hajj, I. N. (2001). Static Timing Analysis Including Power Supply Noise Effect on Propagation Delay in VLSI Circuits. In *Proceedings of the 38th Design Automation Conference* (pp. 295-300). IEEE.

Bálek, D., & Plasil, F. (2001). *Software Connectors and their Role in Component Deployment*. Paper presented at the Third International Conference on Distributed Applications and Interoperable Systems. New York, NY.

Banerjee, A., Venkatasubramanian, K. K., Mukherjee, T., & Gupta, S. K. S. (2012). Ensuring Safety, Security, and Sustainability of Mission-Critical Cyber–Physical Systems. *Proceedings of the IEEE*, *100*(1), 283–299. doi:10.1109/JPROC.2011.2165689

Baraza, J. C., Gracia, J., Gil, D., & Gil, P. J. (2005, November). Improvement of fault injection techniques based on VHDL code modification. In *Proceedings of High-Level Design Validation and Test Workshop, 2005. Tenth IEEE International* (pp. 19-26). IEEE.

Baresi, L. et al. (2013). Formal verification and validation of embedded systems: The UML-based MADES approach. In *Proceedings of Software & Systems Modeling Conference*, (pp. 1-21). Academic Press.

Baresi, L., et al. (2010). *D3.1: Domain-specific and User-centred Verification*. Technical Report. Retrieved from http://www.mades-project.org/

Baresi, L., et al. (2011). *D3.2: Models and Methods for Systems Environment*. Technical Report. Retrieved from http://www.mades-project.org/

Baresi, L., et al. (2012a). *D3.3: Formal Dynamic Semantics of the Modelling Notation*. Technical Report. Retrieved from http://www.mades-project.org/

Baresi, L., et al. (2012b). A logic-based semantics for the verification of multi-diagram UML models. In *Proceedings of SIGSOFT Software Engineering Conference.* (pp. 1-8). ACM.

Baronti, F., Petri, E., Saponara, S., Fanucci, L., Roncella, R., & Saletti, R. et al. (2011, March). Design and verification of hardware building blocks for high-speed and fault-tolerant in-vehicle networks. *IEEE Transactions on Industrial Electronics*, *58*(3), 792–801.

Barrett, C. W., Sebastiani, R., Seshia, S. A., & Tinelli, C. (2009). Satisfiability Modulo Theories. In Handbook of Satisfiability 2009 (pp. 825-885). Academic Press.

Bauer, S., David, A., Hennicker, R., Larsen, K., Legay, A., Nyman, U., & Wasowski, A. (2012). Moving from Specifications to Contracts in Component-Based Design. In *Proceedings of Fundamental Approaches to Software Engineering - 15th International Conference, FASE 2012* (pp. 43-58). FASE.

Becker, S., Grunske, L., Mirandola, R., & Overhage, S. (2006). Performance Prediction of Component-based Systems: A Survey from an Engineering Perspective. In R. H. Reussne, J. A. Stafford & C. A. Szyperski (Eds.), *Architecting Systems with Trustworthy Components: Proceedings of International Seminar* (LNCS) (vol. 3938, pp. 169-192). Berlin: Springer.

Becker, J., Hubner, M., Hettich, G., Constapel, R., Eisenmann, J., & Luka, J. (2007). Dynamic and Partial FPGA Exploitation. *Proceedings of the IEEE*, *95*(2), 438–452. doi:10.1109/JPROC.2006.888404

Bellosa, F. (2000, September). The benefits of event-driven energy accounting in power-sensitive systems. In *Proceedings of the 9th workshop on ACM SIGOPS European workshop: beyond the PC: new challenges for the operating system* (pp. 37-42). ACM.

Benini, L., Bogliolo, A., & De Micheli, G. (2000, June). A survey of design techniques for system-level dynamic power management. *IEEE Transactions on Very Large Scale Integration (VLSI) Systems*, *8*(3), 299–316.

Bentakouk, L., Poizat, P., & Zaidi, F. (2011). Checking the behavioral conformance of web services with Symbolic Testing and an SMT solver. In *Proceedings of the 5th International Conference on Tests and Proofs* (pp. 33-50). Academic Press.

Benveniste, A., Caillaud, B., Ferrari, A., Mangeruca, L., Passerone, R., & Sofronis, C. (2007). Multiple Viewpoint Contract-Based Specification and Design. In *Proceedings of Formal Methods for Components and Objects, 6th International Symposium, FMCO 2007* (pp. 200-225). FMCO.

Benveniste, A., Caspi, P., Edwards, S. A., & Halbwachs, N. L., Guernic, P., & Simone, R.D. (2003). The synchronous languages 12 years later. *Proceedings of the IEEE, 91*(1), 64–83.

Benveniste, A., Caspi, P., Edwards, S. A., Halbwachs, N., Le Guernic, P., & de Simone, R. (2003). The synchronous languages 12 years later. *Proceedings of the IEEE, 91*(1), 64–83. doi:10.1109/JPROC.2002.805826

Berkenkötter, K., Bisanz, S., Hannemann, U., & Peleska, J. (2004). SoftSpez Final Report. In Executable HybridUML and Its Application to Train Control Systems (LNCS) (vol. 3147, pp. 145-173). Berlin: Springer.

Berrojo, L., Corno, F., Entrena, L., González, I., López, C., Sonza Reorda, M., & Squillero, G. (2002). An Industrial Environment for High-Level Fault-Tolerant Structures Insertion and Validation. In *Proceedings of 20th IEEE VLSI Test Symposium*, (pp. 229-236). Monterey, CA: IEEE.

Bersani, M. M., et al. (2010). Bounded reachability for temporal logic over constraint systems. In *Proceedings of the International Symposium on Temporal Representation and Reasoning* (TIME), (pp. 43-50). TIME.

Bersani, M. M., et al. (2013). A tool for deciding the satisfiability problem of continuous-time metric temporal logic. In *Proceedings of International Symposium on Temporal Representation and Reasoning* (TIME) (pp. 99-106). TIME.

Bhattacharjee, A., Contreras, G., & Martonosi, M. (2008, August). Full-system chip multiprocessor power evaluations using FPGA-based emulation. In *Proceedings of Low Power Electronics and Design (ISLPED),* (pp. 335-340). IEEE.

Bienia, G. (2011). *Benchmarking Modern Multiprocessors*. (Unpublished doctoral dissertation). Princeton University.

BitCarrier. (2013). *BitCarrier*. Retrieved Dec 30, 2013, from http://www.bitcarrier.com/

Bjørner, D., & Jones, C.B. (1978). *The Vienna Development Method: The Meta-Language* (LNCS) Vol. 61). Berlin: Springer-Verlag.

Blackman, S. (1999). *Design and analysis of modern tracking systems*. Boston: Artech House.

Blobject. (2013). *CityAnalytics: Statistical Study*. Retrieved Nov 20, 2013, from http://bit.ly/TtnmLn

Blochwitz, T., Otter, T., Akesson, J., Arnold, M., Clauß, C., & Elmqvist, H., … Viel, A. (2012). Functional Mockup Interface 2.0: The Standard for Tool independent Exchange of Simulation Models. In *Proceedings of the 9th International Modelica Conference*. Academic Press.

Bluetooth specification, version 2.1 + edr [vol 0] 1999.

Bodden, E. (2005). *J-lo, a tool for runtime-checking temporal assertions*. (Unpublished Master's thesis). RWTH Aachen University.

Boehm, B. (1986). *Understanding and controlling software costs*. Center for Systems and Software Engineering, University of Southern California. Retrieved from http://csse.usc.edu/csse/TECHRPTS/1986/usccse86-501/usccse86-501.pdf

Bolanos, M. A. (2010). *3D Packaging Technology: Enabling the next wave of applications*. Paper presented at the 34th IEEE/CPMT International Electronic Manufacturing Technology Symposium (IEMT). New York, NY.

Bonabeau, E. (2002). Agent-based modeling: Methods and techniques for simulating human systems. *Proceedings of the National Academy of Sciences of the United States of America, 99*(Suppl 3), 7280–7287. doi:10.1073/pnas.082080899 PMID:12011407

Bowman, K. A., Alameldeen, A. R., Srinivasan, S. T., & Wilkerson, C. B. (2007). Impact of Die-to-Die and within-Die Parameter Variations on the Throughput Distribution of Multi-Core Processors. In *Proceedings of the ACM/IEEE International Symposium on Low Power Electronics and Design*, (pp. 50-55). ACM/IEEE.

Box, G., & Jenkins, G. (1976). *Time series analysis: forecasting and control*. San Francisco: Holden Day.

Bozzano, M., & Villafiorita, A. (2003). Improving System Reliability via Model Checking: the FSAP /NuSMV-SA Safety Analysis Platform. In *Proceedings of 22nd International Conference on Computer Safety, Reliability, and Security, SAFECOMP*, (pp. 49-62). Academic Press.

Brigham Young University. (2013). *BYU EDIF Tools Home Page*. Retrieved 07 29, 2013, from FPGA Reliability Studies: http://reliability.ee.byu.edu/edif/

Britt, J., & The Neurogami Group. (2013). *Test: Unit*. Retrieved January 2014, from http://ruby-doc.org/stdlib-2.1.0/libdoc/test/unit/rdoc/Test/Unit.html

Broenink, J. F., Kleijn, C., Larsen, P. G., Jovanovic, D., Verhoef, M., & Pierce, K. (2010). Design support and tooling for dependable embedded control software. In *Proceedings of the 2nd International Workshop on Software Engineering for Resilient Systems*. ACM.

Broman, D., Derler, P., & Eidson, J. (2013). Temporal Issues in Cyber-Physical Systems. *Journal of the Indian Institute of Science*.

Brooks, F. P. (1975). The mythical man-month. In Essays on Software Engineering. Reading, MA: Addison-Wesley Publishing Company.

Browning, D., & Kessler, G. (2009). Bluetooth hacking: A case study. In *Proceedings of the Conference on Digital Forensics, Security and Law* (pp. 20-22). Academic Press.

Brown, R. (1959). *Statistical forecasting for inventory control*. New York: McGraw-Hill.

Broy, M., Cengarle, M. V., & Geisberger, E. (2012). Cyber-Physical Systems: Imminent Challenges. In *Proceedings of the Monterey Workshop 2012* (LNCS) (vol. 7539, pp. 1–28). Berlin: Springer.

Broy, M., Chakraborty, S., Goswami, D., Ramesh, S., & Satpathy, M. (2011). Cross-layer analysis, testing and verification of automotive control software. In *Proceedings of the 11th International Conference on Embedded Software*, (pp 263-272). Academic Press.

Bruneton, E. (2002). *ASM 4.0: A Java bytecode engineering library*. Retrieved from http://download.forge.objectweb.org/asm/asm4-guide.pdf

Buck, J. T., Ha, S., Lee, E. A., & Messerschmitt, D. G. (1994). Ptolemy: A Framework for Simulating and Prototyping Heterogenous Systems. *International Journal in Computer Simulation, 4*(2).

Burrows, M., Freund, S., & Wiener, J. (2003). Run-Time Type Checking for Binary Programs. In G. Hedin (Ed.), *Compiler Construction* (Vol. 2622, pp. 90–105). Springer. doi:10.1007/3-540-36579-6_7

Cadene, S. (2013). *Embedded Market March 2013*. Retrieved August 2013, from http://www.slideshare.net/StephanCadene/embedded-mar1913

Campagna, S., & Violante, M. (2012). On the Evaluation of the Performance Overhead of a Commercial Embedded Hypervisor. In *Proc. of the First Workshop on Manufacturable and Dependable Multicore Architectures at Nanoscale* (pp. 59-63). Academic Press.

Cancila, D., Terrier, F., Belmonte, F., Dubois, H., Espinoza, H., Gerard, S., & Cuccuru, A. (2009). SOPHIA: a Modeling Language for Model-Based Safety Engineering. In *Proceedings of 2nd International Workshop On Model Based Architecting and Construction Of Embedded Systems*, (pp 11-26). Academic Press.

Cao, Y., & McAndrew, C. (2007). Mosfet Modeling for 45 nm and Beyond. In *Proceedings of the IEEE International Conference on Computer-Aided Design*, (pp. 638-643). IEEE.

Carloni, L., Passerone, R., Pinto, A., & Sangiovanni-Vincentelli, A. (2006). Languages and tools for hybrid systems design. *Foundations and Trends in Design Automation, 1*(1), 1–204. doi:10.1561/1000000001

Castillo, P. A., Arenas, M. G., García-Sánchez, P., Merelo, J. J., & Bernier, J. L. (2012). Distributed Evolutionary Computation using SOAP and REST Web Services. Advances in Intelligent Modelling and Simulation. In J. Kolodziej, S. U. Khan, & T. Burczynski (Eds.), Artificial Intelligence-Based Models and Techniques in Scalable Computing. Series: Studies in Computational Intelligence (Vol. 422, pp. 89–112). Academic Press.

Castillo, P. A., García-Sánchez, P., Arenas, M. G., Mora, A. M., Romero, G., & Merelo, J. J. (2013). Using SOAP and REST web services as communication protocol for distributed evolutionary computation. *International Journal of Computers & Technology, 10*(6), 1659-1677.

Castillo, P. A., Arenas, M. G., Castellano, J. G., Cillero, M., Merelo, J. J., & Prieto, A. et al. (2001). Function approximation with evolved multilayer perceptrons. In N. E. Mastorakis (Ed.), *Advances in Neural Networks and Applications. Artificial Intelligence Series* (pp. 195–200). Tenerife, Spain: Published by World Scientific and Engineering Society Press.

Castillo, P. A., Merelo, J. J., Arenas, M. G., & Romero, G. (2007). Comparing evolutionary hybrid systems for design and optimization of multilayer perceptron structure along training parameters. *Information Sciences, 177*, 2884–2905. doi:10.1016/j.ins.2007.02.021

Cervin, A., Henriksson, D., Lincoln, B., Eker, J., & Arzen, K. (2003). How does control timing affect performance? Analysis and simulation of timing using Jitterbug and TrueTime. *Control Systems, IEEE, 23*(3), 16–30. doi:10.1109/MCS.2003.1200240

Chale, G., Gaudré, T., & Tucci-Piergiovanni, S. (2012). Towards an Architectural Design Framework for Automotive Systems Development. In *Proceedings of the Third International Conference on Complex Systems Design & Management, CSD&M,* (pp 241-258). Academic Press.

Chandra, S., & Orso, A. (2013). *International Workshop on the Future of Debugging*. Retrieved August 2013, from https://sites.google.com/site/futdeb2013/

Chandra, S., Lahiri, K., Raghunathan, A., & Dey, S. (2007). System-on-Chip Power Management Considering Leakage Power Variations. In *Proc. ACM/IEEE Design Automation Conference*, (pp. 877-882). ACM/IEEE.

Chandra, R. (2001). *Parallel programming in OpenMP*. Morgan Kaufmann.

Che, X., Lalanne, F., & Maag, S. (2012). A Logic-based Passive Testing Approach for the Validation of Communicating Protocols. In *Proc. 7th International Conference on Evaluation of Novel Approaches to Software Engineering* (pp. 53-64). Academic Press.

Chen, D., Johansson, R., Lönn, H., Blom, H., Walker, M., Papadopoulos, Y., Torchiaro, S., Tagliabo F., & Sandberg, A. (2011). Integrated Safety and Architecture Modeling for Automotive Embedded Systems. *E&I - Elektrotechnik und Informationstechnik, 128*(6).

Chen, D., Mahmud, N., Walker, M., Feng, L., Lönn, H., & Papadopoulos, Y. (2013). Systems Modeling with EAST-ADL for Fault Tree Analysis through HiP-HOPS. In *Proceedings of 4th IFAC Workshop on Dependable Control of Discrete Systems*. IFAC.

Chen, Y., Xie, L., & Li, J. (2009). An energy-aware heuristic constructive mapping algorithm for Network on Chip. In *Proceeding of the 8th International Conference on ASIC (ASICON)*, (pp. 101-104). Hunan, China: IEEE.

Chen, D., Feng, L., Qureshi, T. N., Lönn, H., & Hagl, F. (2013). An Architectural Approach to the Analysis, Verification and Validation of Software Intensive Embedded Systems. *Computing, 95*(8), 649–688. doi:10.1007/s00607-013-0314-4

Chen, F., & Rosu, G. (2009). *Parametric Trace Slicing and Monitoring. In Proceedings of 15th Tools and Algorithms for the Construction and Analysis of Systems (pp. 246-261). York, UK: Springer-Verlag.*

Chou, C., & Marculescu, R. (2008). Contention-aware application mapping for Network-on-Chip communication architectures. In *Proceeding of the International Conference on Computer Design*, (pp. 164-169). Lake Tahoe, CA: IEEE.

Choudhary, N., Gaur, M., Laxmi, V., & Singh, V. (2011). GA Based Congestion Aware Topology Generation for Application Specific NoC. In *Proceeding of the Electronic Design, Test and Application (DELTA)*, (pp. 93-98). Queenstown, New Zealand: IEEE.

Chun, I.-G., Choon-oh, L., & Duk-Kyun, W. (2007). *Esto NS-Debugger: The Non-stop Debugger for Embedded Systems*. Paper presented at the 9th International Conference on Advanced Communication Technology. New York, NY.

Ciapessoni, E. et al. (1999). From formal models to formally-based methods: an industrial experience. *ACM Transactions on Software Engineering and Methodology*. doi:10.1145/295558.295566

Cimatti, A., & Tonetta, S. (2012). A Property-Based Proof System for Contract-Based Design. In *Proceedings of 38th Euromicro Conference on Software Engineering and Advanced Applications, SEAA 2012* (pp. 21-28). SEAA.

Cimatti, A., Dorigatti, M., & Tonetta, S. (2013). OCRA: A Tool for Checking the Refinement of Temporal Contracts. In *Proceedings of 28th IEEE/ACM International Conference on Automated Software Engineering, ASE 2013* (pp. 702-705). IEEE/ACM.

Cimatti, A., Roveri, M., & Tonetta, S. (2009). Requirements Validation for Hybrid Systems. In *Proceedings of Computer Aided Verification, 21st International Conference, CAV 2009* (pp. 188-203). CAV.

Cimatti, A., Roveri, M., Susi, A., & Tonetta, S. (2012). Validation of requirements for hybrid systems: A formal approach. *ACM Transactions on Software Engineering and Methodology*, *21*(4), 22. doi:10.1145/2377656.2377659

CityAnalytics. (2013). *CityAnalytics*. Retrieved Nov 20, 2013, from http://www.cityanalytics.net/?act=faq

Ciudad2020. (2013). *Ciudad2020: Blobject S.L.* Retrieved Nov 20, 2013, from http://www.cityanalytics. net/?act=nosotros

Clarinox Technologies Pty. Ltd. (2010). *The Clarinox Softframe*. Retrieved August 2013, from www.clarinox.com

Claus, C., Zeppenfeld, J., Müller, F., & Stechele, W. (2007). *Using Partial-Run-Time Reconfigurable Hardware to Accelerate Video Processing in Driver Assistance System*. Design, Automation & Test in Europe. doi:10.1109/DATE.2007.364642

Coburn, J., Ravi, S., & Raghunathan, A. (2005, June). Power emulation: A new paradigm for power estimation. In *Proceedings of the 42nd annual Design Automation Conference* (pp. 700-705). ACM.

Coleman, J.W., Lausdahl, K.G., & Larsen, P.G. (2012). *Co-simulation Semantics, DESTECS Project Deliverable D3.4b*. Retrieved from http://www.destecs.org/

Collander, P., Katzko, C., & Gaborieau, O. (2010). *Packaging technologies for 3D integration*. Paper presented at the 5th International Microsystems Packaging Assembly and Circuits Technology Conference (IMPACT). New York, NY.

Constant, C., Jeron, T., Marchand, H., & Rusu, V. (2007). Integrating formal verification and conformance testing for reactive systems. *IEEE Transactions on Software Engineering*, *33*(8), 558–574. doi:10.1109/TSE.2007.70707

Constantinescu, C. (2003). Trends and Challenges in VLSI Circuit Reliability. *IEEE Micro*, *4*(23), 14–19. doi:10.1109/MM.2003.1225959

Conte, T. M., & Hwu, W. M. (1991, January). Benchmark characterization. *Computer*, *24*(1), 48–56. doi:10.1109/2.67193

Corbet, J. (2007). Process containers. Linux Weekly News, (5). Retrieved from http://lwn.net/Articles/236038/

Corliss, M. L., Lewis, E. C., & Roth, A. (2003). DISE: A Programmable Macro Engine for Customizing Applications. *International Symposium on Computer Architecture (ISCA)*, *31*(2), 362-373. http://doi.acm.org/10.1145/871656.859660

Corno, F., Esposito, F., Sonza Reorda, M., & Tosato, S. (2004, October). Evaluating the effects of transient faults on vehicle dynamic performance in automotive systems. In *Proceedings of Test Conference*, (pp. 1332-1339). IEEE.

Coskun, A.K., Ayala, J.L., Atienza, D., Rosing, T.S., & Leblebici, Y. (2009, April). Dynamic thermal management in 3D multicore architectures. In *Proceedings of Design, Automation & Test in Europe Conference & Exhibition* (pp. 1410-1415). IEEE.

CoWare Inc. (2013). *CoWare Virtual Platform - Hardware/Software integration and testing...without hardware*. Retrieved from http://www.coware.com/products/virtualplatform.php

Cuenot, P., Frey, P., Johansson, R., Lönn, H., Papadopoulos, Y., Reiser, M.-O., ... Törngren, M. (2007). The EAST-ADL Architecture Description Language for Automotive Embedded Software. In Model-Based Engineering of Embedded Real-Time Systems (pp. 297-307). Academic Press.

Czarnecki, K., Helsen, S., & Eisenecker, U. (2005). Formalizing Cardinality-based Feature Models and their Specialization. In *Software Process* (pp. 7–29). Improvement and Practices. doi:10.1002/spip.213

Dadeau, F., Heam, P. C., & Kheddam, R. (2011). Mutation-Based Test Generation from Security Protocols in HLPSL. In *Proceedings of International Conference on Software Testing, Verification and Validation (ICST)*. ICST.

Daigneau, R. (2011). *Service Design Patterns: Fundamental Design Solutions for SOAP/WSDL and RESTful Web Services*. Westford, MA: Addison-Wesley Professional.

Damm, W., & Harrel, D. (2001). LSCs: Breathing life into message sequence charts. *Formal Methods in System Design*, 19(1), 45–80. doi:10.1023/A:1011227529550

Daveau, J. M., Blampey, A., Gasiot, G., Bulone, J., & Roche, P. (2009, April). An industrial fault injection platform for soft-error dependability analysis and hardening of complex system-on-a-chip. In *Proceedings of Reliability Physics Symposium,* (pp. 212-220). IEEE.

de Andrés, D., Ruiz, J.-C., & Gil, P. (2009). Using Dependability, Performance, Area and Energy Consumption Experimental Measures to Benchmark IP Cores. In *Proceedings of Latin-American Symposium on Dependable Computing*, (pp. 49-56). Joao Pessoa, Brazil: Academic Press.

de Andrés, D., Ruiz, J.-C., Gil, D., & Gil, P. (2008). Fault Emulation for Dependability Evaluation of VLSI Systems. *IEEE Transactions on Very Large Scale Integration (VLSI) Systems*, 16(4), 422–431.

Denaro, G., Polini, A., & Emmerich, W. (2004). Early performance testing of distributed software applications. *SIGSOFT Software Engineering Notes*, 29, 94–103. doi:10.1145/974043.974059

Derler, P., Lee, E. A., Torngren, M., & Tripakis, S. (2013). Cyber-Physical System Design Contracts. In *Proceedings of ICCPS '13: ACM/IEEE 4th International Conference on Cyber-Physical Systems*. ACM/IEEE.

Di Natale, M., & Sangiovanni-Vincentelli, A. L. (2010). Moving From Federated to Integrated Architectures in Automotive: The Role of Standards, Methods and Tools. *Journal of the IEEE*, 98(4), 603–620. doi:10.1109/JPROC.2009.2039550

Dick, R. P., Rhodes, D. L., & Wolf, W. (1998). TGFF: task graphs for free. In *Proceeding of the International Workshop Hardware/Software Co-Design*, (pp. 97-101). Seattle, WA: IEEE.

Dijkstra, E. W. (1982). On the role of scientific thought. In *Selected writings on Computing: A Personal Perspective* (pp. 60–66). New York, NY: Springer-Verlag.

Do, R. D. (2011). *New tool for FPGA designers mitigates soft errors within synthesis*. Retrieved 07 29, 2013, from DSP-FPGA.com Magazine: http://dsp-fpga.com/articles/new-errors-within-synthesis/

DO-178C. (2012). *Software Considerations in Airborne Systems and Equipment Certification – RCTA 2012*.

Drake, A., Senger, R., Singh, H., Carpenter, G., & James, N. (2008). Dynamic Measurement of Critical-Path Timing. In *Proc. IEEE Conf. Integrated Circuit Design and Technology and Tutorial*, (pp. 249-252). IEEE.

Druml, N., Menghin, M., Steger, C., Weiss, R., Genser, A., Bock, H., & Haid, J. (2013, February). Emulation-Based Test and Verification of a Design's Functional, Performance, Power, and Supply Voltage Behavior. In *Proceedings of 21st Euromicro International Conference on Parallel, Distributed, and Network-Based Processing* (pp. 328-335). IEEE.

Druml, N., Steger, C., Weiss, R., Genser, A., & Haid, J. (2012, March). Estimation Based Power and Supply Voltage Management for Future RF-Powered Multi-Core Smart Cards. In *Proceedings of Design Automation and Test in Europe Conference and Exhibition* (pp. 358-363). IEEE.

Duato, J., Yalamanchili, S., & Ni, L. (2003). *Interconnection Networks – An Engineering Approach*. San Francisco, CA: Morgan Kaufmann Publishers.

Dumas, X. (2011). *Application des méthodes par ordres-partiels à la vérification formelle de systèmes asynchrones clos par un contexte: application à SDL*. (Doctoral thesis). Université de Rennes 1, Institut Mines-Télécom-Télécom Bretagne-UEB, France.

EAST EEA. (2001). EAST EEA ITEA Project. Retrieved from https://itea3.org/project/east-eea.html

East-ADL Association. (2014). *East-ADL Specifications*. Available from http://www.east-adl.info/Specification.html

East-ADL Consortium. (2013). *EAST ADL language specification*. Retrieved from http://www.east-adl.info/Specification/V2.1.11/EAST-ADL-Specification_V2.1.11.pdf

EAST-ADL. (2012). *EAST-ADL*. Retrieved from http://www.east-adl.info/

EAST-EEA Project. (2004). *Definition of language for automotive embedded electronic architecture*. ITEA.

Ebert, C., & Jones, C. (2009, April). Embedded software: Facts, figures and futurE. *Computer Magazine, 42*(4), 42–52. doi:10.1109/MC.2009.118

Eclipse Foundation. (2014). *Memory Analyzer (MAT)*. Retrieved January 2014, from http://www.eclipse.org/mat/

ECSS. (2009a). *Std ECSS-E-ST-40C Space engineering—Software*. ECSS.

ECSS. (2009b). *Std ECSS-Q-ST-80C Space product assurance—Software product assurance*. ECSS.

ECSS-E-70-41A. (2003). *Telemetry and Telecommand Packet Utilization*. First Issue, January 2003.

ECSS-E-ST-10C. (2009). *Space engineering - System Engineering General Requirements*. Issue 3, 6 March 2009.

ECSS-M-ST-10C. (2009). *Space project management - Project planning and implementation*. Rev. 1, March 2009.

eDIANA. (2011). *ARTEMIS project*. Retrieved from http://www.artemis-ediana.eu/

Edward, A. L., & Sangiovanni-Vincentelli, A. L. (1998). A framework for comparing models of computation. *IEEE Trans. on CAD of Integrated Circuits and Systems, 17*(12), 1217–1229. doi:10.1109/43.736561

Edwards, G., Malek, S., & Medvidovic, N. (2007). Scenario-driven dynamic analysis of distributed architectures. In *Proceedings of the 10th International Conference on Fundamental Approaches to Software Engineering*, (pp. 125-139). Academic Press.

EEMBC. (2013). *AutoBench™ 1.1 Benchmark Software*. Retrieved 07 29, 2013, from The Embedded Microprocessor Benchmark Consortium: http://www.eembc.org/benchmark/automotive_sl.php

Eiben, A. E., & Smith, J. E. (2003). *Introduction to Evolutionary Computing*. Berlin, Heidelberg: Springer-Verlag. doi:10.1007/978-3-662-05094-1

Eidson, J. C., Lee, E. A., Matic, S., Seshia, S. A., & Zou, J. (2012). Distributed Real-Time Software for Cyber–Physical Systems. *Proceedings of the IEEE, 100*(1), 45–59. doi:10.1109/JPROC.2011.2161237

Eireiner, M., Henzler, S., Georgakos, G., Berthold, J., & Schmitt-Landsiedel, D. (2007). Delay characterization and local supply voltage adjustment for compensation of local parametric variations. *IEEE Journal of Solid-State Circuits, 42*(7), 1583–1592. doi:10.1109/JSSC.2007.896695

Eker, J., Janneck, J. W., Lee, E. A., Liu, J., & Liu, X. … Xiong, Y. (2003). Taming Heterogeneity – the Ptolemy Approach. *Proceedings of the IEEE, 91*(1), 127-144.

Elson, J., Girod, L., & Estrin, D. (2004). EmStar: Development with high system visibility. *IEEE Wireless Communications, 11*(6), 70–77. doi:10.1109/MWC.2004.1368899

Emnett, F., & Biegel, M. (2000). *Power Reduction Through RTL Clock Gating*. San José, CA: Synopsys Users Group.

Engel, M., & Spinczyk, O. (2008). Aspects in hardware: what do they look like?. In Proceedings of AOSD workshop on Aspects, components, and patterns for infrastructure software, (pp. 1-6). Brussels, Belgium: AOSD.

Enoiu, E. P., Raluca Marinescu, R., Seceleanu, C., & Pettersson, P. (2012). ViTAL: A Verification Tool for EAST-ADL Models using UPPAAL PORT. In *Proceedings of 17th IEEE International Conference on Engineering of Complex Computer Systems*, (pp. 328-337). IEEE.

Entrena, L., Garcia-Valderas, M., Fernandez-Cardenal, R., Lindoso, A., Portela, M., & Lopez-Ongil, C. (2012, March). Soft error sensitivity evaluation of microprocessors by multilevel emulation-based fault injection. *IEEE Transactions on Computers, 61*(3), 313–322.

Entrena, L., López, C., & Olías, E. (2001). *Automatic Generation of Fault Tolerant VHDL Designs in RTL*. Forum on Design Languages.

ESA ITT AO6523. (2010). *Functional Requirements and Verification Techniques for the Software Reference Architecture*.

Espinosa, J., de Andrés, D., Ruiz, J.-C., & Gil, P. (2011). *Robust communications using automatic deployment of a CRC-generation technique in IP-blocks*. Laguna, Spain: XI Reconfigurable Computing and Applications.

Espinoza, H., Cancila, D., & Selic, B. Gerard, & S. (2009). Challenges in Combining SysML and MARTE for Model-Based Design of Embedded Systems. In *Proceedings of the 5th European Conference on Model Driven Architecture - Foundations and Applications,* (pp 98-113). Academic Press.

Espinoza, H., Dubois, H., Gerard, S., Medina, J., Petriu, D. C., & Woodside, M. (2005). Annotating UML Models with Non-functional Properties for Quantitative Analysis. In J. Bruel (Ed.), *Satellite Events at the MoDELS 2005 Conference: Proceedings of MoDELS 2005 International Workshops Doctoral Symposium, Educators Symposium* (LNCS) (vol. 3844, pp. 79-90). Berlin: Springer.

EyeQ2. (2010). *The MobilEye safety project 2010.* Available: http://www.mobileye.com/node/69

Eyerman, S., & Eeckhout, L. (2010). A Counter Architecture for Online DVFS Profitability Estimation. *IEEE Transactions on Computers, 59*(11), 1576–1583. doi:10.1109/TC.2010.65

Fabre, J.-C., & Pérennou, T. (1998). A Metaobject Architecture for Fault Tolerant Distributed Systems: The FRIENDS Approach. *IEEE Transactions on Computers, 47,* 78–95. doi:10.1109/12.656088

Falkner, K., Chiprianov, V., Falkner, N., Szabo, C., & Puddy, G. (2013). Modeling scenarios for the performance prediction of distributed real-time embedded systems. In Proceedings of MilCIS 2013: Military Communications and Information Systems Conference. Canberra, Australia: MilCIS.

Falkner, K., Chiprianov, V., Falkner, N., Szabo, C., Hill, J., Puddy, G., et al. (2013). Model-driven performance prediction of distributed real-time embedded defence systems. In *Proceedings of the 18th International Conference on Engineering of Complex Computer Systems (ICECCS).* Singapore: ICECCS.

Farokhzad, S., Tanyeri, G., Messiter, T., & Beckett, P. (2010). *Plug-in Based Debugging For Embedded Systems.* Paper presented at the International Conference on Real-Time & Embedded Systems. New York, NY.

Faugere, M., et al. (2007). MARTE: Also an UML profile for modeling AADL applications. In *Proceedings of 12th IEEE International Conference on Engineering Complex Computer Systems,* (pp. 359–364). IEEE.

Ferrucci, L., et al. (2012). A Metric Temporal Logic for Dealing with Zero-Time Transitions. In *Proceedings of International Symposium on Temporal Representation and Reasoning* (TIME), (pp 81–88). TIME.

Fielding, R. T. (2000). *Architectural Styles and the Design of Network-based Software Architectures.* (Doctoral dissertation). University of California, Irvine, CA.

Fielding, R. T., & Taylor, R. N. (2002). Principled Design of the Modern Web Architecture. ACM Transactions on Internet Technology, 2 (2), 115-150.

Finkenzeller, K. (2003). *RFID Handbook: Fundamentals and Applications in Contactless Smart Cards and Identification* (2nd ed.). New York, NY: John Wiley & Sons, Inc. doi:10.1002/0470868023

Fitzgerald, J. S., Larsen, P. G., Tjell, S., & Verhoef, M. (2007). *Validation Support for Distributed Real-Time Embedded Systems in VDM++.* Paper presented at the High Assurance System Engineering Symposium. Dallas, TX.

Fitzgerald, J., Larsen, P. G., Pierce, K., Verhoef, M., & Wolff, S. (2010). Collaborative Modelling and Co-simulation in the Development of Dependable Embedded Systems. In D. Méry & S. Merz (Eds.), Integrated Formal Methods 2010 (LNCS) (vol. 6396, pp. 12-26). Nancy, France: Springer.

Fitzgerald, J. S., & Larsen, P. G. (2009). *Modelling Systems - Practical Tools and Techniques in Software Development* (2nd ed.). Cambridge University Press. doi:10.1017/CBO9780511626975

Fitzgerald, J. S., Larsen, P. G., Mukherjee, P., Plat, N., & Verhoef, M. (2005). *Validated Designs for Object-oriented Systems.* Springer.

Fitzgerald, J. S., Larsen, P. G., Pierce, K., & Verhoef, M. (2013). A Formal Approach to Collaborative Modelling and Co-simulation for Embedded Systems. *Mathematical Structures in Computer Science, 23*(4), 726–750. doi:10.1017/S0960129512000242

Fitzgerald, J. S., Larsen, P. G., & Verhoef, M. (Eds.). (in press). *Collaborative Design for Embedded and Cyber-Physical Systems.* Springer.

Flamand, E. (2009). Strategic Directions Toward Multicore Application Specific Computing. In *Proc. IEEE Conf. Design, Automation and Test in Europe,* (p. 1266). IEEE.

Flinn, J., & Satyanarayanan, M. (1999, February). Powerscope: A tool for profiling the energy usage of mobile applications. In *Proceedings of Mobile Computing Systems and Applications,* (pp. 2-10). IEEE.

Flynn, J., & Waldo, B. (2005). *Power management in complex soc design.* Synopsys White Paper.

France, R., & Rumpe, B. (2007). Model-driven Development of Complex Software: A Research Roadmap. In *Proceedings of Future of Software Engineering (FOSE'07).* IEEE.

Friedenthal, R. S., & Moore, A. (2008). *A Practical Guide to SysML.* Morgan Kaufman OMG Press.

Fritzsche, M., & Johannes, J. (2008). Putting performance engineering into model-driven engineering: Model driven performance engineering. In Proceedings of Models in Software Engineering. Academic Press.

Fritzson, P., & Engelson, V. (1998). Modelica - A Unified Object-Oriented Language for System Modelling and Simulation. In *Proceedings of the 12th European Conference on Object-Oriented Programming,* (pp. 67-90). Springer.

Fussel, J. B., Aber, E. F., & Rahl, R. G. (1976). On the quantitative analysis of priority-and failure logic. *IEEE Transactions on Reliability, 25*(5), 324–326. doi:10.1109/TR.1976.5220025

Gajski & Kuhn. (1983). Guest editor introduction: New VLSI-tools. *IEEE Computer, 16*(12), 11–14.

Gajski, D. D., & Khun, R. (1983). New VLSI Tools. IEEE Computer, 16, 11–14, 19.

Gamma, E., Helm, R., Johnson, R., & Vlissides, J. (1995). *Design Patterns. Elements of Reusable Object-Oriented Software.* Addison-Wesley Publishing Company.

Ganesan, K., John, L., Salapura, V., & Sexton, J. (2008, September). A Performance Counter Based Workload Characterization on Blue Gene/P. In *Proceedings of 37th International Conference on Parallel Processing* (pp. 330-337). IEEE.

García-Sánchez, P., González, J., Castillo, P. A., Merelo, J. J., Mora, A. M., Laredo, J. L. J., & Arenas, M. G. (2010). A distributed service oriented framework for metaheuristics using a public standard. *Studies in Computational Intelligence, 284,* 211–222.

García-Sánchez, P., Merelo, J. J., Sevilla, J. P., Castillo, P. A., Martín, M., & López, M. (2007). Plataforma de integración de servicios para la administración basada en BPEL y SOA. In *Actas de las III Jornadas en Servicios Web Y Soa (JSWEB 2007),* (pp. 111-118). Thomsom Editores Spain S. A.

Gascon, R., Mallet, F., & DeAntoni, J. (2011). Logical time and temporal logics: Comparing UML MARTE/CCSL and PSL. In *Proceedings of Int. Symp. on Temporal Representation and Reasoning (TIME'11)* (pp. 141-148). Lubeck, Germany: TIME.

Gaston, C., Le Gall, P., Rapin, N., & Touil, A. (2006). Symbolic Execution Techniques for Test Purpose Definition. In Proceedings of 18th IFIP Testing of Communicating Systems (pp. 1-18). New York, NY: Springer Berlin Heidelberg.

Gauthier, L., Gray, I., Larkam, A., Ayad, G., Acquaviva, A., & Nielsen, K. (2013). Explicit Java Control of Low-Power Heterogeneous Parallel Processing in ToucHMore. In *Proceedings of International conference on Java Technologies for Real Time Embedded Systems.* Academic Press.

GENIVI. (2014). About GENIVI. Retrieved from www. genivi.org

Genser, A., Bachmann, C., Haid, J., Steger, C., & Weiss, R. (2009, July). An Emulation-Based Real-Time Power Profiling Unit for Embedded Software. In *Proceedings of International Conference on Embedded Computer Systems: Architectures, Modeling and Simulation* (pp. 67-73). IEEE.

Genser, A., Bachmann, C., Steger, C., Weiss, R., & Haid, J. (2011, April). Voltage Emulation Platform for DVFS Voltage Drop Compensation Explorations. In *Proceedings of International Symposium on Performance Analysis of Systems and Software* (pp. 129-130). IEEE.

Gheorghe, L. (2009). *Continuous/Discrete Co-simulation interfaces from formalization to implementation.* (PhD thesis). University of Montreal, Montreal, Canada.

Gheorghe, L., Bouchhima, F., Nicolescu, G., & Boucheneb, H. (2006). Formal definitions of simulation interfaces in a continuous/discrete cosimulation tool. In *Proceedings of the Seventeenth IEEE International Workshop on Rapid System Prototyping,* (pp. 186–192). IEEE Computer Society.

Gheorghe, L., Bouchhima, F., Nicolescu, G., & Boucheneb, H. (2007). A formalization of global simulation models for continuous/discrete systems. In Proceedings of SCSC'07, (pp. 559–566). SCSC.

Ghodrat, M. A., Lahiri, K., & Raghunathan, A. (2007, June). Accelerating system-on-chip power analysis using hybrid power estimation. In *Proceedings of Design Automation Conference*, (pp. 883-886). ACM.

Gil, P., Arlat, J., Madeira, H., Crouzet, Y., Jarboui, T., Kanoun, K., et al. (2002). *Fault Representativeness*. Retrieved July 29, 2013, from Dependability Benchmarking Project (IST-2000-25425): http://www.laas.fr/DBench

Gil, D., Baraza, J.-C., Gracia, J., & Gil, P. (2004). VHDL Simulation-Based Fault Injection Techniques. In A. Benso, & P. Prinetto (Eds.), *Fault Injection Techniques and Tools for Embedded Systems Reliability Evaluation* (pp. 159–176). Springer, US. doi:10.1007/0-306-48711-X_10

Girod, L., Ramanathan, N., Elson, J., Stathopoulos, T., Lukac, M., & Estrin, D. (2007). Emstar: A Software Environment for Developing and Deploying Heterogeneous Sensor-Actuator Networks. *ACM Transactions Sensor Networks, 3*(3), 13. http://doi.acm.org/10.1145/1267060.1267061

Glover, F. (1986). Future Paths for Integer Programming and Links to Artificial Intelligence. *Computers & Operations Research, 5*(13), 533–549. doi:10.1016/0305-0548(86)90048-1

Glover, F. (1989). Tabu Search - Part 1. *ORSA Journal on Computing, 2*(1), 190–206. doi:10.1287/ijoc.1.3.190

Gokhale, A., Balasubramanian, K., Krishna, A. S., Balasubramanian, J., Edwards, G., & Deng, G. et al. (2008). Model driven middleware: A new paradigm for developing distributed real-time and embedded systems. *Science of Computer Programming, 73*(1), 39–58. doi:10.1016/j.scico.2008.05.005

Goknil, A., DeAntoni, J., Peraldi-Frati, M.-A., & Mallet, F. (2013a). Tool Support for the Analysis of TADL2 Timing Constraints using TimeSquare. In *Proceedings of 18th Inter. Conf. on Engineering of Complex Computer Systems,* (pp. 145-154). Academic Press.

Goknil, A., Suryadevara, J., Peraldi-Frati, M.-A., & Mallet, F. (2013b). Analysis Support for TADL2 Timing Constraints on EAST-ADL Models. In *Proceedings of European* Conference *on Software Architecture* (LNCS) (vol. 7957, pp. 89-105). Berlin: Springer.

Goldberg, R.P. (1974). Survey of virtual machine research. *IEEE Computer*, 34-35.

Gonzalez, H., Halevy, A. Y., Jensen, C. S., Madhavan, J., Langen, A., Shapley, R., & Shen, W. (2010) Google Fusion Tables: Data Management, Integration and Collaboration in the Cloud. In *Proceedings of the First ACM Symposium on Cloud Computing, Industrial Track, SoCC2010,* (pp. 175-180). ACM.

Gonzalez, H., Halevy, A. Y., Langen, A., Madhavan, J., McChesney, R., & Shapley, R. et al. (2010). Socialising Data with Google Fusion Tables. *IEEE Data Eng. Bull., 33*(3), 25–32.

Google. (2014). *The Go Programming Language*. Retrieved January 2014, from http://golang.org/

Gottscho, M., Kagalwalla, A., & Gupta, P. (2012). Power Variability in Contemporary DRAMs. *IEEE Embedded Systems Letters, 4*.

Gray, I., & Audsley, N. (2009). Exposing non-standard architectures to embedded software using compile-time virtualisation. In *Proceedings of International conference on Compilers, architecture, and synthesis for embedded systems* (CASES'09). CASES.

Gray, I., & Audsley, N. (2012). Developing Predictable Real-Time Embedded Systems Using AnvilJ. In *Proceedings of IEEE Real-Time and Embedded Technology and Applications Symposium*. IEEE Computer Society.

Gray, I., et al. (2011). Model-based hardware generation and programming - the MADES approach. In *Proceedings of 14th International Symposium on Object and Component-Oriented Real-Time Distributed Computing Workshops*. Academic Press.

Grinschgl, J., Krieg, A., Steger, C., Wei, R., Bock, H., & Haid, J. et al. (2013, March). Case study on multiple fault dependability and security evaluations. *Elsevier. Microprocessors and Microsystems, 37*(2), 218–227. doi:10.1016/j.micpro.2012.05.016

Grochowski, E., Ayers, D., & Tiwari, V. (2002, February). Microarchitectural simulation and control of di/dt-induced power supply voltage variation. In *Proceedings of High-Performance Computer Architecture,* (pp. 7-16). IEEE.

Groenda, H. (2012). Improving performance predictions by accounting for the accuracy of composed performance models. In *Proceedings of the International Conference on the Quality of Software Architectures (QoSA),* (pp. 111-116). QoSA.

Gupta, P., Agarwal, Y., Dolecek, L., Dutt, N., Gupta, R. K., & Kumar, R. et al. (2013, January). Underdesigned and opportunistic computing in presence of hardware variability. *IEEE Transactions on Computer-Aided Design of Integrated Circuits and Systems, 32*(1), 8–23.

Gupta, S. K. S., Mukherjee, T., Varsamopoulos, G., & Banerjee, A. (2011). Research directions in energy-sustainable cyber–physical systems. *Sustainable Computing: Informatics and Systems, 1*(1), 57–74.

Guthaus, M. R., Ringenberg, J. S., Ernst, D., Austin, T. M., Mudge, T., & Brown, R. B. (2001, December). MiBench: A free, commercially representative embedded benchmark suite. In *Proceedings of Workload Characterization,* (pp. 3-14). IEEE.

Guzman-Miranda, H., Aguirre, M. A., & Tombs, J. (2009, May). Noninvasive fault classification, robustness and recovery time measurement in microprocessor-type architectures subjected to radiation-induced errors. *IEEE Transactions on Instrumentation and Measurement, 58*(5), 1514–1524.

Haid, J., Kaefer, G., Steger, C., & Weiss, R. (2003, January). Run-time energy estimation in system-on-a-chip designs. In *Proceedings of the 2003 Asia and South Pacific Design Automation Conference* (pp. 595-599). ACM.

Halbwachs, N., Lagnier, F., & Raymond, P. (1994). Synchronous observers and the verification of reactive systems. In *Proceedings of Third International Conference on Methodology and Software Technology* (AMAST '93), (pp. 83–96). AMAST.

Hall, A., & Chapman, R. (2002, January-February). Correctness By Construction: Developing a Commercial Secure System. *IEEE Software, 19*(1), 18–25. doi:10.1109/52.976937

Han, J., & Kamber, M. (2006). *Data Mining: Concepts and Techniques* (2nd ed.). San Francisco, CA: Morgan Kaufmann.

Harb, N., Niar, S., Saghir, M., ElHillali, Y., & Ben-Atitallah, R. (2011). Dynamically Reconfigurable Architecture for a Driver Assistant System. In *Proceedings of IEEE Symposium on Application Specific Processors (SASP 2011)*. San Diego, CA: IEEE.

Harb, N., Saghir, M., & Niar, S. (2012). A Dynamically Reconfigurable Kalman Filtering Block for an Automotive Multiple Target Tracking System. In *Proceedings of 6th HiPEAC Workshop on Reconfigurable Computing*. Academic Press.

Harb, N., Niar, S., Khan, J., & Saghir, M. (2009). A Reconfigurable Platform Architecture for an Automotive Multiple-Target Tracking System. *ACM SIGBED Review. Special Interest Group on Embedded Systems, 6*(3), 1–4.

Hardebolle, C., & Boulanger, F. (2009). Exploring Multi-Paradigm Modelling Techniques. *Simulation, 85*(11-12), 688–708. doi:10.1177/0037549709105240

Haskins, C. (Ed.). (2011). INCOSE Systems Engineering Handbook: A Guide for System Life Cycle Processes and Activities, (v. 3.2.2, INCOSE-TP-2003-002-03.2.2). International Council on Systems Engineering.

Hastie, T., Tibshirani, R., & Friedman, J. (2009). *The Elements of Statistical Learning: Data Mining, Inference, and Prediction* (2nd ed.). Stanford, CA: Springer Series in Statistics. doi:10.1007/978-0-387-84858-7

Heirman, W., Stroonamdt, D., Miniskar, N. R., Wuyts, R., & Catthoor, F. (2010). PinComm: Characterizing Intra-application Communication for the Many-Core Era. In *Proceeding of the International Conference in Parallel and Distributed Systems,* (pp. 500-507). Shanghai, China: IEEE.

Hemer, D., & Ding, Y. (2009). Modelling Software Architectures using CRADLE. In *Proceedings of the 18th World IMACS/MODSIM Congress,* (pp. 404-410). IMACS/MODSIM.

Henzinger, T. (1996). The theory of hybrid automata. In *Proceedings of the 11th Annual Symposium on Logic in Computer Science (LICS),* (pp. 278–292). IEEE Computer Society Press.

Henzinger, T., & Sifakis, J. (2007). The Discipline of Embedded Systems Design. *IEEE Computer, 40*(10), 32–40. doi:10.1109/MC.2007.364

Herbert, S., & Marculescu, D. (2008). Characterizing Chip-Multiprocessor Variability-Tolerance. In *Proc. ACM Conf. Design Automation Conference*, (pp. 313-318). ACM.

Hill, J., Schmidt, D., Porter, A., & Slaby, J. (2008). CiCUTS: Combining System Execution Modeling Tools with Continuous Integration Environments. In *Proceedings of Engineering Applying System Execution Modeling Tools to Evaluate Enterprise Distributed Real-time and Embedded System QoS of Computer Based Systems,* (pp. 66 –75). IEEE.

Hill, J., Slaby, J., Baker, S., & Schmidt, D. (2006). Applying System Execution Modeling Tools to Evaluate Enterprise Distributed Real-time and Embedded System QoS. In *Proceedings of RTCSA 06: The 12th IEEE International Conference on Embedded and Real-Time Computing Systems and Applications.* Sydney, Australia: IEEE.

Hill, T., & Lewick, P. (2007). *STATISTICS Methods and Applications*. StatSoft.

Hill, J., Schmidt, D., Edmondson, J., & Gokhale, A. (2010). Tools for continuously evaluating distributed system qualities. *IEEE Software, 27*(4), 65–71. doi:10.1109/MS.2009.197

Ho, A., Hand, S., & Harris, T. (2004). *PDB: Pervasive Debugging with Xen*. Paper presented at the the Fifth IEEE/ACM International Workshop on Grid Computing. New York, NY.

Ho, C. W., & Williams, L. (2007). Developing software performance with the performance refinement and evolution model. In *Proceedings of the 6th international workshop on Software and performance WOSP*, (pp. 133 – 136). WOSP.

Holgado-Terriza, J. A., & Viúdez-Aivar, J. (2012). JavaES, a Flexible Java Framework for Embedded Systems. In M. T. Higuera-Toledano, & A. J. Wellings (Eds.), *Distributed* (pp. 323–355). Springer. doi:10.1007/978-1-4419-8158-5_13

Holtz, M., Narasimhan, S., & Bhunia, S. (2008, December). On-Die CMOS Voltage Droop Detection and Dynamic Compensation. In *Proceedings of the 18th ACM Great Lakes symposium on VLSI* (pp. 35-41). ACM.

Hong, S., Narayanan, S., & Kandemir, M. (2009). Process Variation Aware Thread Mapping for Chip Multiprocessors. In *Proceedings of IEEE Design Automation and Test in Europe*, (pp. 821-826). IEEE.

Hredzak, B., & Diessel, O. (2011). Optimization of placement of dynamic network-on-chip cores using simulated annealing. In *Proceeding of the 37th Annual Conference on IEEE Industrial Electronics Society*, (pp. 2400-2405). Melbourne: IEEE.

Huang, L., & Xu, Q. (2010). Energy-Efficient Task Allocation and Scheduling for Multi-Mode MPSoCs under Lifetime Reliability Constraints. In *Proceedings of IEEE Design, Automation and Test, Europe*, (pp. 1584-1589). IEEE.

Huang, L., Yuan, F., & Xu, Q. (2009). Lifetime Reliability-Aware Task Allocation and Scheduling for MPSoC Platforms. In *Proceedings of IEEE Design, Automation and Test, Europe*, (pp. 51-56). IEEE.

Hu, J., & Marculescu, R. (2005). Energy- and performance-aware mapping for regular NoC architectures. *IEEE Transactions on Computer-Aided Design of Integrated Circuits and Systems, 4*(24), 551–562.

Humenay, E., Tarjan, D., & Skadron, K. (2007). Impact of Process Variations on Multicore Performance Symmetry. In *Proc. Conf. Design, Automation and Test in Europe*, (pp. 1653-1658). Academic Press.

IAR Systems. (2013). Retrieved January 2014, from http://www.iar.com/

IEEE BT. (2013). *The IEEE public BT OUI listing*. Retrieved Dec 30, 2013, from http://standards.ieee.org/develop/regauth/oui/oui.txt

IEEE Standards Board. (1999). IEEE Standard for Software Unit Testing: An American National Standard, ANSI/IEEE Std 1008-1987. In IEEE Standards: Software Engineering, Volume Two: Process Standards, 1999 Edition. The Institute of Electrical and Electronics Engineers, Inc.

IEEE. (2008a). *International Standard ISO/IEC 15288:2008(E), IEEE Std 15288-2008 (Revision of IEEE Std 15288-2004) Systems and software engineering — System life cycle processes*. ISO/IEC and IEEE Computer Society.

IEEE. (2008b). *International Standard ISO/IEC 12207:2008(E), IEEE Std 12207-2008 (Revision of IEEE/EIA 12207.0-1996) Systems and software engineering — Software life cycle processes*. ISO/IEC and IEEE Computer Society.

ImapCar. (2006). *Nec Electronics 2006, Nec introduces Imapcar image processor with advanced parallel processing capabilities*. Available from http://www.nec.co.jp/press/en/0608/2501.html

Information Society Technologies. (2009). *OMEGA: Correct Development of Real-Time Embedded Systems*. Retrieved from http://www-omega.imag.fr/

Intelify. (2013). *Intelify: Do it social: CityAnalytics*. Retrieved Nov 20, 2013, from http://www.intelify.net

INTERESTED. (2011). *EU FP7 Project*. Retrieved from http://www.interested-ip.eu/index.html

International Technology Roadmap for Semiconductors. (2001). *2011 edition*. Retrieved from http://public.itrs.net/

International Telecommunication Union. (2010). *ITU-T - Message Sequence Chart. Z.120 recommendation*. Retrieved from http://www.itu.int/rec/T-REC-Z.120/en

International Telecommunication Union. (2014). *ITU-T - Specification and Description Language. Z.100 recommendation*. Retrieved from http://www.itu.int/rec/T-REC-Z.100/en

Intersafe. (2005). *The European FP7, Prevent-Intersafe project*. Retrieved from http://www.prevent- ip.org/en/prevent subprojects/intersection safety/intersafe/

Isa, M. A., & Jawawi, D. N. A. (2011). Comparative Evaluation of Performance Assessment and Modeling Method for Software Architecture. In *Proceedings of Second International Conference, ICSECS*. Kuantan, Malaysia: ICSECS.

ISO. (2008). *System and software engineering (ISO/IEC 12207)*. Retrieved from http://www.iso.org

ISO. (2011). *ISO 26262, Road vehicles – Functional safety*. Author.

ISO. (2012). *Road Vehicles Functional Safety (ISO 26262)*. Retrieved from http://www.iso.org

ISO/IEC 15288. (2008). *System engineering, System life cycle processes*. ISO/IEC 15288:2008(E) IEEE Std 15288-2008.

ISO/IEC/IEEE42010. (2011). *Systems and software engineering - Architecture description*. Author.

ITRS. (2012). Retrieved from http://www.itrs.net/Links/2012ITRS/Home2012.htm

Jackson, D. (2009, April). A direct path to dependable software. *Communications of the ACM, 52*(4), 78–88. doi:10.1145/1498765.1498787

Jenn, E., Arlat, J., Rimen, M., Ohlsson, J., & Karlsson, J. (1994, June). Fault injection into VHDL models: the MEFISTO tool. In *Proceedings of Fault-Tolerant Computing*, (pp. 66-75). IEEE.

Jensen, J. C., Chang, D. H., & Lee, E. A. (2011). A model-based design methodology for cyber-physical systems. In *Proceedings of Wireless Communications and Mobile Computing Conference* (IWCMC), (pp. 1666-1671). IWCMC.

Jeun, W.-C., & Ha, S. (2007). Effective OpenMP implementation and translation for multiprocessor system-on-chip without using OS. In *Proceedings of Asia and South Pacific Design Automation Conference*, (pp. 44-49). ASP-DAC.

Jin, X., & Watanabe, T. (2010). An Efficient 3D NoC Synthesis by Using Genetic Algorithms. In *Proceeding of the Region 10 Conference (TENCON)*, (pp. 1207-1212). Fukouka, Japan: IEEE.

John, L. K., Vasudevan, P., & Sabarinathan, J. (1999). Workload characterization: Motivation, goals and methodology. *Workload Characterization: Methodology and Case Studies*, 3–14.

Joseph, R., & Martonosi, M. (2001, August). Run-time power estimation in high performance microprocessors. In *Proceedings of the 2001 international symposium on Low power electronics and design* (pp. 135-140). ACM.

Kafka, L., Danek, M., & Novak, O. (2007). A Novel Emulation Technique that Preserves Circuit Structure and Timing. In *Proceedings of International Symposium on System-on-Chip*, (pp. 1-4). Tampere, Finland: Academic Press.

Kang, K., Park, S., Roy, K., & Alam, M. (2007). Estimation of statistical variation in temporal NBTI degradation and its impact on lifetime circuit performance. In *Proceedings of the 2007 IEEE/ACM international conference on Computer-aided design*, (pp. 730-734). IEEE/ACM.

Karl, E., Blaauw, D., Sylvester, D., & Mudge, T. (2008). Multi-mechanism reliability modeling and management in dynamic systems. *IEEE Transactions on Very Large Scale Integration (VLSI). Systems, 16*(4), 476–487.

Karnik, T., Hazucha, P., & Patel, J. (2004). Characterization of Soft Errors Caused by Single Event Upsets in CMOS Processes. *IEEE Transactions on Dependable and Secure Computing, 1*(2), 128–143. doi:10.1109/TDSC.2004.14

Kebin, Z., Yu, G., & Angelov, C. K. (2010). *Graphical Model Debugger Framework for embedded systems*. Paper presented at the Design, Automation & Test in Europe Conference & Exhibition (DATE). New York, NY.

Khan, J., Niar, S., Elhillali, Y., Rivenq-menhaj, A., & Dekeyser, J. (2008). An MPSoC Architecture for the Multiple Target Tracking Application in Driver Assistant System. In *Proceedings of IEEE International Conference Application-Specific Systems, Architectures and Processors (ASAP)*. IEEE.

Khan, J., Niar, S., Saghir, M., Elhillali, Y., & Rivenq-menhaj, A. (2009). Driver Assistance System Design and its Optimization for FPGA Based MPSoC. In *Proceedings of IEEE Symposium on Application Specific Processors*. SASP.

Khan, J., Niar, S., Saghir, M., Elhillali, Y., & Rivenq-menhaj, A. (2010). Trade-off Exploration for Target Tracking Application in a Customized Multiprocessor Architecture. *Journal on Embedded Systems, 175043*, 1-21.

Khan, O., & Kundu, S. (2011, September-October). Hardware/software codesign architecture for online testing in chip multiprocessors. *IEEE Transactions on Dependable and Secure Computing, 8*(5), 714–727.

Kiczales, G., Irwin, J., Lamping, J., Loingtier, J.-M., Lopes, C. V., Maeda, C., & Mendhekar, A. (1996). Aspect-oriented programming. *ACM Computing Surveys, 28*(4).

Kirkpatrick, S., Gelatt, C. D., & Vecchi, M. P. (1983). Optimization by Simulated Annealing. *Science, 4598*(220), 671–680. doi:10.1126/science.220.4598.671 PMID:17813860

Kleijn, C. (2006). Modelling and Simulation of Fluid Power Systems with 20-sim. *Intl. Journal of Fluid Power, 7*(3).

Kleijn, C., & Visser, P. (2012). Extension to MATLAB/Simulink. *DESTECS Project Deliverable D3.5*. Retrieved from http://www.destecs.org/

Kolawa, A., & Huizinga, D. (2007). *Automated Defect Prevention: Best Practices in Software Management*. Wiley-IEEE Computer Society Press.

Kolovos, D. S., et al. (2006). Eclipse development tools for Epsilon. In *Proceedings of Eclipse Summit Europe, Eclipse Modeling Symposium*. Academic Press.

Koopman, P., & Chakravarty, T. (2004). Cyclic Redundancy Code (CRC) Polynomial Selection For Embedded Networks. In *Proceedings of IEEE International Conference on Dependable Systems and Networks*, (pp. 145-154). IEEE.

Koudri, A., et al. (2008). Using MARTE in the MOPCOM SoC/SoPC Co-Methodology. In *Proceedings of MARTE Workshop at DATE'08*. Academic Press.

Kozhikkottu, V. J., Venkatesan, R., Raghunathan, A., & Dey, S. (2011, March). VESPA: Variability emulation for System-on-Chip performance analysis. In *Proceedings of Design, Automation & Test in Europe Conference & Exhibition (DATE)* (pp. 1-6). IEEE.

Koziolek, H. (2010). Performance evaluation of component-based software systems: A survey. *Performance Evaluation, 67*(8), 634–658. doi:10.1016/j.peva.2009.07.007

Kraemer, S., Gao, L., Weinstock, J., Leupers, R., Ascheid, G., & Meyr, H. (2007). *HySim: a Fast Simulation Framework for Embedded Software Development*. Paper presented at the 5th IEEE/ACM international conference on Hardware/software codesign and system synthesis. Salzburg, Austria.

Krasner, J. (2009). *Forecast 2010: What Is in Store for Embedded Developers*. Retrieved August 2013, from http://www.embeddedmarketintelligence.com/2009/12/02/forecast-2010-what-is-in-store-for-embedded-developers/

Kreku, J. (2012). Early-phase performance evaluation of computer systems using workload models and SystemC. Acta Universitatis Ouluensis. Series C. *Technica, 435*, 106.

Krieg, A., Bachmann, C., Grinschgl, J., Steger, C., Weiss, R., & Haid, J. (2011, June). Accelerating early design phase differential power analysis using power emulation techniques. In *Proceedings of Hardware-Oriented Security and Trust (HOST), 2011 IEEE International Symposium on* (pp. 81-86). IEEE.

Krieg, A., Grinschgl, J., Steger, C., Wei, R., Bock, H., & Haid, J. (2012, April). System side-channel leakage emulation for HW/SW security coverification of MPSoCs. In *Proceedings of Design and Diagnostics of Electronic Circuits & Systems (DDECS),* (pp.139-144). IEEE.

Krieg, A., Grinschgl, J., Steger, C., Weiss, R., & Haid, J. (2011, July), A side channel attack countermeasure using system-on-chip power profile scrambling. In *Proceedings of On-Line Testing Symposium (IOLTS),* (pp. 222-227), IEEE.

Krieg, A., Grinschgl, J., Steger, C., Weiss, R., Genser, A., Bock, H., & Haid, J. (2012, May). Characterization and handling of low-cost micro-architectural signatures in MPSoCs. In *Proceedings of Test Symposium (ETS),* (pp. 1-6). IEEE.

Krieg, A., Preschern, C., Grinschgl, J., Kreiner, C., Steger, C., Weiss, R., Bock, H., & Haid, J. (2013, May). Power And Fault Emulation For Software Verification and System Stability Testing in Safety Critical Environments. *IEEE Transactions on Industrial Informatics, 9*(2), 1199-1206.

Krishnan, A., Reddy, V., Chakravarthi, S., Rodriguez, J., John, S., & Krishnan, S. (2003). NBTI impact on transistor and circuit: models, mechanisms and scaling effects. In *Proceedings of IEEE International Electron Devices Meeting,* (pp. 14.5.1–14.5.4). IEEE.

Kruchten, P. (1995). The 4+1 View Model of Architecture. *IEEE Software, 12*(6), 45–50. doi:10.1109/52.469759

Kumar, S., Kim, C., & Sapatnekar, S. (2006). An analytical model for negative bias temperature instability. In *Proceedings of the 2006 IEEE/ACM international conference on Computer-aided design,* (pp. 493-496). IEEE.

Kurita, T., Chiba, M., & Nakatsugawa, Y. (2008). Application of a Formal Specification Language in the Development of the "Mobile FeliCa" IC Chip Firmware for Embedding in Mobile Phone. In Proceedings of Formal Methods (LNCS) (pp. 425-429). Berlin: Springer-Verlag.

Kurtev, I., Bezivin, J., Jouault, F., & Valduriez, P. (2006). Model-based DSL frameworks. In *Proceedings of 21st ACM SIGPLAN symposium on Object-oriented programming systems, languages, and applications*. Portland, OR: ACM.

Kwon, S., Pasricha, S., & Cho, J. (2011). POSEIDON: A Framework for Application-Specific Network-on-Chip Synthesis for Heterogeneous Chip Multiprocessors. In *Proceeding of the International Symposium on Quality Electronic Design,* (pp. 1-7). Santa Clara, CA: IEEE.

Lajolo, M., Raghunathan, A., Dey, S., & Lavagno, L. (2002, June). Cosimulation-based power estimation for system-on-chip design. *IEEE Transactions on Very Large Scale Integration (VLSI) Systems, 10*(3), 253–266.

Lalanne, F., & Maag, S. (2013). A formal data-centric approach for passive testing of communication protocols. *IEEE/ACM Transactions on Networking, 21*(3), 788–801. doi:10.1109/TNET.2012.2210443

Larsen, P.G., Fitzgerald, J.S., & Brookes, T (1996). Applying Formal Specification in Industry. *IEEE Software, 13*(3), 48 – 56.

Larsen, P. G., Battle, N., Ferreira, M., Fitzgerald, J. S., Lausdahl, K. G., & Verhoef, M. (2010). The Overture Initiative - Integrating Tools for VDM. *ACM SIGSOFT Softw. Eng. Notes, 35*(1), 1. doi:10.1145/1668862.1668864

Lau, K., & Wang, Z. (2005). A Taxonomy of Software Component Models. In *Proceedings of the 31st Euromicro Conference on Software Engineering and Advanced Applications*. Euromicro.

Le Beux, S. (2006). FPGA Implementation of Embedded Cruise Control and Anti-Collision Radar. In *Proc. 9th Euromicro Conference on Digital System Design (DSD'2006),* (pp. 280-287). DSD.

Leatherman, R., & Stollon, N. (2005). An embedding debugging architecture for SOCs. *IEEE Potentials*, *24*(1), 12–16. doi:10.1109/MP.2005.1405795

Ledeczi, A., Maroti, M., Bakay, A., Karsai, G., Garrett, J., Thomason, G., et al. (2001). The Generic Modeling Environment. In *Proceedings of WISP'2001: IEEE International Workshop on Intelligent Signal Processing.* Budapest, Hungary: IEEE.

Lee, D., Chen, D., Hao, R., Miller, R. E., Wu, J., & Yin, X. (2002). A Formal Approach for Passive Testing of Protocol Data Portions. In *Proceedings of 10th IEEE International Conference on Network Protocols* (pp. 122-131). IEEE.

Lee, E. A. (2008). *Cyber physical systems: Design challenges* (Tech. Rep. UCB/EECS-2008-8). EECS Department, University of California, Berkeley.

Lee, E. A. (2010). CPS foundations. In *Proceedings of the 47th Design Automation Conference* (DAC '10). ACM.

Lee, E. A., & Seshia, S. (2011). Introduction to Embedded Systems: A Cyber-Physical Systems Approach. Academic Press.

Lee, E. A., & Zheng, H. (2005). Operational semantics of hybrid systems. In Hybrid Systems: Computation and Control (HSCC), (LNCS) (vol. 3414, pp. 25–53). Berlin: Springer-Verlag.

Lee, E. A., & Zheng, H. (2007). Leveraging Synchronous Language Principles for Heterogeneous Modeling and Design of Embedded Systems. In *Proceedings of EMSOFT '07*. ACM.

Lee, I., Kim, H., Yang, P., Yoo, S., Chung, E.-Y., Choi, K.-M., et al. (2006, January). PowerViP: Soc power estimation framework at transaction level. In *Proceedings of the 2006 Asia and South Pacific Design Automation Conference* (pp. 551-558). IEEE.

Lee, I., Sokolsky, O., Chen, S., Hatcliff, J., Jee, E., & Kim, B. ... Venkatasubramanian, K.K. (2012). Challenges and Research Directions in Medical Cyber–Physical Systems. *Proceedings of the IEEE*, *100*(1), 75-90.

Lee, K., et al. (2006). Low-power network-on-chip for high-performance SoC design. *IEEE Transactions on VLSI Systems, 14*(2). Cai & Gajski. (2003). Transaction level modeling: An overview. In *Proceedings of Int. Conference on HW/SW Codesign and System Synthesis* (CODES-ISSS), (pp. 19-24). CODES-ISSS.

Lee, E. A. (2009). Computing needs time. *Communications of the ACM*, *52*(5), 70–79. doi:10.1145/1506409.1506426

Lemaire, R., Thuries, S., & Heiztmann, F. (2012). A flexible modeling environment for a NoC-based multi-core architecture. In *Proceedings of High Level Design Validation and Test Workshop (HLDVT)*, (pp. 140-147). Huntington Beach, CA: IEEE.

Leveugle, R. (2000, October). Fault injection in VHDL descriptions and emulation. In *Proceedings of Defect and Fault Tolerance in VLSI Systems*, (pp. 414-419). IEEE.

Leveugle, R. (2002). *Automatic Modifications of High Level VHDL Descriptions*. Grenoble, France: Design, Automation and Test in Europe Conference and Exhibition.

Leveugle, R. (2007, October). Early analysis of fault-based attack effects in secure circuits. *IEEE Transactions on Computers*, *56*(10), 1431–1434.

Liao, W., Pisharath, J., Liu, Y., Choudhary, A. (2005). NuMineBench 2.0. *Center for Ultra-Scale Computing and Information Security Technical Report*, CUCIS-2005-08-01.

Ling, Y., Mallet, F., & Liu, J. (2011). Verification of MARTE/CCSL Time Requirements with Promela/SPIN. In *Proceedings of 16th Int. Conf. on Engineering of Complex Computer Systems* (ICECCS'11), (pp. 65-74). IEEE.

Liu, H., Niar, S., Elhillali, Y. & Rivenq-Menhaj, A. (2011). Embedded Architecture with Hardware Accelerator for Target Recognition in Driver Assistance Systems. *ACM SIGARCH Computer Architecture News*.

Liu, H., Niar, S., Elhillali, Y., & Rivenq-menhaj, A. (2011). Heterogeneous Embedded Architecture for Target Recognition in a Driver Assistant System. In *Proceedings of 2nd International Workshop on Highly Efficient Accelerators and Reconfigurable Technologies (HEART)*. HEART.

Liu, J., Ziwei, L., He, J., Mallet, F., & Ding, Z. (2013). Hybrid MARTE statecharts. *Frontiers of Computer Science*, *7*(1), 95–108. doi:10.1007/s11704-012-1301-1

Liu, X., Liu, J., Eker, J., & Lee, E. A. (2003). Heterogeneous modeling and design of control systems. In *Software-Enabled Control: Information Technology for Dynamical Systems*. IEEE Press. doi:10.1002/047172288X.ch7

Ltd, A. R. M. (2013). *CoreLink System IP and Design Tools for AMBA*. Retrieved July 29, 2013, from http://www.arm.com/products/system-ip/amba

Lukovic, S., Pezzino, P., & Fiorin, L. (2010, April). Stack Protection Unit as a step towards securing MPSoCs. In *Proceedings of Parallel & Distributed Processing, Workshops and Phd Forum (IPDPSW)*, (pp. 1-4). IEEE.

Lutz, R. (1993). Analyzing software requirements errors in safety-critical, embedded systems. In *Proceedings of IEEE International Symposium on Requirements Engineering, RE 1993* (pp. 126-133). IEEE.

LXC - Linux Containers. (2014). Retrieved from http://lxc.sourceforge.net

Lynch, N., & Tuttle, M. (1989). An Introduction to I/O Automata. *CWI-Quarterly*, *2*(3), 219–246.

Ma, X., & Andreeasson, I. (2006). Driver reaction time estimation from real car following data and application in GM-type model evaluation. In *Proceedings of the 85th TRB Annual Meeting*. TRB.

MADES. (2011). *EU FP7 Project*. Retrieved from http://www.mades-project.org/

MAENAD Methodology. (2013). *MAENAD Design Methodology, D2.2.1*. Retrieved from http://www.maenad.eu/public_pw/MAENAD_Deliverable_D2.2.1_V2.0.pdf

MAENAD. (2009). *MAENAD FP7 Project*. Retrieved from http://www.maenad.eu/

MAENAD. (2013). *MAENAD Analysis Workbench, D5.2.1*. Retrieved from http://www.maenad.eu/public_pw/MAENAD_Deliverable_D5.2.1_V3.0.pdf

Maes, P. (1987). Concepts and experiments in computational reflection. ACM SIGPLAN Notices, 22(12), 147-155.

Magureanu, G., Gavrilescu, M., & Pescaru, D. (2013). Validation of static properties in unified modeling language models for cyber physical systems. *Journal of Zhejiang University Science C*, *14*(5), 332–346. doi:10.1631/jzus.C1200263

Mahmud, N. (2012). *Dynamic Model-based Safety Analysis: From State Machines to Temporal Fault Trees*. (Ph.D. dissertation). Department of Computer Science, University of Hull, Hull, UK.

Mahmud, N., Papadopoulos, Y., & Walker, M. (2010). A Translation of State Machines to Temporal Fault Trees. In *Proceedings of the 40th IEEE/IFIP International Conference on Dependable Systems and Networks*, (pp. 45-51). IEEE.

Mahmud, N., Papadopoulos, Y., & Walker, M. (2012). Compositional synthesis of Temporal Fault Trees from State Machines. *ACM SIGMETRICS Performance Evaluation Review*, *39*(4), 79–88.

Mallet, F. (2013). Automatic generation of observers from MARTE/CCSL. In *Proceedings of 23rd International Symposium on Rapid System Prototyping* (RSP'12), (pp. 86-92). RSP.

Mallet, F., Millo, J.-V., & De Simone, R. (2013). Safe CCSL specifications and Marked Graphs. In Proceedings of MemoCode'13, (pp. 157-166). Academic Press.

Mao, S., & Wolf, T. (2010, June). Hardware support for secure processing in embedded systems. *IEEE Transactions on Computers*, *59*(6), 847–854.

Marongiu, A., & Benini, L. (2009). Efficient OpenMP support and extensions for MPSoCs with explicitly managed memory hierarchy. In *Proceedings of the 12th International Conference on Design, Automation and Test in Europe*, (pp. 809–814). Academic Press.

Martijn, O., Vlad, R., Jan, T., De Vries, R. G., & Willemse, T. A. C. (2007). Integrating verification, testing, and learning for cryptographic protocols. In *Proceedings of the 6th International conference on Integrated formal methods* (pp. 538-557). Academic Press.

Martin, P. T., Feng, Y., & Wang, X. (2003). *Detector Technology Evaluation. Technical Report*. Utah Transportation Centre.

Marwedel, P. (2010). *Embedded System Design -- Embedded Systems Foundations of Cyber-Physical Systems*. Springer.

Matragkas, N., et al. (2010). *D4.1: Model Transformation and Code Generation Tools Specification*. Technical Report. Retrieved from http://www.mades-project.org/

Mazzara, M., & Bhattacharyya, A. (2010). On Modelling and Analysis of Dynamic Reconfiguration of Dependable Real-Time Systems. In *Proceedings Third International Conference on Dependability* (DEPEND 2010), (pp. 173–181). DEPEND.

Mazzini, S., Favaro, J., & Vardanega, T. (2013, June). *Cross-Domain Reuse: Lessons Learned in A Multi-Project Trajectory*. Paper presented at The 13th International Conference on Software Reuse. Pisa, Italy.

Mazzini, S., Puri, S., Olive, X., Burte, G., Paccagnini, C., & Tronci, E. (2009, October). *SSFRT Report3: Guidelines for Model Based Space System Engineering*. Issue 1.2.

Mazzini, S., Puri, S., Veran, G., Vardanega, T., Panunzio, M., Santamaria, C., & Zovi, A. (2011, May). *Model-Driven and Component-Based Engineering with the CHESS Methodology*. Paper presented at The International Space System Engineering Conference, DASIA. La Valletta, Malta.

McQueen, S. R. (2010). *Basic DES Cryptography Core*. Retrieved July 29, 2013, from OpenCores: http://opencores.org/project,basicdes

Mehiaoui, A., Tucci-Piergiovanni, S., Babau, J. P., & Lemarchand, L. (2012). Optimizing the Deployment of Distributed Real-Time Embedded Applications. In *Proceedings of International Conference on Embedded and Real-Time Computing Systems and Applications,* (pp. 400-403). Academic Press.

Mehiaoui, A., Wozniak, E., Tucci-Piergiovanni, S., Mraidha, C., Di Natale, M., Zeng, H., et al. (2013). A Two-step Optimization Technique for Functions Placement, Partitioning, and Priority Assignment in Distributed Systems. In *Proceedings of 4th ACM SIGPLAN/SIGBED Conference on Languages, Compilers and Tools for Embedded Systems,* (pp. 121-132). ACM.

Mehta, N. R., Medvidovic, N., & Phadke, S. (2000). *Towards a Taxonomy of Soft-ware Connectors*. Paper presented at the 22nd International Conference on Software Engineering. New York, NY.

Meier, M., Hanenberg, S., & Spinczyk, O. (2012). AspectVHDL Stage 1: The Prototype of an Aspect-Oriented Hardware Description Language. In *Proceedings of 2nd AOSD Workshop on Modularity in Systems Software,* (pp. 3-8). Potsdam, Germany: AOSD.

Mellor, S. J., & Balcer, M. (2002). *Executable UML: A foundation for model-driven architectures*. Addison-Wesley Longman Publishing Co., Inc..

Mendez, F. (2013). *System and method for monitoring people and/or vehicles in urban environments*. US Patent Application No: 2011/0128,127. Serial no 13/56,068. Retrieved Nov 30, 2013, from http://www.google.com/patents/US20110128127

Merle, G., Roussel, J.-M., Lesage, J., & Bobbio, A. (2010). Probabilistic Algebraic Analysis of Fault Trees With Priority Dynamic Gates and Repeated Events. *IEEE Transactions on Reliability, 59*(1), 250–261. doi:10.1109/TR.2009.2035793

Mernik, et al. (2005). When and how to develop domain-specific languages. *ACM Computing Surveys, 37*(4), 316–344.

Michalewicz, Z., & Fogel, D. B. (2004). *How to Solve It: Modern Heuristics. 2 Edition*. Berlin, Heidelberg: Springer-Verlag. doi:10.1007/978-3-662-07807-5

Miclea, L., & Sanislav, T. (2011). About dependability in cyber-physical systems. In *Proceedings of Design & Test Symposium (EWDTS),* (pp. 17-21). EWDTS.

Miller, B. A., & Bisdikian, C. (2000). *Bluetooth Revealed: The Insider's Guide to an Open Specification for Global Wireless Communications*. Upper Saddle River, NJ:Prentice-Hall.

Millo, J.-V., Mallet, F., Couadou, A., & Ramesh, S. (2013). Scenario-based verification in presence of variability using a synchronous approach. *Frontiers of Computer Science, 7*(5), 650–672. doi:10.1007/s11704-013-3094-6

Mitchell, M. (1996). *An Introduction to Genetic Algorithms*. Cambridge, MA: MIT press.

Modelica. (2012). *Modelica: An object-oriented equation based language*. Retrieved from https://modelica.org/

Modelio. (2014). *Open source UML Editor and MDE Workbench*. Retrieved from www.modelio.org

Motoyoshi, M. (2009). Through-Silicon Via (TSV). *Proceedings of the IEEE, 1*(97), 43–48. doi:10.1109/JPROC.2008.2007462

Mousa, H., & Krintz, C. (2005). *HPS: Hybrid profiling support*. Paper presented at the 14th International Conference on Parallel Architectures and Compilation Techniques. New York, NY.

Mück, T. R., Gernoth, M., Schröder-Preikschat, W., & Fröhlich, A. A. (2011). A Case Study of AOP and OOP Applied to Digital Hardware Design. In *Proceedings of Brazilian Symposium on Computing System Engineering*, (pp. 66-71). Florianopolis, Brazil: Academic Press.

Mueller, W., et al. (2010). The SATURN Approach to SysML-based HW/SW Codesign. In *Proceedings of IEEE Computer Society Annual Symposium on VLSI (ISVLSI)*. IEEE.

Mulas, F., Atienza, D., Acquaviva, A., Carta, S., Benini, L., & De Micheli, G. (2009). Thermal Balancing Policy for Multiprocessor Stream Computing Platforms. Transactions on Computer-Aided Design of Integrated Circuits And Systems, 28.

Mura, M., et al. (2008). Model-based Design Space Exploration for RTES with SysML and MARTE. In *Proceedings of Forum on Specification, Verification and Design Languages* (FDL 2008), (pp. 203–208). FDL.

Murillo, L. G., Harnath, J., Leupers, R., & Ascheid, G. (2012). *Scalable and retargetable debugger architecture for heterogeneous MPSoCs*. Paper presented at the System, Software, SoC and Silicon Debug Conference (S4D). New York, NY.

Murphy-Chutorian, E., & Trivedi, M. (2008). HyHOPE: Hybrid Head Orientation and Position Estimation for Vision-based Driver Head Tracking. In *Proceedings of IEEE Intelligent Vehicles Symposium*. IEEE.

Mutyam, M., Wang, F., Krishnan, R., Narayanan, V., Kandemir, M., & Xie, Y. et al. (2009). Process-Variation-Aware Adaptive Cache Architecture and Management. *IEEE Transactions on Computers*, 58, 865–877. doi:10.1109/TC.2009.30

Myaing, A., & Dinavahi, V. (2011, January). FPGA-based real-time emulation of power electronic systems with detailed representation of device characteristics. *IEEE Transactions on Industrial Electronics*, 58(1), 358–368.

Myers, G. J. (2004). *The Art of Software Testing*. Wiley & Sons.

Nagpurkar, P., Mousa, H., Krintz, C., & Sherwood, T. (2006). Efficient Remote Profiling for Resource-Constrained Devices. *ACM Transactions Architecture Code Optimization, 3*(1), 35-66. http://doi.acm.org/10.1145/1132462.1132465

Narayanan, V., & Xie, Y. (2006). Reliability Concerns in Embedded System Designs. *IEEE Computer, 1*(39), 118–120. doi:10.1109/MC.2006.31

Nass, R. (2007). Annual study uncovers the embedded market. *Embedded.com.* Retrieved from http://www.eetimes.com/design/other/4007166/Annual-study-uncovers-the-embedded-market

Ndai, P., Bhunia, S., Agarwal, A., & Roy, K. (2008). Within-Die Variation-Aware Scheduling in Superscalar Processors for Improved Throughput. *IEEE Transactions on Computers*, 57, 940–651. doi:10.1109/TC.2008.40

Nguyen, H. N., Poizat, P., & Zaidi, F. (2012a). Online verification of value-passing choreographies through property-oriented passive testing. In Proceedings of the 2012 IEEE 14th International Symposium on High-Assurance Systems Engineering (pp. 106-113). Washington, DC: IEEE Computer Society. doi:10.1109/HASE.2012.15

Nguyen, H. N., Poizat, P., & Zaidi, F. (2012b). A symbolic framework for the conformance checking of value-passing choreographies. In *Proceedings of the ICSOC*, (pp. 525-532). ICSOC.

Nicolescu, G., Bouchhima, F., & Gheorghe, L. (2006). CODIS – A Framework for Continuous/Discrete Systems Co-Simulation. In C. G. Cassandras, A. Giua, C. Seatzu, & J. Zaytoon (Eds.), *Analysis and Design of Hybrid Systems* (pp. 274–275). Elsevier. doi:10.1016/B978-008044613-4.50051-3

Nielsen, C. B. (2010). *Dynamic Reconfiguration of Distributed Systems in VDM-RT*. (Master's thesis). Aarhus University.

Nisbet, R., Elder, J., & Miner, G. (2009). *Handbook of Statistical Analysis and Data Mining Applications*. Waltham, MA: Academic Press.

Ober, L., et al. (2005). *Projet Omega: Un profil UML et un outil pour la modelisation et la validation de systemes temps reel*. Academic Press.

Object Management Group (OMG). (2011a). *Unified modeling language 2.4.1*. Available from http://www.omg.org/spec/UML

Object Management Group (OMG). (2011b). *UML MARTE profile 1.1*. Available from http://www.omg.org/spec/MARTE/1.1/

Object Management Group (OMG). (2012). System modeling language specification v1.3. Available: http://www.omg.org/spec/SysML/1.3/

Object Management Group. (2007). *Data Distribution Service for Real-time Systems Version 1.2*. OMG Std. Retrieved from http://www.omg.org/spec/DDS/1.2/

Object Management Group. (2007). *MOF QVT Final Adopted Specification*. OMG document ptc/07-07-07. Retrieved from http://www.omg.org/spec/QVT/

Object Management Group. (2008). *Common Object Request Broker Architecture Version 3.1*. OMG Std. Retrieved from http://www.omg.org/spec/CORBA/

Object Management Group. (2011). *UML Profile for MARTE: Modelling and analysis of Real-Time Embedded Systems V1.1*. OMG Std. Retrieved from http://www.omg.org/spec/MARTE/1.1/

Object Management Group. (2014a). OMG - Unified Modeling Language. UML recommendation. Retrieved from http://www.omg.org/spec/UML/

Object Management Group. (2014b). Foundational UML. fUML recommendation. Retrieved from http://www.omg.org/spec/FUML/

OCP-IO Association. (2013). *Open Core Protocol International Partnership (OCP-IP)*. Retrieved July 29, 2013, from http://www.ocpip.org

OMG MARTE. (2011). *UML Profile for Modelling and Analysis of Real-Time and Embedded system*. formal/2011-06-02, Version 1.1.

OMG MARTE. (2013). MARTE profile. Retrieved from. http://www.omgmarte.org

OMG QFTP. (2008). *UML Profile for QoS and Fault Tolerance*. formal/2008-04-05, Version 1.1.

OMG SYML. (2012). *System Modeling Language, formal specification*. 2012-06-01, Version 1.3.

OMG UML. (2011). *Unified Modeling Language*. formal/2011-08-06, Version 2.4.1.

OMG. (2007). *Portal of the Model Driven Engineering Community*. Retrieved from http://www.planetmde.org

OMG. (2009a). *UML Profile for MARTE, v1.0., Novembre 2009*. Object Management Group, formal/2009-11-02.

OMG. (2009b). *Unified Modeling Language, Superstructure, v2.2, February 2009*. Object Management Group, formal/2009-02-02.

OMG. (2011). *Modeling and Analysis of Real-time and Embedded systems (MARTE)*. Retrieved from http://www.omg.org/spec/MARTE/1.1/PDF

OMG. (2011a). *Unified Modeling Language (UML)*. Retrieved from http://www.omg.org/spec/UML/2.4.1/PDF

OMG. (2011b). *Modeling and Analysis of Real-time and Embedded system (MARTE)*. Retrieved from http://www.omg.org/spec/MARTE/1.1/PDF

OMG. (2012). *Final Adopted OMG SysML Specification*. Retrieved from http://www.omg.org/spec/SysML/1.3/

OMG. (2012). *System Modeling Language (SysML)*. Retrieved from http://www.omg.org/spec/SysML/1.3/PDF

OpenACC-Standard.org. (2013, June). *The OpenACC Application Programming Interface, Version 2.0*. Author.

OpenCores. (2010, Juny 22). *Wishbone System-on-Chip (SoC) Interconnect Architecture for Portable IP Cores*. Retrieved July 29, 2013, from OpenCores: http://opencores.org/opencores,wishbone

OpenCores. (2013). Retrieved July 29, 2013, from http://www.opencores.org

OpenModelica. (2012). *Open-source Modelica-based modeling and simulation environment*. Retrieved from http://www.openmodelica.org/

Oracle Corporation. (2013). *Java Platform, Standard Edition 7 API Specification - Future Interface*. Retrieved from http://docs.oracle.com/javase/7/docs/api/java/util/concurrent/Future.html

Organizationally Unique Identifier. (2013). In *Wikipedia*. Retrieved Dec 30, 2013, from http://en.wikipedia.org/wiki/Organizationally_unique_identifier

Palachi, E., Cohen, C., & Takashi, S. (2013). Simulation of cyber physical models using SysML and numerical solvers. In *Proceedings of Systems Conference (SysCon)*, (pp. 671-675). IEEE.

Palermo, G., Silvano, C., & Zaccaria, V. (2009). Variability-Aware Robust Design Space Exploration of Chip Multiprocessor Architectures. In *Proceedings of the IEEE Asia and South Pacific Design Automation Conference*, (pp. 323-328). IEEE.

Panunzio, M., & Vardanega, T. (2010). A Component Model for On-board Software Applications. In *Proceedings of 36th Euromicro Conference on Software Engineering and Advanced Applications, SEAA 2010* (pp. 57-64). SEAA.

Papadopoulos, Y., & McDermid, J. (1999). Hierarchically performed hazard origin and propagation studies. In *Proceedings of 18th International Conference on Computer Safety, Reliability, and Security, SAFECOMP*, (pp. 139-152). Academic Press.

Papazoglou, M., & van den Heuvel, W. (2007). Service oriented architectures: approaches, technologies and research issues. *The VLDB Journal, 16*, 389–415. doi:10.1007/s00778-007-0044-3

PARATOOLS. (2014, March 15). Retrieved from http://www.paratools.com/otf.php

Park, H., Xu, J.-Z., Kim, K. H., & Park, J. S. (2012). On-Chip Debug Architecture for Multicore Processor. *ETRI Journal, 34*(1), 44-54. http://dx.doi.org/10.4218/etrij.12.0111.0172

Parnell, K. (2005, 2nd quarter). The Changing Face of Automotive ECU Design. XCell Journal.

Parr, T. (2103). *The Definitive ANTLR 4 Reference*. The Pragmatic Bookshelf.

Parreira, A., Teixeira, J., & Santos, M. (2003). A Novel Approach to FPGA-Based Hardware Fault Modeling and Simulation. In *Proceedings of IEEE International Workshop on Design and Diagnostics of Electronic Circuits and Systems*, (pp. 17-24). Poznań, Poland: IEEE.

Paschalis, A., Gizopoulos, D., Kranitis, N., Psarakis, M., & Zorian, Y. (2001, March). Deterministic software-based self-testing of embedded processor cores. In *Proceedings of the Conference on Design, Automation and Test in Europe* (pp. 92-96). IEEE Press.

Patel, K., Parameswaran, S., & Ragel, R. G. (2011, September). Architectural Frameworks for Security and Reliability of MPSoCs. *IEEE Transactions on Very Large Scale Integration (VLSI) Systems, 19*(9), 1641–1654.

Paterna, F., Acquaviva, A., Papariello, F., Desoli, G., & Benini, L. (2009). Variability-Tolerant Workload Allocation for MPSoC Energy Minimization under Real-Time Constraint. In *Proc. IEEE Workshop Embedded Systems for Real-Time Multimedia*, (pp. 134-142). IEEE.

Paterna, F., Acquaviva, A., Papariello, F., Desoli, G., Olivieri, M., & Benini, L. (2009). Adaptive Idleness Distribution for Non-Uniform Aging Tolerance in Multiprocessor Systems-on-Chip. In *Proc. IEEE Conf. Design, Automation and Test in Europe*, (pp. 906-909). IEEE.

Paterna, F., Acquaviva, A., Papariello, F., Caprara, A., Desoli, G., & Benini, L. (2012). Variability-Aware Task Allocation for Energy-Efficient Quality of Service Provisioning in Embedded Streaming Multimedia Applications. *IEEE Transactions on Computers*. doi:10.1109/TC.2011.127

Paunov, S., Hill, J., Schmidt, D., Baker, S., & Slaby, J. (2006). Domain-specific modelling languages for configuring and evaluating enterprise DRE system Quality of Service. In *Proceedings of the 13th Annual IEEE International Symposium and Workshop on Engineering of Computer Based Systems*. IEEE.

Peraldi-Frati, M.-A., Goknil, A., Deantoni, J., & Nordlander, J. (2012). A timing model for specifying multi clock automotive systems: The Timing Augmented Description Language V2. In *Proceedings of International Conference on Engineering of Complex Computer Systems*. IEEE.

Phoronix Test Suite. (2014). Retrieved from www.phoronix-test-suite.com

Pierce, K., Gamble, C., Ni, Y., & Broenink, J. F. (2012). Collaborative Modelling and Co-simulation with DESTECS: A Pilot Study, In *Proceedings IEEE 21st International Workshop on Enabling Technologies: Infrastructure for Collaborative Enterprises (WETICE)*, (pp. 280—285). IEEE.

Pnueli, A. (1977). The Temporal Logic of Programs. In *Proceedings of 18th Annual Symposium on Foundations of Computer Science, FOCS 1977* (pp. 46-57). FOCS.

Pohl, C., Paiz, C., & Porrmann, M. (2009). vMAG-IC—Automatic Code Generation for VHDL. *International Journal of Reconfigurable Computing*, 1–9. doi:10.1155/2009/205149

Poole, C., Terrell, J., & Busoli, S. (2007). *NUnit*. Retrieved January 2014, from http://www.nunit.org/

Pooley, R. J., & Abdullatif, A. A. L. (2010). CSAPA: Continuous Performance Assessment of Software Architecture. In *Proceedings of 17th IEEE International conference and Workshops on Engineering of Computer Based Systems*, (pp. 79-87). IEEE.

Poovey, J. A., Conte, T. M., Levy, M., & Gal-On, S. (2009, August). A benchmark characterization of the eembc benchmark suite. *Micro, IEEE*, *29*(5), 18–29. doi:10.1109/MM.2009.74

Popek, G. J., & Goldberg, R. P. (1974). Formal requirements for virtualizable third generation architectures. Communications of the ACM, 17(7), 412–421. doi:10.1145/361011.361073 doi:10.1145/361011.361073

Pradella, M., et al. (2013). Bounded satisfiability checking of metric temporal logic specifications. ACM Transactions on Software Engineering and Methodology, 22(3).

PragmaDev. (2014). PragmaDev Tracer. Retrieved from http://www.pragmadev.com/product/tracing.html

PRESTO ARTEMIS Project. (2014, March 15). Retrieved from http://www.presto-embedded.eu

Pullum, L. L. (2001). *Software fault tolerance techniques and implementation*. Artech House, Inc.

Qiu, W., Liu, X., & Li, H. (2011). A generalized method for forecasting based on fuzzy time series. *Expert Systems with Applications*, *38*(8), 10446–10453. doi:10.1016/j.eswa.2011.02.096

Quadri, I. R., et al. (2012). *D1.6: MADES Tool Set - Final Version*. Technical Report. Retrieved from http://www.mades-project.org/

Quadri, I. R., et al. (2012). MADES: A SysML/-MARTE high level methodology for real-time and embedded systems. In *Proceedings of International Conference on Embedded Real Time Software and Systems* (ERTS2 2012). ERTS2.

Queille, J. P., & Sifakis, J. (1982). Specification and verification of concurrent systems in CESAR. In *Proceedings of the 5th Colloquium on International Symposium on Programming* (pp. 337– 351). Academic Press.

Raccoon, L. B. S. (1995). The complexity gap. *SIGSOFT Software Engineering Notes*, *20*(3), 37–44. doi:10.1145/219308.219315

Rajkumar, R., Lee, I., Sha, L., & Stankovic, J. (2010). Cyber-physical systems: the next computing revolution. In *Proceedings of the 47th Design Automation Conference* (DAC '10). ACM.

Ramsin, R., & Paige, R. F. (2008). Process-centered review of object oriented software development methodologies. *ACM Computing Surveys*, *40*(3), 1–89. doi:10.1145/1322432.1322435

Raspberry Pi. (2013). In *Wikipedia*. Retrieved Dec 30, 2013, from http://en.wikipedia.org/wiki/Raspberry_Pi

Rational Software Corporation. (1998). *Rational Unified Process - Best Practices for Software Development Teams*. IBM.

Rebaud, B., Belleville, M., Beigne, E., Robert, M., Maurine, P., & Azemard, N. (2009). An Innovative Timing Slack Monitor for Variation Tolerant Circuits. In *Proc. IEEE Conf. IC Design and Technology*, (pp. 215-218). IEEE.

Reddi, V. J., Gupta, M. S., Holloway, G., Wei, G., Smith, M. D., & Brooks, D. (2009, February). Voltage Emergency Prediction Using Signatures to Reduce Operating Margins. In *Proceedings of 15th International Symposium on High Performance Computer Architecture* (pp. 18-29). IEEE.

Richardsi, M. A. (2005). *Fundamentals of Radar Signal Processing*. New York, NY: McGraw-Hill.

Rivas, V. M., Merelo, J. J., Rojas, I., Romero, G., Castillo, P. A., & Carpio, J. (2003). Evolving 2-dimensional fuzzy systems. *Fuzzy Sets and Systems*, *138*(1), 381–398. doi:10.1016/S0165-0114(02)00483-9

Rivas, V., Merelo, J., Castillo, P., Arenas, M., & Castellano, J. (2004). Evolving RBF neural networks for time-series forecasting with EvRBF. *Information Sciences*, *165*(3-4), 207–220. doi:10.1016/j.ins.2003.09.025

Rodrigue, J. P., Comtois, C., & Slack, B. (2013). *The Geography of Transport Systems* (3rd ed.). New York: Routledge.

Romani, E. (2007, July 02). *Structural PIC165X microcontroller*. Retrieved July 29, 2013, from The Hamburg VHDL Archive: http://tams-www.informatik.uni-hamburg.de/vhdl

Rosenstiel, W. (Ed.). (2004). Special Issue on IP and Design Reuse. Integration, the VLSI Journal, 37, 191-356.

RTCA. (2013). *Software Considerations in Airborne System and Equipment Certification (DO178C)*. Retrieved from http://www.rtca.org http://www.rtca.org/documents

Ruiz, J.-C., de Andrés, D., & Gil, P. (2009). Design and Deployment of a Generic ECC-based Fault Tolerance Mechanism for Embedded HW Cores. In *Proceedings of IEEE International Conference on Emerging Technologies and Factory Automation*, (pp. 3956-3964). Mallorca, Spain: IEEE.

Ruiz, J.-C., de Andrés, D., Blanc, S., & Gil, P. (2008). Generic Design and Automatic Deployment of NMR Strategies on HW Cores. *IEEE Pacific Rim International Symposium on Dependable Computing*, (pp. 265-272). Taipei, Taiwan: IEEE.

Ruiz, J.-C., de Andrés, D., Gil, P., & Blanc, S. (2008). Using Open Compilation to Simplify the Design of Fault-Tolerant VLSI Systems. In *Proceedings of Workshop on Compiler and Architectural Techniques for Application Reliability and Security*, (pp. B14-B19). Anchorage, AK: Academic Press.

Saastamoinen, J., & Kreku, J. (2011). Application workload model generation methodologies for system-level design exploration. In *Proceedings of Design and Architectures for Signal and Image Processing Conference* (DASIP 2011). DASIP.

SAE. (2009). *Architecture Analysis and Design Language* (AS-5506A). The Engineering Society for Advancing Mobility Land Sea Air and Space, Aerospace Information Report, Version 2.0.

Sami, M., Sciuto, D., Silvano, C., & Zaccaria, V. (2002, September). An instruction-level energy model for embedded VLIW architectures. *IEEE Transactions on Computer-Aided Design of Integrated Circuits and Systems*, *21*(9), 998–1010.

Samman, F. (2010). *Microarchitecture and Implementation of Networks-on-Chip with a Flexible Concept for Communication Media Sharing*. (Unpublished doctoral dissertation). Technische Universitaet Darmstadt.

Sander, I., & Jantsch, A. (2004). System modeling and transformational design refinement in ForSyDe. *IEEE Trans. on CAD of Integrated Circuits and Systems*, *23*(1), 17–32. doi:10.1109/TCAD.2003.819898

Sanwal, M.U., & Hasan, O. (2013). Formal Verification of Cyber-Physical Systems: Coping with Continuous Elements. *ICCSA*, (1), 358-371.

SavariNetworks. (2013). *SavariNetworks*. Retrieved Dec 30, 2013, from http://www.savarinetworks.com/index.html

Schirner, G., Erdogmus, D., Chowdhury, K., & Padir, T. (2013). The Future of Human-in-the-Loop Cyber-Physical Systems. *IEEE Computer*, *46*(1), 36–45. doi:10.1109/MC.2013.31

Schmidt, D.C. (2006). Guest Editor's Introduction: Model-Driven Engineering. *Computer*, *39*(2), 25–31. http://dx.doi.org/10.1109/MC.2006.58

Schneider, S., & Fraleigh, L. (2004). *The Ten Secrets of Embedded Debugging*. Retrieved January 2014, from http://www.eetimes.com/design/other/4025015/The-ten-secrets-of-embedded-debugging

Schoeberl, M. (2007). A Profile for Safety Critical Java. In *Proceedings of 10th IEEE International Symposium on Object and Component-Oriented Real-Time Distributed Computing, ISORC '07*, (pp. 94-101). IEEE.

SDL. (2013). Specification and Description Language. Retrieved from http://www.sdl-forum.org

Selic. (2003). The pragmatics of model-driven development. *IEEE Software, 20*(5), 19–25.

Sendall & Kozaczynski. (2003). Model transformation: The heart and soul of model-driven software development. *IEEE Software*, *20*(5), 42–45.

Shi, B., Srivastava, A., & Bar-Cohen, A. (2012). Hybrid 3D-IC Cooling System Using Micro-Fluidic Cooling and Thermal TSVs. In *Proceeding of the Computer Society Annual Symposium on VLSI*, (pp. 33-38). Amherst, MA: IEEE.

Shigeru, C. (1995). A Metaobject Protocol for C++. In *Proceedings of Tenth annual conference on Object-oriented programming systems, languages, and applications* (pp. 285-299). Austin, TX: ACM.

Shreejith, S., Fahmy, S. A., & Lukasiewycz, M. (2013). Reconfigurable Computing in Next-Generation Automotive Networks. IEEE Embedded Systems Letters, 5(1).

SISO. (2008). *Military Scenario Definition Language (MSDL)*. SISO-STD-007-2008.

Skszek, S. L. (2001). *State-of-the-Art Report on Nontraditional Traffic Counting Methods*. Report FHWA-AZ-01-503. Phoenix, AZ: Arizona Department of Transportation.

Smith, C. U. (2007). Introduction to software performance engineering: origins and outstanding problems. In *Proceedings of the 7th International Conference on Formal Methods for Performance Evaluation*, (pp. 395-428). Bertinoro, Italy: Springer.

Smith, C. U., & Williams, L. G. (2002). *Performance solutions: a practical guide to creating responsive, scalable software*. Reading, MA: Addison-Wesley.

Society of Automotive Engineers. (2014). Architecture and Analysis Description Language. AADL recommendation. Retrieved from http://standards.sae.org/as5506b/

Sonntag, C., Schiffelers, R. R. H., van Beek, D. A., Rooda, J. E., & Engell, S. (2009). Modeling and simulation using the compositional interchange format for hybrid systems. In *Proceedings of MATHMOD 2009 - 6th Vienna International Conference on Mathematical Modelling*, (pp. 640–650). MATHMOD.

Sterman, J. D. (2000). *Business Dynamics: Systems Thinking and Modeling for a Complex World*. Irwin Professional Pub.

Stolz, V. (2010). Temporal Assertions with Parametrized Propositions. *Journal of Logic and Computation, 20*(3), 743–757. doi:10.1093/logcom/exn078

Štuikys, V., Damaševičius, R., Ziberkas, G., & Majauskas, G. (2002). Soft IP Design Framework Using Metaprogramming Techniques. In Proceedings of Design and Analysis of Distributed Embedded Systems (pp. 257-266). Springer.

Suryadevara, J., Seceleanu, C., Mallet, F., & Pettersson, P. (2013). Verifying. MARTE/CCSL Mode Behaviors Using UPPAAL. In *Proceedings of Software Engineering and Formal Methods* (SEFM'13), (LNCS) (vol. 8137, pp. 1-15). Berlin: Springer.

Sweeney, P. F., Hauswirth, M., Cahoon, P., Cheng, A., Diwan, A., Grove, D., & Hind, M. (2004). Using hardware performance monitors to understand the behavior of java applications. In *Proceedings of the 3rd USENIX Virtual Machine Research and Technology Symposium* (pp. 57-72). ACM.

Sylvester, D., Blaauw, D., & Karl, E. (2006). Elastic: An Adaptive Self-Healing Architecture for Unpredictable Silicon. *IEEE Design & Test of Computers, 23*, 484–490. doi:10.1109/MDT.2006.145

Synopsys Inc. (2013). *Accelerate Design Innovation with Design Compiler*. Retrieved 07 29, 2013, from http://www.synopsys.com/Tools/Implementation/RTLSynthesis/Pages/default.aspx

Systematic Paris Competitiveness Cluster. (2014). Retrieved from http://www.systematic-paris-region.org/en/projets/exoticus

Szabo, C., & Chen, Y. (2013). A Model-driven Change Traceability Method in System Modeling Execution. In *Proceedings of the 22nd Australasian Software Engineering Conference*. Academic Press.

Sztipanovits, J., Koutsoukos, X., Karsai, G., Kottenstette, N., Antsaklis, P., & Gupta, V., … Wang S. (2012). Toward a Science of Cyber–Physical System Integration. *Proceedings of the IEEE, 100*(1), 29-44.

Szyperski, C. (2003). *Component Software - Beyond Object-Oriented Programming* (2nd ed.). Addison-Wesley / ACM Press.

Taïani, F., Fabre, J.-C., & Killijan, M.-O. (2005). A multi-level meta-object protocol for fault-tolerance in complex architectures. In *Proceedings of IEEE/IFIP International Conference on Dependable Systems and Networks*, (pp. 207-279). Yokohama, Japan: IEEE.

Takanen, A., DeMott, J., & Miller, C. (2008). *Fuzzing for software security testing and quality assurance. Norwood, MA:* Artech House, Inc.

Tanenbaum, A. S. (2002). *Computer Networks*. Prentice Hall.

Teodorescu, R., & Torrellas, J. (2008). Variation-Aware Application Scheduling and Power Management for Chip Multiprocessors. *ACM SIGARCH Computer Architecture News, 36*(3), 363–374. doi:10.1145/1394608.1382152

Texas Instruments. (2002). *Analyzing Target System Energy Consumption in Code Composer Studio IDE*. Texas Instruments, Application Report

The jQuery Foundation. (2014). *The jQuery API Documentation - Deferred*. Retrieved January 2014, from http://api.jquery.com/jQuery.Deferred/

The Linux Kernel Archives. (2014). Retrieved from www.kernel.org

The Object Management Group. (2011, June). *UML Profile for MARTE: Modeling and Analysis of Real-Time Embedded Systems*. Retrieved from http://www.omg.org/spec/MARTE/1.1/PDF/

TIMMO. (2007). *ITEA2 Project*. Retrieved from http://www.timmo-2-use.org/timmo/index.htm

TIMMO-2-USE project, Deliverable D11. (2012). *TADL2 language semantics and metamodel V2*. Retrieved from https://itea3.org/project/workpackage/document/download/850/09033-TIMMO-2-USE-WP-2-D11Languagesyntax,semantics,metamodelV2.pdf

TIMMO2USE. (2012). *Timing Model – Tools, algorithms, languages, methodology, USE cases, D13*. Retrieved from http://www.timmo-2-use.org/deliverables/TIMMO-2-USE_D13.pdf

Tino, A., & Khan, G. (2011). Multi-Objective Tabu Search Based Topology Generation Technique For Application-Specific Network-on-Chip Architectures. In *Proceeding of the Design, Automation & Test in Europe Conference & Exhibition (DATE)*, (pp. 1-6). Grenoble, France: IEEE.

Tite, T., Vig, A., Olteanu, N., & Cuna, C. (2011). *moviTest: A Test Environment dedicated to multi-core embedded architectures*. Paper presented at the 2011 International Symposium on System on Chip (SoC). New York, NY.

Titzer, B. L., & Palsberg, J. (2005). *Nonintrusive Precision Instrumentation of Microcontroller Software*. Paper presented at the 2005 ACM SIGPLAN/SIGBED conference on Languages, compilers, and tools for embedded systems. Chicago, IL.

Tiwari, A., & Torrellas, J. (2008). Facelift: Hiding and Slowing Down Aging in Multicores. In *Proceedings of the IEEE/ACM International Symposium on Microarchitectures*, (pp. 129-140). IEEE/ACM.

Tiwari, V., Malik, S., & Wolfe, A. (1994, December). Power analysis of embedded software: a first step towards software power minimization. *IEEE Transactions on Very Large Scale Integration (VLSI) Systems, 2*(4), 437–445.

Todorov, V., Mueller-Gritschneder, D., Reinig, H., & Schlichtmann, U. (2013). A Spectral Clustering Approach to Application-Specific Network-on-Chip Synthesis. In *Proceeding of the Design, Automation & Test in Europe Conference & Exhibition (DATE)*, (pp. 1783-1788). Grenoble, France: IEEE.

Tong, H. (1978). On a threshold model. In C. Chen (Ed.), *Pattern Recognition and Signal Processing: NATO ASI Series E: Applied Sc.(29)* (pp. 575–586). Netherlands: Sijthoff & Noordhoff. doi:10.1007/978-94-009-9941-1_24

TOPCASED. (2012). *The Open Source Toolkit for Critical Systems*. Retrieved from http://www.topcased.org/

TraffaxInc . (2013). *TraffaxInc*. Retrieved Dec 30, 2013, from http://www.traffaxinc.com/

TrafficCast. (2013). *TrafficCast*. Retrieved Dec 30, 2013, from http://trafficcast.com/products/

Trafficnow (2013). *Trafficnow*. Retrieved Dec 30, 2013, from http://www.trafficnow.eu/es

Trapp, M., Schneider, D., & Liggesmeyer, P. (2013). A Safety Roadmap to Cyber-Physical Systems. In J. Münch & K. Schmid (Eds.), Perspectives on the Future of Software Engineering, (pp. 81-94). Berlin: Springer.

Trombetti, G., Gokhale, A., & Schmidt, D. C. (2005). A Model-driven Development Environment for Composing and Validating Distributed Real-time and Embedded Systems: A Case Study. In S. Beydeda & V. Gruhn (Eds.), Model-driven Software Development. Springer.

Trubiani, C., Meedeniya, I., Cortellessa, V., Aleti, A., & Grunske, L. (2013). Model-based Performance Analysis of Software Architectures under Uncertainty. In *Proceedings of the International Conference on the Quality of Software Architectures (QoSA)*, (pp. 69-78). QoSA.

Tudoret, S., Nadjm-Tehrani, S., Benveniste, A., & Strömberg, J.-E. (2000). Co-simulation of hybrid systems: Signal-simulink. In M. Joseph (Ed.), FTRTRT 2000 (LNCS) (pp. 134–151). Berlin: Springer-Verlag.

UBM Tech. (2013). *Embedded Market Study*. Retrieved August 2013, from http://e.ubmelectronics.com/2013EmbeddedStudy/index.html

University of Oregon. (2014, March 15). Retrieved from http://www.cs.uoregon.edu/Research/pdt/home.php

Ural, H., & Xu, Z. (2007). An EFSM-Based Passive Fault Detection Approach. Tallinn, Estonia: Springer-Verlag.

Vahidi, A., & Eskandarian, A. (2003, September). Research advances in intelligent collision avoidance and adaptive cruise control. *IEEE Transactions on Intelligent Transportation Systems*, (3), 143–153. doi:10.1109/TITS.2003.821292

Valderas, M. G., Garcia, M. P., Cardenal, R. F., Lopez Ongil, C., & Entrena, L. (2007, June). Advanced simulation and emulation techniques for fault injection. In *Proceedings of Industrial Electronics,* (pp. 3339-3344). IEEE.

Valgrind Developers. (2013). *Valgrind*. Retrieved January 2014, from http://valgrind.org/

Valgrind User Manual. (2013). Cachegrind. Retrieved from http://valgrind.org/docs/manual/cg-manual.html

van Amerongen, J. (2010). *Dynamical Systems for Creative Technology*. Enschede, The Netherlands: Controllab Products.

van Beek, D. A., Hofkamp, A. T., Reniers, M. A., Rooda, J. E., & Schiffelers, R. R. H. (2007). Co-simulation of chi and Simulink models. In *Proceedings of the 6th EUROSIM Congress on Modelling and Simulation*. EUROSIM.

Verghese, N., Rouse, R., & Hurat, P. (2008). Predictive Models and CAD Methodology for Pattern Dependent Variability. In *Proceedings of the IEEE Asia and South Pacific Design Automation Conference*, (pp. 213-218). IEEE.

Verhoef, M., Bos, B., van Eijk, P., Remijnse, J., Visser, E., De Paepe, M., … Van Lembergen, R. (2012). Industrial Case Studies – Final Report. *DESTECS Project Deliverable D4.3*. Retrieved from http://www.destecs.org/

Verhoef, M., Larsen, P. G., & Hooman, J. (2006). Modeling and Validating Distributed Embedded Real-Time Systems with VDM++. In *Proc. 14th Intl. Symposium on Formal Methods* (LNCS) (vol. 4085). Berlin: Springer-Verlag.

Vinoski, S. (2008). Serendipitous reuse. *IEEE Internet Computing*, *12*(1), 84–87. doi:10.1109/MIC.2008.20

Vörg, A. (2003). *ToolIP - Tools and Methods for IP*. Retrieved July 29, 2013, from http://toolip.fzi.de

Walker, M., & Papadopoulos, Y. (2009). Qualitative temporal analysis: Towards a full implementation of the Fault Tree Handbook. *Control Engineering Practice*, *17*(10), 1115–1125. doi:10.1016/j.conengprac.2008.10.003

Walker, M., Reiser, M.-O., Tucci Piergiovanni, S., Papadopoulos, Y., Lönn, H., & Mraidha, C. et al. (2013). Automatic optimisation of system architectures using EAST-ADL. *Journal of Systems and Software*, *86*(10), 2467–2487. doi:10.1016/j.jss.2013.04.001

Wan, K., & Alagar, V. (2011). Dependable Context-Sensitive Services in Cyber Physical Systems. In *Proceedings of Trust, Security and Privacy in Computing and Communications* (TrustCom). IEEE.

Wan, K., Hughes, D., Man, K. L., & Krilavičius, T. (2010). Composition challenges and approaches for cyber physical systems. In *Proceedings of Networked Embedded Systems for Enterprise Applications* (NESEA). IEEE.

Wang, C. (2011). A comparison study between fuzzy time series model and arima model for forecasting Taiwan export. *Expert Systems with Applications*, *38*(8), 9296–9304. doi:10.1016/j.eswa.2011.01.015

Weiglhofer, E. J. M., Aichernig, B. K., & Wotawa, F. (2010). When BDDs Fail: Conformance Testing with Symbolic Execution and SMT Solving. In *Proceedings of 3rd International conference on Software Testing, Verification and Validation* (pp. 479-488). Academic Press.

Weilkiens, T. (2011). *Systems engineering with SysML/UML: modeling, analysis, design*. Burlington, MA: Morgan Kaufmann.

Wendt, M., Grumer, C., Steger, C., Weiss, R., Neffe, U., & Muehlberger, A. (2008, November). System Level Power Profile Analysis and Optimization for Smart Cards and Mobile Devices. In *Proceedings of ACM Symposium on Applied Computing*, November (pp. 118–121). ACM.

Whitehouse, K., Tolle, G., Taneja, J., Sharp, C., Sukun, K., Jeong, J., et al. (2006). *Marionette: Using RPC for interactive development and debugging of wireless embedded networks*. Paper presented at the Fifth International Conference on Information Processing in Sensor Networks, IPSN 2006. New York, NY.

Williams, L. G., Lane, R., & Smith, C. U. (2002). PASA SM: A Method for the Performance Assessment of Software Architectures. *Architecture (Washington, D.C.)*, 179–189.

Wilson, B. (2013). *xUnit.net - Unit testing framework for C# and .NET*. Retrieved January 2014, from http://xunit.codeplex.com/

Wilson, P. R., Johnstone, M., Neely, M., & Boles, D. (1995). Dynamic storage allocation: A survey and critical review. In H. G. Baler (Ed.), *Memory Management* (Vol. 986, pp. 1–116). Springer. doi:10.1007/3-540-60368-9_19

Winters, P. (1960). Forecasting sales by exponentially weighted moving averages. *Management Science*, 6(3), 324–342. doi:10.1287/mnsc.6.3.324

Wolff, S., Pierce, K. G., & Derler, P. (2013). *Multi-domain modelling in DESTECS and Ptolemy – a Tool Comparison* (Technical Report ECE-TR-15). Dept. of Engineering, Aarhus University.

Woo, S. C., Ohara, M., Torrie, E., Singh, J. P., & Gupta, A. (1995). The SPLASH-2 Programs: Characterizing and Methodological Considerations. In *Proceeding of the International Symposium on Computer Architecture*, (pp. 24-36). Santa Margherita Ligure, Italy: IEEE.

Woodcock, J., Larsen, P. G., Bicarregui, J., & Fitzgerald, J. (2009). Formal Methods: Practice and Experience. *ACM Computing Surveys*, 41(4), 1–36. doi:10.1145/1592434.1592436

Woodside, M. (2007). From Annotated Software Designs (UML SPT/MARTE) to Model Formalisms. In *Proceedings of the 7th International School on Formal Methods (SFM'07) for the Design of Computer, Communication and Software Systems*. Academic Press.

Woodside, M., Franks, G., & Petriu, D. C. (2007). The Future of Software Performance Engineering. In *Proceedings of Future of Software Engineering FOSE*, (pp. 171 – 187). FOSE.

Woodside, M., Petriu, D. C., Petriu, D. B., Shen, H., Israr, T., & Merseguer, J. (2005). Performance by unified model analysis (PUMA). In *Proceedings of the 5th International Workshop on Software and Performance – WOSP*. ACM Press.

Wu, X., McMullen, D., & Woodside, M. (2003). Component-based performance prediction. In *Proceedings of the 6th ICSE Workshop on Component-Based Software Engineering*. ICSE.

Xie, T., Taneja, K., Kale, S., & Marinov, D. (2007). *Towards a Framework for Differential Unit Testing of Object-Oriented Programs*. Paper presented at the Second International Workshop on Automation of Software Test. New York, NY.

Xilinx Corporation. (2014, January). *Zynq-7000 All Programmable SoC*. Retrieved from http://www.xilinx.com/products/silicon-devices/soc/zynq-7000/

Xilinx Inc. (2010). *XTMR Tool*. Retrieved July 29, 2013, from http://www.xilinx.com/ise/optional_prod/tmrtool.htm

Xilinx. (2014). *Virtex Series FPGAs*. Retrieved from http://www.xilinx.com/products/silicon-devices/fpga

Xu, T., Liljeberg, P., & Tenhunen, H. (2011). Optimal Number and Placement of Through Silicon Vias in 3D Network-on-Chip. In *Proceeding of the Design and Diagnose of Electronic Circuits and Systems*, (pp. 105-110). Cottbus, Germany: IEEE.

Yagi, H., Rosenstiel, W., Engblom, J., Andrews, J., Vissers, K., & Serughetti, M. (2009). *The Wild West: Conquest of complex hardware-dependent software design*. Paper presented at the 46th ACM/IEEE Design Automation Conference, DAC '09. New York, NY.

Yang, J., Soffa, M. L., Selavo, L., & Whitehouse, K. (2007). *Clairvoyant: A Comprehensive Source-Level Debugger for Wireless Sensor Networks*. Paper presented at the 5th international conference on Embedded networked sensor systems. Sydney, Australia.

Yang, X. S. (2010). *Nature-Inspired Metaheuristic Algorithms* (2nd ed.). Frome, UK: Luniver Press.

Ying, H., Hollstein, T., & Hofmann, K. (2013). GSNoC - The Comprehensive Design Platform for 3-Dimensional Networks-on-Chip based Many Core Embedded Systems. In *Proceeding of the International Conference on High Performance Computing and Simulation (HPCS)*, (pp. 217-223). Helsinki, Finland: IEEE.

Ying, H., Jaiswal, A., Abd El Ghany, M., Hollstein, T., & Hofmann, K. (2012). A Simulation Framework for 3-Dimension Networks-on-Chip with Different Vertical Channel Density Configurations. In *Proceeding of the conference on Design and Diagnose of Electronic Circuits and Systems*, (pp. 83-88). Tallinn, Estonia: IEEE.

Ying, H., Hollstein, T., & Hofmann, K. (2013). Deadlock-free generic routing algorithms for 3-dimensional Networks-on-Chip with reduced vertical link density topologies. *Journal of Systems Architecture*, 7(59), 528–542. doi:10.1016/j.sysarc.2013.03.005

Zhang, L., Bai, L., Dick, R., Shang, L., & Joseph, R. (2009). Process Variation Characterization of Chip-Level Multiprocessors. In *Proceedings of the ACM Conference of Design Automation*, (pp. 694-697). ACM.

Zhang, Y., Dembla, A., & Bakir, M. S. (2013). *Silicon Micropin-Fin Heat Sink With Integrated TSVs for 3-D ICs: Tradeoff Analysis and Experimental Testing. IEEE Trans. on Components, Packaging and Manufacturing Technology.*

Zheng, H., Fan, L., & Yue, S. (2008, December). FITVS: A FPGA-based emulation tool for high-efficiency hardness evaluation. In *Proceedings of Parallel and Distributed Processing with Applications*, (pp. 525-531). IEEE.

Zhong, W., Chen, S., Ma, F., Yoshimura, T., & Goto, S. (2011). Floorplanning Driven Network-on-Chip Synthesis for 3-D SoCs. In *Proceedings of International Symposium on Circuits and Systems (ISCAS)*, (pp. 1203-1206). Rio de Janeiro, Brazil: IEEE.

Zhou, Y., Sheng, W., Liu, X., He, W., & Mao, Z. (2011). Efficient temporal task partition for coarse-grain reconfigurable systems based on Simulated Annealing Genetic Algorithm. In *Proceeding of the 9th International Conference on ASIC (ASICON)*, (pp. 941-944). Xiamen, China: IEEE.

Zot. (2012). *The Zot bounded model/satisfiability checker.* Retrieved from http://zot.googlecode.com

About the Contributors

Alessandra Bagnato is a research scientist and project manager within the Softeam R&D Department. She holds a PhD degree in Computer Science from TELECOM SudParis and Université Evry Val d'Essonne, France and a MSc in Computer Science from the University of Genoa, Italy. She has been at TXT Corporate Research Division headquartered in Milan from 1999 till September 2012 as Project Coordinator, Project Manager and/or Technical Leader in several European research projects in the 5th, 6th and 7th Framework Programme related to embedded systems design, software/service development and security. Among them she was coordinator of project MADES, Model-based methods and tools for Avionics and surveillance embeddeD SystEmS (http://www.mades-project.org/) and of project MOMOCS: Model driven Modernisation of Complex Systems (http://www.momocs.org). In Softeam, she lead the Exploitation efforts within the FITTEST (Future Internet Testing) project and she is currently involved in the FP7 project OSSMETER (Automated Measurement and Analysis of Open Source Software) funded by the European Commission for the improvement of the state-of-the-art in the field of automated analysis and measurement of open-source software and MONDO (Scalable Modeling and Model Management on the Cloud). She is member of multiple international committees and she is the Softeam representative in the OMG SysML 1.5 Revision Task Force.

Leandro Soares Indrusiak was born in 1974 in Santa Maria, RS, Brazil. He graduated in Electrical Engineering from the Federal University of Santa Maria (UFSM) in 1995 and obtained a MSc in Computer Science from the Federal University of Rio Grande do Sul (UFRGS), Porto Alegre, in 1998. He held a tenured assistant professorship at the Informatics department of the Catholic University of Rio Grande do Sul (PUCRS) in Uruguaiana from 1998 to 2000. His PhD research started in 2000 and extended his MSc work on design automation environments for microelectronic circuits. From 2001 to 2008, he worked as a researcher at the Technische Universität Darmstadt, Darmstadt, Germany, where he finished his PhD and then lead a research group on System-on-Chip design. His binational doctoral degree was jointly awarded by UFRGS and TU Darmstadt in 2003. Since 2008, he is a permanent faculty member of the University of York's Computer Science department (Lecturer 2008, Senior Lecturer 2013), and a member of the Real-Time Systems (RTS) research group. His current research interests include on-chip multiprocessor systems, distributed embedded systems, mapping and scheduling of applications over multiprocessor and distributed platforms, adaptive and reconfigurable computing. He currently supervises nine PhD students and two post-doc research assistants, and is always keen to discuss about open problems with potential PhD candidates. He is the principal investigator and technical leader of EPSRC-funded LowPowNoC project and EU-funded DreamCloud project, and a co-investigator in a number of other funded projects. He also coordinates two MSc programmes (MSc in Computing and MSc in Information Technology), serves as the department's Internationalisation Advisor, and is a Senior Member of the IEEE.

Imran Rafiq Quadri is a Senior R&D consultant for EU projects at Softeam, France. He has more than 9 years of working experience including more than five years of consulting and project management experience in EU FP7/ARTEMIS and French national R&D projects related to Embedded Systems and Model-Driven Engineering. He holds a PhD degree in real-time and embedded systems from University Lille 1, Lille-France. In parallel, he was a Research/Teaching Associate at University Lille 1 teaching at undergraduate and Master's levels and carried out research activities in a French national ANR FAMOUS project. Additionally, he was a R&D Consultant at Axilica Limited, from 2009 to 2010, where he worked related to Axilica's Falcon-ML modeling environment and also helped to re-factor Selex Galileo's case studies regarding avionics systems. From 2010, he is working at Softeam in several EU projects such as MADES, ENOSYS and PRESTO. His expertise and interests lie in real-time and embedded systems; systems engineering; model-driven technologies such as UML and related profiles: SysML, MARTE; execution platforms such as dynamically reconfigurable FPGA based System-on-Chips or SoCs.

Matteo Rossi is an assistant professor at Politecnico di Milano. His research interests are mainly in formal methods for safety-critical and real-time systems, with particular reference to architectures for real-time distributed systems. He has previously participated in several national and international projects, including MADES and Green Move. He was the co-chair of the Student Contest on Software Engineering (SCORE) and part of the 33rd International Conference in Software Engineering.

* * *

Andrea Acquaviva is an Assistant Professor in the Department of Control and Computer Engineering of Politecnico di Torino. He received his MSc degree (summa cum laude) at the University of Ferrara, Italy and PhD degree in electrical engineering from Bologna University, Italy. He is currently coordinator of the European FP7 Project TOUCHMORE regarding the design of toolchain for next generation heterogeneous multicore platforms. He is also involved in various FP7 and ARTEMIS European funded projects concerning the design of software for next generation multicore platforms. His research interests focus on multicore and multiprocessor architectures, computer modeling and simulation of biological systems, and wireless sensor networks. In these fields, he is co-author of more than 70 publications and 8 book chapters. He was a member of the Executive Committee of the IEEE DATE conference from 2008 to 2010, and he is a member of the technical program committee of several IEEE/ACM conferences including DATE, SoC, VLSI-SOC, and he was Program Chair of VLSI-SoC 2010.

María I. García Arenas received her PhD in Computer Science and lectures at the University of Granada. She's mainly interested in parallel and distributed computation and has been leader of several local research and innovation projects. During the last years she has had several papers published in important conferences like PPSN, GECCO, CEC, and two indexed papers have been accepted for publishing in two *Journal Citation Reports* journals. She has demonstrated experience with other subjects like Neural Networks or Evolutionary Computation.

Neil Audsley received a BSc (1984) and PhD (1993) from the Department of Computer Science at the University of York, UK. In 2013, he received a Personal Chair from the University of York, where he leads a substantial team researching Real-Time Embedded Systems. Specific areas of research include high performance real-time systems (including aspects of big data); real-time operating systems and their acceleration on FPGAs; real-time architectures, specifically memory hierarchies, Network-on-Chip and heterogeneous systems; scheduling, timing analysis and worst-case execution time; model-driven development. Professor Audsley's research has been funded by a number of national (EPSRC) and european (EU) grants, including TEMPO, eMuCo, ToucHMore, JEOPARD, JUNIPER, T-CREST and DreamCloud. He has published widely having upwards of 150 publications in peer reviewed journals, conferences, and books.

Laura Baracchi is a Senior Analyst at Intecs where she works in the Methodologies and R&D division. She is and has been involved in several EU-funded and ESA-funded projects in the area of Systems and SW Engineering, Requirements Engineering, Model-Driven Development, Model-Based System Verification and Validation, Component-Oriented Design and Development Methodologies, and Safety and Security. She has also many years of experience in the development of Web-based services and in the Lawful Inspection Department for telecommunications. She has been a guest lecturer in support courses on Computer Systems Security within the Computer Science Course at Pisa University. She received her degree in Computer Science from Pisa University in Italy.

Luciano Baresi is an associate professor at Politecnico di Milano, where he got both his Laureat Degree and PhD in Computer Science. Luciano was also junior researcher at the University of Oregon at Eugene (USA) and University of Paderborn (Germany). Luciano was program chair of the ETAPS Conference on Fundamental Approaches on Software Engineering (2006), the International Conference on Web Engineering (2007), the International Conference on Service-Oriented Computing (2009), the Symposium on Software Engineering for Adaptive and Self-Managing Systems 2013) the Joint European Software Engineering Conference, and the ACM SIGSOFT Symposium on the Foundations of Software Engineering (2013). Luciano co-authored some 130 papers, and his work has been cited some 4600 times (according to Google Scholar). Luciano has lead the participation of Politecnico in different European and national projects. His research interests are in software engineering, and currently he is particularly interested in formal modeling notations, dynamic software systems, and software architectures. More detailed information is available at http://home.deib.polimi.it/bares.

Paul Beckett is an Associate Professor in the School of Electrical and Computer Engineering, Royal Melbourne Institute of Technology (RMIT University) in Melbourne, Australia, where he teaches courses in Embedded Systems and microelectronic circuit design and synthesis. He received his B. Eng., M. Eng. and PhD degrees from RMIT University in 1975, 1984, and 2007, respectively. His current research interests include the design and synthesis of low-power computer architecture and the mixed–signal modeling of nano-scale circuits and systems.

Holger Bock received his Masters degree in electrical engineering at the Graz University of Technology in 1994. From 1991 to 1998, he has been working on concepts, software and hardware development, especially on VLSI-Design for cryptographic co-processors for smart cards (DES, ECC) at the Institute for Applied Information Processing and Communications Technologies (IAIK). In December 1998, he joined the team at Infineon's development center in Graz as a core competence for security. Since beginning of 2001, he had been a member of the technology and innovations methodology team at Infineon's business group Chipcard and Security ICs, focusing on secure, especially DPA resistant, design methodologies for cryptographic hardware.

Michel Bourdellès acts as the interface between collaborative projects activities and radio platform products design department at Thales Communications and Security. Michel Bourdellès is involved in projects related to the improvement of the RTES design process as in the ARTEMIS Presto project and protocol resource optimization as in the FP7 Pharaon project. Michel Bourdellès received a PhD degree in Computer Science from the "Ecole des Mines de Paris" in 1999 and joined THALES in 2000.

Etienne Brosse, after a Master degree in Applied Mathematics, joined the Gaspard Monge research team of the IFTS establishment for several years. During this period, he participated in research in CAD, PLM and KBE fields. Since 2007, Mr. Etienne Brosse is an R&D engineer from Softeam where he takes part of several French or EU research projects (MOMOCS, SHAPE, MADES, ENOSYS, Galaxy FIT-TEST) and for the OMG (Model Interchange Working Group and UML Testing Profile).

Salvatore Campagna received an MS from Politecnico di Torino, Italy, where he developed research activities in field of mission critical embedded systems. He recently joined Magneti Marelli, Italy, where he holds a position as a software engineer in infotainment projects.

Pedro A. Castillo-Valdivieso received a BSc degree in Computer Science and a PhD degree, both from the University of Granada, Spain, in 1997 and 2000. He was a Visiting Researcher at Napier University, Edinburg, U.K., in July 1998 and at the Santa Fe Institute, Santa Fe, NM, in September 2000. He has been a leader of several local research projects, and directed four PhDs. His main interests include the optimization of artificial neural networks using evolutionary algorithms. He was a Teaching Assistant in the Computer Science Department of the University of Jaén, Spain. He is currently an Associate Professor at the Computer Architecture and Technology Department, University of Granada.

Ana Rosa Cavalli has obtained her Doctorat d'Etat es Mathematics Science. From 1985 to 1990, she was a researcher in the department of Languages and Switch Systems, at CNET (Centre National d'Etudes des Telecommunications), where she worked on software engineering and formal methods. She has been a Full Professor at TELECOM SudParis since 1990. She is the director of the Software for Networks department. Her research interests are on formal modeling, testing methodologies for conformance and interoperability testing, active testing and monitoring techniques, validation of security properties and their application to services and protocols. She has published more than 200 papers in journals and international conferences.

De-Jiu Chen received his PhD degree in Mechanical Engineering with a research on embedded computer control systems from KTH in 2004. His research interests are on systems and software architecture, model-based engineering, dependability and self-adaptive embedded systems. Since 2006, he has been actively involved in the development of EAST-ADL with the focus on the integration of modeling and analysis technologies for functional safety and behavior. From 2007 to 2009, Dr. DeJiu Chen also worked for Enea Data AB, Sweden, as a senior technical instructor. He is currently an associate professor at KTH.

Vanea Chiprianov is an Assistant Professor at the Université de Pau et des Pays de l'Adour, Mont de Marsan, France. He is a member of the Association for Computing Machinery and of the Institute of Electrical and Electronics Engineers. His research interests cover Software Engineering for complex systems, focusing on Model Driven Engineering, Software and System Architecture, Performance and Security modeling and analysis, Telecommunications systems, large scale Distributed Real-time Embedded systems, and Systems-of-systems.

Alessandro Cimatti received a MS degree in Electronic Engineering from the University of Genova in 1988. He joined the Institute for Scientific and Technological Research in Trento, Italy, in 1990. Within the same institute, he is currently the head of the Embedded Systems research unit. His main research interests concern formal verification, decision procedures, design and verification methodologies, safety analysis, diagnosis and diagnosability techniques for hardware/software systems. He published more than hundred papers in the Formal Methods and Artificial Intelligence fields. Cimatti has been a member of the Program Committee of the major conferences in computer-aided verification, and has been the leader of several industrial research and technology transfer projects in the design and verification of safety critical systems.

Matteo Carlo Crippa is a senior system engineer with 10 years of experience on avionic systems, his specific domain is the flight management system for civil and military aircrafts. Matteo Carlo Crippa got a masters degree in Computer Science at Politecnico di Milano, with a specialization in optoelectronic. He began his experience on the embedded systems with the home automation and quickly moved to safety-critical systems. Now he is team leader for large development teams with the focus onto the definition of software lifecycle for DO-178B (DO-178C) certification; he is interested in development process definition, system architecture, design pattern and more generally in research on safety-critical systems.

Julien Deantoni is currently an associate professor in computer sciences at the University Nice Sophia-Antipolis. After studies in electronics and micro informatics, he obtained a PhD focused on the modeling and analysis of control systems, and had a post doc position at INRIA. He is currently a member of the INRIA-I3S AOSTE team. His research focuses on the joint use of Model Driven Engineering and Formal Methods.

David de Andrés received an MS degree in computer science and a PhD degree in computer architecture and technology from the Universitat Politècnica de Valencia (UPV), Spain in 1998 and 2007, respectively. In 1998, he joined the Fault Tolerant Systems Research Group (GSTF) within the Institute for the Applications of Advanced Information and Communication Technologies (ITACA), UPV. His main research interests include the fields of run-time reconfigurable hardware systems, design of fault tolerance mechanisms for embedded systems, fault- and attack-injection for robustness assessment and dependability/security evaluation, and dependability benchmarking. He has authored over 60 research papers on these topics. Currently, he is an Associate Professor with the Computer Engineering Department (DISCA), UPV.

Robert de Simone is a Senior Researcher at Inria, the French National research Institute in Computer Science and Applied Mathematics. He holds a PhD from the University of Paris 7, and his Habilitation from the university of Nice Sophia-Antipolis (UNS). He is a team-leader of the Aoste project-team, joint between Inria and UNS, dedicated to the modeling and analysis of real-time embedded systems. His interest goes with Formal Methods in Concurrency Theory, Synchronous languages, model-checking, and Model-Driven Engineering for co-modeling and codesign of hardware/software, with mapping adequatiob. He is the author of over 60 articles, several book chapters, and Chair of several conferences.

Norbert Druml received his Masters degree in Telematics from Graz University of Technology in 2011, focusing on embedded systems, and software development. Since 2011, he is carrying out research for his doctoral thesis in the field of Electrical Engineering at the Institute for Technical Informatics at Graz University of Technology in collaboration with Infineon Technologies Austria AG and Enso Detego GmbH. His research interests include low-power hardware/software codesign and emulation-based design analysis techniques.

Jaime Espinosa received his Telecommunications M. Eng. from Universitat Politècnica de València (UPV) in Spain, 2006. After working for nearly 3 years in the medical electronics industry, he returned to the academic world and completed an Electronics Systems M. Eng. in 2010 also in UPV before starting his Ph D in Computer Science. His current research interests include fault tolerance techniques for reconfigurable hardware, fault injection and benchmarking, and the applications of dynamic partial reconfiguration of hardware towards improving the dependability of systems. He has received a grant from the Spanish Ministry of Economy and Competitivity to that purpose. He is currently a member of ITACA-UPV research institute.

Katrina Falkner is an Associate Professor at the University of Adelaide, Adelaide, Australia. Associate Professor Falkner leads both the Defence Information Group and the Computer Science Education Research Group in the School of Computer Science, University of Adelaide. Her research interests include distributed systems, software architecture, model driven engineering in addition to computer science education.

Nick Falkner received his PhD in integrating legacy and modern distributed systems using ontologies from the University of Adelaide. Prior to this, he had worked in network engineering, including routing switching and Voice over IP, as well as working on software and management for embedded systems. He is currently an Associate Dean and Senior Lecturer in the School of Computer Science at the University of Adelaide. He conducts most of his research in the fields of network design (including software designed networking), network interoperation, human factors and computer science education.

Pedro García Fernández received his Technical Engineering degree from the University of Basque Country, Spain, in 1994, and MSc and PhD degrees in Electronic Engineering from the Universitiy of Granada, Spain, in 1997 and 2000 respectively. In 1995, he joined the Department of Electrical Engineering, University of Jaen, as a Lecturer, and since 2002, he has been with the Departament of Electronics and Computer Technology, University of Granada, Spain. His current research interests include digital logic design, distribuited algorithms and data mining where he has actively participated in many research projects.

Antonio Fernández-Ares is a Computer Science and Engineering student at the University of Granada (Spain). He is currently finishing his Masters Degree and is going to continue his scientific career as a PhD student. He has collaborated with some departments at the same university, mainly with the Computer Architecture and Technology department, inside which he has developed his Final Degree and Master Degree Projects. He has participated in several national research projects related data mining and big data and bioinspired algorithms whose results have been published in conferences such as EVO* and IWANN. His interests include bioinspired algorithms, big data, and a computer intelligence applied to videogames.

John Fitzgerald is Professor and Director of Research in Computing Science at Newcastle University, UK, where he heads the Centre for Software Reliability, a group of 45 faculty, research scientists and doctoral students, developing technologies to support the design of trustworthy and resilient systems. His research is on rigorous model-based methods of system design. Over the last 20 years, he has helped to develop several such methods from logical foundations to tool-supported industrial applications. His current research addresses the challenge of cooperative engineering involving multiple disciplines. He recently led work on methods development in the DESTECS project on co-modeling and co-simulation in the design of cyber-physical systems, and now heads the COMPASS consortium, developing model-based methods and tools for engineering Systems of Systems. In new work, he is playing a leading role in Newcastle University's new Cyber-Physical Systems Laboratory, focusing on digital technology for urban sustainability.

Antonio M. Mora García received his PhD in 2009 at the University of Granada (Spain), where he also got his Degree in Computer Sciences in 2001. Currently he is a Teaching Assistant at the Computer Architecture and Technology Department in the same university. He has participated in several funded researching projects, and published a number of papers in top-rated international conferences (such as GECCO, ALIFE, WCCI, PPSN or EVO*). His working areas include Ant Colony Optimization metaheuristic, Multi-Objective Optimization and Genetic Algorithms, and their applications to Pathfinding problems or Video Games among others.

Gérald Garcia has been the head of the on-board software R&D group at Thales Alenia Space France for more than ten years. He is involved in the management and technical lead of several French and international research projects (e.g., European Commission, European Space Agency, French Space Agency). His main topics of interest are process, methods and tools for system and software model-based development for space systems. Mr. Garcia is a graduate specialization engineer from ISIA - Ecole Supérieure des Mines de Paris and graduate engineer from Ecole Supérieure des Mines de Nancy.

Emmanuel Gaudin has a technical background and developed protocol stacks in SDL. He joined a modeling tool vendor in 96, as a Field Application Engineer and as a trainer to finally become technical director of the French branch. Based on that experience, he started PragmaDev in 2001 to develop an SDL-RT tool.

Stefano Genolini has been with TXT since 1989, participating in development of many systems in the embedded mission critical domain, such as on board avionic flight control systems, automotive (test equipment and dash board computers), control systems for industry. He is currently the company reference for applied technology and methodology in embedded and mission critical systems. He is also responsible for the EN9100 and CMMI L3 processes definition and assessments.

Andreas Genser holds a Bachelors and Masters degree in Telematics, and a doctoral degree in Electrical Engineering, all received from Graz University of Technology in 2006, 2008 and 2011. Presently, he works at Infineon Technologies Austria AG in Graz and is responsible for verification concepts of low-power contactless smart-cards. His interests include power estimation and emulation techniques in order to evaluate the effectiveness of low-power measures taken during the design phase.

David George received his BSc in Computer Science from the University of Kent in 2009. Since 2012, he has been a software developer at Rapita Systems Ltd, based in York, UK. His work spans multiple projects, including verification of multi-core real-time systems, development of new and novel tools for runtime constraint analysis, compiler verification and high level software development using Ada. His interests include embedded development in Ada and C, embedded systems architecture and hardware design using FPGAs.

Pedro Gil is a Professor of Computer Architecture and Technology of the Universitat Politècnica de València (UPV), Spain. He has been the head of the Department of Computer Engineering (DISCA) for 4 years, and is the head of the Fault Tolerant Systems (STF) research line of the Advanced Communications and Information Technologies Research Institute (ITACA) of the UPV. His research interest areas include the design and validation of real-time fault-tolerant distributed systems, the dependability validation using fault injection, the design and verification of embedded systems, and the dependability and security benchmarking. He has authored more than 100 research papers and has supervised 11 PhD theses on these topics. He usually serves as a program committee member of the conferences related to fault-tolerant systems, such as DSN, EDCC, LADC, and EWDC. He was general chair of the EDCC 2010, held in Valencia.

Arda Goknil is a research associate at the Software Verification and Validation Lab in the Interdisciplinary Centre for Security, Reliability, and Trust (SnT) at the University of Luxembourg. Between 2011 and 2013, he was a postdoctoral fellow at AOSTE research team of INRIA in France. He received his PhD from the Software Engineering Group (TRESE) of the University of Twente in the Netherlands in 2011. The dissertation title is "Traceability of Requirements and Software Architecture for Change Management." Goknil received his BSc degree in 2003 and MSc degree in 2006, from the Computer Engineering Department of Ege University in Turkey. His current research is about Requirements Engineering and Architectural Design activities with a special emphasis on change management and testing.

Ian Gray is a Research Fellow at the University of York, UK. His PhD, which was completed at York, concerned the use of novel virtualisation techniques to overcome the limitations of traditional programming models for the development of complex embedded systems. This work was further developed as part of the EU-funded MADES project. He has been part of three FP7 research projects, author of three book chapters, and is on the programme committee of EuroMPI 2014. Ian's work is centred around real-time, embedded systems, particularly the use of new programming models and techniques to help the development of systems with complex hardware architectures.

Johannes Grinschgl received his Masters degree in Telematics from Graz University of Technology in 2008, focusing on microelectronics and telecommunications. He received his PhD in 2013 in Electrical Engineering at the Institute for Technical Informatics at Graz University of Technology. His research interests incorporate fault emulation as well as fault modeling. Presently, he is working for Intel as a digital designer and functional verification engineer.

Josef Haid received a Masters degree in Telematics and a doctoral degree in electrical engineering both from the Graz Technical University in Austria in the years 2001 and 2003 respectively. Presently he is a senior staff engineer at Infineon Technologies in Graz/Austria and is responsible for specification of low-power contactless smart cards. His interests include advanced digital design and low power design of hardware and software.

Scott Hansen is the Director for European Projects at The Open Group and has been project leader for 16 previous European Commission funded technology projects with a focus on embedded systems technologies, platform and development tools and security. Based in Brussels, he coordinates the research efforts of The Open Group in Europe amongst European members, as well as with other European standards bodies, and industry consortia. He has set-up and managed industry funded groupings from the banking and retail sectors, as well as technology groupings addressing methodologies for software process improvement and ICT procurement. He holds degrees in computer science, business management and industrial engineering, and has over 25 years' experience working in both large multi-national organisations and smaller start-ups managing technology development and deployment, as well as the financial and administrative disciplines associated with successful market introduction of new technologies.

Naim Harb obtained his PhD in informatics in 2011 at the University of Valenciennes, France. He has been working since October 2011 at the University of Mons (UMONS), Faculty of Electronics and Microelectronics, where he is now a post-doctoral researcher and a project manager. His current research is focused on dynamic partial reconfiguration on FPGAs. He has published more than 10 papers and communications at international conferences in the field of scientific computation and parallel computing. He is particularly interested in porting high demanding applications on new parallel architecture, either local (multicore, GPU) or distant (Clouds and Grids). He acts regularly as a reviewer for research project proposals or Follow ups, either at the Belgian, French, or European level.

Klaus Hofmann received a Dipl.-Ing. Degree in Electrical Engineering from Ruhr-University Bochum and Purdue University, West Lafayette, in 1992, and a PhD degree from TU Darmstadt in 1997. From 1998 until 2009, he held several engineering and engineering management positions at Siemens, Infineon Technologies and Qimonda AG (locations Munich and Suzhou, P.R. China) in telecommunication ASIC and DRAM chip design, project lead of the Infineon-internal semicustom flow, and the inhouse-CAD-tool development. In his last position as Director of DRAM Product Development, he was responsible for interface and technology DRAM lead products. Since 2009, he is a full professor at TU Darmstadt heading the "Integrated Electronic Systems" Lab. His research interests are in the domain of High-Voltage ASICs, Multiprocessor Systems/NoC and High Speed Circuits.

Thomas Hollstein is a Professor in the Department of Computer Engineering at Tallinn University of Technology (TTU). He graduated from Darmstadt University of Technology in Electrical Engineering / Computer Engineering in 1991. In 2000, he received his PhD on "Design and interactive Hardware/ Software Partitioning of complex heterogeneous Systems" at Darmstadt University of Technology. He has an extensive industrial background in the field of embedded HW/SW systems and printable electronics. Since September 2010, Thomas Hollstein is a full professor at TTU leading the research team "Dependable Embedded Systems." His research interests are in the fields Dependable Embedded Systems, System-on-Chip Design, Networks-on-Chip, MPSoCs (Programming Models, APIs, Mixed criticality application mapping and dependability management), Reconfigurable Systems, and Printed Electronics. Thomas Hollstein has published over 70 peer-reviewed papers and is a member of the programme committees of several international conferences and workshops.

Ramin Tavakoli Kolagari works at the Nuremberg Institute of Technology at the faculty of Computer Science responsible for the software engineering field of teaching. He studied computer science and business administration at the Technical University of Berlin and received his PhD at the University of Ulm on the topic of automotive requirements engineering and software product lines. Prof. Tavakoli lectured at the University of Ulm and at the Technical University of Berlin. He researched and published in the area of software reuse in general and specifically in the area of software product lines for the automotive domain. Today, his research focus lies in the area of model-based development for describing the system and software architecture of embedded automotive systems, e.g., with EAST-ADL. After his studies, Prof. Tavakoli worked in the research departments of internationally operative carmakers in Germany and Sweden in the areas software development, software architecture, and model-based development.

Dimitris Kolovos is a Lecturer in Enterprise Systems and will be leading the research and innovation activities in York. He is currently a principal investigator and the technical director of the MONDO project on scalable Model-Driven Engineering and a co-investigator and the technical director of an EU STREP project on model-based analysis and monitoring of open-source software (OSSMETER). Dimitris has previously been a co-investigator and the technical director of a Eurocontrol/SESAR-JU project on model-based safety management in Air Tra_c Management Systems (COMPASS), and a co-investigator in the EU STREP MADES project which focused on Model Driven Engineering for embedded systems. Dimitris has authored more than 80 scientific papers in international journals, conferences and workshops and has been an Eclipse Foundation committer leading the development of the Epsilon open-source project since 2006, and co-leading the Emfatic project since 2010.

Jari Kreku works currently as a senior scientist at VTT in Oulu, Finland. His research interests include early-phase performance and power consumption modeling and simulation methods and tools of embedded computer systems, and mapability methods and tools of algorithms and processor architectures. He has been involved in several European research projects. He has published more than 15 scientific journal or conference articles.

Armin Krieg received his Bachelors and Masters degree in Telematics from Graz University of Technology in 2007 and 2008, focusing on microelectronics and system-on-chip design. From 2010 to 2012 he worked in the POWER-MODES research project at the Institute for Technical Informatics at

Graz University of Technology in collaboration with Infineon Technologies Austria AG and Austria Card GmbH. He received his doctoral degree in Electrical Engineering from the Graz University of Technology in 2013. Currently, he is involved in the specification of authentication devices for the Chipcard and Security department in the design center Graz of Infineon Technologies Austria AG. His research interests incorporate fault emulation as well as fault detection and recovery.

Agnès Lanusse graduated in computer science in 1981 and obtained her PhD from Toulouse III University, France, in 1984. She joined the « Commissariat à l'énergie atomique et aux énergies alternatives (CEA) » were she is conducting currently research on activities on model based safety analysis of systems. Her team is developing the Sophia framework an environment dedicated to support safety assessment of complex systems along the various steps of development life-cycle. This framework is fully integrated with the system modeling tool Papyrus and is based on model driven engineering and UML extensions dedicated to error modeling and safety analysis. Her research interests include system modeling, methods and tools to develop systems correct by construction, and incremental verification.

Peter Gorm Larsen is a professor in the Department of Engineering at Aarhus University, where he leads the software engineering research group. After receiving his MSc in Electronic Engineering at the Technical University of Denmark in 1988, he worked in the industry before returning to complete an industrial PhD in 1995. In his industry career, as a development engineer and manager, he gave industrial courses all over the world and saw the technology he developed being applied in areas as diverse as secure message processing and options trading. He returned to academia in 2005. His prime research goal now is to improve the development of complex mission-critical applications by implementing and applying well-founded technologies, in particular in the design of robust tools that help engineers to leverage models in early design stages to reduce overall product development risk. He is the author of more than 100 papers published in journals, books and conference proceedings, and several books.

Renato Librino graduated in Electronics Engineering. He joined Fiat Research Centre. After an initial phase as an electronics designer for space applications in collaboration with MBB, ESA-ESTEC and NASA, he was involved in research and development of electronic systems for automotive applications in the field of advanced information systems, body systems, including onboard local networks, chassis control and engine management. He was the National Coordinator of research programs in the field of active safety and of electric and hybrid vehicles. In recent years he had the responsibility of developing fuel cell systems and fuel cell vehicle prototypes, as well as electric machines and storage systems for alternative propulsion powertrains. Finally, he has been involved in research for advanced mobility concepts basing on advanced ADAS systems and automated guidance. He held the position of Vice-President of Fiat Research Centre and Director of Electrical Engineering. Co-founder of 4S Srl, he is the Managing Director.

Henrik Lönn has a PhD in Computer Engineering from Chalmers University of Technology, Sweden, with a research focus on safety-critical real-time systems. At Volvo, he has worked with prototypes, architecture modeling, and communication aspects on vehicle electronic systems. He is also participating in national and international research collaborations on embedded systems development. Previous project involvement includes X-by-Wire, FIT, EAST-EEA and TIMMO, and the coordination of FP6 and 7 projects ATESST, ATESST2 and MAENAD.

Gustavo Romero López received a BSc degree in Computer Science and a PhD degree, both from the University of Granada, Spain. He has been working as programmer for CICYT proyect BIO96-0895. He is currently a Lecturer at the Computer Architecture and Technology Department, University of Granada. His main interests in research are in neural networks and evolutionary computation.

Stephane Maag received his PhD degree in Computer Science from the Evry University, France, in 2002. He joined Telecom SudParis as an Associate Professor in 2002 and the CNRS UMR 5157 in 2003. Since 2013, he is a Professor at Institut Mines-Telecom, France. His research and scientific areas are the study of formal approaches for the validation of network protocols and services. He specifically analyzes the networks in order to test in a formal way their protocols through active and passive/monitoring techniques. His main studies were about IMS based protocols and MANET routing protocols. He chaired several conferences/workshops and is an editor and member of several editorial boards. He is also actively involved in several technical and scientific program committees, more than 40 over the years, such as IEEE AINA, ACM SAC, IFIT ICTSS, IEEE ICST, etc. Finally, he published more than 70 papers in refereed conferences and journals.

Gianpaolo Macario is a senior member of the Linux Services team of Mentor Graphics (http://www.mentor.com/embedded). Before joining Mentor Graphics, Gianpaolo worked in the Infotainment and Telematics Business Unit of Magneti Marelli (http://www.magnetimarelli.com) where he was the System Architect for a Linux-based platform development of In-Vehicle Systems units. Gianpaolo has been working with Embedded Linux and In-Vehicle Infotainment for the last several years and had the privilege of seeing and helping Linux evolve from a crazy idea to a solid foundation for delivering IVI services to the vehicle users. Gianpaolo has been involved in the GENIVI Alliance (http://www.genivi.org/) right since its inception, and has been serving as lead Architect of the System Infrastructure Expert Group since January 2012. Gianpaolo has co-authored a few research papers and has given several presentations about Linux and IVI to customers, universities, and other public events.

Nidhal Mahmud received his PhD in Computer Science from the University of Hull, UK, in 2012. He worked on model-based analysis and the design of complex safety-critical systems. The generation of static/temporal fault trees from system behavioral models and the SAFORA compositional method are two core contributions of his PhD thesis, where he also proposed a contribution which enables the automatic optimization of Markov models. Nidhal joined the University of Hull as a postdoctoral researcher in 2012, and his research interests lie in the fields of architectural descriptions, dependability models, and dynamic analysis techniques of complex real-time embedded systems. He has participated in EU projects on safety including ATESST2 and MAENAD.

Frédéric Mallet is currently an associate professor at Univ. Nice Sophia Antipolis. He is a permanent member of the Aoste Team-project, a joint team between INRIA Sophia Antipolis and I3S Laboratory. His work focuses on the design and analysis of real-time and embedded systems. He is one of the designers of the Time and Allocation subprofiles of the MARTE OMG Specification.

Nicholas Drivalos Matragkas is a researcher in the Enterprise Systems Research Group of the Computer Science Department at the University of York, UK. He completed his PhD in Model Driven Engineering (MDE) in 2011. In the past, he has worked as a researcher on the MADES European project with particular focus on the application of MDE to the development of embedded systems. Currently, he is working on the EU-funded OSSMETER project. OSSMETER aims to extend the state-of-the-art in the field of automated analysis and measurement of open-source software. He has published a number of papers on various topics of software engineering such as MDE, embedded systems, and mining of software repositories.

Silvia Mazzini has more than twenty years of experience in the System and Software Engineering field. She has been a senior consultant at Intecs since 1988, where she is involved both in technical leadership and management activities in the context of several international industrial and research projects. She was coordinator of the CHESS ARTEMIS project and currently is coordinator of the SESAMO and CONCERTO ARTEMIS projects. Her main topics of interest are methods and tools for system and software model-based development in the domain of high integrity systems. She is also a member of INCOSE and participates in the European Space Agency SAVOIR-FAIRE, and ECSS E40 and Q80 working groups. She is Methodologies and R&D Manager at Intecs. Mrs. Mazzini took her degree in Computer Science at Pisa University in Italy.

Gundula Meisel-Blohm is an expert for Embedded System and Software Engineering with UML and other model based approaches. She coaches developer teams of various projects in the Defense and Security Systems Division on model based Requirements Engineering and Design and is working in several research and technology projects on system and software engineering improvement of Airbus Group, together with colleagues from Airbus, Astrium and other divisions. She has been working as a software architect since 1991, starting with object oriented development methods in embedded systems in 1998. She gained expertise in numerous naval and ground surveillance (direction finders, radars) and avionic (radar, ELINT, defensive aids, mission management, test facilities) projects as software and system responsible.

Juan J. Merelo received a BSc degree in theoretical physics and a PhD degree both from the University of Granada, Granada, Spain, in 1988 and 1994 respectively. He has been a Visiting Researcher at Santa Fe Institute, Santa Fe, NM, Politecnico Torino, Turin, Italy, RISC-Linz, Linz, Austria, the University of Southern California, Los Angeles, and the Université Paris-V, Paris, France. He is currently a Full Professor at the Computer Architecture and Technology Department, University of Granada. His main interests include neural networks, genetic algorithms, and artificial life.

Manuel Menghin was born 1982 in Rum in Tirol, Austria. He received his Masters degree in Telematics from Graz University of Technology in 2010. After that he worked 1.5 years in a start-up company called NTE-Systems and was responsible for the firmware development of a novel customer oriented solution for solar controllers. Since 2011, he has done his PhD in the field of electrical engineering at the Institute for Technical Informatics at Graz University of Technology in collaboration with Infineon Technologies Austria AG and Enso Detego GmbH (FIT-IT funded project called META[:SEC:]). His research interests include Near Field Communication and system-based power optimization techniques for embedded systems.

Trish Messiter, CEO of Clarinox Technologies, has an Engineering Degree from the University of NSW, Sydney, Australia completed in 1983. Trish has experience across many fields including research, engineering design, computer modeling, software debugging and technical support as well as technical sales and marketing. In her role for Clarinox, Trish has been working with clients implementing innovative wireless designs for 13 years. Trish has provided presentations on short range wireless technologies at a number of conferences including Comms Connect, WiCon USA, WiCon Asia and Industrial Wireless.

José Javier Asensio Montiel received his Degree (2005) and MsC (2010) in Computer Science and Engineering at University of Granada (Spain). He has participated in several national research projects related with industrial automation systems and standards. His research interests include industrial programming languages, consumer robotics, gamification, and machine learning.

Pramila Mouttappa received her Bachelors degree in Electronics and Communication Engineering from Pondicherry University, India, in 2002, and her Masters of Technology degree in VLSI Systems from Sathyabama University, India, in 2005. After her graduation, she worked for three years as a Project Engineer for VLSI Semiconductors at Wipro Technology in India. In 2011, she joined the Institut Mines Telecom/TelecomSudParis, France, to pursue a PhD degree in Computer Science, which was awarded in 2013 for a dissertation entitled 'A Symbolic-based Passive Testing approach to detect Vulnerabilities in Networking Systems.' Her main research interests are the use of formal models and their application to passive testing, as well as performing security related testing for different communication protocols, design and verification of SoC.

Chokri Mraidha is a researcher at the Laboratory of Model Driven Engineering for Embedded Systems of the CEA LIST institute in France. He got a master degree in distributed computing in 2001 and a PhD in Computer Science in 2005. His research and development interests include real-time and embedded systems model driven development, modeling languages design, instrumentation and control architectures design, optimized software real-time architecture synthesis and model compilation. He is involved in UML-based OMG standards for design of real systems like SysML and MARTE and the AUTOSAR standard for automotive. He has supervised 3 PhD theses, and he is working on European and French research projects developing model-based approaches for design and verification of architectures for critical real-time systems for automotive, railway, aerospace, and nuclear power plants.

Smail Niar received his PhD in computer Engineering from the University of Lille in 1990. Since then, he has been a professor at the University of Valenciennes where he leads the "Mobile and Embedded Systems" research group at the "Laboratory of Automation, Mechanical and Computer Engineering," a joint research unit between CNRS and the university of Valenciennes. He is member of the European Network of Excellence on "High Performance and Embedded Architectures and Compilation" (HIPEAC). His research interests are in multi-processor system-on-chip (MPSoC) architectures, power/energy consumption optimization, dynamically reconfigurable embedded systems (FPGA), simulation acceleration techniques for MPSoC design space exploration, and reliability and security issues for embedded systems.

Richard Paige is Professor of Enterprise Systems at the Department of Computer Science, University of York, UK. He leads research on Model-Driven Engineering, agile methods, formal methods, and distributed systems. He is principal investigator on a number of large-scale modeling projects funded by the EU. He was director of the UK Engineering Doctorate Centre in Large-Scale Complex IT Systems from 2009-2013 and currently runs the MSc in Software Engineering course at York. He is on the editorial boards of Empirical Software Engineering, the Journal of Object Technology and Software and Systems Modeling. He has been program chair or co-chair for TOOLS Europe 2008, ICMT 2009, ECMDA 2009, ICECCS 2010, and SLE 2013, was general co-chair for ETAPS 2009, and is general chair for STAF 2014 and SLE 2015.

Marie-Agnès Peraldi-Frati is an associate professor in computer sciences at the University of Nice Sophia-Antipolis. After earning a PHD in automatic and signal processing, she had a post doc position at the Swiss Federal Institute of Technology in Lausanne. She is a member of the INRIA-I3S AOSTE team. She is particularly interested in the modeling and traceability and the verification of non-functional constraints of distributed real-time embedded systems. She taught in different degrees of the University of Nice Sophia Antipolis.

Ken Pierce is a postdoctoral Research Associate in the School of Computing Science at Newcastle University and is a member of the Centre for Software Reliability. His primary interests lie in methods for developing dependable cyber-physical systems (CPS), covering aspects such as faults and fault tolerance and design space exploration (DSE). He worked on developing the methodology of Crescendo in the DESTECS project. Prior to joining DESTECS, he completed a doctorate on rely-guarantee conditions for atomicity refinement. In 2014, he was elected as convener of the Language Board for the VDM community, which oversees the evolution of the VDM family of languages.

Gavin Puddy is currently completing a PhD on Performance Prediction of Evolving Systems. He joined the Defence Science and Technology Organisation in 2005 to work on combat system architecture research for surface and sub-surface platforms. He currently leads up a research program on early evaluation methods into non-functional performances of resource constraint real-time systems within the defence domain.

Stefano Puri received a Computer Science degree from the Pisa University, Italy, in 2000. Since 2001 he worked for Intecs, before as senior software developer and then as senior consultant. He is, and has been involved, in several international industrial and research projects, mainly focusing on the usage and definition of model driven methodologies and the development of supporting tools for the design of high-integrity software systems. He has around 6 years of experience regarding the development of tools around the Eclipse platform. He has around 10 years of experience in the usage OMG standards, and he is part of the Intecs team for training in the OMG modeling languages, in particular regarding the UML, SysML and MARTE.

Shuai Li is a PhD student at Thales Communications and Security and Lab-STICC (UMR CNRS 6285) / Université de Bretagne Occidental (UBO). He is currently preparing to defend his thesis on scheduling analysis of software radio protocols, in November 2014. His area of research includes real-time scheduling analysis and model-driven engineering. He received his Engineering Degree in Computer Science (Master Degree) in 2011, from the Université de Technologie de Belfort-Montbéliard (UTBM).

Mark-Oliver Reiser has studied computer science, psychology, and law in Tübingen and Berlin. After three years working at a research department of Daimler AG he received a PhD in computer science in 2008 and has been working as a research assistant at the Technische Universität Berlin since then. His main research interests include the definition and application of domain specific modeling languages, requirements engineering, product family management and other aspects of model-based development of embedded systems, in particular for the automotive domain. He has been involved in the definition of the EAST-ADL standard, a comprehensive modeling language for automotive embedded systems covering all stages of development from early analysis to implementation based on AUTOSAR.

Victor Rivas is currently an Associate Professor in the Department of Computer Science at the University of Jaen (Spain), after having received a BSc degree in Computer Science and a PhD degree both from the University of Granada, Spain. His main interests in research are related to evolutionary optimization of Radial Basis Function Neural Networks. He was invited by Dr. Mark Schoenauer in October, 1998 to spend two months in the Ecole Polytechnique, in Paris.

Juan-Carlos Ruiz received his PhD from the Institut National Polytechnique of Toulouse (France) in 2002. In 2003, Dr. Ruiz integrated the Fault-Tolerant Systems Research Group (GSTF) of UPV. His current research is focused on, but not limited to, the specification of dependability benchmarks, the definition of fault and attack injection techniques, and the design of adaptive and dynamic fault tolerance mechanisms for embedded and wireless mobile systems. He serves regularly on the program committee at the most important dependability conferences, and he is author of more than 60 papers in the field of dependable systems. Dr. Ruiz is currently an associate professor in the Department of Computer Engineering of the School of Computer Science, where he also acts as Vice-Dean for International Relations. He is also an active member of the Spanish platform of Security and Trust Technologies (eSeC) and the IFIP SIG 10.4 on Dependability Benchmarking.

Andrey Sadovykh holds the M. Sc. degree in Applied Mathematics and Information Technologies of Moscow Institute of Physics and Technology, the Ph. D. degree in Computer Science of Paris 6th University and the MBA degree of HEC Paris Business School. For his Ph. D. he worked in EADS Space Transportation as a research engineer in development of systems for distributed monitoring and supervision. He was involved in the European Space Agency (ESA) projects for ATV spacecraft validation facilities and Hardware in the Loop simulation. At Softeam, Dr. Sadovykh holds the position of the Head of the Research Department. He leads research activities in MDA / MDD - he worked as the project manager and the research engineer for the ENOSYS, MADES, PRESTO, MOMOCS, MODEL-PLEX, SHAPE, REMICS, JUNIPER, and ModaClouds projects. He was the technical coordinator in REMICS and MADES FP7 projects and was the consortium coordinator in the RTE Space (ESA-funded) and ENOSYS FP7 projects. In ModelWare project, Dr. Sadovykh lead development of middleware for integration of model-driven tools. In REMICS project, Dr. Sadovykh proposed an approach on model-driven migration of legacy systems to cloud infrastructures. Dr. Sadovykh is actively involved in the in the standardization activities at the Object Management Group. He contributed to standards on SOA and UI modelling - SoaML and IFML respectively. In ModelioSoft, Softeam's subsidiary, Dr. Sadovykh contributed to the marketing strategy and transformation to open source policies. Lately, in the frame of the MBA program at HEC Paris Business school, Dr. Sadovykh participated in consultancy project for CISCO Systems in the field of business strategy for "Value creation with Big Data at SMB market."

Mazen A. R. Saghir is an Associate Professor of Electrical and Computer Engineering at Texas A&M University at Qatar. He received his BE in Computer and Communication Engineering from the American University of Beirut in 1989, and his MASc. and PhD in Electrical and Computer Engineering from the University of Toronto in 1993 and 1998, respectively. His research interests include reconfigurable computing, computer architecture, compilers and EDA tools, and embedded systems design. He is a senior member of the IEEE.

Pablo García Sánchez is a PhD Student at the University of Granada (Spain). He received his Deegre (2007) and MsC (2008) in Computer Science and Engineering at the same University. He has participated in several national research projects related with e-Health, web-services and optimization, whose results have been published in conferences such as PPSN, EVO* and IWANN. His interests include Service Oriented Computing, evolutionary computation and distributed algorithms.

Christian Steger received a Dipl.-Ing. degree (M.Sc.) in 1990, and the Dr. techn. degree (PhD) in electrical engineering from Graz University of Technology, Austria, in 1995, respectively. He is a key researcher at the Virtual Vehicle Competence Center (ViF, COMET K2) in Graz, Austria. From 1989 to 1991, he was a software trainer and consultant at SPC Computer Training GmbH., Vienna. Since 1992, he has been an Assistant Professor at the Institute for Technical Informatics, Graz University of Technology. He heads the HW/SW codesign group at the Institute for Technical Informatics. His research interests include embedded systems, HW/SW codesign, HW/SW coverfication, SOC, power awareness, smart cards, UHF RFID systems, and multi-DSPs.

Claudia Szabo is a Lecturer at the School of Computer Science, The University of Adelaide, Adelaide, Australia. Her research interests include complex systems, software architectures and model driven engineering.

Gokhan Tanyeri is the cofounder and CTO of Clarinox Technologies Pty Ltd, Melbourne, Australia. He has over 30 years of experience in Embedded Systems Design across many industries including automotive, health, telecommunications and defense and has successfully run the embedded systems arm of several companies in Australia. Prior to Clarinox, Gokhan was a Senior Software Professional and Consultant for Agilent Australia, Fujitsu Australia Ltd and Invetech Pty Ltd. He was a Systems Engineer for Mikes/Loral International Inc. New York and Chief Electronics Engineer for Aselsan Inc., Ankara, a leading Turkish defence electronics company. Gokhan holds a Masters and Bachelors in Electronic Engineering degree in Electronic Engineering from the Middle East Technical University (METU) in Ankara, Turkey.

Stefano Tonetta received a PhD in Informatics and Telecommunications from the University of Trento in 2006. From 2006 to 2007, he was Post-Doc at the Faculty of Informatics of the University of Lugano. In 2007, he joined Fondazione Bruno Kessler (FBK), where he is currently working as a tenured researcher. His research mainly concerns temporal logic and symbolic model checking. He published several research papers in the field of formal verification, in particular on the formalization, the validation and the verification of temporal properties for finite-state, software and hybrid systems. He was a co-recipient of the 2010 Microsoft Research SEIF Award with the project proposal "Formal Methods for Embedded Systems Requirements," of the 2010 FBK Stringa Award, and of the 2012 FMCAD Best Paper Award.

Sandra Torchiaro graduated in Automation Engineering at the "Università degli Studi della Calabria" in 2006. She joined CRF in 2007 focusing his expertise on functional safety for Electrical Electronic Architecture in the group "Functional Safety for Systems Design." She was involved in activities devoted to the application of the Time Trigger Network Protocol "Flexray" in vehicle prototypes. She participates in the Functional Safety Italian Working Group for the ISO DIS 26262 evaluation. She was involved in the developing of the EU Projects ATESST2 and CESAR and will still be involved in MAENAD, OPENCOSS, VeTeSS. Furthermore, she is involved in functional safety efforts related to FIAT and Chrysler Group products. Currently, she holds the role of head of the group "Functional Safety for System Design" of "E/E & Connectivity" department.

Sara Tucci-Piergiovanni is a research engineer at the CEA LIST's laboratory of model-driven engineering. She received her MS and PhD degrees in computer engineering from the Sapienza University of Rome, respectively, in 2002 and 2006. Her masters thesis was awarded in 2002 with the prize of the Confederation of Italian Industry for the best Italian thesis in ICT. At Sapienza, she held a lecturer position teaching a course on distributed systems till 2008. Since her masters degree, she publishes regularly in peer-reviewed scientific forums and journals in the areas of distributed-, real-time-, mission critical-systems and software. She has served as a reviewer in numerous journals (TPDS, JACM, TCS, JSS, SoSym, etc) and as a program committee member in several international conferences (ACM SAC, ETFA, EDCC, etc.). She also co-chaired the International Conference in Distributed Event Systems in 2008. She is also involved in numerous research and industrial projects developing model-driven engineering approaches for the automotive domain. Among these projects, she is leading the tooling workpackage in the EC funded MAENAD project.

Massimo Violante received an MS and PhD from Politecnico di Torino, Italy, where he is now an Associate Professor. Prof. Violante's main research topics are the design and validation of embedded system for safety- and mission-critical applications, with particular emphasis on the use of commercial off-the-shelf components like multicore processors and field programmable gate arrays in automotive and avionic applications. Prof. Violante has published more than 150 papers in the area of testing and designing reliable embedded systems, and he co-authored two books. He served as program co-chair and general co-chair of the IEEE Defect and Fault Tolerance in VLSI and Nanotechnology Systems for 2011 and 2012 and as Program Chair for the IEEE European Test Symposium for 2012. Prof. Violante is scientifically responsible for a number of research projects in the area of embedded systems for space, avionic and automotive applications in collaboration with European Space Agency, Thales Alenia Space, and Magneti Marelli.

Nataliya Yakymets received an MSc degree in Computer Engineering in 2005 and a PhD degree in Computer Engineering (Control Systems) in 2008 from the National Aerospace University, Kharkiv, Ukraine. From 2005-2006, she was a Scientific Researcher and Teaching Assistant with the Kharkiv National Aerospace University (Ukraine). In 2007, she joined the University of Stuttgart in Germany as a Scientific Researcher. From 2009-2011, she held a position of Post Doctoral Researcher at Ecole Centrale de Lyon (France). Since 2012, she has been a Research Engineer at Commissariat à l'énergie atomique et aux énergies alternatives (CEA). Her research interests include system dependability, methods and tools for reliable systems, and model-driven engineering.

Haoyuan Ying received a B.Eng. degree in electronic information engineering from Shenzhen University, China, 2008, and an MSc (Eng.) degree with distinction in microelectronic system engineering from the University of Liverpool, UK, 2009 (MSc thesis is awarded as the best MSc thesis in 2008 – 2009 and also the ARM project prize). He joined the Integrated Electronic Systems Lab, TU Darmstadt, Germany, in 2010 as a PhD researcher. His research interests include 2D and 3D Networks-on-Chip and embedded systems design flow and framework, Mix-Level Simulation and System Modeling and Evaluation.

Index